Everett Delahanty

Systems and Theories in Psychology

McGraw-Hill Series in Psychology

Consulting Editor
Norman Garmezy

Adams Human Memory
Berlyne Conflict, Arousal, and Curiosity
Blum Psychoanalytic Theories of Personality
Bock Multivariate Statistical Methods in Behavioral Research
Brown The Motivation of Behavior
Campbell, Dunnette, Lawler, and Weick Managerial Behavior, Performance, and Effectiveness
Crites Vocational Psychology
D'Amato Experimental Psychology: Methodology, Psychophysics, and Learning
Dollard and Miller Personality and Psychotherapy
Ferguson Statistical Analysis in Psychology and Education
Fodor, Bever, and Garrett The Psychology of Language: An Introduction to Psycholinguistics and Generative Grammar
Forgus and Melamed Perception: A Cognitive—Stage Approach
Franks Behavior Therapy: Appraisal and Status
Gilmer and Deci Industrial and Organizational Psychology
Guilford Psychometric Methods

Guilford The Nature of Human Intelligence
Guilford and Fruchter Fundamental Statistics in Psychology and Education
Guilford and Hoepfner The Analysis of Intelligence
Guion Personnel Testing
Hetherington and Parke Child Psychology: A Contemporary Viewpoint
Hirsh The Measurement of Hearing
Hjelle and Ziegler Personality Theories: Basic Assumptions, Research, and Applications
Horowitz Elements of Statistics for Psychology and Education
Hulse, Deese, and Egeth The Psychology of Learning
Hurlock Adolescent Development
Hurlock Child Development
Hurlock Developmental Psychology
Krech, Crutchfield, and Ballachey Individual in Society
Lakin Interpersonal Encounter: Theory and Practice in Sensitivity Training
Lawler Pay and Organizational Effectiveness: A Psychological View
Lazarus, A. Behavior Therapy and Beyond
Lazarus, R. Patterns of Adjustment
Lewin A Dynamic Theory of Personality
Maher Principles of Psychopathology
Marascuilo Statistical Methods for Behavioral Science Research
Marx and Hillix Systems and Theories in Psychology
Miller Language and Communication
Morgan Physiological Psychology
Mulaik The Foundations of Factor Analysis
Novick and Jackson Statistical Methods for Educational and Psychological Research
Nunnally Introduction to Statistics for Psychology and Education
Nunnally Psychometric Theory
Overall and Klett Applied Multivariate Analysis
Porter, Lawler, and Hackman Behavior in Organizations
Restle Learning: Animal Behavior and Human Cognition
Robinson and Robinson The Mentally Retarded Child
Rosenthal Genetic Theory and Abnormal Behavior
Ross Psychological Disorders of Children: A Behavioral Approach to Theory, Research, and Therapy
Schwitzgebel and Kolb Changing Human Behavior: Principles of Planned Intervention
Shaw Group Dynamics: The Psychology of Small Group Behavior
Shaw and Costanzo Theories of Social Psychology
Shaw and Wright Scales for the Measurement of Attitudes
Sidowski Experimental Methods and Instrumentation in Psychology
Siegel Nonparametric Statistics for the Behavioral Sciences
Spencer and Kass Perspectives in Child Psychology
Stagner Psychology of Personality
Steers and Porter Motivation and Work Behavior
Vinacke The Psychology of Thinking
Winer Statistical Principles in Experimental Design

Systems and Theories in Psychology

Third Edition

Melvin H. Marx
Professor of Psychology
University of Missouri

William A. Hillix
Professor of Psychology
San Diego State University

McGraw-Hill Book Company

New York St. Louis San Francisco Auckland Bogotá Düsseldorf
Johannesburg London Madrid Mexico Montreal New Delhi
Panama Paris São Paulo Singapore Sydney Tokyo Toronto

SYSTEMS AND THEORIES IN PSYCHOLOGY

3 4 5 6 7 8 9 0 DODO 8 3 2 1 0

This book was set in Times Roman by BookTech, Inc. (ECU).
The editors were Richard R. Wright and David Dunham;
the cover was designed by Saiki & Sprung Design;
the production supervisor was Donna Piligra.
R. R. Donnelley & Sons Company was printer and binder.

See Acknowledgments on pages 493-496.
Copyrights included on this page by reference.

Library of Congress Cataloging in Publication Data

Marx, Melvin Herman.
Systems and theories in psychology.

(McGraw-Hill series in psychology)
Bibliography: p.
Includes index.
1. Psychology—Philosophy. I. Hillix, William Allen, date joint author. II. Title.
[DNLM: 1. Psychological theory. BF38 M392s]
BF38.M38 1979 150'.1'9 78-12030
ISBN 0-07-040679-0

Contents

PART TWO CONTEMPORARY THEORIES

Preface

Our purposes in this third edition remain what they have always been: to introduce the student to classical and contemporary approaches to the science of psychology. In the second edition, we added some material intended to help the student to organize all these viewpoints. Our students have convinced us that we did less than an optimum job of presenting these materials.

Thus one of the most important changes in this edition is a reorganization of the introductory materials. The previous editions had three parts (an introductory section of three chapters, a section on systems, and one on contemporary theories). The present edition has only two parts, one on systems and one on contemporary theories. The three introductory chapters have been completely rewritten and placed more appropriately, we think, with the materials they introduce. Now the student need no longer endure three consecutive chapters of unleavened abstraction. In addition, we have tried for a clearer and more complete presentation of introductory materials.

Additions to this edition have been primarily of two kinds. First, there is the usual updating of contemporary theories and the addition of recent historical research, as well as the remedying of some previous omissions and errors. We hope that we have also corrected some errors of perspective, although we may thereby have introduced some new ones. Second, we have tried to add some historical perspective and to make some sections more interesting by adding biographical information. We have not done this at the expense of deleting any substantive materials, except where they were considered redundant or, in a few cases, no longer relevant enough to include. In fact, there is more material in this edition, but we hope it seems like less because it is presented more clearly and interestingly.

This edition is, nevertheless, shorter. With great regret, we report that our appendixes on foreign psychology are no longer included. Despite what we think was their obvious value, publication costs precluded their inclusion in this edition. We take some comfort in the fact that Sexton and Misiak (1976) have published their *Psychology around the world,* making available an up-to-date volume containing far more material than we could have included. Students and teachers can compensate for our unwilling return to provincialism by referring to that book.

We are, therefore, sticking more closely than ever to our enduring objective, which is to provide the essential information about systematic and theoretical psychology any advanced student should have. The book is directed at the senior undergraduate major and the beginning graduate student. It is intended to help students integrate some of the diverse materials and approaches to which they have been exposed in other courses. A number of our students have expressed regret that they could not have taken the course in systems and theories earlier, for they claimed that they would have understood everything else better had they done so. However, we still think the course belongs at the advanced level. Students cannot integrate well until they have something to integrate, and our book presupposes some degree of sophistication.

Part One of the present edition concentrates on the classical systems. The first two chapters set the stage by providing an integrative framework and placing the emergence of psychology in a historical context. Chapters 3 through 8 present the classical schools of psychology—or at least the six schools most often treated as classical by American psychologists.

Part Two examines a small sample of contemporary theories. We have tried to include developments that meet the twin criteria of being important and of revealing the transition from the older schools to our current points of view. It is impossible to present more than a tiny fraction of the important work. However, our concern is not primarily with familiarizing students with the details of any subject matter area. We are presenting an overview, and trying to bring students into contact with the general principles of theoretical development.

The book of readings promised in the preface to the previous edition has now been published (Hillix & Marx, 1974). It should serve equally well as a supplement to this edition for those instructors and students who want more exposure to the original words of psychology's great minds, to whom we express our appreciation for making this book and all like it possible.

We also wish to express our appreciation to our students, particularly to Jon Meeter, who showed us how the book should be organized, to John Thomas, who helped us get started, and to David Little, who helped us to get finished. As usual, our wives have cleaned up the messes we made in the manuscript and elsewhere, in addition to helping in innumerable more specific ways. But particular thanks go to our wily editor, Richard Wright, wise in the ways of authors, who always had one more way of saving a little more production time if we would just meet one last deadline.

Melvin H. Marx
William A. Hillix

Major Figures in the Formation and Development of Six Psychological Systems

1870	1880	1890	1900	1910	1920	1930	1940	1950	1960
	STRUCTURALISM								
	Wundt	Titchener							
		FUNCTIONALISM							
	James	Dewey	Angell		Carr Woodworth	McGeoch	Melton	Underwood	
	ASSOCIATIONISM								
	Ebbinghaus		Pavlov	Bekhterev	Thorndike	Guthrie		Estes	
				BEHAVIORISM					
				Meyer Watson Weiss	Hunter Tolman	Skinner Hull	Miller	Spence	
				GESTALT THEORY					
Mach	von Ehrenfels			Wertheimer Koffka	Köhler				
	PSYCHOANALYSIS								
	Breuer Freud		Adler Jung Rank Ferenczi	Jones	Horney	Sullivan	Fromm	Erikson	

Part One

Systems

In Part One we will present material on the nature of psychological systems. We will then examine how psychology emerged from a general philosophical and scientific background. Six major classical systems of psychology will be presented. For each system, we will first backtrack briefly in order to indicate the origins of the system in the past, usually a philosophical past. Then the founding of the system as a psychological point of view, its major characteristics with regard to content and methodology, and its development and fate are treated. Criticisms and defenses will be offered for each system. The dimensions of R. I. Watson (1967) will be applied where they are most relevant for each system, as well as for each of the more modern viewpoints in the last section of the book. This should help to make comparisons between systems easier, and perhaps also help us to decide whether modern psychology presents any advance over the older systems. The table at the left shows the major figures associated with the origin and development of each system. The names are placed on a common time line, at about the time that they made their first major contributions.

Chapter 1

Systems of Psychology

THE STUDY OF HISTORY

The daily newspaper is history seen through a narrow slit. So is the news on television. Textbooks about psychology are also specialized history, with the width of the slit increased to about 40 years. It used to be necessary to argue that educated students of psychology should widen their temporal perspective, but that may no longer be true. We still sometimes think of ourselves as a brash new country too busy with the present to worry much about the past, but that point of view is harder to sell now that we have celebrated our bicentennial. Alex Haley's book *Roots* (1976) has burned the need for a sense of time and place into the consciousness of whites as well as blacks, and genealogies are selling like McDonald's hamburgers. We are moving into the age of unapologetic history.

For longer than we can remember, psychologists have fondly quoted Ebbinghaus's comment, "Psychology has a long past, but a short history." That statement is getting a little tired, since psychology has its official centennial in 1979. A hundred years is not yet enough to be a long history, but it is too long to be an excuse for lack of progress. We believe, fortunately, that readers of this book will see that we have made progress.

Psychology in the United States has been even shorter on professional historians than it has been on history, but there are many signs that the study of psychological history is becoming an active discipline. Two of these signs are that *The Journal of the History of the Behavioral Sciences* began publication in 1964 and continues to provide a convenient outlet for articles on our history. The International Society for the History of the Behavioral and Social Sciences, established in 1969, holds meetings that increase yearly in size and excitement.

Even some nonpsychologists are becoming interested in the history of psychology. For example, Michael Sokal is a historian who specializes in the history of psychology. He has written about one of our leading early American psychologists, James McKeen Cattell, after finding a treasure trove of historical papers in the Cattell chicken house (1971).

Other scientists also regard the study of the history of their discipline as important. Beveridge, who happens to be a physicist, says:

> In recent years more and more attention is being given to the study of the history of science and every scientist ought to have at least some knowledge of this subject. It provides an excellent corrective to ever-increasing specialization and broadens one's outlook and understanding of science. There are books which treat the subject not as a mere chronicle of events but with an insight which gives an appreciation of the growth of knowledge as an evolutionary process. There is a vast literature dealing with the philosophy of science and the logic of scientific method. Whether one takes up this study depends upon one's personal inclinations, but, generally speaking, it will be of little help in doing research. (1957, pp. 11–12)

Beveridge thus sees the history of science as one discipline (a useful one) and the philosophy of science as another (interesting, maybe, but not very useful). However, many exciting and unexpected things have happened since Beveridge expressed his opinion on these subjects. It now appears that these two subjects can hardly be studied separately, and a study of the history of science has changed many people's opinions of how science proceeds. It is beginning to look like a study of the history of science is as valuable for the philosopher of science as Beveridge thought it was for the scientist.

HOW SHOULD THE PRACTICE OF SCIENCE BE VIEWED?

In 1962 Thomas Kuhn published a book, *The structure of scientific revolutions,* which affected historians and philosophers of science in about the same way that whacking on their nests with a stick affects hornets. Kuhn claimed to be reporting what science was like, and that he had found out by studying the history of science. What was this picture of science which was so remarkable, so upsetting, and so long concealed right under everyone's nose?

Kuhn's most central concept was the *paradigm.* He meant a lot of things by paradigm; Margaret Masterman (1970) found that he had used the term in no fewer than twenty-one ways in his book! Although Kuhn (1970) later made his definition of paradigm more limited and more precise, we will stick to his earlier conceptualization. It is more inclusive, richer, and more relevant for our uses in setting up a framework for studying the history of psychology. A paradigm in Kuhn's inclusive sense involved nearly everything necessary for doing science, all the way from a particular set of metaphysical assumptions "at the top" through particular theories of the subject matter, including very especially particular examples of solved problems (paradigmatic examples), to commitments to apparatus and experimental procedures "at the bottom."

A paradigm is clearly a very large order. But Kuhn demanded even more of his paradigms; the accomplishments of the paradigm had to be impressive enough to attract the allegiance of essentially all of the practitioners of that branch of science. In order to do that, the problems the paradigm had solved had to be convincing examples of the power of the paradigm. Procedures would have to be precise and clearly communicated. The predictions of the paradigm would have to be clear and unequivocal.

Such a paradigm would be very useful indeed. It would tell the scientist what problems were worth studying and how they should be studied. A host of research projects would be at the fingertips of every exponent of the paradigm, for no paradigm provides solutions for every problem of interest. As Kuhn says, the paradigm presents puzzles, much like the crossword puzzles found in newspapers and elsewhere, and the paradigm, like the creator of the crossword puzzle, "guarantees" that the puzzle has a solution. The scientist, however, receives a larger reward when a puzzle is solved, receiving a Ph.D., which may lead to a job, or publishing, which may be instrumental in securing the job. If the puzzle is regarded as a particularly important one, the rewards may be a raise or tenure.

Understandably, a paradigm may come to be regarded with some fondness by its beneficiaries. Textbooks and histories will come to rationalize and glorify the paradigm, albeit unintentionally. After all, history must concentrate upon those developments which led to our current "correct" view, mustn't it? And who cares about those false starts? Textbooks also have a duty to summarize current knowledge efficiently, and again there seems to be little point in reporting inferior alternative views.

Given this background, it is not surprising that those nurtured within the paradigm come to accept it without bothering much about the preconceptions involved, to accept it, so to speak, unconsciously. Neither is it surprising that the paradigm would not be given up easily; when occasional findings do not accord with the expectations demanded by the paradigm, they are easily shrugged off as experimental errors, mistakes in observation, or, as a last resort, unimportant exceptions not affecting the essential correctness of the paradigm.

So long as a paradigm is accepted and scientists can work in this comfortable "puzzle-solving" way, Kuhn says that science is in what he calls a "normal" period. Unfortunately for exponents of the easy life, the paradigm contains the seeds of its own destruction. Those seeds are nurtured by the necessary precision of the paradigm. On the one hand, the precision is an absolutely necessary feature, because imprecise and nonpredictive statements are not attractive to scientists. On the other hand, no body of scientific theory and practice has ever been so perfect that it never makes mistakes in prediction. These unexpected outcomes, which Kuhn calls "anomalies," eventually become so frequent and so obvious that, despite powerful resistance, they intrude upon the consciousnesses of the practitioners of the paradigm. At this point, the paradigm goes into a "crisis" phase. During the crisis, the practitioners will be trying desperately to patch up the old paradigm, and perhaps still to deny the reality of the unwanted results. Other scientists, mostly either new to the science or from some other discipline, will begin to propose alternative paradigms.

Eventually one of the new paradigms will triumph by successfully solving some of the problems presented by the anomalies. It may not solve all of the problems, nor is it likely to be as well developed in the beginning as was the old paradigm. Nevertheless, because the old paradigm is no longer tenable, and the new is therefore more promising, the new one wins out. It does not necessarily do so by converting all of the exponents of the old paradigm; however, new people in the field will be attracted to the new paradigm, and the old scientists will, after all, die off.

Possible examples of alternative paradigms might be Ptolemaic astronomy—the old earth-centered view—which was replaced by Copernican astronomy, which places the sun at the center of the solar system. Another example might be Newtonian physics versus Einsteinian physics. In both cases there were great difficulties in the way of forcing the acceptance of the new paradigm, and only obvious anomalies, according to Kuhn's view, were sufficient to bring about the paradigm switch. These changes in the fundamental beliefs of a whole science constitute what Kuhn calls a scientific revolution, and give his book its title, *The structure of scientific revolutions.*

It can now be made clear why Kuhn's book brought about such a buzzing and humming among historians of science. The traditional view of science has always been that it was carried out at a perfectly objective level. The scientists were supposed to hold opinions very lightly, and abandon them at the first sign of error ("Oh, yes, ho hum, I see that your observations disconfirm my theory, I suppose I shall have to construct a new one"). Anyone familiar with the acrimonious controversies between scientists would recognize the preceding quotation as a humorous parody of the actual behavior of scientists. Yet somehow few before Kuhn had quite realized how subjective and conservative our procedures were. Although there is still great controversy about how important this subjectivity is, one of the greatest proponents of the earlier, more idealistic view, Karl Popper (1970), has said that Kuhn made him realize that something like Kuhn's normal science played a much larger role than he had previously suspected.

Kuhn's picture of science also has other fundamental results. Most important, he sees great difficulty in defining and justifying scientific progress. It is not usually clear that a new paradigm is superior to the one that it replaces. The problems attacked and the natures of the solutions are likely to be so different that it is not easy to compare paradigms on the dimension of "goodness." The world is simply seen *differently,* not *better.*

Later, in Part Two of this book, we will return to the humming historians and listen to the contents of their complaints about Kuhn. Although Kuhn seems to have pointed us much closer to the direction of the truth about the nature of the scientific quest, many of the complaints about him seem to be justified, and we will want to construct the most accurate possible view of the scientific enterprise before embarking on the study of modern psychology. However, the material in Kuhn's book gives us all the background we need for establishing a set of questions to ask about psychology's traditional schools.

We have already seen that Kuhn sees science as proceeding through two phases: *normal* and *revolutionary* science. In this analysis the period of crisis is regarded as a mere transition between the normal and revolutionary phases. There is, however, another genuinely different kind of science: *preparadigmatic science.* For Kuhn, preparadigmatic science was a kind of fumbling activity, in which the practitioners of the science were searching for a way of approaching their problems, of formulating their problems, even of identifying their problems. This preparadigmatic period is therefore predictably marred by disagreements about every aspect of the fundamentals of scientific activity. This is a period of schools, during which each school claims to have the light and the way, and during which no school can produce the evidence required to convince others of the correctness of its claim.

Kuhn believes that the social and behavioral sciences are in this preparadigmatic period. It is always difficult to achieve sufficient perspective to say precisely where one *is;* but it is pretty easy to see that Kuhn is correct about where psychology *was.*

WATSON'S PRESCRIPTIVE SYSTEM

It isn't easy to accept it when someone says, "Look what I've got that you haven't got." The nicest response to "Look at my new bicycle" is being able to say "I've had a new one too, all along, hidden in the back room for this occasion." Unfortunately, that seldom happens; and when Kuhn pointed out that the more developed sciences had paradigms, and psychology didn't, the fact was difficult to deny. However, thanks to Watson, we can now at least say that we are guided by something, and that even paradigmatic sciences still share some of our problems.

Watson accepted Kuhn's judgment that the social and behavioral sciences had not yet developed a sufficiently successful, precise, and unified set of beliefs, theories, and practices to justify the application of the name of paradigm. He then asked himself how we have kept from flying off in all directions, indulging in random and fruitless activity. Psychology admittedly has had plenty of controversy, plenty of flaws and false starts, but we nevertheless seem to have made progress of a sort, and to have some idea of what we're doing. How, in the absence of a paradigm, can that be?

Watson's answer is that our efforts are given direction by a set of persisting questions which are seen as important by all, or at least by most, psychologists. Watson, like Kuhn, arrived at his position after an intensive study of the history of his discipline. He identified eighteen questions which could be expressed as dimensions, with extreme opinions about each question represented as the polar extremes of the dimension, and intermediate opinions represented as intermediate positions on the dimension. The list of dimensions is given in Table 1-1, as taken from Watson (1967, pp. 436–437).

These prescriptions are not something to be assimilated in a moment, but the

Table 1-1 The Prescriptions of Psychology Arranged in Contrasting Pairs

Conscious mentalism—unconscious mentalism (emphasis on awareness of mental structure or activity-unawareness)

Contentual objectivism—contentual subjectivism (psychological data viewed as behavior of individual—as mental structure or activity of individual)

Determinism—indeterminism (human events completely explicable in terms of antecedents—not completely so explicable)

Empiricism—rationalism (major, if not exclusive source of knowledge is experience—is reason)

Functionalism—structuralism (psychological categories are activities—are contents)

Inductivism—deductivism (investigations begun with facts or observations—with assumed established truths)

Mechanism—vitalism (activities of living beings completely explicable by physiochemical constituents—not so explicable)

Methodological objectivism—methodological subjectivism (use of methods open to verification by another competent observer—not so open)

Molecularism—molarism (psychological data most aptly described in terms of relatively small units—relatively large units)

Monism—dualism (fundamental principle or entity in universe is of one kind—is of two kinds, mind and matter)

Naturalism—supernaturalism (nature requires for its operations and explanation only principles found within it—requires transcendent guidance as well)

Nomotheticism—idiographicism (emphasis upon discovering general laws—upon explaining particular events or individuals)

Peripheralism—centralism (stress upon psychological events taking place at periphery of body—within the body)

Purism—utilitarianism (seeking of knowledge for its own sake—for its usefulness in other activities)

Quantitativism—qualitativism (stress upon knowledge which is countable or measurable—upon that which is different in kind or essence)

Rationalism—irrationalism (emphasis upon data supposed to follow dictates of good sense and intellect—intrusion or domination of emotive and conative factors upon intellectual processes)

Staticism—developmentalism (emphasis upon cross-sectional view—upon changes with time)

Staticism—dynamicism (emphasis upon enduring aspects—upon change and factors for making change)

reader can continue to refer back to this table whenever necessary. All the words describing poles of the prescriptions are defined in the glossary. We will apply each dimension to the analysis of the first psychological school to be discussed, associationism, in Chapter 3. We believe Watson has provided a very useful tool for the student of the history of psychology; without an organizing framework, the facts of history sometimes seem to evaporate into a mist of unrelated details.

These prescriptions have a more philosophical tone than one might expect given the fact that they were conceived as replacements for the paradigms of more mature sciences. However, one must remember that psychology was born out of philosophy, and our problems continue to have a philosophical flavor. Accordingly, Watson went back to the philosophers of the seventeenth century to see if he could find in their work the origins of the problems he had identified in a study of the psychology of 1965.

He had considerable success in identifying very similar problems in the dim prehistory of our science. That is excellent for our purposes, for it means that we are likely to succeed in using these problems for the purpose of organizing our historical study, although we will scarcely have time to dwell on the seventeenth century; the nineteenth and twentieth centuries have so bustled with history that we can afford but a moment to pull aside the curtains on the seventeenth and eighteenth for a glimpse of their more fascinating features.

Are Watson's prescriptions all there is to the historical story? Of course not. Watson would be the first to deny that they are. There is always an element of arbitrariness in any such list, and Watson must have wondered whether he should add still other dimensions. A favorite candidate of ours would be a dimension labeled "People are inherently evil—People are inherently good" with a parenthetical explanation like "people suffer from original sin, or are innately hostile and aggressive—people are noble savages perverted by society." Certainly one could trace disagreements on this question from biblical times to this moment, with psychology contributing at least its fair share to the controversy. Readers are free to suggest their own favorite dimension, or a whole new set. Nevertheless, Watson's list represents a thoughtful and useful analysis. It serves to direct our attention to some of the enduring and important issues with which psychology has been concerned.

One very interesting thing that can be done with Watson's prescriptions is to use them as a sort of personality profile to describe individuals and schools that are important in the history of psychology. Your own "psychological personality profile" can be obtained by making a list numbered from 1 through 18, corresponding to Watson's eighteen prescriptive dimensions. Think of each of Watson's dimensions as a range from 1 to 5. For example, in the case of Watson's first dimension, the belief that the only thing psychologically important is the mental structure or activity of which a person is consciously aware would be represented by a 1; if, by way of contrast, you believed that unconscious processes were important, and awareness completely insignificant, you would write a 5 by the number for the first dimension. Intermediate opinions on this dimension, and every other dimension, would be represented by intermediate numbers. This is a very worthwhile exercise for any psychologist to do, since it both familiarizes one with Watson's prescriptions and makes one aware of one's own beliefs—sometimes in surprising ways!

It is more difficult and more problematic to rate the opinions of schools on these dimensions than to rate the opinions of individuals. One individual presumably has only one opinion, although it may be hard enough to decide exactly

Table 1-2 Mean Judgments of the Positions of Six Psychological Systems on Each of Watson's Eighteen Prescriptive Dimensions

	Mean ratings					
Watson's dimensions	**Associationism**	**Structuralism**	**Functionalism**	**Behaviorism**	**Gestalt theory**	**Psychoanalysis**
Mentalism: conscious versus unconscious	2.2	1.2	2.5	4.4	2.3	4.8
Content: objective versus subjective	3.2	4.9	2.1	1.1	3.8	4.2
Determinism–indeterminism	1.3	2.2	2.2	1.1	2.2	1.1
Empiricism–rationalism	1.1	1.7	2.2	1.3	3.2	3.6
Functionalism–structuralism	2.4	4.8	1.1	1.5	3.7	3.1
Inductivism–deductivism	1.5	3.2	1.9	1.7	4.1	4.3
Mechanism–vitalism	1.4	2.0	3.0	1.1	2.9	2.3
Methods: objectivism versus subjectivism	1.9	5.0	2.0	1.1	3.7	4.6
Molecularism–molarism	1.2	1.6	3.2	1.3	4.8	3.3
Monism–dualism	3.3	4.6	4.1	1.1	4.1	4.2
Naturalism–supernaturalism	2.3	1.6	1.4	1.1	2.4	1.9
Nomotheticism–idiographicism	1.3	1.2	2.9	1.0	4.1	3.1
Peripheralism–centralism	2.5	4.4	2.2	1.1	4.7	4.6
Purism–utilitarianism	1.6	1.1	4.9	3.2	2.2	4.6
Quantitativism–qualitativism	1.9	3.2	2.1	1.6	4.7	4.6
Rationalism–irrationalism	1.9	2.0	3.1	4.0	2.8	4.8
Staticism–developmentalism	3.1	1.3	4.1	2.8	2.3	3.6
Staticism–dynamicism	2.6	1.4	4.6	2.6	4.2	4.6

what it is, even when the individual is oneself. When the individual is someone else, known only through writings, it is much more difficult; when one tries to rate a whole school made up of many individuals with varying opinions, one should not take the results too seriously!

Despite these difficulties, Kawash and Fuchs (1974) have asked a number of people who know something about the history of psychology to make such judgments, and have factor-analyzed the results in an attempt to see how Watson's dimensions are interrelated. The present authors will not take themselves so seriously; however, for the sake of our own amusement and that of the reader, we have rated six classical schools of psychology on each of Watson's dimensions. The results are presented in Table 1-2. This table, like the previous one, is not for immediate assimilation; rather, it can be referred to after reading about each of the schools.

SCHOOLS AND SYSTEMS OF PSYCHOLOGY

"So," one might ask, "you have admitted that there is more to psychology than Watson's set of prescriptions. What is that something else?"

Even Kuhn, who denied us paradigms, said that preparadigmatic sciences were guided by something like a paradigm, although he didn't go on to say what it was. That "something like a paradigm" has typically been called a *school* of psychology (if we were paying attention to a group of associated psychologists) or a *system* of psychology (if we were paying attention to a group of ideas that were associated into a coherent opinion about psychology). These schools or systems were, therefore, very like Kuhn's paradigms in that each one furnished the necessary principles for directing the psychologist's study of the subject matter and efforts in a way that would efficiently further knowledge.

Such a school would therefore need to provide statements about what the subject matter in question is or ought to be. Decisions about the subject matter would be related to positions on more philosophical issues, like those making up Watson's prescriptions (look, for example, at Watson's second prescription). The psychologist would also need to be told how the subject matter should be studied. What organisms will be useful in revealing general principles? What general and specific methods will help to uncover their secrets? Should these methods be applied in laboratory or field? What sort of equipment is necessary? And so it goes through a host of questions and answers. They range, just as in the case of the paradigm, all the way from the most metaphysical issues right down to the most mundane questions about preferred types of experimental design and the best place to obtain healthy rats for experimentation.

The directive statements of schools are not so overtly stated as we may have implied above. The process of acculturation into psychology, as into the general culture, is far more subtle and more unconscious. Seldom, if ever, is the student told, "I, your teacher, am a functionalist, and I'm going to try to see that you're one too." The exception to this rule is, of course, psychoanalysis, a school of thought into which one is very explicitly indoctrinated. Usually, the student simply observes how things are done, and much of the training involves imitation during a sort of apprenticeship. After training, most members of the profession simply think of themselves as psychologists, and not as members of a particular school. We may even feel that psychology is becoming too mature and eclectic to have schools any more.

If this has happened, it has probably been quite recently. Krantz (1972) marshaled some evidence indicating that operant psychologists—most of us would probably call them Skinnerian psychologists—form a school. For one thing, the *Journal of the Experimental Analysis of Behavior* cites itself, rather than some other source, quite often. That is some evidence, which Krantz admits is rather weak, that operant psychology is somewhat isolated from other kinds of psychology. It may be more significant that Krantz and nearly everyone else in psychology already knew that "*JEAB* is the operant journal." It is certainly clear that operant psychology has many of the properties to be expected of a school, or even of a paradigm. It includes law, application, instrumentation, a kind of theory, a general philosophy—it has even solved problems! It also presents additional problems and hence stimulates research, to an extent that should warm Kuhn's heart.

In Part Two of this book, we will return to contemporary psychology. Meanwhile, we will be taking a look at six classical systems of psychology, each of which had its own ideas about how psychology ought to proceed. We can phrase the central contentions of each of these systems in a way which makes the directive function of each of them obvious.

Associationism The psychologist should study the principles of association of ideas (or of words or stimulus-response connections), analyzing complex events into simpler ones as the most direct road to understanding.

Structuralism The psychologist ought to study the contents of consciousness through the method of experimental introspection, searching always for the irreducible elements of which consciousness is made.

Functionalism Psychology must be concerned primarily with the functions of mind and behavior in adapting the organism to the environment.

Behaviorism The psychologist must study the behavior of the organism through strictly objective methods; consciousness cannot be part of the data of psychology.

Gestalt The psychologist can arrive at useful and meaningful formulations only through the study of significant wholes; premature analysis is disastrous.

Psychoanalysis The core of psychology is motivation, much of it unconscious and sexual, and must be studied through its manifestations in dreams, errors, symptoms, and free association.

In every school of psychology, classical or contemporary, there is a continuing interplay between the systematic philosophical "prescriptive" content of the school and the empirical findings encountered as the directive policies of the school are followed. Sometimes the findings even precede and give rise to the policies, rather than the other way around. Gestalt psychology, for example, only became a "school" after the results of some experiments on apparent movement had been interpreted in a unique way by its founders. Empirical, theoretical, methodological, and philosophical statements tend to become interrelated (or perhaps just confused), so that the amalgam becomes "the system." This process seems to be precisely analogous in this respect to what Kuhn meant in his inclusive early view of paradigms.

So far, we have put more stress on the similarities between the classical systems of psychology and Kuhn's paradigms than we have on the differences. To prevent giving a distorted view, we ought now to look more closely at the hierarchy of commitments, from the most abstract at the top to the most concrete at the bottom, and see where paradigm-system differences are most likely to be found.

At the top, we find very general presuppositions in both cases, and in both cases these may be difficult or impossible to prove. Some of the presuppositions may even be common to physics and psychology; for example, scientists in both disciplines would be likely to believe that the universe is governed by laws that are humanly knowable, and that these knowable laws are constant as we change places or as time passes. This kind of presupposition is particularly likely to remain unconscious because it seems so appealing and so necessary to all scientific work. Such propositions in such cases would be called *metaphysical* because they could not be directly confirmed through any physical observations, and they certainly would be called *metatheoretical* because such presuppositions lie above the theories of any particular subject matter. Every discipline presumably would accept such presuppositions, and more mature disciplines with paradigms would not differ fundamentally from less mature disciplines in the nature of their presuppositions.

At a slightly lower level of abstraction one finds a set of presuppositions tailored to a particular subject matter, but still at too high a level of abstraction to be part of any theory of the subject matter. Watson's prescriptions, or the positions taken with respect to them, would serve as possible examples of this level. Again, the more mature sciences need and use similar presuppositions, and paradigms and systems should not differ drastically in the "goodness" of their metatheoretical assumptions.

It is at the theoretical level that we find the big difference. Mature sciences have theories specific and predictive enough so that both impressive successes and impressive failures (anomalies) can occur. Without such theories, neither normal science nor crises can occur. In less developed sciences, the theories are usually not precise enough to be disprovable; hence they can't be right in any significant way either.

Systems do *not* lack data. Paradigms organize data better, and more developed sciences may collect more reliable data. However, the differences at this most concrete level are not nearly as dramatic as those at the level of theory. We therefore conclude that systems and paradigms differ primarily in that the former lack the unifying force of strong, precise, well-developed theories.

ORIENTING ATTITUDES TOWARD THE STUDY OF HISTORY

Historians have been around for a long time; Thucydides was a very famous Athenian historian who worked in the fifth century B.C. We'd expect, therefore, that a lot of historians before Kuhn and Watson would have evolved ideas about how they should approach their subject matter, and about the things that are important in determining the direction of historical change.

One important distinction has been that between the *historicist* and *presentist* approaches. The historicist is interested in understanding each period in its own terms, applying only concepts, beliefs, attitudes, and possibilities that were available at that time. The interest of the presentist, obviously, is in the present; presentists want to use a knowledge of history in order to understand the present. Historicists tend to imply that the presentist is naive, and likely to neglect important differences between past and present in making interpretations.

An extreme example is the joke about the tourist, recently returned from Greece, who was boasting about the fabulous old coin he had purchased for a song on the Athenian black market for antiquities; he had cleverly smuggled it out of the country right in his pants pocket along with his other change. "It's priceless," he bragged, "pure gold, and coined in 469 B.C.!" "How could you tell when it was coined?" asked his skeptical friend. "Easy," came the quick reply, "the date was right on it!"

Few of us are such presentists that we would fail to note that no Greek of the fifth century B.C. could know that Christ would be born 469 years later. Not all historical interpretations, however, are so easily kept straight; for example, someone might forget that Charles Darwin had some terrible problems with the theory of evolution because he was completely unaware of the genetic principles already discovered by Mendel. Other problems of historical scholarship can be far more difficult, particularly when a translator must be interposed between the original writer and the historian. A translator who is not a skilled historian could easily translate a word in such a way as to impute concepts to the writer that were not developed until many years later.

The present authors confess to presentism. The present is where our primary interests and skills lie; true historicism is too demanding. We will, however, do our best to avoid buying too much intellectual coin that is labeled "B.C." It can be argued that historicism has its own trap for the unwary; it is possible to be seduced into a sort of necrophiliac antiquarianism, to be buried so deeply in the dusty past that one loses sight of the present. The ideal historical scholar, it seems to us, accepts and interprets the past correctly, and on its own terms, both because the past has its own interest and charm and because it is only by understanding the past on its own terms that one has any hope of extracting wisdom that applies to the present. However, the ultimate use of historical knowledge lies in its present and future application. Thus the hope of presentists lies with historicism, and the uses of historicism lie in presentism.

E. G. Boring, one of psychology's greatest and most beloved figures, helped to perpetuate another distinction in his classic 1950 history textbook. *Zeitgeist* was perhaps Boring's favorite word; literally, it means "time spirit," or, to translate it into more meaningful English, "the spirit of the times." In making the historical connection, however, it became rich in connotation; it referred to a view of history which contrasted with the "great man" view. The *Zeitgeist* view might be compared to a Marxist historical determinism; that is, the spirit of the times decreed, so to speak, that a certain scientific advance would be made when the time was right. Great men (this view would say) seem to be responsible for great advances, but that is an appearance only. If one great man did not appear, another would step forward. Thus Newton and Leibniz both invented calculus independently at nearly the same time, and it matters little who is awarded the larger piece of the garland; more significantly, it would have mattered very little if neither of them had invented it, for then someone else would have done it at nearly the same time.

In contrast with this rather depressing view, the "great man" theory of history says that great men do matter, and that they are in fact responsible for scientific advance. An advocate of this view might say, "It may be true that an advance can only be made when the time is right, but everything you claim is based on the assumption that there are always plenty of great men! Surely Leibniz and Newton were to some extent interchangeable with respect to one particular finding; but take away Leibniz and Newton, and Darwin and Wallace, and Young and Helmholtz, and so on, and then you will see whether or not great men are important in the advancement of science!"

Boring calls the theory of those who emphasize the *Zeitgeist naturalistic,* as opposed to the *personalistic* theory of those who emphasize the great man. One can decline to take sides on this issue. We are realistic enough to recognize the importance of cultural and intellectual preparation in paving the way for any scientific advance; to that extent, we are naturalistic theorists. But great men are great fun, as well as being important in scientific progress. That is plenty of reason for rewarding them with recognition whenever they win their jousts with the dragons of ignorance.

Given this feeling, it becomes redundant to say that we appreciate and respect the people who have played a role in psychology's history. We agree with Boring when he says, "The Greeks were as intelligent as we—there is no evidence that two millennia of evolution have improved man in the dimension in respect of which he excels the great apes" (1950, p. 6). There is not even any evidence that our intelligence is greater than that of Cro-Magnon, whose brain was at least as large as ours. We owe *our* greater preeminence to Cro-Magnon's intelligence and to the achievements of human culture resulting from it, foremost among which is the development of science.

SUMMARY AND CONCLUSIONS

The history of psychology is attracting ever-increasing interest, even as the general culture is becoming fascinated with personal and political history. The history of psychology has recently achieved recognition as a legitimate field of study within psychology. At nearly the same time, the great significance of the study of history for the philosophy of science has been more widely appreciated, largely because of Kuhn's work and the responses to it. Kuhn's key concept is the paradigm, a concrete achievement including theory, law, instrumentation, and application, which unifies a scientific discipline around agreed-upon fundamentals.

The specificity of a paradigm is such that researchable problems are suggested; normal science works out these paradigmatic puzzles. In this process, it is certain that inexplicable observations (anomalies) will occur, forcing a period of crisis for the paradigm. Science then enters a revolutionary phase, and a new, more promising, paradigm will replace the old.

According to Kuhn, psychology and the social sciences have not matured sufficiently so that a unifying paradigm has been developed. Watson, an eminent psychological historian, agrees, but points out that psychology employs a set of guiding problems (which he labels "prescriptions") in a similar role, to suggest how the development of our science should proceed. These prescriptions are prominent concerns of the various schools, or systems, of psychology. They can therefore be used as a framework for comparing the intellectual commitments of the various classical systems of psychology, as well as for understanding our own positions with respect to these earlier systems.

Systems of psychology are like paradigms in that they include a whole range of commitments, from very abstract "world views" to very concrete decisions about the best way to perform experiments, with what instruments. Systems are unlike paradigms in that they have not yet managed to achieve a synthesis of their components in impressive concrete results.

We can approach the study of the history of psychology more efficiently by keeping the conclusions of Kuhn and of Watson in mind. We should also remember the historicistic-presentistic distinction to remind ourselves that history must be understood on its own terms in order that it be applicable to the present; and the naturalistic-personalistic distinction, to remind ourselves that great men—past and present—operate in a context provided by the men, great *and* small, who preceded them.

FURTHER READINGS

Kuhn's *The structure of scientific revolutions* (1962, 1970) is so central to understanding what modern philosophers of science are talking about that everyone should read it. In addition, Kuhn writes so clearly and entertainingly that he provides no excuse for *not* reading him. Watson's *Psychology: A prescriptive science* (1967) provides a full explanation of the relationship of his prescriptions to Kuhn's thinking and to psychology. Hillix and Marx, in their *Systems and theories in psychology: A reader* (1974) reprint Watson's article and an article by Kuhn, "Historical structure of scientific discovery," along with other relevant readings. For those who are motivated enough to want both sides of several issues in the philosophy of science (Kuhn's side and Popper's side, roughly speaking), the more advanced book edited by Musgrave and Lakatos, *Criticism and the growth of knowledge* (1970), is truly excellent. Among other stimulating articles, it includes the one by Masterman, mentioned earlier, a superb anti-Kuhnian article by Lakatos, and a reply to his critics by Kuhn.

Chapter 2

The Emergence of Psychology

In Kuhn's view of science, we have seen three phases: preparadigmatic, normal science, and revolutionary. In our study of psychology, we will recognize three partially overlapping phases of development: a first phase, during which there was no separate discipline of psychology; a second phase which was clearly preparadigmatic in Kuhn's sense; and a third phase, beginning perhaps soon after the end of World War II, in which we believe there has been perceptible movement toward the achievement of at least a near-paradigm in some areas of psychology.

Our roots lie in the earliest period, and we must therefore begin our struggle to understand where we are by tracing the development of some ideas that seemed to be necessary in order that psychology emerge as an independent discipline. We will than outline some more specific, more concrete problems that both motivated and lent a particular form to the new science.

THE GROWTH OF SCIENTIFIC IDEAS

Table 2-1 presents, for ready reference, a summary of the contributions of some of the men who helped to develop the scientific ideas that led to a science of psychology. Ancient birth and death dates may be approximate; the historical record is sometimes incomplete. In addition, multiple calendar changes challenge

Table 2-1 Summary of Major Contributions to the Development of Psychology

Person	Approximate birth and death dates	Contribution
	Philosophy	
Thales	Sixth century B.C.	Naturalistic explanation; universe composed of water
Pythagoras	Sixth century B.C.	Mysticism and mathematics; Pythagorean theorem
Socrates	ca. 470–399 B.C.	Idealistic philosopher; deductive approach
Democritus	ca. 460–370 B.C.	Universe composed of atoms; reductionistic account of complex phenomena
Plato	427–347 B.C.	Rationalistic, dualistic approach
Aristotle	384–322 B.C.	Rationalistic and observational methods; classification systems for biology; laws of associative memory
Euclid	ca. 300 B.C.	Developer of geometry
Roger Bacon	ca. 1214–1294	Emphasis on free empirical observation
Francis Bacon	1561–1626	*Novum organum:* gave philosophical support to empirical science
Descartes	1596–1650	Dualistic interactionism; action of body is mechanistic
Locke	1632–1704	Opposed Descartes' innate ideas; used associationistic principles
Leibniz	1646–1716	Activity as basic; degrees of consciousness; coinventor of calculus
Berkeley	1685–1753	Experience as only source of knowledge; subjective idealism
La Mettrie	1709–1751	Mechanistic explanation applied to human behavior
Hume	1711–1776	Analysis of causality; origins of ideas of God and self in experience
Kant	1724–1804	Importance of native abilities in ordering the data of experience
	Science	
Hippocrates	ca. 460–380 B.C.	"Father of medicine"; an excellent observer; naturalistic view of the human being
Archimedes	ca. 287–212 B.C.	First well-known experimental physicist
Herophilus and Erasistratus	Third century B.C.	First inference of distinction between sensory and motor nerves
Ptolemy	Second century A.D.	Alexandrian astronomer; his view of earth as center of universe held for centuries
Galen	Second century A.D.	Famous physician and anatomist; performed animal experiments
Copernicus	1473–1543	Polish astronomer who placed sun at center of solar system, thus changing the view of the place of human beings in the universe
Vesalius	1514–1564	First thorough treatise on human anatomy
Galileo	1564–1642	Reestablished observation as final court of appeal; made astronomical and physical discoveries
Kepler	1571–1630	Mathematical description of planetary orbits

Table 2-1 *Continued*

Person	Approximate birth and death dates	Contribution
	Science	
Harvey	1578–1657	Demonstrated the circulation of the blood
Van Leeuwenhoek	1632–1723	First effective microscope; discoverer or identifier of protozoa, bacteria, and human sperm
Newton	1642–1727	Coinventor of calculus; set pattern of physics for 200 years
Linnaeus	1707–1778	Binomial system of biological classification
Bessel	1784–1846	Astronomer at Königsberg; worked out personal equations and thus posed a problem for psychology
Weber	1795–1878	Pioneer physiologist; formulated "Weber's law"
J. Mueller	1801–1858	Comprehensive handbook of physiology; doctrine of specific energies of nerves
Fechner	1801–1887	His *Elemente der Psychophysik* believed by some to mark beginning of experimental psychology; modified Weber's law
Darwin	1809–1882	*The origin of species:* primary publication on evolution
Bernard	1813–1878	Concept of the internal environment
Helmholtz	1821–1894	Eminent physiologist; first experimental measurement of speed of nerve impulse; theories of hearing and seeing
Galton	1822–1911	Work in eugenics, statistics, individual differences; set many problems for psychology
Wundt	1832–1920	Founder of first psychological laboratory at University of Leipzig (1879)

the scholar who would like to fix a precise date for ancient events. Some of the contributions of the persons in the table will be discussed at length, but it is helpful, meanwhile, if the reader gets some chronological perspective before examining the key concepts.

Many historians have noted the apparently stepwise progress of the sciences, beginning with those farthest from humans and moving toward those closest to them and their immediate affairs, and the consequent late development of the science of psychology. Astronomy and physics were the first sciences to develop. Archimedes, in the third century B.C., was in some ways a sophisticated physicist. In the early seventeenth century, Kepler's mathematical description of the motions of the planets around the sun was the culmination of a long line of astronomical discoveries. The human body was investigated long before there was a science for the human "mind." Harvey, in 1628, described the circulation of the blood, about 250 years before Ebbinghaus did his pioneer work on memory.

Several reasons have been suggested for this long scientific neglect of human behavior. One is the sanctity of humans as maintained by human institutions, which hindered seeing a person as a natural phenomenon. Another is the complexity of human beings, as proclaimed by most of those who have tried to study them scientifically. A third may be that it is often easiest to be objective about the things that concern us least, and we concern ourselves very much. Finally, it is easy to think that, by virtue of being human ourselves, we already know about all we need to know about people. After all, hasn't everyone read those who know humanity, from Shakespeare to Schulz, in whose comic strip Lucy offers psychiatric help for a price? Thus in saying that the study of people has been neglected, we mean only that the scientific study of people as a formal discipline got a late start. Let us turn to some of the intellectual preparation for that discipline.

Explanation: External and Internal

There was a time in human history when events were typically explained in terms of forces outside the scope of observable natural events. For example, Norse mythology explained storms by saying that the warrior of the gods was angry, and Homer explained victory in war in terms of the favoritism of the Greek gods. From the scientific point of view, there are two very basic things wrong with these explanations: (1) They refer the explanation to unobservables, and (2) the events used as explanations do not fit within the same context as the events to be explained; there is thus no apparent logical connection between the alleged causes and their consequences. Such explanations are therefore called *external,* as opposed to *internal.*

It is not always easy to tell whether a particular explanation is internal. The extremes are easy: theological explanations of natural events are clearly external, and accepted scientific accounts are usually internal. Paradoxically, some of the most sophisticated scientific explanations are the most difficult ones to classify. These sophisticated explanations often depend on postulated but initially unobserved entities like genes, stimulus elements, or charmed quarks. Most scientists accept explanations couched in terms of such concepts as internal because they or their effects are potentially observable, are "observed" indirectly, or have implications for observations at another level. Questions arise, however, if it is not clear that the concept is formulated so that it is potentially observable, if the supposed indirect observation can be accounted for in other ways, or if the implications from the deductive system containing the concept are not clear.

Although there are still people who explain disasters in terms of "the wrath of God," scientific explanation does not have recourse to such descriptions. Thales, a Greek philosopher of the sixth century B.C., is sometimes given credit for initiating attempts to explain natural events in terms of other natural events; he explained the nature of matter in terms of a single basic *natural* element, water. Democritus soon after explained matter in terms of basic particles called *atoms,* and modern science still holds to a similar conception. Whether these men really deserve credit for the swing toward internal explanation, however, is not important; the important thing is that science as we know it depends on the use of explanations which refer to observables within the same natural framework as the observables to be explained.

The Greek culture that developed this idea eventually disappeared. The idealistic skepticism of Socrates and Plato, ingenious as it was, may have contributed to its disappearance. The ensuing Middle Ages showed little concern for internal types of explanations or for scientific problems; perhaps the attitude was that great interest in natural events was bad for the soul. Such science as there was during the medieval period was largely in the East. It remained for the Renaissance, beginning (by the most common convention) with Galileo and his contemporaries, to renew European interest in natural science. An example of the external thinking that was predominant in the Middle Ages is the typical treatment of convulsions by flogging: such action was thought to drive out of the body the demons or evil spirits that were considered to be responsible for convulsive behavior. Today, of course, such treatment is not used because convulsive behavior is generally viewed as determined by organic conditions within the body (an internal explanation). Convulsive electroshock is used in the treatment of psychosis with explanations of its effectiveness which are hardly more satisfying than evil spirits; however, we are *seeking* an internal explanation.

In denigrating external explanations, we are not assuming that the implications of the explanation *necessarily* lead to ineffective treatments. People are frequently "right for the wrong reasons." For example, modern work demonstrates that punishment may serve a purpose in eliminating undesirable behaviors. That would lead us to believe that a medieval treatment, flogging, administered every time an "evil spirit" was seen affecting someone's behavior, might lead to the apparent elimination of the presumed spirit. Watson (1963) gives an interesting case in which a more correct conclusion followed from a kind of evidence we would find altogether unacceptable, while an inferior conclusion about the same issue was derived from an attempt at "internal" explanation, based on observational evidence. Watson says of Aristotle's views:

> In identifying life with the *psyche* and this, in turn, with the heart, he also rejects the Platonic doctrine of the brain as the organ of the soul. He used as one argument for doing so the fact that he found the brain to be insensible to direct stimulation. It is ironical that Plato was right for the wrong reasons. Plato assigned reason to the brain on the basis of several irrelevant reasons typical of which is the fact that the brain was the part of man nearest the heavens. Aristotle, on the other hand, was wrong for the "right," *i.e.,* naturalistic reasons. (1963, p. 52)

If some right decisions follow from the wrong theories, the theories have a greater life expectancy than if all decisions turn out badly. Phrenologists recommended practicing algebra for those who had an inadequate bump in the area responsible, according to their system, for algebraic proficiency. If this "treatment" both followed from the theory and produced algebraic ability, the theory could be regarded as "confirmed;" as a matter of fact, it did take phrenology a long time to disappear.

Such examples bring home the fact that observations cannot logically confirm theories; they can only disconfirm them. In scientific practice, theories are seldom rejected because of a single disconfirmation. They can almost always be saved by finding a flaw in the observation or in the relationship between the observation and the theory. Even if these modes of rescue fail, most theories are complex enough so that a change in a part will bring the theory into line with the observation, and the bulk of the theory can be saved.

On the confirming side, too, the dictates of pure logic are not followed. The logician knows that affirming the consequent, *B,* in a statement of the form "If *A,* then *B*" does nothing toward proving that the antecedent, *A,* is true. Yet if an observation occurs as a theory says it should, confidence in the usefulness of the theory increases, despite the illogic of the increase in confidence. Certainly the illogic is not *altogether* unreasonable; the theory, after all, *has* been demonstrated to be "right" with respect to the observation.

Reliance on Observation

Parallel with the use of internal explanation was an increasing reliance on observation. Most of the earlier Greek thinkers relied more on rationalistic methods than is the case in the modern era. For example, Euclid early developed a deductive geometry, and Pythagoras and his followers had a mystic belief in the efficacy of numbers. Socrates and Plato lent support to a rationalistic approach, Socrates with his logical questioning procedure and Plato with his emphasis on the importance of the ideal world, which he regarded as above and beyond the real world. Both tended to suspect the evidence of the senses as the source of truth and thus helped to turn the tide against what is now regarded as an essential feature of scientific method—a primary reliance on observation.

Aristotle was one early thinker who used observational as well as rational methods. He was an advocate of logic and reasonableness, but did not respect authority. His own authority, however, was accepted during the Middle Ages at the expense of observational methods. Galileo was important in renewing the scientific attitude toward observation and authority. He relied, for example, upon *observation* of the time of fall of bodies of unequal weight, rather than upon the authoritative statement that heavy bodies fall faster than light ones. This is not to say, however, that Galileo made no use of a rationalistic and deductive approach. Pure empiricists and pure rationalists are both as rare as golden fleeces, however hard empiricists or rationalists may try to push the powers of their own methods to their limits.

Francis Bacon, in his *Novum organum* of 1620, did make a powerful appeal for empiricism. He said that science should work strictly by induction, piling observation upon observation until general facts emerged from specific facts. From our objective vantage point, it is pretty clear that Bacon's extreme position was more useful as an antidote against too much rationalism than as a complete description of scientific procedure. Without the intervention of rational human beings, stubborn facts refuse to organize themselves into theories, laws, or even Bacon's "general facts."

The English empiricists who came after Bacon tried to follow his approach to its logical conclusion. Locke denied the innate ideas attributed to man by thinkers like Socrates and Descartes. Berkeley denied that we could be sure of the existence of the external world, since we have only experience to go on. Though he returned the external world to us only slightly used, with the help of the assumption of the existence of God, his skeptical position was more convincing than his retreat, and has been more influential. Finally, Hume applied empiricistic thinking to the notion of causality and maintained that all we really know is that some events are invariably contiguous in space and time. Our notion of causality is based on this observation. (But see Chapter 3 for a fuller discussion.)

Over in the quiet German university town of Königsberg, all this empiricism finally stirred up a tremendous philosophical counterattack. Immanuel Kant was, as he later said, awakened from his dogmatic slumbers by Hume's empiricism. As it turned out, he was stirred into action in time to become one of the greatest philosophers of all time. Although he never in his 80 years of life traveled more than a few miles from his native Königsberg, he embarked upon great voyages of the mind. He saw that the empiricists were right in their claim that knowledge could come only through experience; yet their picture was woefully inadequate in that the empiricists gave no explanation of how experience itself could be possible. Man's mind could not be the tabula rasa, the blank sheet, that the empiricists supposed it to be. There had to be organizing principles, or all would be confusion. Kant proposed a compromise type of theory in which experience remains the teacher, but needs a student who already has the ability to organize that experience. Kant's statements about what is given prior to experience—things like space, time, unity—are no longer very important. However, the problem he raised remains today. Psychologists like Piaget, who try to find out how the mind of the child develops, and the ethologists who try to discover how man and animal organize experience, and the physiological psychologists who try to find out what information is extracted by nerve nets—all of these are working on our modern version of the Kantian problem.

As we have said above, there is no such thing as a *purely* rationalistic or a *purely* empiricistic approach, nor is there a clear-cut line of demarcation between the two approaches. Francis Bacon, in his "discarding" of the rationalistic approach, had to use rationalistic methods in his arguments. The most empirically minded, "hardheaded" scientists eventually make general statements based on their observations—and hence depend on the rationalistic method. On the other hand, rationalistic philosophers very probably take the plausible assumptions with which they begin from some kind of empirical observation. The scientific usefulness of rationalistically derived conclusions depends on their consonance with observations. Though there is no pure approach and no clear method of classifying the techniques of particular individuals as more rationalistic or more empirical, we believe it is reasonable to say that science has tended to emphasize the empirical more than the rational. The final arbiter of truth for a scientist is not what rationally *ought to be* but what observationally *is.* Even that statement is a serious oversimplification, for there is never any final arbiter of truth, and there may be very serious questions about "what is." However, we must stop somewhere in our consideration of this question. It is clear that science relies heavily upon observation.

Simplification

Thales and Democritus tried to simplify the apparent complexity of nature by appealing to simpler elements and to assumptions which allowed them to derive the observed complexity from the assumed simplicity. Their attempts were also *reductionistic,* since they reduced complexity by explanations depending on the existence of phenomena at a different, "lower" level; for example, Democritus supposed humans to be built of particles much like those which compose other forms of matter. Physiological psychologists make similar reductionistic statements when behavioral data are explained in terms of physiological events, which again are at another level of observation. It does not follow that a reductionistic account will also necessarily be a simple account, or even the simplest available. Science seeks and accepts not only simple hypotheses but also the simplest overall theory which adequately explains all the observations made.

Reductionistic explanations offer at least a potential economy of concepts, since a single concept can serve at more than one level of explanation. These economies may serve as the basis for choice between otherwise equivalent theories. Turner says:

> When we turn to the idea of a hierarchy of explanation, we especially realize that there is a guidance implicit within scientific invention. One seeks not only an explanation of a particular set of events but also a theoretical construction that itself is derivable from within some still more basic science. Chemical explanations, for example, were conceived in terms wholly unique to the phenomenology of chemistry itself. But the advantages and the guidance of atomic constructions are now all too apparent. Geneticists could have continued to think in terms of the gross characteristics of genotypes, but the molecular model of biochemistry offered explanations of the duplicative powers of the genes. And psychology can continue to build hypothetico-deductive models in learning theory, knowing (perhaps unconsciously) that issues of alternative theories will be resolved by developments in neuropsychology. (1967, pp. 178–179)

In his later book (1971), Turner continues to favor reductionism but discusses the issues in much greater detail. For example, he considers various alternative routes that might be taken in a reductionistic program: linguistic reduction, mechanical reduction (through computer simulation), and neurological reduction. Despite all the heroic efforts at reductionism, there is probably still not a single case in which an interesting human behavior can be explained, using the concepts of neurophysiology. There seems to be little immediate danger that psychologists will be put out of business! We are not unique in this respect; there is no science which is, at this time, completely explained in the terms of a science which is more basic. However, reductionism still offers the possibility of simplification, and a quest for simplification typifies science.

The Place of Human Beings in Nature

The Greeks seem to have regarded human beings as having no special status apart from the rest of nature. Many of the Greek philosophers would probably have agreed that human behavior is lawful and predictable, just like the behavior of inanimate nature. The Middle Ages, however, took a different view. Human beings were regarded as creatures with a soul, possessed of a free will which set them apart from ordinary natural laws, subject only to their own willfulness and perhaps to the rule of God. Such a creature, being free-willed, could not be an object of scientific investigation.

Even the human body was regarded as sacrosanct. Anatomists had to double as grave robbers, and that made anatomy a highly risky—or very expensive—occupation. The strictures against observation slowed the development of anatomy and medicine for centuries, and allowed incredible misconceptions to persist for over a thousand years. A science of psychology could not flourish in such an atmosphere.

Today a concern for the rights of the living has superseded the superstitious fears connected with the bodies of the dead; and, strangely enough, these rights sometimes constitute almost as great an obstacle to research! No one who has experienced the emotional exchanges of recent years about the treatment of animal and human subjects will be tempted to believe that performance of research is no longer an issue. Related battles continue to rage over the issue of psychological testing. However, we are getting far ahead of our story. Our purpose was to show how a tolerance for research developed, not to demonstrate the contemporary relevance of this historical issue.

Descartes started a trend which favored psychological research. A predictable system is a researchable system. Descartes regarded the human body as a machine which will move and behave in predictable ways if we know what the "inputs" are. He salvaged free will by giving the human being a soul which was free and which decided the actions of the body. Such a view made at least dead (soulless) bodies accessible to scientific investigation; animals, since Descartes regarded them as soulless, were also accessible.

The idea that human beings might be objects of scientific study was furthered by La Mettrie. He was convinced, apparently largely by the deterioration of his own thought processes during a fever, that a person was *altogether* a machine, dependent in mind as in body upon physical events. He espoused this view, despite strong opposition, until his death.

The analogy of comparing a human being to a machine, to which Descartes and La Mettrie contributed, is a good example of the kind of partial analogy which starts persistent controversy. It is clear that human beings are not identical to any existing machine either in their construction or in their mode of operation. Descartes and La Mettrie, both brilliant thinkers, cannot be considered stupid enough to have overlooked this glaring fact. Neither can other mechanistic thinkers. All of them are supporting a limited likeness between the human being and a machine. Human beings construct machines and understand them fairly well; their behavior can be predicted. Human beings, although neither constructed nor understood by themselves, seem also to be creatures of their own construction, and should in principle be predictable like machines. Critics of the "mechanistic" position attack the complete, unintended analogy of the mechanist as often as the partial analogy intended.

There was still resistance to viewing humans within a deterministic, natural framework when Charles Darwin advanced his theory of organic evolution. Evolution itself was not a new idea, but Darwin buttressed the evolutionary theory with so much evidence that it took the scientific community by storm. It restored the continuity between humans and other animals which Descartes had denied when he attributed a soul to humans alone. It also contradicted the biblical account of creation. The theologically based opposition aroused a heated controversy which persisted into the twentieth century and was heard around the world. Today there is little questioning of the correctness of the general outlines of evolutionary theory. Evolution is a fact for the scientific community, if not for all the lay community. Its acceptance has made the science of psychology more acceptable by making it more plausible than ever to view human behavior as lawful. It has also made the study of animals an important part of that science; the assumed continuity between animals and humans supports the belief that knowledge gained in the study of animals will have significance for human behavior.

Let's take a moment to pass the first part of this chapter in review. We've seen that psychology developed late, perhaps because it is complex, but also because people have tended to see themselves as religious objects, to be subjective, and to think that they knew about humankind by virtue of being human. All science tended to develop around the ideas of internal explanation, reliance on observation, and simplification. As humans were placed in nature by virtue of being viewed as more deterministic and as more continuous with other animal forms, it became possible to apply the other scientific ideas to the study of humans as well, and most of the obstacles were cleared from the path that led to psychology. However, an absence of obstacles is not a science. There had to be reasons for starting a new kind of study. Those reasons were provided by the existence of a set of problems, to which we now turn.

PSYCHOLOGY'S LEGACY OF PROBLEMS

Psychology inherited most of its problems from philosophy and physiology; for that reason it is often said that philosophy was the mother of psychology and physiology the father, or vice versa, depending upon one's sexual preferences in this matter. Some of the problems passed on to psychology were of such a nature that no immediate scientific resolution was possible, but that's all right if the impossibility of the solution is not immediately clear. Research was stimulated as scientists tried to find the answers to these elusive questions. We shall consider four problem areas: The mind-body problem, the physiology of perception, the reaction-time problem, and questions related to individual differences.

The Mind-Body Problem

The ghostly apparitions of dreams may have been the convincing factor that there was more to human beings than met the physical eye. The writing of Plato shows that the thinking of his time divided humans into two components. Descartes's dualistic views did not differ greatly from Plato's. Both systems fit into the Christian theology; some unobservable component is necessary if human immortality is logically to be maintained, since the observable portions of human beings are mortal. Even today, the thinking of the lay public separates humans into two components.

If a person has both a mind and a body, then the question naturally arises: "What is the relationship between the two parts?" A long tradition of thought made the question inevitable. Before psychology ever had a formal beginning as a science, a German physicist, Theodor Fechner, started work on the problem. It was his intention to write equations that described the functional relationships between the psychic and the physical realms. The result which he believed he found is the Weber-Fechner law, so named because E. H. Weber had already expressed much the same psychophysical relationship in a simpler, more primitive form. Boring (1950, p. 483) has questioned whether Fechner really intended to take a dualistic position, but certainly his problem was stated in dualistic terms. For example, in his *Elemente der Psychophysik* (1860), Fechner said he was concerned with "the exact science of the functional relations or relations of dependency between body and mind." In order to demonstrate these functional relations, it is necessary to have two separate things to measure. Fechner thought he was measuring two different things. On the one side he had the stimulus which acted on the body. On the other side he had the sensation, which he thought of as a mental event. Fechner wished to demonstrate the identity of the two kinds of events, but it was difficult to reunite the two aspects that had been separated by assumption. He wanted to demonstrate empirically an identity that philosophers, using rationalistic methods, had been alternately proving and disproving for hundreds of years.

The major mind-body positions that have been taken by philosophers are classified and summarized in Table 2-2. Readers should familiarize themselves with the general outline presented here, for the "solutions" reappear in the following chapters. It would be wise to adopt a certain amount of skepticism about our classification; it is not always clear that the different positions are really different, or that we have made the correct decisions about where a given philosopher should be placed. For example, psychophysical parallelism is supposed to assume two separate underlying kinds of reality, while the double-aspect view is supposed to assume two "processes" which are both aspects of one underlying reality. But what if a philosopher is not certain whether the two processes are enough different to "prove" the existence of two kinds of reality? We have already admitted that Fechner's position is not clear. Further, another of psychology's historians, Sahakian (1975) says that Spinoza didn't assume two separate and independent realities. It's probably best to regard our scheme as a set of logical possibilities, into which individual solutions may fit with more or less forcing. The scheme is not even exhaustive; who said there were only *two* realities? What if there were material things, unconscious mind, and conscious mind, in all sorts of possible relationships? It might suit the fancy of some to add superconsciousness, or an immortal soul. Such positions, with more than two kinds of reality, would be called *pluralisms.* But the problem is bad enough as it is, so let's let sleeping dogmas lie.

There is, in any case, no known scientific method for deciding among the suggested solutions to the mind-body problem. Early psychologists nevertheless

Table 2-2 Major Philosophical Solutions to the Mind-Body Problem (An early important exponent of each position is identified in parentheses, with the approximate date of his contributions.)

	Dualism*
Cartesian interactionism (Descartes, 1641)	Two separate and interacting processes assumed
Psychophysical parallelism (Spinoza, 1665)	Two separate, independent, but perfectly correlated processes assumed
Occasionalism (Malebranche, 1675)	Two separate and independent processes assumed; correlated by the intervention of God
	Monism†
Materialism (Democritus, 400 B.C.)	A single underlying physical reality assumed
Subjective idealism (Berkeley, 1710)	A single underlying mental or spiritual reality assumed
Phenomenalism (Hume, 1740)	There are neither minds nor bodies as far as can be known; only ideas resulting from sense impressions exist
	Compromises
Double-aspect view (Russell, 1915)	Two processes assumed to be a function of one underlying reality
Epiphenomenalism (Hobbes, 1658)	Mind assumed to be a noncausal by-product of body

*Any point of view implying a basic difference between mind and body and therefore a relationship to be explained.
†Any point of view ignoring either mind or body or subsuming both under the same rubic.

felt it necessary to take some stand on the problem. Then for several decades it became fashionable to reject the problem as meaningless. Philosophers and psychologists alike repeatedly "proved" that the question was nonsensical in the first place. However, it is not easy to dismiss a question which has so titillated the curiosity of mankind for at least 25 centuries. We are seldom satisfied when someone answers our questions with, "That's a poor question; ask me another." Today, whether it is meaningless or meaningful, soluble or insoluble, the mind-body problem is coming back into the consciousness of psychologists. The word *mind,* which was virtually taboo between about 1920 and 1950 in many circles, has come back into the psychological vocabulary so much that it is almost a "buzz word." We shall return to the mind-body problem repeatedly in the later chapters; here let us merely remember that the problem was bequeathed to us in the beginning by our mother or father, philosophy.

The Psychology of Perception

Other scientists, notably physiologists, were interested in another relationship, that between physiological processes and perception. Hermann Ludwig Ferdinand von Helmholtz is the most famous of those interested in this relationship; he modified Thomas Young's color theory and developed his own theory of hearing. Helmholtz, along with the English empiricists, believed that all knowledge depends upon sense experience. If this is our assumption, then the problem of sense physiology is also the problem of epistemology—the problem of the origins, nature, and limitations of knowledge. Physiological findings in this area of study have philosophical implications. Helmholtz tried to refute Kant's statement that there is innate knowledge. Kant had believed that the axioms of geometry are known independently from any experience of them. Helmholtz asked whether we would have developed the same geometry if we had inhabited that inside surface of a hollow sphere. He discussed non-Euclidean geometries in a spirit which is surprisingly modern.

If the views of Helmholtz and Kant are viewed only in broad outline, however, the two differ less than they may have thought. Although Kant is categorized with nativists and Helmholtz with empiricists, Kant did admit the role of experience. Helmholtz recognized the need for some basic mental faculties to exist in order that the mind be able to develop the concept of space out of the raw materials of experience. There is, of course, a considerable difference in emphasis. Empiricists, by virtue of their philosophy, want to observe and thus want observable things to be as important as possible. The nativist tends to be a rationalist, and it is convenient for rationalists if the uncertain stuff of experience can be assigned as small a role as possible.

It is pretty easy to see the relationship between the philosophical questions of epistemology and the psychological and physiological problems of perception if we pretend that we are philosophers for a moment. We will then want to ask the question, "What kind of knowledge-gathering machine is a human being?" Or alternatively, "What information-gathering equipment does a human being have, and how does it work?" The answers to such questions had to come from a study of the special senses. As in the case of the mind-body problem, we are still seeking the answers, and some are finding fun and fortune in the quest.

The Reaction-Time Problem

The new science of psychology took over a second problem with epistemological implications. F. W. Bessel, an astronomer, was reading about an unfortunate incident which had occurred at Greenwich Observatory in 1796 (cf. Boring, 1950). An assistant's readings did not agree with the readings made by the head astronomer. It is easy to guess whose readings were assumed to be wrong! Maskelyne, the boss, fired Kinnebrook, the assistant.

Bessel recognized, some 20 years too late for justice to be served, that the incident might involve a mystery as well as a misfortune. Seeing a mystery lying under your nose is virtually the hallmark of the great scientist. Bessel saw that the error might have been caused by a difference in the time required for two different observers to react to information presented to different senses—for the readings were complex, and the observer had to coordinate a sound with the movement of a celestial body past a marker.

Bessel checked his hunch by comparing the times at which he recorded star transits with the times at which other astronomers under the same conditions recorded them. There were discrepancies in nearly all cases. Bessel then tried to write personal equations, or correction terms, which would reduce all the readings to a common basis. However, it was obvious that there could be no absolute standard of correctness where the human observer was concerned. Our knowledge was once again shown to depend upon observers and their methods of observing and recording. If the determination of the time at which a star crosses a line is subject to error, then it seems logical that more complex judgments and observations must be even more subject to error. It was not the philosophical point, however, that was important; it was the fact that the theoretical problems of epistemology were shown to be real, practical problems that stimulated Bessel and others after him to action.

It is easy to imagine the difference in urgency between the philosophers' general lament that one cannot be certain of anything, and the astronomers' panic because nobody's readings agreed with anyone else's!

Donders, a Dutch physiologist, and his students developed this general problem. They assumed that complex tasks were made up of a set of simpler components. Thus tasks became more complex as more and more components were required in order to perform them. If the simple operations were carried out one after another, the time for a complex task would be the sum of the times for the simpler operations of which it was composed. The times for a whole set of simple operations could be established by subtracting the times for simpler tasks from those for more complex tasks. For example, Donders asked subjects to respond as quickly as possible with a single stimulus to a single response. Then he asked them to perform a more complex task: to respond in one way to one stimulus, and in another way to a second stimulus. He assumed that the second task required the same operations as the first, plus the operation of "choice." Thus the time for choice could be obtained by subtracting the time for the simpler reaction from that for the just-more-complex reaction.

When Wundt established the first laboratory of psychology, he took over this subtractive procedure. Like Donders, he hoped to use a whole hierarchy of tasks varying in complexity, and thereby to discover the time required for mental operations like sensing, perceiving, discriminating, and the like. Although he sometimes differed from Donders in his beliefs about which operations were included in a complex task, he did not question the assumption that complex tasks are performed via a sequence of simple operations. Few psychologists would still hold this view; for example, it is not clear that perceiving involves sensing plus something else. The whole nature of the process may change as the task is progressively complicated, or "elementary" operations may be carried out in parallel. The subtractive procedure becomes, in either case, invalid.

Individual Differences

Two fields of study that have remained extremely important up to the present day are individual differences and statistics, which was initially taken over and developed by psychology as a method for studying these differences. Much of the American acceptance of psychology may be attributed to the effectiveness of aptitude testing, which is part of the study of individual differences.

Sir Francis Galton pioneered in the development of both statistics and the study of individual differences. He developed the technique of correlation in connection with his inheritance studies. He was led to it by the observation that children typically *regress* toward the mean relative to their parents in such characteristics as height and intelligence; that is, children of extremely tall or short, or bright or stupid, parents *tend* to be closer to the norm in these characteristics than their parents. Correlation is symbolized by *r* because of its development in association with the phenomenon of regression.

The major factor underlying the development of Galton's interests was the Darwinian theory of evolution. Galton, who was Darwin's cousin, was interested in a practical problem—the improvement of the race through eugenics. In order to practice genetic manipulation, he needed to know how traits were inherited. This type of practical concern was in the direct line of conceptual descent that led from evolution to American functionalism. Stress on the organism's adjustment to the environment as a determining condition of survival or nonsurvival became a primary concern of psychology. The intellectual ferment produced by the theory of evolution raised questions that led directly to Galton's interest in individual differences, mental testing and the statistical evaluation of differences, and to the flourishing school of functionalism in the United States.

The theory of evolution also had implications for people's view of the philosophical controversy between rationalism and empiricism. Previously, most rationalists had had to buttress their positions by postulating some kind of far-fetched preestablished harmony between the constitution of the world and the human being's ideas about it. How could it happen that people possess correct innate ideas about the world in which they live? It is not scientifically convincing to suggest that God gives ideas to humans. From the evolutionary point of view, however, it could be suggested that the rational (physiological?) side of the human being has been *pushed into harmony with the world* by the pressures of evolution. We can, according to this argument, count on the outcomes of rational analysis because humans, through evolution, have come to think the right things about the world. People who were mistaken about the world presumably took the wrong course of action and died. Those who were "rational" survived. Evolution solidifies the effects of the world on humans into a kind of physiological rationalism.

PSYCHOLOGY'S INITIAL SUBJECT MATTER

In Chapter 4 we will give a full account of the kind of psychology developed by Wilhelm Wundt, the first "pure" psychologist, and his students. However, this is a good time to relate Wundt's psychology to the prepsychological preparations that we have been describing. What Wundt did was not exactly what one would expect.

Wundt himself was a physiologist who had been trained in a strong scienfitic tradition, partly as an assistant to one of the world's greatest scientists, Helmholtz. Considering this personal background and the problems we have been discussing, one would expect that Wundt's laboratory would study epistemological problems, reaction time, problems in sensation and perception, use experimental techniques. and top everything off with a double helping of physiology. The only real surprise is with the topping; Wundt *called* his psychology an experimental physiological psychology, but there was almost no significant physiological experimentation. Watson (1963, p. 249; 1971, pp. 275–276) notes that Wundt did monitor pulse and breathing rates in studies of feeling; however, such measures played no discernible role in Wundt's system.

Perhaps psychology felt the need of physiology in the beginning primarily for its prestige. Physics and mathematics have often been invoked by psychologists for similar reasons, and controversies have raged about whether the alleged dependence of psychology on the better established disciplines is good or bad. In any case, Wundt seems to have done well by pointing to a presumed continuity with physiology, while at the same time actually working on problems so different that there was no doubt that psychology was an independent discipline.

Wundt was able to justify avoiding physiological experimentation because of his philosophical position on the mind-body problem. He believed that the mind and body run parallel courses but that one cannot say that bodily events *cause* mental events; external events simply give rise to certain bodily processes and, at the same time, to parallel mental processes (cf. Table 2-2). He thought the primary task of psychology was to discover the elements of conscious processes, the manner of their connection, and the laws determining their connection. Since mind and body are parallel, the simplest way to do this, in Wundt's opinion, was to make a *direct* study of the mental events through the method of introspection. Psychology might later turn to the question of just what bodily processes accompany given mental processes, but that problem was secondary. This aspect of Wundt's thought has a modern parallel. Skinner, among others, has insisted that the *direct* study of *behavior* is more likely to be profitable than the attempt to relate it to physiological processes.

Wundt thus brought a kind of problem of dualism to psychology. He also brought a strong belief in the experimental method. His research was laboratory inspection, not armchair introspection. He intended to rule metaphysical speculation out of psychology. He was constantly looking for experimental ways to attack mental processes. Wundt's experimentalism implied that he had accepted the necessary ideas which developed within science and which had to be accepted before a *science* of psychology could become a reality: the necessity for internal explanation, the reliance on observation, and the placement of the human being within the realm of the scientifically knowable. His search for the elements of consciousness also showed his attempt at simplification, or his reductionism, if one prefers.

The Leipzig laboratory, officially founded in 1879, also took over many of the specific problems that were waiting for a psychology. The reaction-time problem has already been mentioned. Problems in sensation and perception were taken over from Helmholtz, Fechner, and others.

There was less at Leipzig to remind one of psychology's predecessors on the other side of the channel. Only through a brash American student, James McKeen Cattell, did the Leipzig laboratory turn out any work on Galton's problem of individual differences. Wundt, with prophetic accuracy, called Cattell's interest *ganz amerikanisch* (typically American). It has indeed turned out to be America's armies, schools, and industries that have placed the greatest emphasis on testing individuals for most efficient placement.

It would be interesting to trace the beginning of psychology farther than this passing glance allows, but our present purpose is simply to place the field of psychology in some kind of perspective relative to its history and role in modern science.

SUMMARY AND CONCLUSIONS

Several scientific ideas had to develop within science before psychology could emerge. Prominent among these were the following propositions: that explanation of an event should be sought within the same system as the one within which the event occurred, that observation is the arbiter of scientific truth, and that human beings are part of the natural order. It follows that human behavior can be studied scientifically to determine the laws governing it.

Certain problems were willed to psychology because of its immediate prehistory within science and philosophy. Among them were relating the mental and physical aspects of the human being, explaining the physiology of perception and the contents of perception, determining the basis for the personal equation, and analyzing individual differences and heredity.

In this context Wilhelm Wundt founded the first formal laboratory of psychology at the University of Leipzig in 1879. Although Wundt took over all of the problems mentioned above, he paid less attention to physiology than might have been expected. He had a powerful, even extreme, bias in the direction of experimentation, and set out to apply that method to the analysis of consciousness.

FURTHER READINGS

The following books are classic works on the general history of science: Conant's *On understanding science: A historical approach* (1947) and *Harvard case histories in experimental science* (1957); Butterfield's *Origins of modern science: 1300–1800* (1957); and Sarton's *Guide to the history of science* (1952). Boring's *History of experimental psychology* (1950) and Watson's *The great psychologists* (1971) are highly recommended as sources of information about the history of psychology; however, so many good books have appeared and are appearing that the best advice may be to browse through the library shelves in the area where history of psychology is kept and see what looks particularly congenial. The six volumes *History of psychology in autobiography* which started to appear in 1930 and continue to appear periodically are very interesting, in addition to providing valuable insights about how careers in psychology are made. Herrnstein and Boring's *A source book in the history of psychology* (1965) provides selected classics from the time of Aristotle up to the time of McDougall for students who like their history firsthand. Hillix and Marx (1974) in *Systems and theories in psychology: A reader* provide original readings coordinated with the present text, along with brief biographies for each of the men represented there.

Table 3-1 Important Figures in Associational Psychology

Antecedent influences	Associationists		Contemporary representatives
	Founder	Developers	
Aristotle (384–322 B.C.)	David Hartley (1705–1757)	Thomas Brown (1778–1820)	William K. Estes-Rockefeller (1919–)
		James Mill (1773–1836)	
Thomas Hobbes (1588–1679)		John S. Mill (1806–1873)	
John Locke (1632–1704)		Alexander Bain (1818–1903)	
George Berkeley (1685–1753)		Hermann Ebbinghaus (1850–1909)	
David Hume (1711–1776)		Ivan P. Pavlov (1849–1936)	
		Vladimir M. Bekhterev (1857–1927)	
		Edward L. Thorndike—Columbia (1874–1949)	
		Edwin R. Guthrie—Washington (1886–1959)	

Chapter 3

Associationism

"Aha," you may say, "the authors have been doing all this historical review, leading up to the first laboratory which clearly was started by Wundt, and all of a sudden they're off onto associationism." This point is well taken. In an earlier edition, we did treat Wundt's structuralistic school first. However, associationism was earlier as a unitary force, and many of its principles were taken over by other schools, especially Wundt's. We therefore found it very awkward to discuss Wundt first, since we had to refer back to associationism and discuss *it* in order to explain what Wundt was doing. Thus, this time we shall discuss the long historical development of the associationistic tradition *before* we turn to Wundt and Leipzig.

Table 3-1 lists the names of the most important figures in this tradition. Associationism is really more a principle than a school of psychology. The principle of association derives from epistemological questions within philosophy. The epistemological question, "How do we know?" is answered by empiricist philosophers, "Through the senses." Immediately the next question arises: "Then where do the complex ideas come from, since they are not directly sensed?" The answer to this second question gives the first principle of association: "Complex ideas come from the association of simpler ones."

Since associationism thus has its roots in philosophy, its history extends back into antiquity; note that we list Aristotle in Table 3-1 as our first associationist. However, the influence of associationism extends right up to today, and some of its guiding principles survive almost unchanged.

The British empiricists probably constituted the closest approach to a "school" of associationism, although it was a philosophical rather than a psychological school. Their attempt to explain mental activity led to the statement of the several factors important in forming associations. In our description of the development of British empiricism, we shall attempt to show the continuity of thinking in which empiricism and associationism were fused. Although these philosophers were concerned more with epistemological than with psychological problems, they definitely anticipated later psychological developments in their attempts to apply the results of empirical observation more directly to the solution of philosophical problems.

Historically, associationistic concepts have served as substitutes for more detailed learning theories. Three men stand out as contributors to this aspect of the associationistic movement. Hermann Ebbinghaus caused a profound shift in the associationistic way of working. Prior to his studies on the learning of nonsense syllables, the tendency had been to begin with the associations already formed and attempt to infer backward to the process of formation of the associations. Ebbinghaus began at the other end, with the study of the formation of the associations; it was thus possible for him to control the conditions under which the associations were formed and to make the study of learning scientific. I. P. Pavlov, the great Russian physiologist, has primary responsibility for shifting the kind of association studied to S-R connections rather than ideas. His research on the conditioned reflex thus helped to objectify psychology. E. L. Thorndike developed an extensive account of psychological phenomena along associationistic lines; we shall treat his system most fully as the representative of associationism.

It is difficult to single out modern associationistic systematists, since they do not belong to any cohesive school. One is considered an associationist to the extent that one uses associationistic principles; but associationistic principles pervade recent and contemporary psychology, so we must select "associationists" according to their tendency to use *only* or *primarily* associationistic principles.

BRITISH EMPIRICISM

The British empiricists used the same principles of association that had been suggested centuries before by Aristotle. He had suggested that items which are similar or opposite or contiguous tend to be associated with one another. The last principle, contiguity, comes closest to winning universal acceptance: If two things are experienced closely in time, they are likely to be associated. Similarity and contrast are accepted by some and rejected by others. The only principle of association added to Aristotle's list by the British empiricists was the principle of causality suggested by Berkeley and treated at length by Hume.

Table 3-2 summarizes the principles of association accepted by the most important figures within the associationistic movement.

Thomas Hobbes (1588–1679) was a political philosopher who helped to

Table 3-2 Principles of Associationism

Author	Date	Principles: Contiguity	Similarity	Contrast	Causality
Aristotle	ca. 330 B.C.	X	X	X	
Thomas Hobbes	1651	X			
John Locke	1700	X	X		
George Berkeley	1733	X	X		
David Hume	1739	X	X		X
David Hartley	1749	X			
James Mill	1829	X			
John Stuart Mill	1843	X	X		
Alexander Bain	1855	X	X		
Herbert Spencer	1855	X	X		

found British empiricism. He saw reason as the dominant guiding factor in human behavior; however, he took a strongly deterministic, mechanical view. Mental content was accounted for by recourse to sensory data only, eliminating the need for innate ideas. The lawful succession of ideas was held to be responsible for all thought and action. Hobbes accounted for this succession in terms of association by contiguity: If an idea had been followed by another previously, it would again tend to lead to the contiguous idea.

John Locke (1632–1704) reputedly "invented" an associationistic position pretty much independently of Hobbes, and is thereby usually regarded as its founder because his position was clearer and more complete (see Boring, 1950, p. 169). We will see that the "founder" of a school, or the "inventor" of an idea is frequently not the first person who had an inspiration, but the first person who does a thorough job with that inspiration.

Locke spent the early years of his adult life in politics, notably as the private secretary of the man who became the Earl of Shaftesbury. The Earl went variously into and out of power, and so of course did Locke. It was not a propitious beginning for a philosopher. If Locke had fallen off his horse on a drunken spree, caught pneumonia, and died, as Shakespeare is rumored to have done at 52, the world would never have heard of him. But Locke was apparently prudent as well as thorough, and his great *Essay concerning human understanding* appeared when Locke was 57, in 1690. It might never have appeared had not the Earl fallen completely from favor and died in exile in 1675; history would then have had little to say about a lifelong private secretary to an earl!

Berkeley, who was very precocious, later wondered patronizingly how Locke could have seen so much when he was so old. As a matter of fact, Locke had been working on his problem for 20 years before he published, so he was not, perhaps, so very old while he was developing his position.

Locke's main concern in his *Essay* was the validity of knowledge. He said that all knowledge comes from experience, either through the senses or through reflection on sensory data. This extreme empiricism with no innate knowledge allowed represented a return to the Aristotelian notion of the tabula rasa (blank tablet, symbolic of the infant "mind," on which sensory experience is presumed to write) and an attack on Descartes' belief in innate ideas.

Locke's ideas on association were also similar to Aristotle's. He added a chapter entitled "Of the association of ideas" to the fourth edition of the *Essay,* in which he pointed out that ideas are combined in experience according to principles very much like those of similarity and contiguity. However, his emphasis on association was not great, and he certainly did not stress it as a universal principle underlying the connection of ideas. He believed that ideas are ordinarily connected by "natural" connections, and he clearly implied that associationistic principles are useful primarily for the explanation of abnormal connections. Locke thus began a sequence of views on association. Berkeley made association more inclusive in scope: Hume characterized it as a "gentle force"; and James Mill made it into an inexorable principle of connection. Within the tradition of associationism the human mind started out free except for a little accidental determination, with Locke, and ended up completely determined with Mill.

Locke also started a trend with his special theory of primary and secondary qualities, which were said to be the basis for sensory "ideas." According to this dichotomy, primary properties are those which inhere in bodies. They offer the main avenue between the mind and the external world. Properties such as solidity, figure, motion, and number are representative of this category. Secondary properties, such as colors, sounds, and tastes, were not supposed to belong to objects, but were instead considered functions of the mind itself. This distinction was soon destroyed by Berkeley (see below), but reappeared as the problem of distinguishing between psychology and physics. As we shall see later, Wundt made the distinction by saying that physics studies *mediate* experience and psychology studies *immediate* experience. Titchener, who brought Wundtian psychology to America, said that physics studies experience as *independent of* the experiencing organism, while psychology studies experience as *dependent on* the experiencing organism. The three men were all making a very similar point; each was dealing with the contribution of the experiencer to the experience, but from a slightly different perspective.

George Berkeley (1685–1753) was Locke's intellectual successor. Although he was born 53 years later than Locke, his most important philosophical work appeared only 20 years after Locke's; Berkeley published his *New theory of vision* (1709) and *Principles of human knowledge* (1710) when he was about 25.

We should not leave the impression, because of Berkeley's comments on Locke's age as contrasted with his own precocity, that Berkeley was nothing but a brash and brilliant young man. Even his comment on Locke may have been intended in a spirit of admiration. In any case, Berkeley had a powerful religious and social sensibility. He wanted to found a university in the New World, and was promised the money to do so by George II. As a consequence of this, Berkeley spent a good bit of time on this side of the Atlantic, 3 years of it in Newport, Rhode Island. George II never came through with the money, so Berkeley's time was wasted, as far as his original plans were concerned. However, we were the beneficiaries; Berkeley left his home, land, and library in the United States to

Yale, and his books to Harvard. We honor his efforts in this country through the name of the city of Berkeley, California, which contains one of the greatest universities in the New World. Berkeley became Bishop of Cloyne, in keeping with his deep religious convictions, and did little that was of interest to the history of psychology after his first burst.

Philosophically, Berkeley was a subjective idealist. For him mind was the ultimate reality. This position is represented by the famous Latin phrase *esse est percipi* (to be is to be perceived). For Berkeley the main problem was not the relation of mind to matter (Descartes) or how matter generates mind (Locke), but how mind generates matter. This kind of position leads, to follow it to its logical conclusion, to a solipsism (belief that there is only one mind, one's own, in which all else, including other minds, exists only as ideas).

Berkeley was an active and ingenious psychological thinker. He used tactual and kinesthetic sensations to break down the distinction Locke had made between primary and secondary qualities. Berkeley pointed out that the alleged primary qualities are really also functions of perception. This argument is congruent with his philosophical idealism. He believed that visual depth perception depends upon experience. He stressed tactual and kinesthetic sensations and their association with ocular movements in looking at near and far objects; the complex association then became "depth." This was a specific psychological attempt to answer his general philosophical question of how mind generates matter. It shows Berkeley inverting the materialistic practice of taking the external world for granted and asking how we come to know about it. Berkeley regarded the data of consciousness as beyond doubt, and the problem was to account for complex ideas, like those of space and external objects.

In line with his theological background, Berkeley attempted to explain the stability, independence, and order of external objects by bringing in the all-perceiving mind of God. His metaphysical position is humorously presented in the following limerick (quoted in Russell, 1945, p. 648, and attributed to Ronald Knox);

There was a young man who said, God
Must think it exceedingly odd
If he finds that this tree
Continues to be
When there's no one about in the Quad.

Reply:

Dear Sir:
Your astonishment's odd:
I am always about in the Quad.
And that's why the tree
Will continue to be,
Since observed by
Yours faithfully,
God.

David Hume (1711–1776), like Berkeley, was brilliantly precocious. His *Treatise on human nature* (1886), on which his reputation was mainly based, appeared in three volumes when Hume was 28 and 29. Unlike Berkeley, Hume seems never to have become too concerned with the welfare of others; he was too busy seeking fame for himself. He never received an adequate measure, according to his own high standards in such matters, until perhaps after the publication of his *History of England,* which was phenomenally successful. Hume may have been irritating as a person; certainly he was irritating as a philosopher. It was his subjective idealism, which was similar to Berkeley's, which stimulated the caustic Samuel Johnson, who was just 2 years older than Hume, to his famous rock-kicking reply. Boswell reports that he once asked Johnson how he could refute Hume's position, that one could not be sure of the existence of the external world. Johnson said, "I refute it thus," and kicked a rock. Opinions vary about the adequacy of Johnson's answer, but few have denied that it makes a good story.

The contrasts between Hume and Berkeley as persons, despite the similarity between their philosophies, should lead us to be very cautious about settling upon what people are like upon the basis of their philosophic or scientific views. Despite millions of counterexamples, it remains common to form prejudices about persons because of their intellectual preferences, just as it is common to form prejudices because of race or religion. The reader can easily think of examples in contemporary psychology, so we will not insult anyone's intelligence and give any.

In his writing, Hume made a distinction between more vivid impressions (what we would call *sensations* or *perceptions*) and less vivid ideas (what we would call *images* or *recollections*). We will see that this distinction was taken over quite directly by Wundt and the structuralists when they began their "analysis of the mind." Their application of introspection to complex mental processes grew very easily out of the empiricistic and associationistic tradition. The epistemological question of the empiricist philosophers, "Where do complex ideas come from?" was attacked directly by the structuralists through introspection.

Hume also applied his analytic tendencies to one of the three principles of association he "discovered," the principle of cause and effect. He found that this principle was closely related to the principle of contiguity and that indeed cause and effect came into being as an idea only if the cause had been contiguous with the effect. In addition, the cause had *invariably* to be followed by the effect. Superficially, it seems that Hume reduced cause and effect to contiguity via his analysis, but the case is not so simple. N. K. Smith (1949), who made a thorough study of Hume's position, concludes that Hume definitely believed that the principle of cause and effect retained its independence despite its close relationship to temporal and spatial contiguity. However, cause and effect were not to be found existing in the things observed, but only in the mind of the observer.

Cause and effect, then, might seem to be a complex idea, one which might have been reduced to simpler ideas had Hume been so inclined. This view, too, is mistaken. Turner (1967) says of Hume's position: "We find, then, that *causation, resemblance,* and *contiguity* are the relations by which we associate ideas. As such, these relations have no existential significance; they represent activities of the imagination, and not ideas reducible in any way to impressions" (p. 34). One must conclude that Hume retained three distinct principles of association.

Finally, Hume's skeptical and antimetaphysical biases have been enormously influential. His famous paragraph from *An enquiry concerning human understanding* reads:

> When we run over libraries, persuaded of these principles, what havoc must we make? If we take in our hand any volume; of divinity or school metaphysics, for instance; let us ask, *Does it contain any abstract reasoning concerning quantity or number?* No. *Does it contain any experimental reasoning concerning matter of fact and existence?* No. Commit it then to the flames; for it can contain nothing but sophistry and illusion. (1902, p. 165; originally published 1748)

This viewpoint is the forerunner of modern positivism and operationism. Psychology from its formal beginnings has had the problem of freeing itself from philosophy, and Hume is one of its heroes.

ASSOCIATIONISM AS A SYSTEMATIC DOCTRINE

Associationism as a system growing out of empiricism was "founded" in the eighteenth century by a scholarly physician, David Hartley (1705–1757). He took Locke's chapter title, "The association of ideas," and made it his thesis. Hartley developed his psychology around associations, thus making associationism a formal doctrine with a name.

In contrast with the earlier politically active philosophers, Hartley led a relatively unexciting, orderly, and leisurely life. His single major publication was *Observations on man* (1749). He was much influenced by Newton and Locke. His theorizing was somewhat similar to earlier, less elaborated speculation by Hobbes on motion as an explanatory concept in brain activity; Hartley postulated vibratory actions within the nervous system which corresponded to ideas and images. More intense vibrations were sensations, and less intense vibrations ideas. He thus gave a physiological interpretation to Hume's distinction between impression and idea. Since vibrations take a little while to die out, sensations persist after removal of the stimulus; this was offered against the then-current view of flow of animal spirits in tubular nerves. Contiguity was stressed as the principle of association, and associationistic principles were used to explain visual depth perception, following Berkeley. Such principles were also said to explain diverse other phenomena, such as emotional pleasure and pain and the meaning of words.

Following Hartley, the next important development in associationism occurred in Scotland. Thomas Brown (1778–1820) rephrased Hartley's principles as principles of suggestion in order to get around the orthodox Scottish school's objection to associationism and its analytic tendencies; however, there was no real difference in the substance of what Brown was saying and what the British empiricists had been saying about the basic principles of mental activity.

Brown is notable because of his emphasis on secondary principles of association. He was concerned with the problem of selection, in a train of associations, of the single association that actually occurred when there were several that might occur. In this sense, he was interested in the problem of improving prediction. He presented several factors that might account for the selection of the particular association: the number of times it had been associated with the preceding mental content, how recently the association had previously occurred, the vividness of the original association, its duration, and the number of ideas now present which had connections with the following idea and thus added to its associative strength. Analogs to several of Brown's principles appear in much more recent learning theories. Concepts like number of trials, recency, stimulus-intensity dynamism, and stimulus summation are obvious parallels to Brown's secondary principles.

James Mill (1773–1836) presented one of the most extreme associationistic positions. His *Analysis of the phenomena of the human mind* (1829), published after 7 years of summer-vacation writing, presents Mill's "mental mechanics." He held that the law of association could account for the most complex mental experience. The idea of "every thing," for example, presumably contains all lesser ideas and is simply their sum. Simple ideas were supposed to coalesce to form more complex ones, which might through long usage become so consolidated that they appeared as a single idea. Once the complex idea appeared thus, it might in turn coalesce with other ideas to form even more complex ideas. Mill's position was the ultimate in simplicity, if not in accuracy, because of his use of simple addition and a single principle of association—contiguity.

John Stuart Mill (1806–1873) and his father James are the most potent philosophical father-son combination we will encounter. James sat John Stuart down at the table with him, while he was writing the *History of India,* and started his infant son reading Greek at the age of 3. John Stuart's educational accomplishments with his father as his only schoolmaster read like something out of Ripley's "Believe it or not"; by the time he was 12 he had gone through geometry, algebra, and Latin, and turned his interest to scholastic logic! Through all of this his perfectionistic father continued to point out how he could and should be a better student, and John Stuart was expected to tutor his eight brothers and sisters.

With this background, it is not surprising that John Stuart did not deviate greatly from the psychological doctrines of his associationistic father; yet he probably felt that his minor changes were veritable revolutions. He transformed the "mental mechanics" of his father into a kind of "mental chemistry." According to his more sophisticated notion, ideas lose their original identity when they fuse into more complex ideas by association. He accepted his father's notion of coalescence of ideas in association, but believed that very rapid combinations result in a loss of some parts. As Mill put it:

> The laws of the phenomena of the mind are sometimes analogous to mechanical, but sometimes also to chemical laws. When many impressions or ideas are operating in the mind together, there sometimes takes place a process of a similar kind to chemical combination. When impressions have been so often experienced in conjunction,

> that each of them calls up readily and instantaneously the ideas of the whole group, those ideas sometimes melt and coalesce into one another, and appear not several ideas but one; in the same manner as when the seven prismatic colors are presented to the eye in rapid succession, the sensation produced is that of white. But in this last case it is correct to say that the seven colors when they rapidly follow one another *generate* white; so it appears to me that the Complex Idea, formed by the blending together of several simpler ones, should, when it really appears simple, (that is, when the separate elements are not consciously distinguishable in it) be said to *result from*, or be *generated by*, the simple ideas, not to *consist* of them. . . . These are cases of mental chemistry: in which it is possible to say that the simple ideas generate, rather than that they compose, the complex ones. (1956, p. 558; original publication 1843)

The younger Mill also treated the problem of how mind creates matter, the problem posed by Berkeley. Mill was willing to admit the power of expectation to the human mind. From this it followed that one might come to expect certain sensations to be possible, given other sensations which arose from a particular "object." Mill named this set of expectations *permanent possibilities of sensation* and thought that these possibilities adequately explained human belief in the material world. We shall see the same general problem reappear later as the problem of meaning in Titchener's psychology.

Alexander Bain (1818–1903) was nominally a logician (at Aberdeen, Scotland), but represents the closest approach we have met to a formal psychologist. Bain was largely a self-made college student and had difficulty in securing Scottish university professorships, finally moving into London circles with John Stuart Mill. He published a comprehensive and systematic two-volume psychology with a strong associationistic basis, *The senses and the intellect* (1855) and *The emotions and the will* (1859). Although at first slow to sell, these books were ultimately very successful, requiring several revisions and remaining the standard psychological text in Britain for almost 50 years. They may be considered a kind of physiological psychology, since they emphasize sensory phenomena. In 1876 Bain founded the first psychological journal, *Mind.* He supported it financially until 1892.

Bain had a well-developed set of laws of association. There were two principles of the formation of associations: contiguity and similarity. In addition, there was a kind of summation effect, whereby "associations that are individually too weak to operate the revival of a past idea, may succeed by acting together" (1886, p. 544). And there was a principle of creativity, whereby "by means of Association, the mind has the power to form *new* combinations or aggregates, *different* from any that have been presented to it in the course of experience" (1886, p. 570). Bain thus accepted Brown's secondary principle that associative strength is increased by several ideas working together and J. S. Mill's notion of the generation of complex ideas. Bain also had a version of the law of effect, which makes the strength of associations depend partially upon the consequences which follow a particular association. We will see later in this chapter that Thorndike made the law of effect the central concept in his psychology, and Skinner has elaborated this law into a virtual system of psychology.

Bain's contributions were therefore to both the professional and the intellectual development of psychology. Because he was himself a psychologist and because he founded the first journal of psychology, he completed the transformation of the philosophical empiricism into the psychological associationism. This transformation was abetted by the bridge that he built between the association of ideas and physiology.

British associationism left a legacy of the utmost significance to the newly developing experimental science of psychology. A major part of this significance lay in the methodological point of view which associationism developed and refined. The stimulus-response type of thinking and experimenting grew more or less directly out of it. This is so much part and parcel of our basic mode of thinking—even for those of us who are most critical of some aspects of modern associationism—that we tend to take it for granted, along with the rest of our cultural heritage.

A somewhat less important part of the heritage of associationism was the content of associationistic theorizing. By and large this contribution consisted of the various laws concerning the formation of associations. Much of the historical content of associationism was more or less directly absorbed into the assumptions and biases of the early psychologists.

We now turn to the kind of associationism that emerged during the last decades of the nineteenth century. Association of ideas was gradually replaced, in psychology, by association of stimuli and responses. The shift was related to the transition of psychology, so long a part of philosophy, into an empirical and natural science in its own right.

THE ASSOCIATION OF STIMULUS AND RESPONSE

Ebbinghaus's Invention of the Nonsense Syllable

Hermann Ebbinghaus (1850–1909) was an extremely capable German experimentalist who published (1885) the first systematic laboratory investigation of memory. He is to be credited as the first psychologist to make a thoroughly empirical study of association, or learning, although his major interest was in memory. He was concerned with controlling the kind of learning whose retention he wanted to investigate and so devised the nonsense syllable in an effort to minimize prior associations (prior, that is, to his laboratory study). The nonsense syllable consisted simply of two consonants separated by a vowel (e.g., WOY, XAM, CIR). Ebbinghaus thought he would be able to obtain more reliable memory curves if his learned materials were more homogeneous than ordinary words, whose associations with other words from prior learning would vary widely. The measure of Ebbinghaus's success is the fact that the negatively accelerated recall curve which he reported for the human subject, with number of syllables retained plotted as a function of time, has not been radically revised over the succeeding decades. Seldom do empirical curves retain their form despite the onslaught of new apparatus and more refined methods.

Ebbinghaus's contribution was particularly important since he was able to show that orderly results could be obtained by means of carefully controlled objective procedures even in so complex and variable a function as human learning and memory. This first laboratory application of strict associationistic principles in the field of learning was a milestone in the history of scientific psychology.

There have been skeptics who have said, "Yes, and the invention of the nonsense syllable was also a milestone in the history of boredom, perhaps the very one William James had in mind when he said that that kind of psychology could never have been produced in a country whose natives could be bored!" But the skeptics are wrong on both counts; in the first place, James was referring to Fechner, not to Ebbinghaus. Ebbinghaus did get his idea for quantifying the study of memory from Fechner (1860), who had already invented quantitative techniques for the study of sensation and perception; but James admired Ebbinghaus. In the second place, the skeptics are correct only on the surface. Truly, nonsense syllables *are* dull, but that misses the point. Science often progresses by learning brilliant things from dull situations. How interesting is a linear accelerator or a cloud chamber? As things-in-themselves, they would bore us silly in a week. And how interesting is a stupid pigeon pecking buttons in a little box? Only the cartoon character, Andy Capp, whose love for pigeons seems boundless, or a mental retardate could enjoy pigeon-pecking-in-itself for long. The charm of all these situations, including the nonsense-syllable situation, is that they tell us something about nature that we did not know before. And each of those situations is very rich in possibilities, in that amazing numbers of different manipulations can be studied within a single controlled environment. The invention of that environment was Ebbinghaus's genius, and his contribution to psychology. The next person we will look at made a similar contribution, and had the good fortune to have a long life in which he could study his situation.

Pavlov's Discovery of the Conditioned Reflex

Ivan P. Pavlov (1849–1936) was a distinguished Russian physiologist, from 1890 to his death director of the physiological laboratory at the Institute for Experimental Medicine. In 1904, he was awarded a Nobel prize for his investigations of glandular and neural factors in digestion. Somewhat earlier, however, he had made an accidental discovery which was destined to change entirely the direction of his scientific career and to have a profound and lasting effect upon the development of psychological science.

Pavlov had developed an apparatus which made it possible to hold and measure the amount of saliva secreted by a dog under various conditions of feeding. In essence, this consisted of a calibrated glass tube inserted through a fistula in the animal's cheek. Pavlov went to some lengths to ensure a very high degree of control over environmental stimuli in the laboratory situation; the animal was harnessed in the apparatus within a relatively isolated experimental chamber, with recording devices outside. Pavlov's discovery consisted of his noting the persistent occurrence of *anticipatory* salivary flow. That is, the stimuli previously associated with the feeding of the animal (e.g., the approach of the attendant or the sight of the food dish) came to initiate salivation in animals as their training proceeded.

Now that we have described how Pavlov discovered the conditioned reflex, we must add that he was not the first person who observed such reflexes. Another of history's lessons is that it almost never happens that anyone discovers something completely new. Robert Whytt (1763) had noted the existence of conditioned reflexes long before Pavlov, and they had even been discovered in America by Twitmyer (1905), who apparently was assured that they were of no interest, and so never followed up on his discovery. Pavlov also knew of the work of Sechenov (1829–1905), who had published a book, *Reflexes of the brain,* in 1863 which accounted for complex behavior in very much the same way that Pavlov came to account for it.

Pavlov's greatness, as is often the case, thus depended to a great extent on tenacity and on the ability to see the importance of a phenomenon which seemed unimportant on the surface. His thinking about the implications of his findings for the adaptive behavior of the animal eventually led Pavlov to a program of active research designed primarily to lead to new insights concerning the physiology of the brain. The term *conditioned reflex* was used, taking account of the acquired nature of the stimulus-response relationship. Pavlov's continuing interest in cortical functions is indicated in his choice of terms to describe the processes he investigated, for example *irradiation,* implying a presumed excitatory brain function. His entire research program was devoted to an exhaustive analysis of the factors involved in conditioning, on the assumption that by investigation of this relatively simply kind of reflexive learning he would be able to penetrate some of the mysteries of the so-called higher mental processes.

Pavlov continued his research on the conditioned reflex throughout the remaining years of his long life. His environmental emphasis accorded extremely well with Marxist ideology, and he received continuing strong support from the communist regime which followed the Russian Revolution. He was able to develop a very complete system of psychology; even language was included as the "second signal system," with the conditioned reflex the first. In his later years, Pavlov also turned his attention to the problems of abnormal behavior. He thought, for example, that catatonic schizophrenia was a matter of protective inhibition, which occurred to keep the organism from being overstimulated. Other psychoses were given similar speculative explanations.

It is somewhat ironic that Pavlov's great influence has been in psychology, a discipline toward which he never seemed to feel too kindly (cf. 1932), rather than in the area of brain physiology, with which he was concerned primarily. This irony has not been perpetrated because of any perversity on the part of either physiologists or psychologists. The reason Pavlov was more honored by psychologists is simply that he was doing psychological work and developing constructs that, though they sounded physiological, were based on behavioral observations. Irradiation, for example, may sound like something that occurs in the cortex, but it was known only through the observation of what we would now call *stimulus generalization.* Kimble (1967) has given a very clear exposition of this facet of Pavlov's thought.

The details of Pavlov's work are beyond the scope of our present endeavor (for some of his own reports in translation see Pavlov, 1927, 1928, 1941, 1955), but they should be familiar, at least in skeleton form, to every student of psychology. His research represents a completion of the shift of the concept of association from its historical application to ideas, to the relations between entirely objective and highly quantifiable glandular secretions and muscular movements, with which the behaviorist was soon to become concerned. John B. Watson, the founder of behaviorism, probably knew of Pavlov's work through the latter's 1906 article in *Science,* which was probably Pavlov's first article on the conditioned reflex in English. We will see in Chapter 6 what use Watson made of Pavlov's research. Interest in Pavlov has outlived the early period of Watsonian behaviorism, and continues to run high among learning theorists particularly.

In Russia, interest in the objective Pavlovian approach has never ceased. Russian psychology has even been "Pavlovinized," in the sense that Pavlovian psychology became official Russian psychology during the early 1950s (Brožek, 1973). Active research on the conditioned reflex has continued, and has filled in a great deal of physiological detail which was generally missing from Pavlov's own research (cf. Cole & Maltzman, 1969, for a review of Russian psychology). There is little doubt that Pavlov has inspired more experimental research than any other single person.

Bekhterev and Motor Conditioning

The third major figure in the shift of associationism away from ideas and toward overt behavior is Vladimir M. Bekhterev (1857–1927). His most significant contribution was the motor conditioned response. Pavlov's research had been almost entirely with glandular secretions, whose direct influence on overt behavior seemed somewhat restricted. Bekhterev, a Russian contemporary and rival of Pavlov, extended the conditioning principle to involve the striped musculature. His major research paradigm involved the application of shock to the paw of a dog or the hand of a person following the presentation of a conditioned stimulus, such as a buzzer (1913).

Bekhterev had studied psychology under Wundt and was much more concerned with psychology than Pavlov. His *reflexology* became the dominant theme in Russian psychology. Although American psychologists have preferred his motor conditioning technique to the salivary conditioning of Pavlov, they have found the latter's comprehensive experimentation and conceptualization more stimulating. Consequently, Bekhterev played a less important role than Pavlov in the further development of associationism as a laboratory technique.

THORNDIKE'S CONNECTIONISM

The systematic stimulus-response psychology of Edward Lee Thorndike (1874–1949) represents the closest approach, besides Pavlov's, to a purely associationistic system since James Mill. Thorndike began his psychological career with the laboratory study of learning in various animal species, but soon shifted his interests to human learning and many aspects of educational and social psychology. Although he did not initiate a school in the same sense that Titchener or Watson did, his mode of thinking was thoroughly associationistic throughout all his investigations in many diverse fields. Thorndike's connectionism offers, therefore, a wide-ranging application of associationism to psychological problems.

Thorndike studied under James at Harvard and under Cattell at Columbia. He began his investigations of animal learning at Harvard, where he trained chicks to run through improvised mazes (formed by placing books on end). He carried on this kind of research at Columbia, then working with cats and dogs in the puzzle box, which he devised, and took his doctorate there in 1898. His dissertation was entitled *Animal intelligence: An experimental study of the associative processes in animals.* It was subsequently republished (1911) together with new material on associative learning in chicks, fish, and monkeys.

Thorndike reveals a typically associationistic attitude in his description of his own career, a description that is deterministic, environmentalistic, and passive in its view of the organism:

> The motive for my first investigations of animal intelligence was chiefly to satisfy requirements for courses and degrees. Any other topic would probably have served me as well. . . . I have recorded my beginning as a psychologist in detail because it illustrates what is perhaps the most general fact about my entire career as a psychologist later, namely, its responsiveness to outer pressure or opportunity rather than to inner needs. . . . Obviously I have not "carried out my career," as the biographers say. Rather it has been a conglomerate, amassed under the pressure of varied opportunities and demands. (Thorndike, 1936, pp. 265–266)

This self-portrait of "Thorndike the passivist" may very well have been exaggerated to show how well his own behavior fit his theory. Boice (1977) relates an incident which gives another side of Thorndike's personality. Thorndike had about 10 minutes left before he had to teach a class. He wondered aloud whether the interests of science would be better served if he used the 10 minutes to prepare for the class, or if he used it to compute another correlation. "I think I'll compute another correlation," he concluded, and proceeded to do so. It does not appear that Thorndike always succumbed to external pressures, although in this case his students probably wished that he had.

Thorndike was appointed an instructor in psychology at Teachers College, Columbia University, in 1899. He stayed there for the remainder of his career. He retired in 1939 after 4 decades, but continued his activities for another decade until his death. Shortly after his original appointment he shifted his interests, at the suggestion of Cattell, to problems of human learning and education. It was in these areas that he spent most of his succeeding years.

Thorndike's fully developed system of connectionism is nowhere presented in a single, comprehensive account. This is understandable: Thorndike did not think of himself as a systematist or of his thinking and writing as contributing to a school. However, some of his later papers and chapters from books are collected in *Selected writings from a connectionist's psychology* (1949), which probably offers the best single source of his work. In our brief sketch of Thorndike's system and of each of the other classical systems, we will follow an outline derived from McGeoch's criteria for a system of psychology (1933). The use of this outline, together with a final discussion of a system's standing on Watson's prescriptive dimensions, should ease the reader's task of comparing systems.

Definition of Psychology

Thorndike's opinion on definitions is suggested by his statement (1949) that "Excellent work can surely be done by men with widely different notions of what psychology is and should be, the best work of all perhaps being done by men such as Galton, who gave little or no thought to what it is or should be" (p. 9). His own definition of psychology is implicit in his writing. Thorndike was a functionalist in his emphasis on utilitarian aspects of psychology. More particularly, however, psychology was for him first and foremost the study of stimulus-response connections, or bonds. But Thorndike's conception of such associations went far beyond the simple connections between discrete, molecular, and highly localized events sometimes assumed to be characteristic of his thinking by his critics. The following excerpt indicates the scope of his interpretation of connections and indirectly gives us a picture of what Thorndike considered to be the subject matter of psychology:

> Connections lead from states of affairs within the brain as well as from external situations. They often occur in long series wherein the response to one situation becomes the situation producing the next response and so on. They may be from parts or elements or features of a situation as well as from the situation as a whole. They may be largely determined by events preceding their immediate stimuli or by more or less of the accompanying attitude, even conceivably by his entire makeup and equipment. They lead to responses of readiness and unreadiness, awareness, attention, interest, welcoming and rejecting, emphasizing and restraining, differentiating and relating, directing and coordinating. The things connected may be subtle relations or elusive attitudes and intentions. (1949, p. 81)

Postulates

Although explicit statements of postulates are not available in Thorndike's writing, some implicit assumptions are clearly made. The most fundamental one is probably that behavior can be analyzed into associations of the kind described by him in the quotation given above. Another is that behavioral processes are quantifiable. He is responsible for the much-cited proposition to the effect that if something exists, it must exist in some amount, and that if it exists in some amount, then it can be measured. An interesting incidental indication of the extent to which Thorndike was prone to practice his preaching on this topic is his estimate, given in his autobiographical sketch (1949), that he had "probably spent well over 20,000 hours in reading and studying scientific books and journals" (p. 7).

Mind-Body Position

Thorndike was too much the matter-of-fact utilitarian to be concerned with this problem, and he adopted no formal mind-body position. He stated (1949): "Under no circumstances, probably, could I have been able or willing to make philosophy my business" (p. 2). His common use of the words *mind* and *mental* therefore has no implication for a mind-body view, but indicates merely that Thorndike was relaxed about the use of ordinary language.

Nature of the Data

Thorndike's data are predominantly objective and very often, as has been noted, quantified. One incidental example of his use of quantified estimates has been mentioned. His research on the "goodness" of cities offers an illustration of the way in which he used quantification and objective data professionally. His own succinct summary of this research follows:

> It seemed to me probable that sociology would profit by studying the differences of communities in the same way that psychology studies the differences of individuals. Therefore I collected nearly 300 items of fact concerning each of 310 cities, studied their variations and intercorrelations, computed for each city three scores for the general goodness of life for good people for each city (G), for the personal qualities of its residents (P), and for their per capita income (I), and studied the causes of the differences among cities in G. (1949, pp. 10, 11)

Principles of Connection

Thorndike's best-known and most controversial contribution to psychological theory is his *law of effect.* In his early research with animals in puzzle boxes, he had been impressed with the gradual learning of the correct response and the gradual elimination of the incorrect one. Although this kind of learning has come to be called *trial and error,* actually Thorndike recognized the primary role of *accidental success* in the fixation of responses. *Exercise,* or frequency of occurrence, was accorded some strengthening powers, but not as much as occurred with the addition of success. He published the following formal statement:

> Any act which in a given situation produces satisfaction becomes associated with that situation, so that when the situation recurs the act is more likely than before to recur also. Conversely, any act which in a given situation produces discomfort becomes disassociated from the situation, so that when the situation recurs the act is less likely than before to recur. (1905, p. 203)

After extensive research on human learning (1931, 1932), Thorndike decided that the role of punishment or dissatisfaction was not at all comparable, on the negative side, to the positive action of reward. He therefore revised his law of effect to give the predominant role to reward; punishment, he said, serves mainly to make the organism try something else rather than directly to dissociate the response from the situation.

With his cautious conclusions on the ineffectiveness of mild punishments (like saying "wrong" following a number guessed by a subject), Thorndike unwittingly gave rise to one of the most incredible psychological dogmas of the twentieth century: that punishment is ineffective in eliminating undesirable responses. This dogma is contrary to so much evidence, naturalistic as well as experimental, that it is about as difficult to believe as that the earth is flat. Nevertheless, it was generally accepted dogma within the psychological community until at least the 1950s, and Lovaas has amusingly described how difficult it was for him to conceive that punishment might be a useful clinical tool (see Chance, 1974). It is still not difficult to find psychologists who maintain that punishment is ineffective.

Two points should be made in this connection. First, Thorndike himself did not generalize to the ineffectiveness of all punishers. Thus, a careful reading of Thorndike would have dispelled the dogma before it had well begun. The second point is that one cannot expect received views to be universally correct anyway; history gives us its mistakes along with its correct decisions, and we must find out which is which.

Thorndike suggested a cerebral function, the so-called confirming reaction (1933b), as the physiological basis of reinforcement, but this suggestion was not closely connected with his strictly behavioral research program. It was typical of Thorndike that he was not timid about making physiological suggestions, but the suggestions were not taken particularly seriously, nor were they critical for either his experimentation or his theorizing.

Nevertheless, one should not overlook Boring's insightful comment on the easy compatibility between the neuron theory which emerged in the last half of the nineteenth century and the associationistic theory which preceded and followed it. Boring says in part:

> The scheme of mind for which the associationists stood is a mental arrangement that much resembles this physical arrangement of the brain. For the associationists, mind is composed of an infinitude of separate ideas, just as the brain is constituted of an infinitude of cells. But these ideas are bound together into more complex ideas or into higher mental processes by a huge number of associations, just as the nerve cells are connected by fibers. . . . The important point is that the new picture of the brain, arrived at unpsychologically by discoveries in histological technique, nevertheless bore a close resemblance to the new picture of the mind that associationism yielded. (1950, pp. 69–70)

The relevance of Boring's comments in the particular case of Thorndike's connectionism is obvious.

In 1933, Thorndike reported an extension of his theory of reinforcement. He had discovered (1933a) what he called an "independent experimental proof of the strengthening after-effect" (p. 2). This was the so-called spread of effect. It appeared that *nonrewarded* stimulus-response connections close to the rewarded connection acquired a strengthening from reinforcement. The closer the nonrewarded connection was to the rewarded one, the greater the strengthening. The observed strengthening was greater than the strengthening that would be produced by exercise alone.

Although the empirical data in support of this phenomenon have been amply verified, Thorndike's interpretation has not been generally accepted (cf. Marx, 1956; Hilgard & Bower, 1975). Alternative explanations in terms of guessing sequences or other types of bias were not eliminated. If an automatic strengthening effect, not dependent on cognitive (rational) factors, is eventually demonstrated, Thorndike's general reinforcement theory will look more attractive. Some published research has suggested that Thorndike's basic explanation may yet prove acceptable (Marx, 1957a, 1957b; Postman, 1961). However, Hilgard and Bower, after reviewing the work on spread of effect, conclude: "What is perhaps so annoying in retrospect is that so much experimental effort was diverted into the controversy over the 'reality' of the spread of effect" (1975, p. 47).

Principles of Selection

Stimulus-response associations account for the selection of behavior as well as for its acquisition. Thorndike's recognition of the problem of selection in behavior is clearly given in the following excerpt from his *Psychology of learning:*

> All man's learning, and indeed all his behavior, *is selective.* Man does not, in any useful sense of the words, ever absorb, or re-present, or mirror, or copy, a situation uniformly. He never acts like a *tabula rasa* on which external situations write each its entire contribution, or a sensitive plate which duplicates indiscriminately whatever it is exposed to, or a galvanometer which is deflected equally by each and every item of electrical force. Even when he seems most subservient to the external situation—most compelled to take all that it offers and to do all that it suggests—it appears that his sense organs have shut off important features of the situation from influencing him in any way comparable to that open to certain others, and that his original or acquired tendencies to neglect and attend have allotted only trivial power to some and greatly magnified that of others. (1913, pp. 111–112)

He interpreted problems of selective behavior, such as creativity in thinking *(learning by influence),* in terms of the same set of principles he applied to all learning, as indicated in this statement from the same source:

> A closer examination of selective thinking will show that no principles beyond the laws of readiness, exercise, and effect are needed to explain it; that it is only an extreme case of what goes on in associative learning as described under the "piecemeal" activity of situations; and that attributing certain features of learning to mysterious faculties of abstraction or reasoning gives no real help toward understanding or controlling them.
>
> It is true that man's behavior in meeting novel problems goes beyond, or even against, the habits represented by bonds leading from gross total situations and customarily abstracted elements thereof. One of the two reasons therefor, however, is simply that the finer, subtle, preferential bonds with subtler and less often abstracted elements go beyond, and at times against, the grosser and more usual ones. One set is as much due to exercise and effect as the other. The other reason is that in meeting novel problems the mental set or attitude is likely to be one which rejects one after another response as their unfitness to satisfy a certain desideratum appears. What remains as the apparent course of thought includes only a few of the many bonds which did operate, but which, for the most part, were unsatisfying to the ruling attitude or adjustment. (1913, pp. 112–113)

If the elimination of mystery is the essence of science, we see Thorndike in this quotation expressing himself as the essential scientist. We can also see his kinship with his forebears in the associationistic tradition: Locke, with his wish to eliminate the mysteries of innate ideas; Berkeley, with his attempt to solve the mystery of space perception; and Hume, who wished to consign all mysterious nonsense to the fire. Certainly the strength of science lies just here, and perhaps its weaknesses lie here too. Either way, Thorndike and the associationists are squarely in the middle of the scientific tradition.

CRITICISMS OF CONNECTIONISM

Elementarism

The essence of an associationistic position is that it is elementaristic. It was through their empiricism, elementarism, and analytic attitude that the British empiricists furthered psychology's progress as a science. It was through his acceptance of these attitudes, as manifested in his specificity, matter-of-factness, and attention to detail, that Thorndike made his most important contributions. Yet such views are open to attack, especially by those who want psychology to concern itself immediately with the "big picture."

Thorndike's theory of transfer of training (Thorndike & Woodworth, 1901) is the epitome of his elementarism. The theory was that improved efficiency at one task, acquired as a result of training, would transfer to another task only insofar as the two tasks had "identical elements." The more identical elements, the greater the transfer of efficiency from one task to another. This is a simple and specific view, one that is open to experimental attack through the manipulation of the number of elements that are similar. It has therefore certainly been of some value. However, in some situations it has appeared that some principle was learned which transferred perfectly to other tasks whose individual elements were quite different; therefore, the theory requires at least some qualifications before it can be accepted as a complete theory of transfer. Gates (1942), in his carefully documented defense of connectionism, has pointed out that Thorndike's elements were never intended to mean only the narrowest S-R connections; rather, they meant such things as principles. "Identical," too, might be modified slightly to allow for degrees of similarity and to allow the theory more flexibility.

Modern theories of transfer (see Hilgard & Bower, 1975, for a review) are much more complex and detailed than Thorndike's and are still wrong. The rightness or wrongness of the identical elements theory, however, is not the issue. All current theories are presumably wrong, but if they lead to clarification, experimentation, and thence to progress, they are good theories. Science typically proceeds fastest when it works on small, researchable problems. Thorndike's elementarism led to such problems.

Trial and Error

Thorndike has been attacked for his emphasis on the randomness of learning, as implied in his characterization of learning as a trial-and-error process. Köhler (1947) and other Gestaltists have been especially active critics of all aspects of Thorndike's connectionism. The Gestaltists have suggested that learning in puzzle boxes and mazes necessarily appears to be random, stupid, and undirected because the animal cannot get an overview of the whole situation. The animal appears stupid because it is in a stupid situation, not because it is really lacking in insight.

Thorndike's supporters might offer several defenses against such criticism. First, the behavior of the animal in the puzzle box is by no means altogether random or stupid; much of the early behavior is directed at the exit, rather than at the device arbitrarily selected by the experimenter to release the animal. Such behavior is not stupid; it is intelligent in terms of the animal's past experience.

Second, there may be a considerable amount of trial-and-error behavior which is not observed or recorded in the more open, less controlled situations which allow the animal an overview of the problem. It may be that Thorndike's situation was designed to reveal more clearly the nature of the basic learning process. Third, and last, there is plenty of evidence from outside the puzzle box to show that learning can be slow, random, blind, and continuous rather than fast, intelligent, and sudden. The psychological clinic or the counseling situation provides many cases which seem to exemplify connectionistic rather than Gestalt learning processes; criticisms of Thorndike's description should be tempered by this consideration.

Exercise

The sufficiency of frequency of occurrence, or the exercise principle per se, was seriously and tellingly questioned by the Gestalt critics. Here so strong a case was made that Thorndike revised his learning theory to add a new principle, *belongingness* (1935). The evidence against exercise came partly from experiments which showed that contiguous terms are not necessarily associated in ordinary learning situations. For example, suppose that a subject has learned a set of paired associates such as A-1, B-2, C-3, D-4. These have been presented in the order indicated. The subject responds perfectly with response terms 1, 2, etc., to stimulus terms A, B, etc.; however, if given one of the response terms—such as 1 or 2—as a stimulus, the subject does not readily respond with the learned stimulus term that actually followed—in this case B and C. But B followed 1 and C followed 2 just as closely in time as 1 followed A and 2 followed B. A similar situation holds for successive sentences, such as "John is tired" and "Jim is hurt." Here the connections John-tired and Jim-hurt are more readily formed and remembered than the connection tired-Jim, even though the purely physical relationship of the latter two terms is more nearly contiguous. Obviously something beyond mere contiguity in these cases is required for an effective association, and belongingness is the concept Thorndike used. He held that it is an important modifying condition of the strength of associations but is not essential to the formation of associations.

Thorndike's own research (1932, p. 184) gave further evidence against the sufficiency of the old law of exercise. Subjects attempting to draw lines of a certain specified length while blindfolded did not show improvement even with many repeated trials. Thorndike's general conclusion was that exercise is a framework within which other conditions, such as effect, can operate.

Law of Effect

The oldest of Thorndike's contributions has been attacked by behaviorists as well as by Gestalt critics. First, some behaviorists objected to what they felt was a mentalistic and subjective concept; they interpreted effect to mean pleasurable sensations or something similar. However, Thorndike met this challenge (1913, p. 2) by pointing out that by a satisfying state of affairs he meant simply a state of affairs which the animal did nothing to avoid, often doing things which maintained or renewed it; by an annoying state of affairs he meant one which the animal often did something to end. Thorndike was not proposing a hedonism; he meant effect, not affect.

Once it became clear that Thorndike was defining terms in a behavioral manner, he was subjected to the accusation that his law was circular. Critics said that acquisition of response would have to be measured in order to determine whether or not the state of affairs was satisfying, and acquisition was just what the law of effect was intended to explain. If justified, this charge would show that Thorndike was saying, "If an animal will learn when its behavior is followed by a given state of affairs, it will learn when its behavior is followed by this state of affairs." This criticism is not fully justified, for the operations that Thorndike specified for satisfaction and annoyance may be different operations from those which constitute a test of new learning. Once satisfiers and annoyers have been determined in some standard situation, they can be used in other situations to test their efficacy as reinforcers. Such tests will be tests of the law of effect. The question, then, becomes one of how generally a given effect will reinforce behavior. Meehl (1950), among others, has directed considerable attention to this point.

Another criticism has been that Thorndike assumed that the satisfier or annoyer had to act backward upon a connection which had already occurred in order to strengthen it. However, it is just as easy to assume that the action is upon the persisting traces that are still active from the occurrence of the stimulus and response that preceded the satisfaction or annoyance. Neobehavioristic Hullian theory (Hull, 1952) has a specific postulate about stimulus traces which assumes that the action of a reinforcer depends upon its temporal relationship to the stimulus traces. This is simply a more sophisticated statement of Thorndike's position. There is no necessary retroaction implied by Thorndike's law of effect.

A last criticism has been of the automaticity of the strengthening which was supposed to occur. Thorndike believed that learning could occur independently of any consciousness about what was being learned or why it was being learned (Thorndike & Rock, 1934). He was particularly gratified by the discovery of the spread-of-effect phenomenon (1933a), since even the most ardent of his critics would not attempt to explain the strengthening of errors as an intelligent or purposive process. The extent to which Thorndike was correct in his emphasis on automaticity cannot yet be determined, so we cannot say whether or not the criticisms of his position were justified; there is currently a considerable body of empirical evidence for both sides. It is interesting, however, that something very much like Thorndike's hypothesized "OK," or confirmatory, reaction is suggested by the intracranial self-stimulation technique (N. E. Miller, 1958a; Olds, 1955); electrical stimulation of certain brain areas apparently has an automatic reinforcing effect on preceding responses.

Mechanistic Determinism

Our final example is related to the last criticism. It concerns the widespread feeling that mechanistic science, such as that represented by Thorndikian connectionism, destroys human values. Thorndike had a characteristic answer to this kind of objection. Here is the way that he posed the problem:

> We must consider one final objection to using the methods of science in the world of values. Science, according to a very popular view, deals with a fatalistic world in which men, their wants and ideals, are all parts of a reel which unwinds year by year, minor whirls in a fixed dance of atoms. Values can have no place in such a world, and efforts to attain them by science must fail.
>
> The truth of the matter, which is rather subtle, may best be realized by considering what I have elsewhere called the paradox of science, which is that scientists discover "causal" sequences and describe the world as one where the same cause will always produce the same effect, in order to change that world into a form nearer their heart's desire. Man makes the world a better home for man and himself a more successful dweller in it by discovering its regular unchangeable modes of action. He can determine the fate of the world and his own best, not by prayers or threats, but by treating it and himself by the method of science as phenomena, determined, as far as he can see, by their past history. (1949, pp. 346–347)

And here, in a nutshell, is his solution:

> Thus, at last, man may become ruler of himself as well as of the rest of nature. For strange as it may sound man is free only in a world whose every event he can understand and foresee. Only so can he guide it. We are captains of our own souls only in so far as they act in perfect law so that we can understand and foresee every response which we will make to every situation. Only so can we control our own selves. It is only because our intellects and morals—the mind and spirit of man—are a part of nature, that we can be in any significant sense responsible for them, proud of their progress, or trustful of their future. (1949, p. 362)

THE CONTRIBUTIONS OF THORNDIKE

Thorndike's 50 years of professional activity at Teachers College were among the most productive that have ever been recorded for a single man. Quantitatively, he accumulated a bibliography which at his death in 1949 had reached the amazing total of 507 items (Lorge, 1949). Many of these were long books and monographs, and many of them were stuffed full of quantitative data. Thorndike worked and published in a remarkably wide range of fields: He initiated the systematic laboratory investigation of animal learning; produced the first formalized associationistic learning theory; proceeded to an exhaustive analysis of human learning, as a result of which he revised his learning theory; became an active leader in the area of mental testing and educational practices; pioneered in the application of quantitative measures to certain sociopsychological problems; and contributed to the development of new techniques in the field of lexicography. All this within the span of a single lifetime!

Thorndike brought to all these fields the same direct and factual kind of approach that was so generally characteristic of his thinking. He was able to cut through to what he saw as the heart of a problem with a minimum of the verbiage and double-talk found in many writers. Whatever one may think of some of his ideas and whatever their eventual fate, we cannot fail to admire the freshness and perseverance of attack that he brought to the discipline.

Systematically, Thorndike's influence has declined, first as the more brash behaviorism took over in the 1920s, and more recently as the more sophisticated versions of neobehaviorism have emerged. But his work remains a bulwark of associationism, especially in the fields of animal and human learning and of educational psychology. As late as 1975, Hilgard and Bower gave over the second chapter of their popular book on learning theory to Thorndike's connectionism, while recognizing the decline within psychology of interest in the system. They quoted Tolman on the importance of Thorndike as a standard; Tolman's judgment was:

> The psychology of animal learning—not to mention that of child learning—has been and still is primarily a matter of agreeing or disagreeing with Thorndike, or trying in minor ways to improve upon him. Gestalt psychologists, conditioned-reflex psychologists, sign-gestalt psychologists—all of us here in America seem to have taken Thorndike, overtly or covertly, as a starting point. (1938, p. 11)

Forty years later, the picture has changed. In particular, B. F. Skinner's psychology is a kind of living monument to Thorndike's system, to which it bears a close intellectual resemblance. We will discuss Skinner in more detail later; but most of our readers will already have recognized that operant psychology relies heavily on a very detailed working out of the law of effect, and that Thorndike's deterministic, automatic-effect attitudes permeate operant psychology. As long as operant psychology lives, Thorndike's psychology lives.

CONTEMPORARY ROLE OF ASSOCIATIONISM

Interpreted most broadly, associationism is practically synonymous with an orthodox interpretation of science: it is a belief that the primary job of science is to relate phenomena, to look for functional relationships. This is a methodological characteristic it shares with functionalism. The two systematic movements have been closely connected in this country, as we have suggested throughout the discussion. Thorndike could well have been considered, along with Hall and Cattell, as a pioneer functionalist. But there is a justification for considering associationism separately. For one thing, it is a special kind of functionalism. And certainly one can be a systematic functionalist without being an associationist (James and Dewey are examples); contrariwise, one can be a systematic associationist without accepting anything but the shared methodological characteristic from functionalism (as is true of many neobehaviorists). The functionalist puts greater emphasis on adaptation in general than the associationist; in addition, functionalists may study this adaptation on a scale of evolutionary time, while associationists tend to limit themselves to the life of the individual organism.

Moreover, most associationists have a more restricted view than the functionalists, attempting to explain behavior with a more limited set of variables. Older associationists attempted to explain complex thought and behavior as *nothing but* the association of ideas. Thorndike was also a "nothing-butter": Behavior was explicable on the basis of nothing but stimulus-response connections, inherited or acquired. Present-day association theorists tend to be more cautious in their objectives and to accept a more restricted domain—a miniature system—for their theory.

Today associationism as a methodological tool, if not as a systematic position, has been fairly well incorporated into the body of psychology; association of variables is generally recognized as a fundamental task of science. However, exactly what is to be associated remains one of the critical problems for psychology. Thorndike's answer emphasized the wide range of possible stimulus and response factors. Whether or not a strict S-R associationism can be effectively applied to explain a broad range of overt behaviors still remains in doubt, although the more refined varieties of associationism now being developed show promise.

There are four interrelated lines of current development. First, research on the conditioned reflex continues, particularly in Russia (Cole & Maltzman, 1969). The Russian work in the tradition of Pavlov and Bekhterev has reached a height of sophistication which surprises most western visitors. In the United States, Gregory Razran (1949) adapted Pavlov's procedure for application to human subjects by using cotton dental plugs to collect the saliva. The amount of salivation can be quantified simply by weighing the plugs before and after each trial. Razran used this procedure to study conditioning involving verbal stimuli.

Second, the neobehavioristic stimulus-response theory of Hull and his many followers and collaborators represents a very important continuing influence. Here again the interest has been mainly in the field of learning, animal as well as human, where in addition to Hull himself, Kenneth Spence (1956, 1960) has been one of the foremost users of strict associationism (see Chapter 10). A more flexible kind of S-R associationism is evident in the work of Neal Miller and John Dollard (Dollard & Miller, 1950; N. E. Miller & Dollard, 1941), where the basic S-R concepts have been extended into the fields of social and abnormal behavior (see Chapter 12). Miller (1959) continued to liberate S-R concepts in more recent publications as well.

A third line is represented by the early associationistic theory of Guthrie (1935, 1952) and the more recent mathematizing of this kind of thinking in Estes' statistical association theory of learning (Estes, 1950). Here associationism is presented in perhaps its boldest form, since the simple principle of contiguity between stimulus and response is utilized as the fundamental law of learning. Within learning theory, Guthrie has long been, almost single-handedly, an articulate supporter of a simple contiguity position wherein learning is seen as fundamentally a matter of associations and nothing else; Estes' mathematical theorizing has given rigorous quantitative expression to this basic associationistic principle. In later writing (1959, pp. 402–405), Estes has indicated some acceptance of reinforcement as a descriptive concept if not as an explanatory principle. These issues are elaborated in Chapters 10 and 13.

Finally, there are some versions of associationism which are somewhat less orthodox than the preceding but which have enjoyed vigorous success. Two important examples are the learning theories of Tolman and Skinner. Tolman's purposive behaviorism (1932) is a cognitive type of learning theory that stresses association between stimuli—a sign-Gestalt or sign-significate theory (see Chapter 11). We have already discussed the close philosophical kinship between

Thorndike and Skinner. The most important distinction between Skinner's position and that of a typical associationist is that Skinner places little reliance on the *stimulus*-response relationship; he is far more concerned with the response-*reinforcement* relationship; this will all be further discussed in Chapter 10.

DIMENSIONAL DESCRIPTIONS OF ASSOCIATIONISM

Now that we have examined the origins of associationism and have discussed one theorist who exemplified it in its finished American form, it is appropriate to see whether we can describe it in terms of the dimensional system provided by R. I. Watson. In order to clarify our thinking about how the dimensions should be applied, we will discuss briefly the mean rating on each dimension and the reason that we thought it a reasonable rating. The left-most position on each dimension, characterized by the first word in Watson's polarity, is rated 1; the right-most position, described by the most extreme emphasis in the other direction, is represented by a 5.

We run into a slight difficulty on the very first dimension. The early associationists put their emphasis on conscious mentalism. This is hardly surprising; although the concept of the unconscious was clear in Leibniz, the publication of his work on this subject occurred 50 years after he had died in 1716. Not a great deal was made of the unconscious until Herbart had published his mathematics of the unconscious in 1824 and 1825. We have seen how Thorndike, 100 years or so after Herbart, shifted his emphasis to the automatic—and thus unconscious—action of the law of effect. Pavlov also had little use for conscious mentalism; his objective emphasis probably left little room for an interest in unconscious mentalism either. Because of this shift over time, we have chosen a nice conservative 2.2 as an average rating, slightly toward conscious mentalism. This could be regarded as a bow of courtesy toward the older associationists.

A very similar problem occurs with respect to Watson's second dimension. There was a clear movement from a concern with subjective content—the association of ideas—to a concern with objective content, with overt stimulus and response. We again leaned in the direction of the older view, by giving a rating of 3.2, somewhat in the direction of the subjective emphasis.

We did not see any such problem with determinism versus indeterminism. Even when the British empiricists were talking only about ideas, they were accounting for them through the use of deterministic principles, and that has been an enduring aspect of the system; hence the 1.3 rating.

One need hardly mention that empiricism was the core characteristic of the system: 1.1.

With respect to structuralism versus functionalism, there seems to be no clear ground for assigning a position. The older, philosophical, association would seem to have a more structuralistic orientation; what is in the mind seemed a more central question than what it was there for. Thorndike and Pavlov were quite concerned with the adaptive functions of S-R connections. It looks like another compromise: 2.4, and don't take that number as representing any individual's position.

Inductivism-deductivism presents no problems at all; from Francis Bacon to Skinner, the associationistic tradition has gone down the line with inductivism; we would have to go all the way back to Aristotle to find a problem. That genius of philosophy used inductive procedures, but also lent his very name to the deductive procedures suggested by the phrase *Aristotelian logic.* Thus, a 1.5, strongly inductive.

On mechanism-vitalism, again no problem: a strongly mechanistic 1.4.

In terms of methods, there is the same problem of objectivism-subjectivism that we found in terms of content: associationism has shifted in the objective direction. However, we felt that even when the concern was with subjective *content,* there was a tendency for the associationist to prefer objective methods; hence we assigned a 1.9 on this dimension.

Associationism began by being molecular, trying to account for complex ideas in terms of their components, and it ended by being molecular, trying to account for complex behaviors in terms of their S-R units. Molecular forever, with a 1.2!

The monistic-dualistic problem, when it comes to assigning a representative rating, is almost insoluble. Locke pretty clearly implied a dualism with his internal and external reality, which he related via his primary and secondary qualities. Berkeley and Hume, although they maintained that only the mental contents could be known directly, did not seem secure in their elimination of the external world. Pavlov and Thorndike, although they made little use of consciousness in their thinking, did not seem at all secure in eliminating the internal world. Therefore we rated associationism as being somewhat tinged with dualism: 3.3.

We rated associationism toward the naturalistic, rather than the supernaturalistic, side with a 2.3. That may be too low; it is hard to find supernaturalism in any measure in any associationist, except for Bishop Berkeley.

It is always confusing to rate the nomotheticism-idographicism dimension, and this is as good a place as any to explain why. There are, of course, the usual difficulties in weighing the positions of individuals who worked at different times, and in interpreting what they meant in the first place. However, the additional difficulty with this dimension is that the dimension itself is complex and confusing. It is all very well to say that nomotheticism puts the emphasis upon discovering general laws, and that idiographicism puts the emphasis upon accounting for the behavior of particular events or individuals. But the minute one asks how general laws can be discovered, it appears that it can be only through the study of individual events or individuals. When one asks how general laws can be tested, it appears that it can be only through the prediction of individual events or the behavior of individuals. On the other side of the coin, it appears that one could only give a scientifically satisfactory account of the individual event by showing how it was explained by general laws. Falk (1956) wrote a long review just on this rather muddled issue. It seems best to look at just what individual psychologists believe about how they should study individuals versus groups, and how they intend to use the information they obtain to explain behavior. It is difficult or impossible to make sense of such a complex issue by assigning a position on a single dimension, but we have pressed on to assign the whole system of associationism a 1.3 because of our belief that all science is really nomothetic, and the associationistic tradition is fundamentally scientific.

Peripheralism-centralism is another "moving" dimension, with the early associationists emphasizing the "centralistic" mental events, and the later ones the peripheralistic stimuli and responses. We assign a perfectly chicken 2.5, nearly in the middle.

We assigned associationism a somewhat utilitarian 1.6, a position which would be a better description of Pavlov or Thorndike than of Berkeley or Hume. We may have overstated the case here, for admittedly there is an aura of pure science about the associationistic tendency to break situations down into very small units, which may not look too significant at a practical level.

There is likely little disagreement that associationism tends to be quantitative. Breaking down complex ideas or behaviors into small units is an invitation to counting, and we see the culmination of this tradition in Thorndike and Pavlov: 1.9, and maybe the number should be smaller.

Again, it is difficult to assign a position on rationalism versus irrationalism. We would not like to imply that there is anything irrational about associationism, and of course that is not the intention of the irrationalism end of the dimension. The meaning is that the system puts the emphasis on irrational factors in accounting for behavior. Locke, very early in this tradition, accounted for some peculiar behaviors in terms of unusual associations; for example, one might have a fear of the dark because ghoulish stories were told about events in the night. Thorndike emphasized such accidental influences, particularly in his claims that errors could "irrationally" be strengthened by their closeness to reinforcement. For these sorts of reasons, we rated associationism as a rather irrationalistic 1.9.

It is in the very nature of an empiricistic view of epistemology that it be developmental; that is, changes occur over time because the organism is influenced by the environment in which it happens to exist. We assigned a 3.3 on this dimension; the number would have been even higher, except that it is not clear that associationists have always put as much emphasis on developmentalism as their philosophical presuppositions might have indicated.

The last contrast, between staticism and dynamicism, is closely related to the immediately preceding polarity of staticism-developmentalism. However, in the preceding case, the focus seems to be more on the progressive development of individuals, versus a cross-sectional view of them; and in the case of staticism versus dynamicism, the focus is on a general fluidity versus permanence, which might be manifested in any direction and even within a very short period of time. We rated associationism an intermediate 2.6 here, since, despite its developmentalism, there seems to be a staticistic (in the second sense) tendency for associationists to assume that associations, once formed, are permanent.

We asked one class of twenty-three graduate students to decide which of Watson's dimensions were most critically involved in the central theses of associationism. They chose, in order, as the three most representative poles: empiricism, determinism, and quantitativism. These choices do seem to describe the essence of associationism, although one should never forget molecularism as another central feature.

That concludes our dimensional analysis of associationism. Now that the reader is more familiar with our intentions and "rational" procedures, we shall analyze succeeding systems much more briefly. Explicit discussion will be confined to critical or problematic dimensions, but we hope that readers will continue to assign their own values and compare them with the mean authors' assignment, as these are presented in Table 1-1.

SUMMARY AND CONCLUSIONS

In this chapter we have traced associationism from its origins and development in British empiricism, where the important tradition of association of ideas was elaborated, through its modification more recently to an association of behavior, and to its emergence in the work of Thorndike as a full-fledged association of stimulus and response. We have treated Thorndike's connectionism as the best representative of associationism, although it was not developed by him as a coherent system. We have tried to indicate the kinds of answers that can be given to some of the major criticisms of Thorndikian connectionism and have presented our evaluation of the significance of Thorndike's work. We have indicated the role of associationism in contemporary psychology, pointing out that in a broad methodological sense, association of variables is the primary task of all science. Finally, we have sketched the major lines of current development of the basic associationistic principle.

It is clear that the associationistic principle must be accorded a key role in psychology, whatever the ultimate fate of the various systems and theories which build upon it as a necessary and sufficient principle. Some kind of associationism is certainly necessary, in a methodological if not a systematic or theoretical sense; whether it is also sufficient as a learning theory is much more doubtful, but still remains to be seen. In any case, it is remarkable that so ancient and simple a notion should persist so long, let alone be accorded an increasingly significant role in contemporary behavior theory. Its long viability attests to its vitality, especially when one considers that empirical tests have been applied since the work of Ebbinghaus and Pavlov. These tests have become increasingly precise and rigorous recently, as mathematical modelers have taken advantage of the quantitative character of associationistic procedures to make exact predictions. It will be most interesting to see whether or not associationistic concepts will continue to serve as the central core of mathematical learning theory.

FURTHER READINGS

Boring's treatment in his *History of experimental psychology* (1950) may always remain a recommended source of information about the important British empiricists and associationists. *A source book in the history of psychology* (1965), edited by Boring with Herrnstein, provides beautifully introduced and organized selected readings from the British empiricists and related theorists in the early part of the twentieth century. In our own book *Systems and theories in psychology: A reader* (1974), we offer a set of selections especially coordinated with the present text. Turner's *Philosophy and the science of behavior* (1967) gives a sophisticated and admiring analysis of the British empiricists, and demonstrates their immediate contemporary significance. *A handbook of contemporary Soviet psychology* (1969) edited by Cole and Maltzman, can be consulted for access to the Russian conditioning literature. As we have already indicated, the easiest access to Thorndike's system is through his *Selected writings from a connectionist's psychology* (1949).

Table 4-1 Important Figures in Structuralism

Antecedent influences	Structuralists	
	Pioneers and founders	**Developers of related positions**
Franz Brentano (1838-1917)	Wilhelm Wundt—Leipzig (1832-1920)	Carl Stumpf—Berlin (1848-1936)
Gustav Fechner (1801-1887)	Edward B. Titchener—Cornell (1867-1927)	G. E. Muller—Gottingen (1850-1934)
H. L. F. von Helmholtz (1821-1894)		Oswald Külpe—Würzburg (1862-1915)
		J. P. Nafe—Washington University (St. Louis) (1888-1970)
		Edward G. Boring—Harvard (1886-1968)

Chapter 4

Structuralism

The highly developed introspective psychology that goes under the name *structuralism* or *existentialism* is represented in its finished American form by the work of E. B. Titchener. In 1898, Titchener so sharpened and dramatized the structural-functional distinction, made almost casually by James in 1884, that he effectively named both systems (see R. I. Watson, 1968, pp. 397–399). He pointed out the analogy between the type of psychology he favored and the study of structure in biology. Titchener's system was a refinement of the psychology of his mentor, Wilhelm Wundt, founder of the Leipzig laboratory. During the early years of psychology, in Germany, structural psychology was *the* psychology. Its purpose was the introspective analysis of the human mind; psychology was to be a kind of chemistry of consciousness. The primary task of the psychologist was to discover the nature of the elementary conscious experiences and, later, their relationships to one another. Introspection by a highly trained person was thought to be the necessary tool.

Table 4-1, on the left, lists the most important persons in structuralism.

The major significance of structuralism has been threefold. First, it gave psychology a strong scientific impetus, getting the name *psychology* attached for the first time to a scientific type of endeavor with formal academic recognition and clearly separated from the two main parental fields, physiology and philosophy. Second, it provided a thorough test of the classic introspective method as the only method for a complete psychology. Third, it provided a strong orthodoxy against which the functional, behavioristic, and Gestalt forces could organize their resistance. The newer schools arose from a progressive reformulation and final discarding of the basic structural problems. This fact alone makes the analytic introspective psychology of Wundt and Titchener a necessary subject for contemporary study.

ANTECEDENTS OF STRUCTURALISM

The Psychology of Wundt

It is customary, at least in America, to cite Titchener as the founder of structural psychology. Certainly he named it, developed it, and buttressed it against functional and behavioristic trends. However, Titchener's system was basically the same as that of Wilhelm Wundt (1832–1920), under whom Titchener had studied. Wundt himself was a self-conscious systematizer and the "father" of the new experimental psychology. He established the first formal laboratory for psychology at the University of Leipzig in 1879. We shall, however, follow American tradition and treat Wundt as a forerunner of the structuralist school, meanwhile recognizing that he was far more than a mere antecedent.

Although Wilhelm Maximilian Wundt thus became the father of psychology in general and of structuralism in particular, he did not have an easy time in becoming the father of anything else, including children. For one thing, Wundt almost died of tuberculosis in 1857, when he was not yet 25 years old. For another, he was so poor that it was not until he reached the age of 40, in 1872, that he made enough money to marry his longtime fiancee, Sophie Mau (Bringmann, Balance & Evans, 1975).

Wundt's relative poverty was initiated by his being born the fourth child of a country pastor who came to the small town of Neckarau, where Wundt was born. The young Wilhelm became very close to his father's young assistant, Friedrich Müller, who tutored and befriended him. The young Wundt apparently had few childhood friends, and perhaps hardly had a childhood. He did not do well in high school away from home and, after failing one year, finished without very good marks. He did finally make friends of his own age, and began to develop an interest in reading and intellectual life. Because of a lack of money, he could not afford to go to the university; he went to medical school instead, and after a miserable first year, he finished and made the top score in the medical board examinations in 1855. Following research, further study, and a stint as an assistant to Helmholtz, Wundt was at last rewarded in 1872 with the appointment to teach Helmholtz's courses temporarily. Helmholtz had left for Berlin, leaving the field at last clear for Wundt, and making it possible for him to marry.

At that point everything suddenly turned good for Wundt. He immediately, in 1872, got a chair in Zurich, followed the very next year by a chair in the more prestigious University of Leipzig (now called the Karl Marx University). It was not long before Wundt was building up the laboratory that made him so famous.

His psychology was to be a sort of experimental mental chemistry, which should remind us of John Stuart Mill's picture of the development of complex ideas.

It seems very likely that Wundt's enterprise received a tremendous boost from the triumphs of chemistry itself, particularly of Mendeleev. In 1871 Mendeleev had revised his periodic table of the elements, first published in 1869, and had predicted from this table the existence of three new, as yet undiscovered, elements. In 1875 the first one of the three, germanium, was discovered; in 1879, the second, scandium, was discovered. That was the very year in which Wundt founded his laboratory.

Even at this distance in time and space, we should be able to imagine the intense excitement and high hopes that attended an enterprise which was to develop a veritable periodic table of the mind. Students flocked to Leipzig from as far away as America, England, and even Japan. It was of course absolutely necessary to follow Wundt's course once one had arrived in faraway eastern Germany. Although some, like America's cynical George Stanley Hall, became disillusioned, most came with a fervor and intensity of purpose which are appropriate when one is part of a new enterprise of high moment.

Wundt lived to the age of 88 and died in 1920. Yet he probably never realized the extent to which the new science was to bear his stamp. I (Hillix) have traced back the academic lineage of the San Diego State University faculty. Of the fifty-five people traced, twenty-eight go back to Wundt. Thus, it appears from this sample that Wundt's American students so preempted the field of American psychology that half of it became theirs, with only half left to students of William James, Carl Stumpf, and all other competitors. Wundt seems to deserve his title of father of psychology very directly, through academic lineage.

Wundt himself had antecedents, some of whom were discussed in Chapter 2. Another antecedent, partly oppositional in its views, may be seen in the phenomenological tradition in German philosophy and psychology at his time. Turner (1967, p. 60) defines phenomenology as a philosophy which regards the entities of experience as possessing an irreducible integrity of their own. Kant, in his *Critique of pure reason,* developed a part of the phenomenological viewpoint. He believed that whatever is known is phenomenon, and that knowing requires an appearance in consciousness. Knowledge was thus restricted by Kant to appearances. This influence is still felt in modern phenomenology; for example, Lauer (1965) says: "If we are to know what anything is—and this the phenomenologist will do—we must examine the consciousness we have of it; if this does not give us an answer, nothing will" (p. 7).

In 1856, Lazarus and Steinthal first distinguished between phenomenology and psychology (see Capretta, 1967). They asserted that the former is concerned with a description of the phenomena of mental life, while the latter seeks to establish causal explanations of these phenomena. Thus when Wundt appeared on the scene opinions were already being expressed on the relationship of phenomenology to psychology. Wundt was not temperamentally a phenomenologist. He thought that psychology needed laboratory experimentation carried out by trained observers, not just the careful observations of phenomenologists.

Wundt's philosophy was neither materialistic nor spiritualistic. He opposed the latter type of view because he thought it erred in trying to establish a science of mental experience in terms of speculations about a "thinking substance." He opposed materialism because he did not think a science of mind could be developed through physical investigations of the brain. Wundt felt that the study of mind must be a science of experience (agreeing on this point with the phenomenologists).

Wundt, however, believed that psychology must be experimental. Schultz (1969) quotes Boring as saying: "The application of the experimental method to the problem of mind is the great outstanding event in the history of the study of the mind, an event to which no other is comparable" (epigraph). We owe Wundt a great debt for establishing psychology as an experimental science. Here is some of what he has to say on the subject:

> It is experiment, then, that has been the source of the decided advance in natural science, and brought about such revolutions in our scientific views. Let us now apply experiment to the science of mind. We must remember that in every department of investigation the experimental method takes on an especial form, according to the nature of the facts investigated. In psychology we find that only those mental phenomena which are directly accessible to physical influences can be made the subject matter of experiment. We cannot experiment upon mind itself, but only upon its outworks, the organs of sense and movement which are functionally related to mental processes. (1894, p. 10)

The subject matter of psychology was to be *immediate experience,* as contrasted to *mediate experience.* By mediate experience Wundt meant experience used as a means of knowledge about something other than the experience itself. This is the usual way in which we use experience in acquiring knowledge about the world. We say, "The *leaf* is green"; the quotation implies that our primary interest is in the leaf, not in the fact that we are experiencing green. Immediate experience for Wundt was experience per se, and the task of psychology was the study of this immediate experience in itself. This distinction looks backward at Locke's distinction between primary and secondary qualities and forward toward Titchener's distinction between the subject matters of psychology and physics. If we attempt to describe the experience we have in connection with a toothache, we are concerned with immediate experience. However, if we, in conjunction with a dentist, start to use the experience to find out about the place and nature of the difficulty which leads us to have the toothache experience, we have switched to the use of mediate experience. It is clear that the experience in each case is, in principle, the same. Only our purposes, and hence possibly the aspects of the experience to which we attend, change.

The physicist is therefore interested only in mediate experience, but the Wundtian psychologist studies immediate experience. The method of study was to be *introspection,* or *Selbstbeobachtung* (self-observation). Introspection was the *controlled* observation of the contents of consciousness under experimental conditions. Nonexperimental introspection was useless for scientific purposes. Wundt clarified his position in the preface to his *Principles of physiological psychology:*

> All accurate observation implies that the object of observation (in this case the psychical process) can be held fast by the attention, and any changes that it undergoes attentively followed. And this fixation by the attention implies, in its turn, that the observed object is independent of the observer. Now it is obvious that the required independence does not obtain in any attempt at a direct self-observation, undertaken without the help of experiment. The endeavor to observe oneself must inevitably introduce changes into the course of mental events—changes which could not have occurred without it, and whose usual consequence is that the very process which was to have been observed disappears from consciousness. In the first place, it (the experimental method) creates external conditions that look towards the production of a determinate mental process at a given moment. In the second place, it makes the observer so far master of the general situation, that the state of consciousness accompanying this process remains approximately unchanged. (1904, p. 45)

Wundt thought that mind and body were parallel, but not directly interacting systems. Thus the mind did not depend on the body and could be studied directly with profit. Psychology was formally called *physiological psychology,* but the task of relating mental events to their bodily parallels could wait until later. Wundt did not think that introspection yielded the only psychological knowledge:

> We may add that, fortunately for the science, there are other sources of objective psychological knowledge, which become accessible at the very point where the experimental method fails us. . . . In this way, experimental psychology and ethnic psychology form the principal departments of scientific psychology at large. They are supplemented by child and animal psychology, which in conjunction with ethnic psychology attempt to resolve the problems of psychogenesis. Workers in both these fields may, of course, avail themselves within certain limits of the advantages of the experimental method. But the results of experiment are here matters of objective observation only, and the experimental method accordingly loses the peculiar significance which it possesses as an instrument of introspection. (1904, p. 5)

Thus Wundt formally recognized methods and areas of psychology other than the particular brand in which he was most interested. Moreover, he did not simply talk about such topics as ethnic psychology; he published ten volumes of his *Völkerpsychologie* (1900–1909) between 1900 and his death in 1920. He did largely "simply talk" about child and animal psychology. The translation of his work *Human and animal psychology* (1894) devotes only 26 of its 454 pages to animal psychology. Wundt's publications and those of his students indicate that he felt these aspects of psychology were of much lesser importance.

Although there are some unevennesses in Wundt's treatment of psychology, there is a much greater unevenness in the modern psychologist's picture of Wundt's psychology. We probably stereotype or parody the position of almost every historical figure, but Wundt and Titchener receive particularly unjust treatment. Anderson (1971) submitted a list of Wundt's statements to a group of graduate students and asked the students to match the quotations to the names of a group of outstanding figures in the history of psychology, one of whom was Wundt. In no case was a quotation attributed to Wundt most often, although they all came from him. It seemed clear that the students regarded many of the statements as too modern or too experimentally or behaviorally oriented to have come from Wundt.

Wundt conceived of the problem of experimental psychology as threefold: To analyze conscious processes into elements, to discover how these elements are connected, and to determine the laws of connection. Wundt's attitude toward the thing analyzed, toward consciousness, left some room for ambiguity. He explicitly talked about mental *process,* not mental *contents* (1894): "As a matter of fact, ideas, like all other mental experiences, are not *objects,* but *processes, occurrences* " (p. 236).

Yet the view of psychology as the science that searches for the elements of process was a difficult one. The result of the lack of clarity was that Wundt was accused of a static elementism—of regarding the contents of consciousness as though they were stationary, structural elements. The name *existentialism* was affixed to the school because it seemed that the elements of consciousness were regarded as existing just as physical objects exist. The experimental work at Leipzig sometimes seemed to justify the critics in their accusations, in spite of the systematic opposition of Wundt to such a view of his psychology. Nevertheless, Boring's (1950) description of the naming of structural psychology is a beautiful summary of the general treatment accorded structural psychology in the United States: "The enemies of this orthodox psychology name it, but always in accordance with what they most dislike in it" (p. 431).

Bringmann, Balance, and Evans (1975) cite Wundt's last assistant, Friedrich Sander, as saying that Wundt as an old man was mellow, tired of controversy, and fond of anecdote, the sort of grandfather that we would all like to have; and, speaking as psychologists, this was the professional "grandfather" that we did have. He probably would not have cared about the opinions of his critics, and, when he thought about it, he could take pride in the fact that he had taught 24,000 students. My wife and I (Hillix) stood at the beautiful graveside of Wundt and his family in the summer of 1977, when a small bird lighted on her hand. "It's Wundt, making us welcome," she said. It is to be hoped that the experimental Wundt never became mellow enough to approve of *that!*

Other European Psychologists

Although Wundt was clearly the most important systematizer and organizer in the early, formative days of psychology, he was by no means the only psychologist in the European tradition who influenced Titchener. Many followed Wundt's lead more or less closely, but others sprang from a different lineage. None of them, however, disagreed with Wundt about the central importance of introspection as *the* methodology to be used in psychology. As Boring (1953) has pointed out in his account of the history of introspection, none of these early psychologists thought of themselves especially as *introspectionists;* they were simply *psychologists,* regarding the importance of introspection as absolutely axiomatic. The only arguments were about the details of the method.

Franz Brentano (1838–1917) was perhaps the most influential of the non-

Wundtians because of the diverse effects he had within psychology. He was originally trained for the priesthood, but took a doctoral degree in philosophy and taught this subject on university appointments first at Würzburg and later at Vienna. He resigned his priesthood because he could not accept the doctrine of infallibility of the Pope. He was known as a great Aristotelian, and he influenced Gestalt psychology and psychoanalysis, in addition to providing a contemporary competitor to Wundt and Titchener.

Brentano's name is associated with *act psychology*. Its major tenet is that psychology should study mental acts or processes rather than mental contents. He believed that mental acts always refer to objects; for example, if we regard hearing as the mental act, it always refers to something heard. In this case, the truly mental event is the hearing, which is an act and not a content. If we see a color, again it is the seeing which is mental, not the thing seen. His *Psychologie* (1874) was the most important of his psychological publications. Brentano was basically a philosopher rather than a scientist and an empiricist rather than an experimentalist. He influenced structural psychology by his opposition rather than by any positive contributions, and he also had a strong influence on phenomenology.

Carl Stumpf (1848–1936) was Wundt's major direct competitor. In 1894, he was awarded the outstanding professorship in German psychology at the University of Berlin, when Wundt, as dean of German psychologists, had seemed the logical choice. It has been rumored that the opposition of Helmholtz prevented Wundt from getting the appointment. There is, however, not a shred of direct evidence to support the rumor, and Wundt's own statements in his autobiography seem to deny it. Thus, like most rumors, this one should not be repeated, and would not be if it were not so delicious.

Stumpf was strongly influenced by Brentano. This influence may have been the cause of his accepting a less rigorous type of introspection than that considered acceptable by Wundt. Their difference of opinion is illustrated by the fact that they carried on an acrimonious argument in a series of publications. The problem concerned tones, and the issue was whether one should accept the results of highly trained introspectors (Wundt) or of trained and expert musicians (Stumpf). Stumpf refused to accept the results obtained in Wundt's laboratory. The disagreement was what one would expect between a man who took a more phenomenological view and one (Wundt) who insisted on a more analytic type of introspection. It was one of Stumpf's students, Husserl, who is usually credited with starting phenomenology as a formal doctrine. Husserl, however, had earlier studied with Brentano, and that association plus his study with Stumpf may have helped to nurture his phenomenological views. He would not have received that nurturance with Wundt or Titchener!

Stumpf's laboratory at Berlin never rivaled Wundt's in scope or intensity of research, but there were many research projects. Stumpf's special field was audition, and his true love was music. Also, there were several men at Berlin who were destined to be of great importance in the development of psychology—notably the three founders of Gestalt psychology, Wertheimer, Köhler, and Koffka; Kurt Lewin, an important field theorist; and Max Meyer, who was an early behaviorist. Stumpf, like Brentano, was of greater significance for his differences from Titchener than for his similarities to him, although he accepted without question the use of introspection.

The most capable and productive experimental psychologist of the time was G. E. Müller (1850–1934). He spent some forty years directing the laboratory at Göttingen. His major work was in the fields of memory, psychophysical methodology, and vision. With Pilzecker, he developed the interference theory of forgetting, and they called the phenomenon wherein new learning interferes with old *retroactive inhibition.* Müller also refined Fechner's techniques in psychophysics and extended Hering's theory of color vision.

More than Wundt or Stumpf, Müller succeeded in cutting free from philosophy and metaphysics, which had been his own early interests. In this respect he was similar to Titchener, who also struggled to free himself of the encumbrance of too much concern for philosophy.

Oswald Külpe (1862–1915) was trained in the Leipzig laboratory by Wundt and for a shorter time in the Göttingen laboratory by Müller. While at Leipzig, Külpe became a friend of Titchener, but the two men were later to have fundamental disagreements; Külpe was not to be a carrier of the Wundtian orthodoxy, and Titchener was.

The first part of Külpe's psychological career was spent in more or less classic research efforts. He published a textbook (1895), which was quickly translated by Titchener, in which he attempted to report only the experimental facts obtained by careful experimental introspection. Very soon thereafter he went to Würzburg, where he directed a series of ingenious and provocative introspective experiments on thought. Classic introspection was found to be incomplete; the continuity in thinking appeared to elude the orthodox introspective analysis. The Würzburg interpretation of the results was that there are *impalpable awarenesses* which do not appear in consciousness as contents usually do, and which should be regarded as functions. They were to be included, however, as genuine conscious data. The points of view of both Brentano and Wundt were accepted by Külpe when he accepted both contents and functions (acts) as conscious experience.

Külpe had a more direct relationship to Titchener in that he made the distinction between psychology and physics on a different basis from the one Wundt used; to Külpe, and later to Titchener, psychology was distinguished by its concern with the dependence of experience upon the experiencing organism. Both men apparently borrowed this distinction from the philosophers Mach and Avenarius, although its relation to Locke's distinction is also clear.

TITCHENER'S STRUCTURALISM

Edward Bradford Titchener (1867–1927) was a native of the English town of Chichester. After receiving an education in his native land, which included training as a physiologist, he joined the students who were beginning to flock to the new mecca of psychology, Leipzig. He studied there with Wundt for 2 years, from 1890 until 1892, when he came to the United States. Wundt left an indelible impression on Titchener in those 2 short years. Titchener's apparent Germanness of personality has become a legend: his autocratic attitude, the formality of his lectures in academic robes, and even his bearded, Germanic appearance. Every lecture was a dramatic production, with the staging carefully prepared by assistants. The presentation began precisely on time, with Titchener sweeping onto the stage in his robes, continued through demonstrations in which Titchener was flanked by his able assistants, and ended with the last period of the lecture in near coincidence with the end of the hour.

Titchener spent all of his years in the United States at Cornell University. During most of those 35 years he was truly a power to be reckoned with, despite the fact that his brand of Wundtian psychology never was accepted well by the pragmatic Americans. However, the greater popularity of the functional and behavioral schools, and perhaps simple fatigue, gradually took their toll. During the last years of his life he turned his interests from psychology toward numismatics, and died relatively young in 1927. He left behind such high goals of scholarship that Boring, his most famous student and the writer of America's best known and best-loved history of psychology, was later to say that there were no scholars in American psychology. A likely guess is that Boring was measuring himself and others against the standards of Titchener.

Titchener's intellectual Germanness is quite as remarkable as his legendary Germanness of personality, although it may not be as much emphasized. There were other non-German students whose exposure to Wundt was more protracted than Titchener's but whose deviations from the line of orthodoxy laid down by Wundt were marked; a number of these students came from America and returned to America. Perhaps the English culture from which Titchener came provided better nurture for a German psychology than did the practical-minded American spirit. Wundt owed a great deal to the English empiricists, and no doubt Titchener in England had already been influenced by these predecessors of Wundt. It is even possible that much of the perceived Germanness of his personal demeanor may have been in the eyes of the beholders—the provincial Americans—who may not have distinguished between a truly German personality and a generally European one. At any rate, psychology for Titchener was very much like psychology for Wundt.

A major theme throughout Titchener's work is the unity of science. It seemed self-evident to him that all sciences were erected from the same foundation—the world of human experience. When this world was observed in different ways, different sciences evolved. For example, Titchener believed that just as physics evolved when people began to view the world as being a vast machine, so did psychology evolve when they looked at it as a mind, a set of experiences subject to psychological laws. To illustrate this idea of scientific unity further, at various junctures he drew analogies between the then-nascent science of psychology and the more established sciences of biology (1898) and of physics and chemistry (1910).

Titchener (1910) felt that the hallmark of scientific method was observation, which in his view subsumed experimentation. He saw an experiment as an observation that could be repeated, isolated, and varied, thereby ensuring clearness and accuracy. He then distinguished between the physical science type of observation (looking at) and psychological observation or introspection (looking within).

States of consciousness were the proper objects of this psychological study. Titchener launched structural psychology in the United States in his paper, "The postulates of a structural psychology," partly as follows:

> Biology, defined in its widest sense as the science of life and of living things, falls into three parts, or may be approached from any one of three points of view. We may inquire into the structure of an organism, without regard to function—by analysis determining its component parts, and by synthesis exhibiting the mode of its formation from the parts. . . .
>
> We find a parallel to morphology in a very large portion of "experimental" psychology. The primary aim of the experimental psychologist has been to analyze the structure of the mind; to ravel out the elemental processes from the tangle of consciousness, or (if we may change the metaphor) to isolate the constituents in the given conscious formation. His task is a vivisection, but a vivisection which shall yield structural, not functional results. He tries to discover, first of all, what is there and in what quantity, not what it is there for. (1898, pp. 449–450; see also Dennis, 1948, p. 366)

It is difficult to tell, from this quotation, just what Titchener thought about mind and consciousness. He changes metaphor, self-consciously, in midsentence. From the context it seems that the bulk of his writing and thinking fits the second metaphor, although he speaks of consciousness as composed of processes rather than elements in his most rigorous, self-conscious writing. Yet by analogy he lends reality status to consciousness, since the word *structure* and the biological attitude toward morphology lend such reality status.

It is not even safe to assume that the founder of America's brand of structuralism rejected functionalism. On this subject, R. I. Watson makes the following flat statement:

> Description of Titchener's system of psychology is sometimes oversimplified. He was a structuralist, critics said, meaning that the static elements of experience were his concern, as contrasted with functional study of the process of experience which had been espoused by James and others. This is simply not true. There is no doubt he utilized functional material; and the findings of psychophysics, which formed one major segment in his system, are readily viewed as depending upon the functions of discrimination and estimation. Unequivocally, he accepted the existence of a functional aspect of psychology. (1968, p. 393)

Still, a stubborn critic might argue that Titchener *regretted* the existence of functionalism, though he *recognized* it.

Consciousness was defined by Titchener as the sum total of a person's experiences as they are at any given time. Mind was regarded as the sum total of a person's experiences considered as dependent on the person, summed from birth to death. Thus:

> "Mind" is understood to mean simply the sum total of mental processes experienced by the individual during his lifetime. Ideas, feelings, impulses, etc., are mental processes; the whole number of ideas, feelings, impulses, etc., experienced by me during my life constitutes my "mind." (1899, p. 12)

Titchener also listed three problems for psychology that were very similar to Wundt's:

> The aim of the psychologist is three-fold. He seeks (1) to analyze concrete (actual) mental experience into its simplest components, (2) to discover how these elements combine, what are the laws which govern their combination, and (3) to bring them into connection with their physiological (bodily) conditions. (1899, p. 15)

Titchener modified Wundt's distinction between psychology and physics much as Külpe did. He could not agree with Wundt that physics studied mediate experience and psychology immediate experience; he thought that all experience must be regarded as immediate. The distinction, rather, was in the *attitude* to be taken toward the study of the ever-immediate experience. The physicist studied the experience as independent of the experiencing person, while the psychologist studied the experience as it *depended* on the experiencing person.

One might object that the astronomers after Bessel were quite concerned with the dependence of experience upon the nature of the experiencing observer and that the physicists would also be prepared to evince concern. The reply to such an objection might be that the physicists' concern with the role of the observer was evinced only so that observations could again be made completely reliable and independent of the observer, and thus illustrated their basic attitude rather than an exception to it.

Titchener's concept of *stimulus error* was related to the distinction between psychology and physics. By stimulus error, Titchener meant the error of paying attention to, and reporting on, the known properties of the stimulus rather than the sensory experience itself. This is probably the most important and the most obvious error made by untrained introspectors. Titchener pointed out that this tendency to describe the conscious state in terms of the stimulus rather than of the experience per se is beneficial and necessary in everyday life. All of us, therefore, grow up with strong habits of this kind, since responses to the objective character of the stimulus are ordinarily the effective ones. But such strong habits must be unlearned if one is to become an adequate psychological observer, and the only way to do this is through a new and intensive learning effort. Thus the trained introspector is one who learns to ignore the objects and events as such and to concentrate instead on the pure conscious experience.

The use of a reduction screen in visual research offers a good illustration of this situation. If the experimenter permits the subject to see the stimulus object and also the illumination impinging upon it, the subject reports that a piece of white paper is white even if it is very dimly illuminated—and is actually reflecting less light energy to the eye than, say, a piece of coal under bright illumination. The common judgment of untrained subjects is that the paper is brighter than the coal. This stimulus error can be eliminated by means of a reduction screen, which permits the subject to see only a small part of the stimulus object through a kind of peephole. Such a device prevents subjects from seeing either the nature of the object or the amount of illumination, and now their judgment follows the "true" character of the isolated sensory experience: a piece of white paper dimly illuminated is called dark gray, and a piece of black coal brightly illuminated is called light gray. These latter judgments are more in accord with the physical energies of the stimuli, although they are less accurate descriptions of the reflectivities of the coal and the paper. Neither type of sensory description need be viewed as more true in any ultimate sense. The structuralists wanted the description that correlated most closely with the local situation. Titchener felt that a kind of functional reduction screen needed to be built into each psychological introspector through extensive practice. Physicists and all other scientists make the stimulus error as a matter of course. They wish to report on observations in such a way that their reports agree with the objective character of the stimulus, regardless of any local or momentary effects that may presently be determining their perception of the stimulus. Only the introspective psychologists want to know the pure character of the present experience.

Titchener thought psychology ought to study experience as it seems to exist when we try to detach it from learning; that is, we should refuse to attribute meaning to it. These meanings become attached to stimuli through learning, and our reactions to the stimuli so directly incorporate the related experiences that the "percept" is no longer a product of the stimulus only.

Titchener exorcised child psychology and animal psychology from the main body, which we saw that Wundt did not do. Titchener did not deny that the study of the behavior of children and animals would yield valuable information; he denied rather that the information would be *psychological* information.

Wundt's hardheaded experimentalism was expressed in perhaps more exaggerated form by Titchener. He held not only that psycholgy must be experimental but also that it must be *pure.* Applied science seemed to Titchener a contradiction. Scientists, as Titchener saw it, must keep themselves free of considerations about the practical worth of what they are doing. He accordingly never accepted the work by Cattell and others on individual differences as making any important contribution to psychology. He decried the notion that the function of psychology is to find ways of ministering to sick minds. He was caustic about the possibility of becoming a psychologist through the process of untrained, morbid self-examination.

Titchener at first accepted Wundt's psychophysical parallelism as his practical solution to the mind-body problem, but philosophy really did not interest him. He accepted it because it allowed him to pursue the study of psychology with the methodology in which he believed. Titchener, like Wundt, boasted about the new freedom of psychology from philosophical speculation. Thus we see in these two practitioners of a fledgling science the full-blown scientific tendency to take philosophy for granted, to view it as irrelevant, and to carry Hume's philosophical antimetaphysical attitude into laboratory practice.

The new freedom from philosophy, they felt, flowed partly from their use of the experimental method. The psychological experiment should be a controlled introspection, with states of consciousness held constant by the external conditions, and the factors within the situation varied one at a time in different experiments. The experimenter need only set up apparatus, devise and explain the problem, and record the trained introspector's comments.

THE METHODOLOGY OF STRUCTURALISM

The technique of investigation for Titchener, as for Wundt, was introspection; but, as indicated above, Titchener's introspection was an even more highly formalized and practiced procedure than Wundt's *Selbstbeobachtung* had been. Introspection, according to Titchener, could be carried on scientifcally only by exceptionally well-trained observers.

One instance of his feelings about naive observers is given in a discussion of phenomenology:

> In the present connection, I mean, by a phenomenological account of mind, an account which purports to take mental phenomena at their face value, which records them as they are "given" in everyday experience; the account furnished by a naive, common-sense, non-scientific observer, who has not yet adopted the special attitude of the psychologist. . . . It is more than doubtful whether, in strictness, such an account can be obtained. (1912, p. 489)

It is clear that Titchener did not favor the use of untrained observers, nor did he at this time favor phenomenology as science.

It is difficult for untrained observers to say just what it is that the trained observers learned to do. Introspection changed to some extent as the years passed. Apparently Titchener thought introspection was becoming more refined and more generally applicable with the passage of time. He commented (1912a): "Our graduate students—far better trained, it is true, than we were in our generation—sit down cheerfully to introspective tasks such as we had not dreamed of" (p. 427).

Still—although we are told that the graduate students were getting better at something—it is hard for an outsider to be sure what that something was. Introspection has been said to be the direct observation of consciousness, of mental processes. However, Titchener said (1912b): "The course that an observer follows will vary in detail with the nature of the consciousness observed, with the purpose of the experiment, with the instruction given by the experimenter. Introspection is thus a generic term, and covers an indefinitely large group of specific methodological procedures" (p. 485).

Even Titchener seems not to have had an easy time finding a satisfactory definition of introspection and to have fallen back on a specification of the experimental conditions, a commendably operational procedure. But are there then no commonalities among the different applications of the term? Surely there is a self-consciousness about introspection, an awareness of observing? Not according to Titchener (1912a): *"In his attention to the phenomena under observation,* the observer in psychology, no less than the observer in physics, *completely forgets to give subjective attention to the state of observing"* (p. 443). Titchener, and Wundt before him, recognized that self-consciousness might interfere with the phenomena under observation and thus invalidate the results (see the criticisms of introspection given later in this chapter).

If Titchener's description of introspection is accurate and complete, we would seem to have little to question. The psychologist's report would be just like the physicist's report of the same thing. But Titchener was speaking of a *trained* introspector. What happens to observers as they undergo training? We note that they give verbal reports from the beginning; we do not deny that we may get interesting results in physics by accepting the reports of other experimenters who describe the things they have seen, and other investigators do not question the fact that we have seen certain things. We accept the words of others' reports with the sole reservation that they must be able to tell exactly what they mean, by pointing to an instance if necessary.

The observer learning to introspect, however, is in a different kind of circumstance. Certain classes of words, which we may call "meaning words," are not accepted. A structural psychologist is not interested scientifically in the statement, "I see a table," for table is a meaning word, based on preknowledge about the aggregation of visual and tactual sensations by which we identify the table. Structural psychologists believe that they are interested in this aggregate as a meaningless aggregate; they do not want the aggregate summarized in a meaning word, for they are interested in the direct contents of experience, not in the inferences made on the basis of the contents. So an observer who says *table* is cautioned against the stimulus error and eventually excludes this type of word from the professional vocabulary. What words are left then? Are only such words left as have no external referents, but referents only in experience? Again it is a difficult question. Wundt and Titchener alike emphasized that the external conditions must be carefully controlled so that the contents of consciousness can be precisely determined and so that more than one observer can experience the same thing and therefore cross-check the results of the experiment. We can then say that a workable vocabulary should be possible, based on the commonalities in experience under the carefully controlled conditions. After all, how else do we agree on a convention for the meaning of the word *table?* A reasonable inference is that we check that part of our experience which consistently occurs in conjunction with the use of the word *table* by others. Therefore, it seems possible to create a language, or language usage, of the type the structuralists required. However, it must be easier to correlate words with objects than with experiences, since we have more useful object languages within science than we have experience languages. It may be too difficult a task for introspectors to isolate that aspect of their manifold experience to which a particular word should apply. Certainly two introspectors cannot reach agreement on the relevant aspect by pointing to it, as one can do in the case of objects. Fingers will not fit in the remoter reaches of the world of experience. The findings of introspection could not always be agreed upon, even with very careful control of conditions. Had it been possible to secure sufficient scientific agreement on introspective statements of findings, the structural school might still be a vital force today.

That it was not possible we shall see later. Meanwhile, we may attempt to delineate introspection by discussing those features of it which a nonintrospective psychologist of today can understand. Introspection may be more, but it involves at least this: A generic term for several types of observation carried out in psychology. Different investigators, for example, at Cornell and Würzburg, tended to use somewhat different subvarieties. The Cornell variety of observation was carried out under laboratory conditions, with the stimulating situation, including instructions, carefully determined by the investigator. Only those subjects were used who had been carefully trained by the investigator or by another investigator who was versed in the method. The training included, among other things, at least the admonition to observe the contents of experience and report on them. It also included punishment when the observer used words that we may designate meaning words or thing words as we ordinarily conceive of these classes of words. The use of words that were considered descriptive of conscious states was no doubt rewarded.

In order to give the reader something of the flavor of the introspective method, as developed by Titchener, we reproduce below part of a representative account of an introspective experiment. In it the subjects, observers (*O*s) C. and P., were instructed to report their memory images; the stimuli used were geometric shapes of various colors. E. Murray's account follows:

> 1 *Introspections.* Manner of appearance of image. As a rule, the memory image appears spontaneously at the beginning of the recording period, or in the preceding after image period. Thereafter it returns at irregular intervals, which usually grow longer toward the end of the minute. On a few occasions, C. reports, the image was apparently evoked by chance twitches of the eyeball or eyelid, by inspiration, or, automatically, by rhythmic pressure of the key. Occasionally, also, the observer reports a faint anxiety at the momentary failure of the image, and a temptation to summon it by movement of the eyes (*O.* C.), by steady fixation, or by recall of detail after detail (*O.* P).
>
> 2 *Localization of image.* The memory image usually appears in the same direction and at the same distance as did the original. P. distinguishes it from the sensory after image by its position outwards on the screen (the after image appearing "on the eyelids"), and remarks that "Its appearance is often accompanied by the feeling of turning toward it." Occasionally it seems to be situated "in the head," but in this case its distinctness is materially lessened.
>
> That this localization is correlated with the presence of motor elements, actual or ideated, has abundant evidence. Thus C., noting that the memory image usually appears as an object with spacial relations, states that in this case "the feeling of accommodation" is present, with "tendency to move the eyes and locate the image directly in space." The less real this feeling (of accommodation and convergence), the less distinct the image. Thus, toward the end of the recording period (C. sometimes reports), the images become less vividly "visual," are accompanied by almost no

> tendency to fixation, and are localized, not in any definite portion of the visual field, but vague, "in the head,"—a type of image described by C. as "more subjective," or "more purely memorial."
>
> It seems probable that P. also refers to the muscular sensations attending fixation in her less concretely phrased account of the semispontaneous recall of images. "I seem to turn my attention toward the place where I expect the image to appear. If I hold my attention on this place, several more images are likely to follow." And again, "my attention vacillates about the place on the board where the image is expected, then settles down, and below unfolds the image, sometimes indistinctly, but as the attention turns more decidedly toward it growing in vividness."
>
> 3 *Incompleteness of image.* Images are rarely complete. The lower right hand portion is most often missing, and the upper left hand portion the most distinct,—a condition possibly correlated with the characteristic grouping of matter on the printed or written page, and the acquired habit of attending primarily to the upper left hand word. In cases *where the outline is complete, it is often doubtful whether* there are not gaps in the main body of the figure. Whether complete or incomplete in relation to the original, the image is usually reported as flashing in and out as a whole, without growth or alteration. (1906, pp. 230–231)

After this examination of the problems in defining introspection, one may have less tendency to laugh at the futile definitional efforts of those who are still vitally concerned with introspection. Natsoulas (1970) shrugs off the problem this way: "Here 'introspection' is a relatively neutral term for the process(es) whereby one arrives on the spot at introspective awarenesses" (p. 90).

EMPIRICAL PROPOSITIONS

In science, not only do observations determine theory, but also theory determines observations. The empirical propositions of structuralism seem today to be mixed with theoretical presuppositions, but to the structuralists their propositions seemed to be based directly on observation.

The three basic elements of consciousness that came down all the way from the English empiricist philosophers seemed to be verified by the introspective observations of Wundt and later of Titchener. These three elements were *sensations, images,* and *feelings.* The elements were thought to be basic and incapable of further analytic reduction.

Images were the elements of ideas, and sensations were the elements of perception. Images were supposed to differ from sensations by being less vivid, less clear, less intense, and sometimes less prolonged. Both images and sensations had certain basic attributes. For Wundt, these were two: intensity and quality. Titchener expanded the list to four: *intensity, quality, attensity,* and *protensity.*

Quality had its usual meaning of a difference in kind; attensity was synonymous with clearness, except that it was understood to mean a type of clearness which varies with attention rather than with the objective characteristics of the stimuli; intensity had its usual meaning of strength; and protensity was a word for the duration in time of the sensation or image. Some sensory modalities produced sensations with the additional attribute of *extensity* in space.

Titchener saw that it was not easy to distinguish image from sensation, but held that there was at least a difference of a quantitative sort; for example, there would be a point along the attensity dimension at which image turned into sensation. An experiment by Perky (1910) at Cornell illustrated the difficulty of deciding what was image and what was sensation. Subjects told to "project" a banana on a blank screen did not report the appearance of a dim picture of a banana actually flashed on the screen, but attributed the sensation to unusually clear imagery on their part at that time; other subjects told to observe the actual banana failed to report when it was turned off, apparently maintaining a sort of equivalent of the dim sensation via their own imagery. We should note that Perky was distinguishing between image and sensation on the basis of the presence or absence of an objective stimulus; this is not a distinction on the basis of conscious contents and seems inconsistent from the point of view of a structuralist. However, Perky's experiment cast doubt on the sensation-image distinction, and as a result there was a tendency to speak more about the attributes of sensations and less about images. Boring (1950, p. 201) cites a later experiment by Schaub (1911) as providing even stronger evidence that images might be more intense than sensations, but he says that Titchener believed Perky's conclusions.

The Würzburg school got into heated controversy with Titchener on the subject of "imageless thought," which they claimed to have "discovered." The admission of such an entity would have necessitated a revision of Titchener's view that images are the elements of thoughts. Accordingly, he rejected the views of Külpe and his students at Würzburg, who were joined in the defense of imageless thought by Binet in France and the functionally oriented Woodworth at Columbia University. Titchener suspected that all their results might have been caused by faulty—that is, incomplete—introspection. He did not find any clear evidence for the existence of this upstart element, this imageless thought. His subjects did not confirm Woodworth's findings. Titchener's verdict was that the so-called thought element was probably an unanalyzed complex of kinesthetic sensations and images, which were always difficult to find in consciousness. The "will" element was also excluded. An *act of will* was simply a complex of images forming ideas in advance of action.

Titchener was able to bring attention into his system by equating it with clearness of sensation. He found in some subjects only a two-part breakdown of clearness, into central and clear versus peripheral and unclear; in other subjects, there was a multistep progression from clear to unclear.

Titchener rejected Wundt's tridimensional theory of feeling. Of the three dimensions—pleasant-unpleasant, strained-relaxed, and excited-calm—he retained only the first. He reduced the other two to sensations and images, especially kinesthetic. They were therefore not to be regarded as special characteristics of feeling; in fact, they were not feeling at all.

Nafe (1927), one of Titchener's students, later reduced even the remaining attribute of feeling to sensations: Pleasantness was regarded as a "bright pressure" localized in the trunk at a higher level than the "dull pressure" of unpleasantness. He suggested that vascular changes might be responsible for these sensations. If Nafe's point of view were accepted, even affect would be reduced to sensation.

So far, we have examined the empirical propositions which had direct systematic relevance for Titchener. In addition, there are more directly empirical propositions (statements of experimental results), which were generally accepted by the structuralists; some of these are asystematic and acceptable to any psychologist regardless of systematic beliefs. For example, Titchener's first "empirical" chapter in *An outline of psychology* (1899) is entitled "The quality of sensation." In it are examined the qualities of visual, auditory, olfactory, gustatory, and other sensations. Each examination of these qualities is based on a relevant experiment or demonstration.

STRUCTURALISM AS A SYSTEM

Definition of Psychology

The structural definition of psychology was "the analytic study of the generalized adult normal human mind through introspection." This summarizes our previous discussion; "generalized" adds the feeling of Titchener and of Wundt before him that psychology is not basically concerned with individual differences, and "normal" excludes the mentally disturbed and defective.

Basic Postulates

The term "postulates" refers, of course, to statements which are to be taken as unquestionable for some purpose; postulates in a formal logical sense would then serve as bases from which other statements, called theorems, would be derived. Psychology, until very recently, has made little use of postulates of this kind, and structural psychology was no exception to this rule. Nevertheless, postulates in some sense have long been a concern of psychologists. Again, the structuralists were no exception; one need look no further than Titchener's 1898 paper, *The postulates of a structural psychology,* for proof of this interest.

What sort of postulates, then, have traditionally concerned psychologists? Most of them have been the "high level" assumptions which guide the behavior of the psychological investigator. For example, the definition of psychology given above serves to direct investigation, and is not to be directly tested. The reader can find other examples of this kind in our discussion of the goals and methods of Wundt and Titchener.

There are, however, still other kinds of statements which have been called postulates. These statements seem to rest upon an empirical foundation, rather than to be simply assumed, but to be universally supported by the relevant observations. We quote Titchener's paper directly for structuralist examples:

> We set out from a point of universal agreement. Everyone admits that *sensations* are elementary mental processes. There is, it is true, diversity of opinion as to the range of contents that the term shall cover. . . . The divergence, however, is not serious. . . . Once more, we set out from a point of universal agreement. "There are two indispensable determinants of every psychical element, quality and intensity." (1898; as cited in Shipley, 1961, pp. 233, 236)

We have already seen that Titchener himself wished to add attensity and protensity to the list of "indispensable determinants." It was thus true that the "basic postulates" of structuralism underwent changes. There is no set of underlying assumptions, nor of universally supported statements, which can be cited. Because the postulates that did exist were not formal, logical, postulates, it is not possible to make any statement about the number, sufficiency, or adequacy of the structuralistic postulates. In this respect, the structuralists are no worse off than the adherents of any other classical system of psychology.

Other examples of the guiding principles that would almost certainly have been accepted by structuralists include the two basic methods of science: control and analysis. They put extreme emphasis on experimentation and excluded other methods as unscientific, and could not affirm too strongly that psychology had won its fledgling wings and was independent of metaphysics. Knowledge was empirical, not a priori. Mind and consciousness were clearly assumed to be useful concepts and the proper province for psychological study. Introspection was assumed to be a valid method for that study and to be a method which required extended training for efficient performance. Consistency and law were assumed to hold for the realm of consciousness, and mind and body were supposed to be parallel systems.

Nature of the Data

To summarize the previous discussion: Titchener believed that the primary data of psychology must be obtained by means of introspection and under strict experimental conditions. Titchener no doubt believed that the data were as objective as any data could be. Were a controversy to arise today about the objectivity of Titchener's data, we would be objective about making the objective-subjective distinction; the data would be referred to a computer for reliability analysis. The intuitive analog of such an analysis condemned introspective data to the subjective category; it is not certain whether this particular judgment was adequately justified.

Mind-Body Position

Titchener's postulate regarding a mind-body position has already been discussed. However, lest we too easily accept the view that Titchener simply accepted Wundt's psychophysical parallelism, we should note another Titchenerian theme (1899): "The metaphysics to which Science points us is rather a metaphysics in which both matter and spirit disappear, to make way for the unitary conception of *experience* " (p. 366). Here, Titchener sounds as though he accepts a monism of experience, or the view that mind and body are two aspects of experience. His view is similar to that of Mach, of whom Titchener was fond and who emphasized experience as the basis of all science. Titchener later elaborated his position. He pointed out that the commonsense conception of mind leads to dead-end questions:

> Where, for instance, on that view, does the body end and the mind begin? Do the senses belong to mind or to body? Is the mind always active and the body always passive? Do body and mind ever act independently of each other? Questions such as

> these arise at once; but it is a hard matter to answer them. Parallelism has no logical pitfalls of this kind. (1910, p. 14)

Principles of Connection

The problem of connection was a secondary one for Titchener; until the detailed nature of the elements to be connected was worked out, there was no point in trying to connect them. His view of connection was similar to his view of function; he recognized the necessity for working out functions eventually, but felt that the study of structure must come first.

To the extent that he concerned himself with connections, he explained them by association. Titchener reworded the principle of association by contiguity as his main law:

> Let us try, however, to get a descriptive formula for the facts which the doctrine of association aims to explain. We then find this: that, whenever a sensory or imaginal process occurs in consciousness, there are likely to appear with it (of course, in imaginal terms) all those sensory and imaginal processes which occurred together with it in any earlier conscious present. . . . Now the law of contiguity can, with a little forcing, be translated into our own general law of association. (1910, pp. 378–379)

His law of association furnished him with a principle of successive connection; that is, item *A* tends to elicit item *B* immediately afterward. There remained the problem of connection of the elements within the cross section which is consciousness. This was to be solved by the presentation of the laws of synthesis. This task seems never to have been completed. From his discussion, it is clear that Titchener recognized the difficulty of synthesis, that the elements did not simply sum to the unitary experience which was there in the first place:

> If the conscious elements were "things," the task of reconstruction of an experience would not be difficult. We should put the simple bits of mind together, as the bits of wood are put together in a child's puzzle-map or kindergarten cube. But the conscious elements are "processes"; they do not fit together, side by side and angle to angle; they flow together, mix together, overlapping, reinforcing, modifying or arresting one another, in obedience to certain psychological laws. (1899, p. 17)

Titchener was never able to give these laws, for his first task of analysis was never finished.

A further kind of connection for Titchener to explain was the problem of meaning: How does meaning become connected with sensation? He regarded the problem as outside psychology, but developed an explanation, his famous *context theory,* anyway. The meaning of a sensation for Titchener's theory was simply the context in which it occurred in consciousness. A simple sensation does not have meaning; it gets meaning only from the other sensations or images accompanying it. The context of the sensation, and hence its meaning, is a result of past experience with the sensation; it is the result of associations between past sensations or images. What we call *meaning* is simply the totality of sensation accompanying the meaningful sensation:

> No sensation means; a sensation simply goes on in various ways, intensively, clearly, spatially, and so forth. All perceptions mean. . . . For us, therefore, meaning may be mainly a matter of sensations of the special senses, or of images, or of kinesthetic or other organic sensations, as the nature of the situation demands. Of all its possible forms, however, two appear to be of especial importance: kinesthesis and verbal images. . . . But is meaning always conscious meaning? Surely not; meaning may be carried in purely physiological terms. (1910, pp. 367–369)

Principles of Selection

The basic problem of explaining why certain stimuli are selected in consciousness was handled by the use of the concept of attention, which was reduced to sensory clearness. Titchener initially believed there were two degrees of clearness, but one of his students at Cornell, L. R. Geissler (1909), found that subjects could rate up to ten gradations along a numerical scale. Wirth, at Leipzig, produced similar findings (see Titchener, 1908).

According to Titchener, there are three general stages of attention: (1) native, involuntary primary attention, where native factors like the intensity and quality of the sensory experience determine attention along with involuntary attentive set or perhaps novelty; (2) voluntary secondary attention after the novelty wears off—this stage is difficult to get through in terms of attempting to maintain attention at a high level of clarity; and (3) derived primary, or habitual, attention, which is the ultimate objective; the attention is again involuntary, this time because of its history of learned development rather than because of native, unlearned factors.

As stages, these three conditions were obviously intended to be viewed as continuous and not as clearly separable. An example of this continuity in stages is the development of interest in reading a certain kind of subject matter, such as that in a psychology text. Originally, attention will be held by factors like novelty and certain expectations generated by presuppositions concerning the subject matter. As reading progresses, however, negative or inhibitory factors may develop as a result of the student's encountering new and unfamiliar terminology, difficult expositions, and the like, and also, perhaps, as a result of disappointment of some of the expectations. The second stage will thus appear, and the student will find it difficult to keep attending clearly. Fixation at this stage of attention is a serious problem in education and might be used to account for much academic difficulty as well as for many students' complaints. If this troublesome stage can be survived, according to Titchener's account, the third stage will emerge. Then familiarity with the material will suffice to maintain a certain level of attention. Reaching this stage of derived involuntary attention in a variety of subject matters is an important objective of education.

CRITICISMS OF STRUCTURALISM

Such was the system called *structuralism.* It made many positive contributions to the science of psychology: It freed it from metaphysics, gave it a careful experimental method and a nucleus to organize around, and contributed experimental facts. Yet perhaps its greatest contribution to psychology was the criticism it elicited.

Introspection

The severest attack on structuralism was on its very heart, the introspective method. Many of these criticisms were recognized as problems by Wundt and Titchener, and they took steps to make sure that the criticism would not remain valid. The following are key problems that were considered.

Introspection must really always be retrospection, since it takes time to report on a state of consciousness. Forgetting is rapid, especially immediately after having an experience, so that some of the experience will perhaps be inadvertently lost. It is also possible that the necessity for retrospection will lead to embellishment or error, especially if the introspector has a vested interest in a theory that will be affected by the experimental results.

This objection was answered partly by having only well-trained observers work within time intervals short enough to reduce forgetting and partly by postulating a *primary memory image,* a kind of mental echo which preserves the experience for the introspector until he can report it. If the report is made within the limits of this immediate memory, before conscious attention has changed, then little of value will be lost.

A second difficulty recognized by structuralists and critics alike is that the act of introspecting may change the experience drastically. The classic example is an introspection regarding anger; if the state is attended to, it tends quickly to disintegrate and may even disappear completely. Thus the measuring technique interferes with experience, as it does with electrons for the physicist. A somewhat analogous situation concerns the role of the cultural anthropologist who wishes to observe in detail the habits and customs of some other culture. The very presence of the anthropologist in the household serves to contaminate the behavior of the subjects. The undesirable effects of such an intrusion can be minimized if the observer comes to live in the household and is eventually accepted; the behavior of the subjects will then become progressively more normal and unaffected by the anthropologist's intrusion. But this process, like that of training oneself to accept the act of introspecting into the mental household, can be accomplished only by long and arduous effort. In the case of the mental household, the state of affairs may be affected by the training process. Wundt postulated an independence of the thing observed with experience, but Titchener apparently did not claim as strong a position; he did feel that the experienced observer becomes unconscious of the act of observation with practice.

A third difficulty is that psychologists relying on the introspective method at different laboratories were not getting comparable results; rather, scientists in one laboratory asserted things that contradicted the results of scientists elsewhere (Boring, 1953). In our discussion previously, we said that it does not seem to be *in principle* impossible to agree on a language describing experience as it is observed by the introspector; this would be possible, however, only because of the control over external elicitors of sensation. It does seem to have been *empirically* impossible to devise a useful, agreed-on introspective language. Titchener continued to maintain that agreement would be reached eventually, presumably when all introspectors had learned to do their work as accurately and carefully as Titchener and his students. That agreement never came.

A fourth argument was perhaps the most decisive. There was growing evidence that data existed which properly belonged to psychology, but which were not accessible to introspection. Titchener himself recognized unconscious meanings. The Würzburg school pressed for the recognition of imageless thoughts as elements; it looked suspiciously like thought went on, blithely oblivious of the "fact" that it could not do so independently of the elements that introspective analysis had revealed. The psychoanalysts claimed that they had demonstrated beyond reasonable doubt that *unconscious* influences played a role in maladjustment and in everyday motivation. Even the animal psychologists joined the opposition; they were getting interesting results altogether without the use of introspection. The rising tide of objection that had been pitching over the wall of structuralist orthodoxy eventually tore it down, and introspection could no longer be accepted as the exclusive psychological method.

Many critics seemingly jumped to the conclusion that, because introspection was not everything, it therefore was nothing, of no value as a psychological method. We have already seen that it is extremely difficult to define introspection. One should not issue a blanket condemnation of something which is undefined. Data which seem to be based on introspection as broadly defined have always been used in psychology, even during our most behavioristic phase. Such data often make it possible to learn something about physiological processes and even structures, sometimes long before observations can be made of the structures themselves. For example, a three-color theory of vision was proposed by Thomas Young (1802) and worked out in detail by Helmholtz over 100 years before microscopic techniques became refined enough to reveal three fundamental types of color receptors within the retina. We believe that the usefulness of some type of introspection is far from ended, and that introspection should therefore not be consigned to the fate suffered by the system which leaned too heavily upon it as its sole support. If by introspection we mean the use of experience and the use of verbal reports based on this experience, then introspection, as Titchener noted, is simply coextensive with science and will presumably always be used. The various contemporary forms of introspection were summarized by Boring (1953), and other authors periodically dust off the issue for a new look.

OTHER OBJECTIONS

There were other criticisms besides those which pertained to method. The narrowness of structural psychology was attacked. Titchener was an outstanding compartmentalizer, and he seemed to prefer putting an area of investigation into a nonpsychological category to claiming it as a new province for psychology. This was not a definitional exclusion; Titchener's catalogue of psychology seemed to include an adequate shopping list of areas. It was a behavioral exclusion. Titchener's personal interests did not include animal psychology and child psychology, nor did he encourage his students to do research in these areas.

When Watson started publishing his behavioral studies, Titchener disclaimed knowing what they were, but he did know what they were not: they were *not* psychology. Even physiological psychology as it is now conceived was a subsidiary problem to be attacked later. This conception of the limits of psychology was too narrow to withstand the explosive pressure of the empiricial interests manifested by a growing band of psychologists.

Structuralism was castigated for its artificiality and its emphasis on analysis. These shortcomings were most vigorously attacked by the Gestaltists, who deplored the loss they felt must be engendered by analysis. They pointed to the primacy of the whole as whole, a whole that they felt could never be recovered by any synthesis of elements. For them, the primary method was phenomenological observation, not the analytic introspection of Titchener.

In order to clarify one final objection, let us recall an incident that was briefly mentioned in Chapter 2. James McKeen Cattell, an American and Wundt's first, self-proclaimed, assistant, had brought the study of individual differences to Leipzig. Wundt had declared the problem *ganz amerikanisch,* which we may translate as entirely, or typically, American. Since the problem arose out of evolutionary theory through Galton, Wundt's comment was not literally true, but Wundt was getting at a deeper truth: the pragmatism of the American temperament (which so far as we can see is still with us). When Titchener brought Wundt's psychology to America, the reaction tended to be symmetrical; Wundt's psychology was regarded as *ganz deutsch.* The "pure science" aspect of structuralism had too little appeal. What difference did the elements of experience make in initiating and guiding action? Beginning with William James, the question was: "What is the function of consciousness in adjustment?" Since structuralism did not propose to give answers to that, or any other, practical question, it never won the hearts of the Americans. If it had, all other obstacles, all criticism, might have been overcome. The fatal objection to structuralism was that its program was not attractive enough.

THE FATE OF STRUCTURALISM

Structuralism, like any other system, was sensitive to criticism and empirical results. It started with an ambiguous view of its subject matter, consciousness, a view which at least failed to deny vehemently enough that consciousness could be thought of as an existent real. This led to an alternative name, existentialism, for the school. The search for the elements of this consciousness finally led to the conclusion that there was but one established element, sensation. In Titchener's posthumous publication, *Systematic psychology: Prolegomena* (1929), he concluded that introspective psychology deals exclusively with sensory materials. Its problem by this time was reconceived as an examination of the dimensions of sensation.

In this reformulation of its problem, structural psychology may be said at the same time to have solved its original problem and to have arrived exactly nowhere. The problem of searching for elements had been eliminated; there seemed to be no laws of combination of elements to look for, since there was but one element to work with. This logical cul-de-sac was brilliantly foreshadowed by James in chapter 9 of his *Principles of psychology:*

> It is astonishing what havoc is wrought in psychology by admitting at the outset apparently innocent suppositions, that nevertheless contain a flaw. The bad consequences develop themselves later on, and are irremediable, being woven through the whole texture of the work. The notion that sensations, being the simplest things, are the first things to take up in psychology is one of these suppositions. The only thing which psychology has a right to postulate at the outset is the fact of thinking itself, and that must first be taken up and analyzed. If sensations then prove to be amongst the elements of the thinking, we shall be no worse off as respects them than if we had taken them for granted at the start. (1890, p. 224)

Evans (1972) points out that Titchener's attitude toward phenomenological description also underwent a gradual change. Despite the general image of Titchener as a rigid traditionalist, he modified his system just as other psychologists have modified theirs. In 1925, he had unbent to the extent of saying: "Phenomenology is not yet, is not of itself, experimental psychology; but it provides today a safe and sure mode of approach to the analysis of our psychological subject matter; and our recourse to it, our realization of its promise may perhaps be taken as a sign of adolescence" (Evans, 1972, p. 179). Had Titchener lived, there is no way of telling how far he might eventually have modified his systematic beliefs to make them more compatible with Gestalt psychology or with functionalism. There is no indication, however, that he could ever have stomached behaviorism, with its denial that consciousness could be the subject matter of psychology. For Titchener, behaviorism was not a school of *psychology* at all.

Time was running out for structural psychology as it ran out for Titchener. He had withdrawn progressively from psychology as the years passed. His early burst of productivity in this country produced about nine papers a year for 7 years, but it diminished thereafter. He withdrew early from the American Psychological Association and formed his own group. His relationships with other psychologists were mixed. He went through a fierce period in his relationship to Thorndike after ripping apart the latter's book (Joncich, 1968). Paradoxically, he was an admirer of Watson, though Watson and Thorndike would not seem to have differed significantly in either brashness or iconoclasm. Moreover, it was Watson's highly successful promulgation of the behavioristic doctrine that served to attract increasing numbers of psychologists and thereby hasten the demise of structuralism. Perhaps the battles were too much, and the old warrior gradually withdrew even from his students and his field and turned to his hobby of numismatics.

E. G. Boring's book *The physical dimensions of consciousness* (1933) was in effect the death throe of structuralism. As a prominent student of Titchener and in some ways his most likely successor, Boring in 1933 was actually concerned chiefly with correlating conscious and physiological processes; this was Titchener's third problem. Boring seems still to have been trying to salvage whatever he could of the structuralist systematic position:

> The doctrine of conscious dimensions, which I believe without proof to be essentially Titchener's way of meeting the challenge of Gestalt psychology and the anti-atomists, seems to me very important and the correct approach to the adequate description of mind. However, I am not willing to stress the doctrine as much as some of its friends would like, because I believe that categories of description, whether they be the psychological dimensions of quality and intensity or the physical dimensions of space, mass and time, are scientifically arbitrary and temporary, matters of the convenience or economy of description. One does not attempt to discover conscious elements, attributes, or dimensions, one makes them up and uses them as phenomenological exigencies require. (1933, p. vii)

At this point, Boring was trying to wed structuralism and the increasing scientific and logical sophistication of his vantage point in time. He recognized the arbitrariness of scientific concepts and the importance of verbal convention even in the communication of introspective results. Yet the influence of Titchener was still strong, and Boring was fighting to salvage consciousness as a fit subject of scientific investigation.

Four years later, he had apparently given up the struggle. He examined the definition of consciousness and the role of private experience. He concluded that private experience could not be scientifically useful until it became public; therefore, it was defined out of science. After arriving at "an awareness of an awareness" as the closest approximation to a definition of consciousness, he had this to say about the word:

> Having understood, tough-minded rigorous thinkers will, I think, want to drop the term *consciousness* altogether. A scientific psychology is scarcely yet ready to give importance to so ill defined a physiological event as an awareness of an awareness. This concept might never have come to the fore had not people tried to interpret others in terms of their own "private" minds—that egocentric Copernican distortion which properly leads to desolate solipsism. (1937, p. 458)

Thus Boring furnished first the capstone, then the tombstone, of structuralism. Structuralism today is dead. For us, it is only a dimly remembered image from our psychological past, not the vibrant sensation which led brilliant young scientists from distant shores to Leipzig and then, for a time, to Cornell. Sad. Yet it died of narrow dogmatism, a disease which no school can long survive in the modern world. Its demise was mourned by few.

Meanwhile, the phenomenological tradition, which furnished part of the matrix from which structuralism sprang, denying its origin as it rose, lives on. Husserl had posited the individual's potential for grasping the "essence" or "central core" of reality, which he thought lies in consciousness. Sartre carries through Husserl's ideas of essences and concludes that phenomena are not appearances of objects, but rather are the beings which objects leave in appearing to consciousness. He regards consciousness as the opposite of objectivity (Lauer, 1965).

Clearly the modern conceptions of phenomenology and existentialism are quite different from the views of our "existentialists," Wundt and Titchener. However, we should not forget that there is at least a surface similarity, a belief that an understanding of consciousness is central to an understanding of the human condition. And, lest we conclude that this is a problem of interest only to philosophers and quaintly outmoded psychologists, let us look at a quotation from a very modern biologist: "The evolution of the capacity to simulate seems to have culminated in subjective consciousness. Why this should have happened is, to me, the most profound mystery facing modern biology" (Dawkins, 1976, p. 63).

DIMENSIONAL DESCRIPTIONS OF STRUCTURALISM

Structuralism is one of the easiest schools to describe, using Watson's dimensions. Systems that tend to be extreme, and that are more often caricatured because we are less familiar with their details, seem to be easier to rate. Readers should rate the system for themselves, referring back to Watson's dimensions, and then compare ratings with those of the authors in Table 1-1.

The twenty-three graduate students mentioned in the previous chapter judged structuralism as putting the heaviest weight on conscious mentalism, structuralism, and empiricism. Other dimensions upon which structuralists took a strong stand would include contentual subjectivism, methodological subjectivism (as judged by us, not by them!), molecularism, nomotheticism, centralism, and purism.

SUMMARY AND CONCLUSIONS

Structuralism was launched in 1898 by E. B. Titchener as *the* psychology. Its problems were the discovery of conscious elements, their mode and laws of combination, and their relation to the nervous system. Its method was introspection, conceived by Wundt as the study of immediate experience and by Titchener as the study of experience as dependent upon the experiencing organism. Both Titchener and his teacher, Wundt, emphasized the indispensability of the experimental method for psychology. The structural school succeeded in winning academic recognition for psychology as an independent science. Titchener tried to free psychology as a method from metaphysics and in general established it as an empirical science, although structuralism as a school was not completely free from some problems that today would be considered metaphysical.

Structuralism was criticized for its methodology and its narrowness in general. The critics prevailed, and today modern psychology tends to accept only the basic scientific attitude of structuralism and the empirical results that were obtained in such a way that they were independent of systematic preconceptions. Various forms of introspection are still in use, but the systematic formulations of structuralism are of historical interest only.

FURTHER READINGS

Wundt's *Principles of physiological psychology* (1904) gives a good picture of the general structuralist systematic position, as the student has already seen in the quotations in the present chapter. This book, supplemented by Titchener's "Postulates of a structural psychology" (1898) and Boring's "History of introspection"

(1953), is adequate to give a very good understanding of the tenor of the structuralist psychology early in the present century. The student might browse through issues of the *American Journal of Psychology* which were printed prior to Titchener's death in 1927, if they are available. These issues give an unbiased view of the everyday experimental implications of the structuralist metatheory which cannot easily be obtained in any other way. Titchener's *Text-book of psychology* (1910); Boring's *Physical dimensions of consciousness* (1933); and Boring's short article with a long title, "A psychological function is the relation of successive differentiations of events in the organism" (1937), will then finish the picture, showing how structuralism developed and why it disappeared. R. I. Watson's *Great psychologists* (1971) is great browsing in connection with every system treated in the present book, as of course is Boring's *History of experimental psychology* (1950).

Table 5-1 Important Figures in American Functional Psychology

British antecedent influences	American functionalists		
	Pioneers	**Founders**	**Developers**
Individual differences, mental tests, statistics			
Sir Francis Galton (1822–1911)	George T. Ladd (1842–1921)—Yale Edward W. Scripture (1864–1945)—Yale James McKeen Cattell (1860–1944)—Columbia G. Stanley Hall (1844–1924)—Clark	John Dewey (1859–1952)—Chicago (Columbia)	Robert S. Woodworth (1869–1962)—Columbia
Evolutionary theory			
Charles Darwin (1809–1882)	James Mark Baldwin (1861–1934)—Princeton William James (1842–1910)—Harvard	James R. Angell (1869–1949)—Chicago	Harvey Carr (1873–1954)—Chicago
Animal behavior			
George John Romanes (1848–1894) C. Lloyd Morgan (1852–1936)	Edward L. Thorndike (1874–1949)—Columbia		

Chapter 5

Functionalism

Functionalism was the first truly American system of psychology. Its development in this country began with William James, who is apparently still regarded as the greatest American psychologist (Becker, 1959), and led directly to Watsonian behaviorism. Part of the early strength of functionalism was drawn from its opposition to structuralism, just as later part of the strength of behaviorism came from its opposition to structuralism and the less extreme functionalism.

Functionalism has never been a highly differentiated systematic position. In fact, according to Woodworth (1948): "A psychology that attempts to give an accurate and systematic answer to the question 'What do men do?' and 'Why do they do it?' is called a *functional psychology* " (p. 13). In terms of such a weak specification, functionalism could not die until our linguistic habits of asking what, how, and why had been replaced by others. But this is probably an inadequate specification of functionalism. Though its definition must remain as loose as the system, we can at least add that a functionalist is characteristically concerned with the function of the organism's behavior and consciousness in its adaptation to its environment. The functionalist is also likely to be concerned with functional, or *dependency,* relationships between antecedents and consequents; here function is used in its mathematical sense. American psychology, influenced by evolutionary theory and a practical spirit, has been concerned with the utilities of consciousness and behavior. Thus it has tended to be functional.

Table 5-1 (facing) shows that three groups of psychologists contributed to the development of functionalism. The *pioneers* are early psychologists who laid the groundwork for the later growth of functionalism by opening up a wide variety of new fields of inquiry, such as child and animal behavior. The *founders,* John Dewey and James Angell, established functionalism as a system. And the *developers,* Harvey Carr and Robert S. Woodworth, were responsible for the maturation and further elaboration of the system.

Three primary antecedent influences, all British in origin, are also shown at the left of Table 5-1. Charles Darwin (1872) engaged in the study of animal behavior as well as in the development of the modern theory of organic evolution. Galton was influenced by evolutionary theory and initiated the scientific study of human capacity. Romanes and Morgan gave additional impetus to the study of animal behavior. James, Hall, and Baldwin were directly influenced by evolutionary theory, and Hall was also interested in testing and individual differences. Carr was more interested in animal studies than was his most direct predecessor, Angell. Baldwin, Ladd, and Scripture are included because they had a hand in setting the stage for the development of functional psychology; they are not considered important enough to the basic tenets of functionalism to require treatment in this text. Early in his career E. L. Thorndike had strong interests in animal research and was related closely to both James and Cattell. His connectionism might have been included in this chapter as a special kind of functionalism rather than in Chapter 3 on associationism.

Table 5-1 excludes two men who, although originally trained by functionalists, were subsequently involved in the development of other schools. John B. Watson was functionally trained and later turned behavioristic; he took his degree with Angell. Bergmann (1956) goes so far as to regard Watson as the last and greatest functionalist. Walter S. Hunter is another product of the Chicago school, although he also tended to regard himself as a behaviorist. Nevertheless, his development and guidance of a small but very active and productive laboratory at Brown University justifies at least mention in the present overview. The research produced for many years at Brown had a strong functionalist flavor and would certainly rate with that produced at Columbia and Chicago in general excellence if not in quantity or scope.

Thus it seems that we almost have a rule of systematic evolution: Most of the American students of Wundt—notably Cattell and Hall—returned to the United States and became functionalists, or at least moved in that direction. The students of functionalists, like Watson and Hunter, moved further in the direction of objectivism and became behaviorists or near-behaviorists. Of course, in any generation of organisms or of systematists, most individuals will not move very far; but there seemed to be a clear direction of movement for those who did move.

ANTECEDENTS OF FUNCTIONALISM

Charles Darwin (1809–1882) created one of the greatest controversies in intellectual history, one whose reverberations have not fully died out in the current year of our Lord. The Lord, of course, had a great deal to do with the controversy, since evolution shook religion to its foundations.

Ironically, Darwin was such a cautious scientist, not to say a timid and withdrawn recluse, that he might never have published and started the controversy had Alfred Russell Wallace (1823–1913) not sent him a report which outlined exactly the same theory of evolution on which Darwin had been working for twenty years. As Irvine says:

> Wallace's next letter, containing the famous paper on evolution and natural selection, struck him like a bombshell. Within a single week, while lying ill with malarial fever in the jungles of the Malay peninsula, Wallace had leaped from his earlier position to Darwin's most advanced conclusions. What Darwin had puzzled and wondered and worried and slaved over with infinite anxiety and pain for two decades, Wallace had investigated and explained—far less elaborately but still to precisely the same result—in some three years. The familiar ideas, the older man could not help noticing, were conveyed with un-Darwinian force and clarity. (1963, pp. 98–99)

Characteristically, Darwin was unable to resolve the dilemma presented by his receipt of Wallace's paper. Two friends of his, Lyell and Hooker, resolved it for him by reading both Wallace's report and a sketch of Darwin's ideas before the same meeting of the Linnaean Society. It is to the credit of both men that they were lifelong friends, their mutual respect emerging unscathed from a situation which could have become extremely acrimonious.

Darwin could not personally respond to the furor which arose over this paper and reached a climax with the 1859 publication of *The origin of species.* The battle fell to the lot of Thomas Henry Huxley (1825–1895), Darwin's fierce, brilliant friend and fellow biologist. That Huxley eventually carried the day for evolution (with the scientific community, at least) is now history. Darwin, when unpleasantness threatened, always found it necessary to withdraw to a spa for the sake of his uncertain health.

Despite his eccentricities, this English scientific bulldog was one of functionalism's most important antecedents. He was an acute observer of animal behavior as well as of animal morphology. His theory established a continuity between human beings and animals that was necessary to justify the extended study of animal psychology. Finally, the evolutionary emphasis on adaptation to the environment was imported directly as an "explanation" of behavior via instinct, and perhaps indirectly as the principle of reinforcement.

Sir Francis Galton (1822–1911) was inspired by his cousin, Darwin, to study the problem of heredity in human beings. It was his aristocratic wish to control heredity, but first he had to demonstrate its effectiveness as an agent of change. He was led by this necessity to study the inheritance of human intelligence, of which Galton himself is said to have had plenty (his estimated IQ was 200; see Boring, 1950, p. 461). Such quasi-quantitative estimates are, of course, nonsense. However, if they are not taken seriously they are amusing nonsense, and they may remind us once again that in studying history we are studying the exploits of brilliant people.

Galton's *Hereditary genius* (1869) contained studies of individual differences in intelligence. We have already noted briefly how Cattell followed up in this area; it was not long before the field of mental testing was opened up, to come into full blossom in the testing of recruits for the United States Army during World War I. This field has done a great deal to justify the existence of psychology with the public during its childhood years, although it is now beginning to plague our adulthood. For some reason—and we will discuss one possible reason very soon—Galton has received relatively little credit for his accomplishments.

Romanes (1848–1894) and Morgan (1852–1936) are important to psychology because of their work in the field of animal behavior. Each represents an attitude toward the relationship between man and the lower animals. Darwin was castigated by theologians because of their belief that he was bringing humanity down to the level of the animals; they admitted apelike ancestry only with great, high-collared resistance. From the contemporary point of view, however, it appears that both Darwin and Romanes were overgenerous in the other direction. Each of them was disarmingly willing to attribute human faculties to animals. Morgan would have none of their childish enthusiasm and demanded strict evidence before according humans or animals a "higher" phyletic faculty on the basis of a particular performance. Romanes and Morgan thus defined a polarity which is still visible, but both men lent support to the study of animals.

In the 1970s, interest in animals seems to have hit an all-time peak. Popular TV portrays animals as having abilities that make the claims of Romanes seem ultraconservative. In the opposite direction, we have a host of books likening humans to apes or antelopes, and accounting for our problems by pointing to the origins of our aggression, or sexuality, or territoriality in our animal past (Ardrey, 1966, 1970; Lorenz, 1966; Morris, 1967). However questionable these efforts may be, they indicate a deep acceptance within the popular consciousness of the evolutionary perspective. The theory of evolution seems to have been a necessary intellectual step in preparing ourselves to see ourselves as a part of all nature, and thus to have a serious concern for all nature.

Herbert Spencer (1820–1903) had a somewhat different perspective on nature; he saw evolution as a continuous battle of tooth and claw, with the victory going to the stronger. He thought that society must not interfere with the human part of this battle by helping the weak; it was nature's law that the weak must perish. Spencer was, in a slightly different guise, expressing Galton's eugenic concern with the betterment of the species. The reputations of both men have probably been worsened by this aspect of their thought; this is the reason we referred to earlier, in connection with Galton's receiving less credit than he seemingly deserves. The notion of eugenics has never been popular in democratic societies, and is even less popular following Hitler's attempt to "improve the species" by murdering millions of Jews. Thus Spencer and Galton, both brilliant men and strong supporters of evolutionary theory, probably did as much in the long run to impede the development of functional psychology as they did to advance it.

Spencer would be featured even in a catalogue of eccentric geniuses. He anticipated Darwin with a theory of evolution which had the misfortune of being Lamarckian and thus not influential for long. Also unfortunately, Spencer did not tend to base his views on a thorough perusal of the facts. According to Irvine:

> No modern thinker has read so little in order to write so much. He prepared himself for his *Psychology* chiefly by perusing Mansel's *Prologomena Logicae* and for his *Biology* by going through Carpenter's *Principles of Comparative Physiology.* He produced a treatise on sociology without reading Comte, and a treatise on ethics without apparently reading anybody. . . . He had discovered that his "head sensations," with their attendant ramifications, were due to an impaired circulation of the blood to the brain . . . therefore. . . . Some of the most abstruse chapters of the *Psychology* were dictated . . . during the intervals of a tennis game near London. His rational life had not become less eccentric with the passing of years. (1963, pp. 287–288)

Despite his eccentricities, of which the foregoing gives but a hint, Spencer produced the first completely evolutionary psychology. Darwin specifically mentions Spencer's *The principles of psychology* (1855) as laying down the lines along which evolutionary psychology must develop. That is a little strange, since Darwin makes that comment in *The origin of species* (1859), which was the first complete exposition of Darwin's own theory!

Moreover, as we have seen, Spencer did not hesitate, like the cautious Darwin, to make broad characterizations of evolutionary theory and to draw analogies to society (see Spencer, 1961; first published 1863). His influence was, accordingly, pronounced if not always favorably regarded in social thought, sociology, and social psychology (see Hofstadter, 1955). Spencer saw clearly that the kinds of changes that occur through learning in the life of the individual could occur through selection in the life of the species. Unfortunately, he decided that associations acquired by the individual organism could be genetically transmitted; that is, he believed that Lamarck was correct. He had been persuaded of Lamarck's correctness by reading the arguments against his theory, which indicates that Spencer's stubbornness did not always pay off. Had Spencer rejected Lamarck, or even suspended judgment, he might have been considered a great psychologist rather than one among many of functionalism's antecedents. Even so, the idea of referring evolutionary changes and changes with learning to a common framework, but with a different time scale, is a very important one (see Fisher, 1966, for a discussion). We may hope that modern psychology and biology will be able to show that common mechanisms are even involved, perhaps by implicating genetic materials like DNA or RNA in the learning process.

THE PSYCHOLOGY OF JAMES

William James (1842–1910) was the leading American antecedent of functionalism, if we do not choose to regard him as its founder. His two-volume work, *The principles of psychology* (1890), was a classic virtually before it was published, since much of the book had appeared in periodical form as the chapters were completed. Watson (1968) is among those who have pointed out that the book is still read by people who have no necessity to do so—a rare tribute for a textbook! James was also voted the greatest American psychologist by his fellow psychologists in a poll taken after 1950. Not bad for a one-book man who did almost nothing in psychology after 1890!

Part of the reason for James's popularity was the urbane but enthusiastic personality which comes through in his writing. Joncich (1968) says of James that "the last book he read was always a great work and the last person seen a wonderful man" (p. 434). Considering what James said about the Fechnerian type of psychology (we will look more closely at that in a moment), Joncich may have been engaging in a bit of hyperbole. James also at times called Herbert Spencer an ignoramus, and said he had no ability to work out anything in detail. But Joncich is essentially correct; James was enthusiastic even about his dislikes, and no doubt was happy whenever he found something on which to exercise them.

Such a personality did not lead James to be a great experimentalist. His contribution to the development of psychology was through his ability to synthesize psychological principles suggested by the experiments of others, to make intuitive guesses where knowledge was missing, and to present the results in an incredibly attractive verbal package. A favorite saying of psychologists for years has been that William James was a psychologist who wrote like a novelist, while his brother Henry was a novelist who wrote like a psychologist.

Chronologically, James belongs between Wundt (who was 10 years his senior) and Titchener (25 years his junior). As has been pointed out (Heidbreder, 1933), he both precedes and succeeds Titchener—in the sense that his ideas reach further back into the past for metaphysical roots and at the same time have lost so little of their freshness that James is still not only readable but also surprisingly modern, although necessarily outmoded in most details. He had an unusual talent for being practical, readable, interesting, and popular—and at the same time commanding scientific respect. His writing was by no means mere popularization; a great deal of original thought and interpretation went into it.

James came from a well-known New England family. He began rather early to manifest a genius for finding out what he was not; he studied art for a year, and decided that he was no artist; went collecting with the great naturalist Louis Agassiz, and discovered that he was no collector; and went through the course of study for an M.D. with many interruptions because of poor health, only to find that he was no doctor. He did obtain an appointment from Harvard in order to teach anatomy, and actually taught physiological psychology, for which he established a small demonstration laboratory in 1875, at almost exactly the time that Wundt was doing the same thing in Leipzig. Soon thereafter, he embarked on his last great adventure in finding out what he was not; he started writing his great *The principles of psychology* (1890), which led him upon its completion to decide that there was really no such thing as a science of psychology. He then turned increasingly to philosophy (he was a philosopher at heart throughout his life), and was soon successful in getting Hugo Munsterberg to come to Harvard and assume the responsibilities connected with the psychological laboratory. After Munsterberg's arrival in 1897, James continued to write prolifically, and his *Talks to teachers* of 1899 and his *Varieties of religious experience* of 1901 and 1902 are of interest to psychologists.

James as a Critic

James rebelled against what he considered to be the narrowness, artificiality, and pointlessness of the German, or Wundtian, tradition in psychology, as exemplified in Titchener and the Cornell school. James was a most important factor leading to the more general protest that the functionalists were later to make. It is best to let James speak for himself, as in the following two quotations from the *Principles,* to demonstrate the forcefulness of his criticism as well as the fluency and the persuasiveness of his literary style. Of Fechner, for example, he said:

> But it would be terrible if even such a dear old man as this could saddle our Science forever with his patient whimsies, and, in a world so full of more nutritious objects of attention, compel all future students to plough through the difficulties, not only of his own works, but of the still drier ones written in his refutation. (1890, I, p. 549)

And, speaking more generally of the subsequent Wundtian psychology:

> Within a few years what one may call a microscopic psychology has arisen in Germany, carried on by experimental methods, asking of course every moment for introspective data, but eliminating their uncertainty by operating on a large scale and taking statistical means. This method taxes patience to the utmost, and could hardly have arisen in a country whose natives could be *bored.* Such Germans as Weber, Fechner, Vierordt, and Wundt obviously cannot; and their success has brought into the field an array of younger experimental psychologists, bent on studying the *elements* of the mental life, dissecting them out from the gross results in which they are embedded, and as far as possible reducing them to quantitative scales. The simple and open method of attack having done what it can, the method of patience, starving out, and harassing to death is tried, the Mind must submit to a regular *siege,* in which minute advantages gained night and day by the forces that hem her in must sum themselves up at last into her overthrow. There is little of the grand style about these new prism, pendulum, and chronograph-philosophers. They mean business, not chivalry. What generous divination, and that superiority in virtue which was thought by Cicero to give a man the best insight into nature, have failed to do so, their spying and scraping, their deadly tenacity and almost diabolic cunning, will doubtless some day bring about. (1890, I. pp. 192ff.)

The Positive Program

It would be a mistake to assume that James was merely a clever critic of elementarism and Wundtian introspectionism. On the contrary, he had an extensive positive program for psychology. While he himself preferred not to experiment, he recognized the value and the necessity of the experimental method, for psychology as well as for the older disciplines. More broadly, however, the keynote of his program is his emphasis on *pragmatism,* which implies that the validation of any knowledge must be in terms of its consequences, values, or utility. Useful knowledge for psychology, James felt, would come from a study of behavior as well as consciousness, of individual differences as well as generalized principles, of emotion and nonrational impulses as well as intellectual abilities.

Underlying all this kind of study was the general assumption that psychology must study *functions*—that psychology is a part of biological science and that human beings must be considered in their adaptation and readaptation to the environment. In keeping with the newly influential evolutionary theory, James felt that human behavior, and especially the mind, must have had some function to have survived. The effects of James's early medical training are also evident throughout his writings in his stress on the importance of the *conditions* of mind and behavior; conditions for him meant the nervous system. James retained an active interest, on a literary level at least, in neurophysiological theorizing. His most famous original theoretical contribution—his theory of emotion—is a nice illustration of this tendency, since James makes the sensory feedback from bodily actions the focal point of the emotional process.

James on Consciousness

The breadth of James's view on consciousness, when contrasted with that of Titchener, is especially instructive as a cue to the difference between the structural and functional approaches to psychology. First, James pointed out the *characteristics* of consciousness, which are studied only by psychology: It is *personal,* individualistic—belongs only to a single person; it is *forever changing*—is essentially a process and and should be studied first as such (his famous phrase "stream of consciousness" was coined to express this property); it is *sensibly continuous*—in spite of gaps, individual identity is always maintained; it is *selective*—it chooses, with attention providing the relevance and continuity for choice; and it occurs in *transitive* as well as *substantive* form.

This last point, the dichotomy between clear content and so-called fringe states of consciousness, is one of James's more noteworthy emphases. James held that transitive conscious processes are less easily noticed but are very important, and that they had not been given sufficient credit or study. He thought that all ideas enter consciousness as transitive, marginal in attention, and often fleeting and that they may or may not then proceed to substantive form, in which the idea has more stability, more "substance." In any case, transitive or fringe ideas (as of unfamiliarity, relation, and the like) account for much meaning and behavior.

Second, James emphasized the *purpose* of consciousness. Here, as suggested above, he was much influenced by the new evolutionary theory and felt that consciousness must have some biological use, or else it would not have survived. Its function is to make the human being a better-adapted animal—to enable humans to choose. Conscious choice is to be contrasted with habit, which becomes involuntary and nonconscious. Consciousness tends to become involved when there is a *new* problem, the need for a *new* adjustment. Its survival value, as James reasoned, is in relationship to the nervous system (1890): "The distribution of consciousness shows it to be exactly such as we might expect in an organ added for the sake of steering a nervous system grown too complex to regulate itself" (p. 144).

Third, James thought that psychology had to study the conditions of consciousness. In contrast to Titchener, with his psychophysical parallelism, James felt that consciousness could not be considered apart from the body. In the *Principles* James examined in detail the mind-body solutions of his time and found that he had to reject them all. However, his functional view of consciousness seemed clearly to imply an interactionism; how could consciousness "control" the nervous system unless it could interact with it?

James's speculations about ideo-motor action seem to confirm this interpretation. James said that sensory processes tend to express themselves in motor processes unless something inhibits them; thus it is to be expected that any idea, unless inhibited by other ideas, will lead more or less directly to action. James's own example of the value of this hypothesis was that if one has trouble getting out of bed in the morning, one has simply to keep getting up in mind and clear out all conflicting ideas. According to the hypothesis, one will soon find oneself standing up.

We have mentioned that James experienced the usual textbook writer's disgust with his product, saying when he finished that his book proved only "that there is no such thing as a science of psychology" and that psychology is still in "an ante-scientific condition" (Boring, 1950, p. 511). Yet even today James seems sometimes to have had an incredible modernity. Herrnstein and Boring (1965, pp. 483–495) present a selection from James in which we see him brilliantly refuting the arguments that were to be produced by John B. Watson about 25 years later as the foundations of behavioristic psychology. This demonstrates that such issues were already in the air of 1890, but it also shows James at his usual high pitch of incisiveness, recognizing and surgically exhibiting the most critical methodological issues. We shall see the same characteristics again when we look for the antecedents of Gestalt psychology!

We shall now take a brief look at other early American psychologists who were important parts of the functional tradition. It is a peculiarity of our history that, after James, there was a tendency for functional psychology to become less functional as it developed. No one can be certain why this happened; however, we can advance a reasonable hypothesis. Functional psychology is a child of evolutionary theory, and the basic focus of such a psychology should be on the adaptation of the organism to its environment. Keeping that focus in the center of our attention requires study of the organism *in its environment.* However, most of the pioneers of American functionalism had some exposure to Wundt, with his emphasis on pure science and on the almost exclusive virtues of the experimental approach. Thus functionalism between James and very recent times has tended to be an uneasy marriage between an evolutionary *philosophy* and an experimental *methodology.* When there were conflicts in this marriage, it usually turned out that methodology was the head of the household.

PIONEER AMERICAN FUNCTIONALISTS

G. Stanley Hall

Granville Stanley Hall (1844–1924) could in some ways serve as a prototype of the sort of hybrid psychologist who combined the features of Wundt and James. He took the first American doctorate in psychology under James in 1878; then he went to Leipzig to study for 2 additional years under Wundt, lived next door to Fechner, and studied physiology under Ludwig. Very soon after his return, he founded one of the first psychological *laboratories* at Johns Hopkins University, in 1883. We should not push Hall's hybrid side too far, however; he was not too much of an experimentalist, and made most of his contribution to psychology via the eminently practical administrative route. But before we go on with that story, let us take a very brief look at Hall's early life.

Hall was born in Ashfield, Massachusetts. As reported in Dorothy Ross's excellent book (1972), Hall's father farmed after Hall's birth, although he had earlier spent time as a schoolteacher, and emphasized intelligence and innovation in his farming. Hall's mother and father shared strong religious convictions, which had a great deal to do with Hall's going to Williams College to prepare for the ministry. He then went to Union Theological Seminary to complete his preparations, but there turned toward philosophy, and soon left for Germany, where he studied at the University of Berlin until, upon running out of money, he returned to Union and finished his divinity degree. However, he had been irreparably tainted with liberalism by his contact with philosophy, and he managed to preach for only 10 weeks before resolving his religious conflicts sufficiently to turn toward an academic career.

We have seen that it took some time before he ended up receiving his degree from James at Harvard, by which time he was already 34. He was 36 by the time he had returned from Leipzig to embark upon the main business of his life. Nevertheless, he had one of the most amazingly busy and varied careers of any professional psychologist. In 1887 he founded the *American Journal of Psychology*. In 1888 he was called to the presidency of a new graduate school, Clark University, in Massachusetts. In 1891 he founded the *Pedagogical Seminary* (now the *Journal of Genetic Psychology*). In 1892, the same year that Titchener arrived in America, the American Psychological Association was planned in a conference in his study, and he became the first president.

Hall's development of psychology as a scientific academic discipline at Clark is of considerable interest; it resulted in the then unusual situation of having the newest of the scientific disciplines assuming the most important part in this graduate school established primarily for scientific training. He brought in E. C. Sanford from Hopkins to head the laboratory and maintained an active personal interest in psychology.

Hall was responsible for the most famous photograph in the history of psychology. Clark University was to have a celebration of its twentieth anniversary. Hall, ever open and alert to the newest developments, managed to get Freud, Jung, and Ferenczi, three of the leading psychoanalysts, to come from Europe to the celebration in 1909. Naturally, with such bait, the event was also attended by many of America's most famous psychologists—Williams James in the year before his death, Hall himself, and so on. The resulting group portrait is one of the best known to those with an interest in the history of psychology.

Hall continued to develop new areas in psychology, proceeding from child psychology—where he popularized the use of the questionnaire as a research tool—through adolescent psychology—where his two huge volumes, *Adolescence* (1904), are probably his most influential publications—and on into the psychology of old age, publishing *Senescence* (1922)—appropriately, at the age of 78! In addition, he worked in the fields of applied psychology; educational psychology; sex (after his discovery of Freud); religious psychology (his book *Jesus, the Christ, in the light of psychology* [1917] representing a revival of his early theological interests); and even alimentary sensations!

Hall's influence was felt mainly indirectly, in that he stimulated interest and activity in such a great variety of fields. All these fields were more applied than the strict introspectionism of Titchener. Although he turned out eighty-one Ph. D.s at Clark (as contrasted with the fifty-four produced at Cornell by Titchener), only a few of these became prominent in psychology. Lewis Terman, long an American leader in the field of testing and individual differences, is perhaps the best known of them. It is suggestive of Hall's personal influence that fully a third of his doctoral candidates eventually went, like himself, into administrative positions. In any case, the career of this most remarkable man had much to do with the variegated development of early American psychology and particularly with the strong tide toward functionalism.

James McKeen Cattell

We have already met James McKeen Cattell (1860–1944) as the brash young American who appointed himself Wundt's first assistant. That happened in 1883, the year Hall had started the laboratory at Johns Hopkins after returning from Leipzig. Cattell continued to show his aggressive, opinionated, and forceful nature by refusing to accept wholeheartedly Wundt's definition of psychology.

After three years, Cattell returned to the United States and founded the psychology laboratory at the University of Pennsylvania. In 1891, he moved on to Columbia University and again founded a laboratory. He was there when Thorndike arrived with his basketful of trained chickens, hatched and educated in the James basement.

Columbia fired Cattell in 1917 because of his outspoken pacifism; apparently Cattell remembered Wundt and his colleagues in Leipzig all too well, even though he had never accepted authoritative pronouncements from them either.

Cattell did not find it necessary to starve after his discharge from the academic world. He simply spent all his time in running the profitable ventures he had already founded: the Psychological Corporation; *Science* magazine, which is still the official organ of the American Association for the Advancement of Science; the periodical biographical publication, *American Men of Science;* and the *Psychological Review,* which he had founded with James Mark Baldwin in 1894. All these ventures contributed in one way or another to the development of psychology, and the Psychological Corporation in particular demonstrated that psychology could be applied outside the classroom and the clinic.

Of more direct importance to the development of functionalism was Cattell's promotion of mental tests. He was giving mental and physical tests, of a relatively simple sort, to Columbia University students in the 1890s, before the Binet-Simon Scale had been produced. However, the success of this more comprehensive battery eclipsed the earlier work at Columbia. Cattell continued his activity in the field of individual differences and capacity (for example, in perception and reading, in psychophysics, and in free and controlled association), working in later years mostly through the Psychological Corporation.

THE FOUNDING OF FUNCTIONALISM

Functionalism as a school started at the University of Chicago under John Dewey and James Angell, both of whom came in 1894 to teach at the new university.

Angell had previously studied under Dewey, at the University of Michigan; James, at Harvard; and Erdmann, in Halle, Germany.

John Dewey

John Dewey (1859–1952), a philosopher, educator, and psychologist, was one of the eminent Americans of recent times. He studied with Hall at Hopkins, taking his doctorate there, and taught at Minnesota, as well as Michigan, before going to Chicago. It was Dewey who sent Angell from Michigan to Harvard to study with James. Sometimes we are surprised at the many interrelationships which detailed study reveals among prominent figures in the history of psychology. This is probably not as true of the men just mentioned, who belonged to a common tradition, as it is of Watson and Titchener, discussed in the previous chapter. Our conceptual categories seem to make us visualize the American Psychological Association meetings of the past as though they took place in a great hall in which there were signs reading "Structuralists register and meet here," "Functionalists register and meet here," etc. Yet a moment's thought should tell us that were such a meeting held today, psychologists would be simply visiting with other psychologists, whatever their systematic persuasions. So would the last generation have done; although psychologists doubtless associated selectively to some degree, there was much mingling, and well-known psychologists knew one another's work well.

Having the groups separated would not have helped in personal relationships, anyway. Titchener would have missed his friend Watson—except that Titchener had nothing to do with the American Psychological Association after the first years, and would not have come. Dewey would have had to meet with G. Stanley Hall, his teacher and fellow functionalist—but the two disliked each other intensely. Dewey would have missed sharing his feelings with Wundt, who was very angry with Hall for having written a biography of Wundt which Wundt described as "fabricated from beginning to end." So it seems just as well that we have never had to be segregated on systematic grounds!

To return to Dewey, we find him in 1886 happy with the publication of his new book, *Psychology*. His happiness was justified, because the book was at first very popular; but it was short-lived, for, as we know, James was about to publish his *Principles* of 1890, a book against which nothing could compete.

Ten years after his book appeared, Dewey made what was to be a more influential contribution to psychology in a short paper, "The reflex arc concept in psychology" (1896). The paper became a classic and is considered to be the most significant landmark in the beginning of the functionalist movement. Dewey objected to the reflex-arc analysis, which broke behavior down into the separate stimulus and response units and assumed that the sensory and motor nerves that participate in reflexes thus behave separately. According to the reflex-arc schema, the behavior chain can be broken down into (1) an afferent, or sensory, component, initiated by the stimulus and mediated by sensory nerves; (2) a central, or associative, component, mediated by the spinal cord and the brain; and (3) an efferent, or motor, component, mediated by motor nerves and culminating in a response.

Dewey took examples from James and from Baldwin to show the inadequacy of their formulations of behavior in terms of reflexes. He developed an organismic position, stressing behavior as a total coordination which adapts the organism to a situation. He followed the spirit of James when James urged the continuity of consciousness rather than when James talked about reflex action. Dewey regarded stimulus and response as convenient abstractions rather than as realities and pointed out the necessity for having a response before we can meaningfully say we have a stimulus; the overall reflex is not a composition made of successive stimulus and response, for there is no such successive relationship involved. The stimulus-response distinction is artificial; it is a result of the holding over of the old mind-body dualism. (Dewey said this in 1896!) The two main points Dewey made were that behavior should be considered as it functions and that molar units of analysis should be used in order to prevent too much elementaristic analysis. The first point marked the beginning of the Chicago school of functional psychology, and the second was a Gestalt point made twenty years before Gestalt psychology existed.

The functional side of Dewey's paper is revealed in the following statement:

> The fact is that stimulus and response are not distinctions of existence, but teleological distinctions, that is, distinctions of function, or part played, with reference to reaching or maintaining an end. . . . There is simply a continuously ordered sequence of acts, all adapted in themselves and in the order of their sequence, to reach a certain objective end, the reproduction of the species, the preservation of life, locomotion to a certain place. The end has got thoroughly organized into the means. (1896, pp. 365–366)

Unfortunately, the reflex-arc paper was one of the last of Dewey's contributions to psychology proper. During his stay at Chicago, he worked mostly in education and philosophy. He laid out the program for the progressive education movement in an address, "Psychology and social practice" (1900), delivered upon his retirement as president of the American Psychological Association. Dewey remained the titular head of this movement until his death. He, more than anyone else, was responsible for the application of pragmatism to education—the notion that education is life, learning is doing, and teaching should be student-centered rather than subject-centered. We should not hold Dewey responsible for the occasional excesses of his followers in the progressive education movement. Leaders are seldom asked by their followers to approve new interpretations and applications before they are put into practice. Dewey simply paid the usual price of fame in being saddled with the errors of others. In 1904, Dewey went to Columbia University Teachers College as professor of philosophy, and he remained there for the rest of his career.

Dewey, like William James, was always the philosopher in reality, whatever academic title he happened to be assuming at the time. Thus his importance to psychology does not come primarily from his contributions to the subject matter of psychology. He is remembered for his stimulation of others, particularly through his delineation of the philosophical foundations of functionalism.

James Rowland Angell

One of the men most influenced by Dewey was J. R. Angell (1869–1949). Angell's interest in academic life was first awakened by reading Dewey's *Psychology,* and Angell later studied under Dewey at the University of Michigan. Angell's father was president of that institution, and it was there that Angell received his M.A. with a major in philosophy.

After studying with Dewey, Angell went to Harvard to study with James for a time, after which he departed for Germany. He hoped to study with Wundt, but the laboratory was full, and Angell settled for a semester at Berlin and then one at Halle under Erdmann. With his thesis in philosophy nearly finished, Angell received an offer to assume a teaching position immediately at the University of Minnesota. Accepting the position would make it possible for him to marry his fiancee of 4 years. At that point, Angell showed his true evolutionary heritage by returning posthaste to Minnesota; he never found the time in a hectic life to return for a Ph.D., although honorary degrees later were conferred upon him. Angell spent only 1 year at Minnesota before receiving an offer to come to the University of Chicago, where he would be rejoining his beloved teacher, John Dewey. That was naturally an offer that he could not refuse, and a move of which a school of psychology was the result.

Angell came to Chicago in 1894. His first paper, with A. W. Moore (1896), appeared in the same volume of the *Psychological Review* as Dewey's reflex-arc paper. It was an experimental study of reaction times. The Angell-Moore paper attempted to resolve the controversy between Titchener and Baldwin. Titchener had held that reaction times are faster when the subject concentrates on the response (*motor* condition); Baldwin had claimed that, on the contrary, they are faster when the subject concentrates on the stimulus (*sensory* condition). Angell and Moore reported that there were wide individual differences in reaction times among naïve subjects, with some giving faster sensory times (supporting Baldwin), but that with continued practice motor times generally were faster (supporting Titchener). This resolution pointed up the basic difference between the structuralist position, with its emphasis on the highly trained observer, and the developing functionalist position, with its acceptance of data from naïve as well as from trained observers.

In his paper replying to criticism of his type of psychology, Titchener borrowed from James the term *structural psychology* as opposed to *functional psychology.* The terms *structural* and *functional* were used as the basis of the newly defined "isms" in psychology; Titchener was thus responsible for the naming of both systems.

As we have already observed, Titchener was fighting a losing battle. As the century ended, developments in educational psychology, animal psychology, mental testing, and related fields were helping to strengthen the basic functionalist position. It was James Angell who became the leading champion of the new trend. He published a paper on the relations between structural and functional psychology (1903), a textbook (1904), and finally the clearest expression of the functionalist position in his 1906 address as president of the American Psychological Association, "The province of functional psychology":

> Functional psychology is at the present moment little more than a point of view, a program, an ambition. It gains its vitality primarily perhaps as a protest against the exclusive excellence of another starting point for the study of the mind, and it enjoys for the time being at least the peculiar vigor which commonly attaches to Protestantism of any sort in its early stages before it has become respectable and orthodox. The time seems ripe to attempt a somewhat more precise characterization of the field of functional psychology than has as yet been offered. (1907, pp. 61–94)

Angell proceeded in his address to outline three separate conceptions of functional psychology. First, functionalism might be considered a psychology of mental operations in contrast to a psychology of mental elements. This view presents a direct antithesis between the structuralist and the functionalist positions. From the functionalist point of view, Angell notes, the complete answer to the question "What?" with respect to the mind must include answers to the corollary questions "How?" and "Why?" Second, functionalism might be considered the psychology of the fundamental utilities of consciousness. Angell presents in this second connection a view very similar to James's, with the mind functioning to mediate between the organism and its environment and becoming active primarily in accommodating to the novel situation. Third, functionalism might be considered the psychology of psychophysical relations. Here functionalism is the psychology of the total relationship of organism to environment, including all mind-body functions. This third view leaves open the study of nonconscious, habitual behavior.

Angell believed that the first and second views were too narrow; each of them restricted functionalism to the study of conscious experience, and the first put too much emphasis on opposition to structuralism. The third view was most satisfactory, although Angell felt that the three views of functionalism were interdependent.

At Chicago, Angell got the department separated from the department of philosophy and became its chairman when Dewey left for Columbia. He made it a center for functional studies, with the help of outstanding students like John B. Watson and Harvey Carr, among others. Then Angell left Chicago to head the Carnegie Corporation, after much agonizing. As he had at Minnesota, Angell again received an offer that he could not refuse, to become president of Yale University, a job that he ably filled from 1921 until his retirement in 1937. It was inevitable that he give up his active role in psychology during these years because of the pressure of administrative affairs.

THE CHICAGO SCHOOL: HARVEY CARR

It was also inevitable that psychology should miss the leadership of a man like Angell, but he was replaced by another able, quiet, modest, and underrated man, Harvey Carr (1873–1954). Carr, as a country boy from Indiana, did not have an easy time in making his way to the University of Chicago. He very gradually developed intellectual interests, first attending preparatory school and two years of college at DePauw University. He then fell ill and had to stay out of school while he recovered first his health and then his financial equilibrium by teaching in a nearby country school. Carr finally completed his degree at the University of Colorado, and went ahead to get a master's degree before, at the age of twenty-nine, going to Chicago to study experimental psychology. In 1905, Carr got his Ph.D. degree, but no job to go with it. At last, near the end of the summer, he got a job teaching in a high school in Texas, from whence he went to the Pratt Institute for 2 years, and then finally back to the University of Chicago to take the place of the departing Watson. Eleven years later, he in fact succeeded Angell as head of the psychology department, although his appointment was not formalized for 2 additional years. Harvey Carr had found a place, and he had earned it. Since it was under Carr that Chicago functionalism flourished and took on as much definition as it ever had, we have chosen to consider his system in some detail as the most comprehensive representative of functionalism.

The attitude at Chicago under Carr was not such that it encouraged much systematic fuss or bother. What was being done at Chicago was regarded as *the* psychology of the time, and there was apparently little need felt for formal systematizing. Marx (1963, pp. 14ff.) has placed functional theorizing between the extremes of the large-scale deductive approach and the purely inductive approach. The functional tendency has been to construct very limited, data-bound theories. In this respect, the functionalists anticipated the modern trend toward mathematical miniature systems. Since the functionalists did not attempt to build a cohesive system, they had no need to ignore any particular data or approach to psychology.

The functionalists also tended to share the feeling that other "new" systematic positions like behaviorism, Gestalt psychology, and psychoanalysis had little to offer. These movements were seen as exaggerated, overdramatized emphases on relatively limited aspects of psychology. Thus the behaviorist, with a stress on, and use of, measurements of overt behavior, was merely taking up where the functionalist had already more quietly broken the ground. The Gestalt psychologist was emphasizing points about the stimulus field which the functionalist had been investigating all the while. The psychoanalyst was pointing to the great importance of motivation, a concept that had been basic all along to the functionalist stress on purposive and adaptive behavior. The functionalists felt that the new schools added little beyond what their own all-embracing psychology had always included in its scope.

We will briefly discuss Carr's functionalism as it was described in his 1925 textbook, *Psychology,* again following the outline derived from McGeoch's criteria for systems of psychology. Carr's central theme is organismic adjustment, which qualifies him as a functionalist in the broadest sense.

Definition of Psychology

Psychology is the study of *mental activity,* which is the generic term for adaptive behavior. According to Carr (1925, pp. 72ff.), the adaptive act is a key concept for psychology. It involves three essential phases: (1) a motivating stimulus, (2) a sensory situation, and (3) a response that alters the situation to satisfy the motivating conditions. The motive is a stimulus that dominates the behavior of the organism until the organism reacts in such a way that the stimulus is no longer effective. Motives, as thus defined, are not conceived of as necessary to behavior but as directive forces that in general determine what we do. There are three ways in which a motive may be resolved by an adaptive act: The act may remove the stimulus, disrupt it by introduction of a stronger stimulus, or resolve it through sensory adaptation to the stimulus.

Carr felt that adaptive behavior was the subject matter of both psychology and physiology. The two disciplines were to be distinguished, however, in terms of the kinds of variables studied. Carr made the following distinction:

> Psychology is concerned with all those processes that are directly involved in the adjustment of the organism to its environment, while physiology is engaged in the study of vital activities such as circulation, digestion, and metabolism that are primarily concerned with the maintenance of the structural integrity of the organism. (1925, p. 7)

On the role of a strictly introspective psychology, Carr took a definite stand. Consciousness, he held, is an artificial abstraction, an unfortunate and unnecessary reification; something is supposed to exist, whereas all that exists in reality is a set of processes. The concept of consciousness is similar to other abstract concepts like intelligence, willpower, and crowd mind; none of these concepts exist apart from the acts and processes that give them meaning, and none of them can serve directly as the subject of empirical investigation.

In this respect, Carr's position differs from that of other functionalists. Angell, for example, insisted that a kind of introspection was absolutely necessary if psychologists were to arrive at meaningful results, and we have seen the role accorded to consciousness by James in his *Principles.* On this point, Carr was closer to his fellow student, and a man he much admired, John B. Watson.

Postulates

The postulates of functionalism, as in the case of all early psychological systems, were not explicitly stated. However, several assumptions stand out clearly: (1) Behavior is intrinsically adaptive and purposive. (2) All sensory stimuli affect behavior—not just motives, as defined above. For Carr, there was no absolute difference between a motive and any other stimulus; a motive might become an ordinary stimulus after it was resolved as a motive. (3) All activity is initiated by some sort of sensory stimulus; no response occurs without a stimulus. (4) Each response modifies the stimulus situation. Behavior, as earlier pointed out by Dewey, is essentially a continuous and coordinated process.

As in the case of all the other systems, functionalism also had its share of quasipostulational methodological preferences. Two that seemed characteristic of the Chicago school, although they seem not to derive from an evolutionary viewpoint, were that the experiment was clearly to be preferred to the naturalistic observation, and that learning was the key area for study. Thus functionalism as it actually developed historically in the United States tended toward environmentalism, when philosophically we might have expected it to tend toward nativism.

Mind-Body Position

Here Carr followed Dewey, rather than James, and minimized the problem (see Table 2-2 for a summary of mind-body positions). He felt that there was no need for a detailed solution because there was no real problem. The psychophysical integrity, or integration, of the organism was simply assumed. Functionalism thus tends to adopt either a monistic or a double-aspect position, but has no elaborate or strongly held position of any kind. The earlier functionalists, like Angell, might tend toward a parallelism or might even take a position that seemed to imply interactionism, like James; but Carr felt that psychology as an empirical and natural science did not need to concern itself with metaphysical problems. Carr did point out the inadequacy of psychophysical parallelism as adopted by Titchener, and the general functionalist position was in turn vigorously attacked by Watson as being in reality interactionist. Angell had earlier made the point that an epiphenomenal position must be rejected if one accepts the functionalist belief that consciousness has adaptive value, a belief that does seem to imply interactionism.

Nature of the Data

Although in its stress on organismic adjustment to the environment functionalism has a behavioristic flavor, functionalism does not eliminate introspection as a method of obtaining data. Its data are thus both objective and subjective, with increasingly more stress on the former kind as functionalism matured as a system.

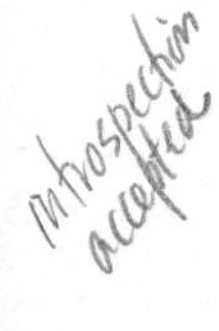

There are ample studies of animals in the functionalist experimental literature to illustrate the use of objective data. On the other side, Carr's interests in perception and thinking illustrate his use of concepts that might not fit within a behavioristic framework. *Perception* as Carr used the word referred to the apprehension of the immediate environment through present spatial stimuli; *thinking* referred to apprehension of a situation that was not immediately present in the environment. Introspective data were acceptable in the study of either.

In this respect we see Carr in a position which has mystified many psychologists; he is accepting introspective data, while denying the usefulness of consciousness as a scientific concept. No doubt he resolved the difficulty by assuming that introspection did not really consist of a study of a reified "consciousness"; it simply reported on perfectly objective states of affairs, like the distances of objects (in studies of space perception) or the firings of neural circuits (in studies of learning, thinking, and the like).

Principles of Connection

The principles of connection are the principles of learning and as such were the heart of the functionalist research program. Learning, basically, was a process of establishing associative connections or of organizing elements of behavior through association into new and larger units. Most functionalists, like Carr, were willing to take over associationistic principles in their explanations of learning. Much of the work that followed from the Chicago tradition could not be distinguished from work that might have followed from the associationistic tradition. Notable examples are the verbal learning work done by McGeoch, Melton, and Underwood (see below). Their work on nonsense syllables follows logically from the work of Ebbinghaus, who was listed as an associationist. The diffuse "schools" of associationism and functionalism are often difficult to distinguish!

The functionalists usually preferred the *relative* approach to the interpretation of learning. They avoided what Carr called the "quest for constants" and emphasized instead a *dimensional* analysis through structuring a total learning situation into specific continua which could eventually be measured. As Underwood put it (1949): "When any phenomenon can be demonstrated reliably (consistently) to vary in amount with respect to some specific characteristic, we have a *dimension*" (p. 7). His books on experimental psychology (1957, 1966) are generally illustrative of the functionalist approach. Carr's student and friend, J. A. McGeoch (McGeoch & Irion, 1952), also provides an excellent example of this general approach to the problems of learning. The position taken on the problem of the learning curve, which was a controversial and apparently exciting issue to the early generations of experimental psychologists, is representative. Until dimensional analyses could be completed, the functionalist was willing to accept gracefully the fact that there is no curve that can be called *the* learning curve; there is too much dependence of results upon the influence of the specific situation.

In an unpublished letter replying to a question about graphology (1931), McGeoch once expressed the functionalist willingness to suspend judgment until the facts were in:

> Before your craving for information anent graphology I bow in ingorance . . . but until I know, I doubt with good and hearty doubt. In the meantime I shall hold unto my bias that, when another few hundred years of fundamental work has been done upon the complexities of the interwoven functions we call mind, it will be time to attack the hinterlands where molar forecasting and proximal necromancy abide. But by that time Robert may have become long since a saint and Mr. Rhine, who has recently sprinkled salt on the tail of telepathy, may be an archangel, while I am running memory drums in hell for their amusement.

Functionalist research has dealt with factors influencing the rate and course of learning rather than with the basic nature of the learning process; it has also dealt with problems of retention and transfer. McGeoch's (1942) attitude typifies the usual atheoretical stand, accepting the empirical law of effect as an adequate explanatory principle and refusing to take a stand on the theoretical necessity of effect. A summary of functionalist learning theory and research is given by Hilgard (1956) and Hilgard and Bower (1966, 1975).

Principles of Selection

The main agents of behavior selection for Carr were *attention, motives,* and *learning.* Attention is conceived of as a preliminary act or sensorimotor adjustment, whose major function is to facilitate perception. Motives, defined as persistent stimuli, direct action and so have a major role in determining which behavior occurs. Learning operates in three main ways: (1) Certain adaptive mechanisms must be acquired by necessity in living; (2) as adjustive mechanisms are thus acquired, other aspects of the stimulating situation come to be associated with the response (as in conditioning) and thus capable of eliciting it; and (3) certain associations are imposed by society (for example, fear of the dark or of thunderstorms and dislike of particular ethnic groups).

The Experimental Program

Laboratory experimentation, as we have suggested, was the keynote of functional psychology under Carr at Chicago. One example of Carr's own research interests stands as an important contribution in its own right and as an interesting indication of how the functional principles were actively implemented in the experimental program. Research on guidance, or tuition, was a persistent laboratory problem. The main problem here was under what conditions and at what time active guidance should be introduced. Research on the rat in the maze was utilized to develop important and far-reaching principles. For example, it was concluded that, as far as possible, the animal's own initiative should be utilized, with active guidance used sparingly, and that such guidance as is given should be administered early in training. Carr's attempt to apply such principles to human teaching and learning (1930) represents a good early example of how results on animals may, with caution, be generalized to human problems.

Besides Carr, the two most important figures in the experimental program at Chicago were Karl S. Lashley, an early behaviorist whose best-known contribution was his program of brain extirpation related to learning efficiency (see Chapter 11), and L. L. Thurstone, best known for his contributions to factor analysis and the study of primary human abilities. In addition, prominent psychologists from all over the country were brought into Chicago for short periods, especially during the summer sessions, so that during the 1930s, the university developed into one of the leading centers in American psychology.

THE COLUMBIA SCHOOL: ROBERT S. WOODWORTH

Robert Sessions Woodworth (1869–1962) was one of psychology's most remarkable men. His career spanned the period from Thorndike's early work with cats in puzzle boxes to the present era. He received the first American Psychological Foundation Gold Medal Award in 1956; published *Dynamics of behavior* in 1958, when he was 88; and started revising his popular *Contemporary schools of psychology* (1964), no doubt in the midst of a busy schedule of other activities. It was jokingly said at the 1956 convention of the American Psychological Association that Woodworth, then 86, was having an affair with his secretary; although this was not an accurate reflection of Woodworth's behavior, it did accurately reflect the genial and loving awe accorded Woodworth and his continuing accomplishments. In this context, it is amusing that Murchison got Woodworth to write his autobiography for the 1932 edition of *A history of psychology in autobiography;* it is assumed that such an autobiography is a backward look, shared by a man at or near the end of his professional career. Woodworth was obviously a man who spent little time in looking back, and he actually had nearly half his career still before him when he wrote that premature autobiography. The person who writes Woodworth's comprehensive biography will be taking on a big job!

Woodworth was born in Massachusetts, the son of a minister and a schoolteacher; he spent 6 early years in Iowa, 6 in a small Connecticut village, and the balance of his early youth in Boston. He studied mathematics and taught it in high school, studied psychology and philosophy with James and Royce at Harvard, took a Ph.D. with Cattell, and studied physiology for 5 years, last with Sherrington at Liverpool, before finally making a decision for psychology. By that time, 1903, Woodworth was 34 years old. We have already seen that he had nearly 60 years of active professional life ahead of him when he returned to Columbia University and the department headed by James McKeen Cattell, Woodworth's beloved professor.

Woodworth's systematic viewpoint was first expressed in his *Dynamic psychology* (1918). There are many close resemblances between Woodworth's position and that of the Chicago functionalists; however, to a great extent he developed his position independently, and dynamic psychology might be considered an independent school. We shall follow the example of Boring (1950) and Hilgard (1956) in including it as a branch of functionalism.

Woodworth shares common antecedents with Chicago's functionalists: James and Dewey, Hall and Cattell. His system, like theirs, is moderate and unassuming, with no pretensions to finality or completeness. Both views are experimentally oriented, with very restricted theoretical superstructure. Woodworth shows the functionalist eclecticism in extreme form, seeking to take the best features from each system. Mowrer tells a story about Woodworth which illustrates this attitude:

> There is a story, perhaps apocryphal, to the effect that a colleague once good-naturedly chided Professor Woodworth for having "sat on the fence" during much of his professional lifetime, instead of getting down and becoming involved in prevailing controversy. To which Woodworth, after a moment's reflection, is supposed to have replied: "I guess I have, as you say, sat on the fence a good deal. But you have to admit one gets a good view from up there—and besides, it's cooler!" (1959, p. 129)

This point of view may not be true of his 1958 book, but is certainly true of Woodworth's earlier eclecticism; he tended to accept contributions irrespective of their origins. Even in Woodworth's last work (Woodworth & Sheehan, 1964), one gets the impression that he evaluated new experiments as follows: "If it is good work, then it is functional. If it is functional, it is acceptable."

Woodworth's dynamic psychology was less a protest against Titchenerian structuralism than the Chicago functionalism was. Woodworth accepted introspective techniques to a greater extent and was even at times a staunch defender of introspection. Nevertheless, he rejected structuralism as well as behaviorism as providing an adequate methodology for psychology. He was less influenced by associationism and a strict stimulus-response approach. The S-R theorists have often talked as though the stimulus led directly to a response, without mediation of the organism or dependence upon the organism to determine the response; this is the basis of the complaint that much psychology deals with the "empty organism." Woodworth emphasized the importance of considering the organism and insisted upon putting the organism into the basic formula which expressed the relationship psychology dealt with. Thus he wrote not S-R, but S-*O*-R. As a partial corollary to his emphasis on the organism, Woodworth gave more emphasis to motivation than the Chicago functionalists did. Carr might define motivation as a persisting stimulus, but Woodworth insisted on considering the physiological events which underlie motivation.

The heart of Woodworth's system is his concept of *mechanism,* which has more or less the same meaning as Carr's *adaptive act.* Mechanisms for Woodworth were purposive responses or sets of responses. He made the same distinction as Sherrington (1906) between preparatory and consummatory reactions; the former prepare for oncoming reactions, while the latter carry out the intention. Thus we open our mouths (preparatory reaction) before we can receive the food and swallow (consummatory reaction).

Drives for Woodworth were closely related to mechanisms. Although drives are generally defined as internal conditions that activate mechanisms, Woodworth preferred to think of internal drive processes as being themselves kinds of responses. The reverse was also true: Mechanisms, the overt behavioral ways in which drives are satisfied, could become drives! Woodworth felt that practically all mechanisms could become drives and thus run under their own power, so to speak. G. W. Allport (1937) later advanced a similar notion in his theory of the "functional autonomy of motives."

A later contribution of Woodworth offers another illustration of this kind of thinking. This is his suggestion that the act of perceiving is intrinsically reinforcing, which was proposed in an unpretentious paper entitled "Reënforcement of perception" (1947). Perception is here interpreted as an adaptive behavior whose successful performance is reinforcing without the operation of either extrinsic drive conditions or extrinsic reward conditions. This paper and his latest book seem to put him more in the cognitive camp than in the S-R-reinforcement camp, since he does not see any necessity for external reinforcing operations in order that behavior be maintained.

CRITICISMS OF FUNCTIONALISM

Definition

It was said by some that functionalism was not a well-enough-defined position to constitute a meaningful system. A Titchener-trained psychologist, C. A. Ruckmick (1913), objected to what he saw as the vague and vacillating use of the term *function.* He found it used in two senses: first, to mean an activity or a use, and second, in the mathematical sense, to indicate a dependence of one variable on another (a functional relationship). Although it may be true that there was some vagueness in the functionalist's usage of the word *function,* there is nothing wrong with using a word in two different ways, as long as the two usages are generally acceptable and are not illegitimately interchanged. The functionalists probably were trying to keep the best parts of two worlds in their multiple definitions; they did retain a generally evolutionary view (first definition above), but wished to emphasize their "scientific" reliance on experimentation, which provides us with functional relationships between independent and dependent variables (second definition above). Carr said, correctly we believe, that the mathematical meaning could be shown to include the others. This meaning of "function" is in fact so general that there is nothing peculiarly functional (in the sense of functional psychology) about it.

Applied Science

The fact that functionalists, with their multiple interests in utilitarian activities, did not distinguish carefully between pure and applied science was disturbing to some of the early critics. Contemporary psychologists take a position much like that of the functionalists. It is now generally accepted that the essential scientific procedures are identical and that pure and applied science can be distinguished only with respect to the intent of the investigator (i.e., the degree to which the investigator has an application in mind). Many important basic relationships have been discovered as a result of strictly applied efforts, and it is perhaps more significant that some of the *most* important applied findings have been incidental results of the carrying out of pure research. Thus the contemporary position would be that the pure-applied distinction is not absolute or even very important and that the functionalist should be congratulated rather than criticized for deemphasizing the distinction.

Teleology

Functionalists, with their interest in utility and purpose, were accused of using the ultimate consequences of behavior to explain behavior; in the absence of relevant evidence, such an explanation is generally referred to as *teleological.* This criticism may apply to some functionalists, but not to Woodworth or Carr; Carr was particularly careful to disclaim teleology and to postulate only proximate stimuli as causal. He recognized that an explanation in terms of the effects of behavior was incomplete at best, tending to stop investigation before the detailed nature of the relationship between the stimulating situation, the physiology of the organism, and the behavior was worked out. The tree-climbing behavior of certain larvae may be taken as an example. Their climbing has the effect of taking them up to a place where they feed on leaves. Thus the behavior may be an important factor in the evolutionary survival of the species; but if we say that they climb up the trees in order to eat leaves, we are giving a teleological explanation that really tells us nothing about the "why" of the behavior of the individual organism. As Carr (1925) said: "Each act must be explained in terms of the immediate situation and the animal's organization in reference to it" (p. 81). Thus, if we can point out that the larvae always make a positive response to light and that there is a gradient of brightness which leads them up the tree, we have escaped from the illusory finality of the teleological explanation and are on the way to an explanation of the behavior in terms of proximate factors.

There is some similarity between the teleological accusation made against the functionalist in this context and the accusation made against Thorndike and other reinforcement theorists that their explanation of reinforcement requires that a cause work backward to an effect that preceded it in time. In the case of both "instincts" and "behaviors learned through the action of reinforcement," however, the cause acts forward in time. When only the fittest survive, the effect is to select behaviors that are already adaptive. When reinforcement occurs, the effect is seen on subsequent trials and is presumed to be mediated through effects on activity contemporaneous with or following the reinforcement.

Because the problem of teleology so often comes up in any discussion of the marvelous adaptations of organisms to their environments, let us try to examine the question with the use of an analogy from another field. Assume that a believer in teleology points to the heavens, and notes the marvelous adaptation of the planets to their task of revolving about the sun. "How," this person might ask, "could this have happened unless the orbits were *designed* to fulfill the final purpose, revolution about the central star?" The answer of the consistent nonteleologist in this case should be simple. All the planets or potential planetary components which were not adapted to this task fell into the sun, or fell away from it. The fittest planets survived. They were fittest only in the sense that they were fittest to revolve for a long period about the sun; that is, only given a criterion for fitness, and only given a set of gravitational laws determining which ones meet the criterion.

So it is with organisms. We see only the survivors, and they are marvelously fitted to their environment; but again, we cannot conclude that any teleological mechanism was needed to lead them to their present adaptation. The results of most behaviors of surviving organisms are either adaptive or not seriously maladaptive, but that is a result of selection, not of teleology.

ECLECTICISM

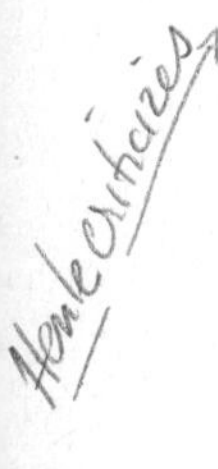

Because functionalists have generally been willing to accept so many different kinds of problems and techniques of investigation, they have often been accused of being vapid and nondescript eclectics. Henle (1957) has criticized the eclectic position, directing her attention mostly to Woodworth. She maintains that an eclectic tends to accept the good features of contradictory positions at the expense of blurring the differences between them. However, she does not distinguish clearly between different possible types of eclecticism.

Henle is speaking of eclecticism at a theoretical level. She maintains that when there are alternative deductive systems for deducing empirical statements, we cannot afford to fall between them, lest we lose deductive capacity. Thus, the eclectic must choose a theory or devise one. But there are other *levels* of eclecticism and other eclectic positions regarding theories even at this level.

First, one may be an eclectic at the level of rules for theory building as well as at the level of theory itself. That is, one may accept both Gestalt and behavioristic methodological pronouncements and do work typical of both schools. Both subjective and objective data may be accepted. An eclecticism of methodology we shall call a *metatheoretical eclecticism.* In the present state of uncertainty about the specifics of methodology, especially in psychology, a certain degree of tolerant but skeptical metatheoretical eclecticism is a necessity, not a handicap. We have already seen how too narrow a metatheory contributed to the downfall of structuralism. Failure to attack problems because they do not fit into a fixed methodological framework is always dangerous in science. Only the most basic and general premises of science are sufficiently well established to accept even tentatively, and these are accepted within all systems.

Even at a theoretical level, eclecticism may be safe; that is, the eclectic may admire many theories for their successes and be sorry for their failures, ideally while trying to improve on them. The eclectic may accept *no* theory rather than all, and, belonging to no system, is freer to reject than people who do belong to systems. The eclectic misses some of the stimulation, as well as the acrimony, of controversy; personal temperament will determine whether or not this is good.

Functionalists have tended to take a more inductive viewpoint than exponents of other systems. They have therefore tended to ignore theory construction, paying greater relative attention to empirical findings. Thus, if one does not like eclecticism, a criticism of functionalism on the ground that it is too eclectic is justified. Henle is such a critic. However, eclecticism may be made the grounds for a compliment rather than a criticism. Certainly, the eclecticism of the Chicago and the Columbia functionalists must not be considered evidence of soft-mindedness or weakness. On the contrary, these functionalists generally tended to be very astute and tough-minded critics, particularly with regard to empirical problems.

Finally, there is an entirely different defense available against those who bemoan eclecticism. It is that functionalism is not necessarily eclectic. One can easily imagine an eclectic structuralism under the quiet and modest Carr and a rigid functionalism under the autocratic Titchener (once over the hurdle of imagining the two gentlemen in question switching other aspects of their systematic positions, that is). The point is that eclecticism is a function of the personalities of a school's leaders, as well as of the systematic precepts of the school. There is nothing in functionalism to make it permanently atheoretical, nor is there any stipulation that it must forever have a wider range of experimental interests than other schools. Eclecticism appears to have a partially subsidiary, partially accidental relationship to the functionalistic position.

THE CONTRIBUTION OF FUNCTIONALISM

Because of the moderation and lack of presumption with which functionalism has gone about its business, it is easy to overlook the importance of its contribution to psychology. True, it has erected no fancy theories; it has not even been much of a school or system, in a formal sense. But its early opposition to the stifling restrictions of structuralism provided a real service to American psychology at a time when the embryonic outlines of the new discipline were just emerging.

Functionalists have continued actively to stimulate and to perform experimental research in all the fields where the early functionalists pioneered; learning in animals as well as humans; psychopathology; mental testing; and genetic and educational psychology.

Two research products may be cited as good illustrations of the functionalist program. Woodworth's scholarly manual, *Experimental psychology* (1938; Woodworth & Schlosberg, 1954), is a classic of its kind. It is a scientific handbook in the old style, dealing intensively and comprehensively with the data and theories of a large variety of experimental problems. The other example is the extended series of researches, lately reaching twenty-four in number, on the phenomenon of distributed practice in human verbal learning by Underwood (Underwood & Ekstrand, 1967). Underwood's persistent and patient productivity in research nicely illustrates the functionalist's tendency to deal intensively with interdependencies of empirical variables (even though, theoretically, Underwood himself may well be considered an associationist in functionalist's clothing).

Among the functionalists actively conducting research were some of the Chicago graduates who worked under Carr: John McGeoch, with his extensive set of human verbal learning and retention studies (and his own protégés and students, A. W. Melton, B. J. Underwood, and A. L. Irion); M. E. Bunch, with his long-time program of human and animal research on transfer and retention; Fred McKinney, who shifted his interests from learning to mental health and counseling, and subsequently to television instruction and the problem of values in teaching; and Henry N. Peters, who similarly shifted from early research on a judgmental theory of emotion to the application of basic learning techniques to the motivating of chronic schizophrenics. None of these men have produced anything like the elaborate theoretical superstructure characteristic of Hull and some others, but they have pursued empirical problems carefully and intensively.

THE REBIRTH OF FUNCTIONALISM

The best current guess seems to be that functionalism is undergoing a renaissance. In 1973, Arnold Buss produced one piece of evidence that this might be so by attempting an introductory psychology textbook, *Psychology: Man in perspective,* in which he expressed the opinion that evolutionary theory was the only one sufficiently encompassing that one could organize all of psychology around it. The geneticists, the ethologists, and the sociobiologists have filled in so many pieces of the evolutionary puzzle that one *can* begin to believe that a comprehensive framework may be coming into view. We will discuss this development of a biological psychology in somewhat more detail in our epilogue, but at the present we will merely reiterate that functionalism not only still lives, but also shows some indication of becoming the most widespread general approach to psychology.

A DIMENSIONAL DESCRIPTION OF FUNCTIONALISM

The eclectic and diffuse nature of functionalism as it has existed in the United States might lead us to expect difficulty in placing it on Watson's dimensions, and those expectations are not disappointed. There were the usual differences between individuals who held the same general position; for example, there seems to be a rough progression between the positions of James, Woodworth, and Carr. One helpful feature of functionalists is that they did not usually take extreme positions; thus they should usually be found somewhere near the middle of the dimensions. Again, students should make their own ratings, and compare them with those of the authors. It is also quite illuminating to compare ratings of one school with another. A very striking way of doing this is to plot all the ratings in different colors on a single sheet of graph paper.

Although it is difficult to place functionalists on *any* dimension, the difficulties do not seem to be any more pronounced in one dimension than in any other. Monism—dualism can be taken as a representative dimension; if one chooses James as a representative, or perhaps Angell, than one may rate toward the dualistic end; but Carr leads us in the opposite direction.

The dimensional characteristics chosen as most important by our graduate students were functionalism, utilitarianism, and molarism; the latter was rated just to the molar side of center, but the dimension was probably regarded as important by the majority of the students because it was dramatized by the contrast with structuralism.

SUMMARY AND CONCLUSIONS

We have been concerned in this chapter with the diverse origins and manifestations of functionalism in psychology. Functionalism has been described as a loose and informal systematic development, but one that represented, more than any other, the mainstream of American psychology. Its major antecedents and pioneers were William James, G. Stanley Hall, and James McK. Cattell; its founders were John Dewey and James Angell; its mature representatives were Harvey Carr at the University of Chicago, where the more formal development occurred, and Robert S. Woodworth at Columbia University, where a collateral branch flourished as dynamic psychology. Functionalism as a systematic movement arose in opposition to Titchener's structural psychology. It emphasized learning, mental testing, and other utilitarian subject matters. Functionalism declined in systematic importance as the need to oppose structuralism disappeared. However, its characteristics fit many psychologists, and functionalism has therefore continued to go its unpretentious way even after its systematic decline. Today there are strong indications that a more sophisticated modern functionalism is enjoying a dramatic renaissance in a modified form.

Functionalism, especially as represented in the psychologies of Carr and Woodworth, has been identified as basically experimental; concerned more with functional interrelationships of variables than with theoretical superstructures; accepting both introspective and behavioral data but utilizing mainly the latter; stressing adaptive behavior and purposive, motivated activity within either an S-R (Carr) or an S-O-R (Woodworth) framework; and revealing always an active, systematic eclecticism in combination with a tough-minded approach to experimental problems. It has made and will continue to make a most important contribution to the advance of psychology as a science.

FURTHER READINGS

Our favorable allusions to Irvine's delightful *Apes, angels, and Victorians* (1963) should already have convinced the reader that it furnishes an easy entrée to the world of functionalism's English antecendents. James's *Principles*, too, needs no further advertising from us as a source of information about our American genius. Dewey's paper (1896) is also brilliant and blessedly short, since it is not easy reading even for us sophisticated moderns. Carr's *Psychology* (1925), for the Chicago school, is a good historical source. For the Columbia development, Woodworth's early *Dynamic psychology* (1918) and his more recent *Dynamics of behavior* (1958) are excellent sources. In addition, Woodworth's systematic textbook, *Contemporary schools of psychology* (1948), expresses the functionalist, or middle-of-the-road, point of view very well. Woodworth's *Experimental psychology* (1938), revised by Woodworth and Schlosberg (1954), should also be mentioned; this book stands as a classic experimental approach to the older problems of psychology. For the more recent developments, Underwood's two books, *Experimental psychology* (1949) and *Psychological research* (1957), offer prime examples of a thoroughly functionalistic approach to experimental problems and methodological issues. McGeoch's *Psychology of human learning* (1942), revised as McGeoch and Irion (1952), summarizes much of the early type of functionalist research utilizing verbal human materials and subjects. Finally, for the last reading, what could we suggest except the last word of the last great functionalist, Woodworth's *Contemporary schools of psychology* (as revised by Woodworth & Sheehan, 1964)? In later chapters, we will suggest readings relevant to the rebirth of functionalism.

Table 6-1 Important Figures in Behaviorism

Antecedent influences	Behaviorists		
	Pioneers	**Founders**	**Developers**
Evolution and animal behavior			
Charles Darwin (1809–1882)	James McKeen Cattell (1860–1944)—Columbia	John B. Watson (1878–1958)—Hopkins	Albert P. Weiss (1879–1931)—Ohio State
C. Lloyd Morgan (1852–1936)	Edward L. Thorndike (1874–1949)—Columbia		Walter S. Hunter (1889–1953)—Brown
Jacques Loeb (1859–1924)			Karl S. Lashley (1890–1958)—Chicago
Extensions of mechanistic explanations			
Descartes (1596–1650)	Ivan P. Pavlov (1849–1936)—St. Petersburg		Edward C. Tolman (1886–1961)—California
La Mettrie (1709–1751)	Vladimir M. Bekhterev (1857–1927)—St. Petersburg		Edwin R. Guthrie (1886–1959)—Washington
Cabanis (1757–1808)	James R. Angell (1869–1949)—Chicago		
Positivism			
Auguste Comte (1798–1857)	Max Meyer (1873–1967)—Missouri		Clark L. Hull (1884–1952)—Yale
			B. F. Skinner (1904–)—Harvard

Chapter 6

Behaviorism

The system of objective psychology called *behaviorism* by its founder, John B. Watson, is by far the most controversial of all the American schools. Behaviorism came to play a prominent role not only in psychology but also in general cultural affairs, where its influence has rivaled that of the European import, psychoanalysis.

Watson had one main positive and one main negative interest. On the positive side, he proposed a completely objective psychology. He wished to apply the techniques and principles of animal psychology, in which he had been working, to human beings. This positive aspect of behaviorism has been called *methodological* or *empirical* behaviorism. His main methodological point—insistence on the primacy of *behavior* as the source of psychological data—has been dominant and is still well accepted today; however, the recent rise of phenomenology and existential psychology has again made it controversial.

Watson's negative emphasis was his inveighing against mentalistic concepts in psychology. He protested against both the introspective psychology of Titchener and what he considered the inadequacies of Angell's functionalism; Watson alleged that Angell had retained an interactionistic bias and still accepted introspective data. Though Watson deplored the prominence of metaphysical problems in psychology, he took a definite metaphysical position by denying, by implication at least, the existence of mind. This denial constituted his *metaphysical,* or *radical,* behaviorism, which has been less widely accepted. Radical behaviorism has been the center of much of the controversy that has raged around Watson and his ideas.

The present treatment begins with a consideration of the three major trends out of which Watsonian behaviorism developed: the philosophical traditions of psychological objectivism (whose direct influence on Watson is questionable), animal psychology, and functionalism. We then describe the founding of behaviorism; outline Watson's system, with special emphasis on the mind-body issue; consider some of the secondary characteristics of Watson's thinking; and discuss some of the more important of the early behaviorists other than Watson. We conclude with a treatment of the various criticisms offered against Watsonian behaviorism, an analysis of the factors responsible for the acceptance of behaviorism, and finally an evaluation of Watson's contribution.

Table 6-1 (page 124) lists the most important persons in behaviorism.

EARLY TRENDS TOWARD PSYCHOLOGICAL OBJECTIVISM

Watson was by no means the first to stress the need for objectivity in psychology. There is a long history of such efforts, involving mainly philosophers. Our treatment of this history is indebted to the classic review by Diserens (1925), who defines psychological objectivism as including "any system in which the effort is made to substitute objective data and the universal method of science, direct observation, for subjective data and the special method of introspection" (p. 121).

We have already seen how Descartes and La Mettrie took some of the first steps toward the use of objective data in psychology by extending mechanistic explanations to the human body, and finally the human mind. Cabanis (1757–1808) then attempted to define mind in terms of objective factors, especially physiological functions. According to him, "mental" events are functions of the total organism and not simply of the mind (see Boring, 1950).

The most important name in this series is that of another Frenchman, Auguste Comte (1798–1857), who founded a movement called *positivism.* All varieties of positivism emphasize positive (i.e., not debatable) knowledge; there is sometimes disagreement about what kind of procedure gives such knowledge. Comte believed that only social, objectively observable knowledge could be valid; introspection, which depends upon a private consciousness, could not provide valid knowledge. He denied the importance of the individual mind and vigorously criticized mentalism and subjective methodology. He believed that human critical thinking advanced through three stages, from the theological through the metaphysical to the positivistic, or scientific, mode of thought. Comte referred to traditional psychology as the last phase of theology. He stated (1896; first published 1824) that "In order to observe, your intellect must pause from activity, and yet it is this very activity you want to observe. If you cannot effect the pause, you cannot observe; if you do effect it, there is nothing to observe. The results of such a method are in proportion to its absurdity" (p. 11). More constructively, Comte emphasized two types of study of affective and intellectual functions: (1)

determination with precision of the organic conditions on which they depend and (2) observation of the behavioral sequence. These two types of study certainly should provide data acceptable to Watsonian behaviorists.

Subsequent French and British materialists, followers of Comte, carried on in this tradition. The most important of these were Antoine Cournot, G. H. Lewes, and Henry Maudsley.

ANIMAL PSYCHOLOGY

We have already seen how important Darwinian evolutionary theory has been in the development of psychology as a science and particularly as a background factor determining the form of functional psychology. The theory also gave great impetus to the study of animal psychology, which in turn was perhaps the most important single factor which led Watson to formulate his behavioral psychology.

Animal psychology grew more or less directly out of evolutionary theory. Darwin's theory had a great influence among British intellectuals, but strong opposition to the theory arose, particularly among the clergy and theologians. A primary objection was to Darwin's assumption of mental continuity between man and the lower animals. The most effective answer to the objection was to demonstrate such mental continuity in somewhat the same way as Darwin's evidence had already demonstrated the physical continuity. This demonstration necessitated an animal psychology. One way to defend Darwin's theory was therefore to show the presence of mind in infrahuman organisms (contrary to Cartesian tradition) and to exhibit its continuity with the human mind.

Charles Darwin himself began the defense. His main theme in *Expression of emotions in man and animals* (1872) was that human emotional behavior is the result of the inheritance of behavior once useful to animals but now useless to human beings. Darwin's great wealth of observation on animals was drawn upon for many examples. One of the most famous is the way people curl their lips in sneering; this was held to be a remnant of the baring of the canine teeth in rage by carnivorous animals. The tendency found in the dog to turn in a circle several times before sitting down was likewise held to be an evolutionary remnant of behavior once useful in the more primitive stage of its ancestors; presumably, the dog performed the motion as a precautionary measure against snakes and the like and to flatten out a bed.

We have already seen that one of Darwin's personal friends, George John Romanes, later undertook the defense. Romanes culled the literature for all sorts of stories, both scientific and popular, on animal behavior. He accumulated a great mass of material from which he wrote the first comparative psychology, *Animal intelligence* (1886). Romanes's method of gathering data is now called the *anecdotal method.* In spite of the fact that he had explicitly laid down rules for using the stories, Romanes was unable to avoid using some inadequately controlled observations, since he had no way of checking on the original sources. The tendency to anthropomorphize—to read human motives and abilities into animal behavior—played into Romanes's hands, since he wished to demonstrate a con-

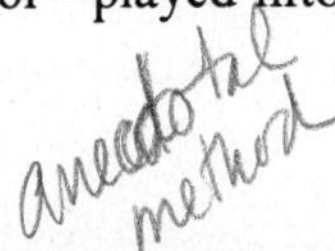

tinuity between humans and animals. Anthropomorphizing, like the anecdotal method, is today thoroughly disapproved of in psychology. In spite of the limitations of his methodology, Romanes deserves credit for stimulating the initial development of comparative psychology and preparing the way for the experimental methodology that followed.

C. Lloyd Morgan used a semiexperimental methodology and partly controlled observations in the field in his studies on lower animal forms. He is better known today for his methodological contributions than for his substantive findings. Morgan adapted the law of parsimony (also called, more picturesquely, *William of Occam's razor*), to comparative psychology. In what came to be known as *Lloyd Morgan's canon,* he expressed this position (1899): "In no case may we interpret an action as the outcome of the exercise of a higher psychical faculty, if it can be interpreted as the outcome of the exercise of one which stands lower in the psychological scale" (p. 59). This dictum was intended to counteract the tendency to anthropomorphize, and the point was well received. (See Newbury, 1954, for an extended discussion of Lloyd Morgan's canon in its various interpretations.)

If one does not anthropomorphize, how does one demonstrate the desired continuity? For one thing, Lloyd Morgan's canon applied not just to animals but also to human beings; in the latter case it implied that we have a tendency to "anthropomorphize" when interpreting the behavior of others, in the sense that we may give them too much credit for higher mental functions. Romanes was demonstrating continuity by finding mind everywhere; Morgan also wished to demonstrate continuity, but suggested that it might be done as well if we could find mind nowhere. Morgan's appeal to simplicity and rejection of anthropomorphism would seem, from a modern perspective, to have made the development of a scientific behaviorism inevitable.

Morgan relied upon habits, rather than upon intelligence, as the main explanatory factor, and trial-and-error learning was stressed. He assumed that human and subhuman learning processes were continuous. Thorndike's later laboratory experimentation is closely related to Morgan's work in both content and outlook; Watson also was stimulated in his animal research by reading Morgan's reports. It is interesting that all three tended to explain all learning in terms of a few simple principles which apply to humans as well as to animals low on the phyletic scale. Others, like the Gestaltists, are more like Romanes in their tendency to see insight, characteristic of human learning, even in animals lower on the scale.

Lloyd Morgan's canon has been attacked by some psychologists who recognize, correctly we believe, that in many cases the more complex of two alternative interpretations is the appropriate one. However, this does not invalidate Morgan's canon or the principle of parsimony; these rules apply only to cases in which all the alternatives are about equally supported by the available data. Naturally, if there is a flaw in the simpler explanation, it is not acceptable, and there is no issue at all. But it is incumbent upon the proponent of the more complex account to show why his account must be accepted over the simpler one; if he cannot, the simpler account is preferable.

Jacques Loeb (1859–1924) is the next important figure in the development of animal psychology. Loeb, a German biologist, came to the United States in 1891 and spent the greater part of his professional career here. Loeb is responsible for the wide acceptance of the concept of the *tropism,* or forced movement, as an explanatory factor in animal behavior. In a tropism, the response is a direct function of the stimulus and is in this sense forced. Loeb felt that all the behavior of the lowest of animal forms is tropistic and that a considerable proportion of the behavior of higher forms is also. One familiar example of a tropism is the apparently mechanical and irresistible movement of certain moths into light (positive phototropism), even though flight directly into a flame results in their destruction. Naturally, not all tropisms are so maladaptive. In modern usage, forced movements of animals are most often called "taxis" to distinguish them from the slower forced movements of plants.

Loeb was not reacting against Darwinism but against the anthropomorphic tendency which we have seen represented by Romanes. Despite the fact that Loeb felt tropistic factors could account for a great deal of the behavior of higher forms, he did not attempt to deal with human problems. He did, however, contribute to a problem arising from the human being—the problem of consciousness. He suggested an objective way to determine whether a given organism was conscious. His criterion was whether the organism manifested associative memory. Certainly this criterion is not very exclusive; protozoa, for example, have been said to show evidence of associative learning, though the evidence has also been seriously questioned. The question of what organisms are conscious can be given only an arbitrary answer; our operational criterion of consciousness in animals can be chosen at will, and we should be quite clear that various answers to the problem are possible. Any other attempt at solution would have to fall back on our tendency to anthropomorphize.

By this time the study of animal behavior within the biological sciences was becoming widespread. In support of Loeb's position, the biologists Thomas Beer, Albrecht Bethe, and Jacob J. von Uexküll came out strongly for the elimination of psychological terms and the substitution of objective ones. The biologist H. S. Jennings, on the other hand, obtained evidence for the modifiability of behavior in the protozoan *Paramecium* and opposed Loeb's mechanistic interpretations of animal behavior. Hans Driesch also opposed Loeb and maintained a vitalistic position (i.e., there is something qualitatively different about living organisms, and they are not reducible to physicochemical reactions). Sir John Lubbock was studying ants, wasps, and bees, and the Frenchmen Fabre and Forel were also studying insects. Albrecht Bethe published a mechanistic interpretation of the social life of ants and bees. Certainly animal psychology was a going concern. The pressure of these various researches was beginning to push objective psychology to the fore long before behavioristic psychology was founded as a school in America.

Watson, who studied under Loeb at the University of Chicago, was thoroughly exposed to this objective tradition within biology. Then, several years later, he found Jennings at Johns Hopkins when he arrived, and took his courses, even though he went to Hopkins as a full professor.

We have already seen how systematically E. L. Thorndike was working with animals. In this he was not alone. Robert M. Yerkes (1876–1956) began his animal investigations in 1900. Yerkes studied crabs, turtles, frogs, dancing mice, rats, worms, crows, doves, pigs, monkeys, apes, and finally humans. His research on the apes is the most significant; it is comprehensively summarized in *Chimpanzees: A laboratory colony* (1943). Yerkes at one time collaborated with Watson in the development of visual testing techniques for animals. However, Yerkes was not a behaviorist by persuasion, despite the fact that he did work in comparative psychology that was typically behavioristic in method. Yerkes was an admirer of Titchener and felt that the investigation of experience was one of the most interesting of psychology's problems. Yerkes's contribution to behaviorism was simply in strengthening the position of comparative psychology, especially through his establishment of the chimpanzee experimental station at Orange Park, Florida; the station was named the Yerkes Laboratories of Primate Biology when he retired from active administration in 1941. The laboratory has since been moved to Atlanta, where it is associated with Emory University. The federal government now supports several independent regional primate centers scattered about the nation. Yerkes made a great contribution to the advancement of the application of psychology during World War I when he was a leader in developing the program of testing of Army recruits.

W. S. Small at Clark devised the first rat maze in the same year that Yerkes began his animal investigations—1900. The albino rat was so well adapted to being studied in the maze that it has ever since been the outstanding laboratory animal in psychology, and the rat-in-the-maze has been a standard situation for the study of learning. Since the 1930s, it has become clear that the rat is equally well adapted to life in the Skinner box (or, as Skinner seems to prefer, life in the operant chamber). Growth of the study of animals was so rapid between 1900 and 1911 that the *Journal of Animal Behavior* was founded then. Finally, Titchener's first doctoral student, Margaret Floy Washburn, published a compendium of animal psychology (1908). The book was essentially an analogical study of human and animal mental processes, but it contained a great deal of factual information and became a classic in the field. Thus, some of the impetus for a behavioral psychology came from the camp of the structuralists.

AMERICAN FUNCTIONALISM: 1910

American functionalism was the third of the important trends that led toward behaviorism. Several psychologists who were functionalists only partially or indirectly were also leaning toward an objective orientation. We have already mentioned Cattell and Thorndike; Herrnstein (Watson, 1967, pp. 18–20) even argues that Thorndike's position was more like that of modern behaviorists in some respects (the roles of learning and of reinforcement) than Watson's was. In 1904, Cattell said (as quoted by Woodworth & Sheehan, 1964, p. 114): "It seems to me that most of the research work that has been done by me or in my laboratory is nearly as independent of introspection as work in physics or in zoology. . . ." Watson's old opponent, William McDougall (1871–1938), had defined psychology as the positive science of conduct. He made experimental observations on

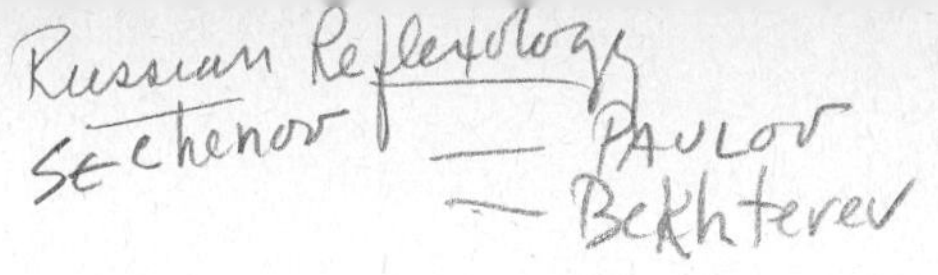

color discrimination in infants in 1901, and his books (1905, 1912) contain objective data; the latter book was even named *Psychology: The study of behavior.* However, McDougall was an outspoken purposivist, accepted consciousness, and used introspective data—in short, he was the antithesis of Watson in the most critical respects one can think of, and thus he cannot be considered a serious rival to Watson in the formulation of an exclusively objective psychology.

Max Meyer (1873–1967) would be a more serious candidate. He published *The fundamental laws of human behavior* in 1911, a book which reflects his thoroughgoing objectivism; this was 2 years before Watson published on the subject. By 1921, he had indicated his behavioristic inclinations more overtly by titling another book *The psychology of the other one.* However, by this time Watson's contributions had already been universally recognized. Meyer was a "scientific isolate" (Esper, 1967), who feuded with his teacher, Carl Stumpf, had exactly one Ph.D. student, A. P. Weiss, and finally got himself fired from the University of Missouri, partially because of his own self-righteous stubbornness. Fame does not seek out those whose personalities are not right!

We have also mentioned the Russian reflexology school, initiated by I. M. Sechenov and developed by Pavlov and Bekhterev; the latter entitled one of his major books *Objective psychology* (1913); the book was published in Russia in 1910. Sechenov (1965) published his *Reflexes of the brain* in book form in 1873 and in monograph form in 1863! This is truly amazing when one considers that Sechenov's basic philosophical and methodological position was nearly identical to Watson's in its objectivity.

In America, the most prophetic psychologist was probably James Angell, with whom Watson was associated at Chicago before 1908. We have already met Angell as a founder of functionalism. He seemed to recognize that psychology, already largely functional in character, was about ready for a further step in the direction of objectivity. Two expressions of his changing point of view preceded Watson's first published behavioristic pronouncements. In 1910, at the Minneapolis meetings of the American Psychological Association, Angell said:

> But it is quite within the range of possibility, in my judgment, to see consciousness as a term fall into as marked disuse for everyday purposes in psychology as has the term soul. This will not mean the disappearance of the phenomena we call conscious, but simply the shift of psychological interest toward those phases of them for which some term like behavior affords a more useful clue. (1913, p. 255)

Two years later, at the Cleveland meetings of the association, he presented a paper on this topic which was written just before Watson's first systematic paper. He now spoke at more length:

> The comparative psychologists have from the first been vexed by the difficulty of ascribing to animals conscious processes of any specific kind in connection with intelligent behavior. . . . Obviously, for scientists engaged in this field of investigation, it would from many points of view be a material gain, in convenience at least, if the possible existence of consciousness might be forgotten and all animal behavior be described objectively. Nor has there been, so far as I am aware, any general

> objection to this proposal. . . . It is furthermore not unnatural that finding it practicable and convenient, as undoubtedly it is, to waive reference to consciousness in matters relating to animal behavior, the tendency should manifest itself to pursue a similar line of procedure in dealing with human conduct. This tendency does not so much represent any formally recognized program like that of our world-reforming realists, as it does a general drift occasioned by several different sources. Its informal and unselfconscious character is probably indicative of a more substantial and enduring basis than belongs to movements more carefully and more purposely nurtured. (1913, pp. 256ff.)

Boring (1950) has summarized the situation in American psychology just prior to Watson's founding of behaviorism: "America had reacted against its German parentage and gone functional. . . . Behaviorism simply took from functionalism part but not all of the parental tradition . . . the times were ripe for more objectivity in psychology, and Watson was the agent of the times" (p. 642).

THE FOUNDING: JOHN B. WATSON

John Broadus Watson (1878–1958) was born near Greenville, South Carolina. He early showed a personal rebelliousness, which later surfaced in the iconoclasm of his behaviorism. According to Watson's own account (1936), he never made more than a passing grade during his early years in school, and was twice arrested, once for discharging a firearm within the city limits of Greenville. Later at Furman University, one of his professors said that if a man ever handed in a paper backwards, he would fail him. Watson "accidentally" handed in his paper "backwards" (whatever that meant), was duly failed, and had to stay for an additional year of school and got a master's degree instead of a bachelor's because of it. Even after he had fathered behaviorism, he managed to so incense the authorities in the United States Army during World War I that they consigned him to a school for "positive intelligence" which virtually guaranteed death to its successful graduates, once they reached the front. The armistice came while Watson awaited his orders to go to the front.

Before this latter incident, Watson went to the University of Chicago to study philosophy under Dewey. Angell, however, preempted his interest, and steered him into experimental psychology. He also studied physiology and neurology under H. H. Donaldson and Jacques Loeb. He considered doing his dissertation under Loeb, but the latter was not considered "safe" enough by Angell and Donaldson, so they supervised his work themselves. Watson finished his Ph.D. work after just three years and three summers in 1903, the youngest man to receive a Ph.D. from Chicago up to that time (Watson, 1936).

Although he had developed an undergraduate interest in philosophy and had taken graduate work in it, apparently this kind of thinking "wouldn't take hold." Watson explained briefly:

> I got something out of the British School of philosophers—mainly out of Hume, a little out of Locke, a bit out of Hartley, nothing out of Kant, and strange to say, least of all out of John Dewey. I never knew what he was talking about then, and unfortunately for me, I still don't know. (1936, p. 274)

While at Chicago, Watson worked mainly with animal subjects. Some three decades later, he put his feelings this way:

> I never wanted to use human subjects. I hated to serve as a subject. I didn't like the stuffy, artificial instructions given to subjects. I always was uncomfortable and acted unnaturally. With animals I was at home. I felt that, in studying them, I was keeping close to biology with my feet on the ground. More and more the thought presented itself: Can't I find out by watching their behavior everything that the other students are finding out by using *O*'s [observers]. (1936, p. 276)

Watson's doctoral dissertation was accordingly done with animal subjects. Directed jointly by Donaldson and Angell, it involved the correlation between the increasing complexity of behavior in the young albino rat and the growth of medullation in the central nervous system. A somewhat better-known piece of research completed at Chicago was his analysis of the sensory cues used in maze learning by the rat. Here Watson followed the techniques of Small, Morgan, and Thorndike and concluded, after systematic elimination of the various senses, that kinesthesis (which he could not completely eliminate) was the most basic to maze learning.

In 1908, Watson accepted a professorship in psychology at Johns Hopkins University. There he continued his experimental laboratory research on animals, collaborating with Yerkes (who was for a short time at Hopkins in the medical school) on an apparatus for testing animals' visual abilities, taking course work and laboratory work with Jennings, and apparently making satisfactory professional progress.

According to his own statement, Watson had early begun to think in more thoroughly objective terms. His animal researches at Chicago stimulated him to his first formulation in connection with a colleague at the University of Chicago in 1903 (J. B. Watson, 1929, preface); this formulation was not encouraged. Apparently the chief objection at that time was that the formulation applied to animals but not to human beings. His first public expression came in a lecture given at Yale Univeristy in 1908, when he was again discouraged, this time on the grounds that his formulation was descriptive and not explanatory. Finally, in 1912, he gave a more definitive expression in the course of some public lectures delivered at Columbia University. The first published polemic, a paper entitled "Psychology as the behaviorist views it," appeared the following year in the *Psychological Review* and marked the official launching of the behavioristic school.

Here is the keynote of Watson's original position:

> Psychology as the behaviorist views it is a purely objective experimental branch of natural science. Its theoretical goal is the prediction and control of behavior. Introspection forms no essential part of its methods, nor is the scientific value of its data dependent upon the readiness with which they lend themselves to interpretation in terms of consciousness. The behaviorist, in his efforts to get a unitary scheme of animal response,recognizes no dividing line between man and brute. The behavior of man, with all its refinement and complexity, forms only a part of the behaviorist's

> total scheme of investigation. . . . The time seems to have come when psychology must discard all reference to consciousness; when it need no longer delude itself into thinking that it is making mental states the object of observation. (1913b, p.158)

This first paper on behaviorism was followed shortly by a second one on the concepts of image and affect (1913a). He reduced images to implicit language responses and affect to slight vascular changes in the genitalia. We shall see later that he was severly criticized for these reductions. These two early papers were combined into the introductory chapter of his first book, *Behavior: An introduction to comparative psychology,* which appeared in 1914. This book has been reissued (1967) with an introduction by R. J. Herrnstein, who shows especially clearly how Watson first ignored and then embraced Pavlov. Herrnstein also outlines particularly well the relationship of Watson's thought to that of Tolman, Hull, and Skinner.

In 1919 Watson published another book, *Psychology from the standpoint of a behaviorist.* This volume completed the program outlined in his earlier papers. Objective methods were definitely extended into human behavioral problems. Verbal behavior was to be accepted as data, but introspection was rejected. (This distinction led his critics to heated charges of inconsistency.) The stress was on developmental factors, and the 1924 revision gave detailed results of Watson's work at the Johns Hopkins Hospital on infantile emotions and emotional conditioning.

Watson felt that psychology as a scientific discipline needed to make a complete break from the past. He declared:

> [Psychology] made a false start under Wundt . . . because it would not bury its past. It tried to hang on to tradition with one hand and push forward as a science with the other. Before progress could be made in astronomy, it had to bury astrology; neurology had to bury phrenology; and chemistry had to bury alchemy. But the social sciences, psychology, sociology, political science, and economics, will not bury their "medicine men." (1929, p. 3)

Watson resigned from the faculty at Johns Hopkins before the beginning of the 1920–1921 school year. On November 20, 1920, Watson's wife, Mary Ickes Watson, sued him for divorce. Rosalie Raynor, the girl with whom Watson did his famous experiment work on infants, was named as a correspondent in the divorce suit. On January 1, 1921, the *Baltimore Sun* reported that John B. Watson and Rosalie Raynor had been married on the previous Friday. Watson's own two-line account of these events is somewhat misleading: "All of this work came abruptly to a close with my divorce in 1920. I was asked to resign" (Watson, 1936, p. 279).

However it happened exactly, Watson was forced out of academic life, never to return. He was displeased with the way the academicians had let their opinions of his personal life ruin his scientific career. He went into the field of advertising, where he stayed until his retirement from active life. For several years, however, he continued to lecture in New York City and to publish on psychological topics. In 1925 his *Behaviorism* appeared, as a series of lectures, with a strong environmentalist position and a positive program for the improvement of human beings. This was the book that provoked the most attention from the nonpsychological public, both favorable and unfavorable. Watson continued to publish occasionally, producing one book on child care and a number of popular articles. However, he was careful to point out the scientific inadequacy of these in his autobiographical statement (1936). Nothing new or significant was produced by him following the mid-20s; this man, whose systematic pronouncements did so much to influence the course of psychology, dropped completely out of professional activity. Whatever our systematic position, we must regret the untimely and unnecessary loss of a figure whose vitality and clarity of expression commanded so much attention and (depending on one's bias) admiration or amazement. Watson was essentially relegated to the scientific scrap heap at the age of 42, when many famous psychologists have just been reaching the height of their powers.

WATSONIAN BEHAVIORISM: SYSTEMATIC CRITERIA

Definition of Psychology

Psychology for Watson was (1929) "that division of natural science which takes human behavior—the doings and sayings, both learned and unlearned, of people as its subject matter" (p. 4). No mention need be made of the psychic life or consciousness—these are "pure assumptions." Watson clearly included verbalization as a kind of behavior (1925): "*Saying* is doing—that is, *behaving.* Speaking overtly or to ourselves (thinking) is just as objective a type of behavior as baseball" (p. 6).

Watson's behaviorism had two specific objectives: to predict the response, knowing the stimulus, and to predict (really *postdict*) the stimulus, knowing the response. The terms *stimulus* and *response* represented for Watson broader concepts than their usual definitions allow:

> The rule, or measuring rod, which the behaviorist puts in front of him always is: Can I describe this bit of behavior I see in terms of "stimulus and response"? By stimulus we mean any object in the general environment or any change in the tissues themselves due to the physiological condition of the animal, such as the change we get when we keep an animal from sex activity, when we keep it from feeding, when we keep it from building a nest. By response we mean anything the animal does—such as turning toward or away from a light, jumping at a sound, and more highly organized activities such as building a skyscraper, drawing plans, having babies, writing books, and the like. (1925, pp. 6, 7)

Postulates

Watson's assumptions were stated directly and carefully, although not necessarily in the form of postulates. The major ones may be summarized as follows:

1 Behavior is composed of response *elements* and can be successfully *analyzed* by objective natural scientific methods.

2 Behavior is composed *entirely* of glandular *secretions* and muscular *movements;* thus it is reducible ultimately to physicochemical processes.

3 There is an immediate response of some sort to every effective stimulus; every response has some kind of stimulus. There is thus a strict cause-and-effect *determinism* in behavior.

4 Conscious processes, if indeed they exist at all, cannot be *scientifically* studied; allegations concerning consciousness represent supernatural tendencies, and as hangovers from earlier prescientific theological phases of psychology must be ignored.

A number of secondary assumptions, having to do with the nature of thinking, the role of the environment, and the like, are discussed in a later section because they are not essential to the central behaviorist argument.

Nature of the Data

The character of the data for behaviorism has already been fairly well indicated in the material included under the two preceding headings. Briefly, they are always objective reports—of muscular movements or glandular secretions in time and space; these must be, at least in principle, quantitatively analyzed, and stimulus-response relationships are the units of description (although they may be rather large-scale units, such as "building a skyscraper," and not merely "muscle twitches").

Principles of Connection

Here Watson adopted, at first, merely an older version of associationism—the laws of frequency and recency minus the "effect" aspect that Thorndike had added. Apparently he saw in effect too much of the old mentalistic attitudes, although, as we have noted, a strictly objective and operational interpretation is possible. Watson emphasized that the successful response must always occur and terminate the behavior; Thorndike's retort was that very often certain errors, such as entrances into the more popular blind alleys in a maze, were much more frequently made than the corresponding correct response. Watson subsequently shifted his emphasis to classical conditioning as demonstrated in the laboratory by Pavlov and Bekhterev (see Chapter 3). This he came to recognize as the basis for all learning; the most complex habits could be most appropriately conceived of as combinations and chainings of simpler reflexes. It is interesting, as Woodworth notes (1948, p. 88), that in spite of his enthusiasm for classical conditioning Watson apparently never recognized the very great similarity between Pavlovian reinforcement and Thorndikian effect; he continued to hold to an exercise law (frequency and recency factors) while accepting classical conditioning principles and even using them himself in his experiments on emotional conditioning in infants.

Principles of Selection

Watson assumed a large number of inherited reaction tendencies to stimulation and the "almost immediate" modification of these through conditioning into more and more complicated and individually differentiated tendencies. Thus he wrote:

> One of the problems of behaviorism is what might be called the ever increasing range of stimuli to which an individual responds. Indeed so marked is this that you might

be tempted at first sight to doubt the formulation we gave above, namely that response can be predicted. If you will watch the growth and development of behavior in the human being, you will find that while a great many stimuli will produce a response in the new-born, many other stimuli will not. At any rate they do not call out the same response they later call out. For example, you don't get very far by showing a new-born infant a crayon, a piece of paper, or the printed score of a Beethoven symphony. . . . It is due to conditioning from earliest childhood on that the problem of the behaviorist in predicting what a given response will be is so difficult. (1925, p. 13)

Thus Watson maintained that selectivity of response and of the sufficient stimulus depends only on innate and acquired S-R connections. Selection does not constitute a unique problem. The older mentalistic concepts of purpose and value are eliminated as explanations.

THE MIND-BODY PROBLEM

The mind-body solution proposed by Watson is at the heart of what has been called *radical* or *metaphysical* behaviorism. Historically, the mind-body issue has been of considerable importance, especially with respect to the controversy about behaviorism. We therefore treat the problem at some length. Twenty years ago the issue seemed to have become noncontroversial, with the behaviorist position completely dominant within psychology. However, the issue has been revived (cf. Wann, 1964) by humanists, phenomenologists, and existentialists, and the completeness of the behavioral position is again in question. Nevertheless, we agree with the weaker view (to which Watson and other behaviorists sometimes subscribed) that there is presently no method through which the mind can be made the direct object of study.

Many avowed behaviorists, however, felt a need to accept some more positive position. They did not wish to study consciousness or mind and therefore wished to deny its importance; this they could do only if they accepted some appropriate mind-body position. Of the available positions (see Table 2-2), two were best fitted to their purposes. First, an epiphenomenal view would imply that consciousness had no causal efficacy and therefore little interest for science; it might or might not attend bodily events and would be of little importance. According to this position, mind would have a role comparable to that of a shadow; it would often, but not always, accompany and more or less follow the outline of the physical object (body) to which it related but would itself have no substance and accomplish no causal effects upon the physical objects producing it (i.e., would not interact). This analogy, like all analogies, is not perfect but is useful in clarifying the general nature of the epiphenomenal view.

Second, a completely physical monism would deny the very existence of mind and would from this point of view serve the purposes of behaviorism admirably.

Watson's early pronouncements were of a less extreme sort. For example:

Will there be left over in psychology a world of pure psychics, to use Yerkes' term? I confess I do not know. The plans that I most favor for psychology lead practically

> to the ignoring of consciousness in the sense that that term is used by psychologists today. I have virtually denied that this realm of psychics is open to experimental investigation. I don't wish to go further into the problem at present because it leads inevitably over into metaphysics. If you will grant the behaviorist the right to use consciousness in the same way as other natural scientists employ it—that is, without making consciousness a special object of observation—you have granted all that my thesis requires. (1913b, p. 174)

Other expressions of this point of view may be found in papers by Walter Hunter and A. P. Weiss. Hunter, for example, said:

> A brief inspection of the writings of any behaviorist will convince you that he is neither blind, deaf, anosmic, ageusic, or anaesthetic. He lives, and admits quite frankly that he lives, in the same world of objects and events which the psychologist and the layman alike acknowledge. Let us, therefore, hear no more from the psychologist that his opponent denies the existence of these things. (1926, p. 89)

Weiss also accepted conscious processes as real, even if no more than epiphenomenal. He held (1917) that ". . . consciousness (the totality of our sensations, images, and affections) is a purely personal experience and has no scientific value or validity unless it is *expressed* in some form of behavior, such as speech or other form of representation" (p. 307). The general position here clearly stated is that the physical facts of behavior are sufficient; the "mental" correlates to these facts are unreliable and superfluous.

Acceptance of this methodological behaviorism put the behaviorist into the somewhat embarrassing position of admitting that experience exists, even if in a most shadowy manner, and yet cannot be attacked by scientific tools. Thus, faced with the dilemma of either admitting that there are some psychological facts which he cannot explain by natural scientific techniques or denying the existence of such alleged facts, the radical behaviorist, following Watson, chose the latter course: the explicit denial of the existence of any conscious correlates to introspective reports.

By 1924 Watson seems to have come to this alternative. For example, in his debate with McDougall (J. B. Watson & McDougall, 1929), he said that consciousness "has never been seen, touched, smelled, tasted, or moved. It is a plain assumption just as unprovable as the old concept of the soul" (p. 14). And, more at length:

> He then who would introduce consciousness, either as an epiphenomenon or as an active force interjecting itself into the physical and chemical happenings of the body, does so because of spiritualistic and vitalistic leanings. The Behaviorist cannot find consciousness in the test tube of his science. He finds no evidence anywhere for a stream of consciousness, not even for one so convincing as that described by William James. He does, however, find convincing proof of an ever-widening stream of behavior. (p. 26)

Another early behaviorist, K. S. Lashley, likewise supported an extreme position. In his single excursion into such polemic, he wrote:

> There can be no valid objection by the behaviorist to the introspective method so long as no claim is made that the method reveals something besides body activity. . . . The attributes of mind, as definable on introspective evidence, are precisely the attributes of the complex physiological organization of the human body and a statement of the latter will constitute as complete and adequate an account of consciousness as seems possible from any type of introspective analysis. (1923, pp. 351–352)

This view reduces mind entirely to physiological functions and thus represents a radical behavioristic position.

There were several common behavioristic arguments against the existence of consciousness. Though we present them, we do not vouch for their validity. First, the critics asked how the so-called gaps in consciousness, such as allegedly occur during sleep, can be explained? What is lost? What returns? There appears to be no measurable, physical loss. But there are behavior differences. The behaviorists answered that unconsciousness (as in sleep or anesthesia) simply means that certain neural pathways are blocked off so that the person is unable to report stimulation.

Second, the behaviorists maintained that the stimulus is really the important thing in introspection, not the alleged conscious correlates. Introspection is simply a way of reporting what has been learned by language training. Situations in which the "wrong" terms are learned are instructive: for example, the calling of a "red" stimulus "gray" by a color-blind person is wrong only because it is not consistent with most other language reports on the stimulus.

Third, and most important, the behaviorists argued that the assumption of nonphysical events interacting with physical events clearly violates the conservation-of-energy principle. Physics tells us that energy is neither created nor destroyed in physical systems; it is only transformed. All the energy within physical systems can be accounted for physically; none is gained from, or lost to, any nonphysical system. If conscious events affected the body or its physiological processes, they would have to do so by adding or subtracting energy or mass. But this is impossible, according to the conservation-of-energy principle, which is scarcely to be overthrown on the basis of old theological and philosophical dogma. Thus the fact of experiencing the allegedly mental process, cannot influence even the muscular efforts necessary to speech. And if ideas *can* influence muscles, then they must themselves be physical events occurring in the nervous system—and therefore nonmental.

To follow up the implications of this argument, the radical behaviorist next disposed of both major dualistic positions in the following manner: If mind is granted, for the sake of argument, then it must either (1) affect behavior (interactionism) or (2) not affect behavior (parallelism). But if (1) is true, then the law of the conservation of energy, otherwise inviolate in physics, is violated. If (2) is true, how can one *say* that one has an "idea," unless so saying is induced by the "idea" itself, as according to (2) it cannot be. Belief in such a well-coordinated set of coincidences overstrains credulity, and the assumption of some outside coordinating force—such as God (occasionalism)—is scientifically unacceptable. Thus ideas cannot be proved unless they affect the nervous system, but to do this they must be within the physical system, and this is quite satisfactory to the behaviorist because it means that ideas are no longer "mental."

Finally, the behaviorists insisted, the conservation-of-energy principle can be applied to the epiphenomenal view. If conscious correlates are accepted as strictly noncausal events, they must nevertheless be produced by physical events. But this means that energy is used to produce them; how else could the physical events operate? Such expenditure of energy without demonstrable physical loss of energy or mass is likewise incompatible with generally accepted physical principles.

The radical behaviorist therefore turned to a strict physical monism, according to which "mental" is merely a description of the way the physical events function and consciousness has no independent or unique existence.

WATSON'S EXPERIMENTAL PROGRAM

Although Watson's early work was with animal problems, as indicated above, the best example of his experimental behavioristic program is probably the research he conducted on conditioning and reconditioning of emotional responses in infants. This work also represents the best example of the application of the conditioning technique by any of the early classical behaviorists. The early research is most comprehensively described by Watson in three papers in the volume *Psychologies of 1925,* (1926a) from which the following exposition is mainly derived.

Starting from the vantage point provided by the extensive studies of behavior during the fetal and early postnatal periods in animals, Watson began the comparable study of very young human infants in an effort to determine the kind and variety of congenital behavior which could be reliably identified and which was presumably inherited. He states that "almost daily observation" was made of several hundred children through the first 30 days of postnatal life and of a smaller number for longer periods ranging into early childhood. The result of these observations was a catalog of the "birth equipment of the human young," as Watson called it. A long list of behaviors was developed, with objective descriptions for each, but the only experimental, or semiexperimental, observations at this time involved some interesting work with twenty babies on the causal factors in handedness. Watson's conclusion (1926a) was that ". . . there is no fixed differentiation of response in either hand until social usage begins to establish handedness" (p. 29).

Watson was also concerned with the genetic (longitudinal) study of the emotional life of the infant and child. Again the fully objective technique of behavior description was applied, this time intensively to a sample of 3-year-olds. Watson found, not too surprisingly, that most 3-year-old children are shot through with useless and actually harmful emotional reactions. Not content with what he described as the historically orthodox interpretation of such emotional behavior as inherited, Watson saw the need for new experimental techniques. He early discovered that children taken from typical homes did not make good subjects for the study of the origin of emotions. The obvious need for controlled emotional backgrounds in such subjects was met by use of "strong healthy children belonging to wet nurses in hospitals, and other children brought up in the home under the eye of the experimenters" (1926a, p. 42). With these subjects he instituted a prolonged series of simple tests, made primarily by the introduction of various kinds of animals, at the zoological park as well as in the laboratory. He was unable to find evidence of fear and concluded that accounts of the inheritance of emotional responses to such stimuli were false.

One of the best-known contributions of this phase of the research program was Watson's description, as a result of further semiexperimental observations, of the basic conditions that could be depended upon to produce fear, rage, and love in infants. Watson found fear produced by loud sounds and sudden loss of support; rage, by hampering of bodily movement; and love, by tickling, rocking, patting, and stroking of the skin.

This pioneer research of Watson's constituted an advance and a stimulation to further research. Bridges (1932) questioned the ability to discriminate different emotions in the infant, and her results showed that the only sure distinction is between a generally excited state and a quiescent one. It is now generally conceded that adults cannot make reliable judgments of the emotion being shown by an infant unless they have knowledge of the stimulating situation (e.g., pinprick versus stroking). Despite the modification of Watson's conclusions suggested by later research, his basic point that infants show very few varieties of innate emotional behavior has not been contradicted.

From 1918 on, Watson reported, he conducted experimentation designed to determine some of the factors underlying the acquisition and loss of emotional responses in children. "We were rather loath at first to conduct such experiments," he said (1926b), "but the need of this kind of study was so great that we finally decided to experiment upon the possibility of building up fears in the infant and then later to study practical methods for removing them" (p. 51). Watson found it relatively easy to establish fear in a subject through a simple conditioning procedure. This aspect of the research was completed by the demonstration of spread, or generalization, of the conditioned fear response to similar but previously neutral stimuli, in a manner comparable to that found for other kinds of conditioned responses without emotional components.

Finally, Watson turned to the problem of eliminating conditioned fears. A variety of commonly used techniques was first tried experimentally on subjects in whom conditioned fears had been produced: disuse, verbal appeal, frequent application of the fear stimulus, and use of a social (unafraid) model. None of these was effective. Then, in experimentation performed by Mary Cover Jones under Watson's direction, clear evidence for the effectiveness of the unconditioning, or reconditioning, technique was obtained from an infant named Peter, with whom intensive work was done. This was achieved by bringing in the conditioned fear stimulus at some distance, so as not to elicit the fear response, while the child was eating. After daily introductions of the stimulus (a rabbit) at progressively closer points on the long lunchroom table, the child was finally able to handle it without fear while continuing to eat. Generalized fear responses to similar objects were also found to be eliminated by this procedure.

Many years later in reminiscing about this research and about Watson, Mary Cover Jones concluded her article with the final mild comment: "We now use the term *behavior modification therapy* to describe the practical approach of John B. Watson and his followers. I welcome this opportunity to acknowledge with gratitude our indebtedness to this impressive figure in American psychology" (1974, p. 583).

There was about a 30-year lag between Jones's report (1924) of the successful elimination of fear in Peter and the development of any significant body of work in behavior modification. This provides us with a good chance to find out whether we are *Zeitgeist* theorists or great-man theorists of the history of psychology. Would it have made a significant difference in the development of behavior modification if John B. Watson had not been asked to resign his position as professor at Johns Hopkins some time before the beginning of the fall semester, 1920?

SECONDARY CHARACTERISTICS OF WATSONIAN BEHAVIORISM

Today, the methodological characteristics of the behavioristic position are felt to be the most basic because of the wide acceptance of the methodological point and the rejection of, or controversy about, the other points. The secondary aspects of Watson's thinking are not implied by the word *behavioristic.* However, much of the attack on behaviorism has been directed at these secondary points, and they are many times confused or mixed indiscriminately with the primary characteristics (see Koch, 1954, pp. 5–6).

It is safer to distinguish the critical and secondary propositions. For example, although it is natural for the behaviorist to view thinking as a peripheral process that is easily accessible to behavioral observation, it is not necessary that one accept Watson's peripheralism in order to remain a "good" methodological behaviorist. Characteristics like this one are treated as secondary. We shall discuss language development and thinking, the role of environmental factors in behavior, and determinism and personal responsibility as examples of the secondary characteristics.

Language Development and Thinking

Because of its use as an example of a behavioristic interpretation of a mentalistic concept, the theory of language development plays a key role in behavioristic thinking. It goes as follows: First, many separate syllables are naturally produced by the normal vocimotor apparatus of any human child. The normal instigation for the first of such mouthings—for example, the common sound *da*—is probably some obscure physiological stimulus. A *circular conditioned response* eventually becomes established as a result of the concurrence of the sound *da* with the saying of it. That is, infants hear *da* as they say it, and the sound itself becomes a conditioned stimulus to the saying—circular because it is obviously self-perpetuating. The kind of babbling that is characteristic of early vocalization thus develops, with the infant stopping the sequence of repeated syllabizing only when distracted by some other stronger stimulus or when fatigued. Second, the mother or some other adult hears this kind of babbling and repeats the sound, thus producing the conditioned stimulus and causing the child to repeat it. In this manner the child soon learns to imitate many of the sounds the mother makes—or at least to approximate them. Finally, the mother shows the child an object, such as a doll, while repeating the appropriate syllable. In this way new connections between visual stimuli and established sounds are developed. The further process of language development is a long-continued elaboration and refinement of this basic process.

Evidence for the soundness of this general interpretation was adduced from the case histories of deaf-mutes—babies born deaf whose initial babblings are not continued and who do not learn to speak, presumably because of the absence of normal auditory conditioned stimuli. Also, with normal children, the behaviorist can point to the common occurrence of parents using so-called baby talk in communicating with their infants.

In all this, the behaviorist takes pains to point out, there is nothing save brain connections and reconnections; no mental events are necessary. The child learns to say *blue* or *red* or *green,* or *loud* or *shrill* or *bass,* because of the conditioning of brain events and not because of sensory experience such as sensations. Watson himself preferred to avoid the old terminology as contaminated with mentalistic connotations, but Weiss and some of the less radical behaviorists were willing to use the old terms with new behavioristic meanings.

Watson extended this interpretation into the field of thinking, considered as implicit, or covert, behavior. Such behavior consists of tendencies toward muscular movements or glandular secretions that are not directly observable by the usual techniques of observation but may nonetheless play an important role in activating or mediating other, more overt behavior (e.g., *action currents* detectable in musculature by electronic devices in the absence of any overtly observable movements). As language functions develop in young children, from 2 years or so on, much of their motor activity tends to be accompanied by a more or less complete language description. For example, a child will tend to say "Sally eats"—or some approximation thereof—as she eats. Under parental and other adult pressures, however, a child is gradually forced to reduce this overt speech, which is generally regarded with disfavor. It then tends to turn into silent speech—or thinking—in adulthood.

Past training in the form of conditioning accounts for both overt body behavior and language responses, overt and implicit. If the overt behavior aspects are inhibited, the implicit language responses may still be kept; the person is then said to be thinking. Thinking is thus primarily trial-and-error behavior of the laryngeal mechanism (or, as a humorist epigrammatically put it, Watson made up his windpipe that he had no mind). Watson further pointed out, however, that under certain conditions, language behavior of this sort might also be suppressed, and then thinking could continue in the form of either overt body activity or visceral reactions. A later Watsonian position was thus that we think with our whole bodies. Because of the poor connections between the visceral and the laryngeal series of muscle changes, visceral thinking responses are largely unverbalized. They are therefore fundamentally important in thinking of an unverbalized sort (determining tendencies, hunches and intuitions, and feelings of unfamiliarity, familiarity, approaching familiarity, certainty, and the like). Although thinking occurs primarily in verbal terms, it may go on in other forms.

Watson's position on the developmental control of unverbalized thinking is well summarized in the following statement:

> I want to develop the thesis sometime that society has never been able to get hold of these implicit concealed visceral and glandular reactions of ours, or else it would have schooled them in us, for, as you know, society has a great propensity for regularizing all of our reactions. Hence most of our adult overt reactions—our speech, and movements of our arms, legs, and trunk—are schooled and habitized. Owing to their concealed nature, however, society cannot get hold of visceral behavior to lay down rules and regulations for its integration. It follows as a corollary from this that we have no names, no words with which to describe these reactions. They remain unverbalized. (1926b, p. 56)

Although Watson held an essentially peripheral theory of thinking, with stress on muscular reactions and tendencies toward them as the basis of thinking, other behaviorists carried the assumption of progressive suppression of muscular actions on to its logical conclusion. This means a central theory of thinking, with only brain states involved. However this problem is eventually decided, it will not affect the methodological tenets of behaviorism, but only Watson's elaboration of them. B. F. Skinner's treatment of verbal behavior (1957) shows that Watson's basic behavioristic position regarding language and thinking is very much alive today. Recent multiple successes in teaching a kind of language to chimpanzees all seem to be based on a view of language as just another behavior, which should therefore be teachable to lower organisms once an appropriate response is found. Presumably each organism has some practical limitations on the complexity of the language which it can learn and produce.

Emphasis on the Environment

Although in his earlier writing Watson accepted the importance of inherited behavioral tendencies, in his later work he placed the major emphasis on the role of the environment in the molding of adult human behavior. He declared that the concept of instinct was no longer needed in psychology, but took pains to make it clear that he did not doubt the important role of inherited *structures*. Performance, then, was dependent upon the way in which the environment acted on such structures. In the following example, he attempts to clarify his position:

> The behaviorist would *not* say: "He inherits his father's capacity or talent for being a fine swordsman." He would say: "This child certainly has his father's slender build of body, the same types of eyes. . . . He, too, has the build of a swordsman." And he would go on to say: ". . . and his father is very fond of him. He put a tiny sword into his hand when he was a year of age, and in all their walks he talks sword play, attack, and defense, the code of duelling and the like." A certain type of structure plus early training—*slanting*—accounts for adult performance. (1926a, p. 2)

In his emphasis on the importance of the environmental factors, Watson pointed to the very great variety of human traits and habits associated with different climates and different cultures. Although recognizing the limitations of available data, he felt that every normal human baby has within it essentially similar potentialities. This presumption led him to make predictions for which he has been strongly attacked. For example, he stated (1926a): "I would feel perfectly confident in the ultimately favorable outcome of careful upbringing of a *healthy, well-formed* baby born of a long line of crooks, murderers, thieves and prostitutes. Who has any evidence to the contrary?" (p. 9). Then, admittedly going beyond the facts, Watson went on to state a challenge for which he is famous:

> I should like to go one step further tonight and say, "Give me a dozen healthy infants, well-formed, and my own specified world to bring them up in, and I'll guarantee to take any one at random and train him to become any type of specialist I might select—a doctor, lawyer, artist, merchant-chief, and yes, even into a beggarman and thief, regardless of his talents, penchants, tendencies, abilities, vocations and race of his ancestors." . . . Please note that when this experiment is made I am to be allowed to specify the way they are to be brought up and the type of world they have to live in. (1926a, p. 10)

Determinism and Personal Responsibility

In the long-standing disagreement between science, with its acceptance of a strictly determined natural world, and theology and various types of philosophy, in which freedom of the will is generally accepted, there is no question at all about where Watsonian behaviorism stands. Since all behavior, including that called *voluntary* and involving choices, is interpreted in physical terms, all acts are physically determined in advance.

Watson's own interest was less in the theoretical problem of determinism per se than in the consequent or corollary question of personal responsibility. Along with many other behavioristically inclined psychologists and sociologists, he argued strongly against the assumption that individuals are personally responsible for their actions in the free-will sense. The implications of this belief are especially important in relation to such social problems as crime. The behaviorist would accept punishment of criminals as a part of a general system of social control but not on the basis of a theory of retribution. Instead of retributive treatment by which an errant individual is made to pay for violations, Watson argued for treatment on the basis of the individual's need for reeducation. He conceded that if criminals could not be salvaged for society—that is, if satisfactory reconditioning could not be achieved—then they should be kept under restraint or destroyed.

Watson himself developed quite a visionary program for social improvement—a so-called experimental ethics to be based on behaviorism. At the very end of his *Behaviorism,* he states:

> I think behaviorism does lay a foundation for saner living. It ought to be a science that prepares men and women for understanding the first principles of their own behavior. It ought to make men and women eager to rearrange their own lives, and especially eager to prepare themselves to bring up their own children in a healthy way. I wish I had time more fully to describe this, to picture to you the kind of rich

> and wonderful individual we should make of every healthy child; if only we could let it shape itself properly and then provide for it a universe in which it could exercise that organization—a universe unshackled by legendary folk lore of happenings thousands of years ago; unhampered by disgraceful political history; free of foolish customs and conventions which have no significance in themselves, yet which hem the individual in like taut steel bands. (1925, p. 248)

OTHER PROMINENT EARLY BEHAVIORISTS

Although Watson was without question the first and foremost systematic behaviorist, he had a number of important and sometimes vociferous supporters. One, Albert P. Weiss (1879–1931), was born in Germany but came to the United States at an early age. He was appointed an assistant to Max Meyer, who himself had come from the University of Berlin in Germany to establish the psychology laboratory at the University of Missouri in 1900. Meyer has already been mentioned as an early objectivist whose "psychology of the other one" antedated Watson's behaviorism. Weiss took his Ph.D. with Meyer at Missouri in 1916 and pursued an active career at Ohio State University. Weiss's *Theoretical basis of human behavior* was first published in 1925. Weiss saw behavior as ultimately reducible to physicochemical terms. Psychology was thus a branch of physics. The first chapter of his book, for example, is entitled "The ultimate elements" and consists of a discussion of the structure of matter, the nature of energy, the concept of force, and the like.

The reader should not be misled into assuming that Weiss was merely a farfetched and unrealistic theorist. On the contrary, he was among the most careful and ingenious of the early behaviorists, certainly far more careful than Watson in the matter of defining terms and developing concepts. A single example will suffice to indicate this quality of his theoretical thinking: his attempt to explain voluntary activity (a problem whose resolution Watson did not bother to attempt). The problem for Weiss was to determine what kind of behavior is conditioned to the word *voluntary*. Whereas the mentalist says that the mind does the choosing, the behaviorist says that physiological brain states operate and that the term *voluntary* is applied when there is some conflict, or at least potential conflict, between the tendencies to action associated with different sets of stimuli. One set of stimuli eventually achieves a clear physiological channel, and the individual makes a "choice." This is of course determined by past experience as it has shaped the brain connections. "Willpower," which is allegedly exercised on difficult choices, was for Weiss merely the spilling over of brain excitations into motor tensions which build up because they are not allowed immediate outlet. The effort of the "will" is assumed from the muscular contractions that are themselves by-products of brain action. Voluntary behavior is thus basically no different from other types, but does have this apparently additional characteristic of muscular tension.

Weiss regarded psychology as a biosocial discipline because of the nature of the variables with which it was concerned. He set up an experimental program of research on child behavior, but his early death prevented its consummation.

Edwin B. Holt (1873–1946) was influential mainly through his books, in which he gave strong philosophical support to the behavioristic movement. As Boring (1950) has noted, Holt's greatest specific influence in contemporary psychology has probably come through his role in stimulating E. C. Tolman to a behavioristic combination of purposivism and cognitive theory. Holt published *The Freudian wish and its place in ethics* in 1915, and *Animal drive and the learning process* appeared in 1931. Holt was a philosophical neorealist who attempted to integrate the essential parts of the behavioristic and the psychoanalytic ("dynamic") movements. He took his Ph.D. at Harvard in 1901 and subsequently taught both there and at Princeton.

Walter S. Hunter (1889–1953) made some of the most important methodological contributions to the field of animal learning. Like Watson, Hunter was trained in functionalism at Chicago, taking his Ph.D. there in 1912 with Angell and Carr. After teaching at Texas, Kansas, and Clark Universities, he was at Brown University from 1936 until his death. At Brown, he developed and maintained a small but active department of experimentalists. His methodological innovations included the delayed-response and double-alternation tasks, which were devised for the investigation of higher symbolic abilities in animals. Hunter was interested primarily in laboratory research rather than in theory, but he did attempt to push his new name for the science of behavior, *anthroponomy* (1926). Like most terminological innovations, this one did not stick.

Karl S. Lashley (1890–1958) was a student of Watson and received his Ph.D. at Hopkins in 1914. He was later at the Universities of Minnesota and Chicago, then at Harvard, and finally at the Yerkes Laboratory of Primate Biology. Lashley was a leading physiological psychologist and ventured only occasionally into systematic problems. He is best known for his work on brain extirpation in the rat, which demonstrated the limits of localization.

Lashley developed several principles of cerebral action on the basis of his extirpation work. The two most famous ones were the principles of equipotentiality and of mass function. The first designated the apparent capacity of parts of a functional area to take over the function previously carried out by an extirpated part. The principle of mass function limited the previous principle by pointing out that there would be a loss of efficiency proportional to the extent of the brain injury; thus equipotentiality was not complete in the sense that altogether efficient performance could be produced by whatever parts remained, however small.

Although Lashley's principles pointed away from localization, Lashley by no means denied that localization existed. In fact, he discussed individual differences in localization in the same book (1929) in which the other principles were being discussed. Thus Lashley's shift was quantitative, rather than qualitative.

Lashley moved away from a stimulus-response toward a field-theory frame of reference (see Chapter 11), partly as a consequence of the theoretical import of his own findings on brain functions. This shift should not be construed as implying that Lashley's attitude toward a basic behavioristic psychology changed; rather, he changed his position with respect to some of Watson's secondary points. He no longer believed that the most fruitful analysis was to be made in terms of discrete S-R connections which were strengthened via some kind of conditioning process.

Floyd H. Allport (1890–) took his Ph.D. in 1919 at Harvard and went on to popularize behavioristic concepts (for example, the circular-conditioned-reflex theory of language development, described above) in his social psychology text (1924). Allport has continued, at Syracuse University, to apply behavioristic principles to social psychology. More recently, he has turned to the psychology of sensory processes (Allport, 1955).

Z. Y. Kuo (1898–1970) was a Chinese psychologist who was trained in this country (Columbia University). He adopted an extremely environmentalistic position (1922, 1924), far more radical even than Watson's. All alleged instincts were to be explained on the basis of inherited structure and environmental influences. Kuo was far from an armchair speculator on the problem. He watched the development of behavior in the embryo chick by replacing part of the shell with a small transparent window (1932a, 1932b, 1932c, 1932d, 1932e). He found that much chick behavior which may appear to be instinctive is really learned during the embryonic period as a function of conditions within the egg. For example, the alternate stepping behavior of the normal newly hatched chick was shown to be dependent upon certain mechanically induced alternate hind-limb movements inside the shell. Cramping from the yolk sac often acted as a stimulus to the movements. Kuo differed from Watson in that he preferred to think of continuities in behavior rather than conditioning as a basic explanation of behavior changes.

In other research Kuo showed that the cat's reactions to rats are not strictly determined by heredity but can be easily altered from the normal predatory form by appropriate experiences (1930, 1938). These results all fit well into his environmentalism. Kuo concluded that inherited structures are important but that even these can be molded via environmental influences. He did not believe in any direct native behavior tendencies beyond those which are strictly the result of structural factors.

Kuo came back into print late in life (1967), apparently in response to the new ethological emphasis on inherited behaviors. At that time, his view on exogenous and endogenous behaviors was considerably moderated with respect to his earlier view, but he continued to emphasize the influence of learning, and to be the hardheaded antimentalist. His book is interesting because it is the product of a truly early behaviorist, and because his brief recital of the woes he suffered in the maelstrom of Chinese history of his times makes us appreciate our own stability.

CONTEMPORARY BEHAVIORISTS

A list of contemporary psychologists who accept the behaviorist methodological point would be a large one indeed. There are four men, however, who have bridged the gap between Watson and the present; they were important during Watson's lifetime and are still important. These four men are E. C. Tolman, E. R.

Guthrie, C. L. Hull, and B. F. Skinner. Their contemporary importance is such that their systems are discussed later in the present book. Their past role has been one of winnowing Watson's behaviorism for the good that was in it and adding their own personal contributions. In addition, we note the important role of such men as C. H. Graham (1951, 1958) and W. R. Garner (Garner, Hake, & Eriksen, 1956) in applying the basic behavioristic notions to the experimental psychology of visual perception, and of D. O. Hebb (1949) and R. C. Davis (1953) in applying these notions to physiological psychology. The psychology that has emerged because of the creative efforts of all these men is far more sophisticated than anything Watson himself produced.

WATSONIAN BEHAVIORISM: CRITICISMS AND REPLIES

The critical attacks made upon Watson and his brand of behaviorism hit all aspects of the system. Since we cannot consider them all, we shall select those which refer to the methodological and metaphysical points that are most crucial. In addition, the criticisms of Watson's experimental ethics are presented as representative of the attacks upon the more peculiarly Watsonian aspects of behaviorism.

Methodological Behaviorism

Although psychology was reasonably well prepared for the stress on objectivity, not all psychologists were satisfied with Watson's pronouncements. An immediate objection was that Watson's extreme formulation left out important components of psychology. This point was made even by those who in general supported much of the objective program. Woodworth, for example, has complained that the early behavioristic emphasis upon strict objectivity hindered the development of research into sensory and perceptual processes by turning the attention of younger men away from this problem area. Acceptance by Watson of the "verbal report" was not satisfactory. For example, Woodworth criticized Watson for attempting to deal, within the strictly objective framework, with the phenomena of afterimages. He stated:

> The "phenomena" which Watson finds so interesting and valuable in the after-image experiment are the after-images themselves, not the subject's speech movements. We may conclude that verbal report is not a behavioristic method and that Watson's use of it is practically a confession of defeat for methodological behaviorism. (1948, p. 84)

A broader and more vigorous attack was made by McDougall, who presented himself, as we have noted, as an earlier proponent and user of the strictly behavioristic experiment. McDougall's strictures of this methodological incompleteness of Watson's position may be summarized in the statement that a completely objective approach cannot obtain an adequate account of (1) the functional relations of conscious experiences (e.g., their dependance on external or bodily conditions), (2) the accuracy of verbal report (e.g., whether or not a subject is malingering, as in military service), and (3) the meaningfulness of the verbal report (e.g., in regard to the analysis of dreams). He was particularly eloquent in regard to the incompleteness of the behavioristic account of the finer things in life, specifically music:

> I come into this hall and see a man on this platform scraping the guts of a cat with hairs from the tail of a horse; and, sitting silently in attitudes of rapt attention, are a thousand persons who presently break out into wild applause. How will the Behaviorist explain these strange incidents: How explain the fact that the vibrations emitted by the cat-gut stimulate all the thousand into absolute silence and quiescence; and the further fact that the cessation of the stimulus seems to be a stimulus to the most frantic activity? Commonsense and psychology agree in accepting the explanation that the audience heard the music with keen pleasure, and vented their gratitude and admiration for the artist in shouts and handclappings. But the Behaviorist knows nothing of pleasure and pain, of admiration and gratitude. He has relegated all such "metaphysical entities" to the dust heap, and must seek some other explanation. Let us leave him seeking it. The search will keep him harmlessly occupied for some centuries to come. (J. B. Watson & McDougall, 1929, p. 63)

Watson would argue that McDougall and Woodworth, despite their objections, must use behavior as their datum. Whenever their metaphysics makes them try to use something else, they get into trouble; and we find those who try to use consciousness as the basic datum involved in useless squabbles about what they find there. Consciousness is a tool for scientists, not an object of study. They use it to study *both* afterimages and concrete blocks, but do not study it in itself.

As an example of the behavioristic attitude, consider a blind person who is interested in studying visual afterimages. Given someone to set up the equipment, this person could successfully conduct research by writing down the verbal responses emitted by an assistant and by subjects. Unable to use direct personal experience for obtaining data, a blind person would use the behavior of others. Those who themselves can respond to light might use their own responses as data, but would not use their own experience directly. The blind person would be truly objective in collecting data, for the data, which anyone could study, would include no private data stemming from the researcher's own response to light. Skeptical experimenters might doubt that the subjects' *consciousness* of their response to light differed in any respect from the experimenters' own, though the subjects respond differently. Even that belief would not change the data. As Washburn (1908) early pointed out, the situation is exactly the same for animals as for people other than ourselves; we can only *infer* that others are conscious, and the inference is of no scientific use.

On a somewhat different level of argument, Boring has also criticized Watson for his acceptance of verbal report:

> [Watson] wished to let in discriminatory verbal report when it was accurate and verifiable, as it is, for instance, in the observation of difference tones, and to rule it out when it was unverifiable, as it is when it consists of statements about the nature of feeling or about the impalpable contents of imageless thinking. . . . The admission of verbal report was a damaging concession, for it made it appear that behaviorism was asking only for verbal changes and not for a reform in scientific procedures. (1950, p. 645)

The modern behaviorist's answer to Boring's objection is simply agreement. The point basic to the whole behaviorist revolution was to use only verifiable, accurate data in psychology. The thing that furnishes such data is behavior and only behavior. Verbal behavior is behavior and constitutes valuable data if it is verifiable and repeatable. Not all behavior, and hence not all verbal behavior, furnishes useful data; the behaviorist is not obliged to accept data indiscriminately. Boring himself (1964) reports on a senseless controversy between Wundt and Stumpf concerning ". . . whether a perceived tonal interval is bisected psychologically by the arithmetic or by the geometric mean of its tonal stimuli" (p. 683). The behaviorists believed, rightly or wrongly, that these disagreements arose partly because of the type of data used.

Woodworth and Sheehan (1964) present the basic enigma in two moderate, eloquently understated paragraphs which quietly communicate despair of a final answer:

> For one group of psychologists the proper content seemed reasonably to be man's conscious experience, which they held could be investigated through introspection. This is a method of self-observation which, as we shall see later, may take a variety of forms, ranging from the simple reporting of one's immediate sensory impression of a stimulus to long-extended probing, during analytical therapy, of one's emotional experiences. Unlike as these "introspections" may seem, they have in common a private quality which appears to distinguish them from the methods of physics or chemistry or biology. In these sciences any number of observers can report on what is visible in the test tube or under the microscope, whereas the psychological "experience" can be reported by only one observer.
>
> How real this distinction is remains a perplexing epistemological problem. Does each observer see in the test tube or under the microscope a bit of the real external world, or does each merely report on his subjective experience resulting from some emanations of the real world? If the latter is the case a sharp line cannot be drawn between the data of the "objective" sciences and the subjective data of psychology. In all cases the observing subject would be reporting the private content of his own "consciousness." (pp. 3–4)

Still more recently, O'Neil (1968) has tried to clarify the behaviorist's position on consciousness by relating behaviorism to realism in philosophy, and he does succeed in showing that consciousness is not a problem for radical behaviorists; but it may remain a problem for others.

Watson's initial attempts to translate some of the older mentalistic concepts of psychology into behavioristic language have been criticized from two points of view. On the one hand, some have contended that the acceptance of any mentalistic terms weakened his strictly objective system. On the other hand, Heidbreder has taken Watson to task for:

> . . . a tendency to indulge in feats of translation, and apparently at times to regard translation as an explanation. It is difficult, when reading some of the behavioristic accounts, to escape the impression that the writers regard it as an explanation to say that a wish is an organic set, that a meaning is a bodily attitude, that thoughts are language mechanisms. Yet little is added to the knowledge of wishes, meanings, and

> thoughts by these statements, which after all consist largely in taking over what is known about these happenings from common sense and the older psychology and devising, often not on the basis of known facts, some possible physiological explanation of them. (1933, p. 275)

Although we agree with Heidbreder that Watson actually did little with such translations, we think they can be regarded as starting points in the objectification of psychological problems. While Watson was guilty as charged of premature enthusiasm, final evaluations of the success of the fully objective program need to await more extensive applications of detailed research like that which Watson himself initiated on emotional conditioning in infants and children. No behaviorist would today rest content with such a purely verbal translation, and probably that is not what Watson really intended either. The point is that the mentalistic terms as they were used had no behavioral meaning, and the translation was really a definition. The concept was then not explained but defined and made workable. Wishes and thoughts did not need translating; they needed *some* meaning that would be useful in a natural scientific framework. Skinner's book *Verbal behavior* (1957) makes its chief contribution through such a reformulation rather than through the presentation of new empirical results. This book presents many independent variables which seem likely to be useful in the explanation of verbal behavior. It does not, as one example, translate ideas into other terms; ideas are simply not part of the formulation. Watson himself was often content simply to let mentalistic terms disappear rather than translate them into some other language. This elimination of fruitless concepts and the hardheaded attitude toward all concepts were behaviorism's outstanding contributions.

Another line of methodological criticism involves the charge that Watson was backtracking on his own restriction of psychology to observables by including implicit behavior tendencies, which were not directly observed, albeit in theory observable. Woodworth, for example, has complained that Watson, even while postulating such implicit behavior, restricted his own research on emotion to the directly observable overt aspects of behavior and made no effort to investigate the presumably important visceral components.

The answer to this objection is similar to that given to the previous one. Certainly Watson, in his impatient enthusiasm to get to a new and thoroughly objective psychology, went beyond the available data in drawing conclusions and did not himself begin all the necessary research to back up his assumptions. Nevertheless, there is no necessary inconsistency in the assumption of implicit behavior tendencies and the holding to a strictly objective systematic and experimental framework. No one can do everything. Attempts were made to observe the implicit responses, for example, tongue, mouth, and larynx movements in implicit speech, and much later even muscle potentials in deaf-mutes. Watson's own research utilized observable responses for its data. It was only natural to make the explanatory system of behaviorism consistent with the data system, and the responses were not expected to *remain* unobservable.

This tendency may be seen throughout psychology. For example, Freud's explanation of the subconscious processes grows out of the kind of data available to the psychoanalyst, and Hull's theory of learning was taken directly from experimental results. Watson's theorizing about internal changes, especially with emotion, seems amply vindicated by results of recent studies on the learning of visceral and glandular responses (N. E. Miller, 1969). Such is the success of this work that society may, after all, eventually be able to regularize these responses, the ones whose freedom from control Watson seemed to be bitterly celebrating in 1926.

A related criticism has been developed strongly by another avowed behaviorist, E. C. Tolman, who finds in overt behavior a purposiveness that Watson did not admit. Tolman early criticized Watson's research on emotions and stated his position most succinctly as follows:

> In short, our conclusion must be that Watson has in reality dallied with two different notions of behavior, though he himself has not clearly seen how different they are. On the one hand, he has defined behavior in terms of its strict underlying physical and physiological details. . . . We shall designate this as the *molecular* definition of behavior. And, on the other hand, he has come to recognize . . . that behavior, as such, is more than and different from the sum of its physiological parts. Behavior, as such, is an "emergent" phenomenon that has descriptive and defining properties of its own. And we shall designate this latter as the *molar* definition of behavior. (1932, pp. 6–7)

Tolman's psychology is proof that he prefers the molar definition of behavior, that he thinks purposiveness must be introduced in order to have a useful psychology. Purpose generally alludes, in Tolman's usage, to some influence of the animal's behavior on the environment; for instance, we may speak of the purpose of an animal's behavior as being the release of a food pellet or the depression of a bar. Usually, the bending of a limb would not be considered a purpose, although this would be a purposeful description compared with the flexion of a muscle. Tolman contends that it is more useful to define responses in molar behavioral than in molecular physiological terms. Watson, like most psychologists before and after him, agreed in practice with this point. He wished to make the additional point that purposive behavior is in principle reducible to the physiological level, although he did not actually work on this level. Other behaviorists, like Guthrie (1952), have attempted to work on a more molecular level. If the problem of psychology is to explain the behavior of the animal in its environment, then it seems that a complete psychology must consider purpose as so defined. Watson would no doubt be a purposivist when purpose is so defined. Tolman's quoted statement suggests that he believes Watson recognized this kind of purposivism, since he rightfully accuses Watson of using the term *behavior* in both senses. However, Watson would not agree, nor would most contemporary behaviorists, that purpose as an explanatory concept in the McDougallian sense is legitimate.

The Gestalt psychologists have been vociferous in their complaints against the allegedly molecular brand of S-R psychology, as we shall see in the following chapter. But, again, a particularly telling argument came from within the behavioristic camp itself. As suggested above, K. S. Lashley began his professional career as an avowed and enthusiastic behaviorist. His own research, however, convinced him that some of the behavioristic assumptions were in error. As he himself has told the story:

> I began life as an ardent advocate of muscle-twitch psychology. I became glib in formulating all problems of psychology in terms of stimulus-response and in explaining all things as conditioned reflexes. . . . I embarked enthusiastically upon a program of experiments to prove the adequacy of the motor-chain theory of integration. And the result is as though I had maliciously planned an attack upon the whole system. . . . The conditioned reflex turned out not to be a reflex, not the simple basic key to the learning problem. . . . In order that the concept of stimulus-response should have any scientific value it must convey a notion of how a particular stimulus elicits a particular response and no other. . . . When viewed in relation to the problems of neurology, the nature of the stimulus and of the response is intrinsically such as to preclude the theory of simple point-to-point connection in reflexes. (1931, p. 14)

Watson's own research efforts were certainly not of the muscle-twitch variety, with which he is so often identified; much of the debate over behaviorism has resulted from the discrepancy between the actual behavioristic experimental program and the theoretical framework. According to the framework of theorists like Watson and Weiss, all complex behavior is ultimately reducible to combinations and chainings of simple reflexes and even to the terms of physics and chemistry. It is this kind of aspiration that is responsible for much of the opposition. But it would be a mistake to assume that behaviorism is tied to a muscle-twitch view of psychology. It would even be a mistake to assume that Lashley became less a behaviorist because of his findings. In the methodological sense, one can be a field theorist and a behaviorist at the same time; a good example is Tolman himself. The issue between the orthodox S-R behaviorists on the one side and the S-S (Tolman) behaviorists and the field theorists on the other side is still a source of systematic controversy, but its outcome should have little to do with the acceptance of behaviorism.

Metaphysical Behaviorism

Criticisms of Watson's rejection of the introspective technique were blunted by his acceptance of the verbal report as behavior, as indicated above. The argument that he was neglecting useful data was therefore not valid. The brunt of the critical attack upon his system was transferred to the essentially metaphysical argument against interactionism and against his denial of the existence, and not merely the scientific usefulness, of mind.

Early attacks upon the extreme behavioristic position on mind were made by behaviorists and nonbehaviorists alike. Angell, for example, cautioned:

> After all is said and done, something corresponding to consciousness in its vague common meaning does exist and it is within its compass that the problems of science arise. We must be cautious therefore that in seeking for bettered means of knowing human nature in its entirety we do not in effect commit the crowining absurdity of seeming to deny any practical significance to that which is its chief distinction—the presence of something corresponding to the term mind—the one thing of which the fool may be as sure as the wise man. (1913, p. 267)

And the behaviorist Hunter (1924) likewise expressed doubt about the radical position in his conclusion that ". . . no mere denial of the existence of 'consciousness' can permanently win a wide following among psychologists" (p. 4). In this prediction Hunter would seem to have been fairly well borne out, since the radical behavioristic position has never been generally accepted.

Some of the attacks upon methodological behaviorism may be more or less directly traced to the underlying assumption of the monistic metaphysical position. A good example is the criticism by Heidbreder. She pointed out that if the behaviorist makes an outright denial of consciousness

> . . . he finds it extremely difficult to explain what he means by some of his terms. When he says that thinking is merely a matter of language mechanisms, or emotion an affair of visceral and glandular responses, he is at a loss to tell where he gets the terms "thinking" and "emotion." He cannot get them from his own awareness of his own inner speech or disturbed heart-beat, for, by hypothesis, such awareness is impossible. The heart and the larynx, to be sure, belong to the physical world, but one's immediate awareness of their action can be based only on one's personal and private sensations. Does the behaviorist mean, then, that a person cannot be aware of his own anger except by means of kymograph tracings, or blood-analysis, or some other evidence of his bodily reactions that is accessible to others as well as himself—by catching sight of his flushed face, in a mirror, for example, or by seeing directly his own clenched fist? (1933, p. 281)

Heidbreder also pointed out (1933) that ". . . in actual practice, behaviorism rejects awareness that arises through the interoceptors and proprioceptors; awareness which arises through the exteroceptors it accepts without question. In this fact lies the clue to the acceptances and rejections that characterize behaviorism" (p. 218).

The behaviorist's reply would probably be to point out that it is difficult for anyone to say how one attributes meaning to words like *thinking* and *emotion.* Actually, the behaviorist would urge, they are not learned by some kind of connection to internal events; we learn to say *pain* in certain situations, such as when we observe blood on others or ourselves, or *thinking* when a problem has been presented and the person is oriented toward the problem but otherwise quiescent. We do not actually learn these things on the basis of the contents of our own consciousness alone; otherwise our language would be private. It is not surprising that the awareness which arises through the interoceptors is rejected, while that which arises through the exteroceptors is accepted. For the language of exteroceptors is based on public events, observable at the same time by anyone. The language of interoceptors is based on private events, observable only by one individual. Science is a public enterprise, and only a public language, only public events, are appropriate for its subject matter.

The more recent criticism of Watson's extreme metaphysical position is represented by Bergmann's professional philosophical evaluation (1956): "Watson's particular mistake was that in order to establish that there are no interacting minds, which is true, he thought it necessary to assert that *there are no minds,* which is not only false but silly" (p. 266). Bergmann suggests that Watson failed to keep out of trouble because he saw himself as a champion of the revolt not only against structuralism but also against functionalism; for this reason, presumably, he was not willing to stay with the more moderate metaphysical positions of the earlier systematists.

Bergmann's view is probably fairly representative of the modern attitude toward Watson's metaphysics. Watson seems to have felt it necessary to do more than divorce psychology from metaphysics; others within the school that he opposed had already tried to do that. He felt it necessary to destroy the very existence of mind in order that psychologists be freed from the methodological error of attempting to study this presumed entity. Part of Watson's contribution, then, is that he was wrong on a metaphysical point—wrong so courageously and forcefully that he was able to lead psychologists out of the wilderness on the planks of a false platform. (The above, of course, is not to be taken as a literal description of Watson's motivation.)

Criticisms of Secondary Properties

There has been a plethora of attacks upon the more specific positions that Watson himself took on psychological problems. One particular issue is of sufficient generality and interest to justify a detailed account as representative of such arguments. This is Watson's stand on determinism and personal responsibility as it relates to his espousal of experimental ethics.

To begin with, it was pointed out that there is a paradox in the situation where a strict determinist talks as though he is trying to tell people what they should do—as though they could choose for themselves! A related argument is directed against the assumption by the behaviorist of a strict S-R interpretation of behavior, which is seen as mechanistic and therefore of dubious explanatory value in practical problems. McDougall, for example, said:

> If all men believed the teachings of the mechanical psychology (and only beliefs that govern action are real beliefs) no man would raise a finger in the effort to prevent war, to achieve peace or to realize any other ideal. So I say that the mechanical psychology is useless and far worse than useless: it is paralyzing to human effort. (J. B. Watson & McDougall, 1929, pp. 71–72)

Before describing the behaviorist answer to such attacks, we should like to clarify one confusion that is well represented by the excerpt from McDougall. This is the confounding of determinism and mechanism. Now, the defense of mechanism aside, there is no good reason why a basically deterministic position should be any more mechanistic than nonmechanistic. It is true that people like Watson, who hold what appears to be a mechanistic view, are also determinists; but so are most field theorists, at least ones like Köhler and Lewin. They do share the general belief that behavior as a process is lawful, but they diverge markedly with respect to the type of lawfulness involved. Mechanism involves a belief that organisms behave in a machinelike fashion and therefore implies a particular subtype of determinism. Determinism requires only that events occur according to *some* kind of natural law, and hence it is not necessarily mechanistic.

The behaviorist would also note that the existence of practical difficulties such as McDougall mentioned does not break down determinism or establish free will. It might be true that man cannot work for his own betterment, undesirable as this may seem. The behaviorist would argue further that the claim of many opponents of determinism that they are for freedom is an illusory one; what they are actually for is not a true freedom but a determinism of another sort than the scientist endorses. Generally, at least in the case of most of those opponents who have a fundamentalistic theological background, this is a determinism by some divine force: individuals are free only in order that they can accept the fully determined rule of God.

Finally, the behaviorist would take note of one mistaken claim of those who hope to establish the existence of free will. The Heisenberg principle of uncertainty, or limited measurability, has often been invoked as a proof that free will must exist for the human being, since it presumably exists for the electron. It is simply a mathematical demonstration that the simultaneous precise measurement of the position and the momentum of an electron is impossible. There is disagreement within physics about the philosophical implications of this demonstration; Einstein, for example, would not forsake a strictly deterministic picture of even the behavior of the electron on the basis of this principle. Even if behaviorists accepted their own positivistic medicine regarding the meaningfulness of determinacy in electrons under these circumstances, they would still have a way out. Before the principle could be applied to behavior problems, it would need to be shown that behavioral variables are influenced by the indeterminacy of electron behavior. It may be that the indeterminacy at the atomic level disappears in going to the far more molar level of behavior; certainly indeterminacy has only minute and utterly insignificant effects on molar physical events, such as the flight of golf balls. A behaviorist's conclusion would be that there is thus no really sound scientific basis at the present time for attempting to utilize the Heisenberg principle in relation to psychological problems.

We should like to add some final comments to this discussion. Determinism amounts mostly to a kind of faith, since at best our knowledge can be only partially complete. A test of complete determinism cannot be obtained. This does not constitute any support for the opposite contention that there is some kind of free will. Our own position on this problem is similar to that earlier stated in connection with the ancient mind-body issue: It will take a great deal more relevant data than we presently have or can even envisage before a sound scientific position can be taken on the problem.

To return to the problem originally posed by the paradox of the determinist attempting to influence people, we must concede that there is really no completely logical and satisfactory answer to it. The determinist will most probably agree with Thorndike's point of view as earlier presented (Chapter 3). Essentially, we are free only if determined; we can determine the behavior of other people and build a better world only if the world is lawful. Yet if everything is determined, including our efforts to make changes in nature, as we assume, the behaviorist can only hope that it is favorably determined, and that the world will get better. Certainly McDougall's statement that mechanists (he really means determinists) will not raise a finger to prevent war, etc., is false. People who hold this view strongly, like Watson and Thorndike, *do* attempt to make the world better. This is simply a matter of observation.

Two other aspects of Watson's individual position suffered heavy attack. One was his environmentalism. Though there is nothing morally reprehensible about being an environmentalist, it is probably true that innate factors in behavior were neglected more than they needed to be during the period of ascendance of Watsonian behaviorism. We may be seeing that common phenomenon, the swing of the intellectual pendulum to the other side of center, with the rise of ethology and sociobiology. The second point of attack centered on Watson's use of the term S-R. His definitions were too casual and flexible and lent themselves easily to a certain amount of post hoc bending to account for results—whatever results there were! This issue will be discussed further in Chapter 10, where we shall examine the Skinner-Chomsky controversy over language.

To rebut these arguments against Watson, it might be argued that an infant science must sometimes exclude areas and be a bit cavalier about definitions if it is to get off the philosophical ground where it finds itself stranded. Here, too, Watson's prescriptions can be defended on the basis of their results.

THE APPEAL OF BEHAVIORISM

The response to Watson's plea for complete objectivity in the methods and facts of psychology was far from predominantly negative. Both within psychology and without, he was greeted with acclaim of the kind accorded outspoken men of great vision.

The primary reason for the appeal of Watsonian behaviorism is that American psychologists were ready and willing to leave the cramping confines of introspective study. Watson's call for an explicit extension of natural scientific methodology into the field of behavior was bound to be welcomed enthusiastically by many of the younger generation. An indication of the extent to which this enthusiasm went is given by E. C. Tolman, who said:

> This paper should have been called "The frantic attempt of a behaviorist to define consciousness." In fact, the doctrine I shall present seems to me quite unprovable and to you it will no doubt seem something far worse. And yet so great is my faith that behaviorism must ultimately triumph that I should rather present even the following quite doubtful hypothesis than hold my mouth and say nothing. (1927, p. 433)

Tolman's faithful adherence to his doctrine shows that scientists do not always meet the standards of objectivity that they set up as ideal. In Tolman's case, however, his disarmingly human honesty tells us that, at a higher level, he has reached the ultimate degree of objectivity required to recognize his own prejudices.

Strong supplementary support for the behavioristic doctrine came from the operational movement in physics, which was very quickly welcomed and adapted to psychology, and from the new positivism in philosophy as represented by the

Vienna Circle. The relationships of these movements to behaviorism are well discussed by Stevens (1939). The relationship is roughly one of equivalence to methodological behaviorism. All result in an insistence upon the use of the same kind of data and the same attitude toward the data.

There are a number of secondary reasons for the striking success of Watson's call to arms. These have been well summarized by McDougall in his polemic directed against Watson. First, behaviorism was so simple as to be easily understood and undertaken, in contrast to Gestalt psychology and structuralism particularly; McDougall's further comment was that Watson's views:

> . . . abolish at one stroke many tough problems with which the greatest intellects have struggled with only very partial success . . . by the bold and simple expedient of inviting the student to shut his eyes to them, to turn resolutely away from them, and to forget that they exist. This naturally inspires in the breast of many young people, especially perhaps those who still have examinations to pass, a feeling of profound gratitude. (J. B. Watson & McDougall, 1929, pp. 41–42)

Second, in addition to its natural simplicity, Watsonian behaviorism had the advantage of being a peculiarly American product and so of being readily comprehended in this country. Third, Watson's own forceful personality was a factor in the spreading of his gospel.

Two additional factors were suggested by McDougall. First of all, behaviorism was said to be attractive because some people are attracted by anything which is bizarre and preposterous. Second, some were attached to behaviorism out of pity for what they saw as Watson's misguided efforts, especially if they themselves were well informed. These explanations of behaviorism's appeal are more entertaining than serious; McDougall, although he seems to have regarded behaviorism as bizarre enough, certainly showed it little pity. In this he was typical of behaviorism's opponents; there was little relenting on either side.

The response to Watson's appeal was in some ways even more striking outside psychology and the academic-scientific sphere. Woodworth (1948, pp. 93–94) gave some interesting specimen comments from newspaper and magazine reviews of Watson's *Behaviorism,* which called for social reforms. Most instructive are the brief quotations from the *New York Times* ("It marks an epoch in the intellectual history of man") and the *New York Herald Tribune* ("Perhaps this is the most important book ever written. One stands for an instant blinded with a great hope"). Woodworth concluded that Watson's behaviorism was "a religion to take the place of religion." There is no question but that in its fervor and faith it had some of the aspects of religion and that these were partly responsible for its great appeal.

Watson's environmentalism fitted well into the framework of our political system, whose self-evident truths include the claim that all are created equal. Watson's claim to be able to make anything of any healthy child supported the American dream that anyone can become president. Environmentalism has always been a more hopeful position than nativism, since there is (or at least has been) little that we can do about our heredity.

THE CONTRIBUTION OF WATSONIAN BEHAVIORISM TO PSYCHOLOGY

By now we have probably made clear our opinion that, in spite of his shortcomings, Watson made a very great contribution to the development of a scientific psychology. The primary contribution is the one that we cited as responsible for the welcome reception with which many psychologists greeted behaviorism: It called out plainly and forcefully for a strictly objective study of behavior. The influence of Watsonian behaviorism in objectifying psychology, as to both methodology and terminology, has been enormous. Methodological behaviorism has been so well absorbed into American psychology that it no longer need be argued. As Bergmann said (1956): "Methodological behaviorism, like Functionalism, has conquered itself to death. It, too, has become a truism. Virtually every American psychologist, whether he knows it or not, is nowadays a methodological behaviorist" (p. 270).

An appreciably smaller number would care to be listed as Watsonian behaviorists. Woodworth's 1924 comment is still relevant and applicable to many psychologists:

> In short, if I am asked whether I am a behaviorist, I have to reply that I do not know, and do not much care. If I am, it is because I believe in the several projects put forward by behaviorists. If I am not, it is partly because I also believe in other projects which behaviorists seem to avoid, and partly because I cannot see any one big thing, to be called "behaviorism"—any one great inclusive enterprise binding together the various projects of the behaviorist into any more intimate union than they enjoy from being, each and severally, promising lines of work in psychology. (1924, p. 264)

Watson's extreme metaphysical position, which we believe was unnecessary, made a kind of contribution. Just as Titchener's strenuous effort to develop Wundtian structuralism gave a thorough trial to that brand of psychology, so Watson's insistent laboring of the mind-body issue has helped to point up the scientific fruitlessness of the problem. There is no necessary relation between one's mind-body position and his experimental or theoretical research. One's mind-body position usually is not specific enough to direct research; however, the type of research persons engage in may influence their mind-body position. The latter, after all, is easier to change. Even Titchener apparently was little concerned with the problem and behaved as though he wished the issue would go away and leave him to his research on more strictly psychological problems. Watson helped to eliminate the problem for today's experimenters. A mind-body position seems to have little influence on research even in fields like psychosomatic medicine, where there is a superficial plausibility to such a relationship. Examination of the actual operations of the researcher, however, will soon indicate that the relationship is an illusory one.

Watson's own personal contribution was primarily, as Boring put it (1950), "as a dramatic polemicist and enthusiastic leader" (p. 645). In addition, we have described several pieces of important research, both with animals and with human young. Nevertheless it is true that he himself contributed little of importance in the way of new technique or new substantive theory; even his loosely formulated notions of thinking and the like were mostly revisions of older ideas. Bergmann went so far as to say of Watson (1956): "As I see him, Watson is above all a completer and a consummator—the greatest, though not chronologically the last, of the Functionalists" (pp. 267–268). It is difficult ever to say that anyone is really an originator. But one who states issues for the first time clearly and unequivocally, as Watson did, is at least in this much an innovator. Seldom has a person had such an impact upon the general method and formulation of a science.

Watson combined his own clear and forceful personality, his extreme metaphysics, and his work in the laboratory to convince psychologists that they would be better off doing the type of work he advocated. It was as if he had said, "It is better to light one candle than to curse the darkness; better to do behavioral studies in which we can be certain of what we have found than to introspect, possibly to end up with nothing."

Bergmann, as we have seen, thought that Watson's most important contribution was his insistence that there are no interacting minds. We agree, but Bergmann's statement should be further clarified. It could, on the face of it, mean either (1) there are no minds that interact with bodies, or (2) there are no minds that interact directly with each other. Bergmann and Watson would agree that both (1) and (2) are true. Even critics of behaviorism would probably accept (2); minds could not interact directly except through some kind of extrasensory perception, which would not be seriously considered by many psychologists. The other alternative, (1) is disproved by our consideration of the conservation of energy principle. Thus, as Bergmann puts it, it must be possible in principle to predict the behavior of organisms given sufficient knowledge of three classes of antecedent variables: behavioral, physiological, and environmental. "Mental" variables are *not* included.

Margaret Washburn believed that consciousness is a useful concept and introspection a useful method. Yet she would have agreed with the point of the preceding discussion in that she recognized that the existence of consciousness in any other organism must rest upon an analogy. That is, there are no interacting minds! Mind must remain an inference based upon behavioral observations.

The great import of the Watsonian revolution in psychology was to clarify and elaborate this point: The only interaction between minds is through physical events like words or other forms of overt behavioral cues. Since Watson wished to relegate the mystical minds to the dust heap, we would do him more justice to say that *organisms* interact only through physical processes. Since science is made by human organisms, and since they have defined it as *public* knowledge, the subject matter of science must be observable by more than one member of the species. It must be *objective.*

In conclusion, Watson's own comments on his contributions are interesting. We quote both from his first polemic statement and from what is probably his last professional word:

> In concluding, I suppose I must confess to a deep bias on these questions. I have devoted nearly twelve years to experimentation on animals. It is natural that such a one should drift into a theoretical position which is in harmony with his experimental work. Possibly I have put up a straw man and have been fighting that. There may be no absolute lack of harmony between the position outlined here and that of functional psychology. I am inclined to think, however, that the two positions cannot be easily harmonized. Certainly the position I advocate is weak enough at present and can be attacked from many standpoints. Yet when all this is admitted I still feel that the considerations which I have urged should have a wide influence upon the type of psychology which is to be developed in the future. (1913b, p. 175)

And, in his brief autobiographical statement, he concluded:

> I still believe as firmly as ever in the general behavioristic position I took overtly in 1912. I think it has influenced psychology. Strangely enough, I think it has temporarily slowed down psychology because the older instructors would not accept it wholeheartedly, and consequently they failed to present it convincingly to their classes. The youngsters did not get a fair presentation, hence they are not embarking wholeheartedly upon a behavioristic career, and yet they will no longer accept the teachings of James, Titchener, and Angell. I honestly think that psychology has been sterile for several years. We need younger instructors who will teach objective psychology with no reference to the mythology most of us present-day psychologists have been brought up upon. When this day comes, psychology will have a renaissance greater than that which occurred in science in the Middle Ages. I believe as firmly as ever in the future of behaviorism—behaviorism as a companion of zoology, physiology, psychiatry, and physical chemistry. (1936, p. 281)

DIMENSIONAL PROPERTIES OF BEHAVIORISM

Behaviorism had the charm of clarity. The later behaviorists may have taken less extreme, and hence less clear, positions on R. I. Watson's dimensions than John B. Watson took; even so, there seems to be less philosophical disagreement between behaviorists than we have seen within functionalism.

It is again recommended that students make their own ratings and compare them with the authors' ratings to reveal any sources of disagreement.

One problematic dimension is, surprisingly, that of conscious versus unconscious mentalism. The behaviorists did not emphasize either, and on this basis should be assigned a neutral position. However, if one is to assign them a position at all, one could well decide that it should be in a direction *away* from conscious mentalism! Unconscious *factors,* but not unconscious *mentalism,* are important in the causation of behavior.

The dimensions our students selected as most strongly emphasized were contentual objectivism, methodological objectivism, and determinism, in that order. All of our preceding discussion confirms the importance of these dimensions.

SUMMARY AND CONCLUSIONS

Behaviorism, like all other schools, has a long past. It goes back directly to Descartes, who viewed the human body as a complex machine. Watson's real contribution was the consistency and extremity of his basic viewpoint; he simplified and made objective the study of psychology by denying the scientific usefulness of mind and consciousness. He espoused a metaphysics to go with his methodology and felt it necessary to deny the existence as well as the utility of consciousness, or at most to regard it as an epiphenomenon with no causal effects on behavior. His methodological point today is accepted, either wittingly or unwittingly, by nearly all experimental psychologists. Most other psychologists also are methodological behaviorists, but the indication at present is that unanimity is no longer being approached, and may be decreasing.

His metaphysical point, like most metaphysical points within science, is neither accepted nor rejected for scientific purposes, but simply called irrelevant. There seems to be little evidence that a mind-body position has a marked influence on the work done by psychologists. Rather, scientists seem more likely to accept a mind-body position which harmonizes with the work they are already doing.

Watson's secondary positions on issues like environmentalism and peripheralism have served to encourage research. However, they are today regarded as preliminary formulations and no longer useful or meaningful as originally phrased.

The reasons for the acceptance of Watsonian behaviorism are related to the clarity and force of Watson himself. The close relationship of his psychology to the American tradition also made his credo more desirable. Contemporaneous and somewhat later developments in physics (operationism) and philosophy (positivism) accorded so well with behaviorism that the conjunction of the three movements added power to all. The confining influence of structuralism also added impetus to any movement that was away from it.

Criticisms of behaviorism have been and continue to be vociferous. They have swept away most of the excesses of behaviorism and changed its form markedly. Metaphysical behaviorism, many of Watson's secondary tenets, and any mechanistic views that may have been associated with too rigid an S-R reflex formulation have disappeared in the storm of protest. The foundation stone, behavioristic methodology, has stubbornly resisted and must today be regarded as a solid and apparently enduring contribution of John B. Watson. However, a stone is not a house, and a methodological restriction is not a system; so today, as there is no structuralism, there is no complete system called *behaviorism.*

FURTHER READINGS

Diserens's (1925) paper on psychological objectivism is a classic historical treatment of behavioristic antecedents. The most useful primary publications of a behavioristic sort are Watson's *Behaviorism* (1930), Meyer's *Psychology of the other one* (1921), and Weiss's *Theoretical basis of human behavior* (1925). Watson's *Behavior: An introduction to comparative psychology* has been reprinted with an introduction by Herrnstein (1967). Tolman's *Purposive behavior in animals and men* (1932) represents an important broadening of the basic behavioristic doctrine. For the flavor of the early polemics, the student will do well to consult the interesting little volume reporting the debate between Watson and McDougall,

The battle of behaviorism (1929). A comprehensive volume on the various facets of the mind-body problem is edited by Feigl, Scriven, and Maxwell (1958). Secondary sources, mostly critical, are Woodworth's *Contemporary schools of psychology* (1948), Heidbreder's *Seven psychologies* (1933), Murphy's *Historical introduction to modern psychology* (1949), and Roback's *History of American psychology* (1952). Stevens's classic (1939) paper, "Psychology and the science of science," relates the behavioristic trend to logical positivism and operationism and is a most useful historical treatment. An especially interesting and provocative paper, utilizing Kuhn's concept of paradigm clash, is that by Burnham (1968). Finally, a treatment of behaviorism from a highly sympathetic point of view is found in Spence's paper "The methods and postulates of behaviorism" (1948). Other more recent treatments are cited in Chapter 10.

Table 7-1 Important Figures in Gestalt Psychology

Antecedent influences	Gestaltists		
	Pioneers	Founders	Developers
Franz Brentano (1838–1917)	G. E. Müller (1850–1934)—Göttingen	Max Wertheimer (1880–1943)—Frankfurt	Kurt Lewin (1890–1947)—Berlin
Ernst Mach (1838–1916)	Erich R. Jaensch (1883–1940)—Göttingen	Wolfgang Köhler (1887–1967)—Frankfurt	Raymond H. Wheeler (1892–1961)—Kansas
Christian von Ehrenfels (1859–1932)	David Katz (1884–1957)—Göttingen	Kurt Koffka (1886–1941)—Frankfurt	Kurt Goldstein (1878–1965)—Berlin
Alexius Meinong (1853–1920)	Edgar Rubin (1886–1951)—Göttingen		
G. F. Stout (1860–1944)			
William James (1842–1910)			
John Dewey (1859–1952)			

Chapter 7

Gestalt Psychology

Gestalt psychology was born with Max Wertheimer's (1880–1943) paper (1912) on apparent movement. The paper was a report of work by Wertheimer, Wolfgang Köhler (1887–1967), and Kurt Koffka (1886–1941), the cofounders of the new school. Like most new schools, Gestalt psychology cleared away some of the old problems in psychology and pointed the way to new ones. Its rejection of the artificiality of much of the psychological analysis of the day led to a collateral concern for problems closer to everyday-life experiences. The problem of the organization of elements into wholes and the laws of such organization were emphasized. The Gestalt type of examination and explanation of perceptual phenomena, such as afterimages and apparent movement, was begun. Learning theorists were forced to consider Gestalt principles, such as organization and insight, in the formulation of their theories. We have already seen Thorndike's belongingness as an example of such a concession to Gestalt principles.

Gestalt psychology was and is especially prone to be misunderstood. It was the product of European culture (see Table 7–1, which lists the names of the most important persons in the school), with its credo originally published in German. Fortunately, Gestalt psychology had founders who remained active in psychology. The sojourns of the three founders in the United States after they fled Nazism helped to clarify the Gestalt position and to make its principles available in

English. The early misunderstandings are beginning to dissipate. Köhler's book (1947) has been especially helpful. For example, he has pointed out (p. 168) that Gestalt psychology does not reject analysis in general. Many American psychologists had felt that the Gestalt derogation of artificial introspective analysis implied a rejection of all analysis. Köhler has also pointed out that the Gestalt opposition to quantitative statements was a prescription for psychology because of its youth, not an objection to the ultimate desirability of such formulations.

This improved understanding of the Gestalt position and the interaction of Gestalt psychology with the more Americanized brands have resulted in the general acceptance of several fundamental Gestalt ideas even in the relatively unfriendly climate of American psychology. An acceptance of the Gestalt point that there are wholes which lose much of their identity and importance by an analysis into parts has helped make the study of relatively unanalyzed, global variables more respectable in experimental psychology. The size of the unit of analysis is now seen as arbitrary and a matter of convenience. This position is quite different from the Watsonian theoretical tendency to reduce every molar act to chained reflexes, using only relatively molecular units of analysis. An "atomistic reductionism" is no longer the exclusive concern of psychology. If the psychologist does analyze situations into a number of simpler variables, he recognizes the need for what may be called *combination laws.* These combination laws specify the relationships between the several simple variables and tell how they combine in the production of the final behavior. It is no longer considered sufficient to specify the relationships between single independent variables and the dependent variable, "other things being equal." Situations can be completely understood only when we know how the several relevant variables interact. The Gestalt point that new phenomena are created *(emerge)* in complex situations is accepted.

The Gestalt emphasis on phenomenology makes it difficult for present-day users of introspection to ignore the phenomenological contents of experience, that is, the direct, naïve reports of untrained observers. Since the phenomenological report contains meanings directly, it is no longer necessary to quibble about stimulus errors, which presumably arise from prior knowledge about the stimuli. The report, with its meaning, can be accepted as such. Since the wholes given in phenomenological experience are assumed to be legitimate phenomena in their own right, there is less concern with an attempt to break every experienced whole into its constituent elements. The concept of constancy in perception has been re-thought. The old concept, which was based on constancy in response when local stimulation varied (as when you move away from a person and the retinal image changes, and yet the person continues to appear to be the same height), was no longer meaningful. The Gestaltists insisted that *local* stimulation should not be expected to coincide with *local* response, for both are parts of a total field whose influence would be expected to change the nature of the response to every local stimulation present. Thus the person should be *expected* to remain the same perceptual height, being part of a field which retains many of its relationships through the shift in distance.

J. J. Gibson has, over the years, worked out in impressive detail the nature of the properties that remain invariant under certain kinds of shifts. His point of view is that the senses exist for getting information; they have evolved as effective systems for carrying out this function. One desirable property in an information-gathering system would be to have it extract constant features from the flux of experience. Along these lines, Gibson (1966) says: "Above all, it should be remembered that the informative variables of optical structure are *invariant under changes in the intensity of illumination and changes in the station-point of the observer*" (p. 242). If one considers the infinitude of changes in illumination and station-point that take place during the life of a human being, it is clear that a system which preserved the results of such changes would very quickly find itself overloaded. From this point of view, it becomes clear that the structuralist concern with the analytic details of local stimulation was misguided if scientific interest is to be focused on the same things that are important in the life of the organism. The organism, in order to function through a reasonable lifetime, must be constructed so that it focuses on invariants, and these invariants turn out to be fairly complex, relational properites of wholes. Thus efficient stimulus definition must be molar stimulus definition.

THE ANTECEDENTS OF THE GESTALT MOVEMENT

When one speaks of antecedents of modern psychological systems, Wundt comes readily to mind. He was the villain against whom the systematists rebelled, and his role was necessary. His elementaristic position was a target for Gestalt psychology just as it was for functionalism and behaviorism. However, he was an antecedent in a more direct sense; his principle of creative synthesis was an early concept that implied some recognition of the difference between wholes and the sum of their parts. This concept was much like John Stuart Mill's mental chemistry. Both men recognized that new characteristics might emerge from the combination of elements into wholes. Neither, however, did enough about his notion to satisfy the founders of Gestalt psychology.

Franz Brentano, whom we have discussed in relation to Wundtian psychology (Chapter 4), believed that psychology should concentrate upon the process or act of sensing rather than upon the sensation as an element. He used introspection, but his introspection tended toward the naïve phenomenological variety. He considered Wundt's introspection artificial and strained. Thus he anticipated the Gestalt method of introspection and made the direct, naïve expression of experience respectable. However, he did not recognize the emergence of new phenomena with increasing complexity.

Carl Stumpf (1848–1936) was another antecedent of Gestalt psychology, but he bore a very peculiar relationship to its founders. Köhler (1920) dedicated a book to Stumpf, from whom he had received his Ph.D.; Koffka was also a student of Stumpf, as was Kurt Lewin, a developer of a kind of Gestalt psychology. Wertheimer got his degree with Külpe at Würzburg, but studied with Stumpf and was associated with him for years at the University of Berlin. Yet Stumpf, so closely associated with these four chief figures in Gestalt psychology, denied having any direct systematic influence on the new movement (Hartmann, 1935, p. 32). It seemed that Stumpf was positively anxious to disown any influence.

Both Stumpf and Külpe, however, deviated in important ways from structuralist orthodoxy. Both used some variation of the introspective techniques or problems, and Stumpf in particular may have helped transmit Brentano's more tolerant style of introspection to the Gestaltists. Boring (1950, p. 595) reports that Brentano and Husserl had won Stumpf over to phenomenology.

Most of the other antecedents had some more direct intellectual relationship to Gestalt psychology, although none of them could have had a closer *personal* relationship than Stumpf. Ernst Mach (1838–1916) was a physicist who came into the history of psychology by the back door. He was interested in the new psychology and contributed to it both in theory and in experiment. He insisted that sensations form the basis of all science. This was a point that a physicist could make as well as a psychologist, for it relates to the general question of epistemology. Yet in his specification of the nature of sensations, he was led to postulate the existence of two entirely new types of sensation: sensation of space form, as in a circle or any other type of geometrical form, and sensation of time form, as in a melody. These sensations of space form and time form Mach correctly (according to the Gestalt psychologists) stated to be independent of their elements. For example, circles can be red, blue, large, or small and lose nothing of their circularity. Similarly, the notes of a melody can be played in another key without any alteration of their time form.

Christian von Ehrenfels (1859–1932) shared with Mach an interest in the new psychology. Although he was a philosopher for the most part, he elaborated Mach's psychological notions of the new elements into a theory and called it *Gestaltqualität.* In his analysis of the new sensational elements, he was faced with the problem of whether they were really new. Could the new qualities be reduced to combinations of the other qualities? He decided that although the qualities depend upon the elements arranged in a certain pattern, they are nevertheless immediately experienced and do not inhere in any of the component elements. They are present in the mind and not in the physical events.

According to Boring (1950), "At first the Gestalt psychologists did not realize what a respectable and competent ancestor they had in von Ehrenfels, but presently they discovered him, and when he died in 1933 the *Psychologische Forschung* printed a brief but fitting recognition of his role" (p. 608). Similarly, Heider (1973) says that the Berlin Gestaltists singled out von Ehrenfels as a significant forerunner of their own theories. However, the original development by Wertheimer, Köhler, and Koffka seems to have occurred before they were aware of Ehrenfels and his work.

These figures postulated new elements, but they were not Gestalt psychologists. We miss the point of the Gestalt revolution unless we see that its precursors, like Mach and von Ehrenfels, were in reality merely carrying on in the old atomistic tradtion. They simply discovered new elements rather than eschewed elementarism, as the Gestaltists did. They pointed out the problem but gave an entirely wrong solution. They complicated rather than simplified.

Alexius Meinong (1853–1920) gave the same wrong answer that von Ehrenfels had. He was a pupil of Brentano and the leader of the Graz school of psychology. He elaborated the ideas of von Ehrenfels and changed his terminology, but added nothing essentially new. His methodology tended toward the phenomenological, again anticipating Gestalt. The break of act psychology and the psychology of the Graz school with the academic tradition was not clean enough.

Helson (1969), in his article "Why did their precursors fail and the Gestalt psychologists succeed?" makes nearly the same point: "First and foremost, it was a radical movement. I once referred to the Benussi group as the left-wing Gestalters with their assumption of higher level processes to account for whole qualities, and Koffka said: 'No, we are the radicals in rejecting such processes,' and he was, of course, right" (p. 1007).

The Benussi group to which Helson was referring was made up of students and other associates of Benussi, who was himself a student of Meinong. They, like the other predecessors, failed to take the radical step; they failed to reject elementarism. However, Benussi did do a long series of experiments on perception in an attempt to clarify the question whether Gestalt properties were really different from sensations. Had he rejected the question and accepted Gestalts as given in perception, he would have been the founder of the Gestalt school. As it was, he became a respected and friendly opponent of the Gestaltists (Heider, 1973).

Thus these schools did not flourish and gain adherents as Gestalt psychology did later. They did not satisfy one of Kuhn's conditions for having a paradigm, and they established no real school, since schools need "students." And, although we can see them now as antecedents in the intellectual, systematic sense, there was no real continuity of the personnel of these earlier schools and the originators of Gestalt psychology. The origin of Gestalt psychology can therefore be thought of as occurring by the very process that Gestalt psychology later was to advocate as the basis of learning—an insight!

Several psychologists at Göttingen were important precursors and supporters of Gestalt psychology. G. E. Müller directed the laboratory there and supported a program of introspective research that savored of the Gestalt phenomenological approach. He was later to claim (Müller, 1923) that there was really nothing new in the Gestalt approach to perceptual theory. The research of three other men in his laboratory lent support to his contention. Had these men had the inspiration to make their results the ground for a school, the names of Gestalt psychology's founders might have been Erich R. Jaensch (1883–1940), David Katz (1884–1957), and Edgar Rubin (1886–1951). All three men were working on and publishing phenomenological investigations in 1911 or 1912, which was the year Wertheimer published his results and launched Gestalt psychology.

Jaensch was working with visual acuity, and he showed that large interacting systems had to be considered in the discussion of acuity; the elementary atomistic approach would not do. Katz had already published an investigation of color in 1907, and in 1911 he published an extensive monograph on color. It contained a careful phenomenological description of the different kinds of colors: surface colors, volumic colors, and film colors. He described the conditions under which each type of color could be observed and did *not* try to explain the different types of colors by recourse to the combination of sensations of color with some other elements, as the Wundtians would have. Rubin did not begin his work until 1912, the year the Gestalt school was founded. He developed the distinction between figure and ground in his phenomenological investigation. He noted that commonly part of the total stimulus configuration stands out, while part of it recedes and is more amorphous. He produced several demonstrations in which the figure and ground can be reversed. He did not publish until 1915; the Gestaltists pounced on his work immediately and appropriated it to their system, since it was another instance of evidence which required the consideration of the totality of stimulation for its explanation.

Meanwhile, others were being beckoned by problems similar to the one so ingeniously solved by the Gestalt triumvirate. In England, G. F. Stout (1860–1944) in 1896 raised questions about the whole-part relationship. He was concerned chiefly with form and concluded (1902) that ". . . an element which is apprehended first as part of one whole, and then as part of another, is presented in two different points of view, and so far suffers transformation" (p. 71). He had stated clearly the Gestalt point that there exist wholes which influence the mode of existence of the parts.

Even earlier, William James in the United States had challenged psychological atomism (1890). He said "The traditional psychologist talks like one who would say a river consists of nothing but pailsful, spoonsful, quartpotsful, barrelsful, and other moulded forms of water. Even were the pails and the pots all actually standing in the same stream, still between them the free water would continue to flow" (vol. I, p. 255). Like the water, the stream of consciousness for James had a reality independent of its atomistic analysis.

Curiously, James also used an analogy that was almost exactly like one used by Köhler many years later:

> In a sense a soap bubble has parts; it is a sum of juxtaposed spherical triangles. But these triangles are not separate realities. Touch the bubble and the triangles are no more. Dismiss the thought and out go its parts. You can no more make a new thought out of ideas that have once served you than you can make a new bubble out of old triangles. Each bubble, each thought, is a fresh organic unity, sui generis. (James, 1890, vol. I, p. 279, footnote)

Had James seen fit to elaborate his point sufficiently, Gestalt psychology might have had an earlier founding.

We have already met another American who was surprisingly close to Gestalt principles, although his point was made relative to quite another empirical area. John Dewey, in his reflex-arc paper (1896), was advocating a field approach, a study of the whole situation in itself, a discarding of the artificial analysis into stimulus and response. The reflex arc was seen to be an organic unity, losing its meaning and reality in the analysis (cf. Chapter 5).

The very atmosphere of thought just prior to the founding of Gestalt psychology seemed to be permeated with the notion of fields, the notion of organic wholes. And thought of this sort was not limited to psychologists and philosophers. For example, E. B. Wilson, a leading biologist, said that the cell must not be regarded as an independent unit, the only real unity being that of the organism.

THE FOUNDING OF THE GESTALT SCHOOL

Max Wertheimer, the oldest of the three founders, was born in Prague in 1880, and studied law there before turning to psychology (Boring, 1950). He studied with Stumpf and Schumann before taking his degree with Külpe at Würzburg. After that, he rather dropped from historical notice for about 6 years; he was apparently "financially independent" so that he could afford to work only wherever and whenever he wished. He bobbed back to the historical surface in 1910, with his arrival at the Psychological Institute in Frankfurt am Main. He had obtained a toy stroboscope upon leaving the train, and made some observations in his hotel room; then he went to the institute to find more subjects. Schumann, his friend from Berlin, was there. He gave Wertheimer a tachistoscope, and two other graduates of Berlin—Köhler and Koffka—were soon helping Wertheimer study apparent movement. No doubt the young assistants were happy to help the aged Wertheimer, who was then 30, by serving as subjects. The three of them afterward had long discussions of the results of their research. The phenomenon which gives us motion pictures had long been difficult for psychologists to interpret. In essence, the problem was how to explain, using sensations as elements, the perception of movement which arose from a series of stimuli, none of which moved.

Wertheimer worked with two slits, one vertical and the other inclined 20 or 30 degrees from the vertical. When light was thrown first through one slit and then through the other, the slit of light appeared to move from one position to the other if the time between presentations of the two lights was within the proper range. Wertheimer worked out the range within which movement was perceived. The interval of around 60 milliseconds was optimal. If the interval between presentations was longer than about 200 milliseconds, the light was seen successively first at one, then at the other position. If the interval was too short, 30 milliseconds or less, both lights seemed to be on continuously. Wertheimer gave one type of movement the name *phi*; he wished to give it a name that would emphasize its independent character as a phenomenon in its own right. It was a phenomenon which could not result from the summation of individual stimulations, for certainly an elementarist could not argue that the addition of a second stationary stimulation to a first stationary stimulation could yield, by summation, a sensation of movement. The founders of Gestalt psychology were perhaps fortunate in working with an experimental paradigm which made it so crystal clear that the overall situation was critical in determining what was perceived.

Wertheimer's monograph (1912) describing the research contained an explanation of apparent movement so simple, yet so ingenious, that it served as the basis of the new school of psychology. The explanation was essentially that apparent movement does not need explaining! It exists simply as a real phenomenon in its own right, a phenomenon irreducible to simpler sensations of any kind.

An attempt to analyze it into simpler sensations, in the orthodox Wundtian manner, would destroy the reality of the phenomenon as such. Apparent movement would not be found to exist except in situations where prescribed *relationships* between elements held. Wertheimer said, "There is no internal reason why something that is psychologically 'dynamic' should have to be deduced á priori from something 'static' " (Shipley, 1961, p. 1082; translated from Wertheimer, 1912).

This apparently simple beginning of Gestalt psychology was really not so simple as it might now seem. Its principles were completely counter to most of the academic tradition of German psychology. To regard a complex experience as having an existence of its own amounted to revolution. To maintain, as Wertheimer did, that the *primary* data of perception are typically structures *(Gestalten)* was heresy to the German introspectionistic tradition and to its American counterpart, which was flourishing under Titchener. Structures, for these psychologists, were things to be broken down into the elements, which were primary.

In addition, Wertheimer thought that it was legitimate for introspection to use simple, naïve descriptive words. He maintained that local sensations should not be expected to concur with local stimulation because both are part of a field, a whole, which influences the individual parts in a way depending on the structure of the whole.

Not only did Wertheimer advocate these things, but Köhler and Koffka advocated them vociferously. As Köhler said in his obituary for Koffka:

> Those were years of cheerful revolt in German psychology. We all had great respect for the exact methods by which certain sensory data and facts of memory were being investigated, but we also felt quite strongly that work of so little scope could never give us an adequate psychology of real human beings. Some believed that the founding fathers of experimental psychology had done grave injustice to every higher form of mental life. Others suspected that at the very bottom of the new science there were some premises which tended to make its work sterile. (1942, p. 97)

This last point concurs with one stated brilliantly by James and cited in Chapter 4 (see p. 89).

With such cheerful revolutionists, the movement gained momentum. There were many in Germany, as in America (e.g., Helson, 1925, 1926), who were dissatisfied with the artificiality and paucity of results of the older psychology. Gestalt psychology quickly gained support from them. Many psychologists were happy to find a way to avoid the proliferation of elements needed to explain each new complex experience. They did not believe that the legitimacy of the phenomenological approach, or of emergent real phenomena, could any longer be denied. This was the primary assumption of the developing school. Let us look further at the set of tenets developed by the new psychology.

THE TENETS OF GESTALT PSYCHOLOGY

The Whole-Part Attitude

Examples Illustrating the Problem The attitude of Gestaltists toward wholes is one of the most difficult to grasp in all psychology. We must therefore

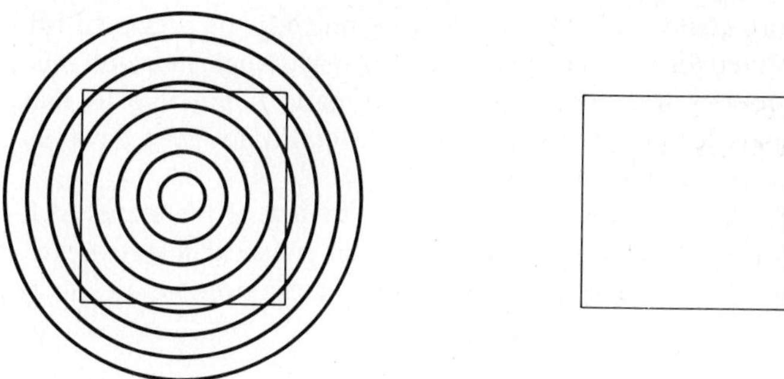

Figure 7-1 An illustration of the dependence of perception of a part upon the pattern of the whole. *(Adapted from Orbison, 1939, p. 42.)*

devote the most careful attention to it. Certainly the distinction they make between a whole and the sum of its parts is not new. The Chinese sage Lao-Tse is said (G. W. Hartmann, 1935, p. 9) to have expressed in 600 B.C. the notion that the sum of the parts is different from the whole. Also Skinner (1938, p. 29) has contended that the question of whether the whole is different from the sum of its parts is a pseudoproblem. On the other hand, Weiss (1967) has entitled a long and beautifully illustrated article "$1 + 1 \neq 2$ (One plus one does not equal two)," and there is no doubt whatever that he considers it a meaningful problem. Many have been concerned with it, and it may justify as much investigation as that other long-lived puzzle, the mind-body problem, in order to find out whether it is a profitable question to ask.

Max Wertheimer had this to say about the whole-part problem as it occurs with respect to the given in experience (Wertheimer, 1938): "*The given is itself in varying degrees structured* (Gestaltet), *it consists of more or less definitely structured wholes and whole-processes with their whole-properties and laws, characteristic whole-tendencies and whole-determinations of parts. Pieces almost always appear as parts in whole processes*" (p. 14).

Wertheimer is of course pointing to the importance of structure, but he is doing more than that. Even an associationist or a structuralist could accept that. Wertheimer is indicating a kind of logical *priority* of the whole. Consider an example provided by Orbison (1939) and reproduced here as Figure 7-1. The two squares are "objectively" identical in size, with all sides straight. Yet in perception the structure of the whole makes them appear as different parts. It does not make sense to a Gestaltist to say that the two squares appear first as parts, and then make up different wholes. The very nature of their existence as parts is determined by the wholes.

Analogies from other fields which demonstrate the importance of structure and the difference between wholes and the sums of parts are common. One of the oldest and most familiar is water, which is quite different from a simple mixture of its elements, hydrogen and oxygen. Water has emergent qualities, that is, qualities that emerge only in the combination of its elements. We can know about the characteristics of the compound, water, only by studying water directly; the characteristics could not, at least until very recently, be predicted by a knowledge of the characteristics of the elements alone. Although new advances in theories and techniques of wave mechanics have made it possible to make such predictions, it can be argued that the advances could not even have occurred in the absence of observations of wholes.

C. S. Smith, a materials scientist, in a review of the status of his own field, makes several statements which indicate that physical scientists are increasingly being forced to recognize the importance of organized wholes in their study of materials:

> The main characteristic of today's science of materials is a concern with properties and the dependence of properties upon structure. This is exactly where the story began. The history of materials has been a long journey in search of knowledge in strange and difficult terrain, finally to return to the familiar scene with vastly better understanding. . . . Matter cannot be understood without a knowledge of atoms; yet it is now becoming evident that the properties of materials that we enjoy in a work of art or exploit in an interplanetary rocket are really not those of atoms but those of aggregates; indeed they arise in the behavior of electrons and protons within a framework of nuclei arranged in a complex hierarchy of many stages of aggregation. It is not stretching the analogy much to suggest that the chemical explanation of matter is analogous to using an identification of individual brick types as an explanation of Hagia Sophia. The scientists' laudable striving to eliminate the evidence of the senses has sometimes produced a senseless result. (1968, p. 638)

To eliminate any doubt that Smith is talking about the whole-part problem, look at a later excerpt:

> The immense understanding that has come from digging deeper to atomic explanations has been followed by a realization that this leaves out something essential. In its rapid advance, science has had to ignore the fact that a whole is more than the sum of its parts. (1968, pp. 643–644)

Polanyi (1968) has strongly argued that biology is not reducible to physics and chemistry since the existing morphology of an organism, which provides the boundary conditions within which the physical or chemical laws operate, is physically and energetically indistinguishable from other no less probable morphologies that have not happened to come into existence. This argument is valid and applies even to the much simpler aggregates of the materials engineer.

Köhler's *Die physischen Gestalten* (1920) is a relatively clear statement of the Gestalt view of the whole-part relationship, although such a complex problem with so many facets is never really simple. Here Köhler said in part:

> Let us consider under what conditions a physical system attains a state which is independent of time (i.e., a state of equilibrium or a so-called stationary state). In general we can say that such a state is reached when a certain condition is satisfied for the system *as a whole.* The potential energy must have reached a minimum, the entropy a maximum, or the like. The solution of the problem demands not that forces or potentials assume particular values in individual regions, but that their total arrangements relative to one another in the whole system must be of a certain definite

> type. The state of process at any place therefore depends in principle on the conditions obtaining in all other parts of the system. If the laws of equilibrium or stationary state for the individual parts can be formulated separately, then these parts do not together constitute a *single* physical system, but each part is a system in itself.
>
> Thus an electric circuit is a physical system precisely because the conditions prevailing at any given point are determined by those obtaining in all the other parts. Contrariwise, a group of electrical circuits completely insulated from each other constitutes a complex of independent, single systems. This complex is a "whole" *only* in the mind of one who chances to think of it as such; from the physical standpoint it is a summation of independent entities. (Köhler, 1920, as translated in Ellis, 1938, pp. 18–19)

Weiss (1967) gives several commonplace examples of complexly interrelated systems best regarded as wholes. One is a spider web. Changes made by the spider near the center of the web have effects that literally *can be seen* to reverberate throughout the web, as when a garden spider vibrates its web in response to an intruder. Multiple interconnections between all parts of the web can be seen to account for its action, but these interconnections defy analysis into parts—hence, "the whole is different from the sum of the parts."

As a contrasting type of example, consider a collection of 500 marbles scattered on a floor. Assume that an outside marble hits one of the collection. Multiple hits would follow, provided the mass and velocity of the first marble were great enough. Nevertheless, this "system" is quite different from the first one, and the changes in marble position would seem to be potentially analyzable into a collection of interactions between individual pairs of marbles. In contrast, the spider web provides no place for sinking in our analytic teeth and constitutes a real system rather than the kind of pseudosystem provided by the marbles.

Implications for a World View G. W. Hartmann has pointed out that there are two extreme views of the physical world and the role of systems in it. One view is that the world is composed of independent additive parts whose total constitutes reality. The other view is that everything is related to everything else, and there are no independent systems. The Gestaltists held neither of these extreme views, although they leaned toward the latter. They recognized that there are systems which may be considered independent for practical (including practical scientific) purposes. Hartmann has concluded (1935): "Both evils are avoided as soon as one recognizes that *the laws of science are the laws of systems,* i.e., structures of finite extent—a generalization applicable to both physics and psychology" (p. 42).

The Gestaltists, then, wished to extend these ideas about physical systems to psychology. They maintained that in biology and psychology as in physics, there are phenomena whose character depends on the character of the whole field. In visual perception, for example, the thing seen was thought to be a function of the total, overall retinal stimulation rather than of the stimulation of any specific local point. Unfortunately, the nature of the psychological field is not always clear.

In 1955, at the American Psychological Association meeting in San Francisco, the physicist Robert Oppenheimer (1956) said he had no idea what a "psychological field" could mean. The statement drew laughter and applause from the audience of American psychologists. Apparently many of them did not know either and felt either that there is no such thing or that it is an overworked and ill-defined concept. Yet Köhler's analogy, quoted above, seems simple and reasonable enough. The real question is whether or not the application can meaningfully be made to psychology. Let us examine this question: "What meaning can wholes, systems whose parts depend on the whole, or fields, have in psychology?"

One of the key issues is the determination of what constitutes an isolated system. The Gestalt contention has been that fields or systems are widespread in psychology and that the elementaristic analysis of structuralism or behaviorism destroys the meaningful relationships these fields might have in psychological laws. At the same time, the Gestaltists have not denied that the proper use of analysis is necessary. How can we determine whether a particular field can be further analyzed without destroying the very relationships we intend to study? It seems that the only way to do so is by attempting both analysis and the use of the unanalyzed field in the construction of psychological laws. The decision about which method should be used will eventually be made on a pragmatic basis. If the molar, Gestalt approach leads to more useful laws, and if no further analysis is necessary, then this approach will be adopted for the particular purpose. On the other hand, if this approach does not succeed, further analysis may be indicated.

A very important tool for determining the degree and kind of system one is dealing with is factor analysis. If various measures of system behavior can be taken, the matrix of intercorrelations may reveal significant aspects of the system's structure. There seems to be a trend in Germany for present-day psychologists to return to some of the qualitative Gestalt problems using multivariate analysis. Thurstone, though certainly not a Gestaltist, was well known for his multivariate analysis. Gulliksen says of him:

> Neither could the experimenter hope to learn very much from an experiment involving only two or three variables. For the last 25 years of his study, Thurstone typically investigated 40–60 variables at a time in order to get good leverage on the interrelationships among them. It may be said that this is the greatest legacy he has left us: the emphasis on both accurate experimentation and accurate analyses in the multivariate situation that is essential to psychology. (1968, p. 800)

Modern mathematical techniques for studying dynamic systems involving several variables demonstrate that Köhler was quite correct in his contention that equilibrium conditions depend upon some condition in the system as a whole. These mathematical techniques are quite powerful when they can be applied. Specifically, some systems can be represented by a set of linear differential equations. The coefficients of the equations can, in turn, be represented in a matrix. It is then characteristics of the *matrix as a whole* that determine whether or not the system will be stable and, if it is, what kind of stability it will manifest. Thus some of the Gestalt contentions have a very precise interpretation, and the contentions are correct.

The Gestalt psychologist proceeds on the assumption that the unit of description should be chosen by the organism being studied; that is, the organism's responses determine what constitutes a meaningful whole. For example, if in a study of perception an observer reports that he sees a tree, then "tree" will become a unit of description, rather than some combination of greens, browns, textures, and the like. For this particular analysis, the tree as perceived will be assumed to be a reasonably isolated system and a meaningful unit of analysis. The acceptance of phenomenological description implies an acceptance of the units decided upon by the phenomenological describer.

Many times, the unit is chosen that seems most natural to the scientist, who will simply make a phenomenological decision. For example, one may decide to choose as a response unit any depression of a bar by a rat. This is the unit of response that seems most useful to the scientist. Since people make science, some such method seems inevitable. The Gestaltist, in voluntary acceptance of phenomenological description, has recognized that knowledge will always depend in part on the nature of the perceiving organism and at the same time has decided to live graciously with that limitation.

GESTALT PSYCHOLOGY AND PHYSIOLOGY

In his 1912 paper Max Wertheimer had no sooner said that apparent movement need not be explained in terms of its "elements" than he turned to an explanation in terms of presumed underlying physiological events. He suggested that when the temporal relationships were within the right range, excitation from one object jumped over to the excitation generated by the object next presented. Thus Gestalt psychology revealed its deep interest in physiology at the very beginning.

Unfortunately, all too often physiology served a purely hypothetical role. In the absence of direct observation, it was easy to hypothesize just the physiological "field" needed to "explain" the observed results. In physics, a field is simply an inference made directly from the movements of particles within a portion of space. From Oppenheimer's remarks, cited earlier, we may infer that field does not always mean exactly the same thing in psychology that it does in physics. If it did, we would have in both cases a mathematical description which would predict the phenomena in question, and that is all we would have. The physical field has only these mathematical properties; it has no existential properties.

In psychology, a similar situation *may* obtain. By *perceptual field,* the careful psychologist may mean nothing more than certain antecedent-consequent relations and the verbal or mathematical description of a state of affairs which would allow the derivation of the observations. The concept of field is most likely to be used where the consequent (verbal report or other behavior) does not depend in a point-to-point fashion upon the local characteristics of the stimulus. If field is used in this strict sense, as a mathematical device for describing relationships, there is a considerable kinship between psychological and physical fields. Of course, if the psychological field does not allow predictions, it is essentially meaningless. A psychological field, used thus strictly, is many times more "physical" than most physiological fields, which are quite likely to be pure assumptions, especially when used by psychologists. That is, there will often have been no observations of any kind at the physiological level. If the physiological field is recognized as a model which helps in making predictions, there is nothing wrong even with this usage, for it makes no difference to its predictive power whether the field is thought of as physiologically localized or not. The unfortunate thing is that the reader may be misled into thinking that the physiological field is based on some physiological evidence.

As yet, the picture of cerebral action is quite incomplete. The early ablation work of Franz and Lashley, referred to in Chapter 6, demonstrated that the mode of action of the brain must be extremely complex, a conclusion that has never been brought into question. Lashley generally favored the view that a whole pattern of neural activity, rather than localized activity, determines behavior (see Chapter 11 for a fuller discussion of Lashley's views). Yet Lashley, Chow, and Semmes (1951) performed experiments whose results brought into question the whole Gestalt view that electrical field activity in the brain underlies perception. Lashley and his coworkers simply took the Gestalt position seriously and undertook to short out field currents in the visual cortex of the monkey by placing silver foil on the cortical surface or by placing metal pins in the striate cortex. They found no deterioration of visual discrimination and concluded that cortical fields are probably not related to visual perception. This type of experiment was later extended (Sperry & Miner, 1955; Sperry, Miner, & Myers, 1955), again without affecting visual discrimination.

Köhler (1958) did not think Lashley's procedures had been adequate to short out the cortical currents, but he was more concerned with the more thorough tampering which had occurred in the Sperry experiments. However, Köhler maintained that the latter results were not consistent with *any* theory of cortical mechanisms, since the damage had been so extensive that visual discrimination should have deteriorated. He suspected that some extraneous cues might have accounted for these results, with visual discrimination essentially bypassed.

The attempt to explain brain action without the invocation of a field concept has not been abandoned (Hebb, 1949, 1959). And, whatever the final explanation, there is certainly no detailed field explanation which is accepted at the present time. The description of brain fields given by the Gestalt psychologists depends largely upon data from perceptual, not physiological, experiments. Prentice (1959, p. 451) cites physiological research which provides some exceptions to the above statement, but the physiological results thus far are not overwhelmingly impressive.

We must conclude that the Gestaltists' physiological statements should be regarded as models which presumably make possible the predictions of results on the psychological (behavioral) level, although it is not clear that these predictions would actually be possible in all cases.

An instructive instance is the theory of cohesive and restraining forces. Cohesive forces are tendencies of excitations in the cortex to attract one another if nothing restrains them. Restraining forces prevent such movement and are generally the result of present stimulation. When stimulation is presented and then removed, cohesive forces are free to manifest themselves. Brown and Voth (1937) demonstrated cohesive effects in an experiment on apparent movement. Four lights were arranged in a square pattern and flashed on, one at a time, successively around the square. As the rate of succession increased, apparent movement was perceived from one position to the succeeding position. As the rate increased further, the path of the movement became curved until the path followed finally became circular. The perceived path of movement had a diameter too small for the path to intercept the actual positions of the lights! A circle, in order to pass through the lights, would have to have a considerably larger diameter than the path of the perceived movement.

This phenomenon was explained by invoking cohesive forces. The excitations begun by the flashes of light attract one another, thus constricting the path of the perceived movement. The locus of the attraction is presumably the brain. However, it is clear that the inference about cohesive forces is made from observation of a stimulus-response relationship, and the cohesive forces would be equally useful as an explanatory concept if they were presumed to occur in the stimulus field, or a psychological field.

Isomorphism

Gestalt theorists have tended to make easy inferences from stimulus-response observations to physiological events because they accept the principle of isomorphism. An isomophism is a 1:1 relationship, assumed in this case to hold between brain fields and experience. The structural properties of brain fields and experience are assumed to be topographically identical; that is, we may think of the relationship between the two as being identical as to order.

Köhler stated an isomorphism with respect to experienced space as follows (1947): "*Experienced order in space is always structurally identical with a functional order in the distribution of underlying brain processes*" (p. 61). Woodworth (1948, p. 135) used an analogy to the relationship between a map and the country it represents to clarify what the Gestaltists mean by isomorphism. The map and the country are not the same, but their structure is identical in the sense that we can read off the characteristics of the country from the map, and vice versa. The identity is a very restricted one. All that the Gestaltist seems to demand is that the physiological and experimental fields have *some* identity, perhaps not one as strong as that between a map and a country. To extend Woodworth's analogy, the "scale of miles" involved in going from physiology to experience and back may not be the same for all parts of the map or country. In addition, the map may be folded or wadded up without destroying the isomorphism. Nevertheless, the Gestaltist assumes that we shall eventually be able to read off information about physiology from what we know of experience, and vice versa; we just need more directions for reading and need to open the physiological events to easier view.

The doctrine of isomorphism leads easily to another way of approaching the whole-part problem. To recapitulate, the Gestaltists emphasized whole properties and a phenomenal approach to perception. Gibson showed that the informational properties of our stimulus world require a complex "holistic" description. These facts have their counterparts in physiological observations made years after the doctrine of isomorphism was proposed. In their now classic article, Maturana, Lettvin, McCulloch, and Pitts (1960) described units in the frog's optic tract which responded when stimuli had certain complex characteristics, such as a particular degree of curvature, but which did not respond when those characteristics were absent. It is clear that a physiology or a psychology which studied only local responses to local stimulation would find it impossible to deal with such complex properties. There are probably large numbers of examples of such nerve nets that extract complex features from stimuli, in man as in frogs. These nets may extract precisely the kinds of information-bearing features that Gibson stresses.

The doctrine of isomorphism reflects a view of the value of introspection which is quite different from that of the behaviorist. For Gestaltists, experience is just the other side of physiology, and therefore becomes their "royal road" to knowledge of physiology. The same attitude could be deduced from an interactionistic, or a double-aspect, view of the mind-body problem. However, the Gestalt statement of isomorphism was clearer and more specific than the loose and general notions of mind-body correspondence implied by the philosophical mind-body "solutions."

Nativism-Empiricism and the Contemporaneity Principle

Both the components of the Gestaltists' isomorphism are components that presently exist. Both the physiology and the correlated experience are available for present study. Thus present experience is explicable solely on the basis of its relationship to the present state of the physiological field. It is only natural that this relatively ahistorical point of view led the Gestaltists to show less interest in past experience than had the members of the other schools. They did not deny that past experience might play a role in perception and behavior, but they tended to deemphasize its role. They argued that the past experience must have modified the *present* condition of the organism before it could have any effect. Thus a complete knowledge of the present would leave nothing out of the immediate causal account, while a study of the past would be handicapped by the distortions worked upon earlier events by later ones, as well as by the complexities introduced by the participation of the historical effect in the present field.

Köhler stated part of the case against past experience as an exclusive explanatory principle as follows:

> It would be extremely unfortunate if the problem were thrust aside at this point as being after all only another case of the influence of past experience. No one doubts that past experience is an important factor in *some* cases, but the attempt to explain all perception in such terms is absolutely sure to fail, for it is easy to demonstrate instances where perception is not at all influenced by past experience. Fig. 1 is an example. We see a group of rectangles; but the figure may also be seen as two H's with certain intervening lines. Despite our extensive past experience with the letter H,

> it is, nevertheless, the articulation of *the presented object* which determines what we shall see. (1938, p. 58)

Here is Köhler's figure 1:

Köhler was not insisting that past experience is irrelevant to present perception, nor was he insisting that perceptual behavior is innate. There are three types of variables that may influence perception: genetic, historical, and present. Nativism is commonly understood to be the position that genetic variables completely determine present perceptual responding. The Gestalt position is not nativistic in this sense. The Gestaltists have simply insisted that the historical variables do not completely determine perceptual responding and concomitantly have emphasized the two other classes of variables.

Egon Brunswik was a psychologist with Gestaltlike leanings (see Chapter 11). Yet he apparently did not see anything contradictory in the position that the Gestalt laws of organization, which were concerned with features of the presented stimulus, might be learned. Brunswik and Kamiya (1953) did a preliminary study of photographs of natural objects to see whether it was conceivable that elements in proximity might be seen as parts of the same object because people had *learned* that elements in proximity belonged to the same object. If elements in proximity within the stimulus tended to belong to the same object, then people could learn to organize proximate elements into the same whole because other experiences had shown that they (the perceptual elements) probably arose from the same object. Brunswick and Kamiya found that there is a tendency, relatively weak, for proximate elements to belong to the same object. Their conclusion was that the principle of proximity could be learned by the individual, although to show that it is would require further investigation. The possibility that the visual system had "learned" the principle through the process of evolution would have to be eliminated.

The Attitude toward Analysis

Gestalt psychology began partly as a revolt against the allegedly artificial analysis of the introspectionist. Still, the Gestalt psychologists recognized that analysis is at the very heart of science. The objection was not to analysis as such but to a particular kind of analysis. Köhler (1947) said that if we analyze as the orthodox introspectionists do, then those experiences that are most important will be neglected completely. Common experience, the experience of everyday life, is not to be found in the introspectionist's psychology. Köhler did not argue that the introspectionist's findings are unreal, just that the reality is contrived and artificial. Gestalt psychologists have objected not to the artificiality of the laboratory as such but to the artificiality of a stilted type of method and a sterile conception. Gestalt psychology is not an applied psychology, but the Gestaltists have tried to make it a psychology whose results apply to real experience.

Gestaltists have also been interpreted as rejecting quantification within psychology. Their feeling was not that quantification is illegitimate or unnecessary, but that it is often premature. They have held that psychology should first concern itself with important qualitative discoveries. The attitude toward quantification *as such* was not negative, but the attitude toward quantification *for its own sake* was quite negative. The feeling is summed up in Köhler's statement (1947) that ". . . one can hardly exaggerate the value of qualitative information as a necessary supplement to quantitative work" (p. 49). He went on to say, of his own work on learning: "Everything that is valuable in these observations would disappear if 'results' were handled in an abstract statistical fashion" (p. 50). It is not often that an opportunity arises to point out an analogy between the attitude of the Gestalt psychologist and that of the operant conditioner, but here we find an exception!

Koffka (1935, pp. 13–15) gave a more thorough and sophisticated treatment of quantification, making essentially the same points. He destroyed the antithesis felt by some to exist between quantity and quality, concluding that ". . . the quantitative, mathematical description of physical science, far from being opposed to quality, is but a particularly accurate way of representing quality" (p. 14). Koffka would therefore agree that psychology must eventually express its laws in quantitative form in order to reach maximum precision.

EMPIRICAL STATEMENTS

Principles of Organization

The best-known empirical statements made by the Gestalt psychologists are the principles of perceptual organization put forth by Wertheimer (1923). These principles are typically given a demonstrational type of proof, and that precedent is followed here. Hochberg and McAlister have commented on the status of the laws of organization (1953): "Empirical study of the Gestalt principles of perceptual organization is, despite their great heuristic value, frequently made difficult by their subjective and qualitative formulation" (p. 361). Thus, if readers sometimes have difficulty in understanding the following laws, they need not feel that the inadequacies are all theirs; even the more emphasized perceptual factors, outlined below, are lacking in precision of statement.

1 *Proximity.* Elements close together in time or space tend to be perceived together. For example, the lines in Figure 7-2*a* tend to be seen as three pairs of lines rather than in some other way.

2 *Similarity.* Like elements tend to be seen together in the same structure, other things being equal, as in Figure 7-2*b*.

3 *Direction.* We tend to see figures in such a way that the direction continues smoothly. This factor is illustrated in Figure 7-2*c*.

4 *Objective set.* If one sees a certain type of organization, one continues to do so even though the stimulus factors that led to the original perception are now absent. Consider the series shown in Figure 7-2*d*. As one looks at the dots progressively from left to right, one tends to continue to see the pairs of dots as on the left, even thought on the right the proximity factor no longer favors this organization.

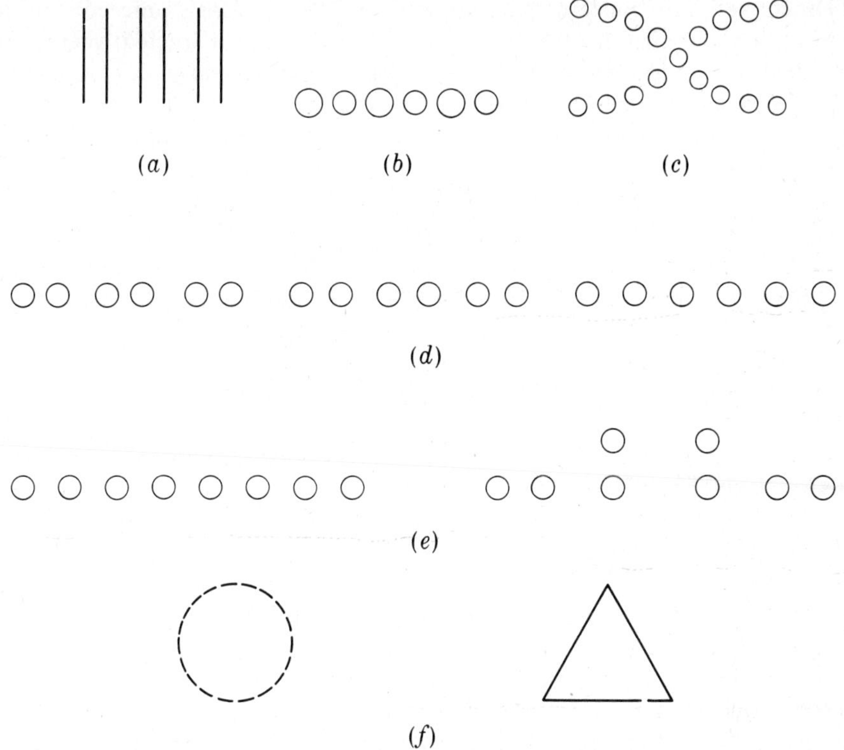

Figure 7-2 Examples of perceptual factors in Gestalt psychology.

5 *Common fate.* Elements shifted in a similar manner from a larger group tend themselves to be grouped, as in Figure 7-2*e*.

6 *Prägnanz.* Figures are seen in as "good" a way as is possible under the stimulus conditions. The good figure is a stable one. For example, as shown in Figure 7-2*f*, gaps in a figure are frequently closed because the resulting figure is more "pregnant" (subprinciple of closure). A good figure is one which cannot be made simpler or more orderly by a perceptual shift.

Wertheimer recognized that the laws of organization were far from final or even completely stated. He suggested by implication some of the work that needed to be done to improve them (1923, as translated in Ellis, 1938): "What will happen when *two* such factors appear in the same constellation? They may be made to cooperate; or, they can be set in opposition. . . . In this way, it is possible to test the strength of these factors" (pp. 76–77).

Koffka, writing 12 years later still could say (1935): "A measurement of the relative strength of these factors would be possible, as Wertheimer has already suggested, by varying these relative distances" (p. 166).

This kind of situation is, unfortunately, a common one in psychology. The effective variables, or at least some effective variables, are often known, but the exact functional relationships relating the effective independent variables to the dependent variables concerned are not known. The Gestaltists proceeded in just the way they criticize in others. Demonstrations were constructed wherein the individual factors can clearly be shown to operate, *other things being equal.* The laws of combination of the factors, their relative strengths, and even precise definitions of the meanings of the variables were and are missing.

Learning Principles

Gestalt psychologists have not worked nearly so extensively in learning as in perception. However, they have done some highly suggestive studies. Köhler's *Mentality of apes* (1925) was based largely on his study at the anthropoid station at Tenerife in the Canary Islands, where he had been marooned during World War I.

It was natural that Köhler saw the problem-solving process in quite a different way from the way the behaviorists and associationists or even the functionalists saw it. Gestalt psychology is based on the premise that perception is determined by the character of the field as a whole. What is more natural than that the Gestaltists should explain learning and problem solving in an analogous fashion? That is just what Köhler did. Problem solution for him became a *restructuring* of the perceptual field. When the problem is presented, something necessary for an adequate solution is missing. The solution occurs when the missing ingredient is supplied so that the field becomes meaningful in relation to the problem presented. For example, one of the chimpanzees in Köhler's experiment was given two sticks which could be joined, enabling him to reach a banana that could be reached in no other way. After many futile attempts to reach the banana with one stick by itself, the chimp gave up and continued to play with the sticks. When he accidentally (or at least idly) joined the two sticks, he immediately reached out and got the banana. The missing perceptual ingredient for the solution had been supplied. The perceptual field had been restructured.

The Gestaltist would want us to notice that the missing *ingredient* in the solution was not a missing *element.* All the elements were always present, but they were not "seen" in the right way. Our very language, in using the word seen in this context, tells us what a close analogy exists between perception and problem solving.

Just as "good" perceptual figures are stable, so learning, once achieved through this insightful restructuring, is stable. The Gestaltists regarded some kinds of learning as requiring a single trial, with the performance being easily repeatable without further practice.

Much Gestalt work has concerned problem solving rather than learning. The two areas are distinguished roughly. Problem solving involves the combination of already learned elements in such a way that a solution is achieved. Learning is usually concerned with the acquisition of relatively simpler, more discrete responses. The distinction is to some extent arbitrary, as is certainly clear from Köhler's experiments with apes, which could be considered either learning or problem solving.

Wertheimer's *Productive thinking* (1945) suggested effective methods for problem solving. He applied the Gestalt principles of learning to human creative thinking. He said that thinking should be in terms of wholes. One should take a broad overview of the situation and not become lost in details. Errors, if inevitable, should at least be good errors, errors with a possibility of success, not blind errors made without regard to the limitations of the situation as a whole upon acceptable solutions. Just as learners should *regard* the situation as a whole, so teachers should *present* the situation as a whole. They should not, like Thorndike, hide the true solution or the true path and require errors. One should not be required or even allowed to take a single blind step, but rather should always be required to keep the goal and the requirements for success in view.

Very modern techniques of programmed, or individualized, instruction usually are designed to eliminate errors, in accordance with Wertheimer's suggestion. These techniques are not based on Gestalt theory, but on repeated experiences with what works best. One could even, with a mighty stretch, point out that "errorless discrimination" as developed by Terrace (1966) is a very effective way to teach simple sensory distinctions, and it, too, is designed to eliminate errors. The mighty stretch is needed in relating this to Wertheimer's suggestions because the Terrace situation is clearly much simpler than the situations Wertheimer was treating.

Duncker (1945) performed an extensive Gestaltist analysis of the problem-solving process. He analyzed the factors in the situation and in the problem-solving procedure which determine difficulty of solution. Like Wertheimer, he believed that the tendency of the subject to narrow the possible solutions is one of the most serious obstacles to successful performance. He devoted a great deal of attention to discussion of fixedness of response. Errors were regarded as helpful in the sense that thinking does not regress to the original ideas about possible solutions when leads are found to be false. Thus errors direct further responses, serving a positive function as well as simply being eliminated. The requirements of the problem situation "ask for" a solution with the required attributes; that is, responses are determined by the total situation, the problem field. Duncker's classic monograph contains many ingenious ideas and examples, but has the usual Gestalt characteristic of being largely nonexperimental and programmatic.

The Gestaltists have generally emphasized the *directed* character of behavior in problem-solving situations. Thorndike emphasized trial-and-error learning, as though the behavior of the animal in the situation were blind and random. Köhler and Wertheimer pointed out the blindness of Thorndike's situation. They believed that the random nature of the activity inhered not in the animal but in the situation. A good solution is possible only if the whole situation is available to the animal. In Thorndike's puzzle-box situation, only the experimenter can see the overall situation. The animal is *reduced* to trial and error by the situation, but to say that learning in general is by trial and error is itself an error.

Thorndike, a favorite Gestalt target (see Chapter 3), had stated that learning is a gradual process of elimination of errors with the accompanying fixation of the correct response. The Gestaltists said that more frequently, learning is not gradual at all, but is rather a process involving insight. We might think of insight as a sudden shift in the perceptual field. There seems to be no basic theoretical reason why the Gestaltists should say that the perceptual shift should be sudden rather than gradual, but Köhler's empirical observations indicated to him that sudden learning does occur. Four behavioral indices of insight learning are usually cited: the sudden transition from helplessness to mastery, the quick and smooth performance once the correct principle is grasped, the good retention, and the immediacy with which the solution can be transferred to other similar situations involving the same principle. Once the sticks had been joined to reach the banana, they would be joined in other situations for reaching other objects if insight were truly involved.

The disagreement about whether learning is continuous, as Thorndike thought, or sudden, as the Gestaltists stated is typically the case, gave rise to the continuity-noncontinuity controversy in learning. According to the continuity position, each trial or reinforcement contributes some increment of response strength. This assumption is denied by the noncontinuity position, which emphasizes sudden discontinuous increments, such as are associated with insights, rather than a slow building up of strength.

This controversy, like many such controversies, is no longer regarded as answerable in a simple yes-or-no fashion. Both continuous and discontinuous improvements in performance occur. A complete learning theory will define all the variables affecting learning and give their functional relations to performance. Both continuous and discontinuous learning curves will be possible, depending upon the values of each of the effective variables over successive trials.

Spence (1940) has shown that Hull's theory, which treats *learning* as continuous, can predict sudden increments of *performance* if the constants in his equations are chosen properly. Then, if there is a sudden shift in a parameter like hours of deprivation from one trial to the next, there will be a sudden increment in performance. The Gestalt assertion is just that such sudden changes can occur, although presumably as a function of other variables besides shifts in deprivation. The Gestalt learning theorist is now faced with the task of writing the equations needed to make a Gestalt learning theory as sophisticated as its competitors, which can now predict the same phenomena. The occurrence of insight, however, is not as critical as some of the more basic tenets of Gestalt theory.

Insight involves structuring, or restructuring, the situation as a whole. Thus it is predicted, from Gestalt theory, that there will be occasions when an animal will respond not absolutely to the local stimulus but to a relationship between stimuli. This is exactly the situation that is said to hold for perception, where the perception accords with the whole field rather than with the local, elementary stimulation. So behavior should depend on the situation as a whole.

The transposition experiment is an example of this principle. An animal is trained to respond to the darker of two gray cards; food is always found behind it. The traditional associative explanation of what has happened in training is that the dark card is now associated with reward, so that the animal approaches it. The lighter card has no association with reward, and it is not approached. However, when the dark card is put with a still darker card, the animal under some conditions chooses the new darker card, even though responding to it has never been reinforced. Koffka (1935) said that in looking at the two cards, a *step* is perceived from lower to higher brightness, and the animal responds to the lower step. Thus, the whole field must be considered in making predictions.

Spence (1937b) has derived the observed relational responding by introducing gradients of generalization of reinforcement from the reinforced card to other values of gray and of inhibition from the lighter card to other values. If the generalization curves are given appropriate shapes, the animal should respond to the new card, according to associative principles. The significant aspect of Spence's transposition demonstration is that it not only allowed for prediction of the Gestalt phenomenon, but also predicted and found failures of transposition when the test stimuli were too different from the training stimuli. The original Gestalt account could not handle these failures.

Hearst (1968) has showed that empirically derived gradients of inhibition and excitation *can* be used to predict discrimination behavior successfully. Even so, the general Gestalt point is again made—that the combination of simple elements presents a complexity requiring new laws for its description (in this case, new equations describing generalization gradients and methods for combining them).

Krechevsky (1932) noted that animals tended to persevere over a number of trials with systematic responses. For example, the animal might respond in terms of a position habit and then suddenly shift to a choice of the brighter of two stimuli. These consistent tendencies he called *hypotheses,* by analogy with a situation in which a human being tries out various alternative solutions until the correct one is found. This finding lent some support to the Gestalt contention that animals were not responding blindly or randomly in their solution of problems. Spence (1936) observed that *hypothesis* is just a name for a persistent response tendency whose history of reinforcement we do not know. Harlow (1951) pointed out that the typical paradigm for insight learning is one in which we do not know the past experience of the animal with the component parts of the problem. Insight did not occur in some experiments in which the subjects were animals without such previous experience.

Levine (1970) has demonstrated that human subjects who are led into generating misleading hypotheses may persist for 100 trials or more in making errors. If these subjects were responding in terms of a simple reinforcement theory, the problem should be solved immediately; the answers can be very simple, for example, "The black card is correct, and the white card is incorrect." Levine's experiments convincingly indicate that human beings, at least, often behave in a way more consistent with a Gestalt view of learning than with more behavioristic alternatives.

Thus Gestalt psychology has pointed to interesting phenomena in the field of learning, but it has not worked out many detailed answers, and the experimentation carried out has often lacked any control of critical background factors that might influence the outcomes. The Gestaltists' theorizing has been highly general, and their explanations usually ad hoc.

Lewin is a case in point. He is a field theorist, and his is the most sophisticated of the field theories of learning. Even so, examination of the theory (Estes, 1954) has revealed that its usefulness is severely curtailed because of its failure to make specific predictions capable of verification or disproof. If the most sophisticated of the Gestalt learning theories suffers from this evaluation, the less sophisticated ones suffer still more from a lack of any predictive power. Lewin's theory will be treated in greater detail in Chapter 11.

GESTALT PSYCHOLOGY AS A SYSTEM

Definition of Psychology

The Gestaltists tended to define psychology as the study of the immediate experience of the whole organism. They intended to include all the areas of psychology within their scope, but they began with perception and emphasized perception more than the other areas. Thus the Gestaltists and those following them have tended to pay more attention to the relationships between antecedents and perception than to those between perception and behavior. They contrast markedly with the behaviorists, who skipped the way station of perception to study the relationships between antecedents and behavior directly.

Postulates

We present here only the few postulates that we feel are most basic, and even these are divided into a primary and a secondary set. The reader can find a more complex list in Helson (1933) or in the original sources.

Gestalt psychology, like behaviorism, seems to have only one really primary postulate which relates to its name and which has finally commanded wide acceptance. This is the postulate related to the whole-part attitude. Any shorter discussion than the one given earlier in this chapter must fail to do it justice, but the following sentences indicate this attitude. The whole dominates the parts and constitutes the primary reality, the primary datum for psychology, the unit most profitable to use in analysis. The whole is not the sum, or the product, or any simple function of its parts, but a field whose character depends upon all of itself.

The secondary postulates, like those of behaviorism, are not necessary to a Gestalt psychology, although the founders made them a part of *the* Gestalt psychology that has developed. The most important of these is the isomorphism principle. A related principle, or perhaps a corollary, is the contemporaneity principle. More specific secondary principles related to the whole-part attitude are the laws of organization. The noncontinuity postulate regarding learning has been discussed as secondary.

None of the Gestalt postulates were entirely new. Even the basic postulate had been anticipated. The thing that made Gestalt psychology new was itself a Gestalt. It was the organization, pattern, or structure of things that Gestaltists said about the whole-part attitude that distinguished their psychology from the philosophical forerunners which had made a case for emergence and from the psychological forerunners which had made a case for phenomenology.

Mind-Body Problem

The Gestaltists, like most psychologists, tried to evade this issue by pointing to the unity of the organism and maintaining that there was no real problem. However, their recognition of experience and their use of the principle of isomorphism implied some kind of dualism, for isomorphism must be a relation between two different sets of events. Isomorphism itself says nothing about the particular subvariety of dualism that should be chosen. Since the Gestaltists attempted to make light of the problem, and since their whole-part attitude emphasized the emergence of new levels of description, new *aspects* of complex phenomena, the mind-body position that seems most consistent with their general position is a dual-aspect view. This view gives two aspects that can be isomorphic, and yet it allows the statement that there is somehow really only one basic reality seen in two views—that the organism is really unitary and integrated.

Prentice expressed the Gestalt desire to avoid the issue:

> Let me say once for all that the concept of isomorphism is not an attempt to solve the mind-body problem in its usual metaphysical form. It takes no stand whatsoever on the question of whether "mind" is more or less "real" than "matter." Questions of reality and existence are not raised at all. Mind and body are dealt with as two natural phenomena whose interrelations we are trying to understand. . . . It comes nearest, perhaps, to what has sometimes been called the "double aspect" theory, the view that cortical events and phenomenal facts are merely two ways of looking at the same natural phenomenon, two faces of the same coin, as it were. (1959, p. 435)

However, Prentice has apparently not been allowed to have his say "once for all," since R. I. Watson says (1968): ". . . by his statement of isomorphism Köhler was offering his particular solution to the age-old mind-body problem. Isomorphism was his way of integrating the mind with the rest of the world" (p. 448). Obviously, it is not easy to agree on just what kind of stand is required to constitute a mind-body position.

Nature of the Data

Immediate, unanalyzed experience obtained by naïve introspection furnished the bulk of the data for Gestalt psychology. The "given," as they called such experience, was used as data. Behavioral data were also used, notably in the fields of learning and problem solving, but behavioral data were less important because of the larger number of perceptual studies.

Because the behaviorists were making a different point and because they deemphasize experience, it is easy to miss the fact that both schools tended to accept the same types of data and that both schools were making a point that converged on the same criterion for acceptability of data. The behaviorists, although they rejected consciousness, accepted verbal behavior as data when there was consistency and agreement within the given experimental condition. The Gestaltists, although accepting experience and consciousness, rejected a certain kind of analysis of that experience. They retained the given in consciousness. Now, that given was generally very nearly coterminous with the class of verbal behavior which was acceptable to a behaviorist. Wertheimer, when he talked about the given, talked about trees and windows. Watson, when he wished to make the point that consciousness was not part of science, contrasted it with things that were—contents of test tubes, things that he could see and feel and lift. Both were using primarily an object language. A long history of usage has demonstrated that we can agree about the meaning of such a language. Thus, although the two schools started from quite different points, they tended to accept about the same kinds of data as being of interest in their kind of psychology. The Gestaltists were more tolerant; they could afford to accord a kind of reality to the results of the old introspection, while the behaviorists, whose whole existence was based on this methodological point, could not.

Principles of Selection

For the Gestalt psychologist, every part of the field played some role in perceptual structuring. Thus the problem for the Gestaltist was not so much how the given was selected as how it was structured. Why, out of all the possible alternatives, did the actual structure emerge? One principle was that in a given perceptual whole, part of the perception will be figure, and part ground. Rubin's laws governing the selection of the figure state how this segregation takes place. Wertheimer's laws of organization are also laws of selection in the same sense; they explain the particular form taken by the figure. Neither Rubin nor Wertheimer worked out the laws in great detail, as we have already seen in the case of Wertheimer. J. J. Gibson's later work (1966) has done much more to specify the properties of stimuli which make them available as invariants for the organism's stimulus processing. Maturana et al. (1960) used objective physiological responses to discover some of the properties of stimuli that were responded to by the frog's eye. Maturana and his coworkers found that the frog's eye contains cells that respond only to small curved moving objects within a circumscribed receptive area; that is, these cells "select" only those objects possessing the right *set* of complex properties. Gibson argues that such complex "invariants" are the primary stimuli for most human perception. Such work fits neatly into the Gestalt tradition. None of this leads to a denial of the role of experience in determining which perception or which behavior would be selected. However, it does place more emphasis on the current situation, and it does demand attention to the complex relational properties of the situation in determining response to it.

Principles of Connection

The form of the problem of connection was also different for a Gestaltist. Since elementarism was rejected, one form of the question of connection could also be ignored. It is not meaningful to try to reconstruct wholes by connecting elements which are supposed to be the parts of the whole. The Gestaltists believed that the *bundle hypothesis* was completely fallacious. The bundle hypothesis treated complex perceptions as though they were a bundle of simple perceptions and treated meaning as though it arose from such a bundling. Thus one of the Gestalt principles was negative; it was that the bundle hypothesis is invalid, and therefore one of the problems of connection is an artificial problem arising from an artificial analysis. The laws of organization are not principles of connection, for organizations are not elements connected. The laws state what structures will arise, not what elements will be connected.

It follows that Gestalt psychology would have more to say about how elements would be *related* in a particular whole than about how elements would be connected. The extensive work of Johansson (see Hochberg, 1957) on relative movement in two or more objects provides an interesting example. The general and surprising finding is that when the objects have a common component of movement, that component will be "partialed out" of the total movement, and seen as a movement of a common frame; the remaining component of the total movement will be seen as movement of the separate objects relative to each other. What makes this surprising from a non-Gestalt point of view is that the perceived movement of the "frame" does not necessarily exist in the objective stimulus, nor need the remaining relative movement component! However, this makes for a simple description of the total movement, as (the Gestaltists would say) should be expected.

Another form of the problem of connection cannot be avoided by any system. This is the problem of the connection or relationship between antecedents and consequents in laws. The Gestaltists have stated that the relationships are dynamic and that the significant relationships are between fields. Their experiments have illustrated a few of these relationships, and their principle of isomorphism states another relationship in advance.

CRITICISMS OF GESTALT PSYCHOLOGY

Gestalt psychology has been criticized chiefly for its nebulous character. Many hardheaded scientists have maintained that it does not really assert anything. This criticism seems to be at least partially justified. Harrower, one of Koffka's students, may be typical of the Gestalt school in her attitude toward the problem of definition of terms in psychology:

> Much criticism has accrued to Gestalt theory for its use of the term "organization," which has not yet been sufficiently rigorously defined to meet the demands of many psychologists. And if, in the realm of perception, where as yet it has been predominantly employed, one meets with the criticism of its vagueness and ambiguity, how much more open to attack will be its preliminary appearance in investigations concerning the higher mental processes.
>
> And yet we deliberately give no precise definition of our use of the term, for with Dewey we believe that "Definitions are not ends in themselves, but instrumentalities for facilitating the development of a concept into forms where its applicability to given facts may best be tested." And since we believe that the concept is already in such form as to make it applicable to our facts, we leave more precise definition until experimental results can contribute towards it. (1932, p. 57)

Harrower's cool bow in the direction of definition does not help in bringing experimental facts to bear. Psychologists need to have some way of distinguishing a situation that is an organization from one that is not if they are to carry out empirical investigations on the subject. We have seen nearly the same criticism raised in reference to the principles of organization. However, Gestaltists can certainly defend themselves by pointing their fingers at other psychologists, who are also often obscure or incomplete in their definitions, although presumably much concerned with problems of definition. The often conflicting usages of the basic words *stimulus* and *response* are examples; Koch (1954) gives a specific treatment of conflicting usage by a single author, which could easily be applied to many others. The Gestaltist, perhaps, has been more cautious, preferring to await more results before rigidifying meanings of words.

Gestalt psychology has been criticized for having too high a ratio of theory and criticism to experiment and positive empirical statements. Gestalt psychology has certainly been experimental, but the devastation wrought by its criticism has not always been repaired quickly by its positive statements. A closely related criticism is that Gestalt psychology has not furnished a system with predictive power. Gates, in defending Thorndike's identical-elements theory of transfer of training, has presented a criticism which, if justified, invalidates the Gestalt theory of transfer:

> The Gestaltists somewhat similarly insist that transfer depends upon "insight." The objection to these views is not that they are wrong, but merely that they are too vague and restricted. To say that one transfers his learning when he generalizes is not saying much more than "You generalize when you generalize." "You get transfer when you get it." We must go deeper than that. In a scientific sense, no theory of transfer is a full or final explanation, but the Thorndike formulations at least point to a number of factors, observation and study of which enable us to improve learning. (1942, p. 153)

Gates's criticism can probably be generalized to other areas, but is especially true of learning, where the associationists, functionalists, and behaviorists have been able to present some fairly specific theories. The Gestaltist has said, in effect: "Your theory is necessarily inadequate for the following reasons, and an adequate theory must take the following form." But the Gestaltist has not often said what the specific statements of this programmatic theory shall be. Thus, the proponent of the theory attacked can often say that the Gestaltist's criticism may be correct but that the Gestaltist has done no better or has in fact presented *nothing but* criticism. But this is true of most critics. They do not have time to present correct theories in detail, especially where such theories must wait upon empirical spadework.

These first two criticisms picture Gestalt psychology as more nebulous and programmatic than most systems. Even if there is at least a grain of truth in these criticisms, the third one, that Gestalt psychology has been metaphysical and mystical, is certainly not justified. The feeling that it is mystical probably comes largely from the difficulty of presenting its central points clearly. This difficulty was initially compounded in the United States by problems of translation and by the fact that Gestalt psychology arose from a cultural background somewhat foreign to Americans. When Gestalt psychology is properly understood, it seems to be as much a natural science as behaviorism and often is more sophisticated. Gestaltists universally reject vitalism, which is often a mark of some degree of mysticism. Sometimes certain behaviorists who cannot think in other than mechanistic terms make the accusation that those who reject mechanistic explanations are vitalists, and certainly a part of Gestalt psychology's paradigm is a rejection of a simple view of mechanism. Heider states the actual Gestalt attitude very strongly (1973): "They abhorred vitalism because it implied the presence of a mysterious metaphysical agency that reaches into the world of nature from outside and is somehow made responsible for the order of the world as we perceive it" (p. 68).

Weiss sums up the source of, and reply to, this kind of objection as follows:

> The unorthodox dissenters usually phrased their argument in the age-old adage that "the whole is *more* than the sum of its parts." Look at this phrasing and you will discover the root of the distrust, and indeed, outright rejection, of the valid principle behind it. What did they mean by stating that "an organism is *more* than the sum of its cells and humors"; that "a cell is *more* than its content of molecules"; that "brain function is *more* than the aggregate of activities of its constituent neurons"; and so on? As the term "more" unquestionably connotes some tangible addition, an algebraic plus, one naturally had to ask: "More of what? Dimensions, mass, electric charges?" Surely none of those. Then what? Perhaps something unfathomable, weightless, chargeless, nonmaterial? All sorts of agents have indeed been invoked in that capacity—entelechy, *élan vital,* formative drive, vital principle—all idle words, unpalatable to most scientists for being just fancy names for an unknown X.
>
> Unfortunately, in their aversion to the supernatural, the scientific purists poured out the baby with the intellectually soiled bath water by repudiating the very aspect of wholeness in nature that had conjured up those cover terms for ignorance. (1967, p. 801)

A common and serious objection to Gestalt psychology has involved its usage of "field" analogies from physics. These criticisms are discussed more fully in Chapter 11, where the central issue is the notion of field. Here we shall preview that discussion by pointing out that physicists (Oppenheimer, 1956) and psychologists (Estes, 1954; Spence, 1948) alike have seriously questioned whether the analogy between the term *field* as it is used in physics and as it was used in psychology by the Gestaltists is close enough to be useful.

One of the specific objections to the speculation found in the Gestalt system has been to its physiological assumptions. As we have previously pointed out, the principle of isomorphism has made these speculations easy. However, speculation is a part, and a useful part, of every system. The Gestaltists have frankly admitted, in most cases, that their physiologizing is speculative. It has no effect on the validity of their experimental results and has in fact stimulated or suggested experimentation. Prentice (1959) gives one vivid account of the relation between theory and experiment. Besides, orthodox physiologizing, like Thorndike's assumptions about synaptic changes with learning, is just as speculative and no more likely to be correct.

The criticism that Gestalt psychology is antianalytic has already been countered in the discussion of the Gestalt attitude toward analysis.

The experimentation of Gestalt psychologists has been criticized for being poorly controlled, nonquantitative, and nonstatistical. Experimenters have been accused of giving the subjects cues which affected learning in unknown ways and of ignoring possible effects of past experience. It is true that the Gestaltists' level of sophistication in experiments has not been up to the level of their criticism and metatheory construction. However, they consciously feel that qualitative results must come first. Thus the experiments have purposely been nonquantitative and nonstatistical. Since new areas have been explored, or old areas explored from an entirely new point of view, it is natural that the experiments performed have often been of a preliminary, tentative sort. Anyway, such a criticism of experimentation, if valid in some individual cases, is not a criticism of Gestalt psychology but of particular Gestalt psychologists. Gestalt psychology certainly does not advocate poorly designed experiments. Poor experiments have been done under the aegis of every school, but with the sanction of none.

Other criticisms can be treated very lightly. One is that Gestalt psychology is not new. This can always be said, but (1) Gestalt psychology is as new as any school ever is, a point almost too obvious to discuss, and (2) the criticism is not even relevant to the merits of the system as it stands. The criticism that Gestalt psychology sets up straw men to attack in each of the older systems is also irrelevant; it applies to Gestalt psychology as an objection to other systems, but not to its positive program.

THE CONTRIBUTIONS AND PRESENT STATUS OF GESTALT PSYCHOLOGY

The experiments done by Gestaltists are an unquestioned contribution to psychology. This is the statement that is safest about any system. Gestalt psychologists have often done experiments which challenged the cherished beliefs of others. For example, latent learning and Zeigarnik effects (see Chapter 11), experimentally demonstrated, contributed to the difficulties of associationistic learning theorists and stimulated much research. Sometimes Gestalt psychology itself could not have predicted the results, but a fresh-thinking upstart can afford to create difficulties for himself as well as for others.

Hochberg (1957) reviewed a number of experimental results in his report of a symposium on the Gestalt revolution; we have already mentioned the Johansson experiments on perceived motion. Another set of experiments by Ivo Kohler of Innsbruck is also particularly interesting. He created several types of disturbances to normal stimulation and observed perceptual and behavioral adaptations to the disturbances. In one rather representative experiment, the left half of each of a pair of spectacles was made blue, and the right half yellow. Then, when the spectacles were worn, white objects to the left of center were seen as blue, and white objects to the right as yellow. After long adaptation, objects remained constant in color despite eye movement. Then when the glasses were taken off, the world appeared yellow with eyes left and blue with eyes right! This fact illustrates a relational determination of color which is *completely* independent of local stimulation. Gestalt psychology could hardly have asked nature to provide a clearer demonstration of the inadequacy of the "mosaic hypothesis."

It was suggested that Kohler's results could be summed up as an elimination of invariable relations in order to achieve a maximum amount of information via a description which eliminated unneeded complexity. Thus in the blue-yellow spectacles experiment, it would invariably be the case that blue light would be received with eyes left, and yellow light with eyes right. This common blue or yellow bias could be filtered out in perception without loss of information, and it was. The resulting "normal" perception was quite relational, and thus very much in keeping with the older Gestalt views.

These experiments and others provide abundant illustration that local stimulation may not be well correlated with local sensation. Though Kohler's observations emphasize the importance of perceptual learning, this direction of emphasis is by no means diametrically opposed to Gestalt precepts. The Gestalt position tended toward nativism because an antidote was needed. The structuralists had tended too often to hide behind the skirts of past associations whenever empirical facts belied what their elementaristic anlaysis led them to expect. Now that structuralism is gone and the nebulous past associations are passé as a refuge, the Gestalt position on nativism-empiricism can relax to a more natural neutral position.

The evidence gathered by Land (1959), apparently independently of any systematic preconceptions, gives additional support to the Gestalt antimosaic hypothesis. Color perception, according to Land, is to a large extent independent of the nature of the stimulation of the individual retinal receptors; the perception of color depends, rather, upon relationships over the whole retina. Land believed that information about colors is gathered, and that colors are therefore seen, because objects of different colors reflect different proportions of "warm" and "cool" light. Thus negatives exposed through filters that screen long (warm) and short (cool) parts of the spectrum differently contain information about the colors of the objects present.

A very interesting demonstration follows. Land exposed two black-and-white negatives to the same scene, one through the long filter and one through the short. Then each developed negative was put into a projector, and the images from the two projectors were precisely super-imposed upon the screen. Viewers reported seeing a wide range of colors, despite the use of the black-and-white film! Land's findings could not give better support to the Gestalt antimosaic hypothesis if they had been especially made up for that purpose. This does *not* mean they supported the details of Gestalt color theory, for Land believed that his results demanded a reformulation of all color theories. Walls (1960) disagreed with Land, and held that traditional explanations in terms of contrast and induction were adequate to explain the observations. Regardless of who turns out to be closer to the truth with respect to the details, Land's redirection of attention to these color phenomena again vindicates the general Gestalt methodological emphasis on fields.

Gestalt psychology, then, is not a useful failure like structuralism. It is a going concern. It is more actively a school today than any of the systems we have discussed so far. One of its founders, Wolfgang Köhler, in 1956 received a Distinguished Contribution Award from the American Psychological Association, and in 1959 he served as its president. One of the reasons Gestalt psychology still has some of its school character is probably that its main points are not quite as well assimilated into psychology as the main points of the older schools and the more native (to America) behaviorism. Until Köhler's death in 1967, it still had a founder to organize around. Its propositions, especially those which concerned the whole-part relationship, involved complexities that still require working out, and that has kept scientists interested. Modern systems theory is just developing some of the techniques required for dealing with organized wholes.

Wellek (1968), in discussing the German immigration into the United States before World War II, hypothesized that the impact of Gestalt psychology would have been much less if the immigration had not occurred. Perhaps, says Wellek, it would have been no greater than that of the Würzburg school. We believe that America did indeed profit from the influx of brilliant minds, but that the influence of Gestalt psychology would have been almost as great, though delayed, without the immigration. American psychology needed, although it did not want, the Gestalt ideas. The Gestalt psychologists needed a haven from the terror of Naziism, either because (like Wertheimer) they were Jewish, or (like Köhler) because they were too courageous to walk away from defending their friends, even though they risked their lives to do so (Crannell, 1970).

Köhler lived to see the Gestalt whole-part attitude accepted as at least theoretically correct. Psychology has also accepted the theoretical correctness of the contemporaneity principle, although many psychologists still study historical variables because of their easier availability. The primacy of perception and the methodological dependency of sensation on perception are also accepted. Moreover, Gestalt psychology has led directly to stimulating and significant work within orthodox areas of general psychology (e.g., Asch, Hay, & Diamond, 1960, on verbal learning; Katona, 1940, on memory).

The attitudes of Gestalt psychology have been easily assimilated by cognitive psychologists, particularly by those working with computer models of learning, memory, and performance. Gestaltists tend to be centralistic, to emphasize organization in memory, and to concentrate on the use of principles rather than on the influence of habits. All of these tendencies are very consistent with modern developments in computer modeling. We cannot credit the Gestalt position directly with the development of the cognitive or computer-oriented approaches, but it is easy to see the intellectual similarities. Thus the current great activity in these areas strengthens our belief in the importance of the conceptions originally presented by the Gestaltists.

Lastly, Gestalt psychology has contributed to psychology even where its tenets were rejected. Its sharp criticism has required some reexamination and revamping on the part of every system which wished to stand in opposition to it. It has pointed to phenomena which existing systems could not incorporate, and these systems were energized by an order of criticism and competition that they might not otherwise have had.

A DIMENSIONAL DESCRIPTION OF GESTALT PSYCHOLOGY

It is pretty clear that the most important of Watson's dimensions for Gestalt psychology is molarism-molecularism. Our student survey put centralism in second place, and that is certainly a good choice when one considers the Gestalt emphasis on perception, which is a central process. Purism was voted a third place, but with a very moderate rating. Other reasonable choices of important dimensions might include dynamicism as opposed to staticism, since the Gestaltists placed so much stress on restructuring of fields as underlying learning, and the dynamic structuring which presumably organizes our perceptions. We would say, however, that Gestalt psychology tended toward staticism when that dimension opposes developmentalism, for the Gestaltists opposed the exclusive reliance on past experience as a sufficient account of perceptual organization and learning ability.

A dimension which presents some difficulty is the complex nomothetic-idiographic opposition. The idiographic approach tends to involve an insistence on "realism" and therefore to study situations in which many variables are free to act, as contrasted to a tightly controlled laboratory situation. The idiographicist also is likely to look closely at individual data, rather than to go quickly to statistical summaries of group characteristics. In these two senses, Gestalt psychology looks idiographic. However, the key distinction is that the nomotheticist seeks general laws, while the idiographicist seeks to explain individuals—to understand them in their uniqueness. In this sense, the Gestaltists were just as nomothetic as the structuralists with their "generalized human mind," and therefore "qualify" as nomotheticists. In looking at the table of the authors' ratings, therefore, the reader should probably regard our rating on this dimension as too idiographic.

Finally, disagreements sometimes arise with respect to the Gestalt position on rationalism versus irrationalism. We believe that the Gestalt emphasis on intellectual ability, even to the extent that insight becomes typical of learning in the chimpanzee, gives Gestaltists a very clear rationalistic bias. Further, the Gestaltists had a nativistic tendency, and that is usually associated with rationalism because our at-birth equipment should have evolved to give us "rational" responses to our environments. Wertheimer's book, *Productive thinking,* (1945) like other Gestalt publications, stressed the open presentation of a total problem situation, plus taking a *reasonable* approach to solving the problem.

SUMMARY AND CONCLUSIONS

Gestalt psychology originated in Frankfurt am Main, Germany, between 1910 and 1912. Wertheimer, Köhler, and Koffka arrived at their basic position after an examination of the experience of apparent movement (phi phenomenon). Their psychology was more phenomenological than that of Wundt; they accepted introspection but changed its character. One of their basic objections to the old psychology concerned its artificiality of analysis. They disliked the quest for the elements of experience and noted that the simple combination of elements was inadequate to produce the features of the whole. The *whole* in psychology, as in physics, required laws of its own, and psychology should try to find these laws.

For the Gestaltists, the laws of science were the laws of systems. They set out to apply their points of view to the fields of perception and learning. In perception, they put forth the laws of organization. In learning, they found the same kinds of principles. They objected to the overuse of past experience as an explanatory concept both in perception and in learning. Learning and problem solving were seen in relationship to restructuring of the perceptual field. Only influences on this field that were presently active could be used in the explanation of perception and behavior. Gestalt psychology has been accepted in part in America. Many of its criticisms of structuralistic and behavioristic psychology have been accepted as cogent, and these criticisms have forced the reformulation of those theoretical positions. Gestalt psychology is still itself an active force.

FURTHER READINGS

G. W. Hartmann's *Gestalt psychology* (1935) is a fine source for the student who seeks information about, and appraisal of, Gestalt psychology in the same book. It gives excellent historical background and a good explanation of the basic position. Köhler's *Gestalt psychology* (1947) is the most readable of the primary sources by the three founders; Koffka's *Principles of Gestalt psychology* (1935), while less readable, is more thorough. Koffka's book is the most comprehensive treatment in English by one of the founders. Wertheimer is represented in English by the posthumous *Productive thinking* (1945), which is brief and incomplete. For translations of early papers, Ellis's *Source book of Gestalt psychology* (1938) is, as the title suggests, a classic source for some of the most important of the basic Gestalt writings. Henle's *Documents of Gestalt psychology* (1961) also provides a useful source for many of the basic Gestalt writings. Prentice's article entitled "The systematic psychology of Wolfgang Köhler" (1959) is an easily available summary. Köhler's *Task of Gestalt psychology* (1969), prepared for posthumous publication by Solomon Asch, Mary Henle, and Edwin Newman, presents a broad review of the Gestalt movement (including an introductory eulogy by Carroll Pratt). Henle has recently (1971) edited a new collection of papers by Köhler. An article by Crannell (1970) is interesting for its description of Köhler's personal courage in the face of Nazi persecution. Fritz Heider (1970) provides some good background for Gestalt theory, including descriptions of Meinong and Benussi. Hochberg's summary of the Cornell symposium (1957) is a succinct appetizer for those who are curious about the kind of perceptual work which is now being done with a methodology which is Gestalt in orientation. Finally, Weiss's (1967) article can be unhesitatingly recommended for those who still do not believe that, under some conditions, $1 + 1 \neq 2$.

Table 8-1 Important Figures in Psychoanalysis

Antecedent influences	Psychoanalysts		
	Pioneers	Founder	Developers
G. W. Leibniz (1646–1715)	Johann Friedrich Herbart (1776–1841)	Sigmund Freud (1856–1939)	Alfred Adler (1870–1937)
Johann Wolfgang Goethe (1749–1832)	Arthur Schopenhauer (1788–1860)		C. G. Jung (1875–1961)
Gustav Theodor Fechner (1801–1887)	Jean Martin Charcot (1825–1893)		Sandor Ferenczi (1873–1933)
Charles Darwin (1809–1882)	Joseph Breuer (1842–1925)		Otto Rank (1884–1939)
			Karen Horney (1885–1952)
			Harry S. Sullivan (1892–1949)
			Erich Fromm (1900–)

Chapter 8

Psychoanalysis

Psychoanalysis is the most widely known psychological system, especially among nonpsychologists. Although it has long been rejected by some academic psychologists, it has been more popular in other scientific and technical areas, in literary circles, and with the lay public. More recently, it has become a growing concern within some of the previously recalcitrant groups of academic psychologists.

The body of psychoanalytic writing is enormous. Freud's collected works alone, in their English translation, run to twenty-four volumes. We must therefore present a synoptic treatment.

The fact that discussion of psychoanalysis has a critical tone cannot be taken as a denial that Freud and his followers made an enormous contribution to psychology. Despite all objections to his theory, Freud has been rated by American psychologists as by far the most eminent pyschological theoretician of all time (Coan and Zagona, 1962). The reader should bear this in mind when reading the critical parts of the present chapter. These criticisms should be regarded not as an attempt to belittle the psychoanalytic contribution, but as an indication of flaws which need to be eliminated before psychoanalytic theory can gain complete acceptance by the scientific community.

Table 8-1 lists the more important names associated with psychoanalysis.

HISTORICAL ANTECEDENTS OF PSYCHOANALYSIS

Psychoanalysis fell upon the world like a bomb. The shock of some of its concepts and principles was so great that most people regarded it as entirely new. Yet it, too, had many antecedents—so many that they again resign us to the fact that there is rarely anything entirely new in the world of ideas.

In the development of psychoanalysis, there were two kinds of influences. There was an intellectual tradition in which Freud can be placed, as Bakan (1958) has suggested, and there was another set of more direct, personal influences on Freud. Let us consider the former first.

Early in the eighteenth century, Leibniz developed a theory about the elements of reality that differed in kind from most of the previous theories. His elements were called *monads,* and they were extremely unlike the mechanistic atoms of Democritus. They were not even material in the usual sense, but could better be described as centers of energy. Each such center was independent of the others, with a source of striving within itself; a monad might be regarded as a center of motivation, a self-moved entity. Activity was the basic condition for being. Freud took a decisive step in his career when he turned away from the mechanistic tradition, in which he had been nurtured scholastically, to the more dynamic tradition represented by Leibniz.

Leibniz also pointed to the unconscious and to degrees of consciousness. A century later, Herbart took over some of Leibniz's ideas and worked out a mathematics of the conflict of ideas as they strive to become conscious. Freud, then, was not the first to "discover" the unconscious; his unique contribution was his detailed characterization of the unconscious and its mode of operation. Freud (1938, p. 939) yielded precedence to Schopenhauer for the idea of repression into the unconscious and resistance to recognizing repressed material; however, he said that he developed the same ideas without having read Schopenhauer.

Freud attended the lectures of Franz Brentano, who was at the time a very popular lecturer in Vienna. No doubt Brentano introduced him to the Leibnizian mode of thought, for Brentano based his own psychological ideas on *activity* rather than on elements.

The German romantic scientific tradition played a somewhat more direct role for Freud. Schelling and Goethe were two of the most important figures in this tradition. Freud said that he decided upon a scientific career after hearing a poem of Goethe's called "Nature." Jones (1953) suggested that Freud saw his way to power through an extremely deep understanding of nature.

Freud's formal training put him in quite another tradition, the more mechanistic school of Helmholtz. For Freud, its direct representative was Ernst Brücke, with whom he was closely associated for years at the Vienna Physiological Institute. Brücke, Ludwig, and Du Bois-Reymond had formed an antivitalistic pact with Helmholtz when all were in their twenties (Boring, 1950, p. 708). They intended to force acceptance of the notion that there are no forces within living bodies that are not to be found in nonliving bodies. Part of what motivated Helmholtz to write his earlier paper on the conservation-of-energy principle was a desire to show that there is no unique energy unaccounted for within the organism considered as a physical system. Perhaps contact with this tradition later helped Freud to view the dreams and fantasies, wit and errors, of humans as determinate and to formulate his own version of the determinacy of human behavior, which he called *psychic determinism.* It is possible that a familiarity with Helmholtz's concept of "unconscious inference," used as a way of describing how we reach conclusions in perception in the absence of identifiable cognitive processes, may have been of more direct help in pointing Freud toward the importance of unconscious processes.

Freud was no doubt reinforced in his determinism by his reading and discussion of Charles Darwin's evolutionary thesis with others in the institute and in the hospital where he studied during the course of obtaining his medical degree. He tended to take a biological view of man in accord with Darwin's biological view, and many of his ideas drew directly upon evolutionary theory; an example is the death instinct, which he said depends upon speculation about the origins of life. Freud's ideas about the almost exclusive importance of sexual motives can hardly have been completely independent of evolutionary thinking, in which reproduction is necessarily the central issue.

Hughlings Jackson combined a physiological and an evolutionary outlook in his influence on Freud. He conceived the notion that nervous systems achieve, through evolutionary development, a hierarchical structure in which the higher structures are more complex, but less completely determined in structure. The precise interconnections of the higher structures are then developed during the life of the individual. In nervous diseases, Jackson thought there is a process which he called *dissolution,* the approximate opposite of the process of evolutionary development. Freud, in turn, apparently patterned his idea of regression after Jackson's dissolution (Herrnstein & Boring, 1965, p. 248).

Two somewhat conflicting traditions, which we may refer to as the romantic and the mechanistic, thus had some influence on Freud. The romantic and mystical side was strengthened by Freud's Jewish religious background, which contained strong mystical components. The Jewish writings also attributed a mystical significance to sex. Bakan (1958) has documented this influence.

One man, Gustav Fechner, seems to have shared the mechanistic-romantic conflict with Freud and finally to have solved it by being rigorously scientific about an essentially mystical, romantic problem—the mind-body issue. It seems that the kind of genius most peculiar to psychology has been of just this type. Among others who have "naturalized" some kind of theretofore mystical phenomena, we may mention Darwin (natural selection and evolution), Ebbinghaus (memory), Pavlov (associations in behavior), and Skinner ("superstitious" behavior). Ellenberger (1956), among others, has shown in some detail that there was a direct relationship between Fechner and Freud. Freud confessed to an admiration of Fechner and was familiar with his writings. Freud's concern with the intensity of stimulation, with mental energy, and with the topographical concept of mind was related to Fechner's prior work.

THE LIFE OF SIGMUND FREUD

Sigmund Freud (1856–1939) is almost universally considered a giant among psychologists, even by those who think he was a misguided giant. For that reason, and because his system was based to an appreciable extent on his observations of himself, his life deserves a closer look than we have afforded most of our "founders."

Freud was born in what is now Pribor, Czechoslovakia on May 6, 1856. His father, Jacob, was primarily in the business of dyeing and dressing wool cloth at that time; there is no direct evidence as to how he supported his family later, after they moved to Vienna by way of Leipzig. Pribor was at that time Freiberg, Austria, and the family had arrived in Vienna by the time young Sigmund was 4.

It soon became clear that Sigmund had great academic aptitude. He eventually decided upon medicine as a career, although he neither liked the practice of medicine nor identified himself closely with the medical profession. He postponed the taking of the medical examinations while he spent his time working under Brücke in the institute on problems that were purely scientific and thus more friendly to his temper. He hoped eventually to become a professor of anatomy, rather than a physician. He finally gave up hope of academic advancement and decided to take his medical examinations and training at the hospital in order that he might enter private practice as a physician. Brücke had apparently helped him to arrive at this decision. Freud's Jewishness may have impeded his advancement, but another factor was apparently the great length of time that might elapse before a position became available.

Even prior to his taking the examinations for the M.D. degree, Freud felt an interest primarily in neurology or psychiatry among the medical specialties. In the hospital, his feelings were reinforced. From 1880 on, he wavered between study of the anatomy of the nervous system and study of psychiatry. He published many papers on anatomy, among them one concerning a new method of staining nervous tissue and a paper containing the germ of the neuron theory. At one time he became interested in cocaine and suggested its efficacy to one of his colleagues, who discovered its anesthetic properties. Freud was intensely disappointed that he had missed the opportunity to make this discovery and achieve the fame that attended it. He was more interested in cocaine's potency as a tranquilizer, and recommended its use to friends. One substituted a cocaine addiction for a prior addiction, and Freud received reprimands from his colleagues rather than the recognition he so much desired.

From the 1870s to the early 1890s, Freud was befriended by Josef Breuer, a practicing physician. Breuer gave his impoverished younger colleague money as well as advice and friendship. The two later were estranged at about the time Freud became closely attached to another physician, Wilhelm Fliess. The Fliess association led to an unusually close relationship during the years when Freud was first formulating his notions on psychoanalysis.

In 1885, Freud obtained a grant to study in Paris. He studied under Charcot, a famous Parisian hypnotist, teacher, and authority on hysteria. Freud already had some interest in hypnosis as a method of treatment, and the interest was strengthened by Charcot. Back in Vienna, he reported to his colleagues what he had seen and learned about hysteria and hypnosis. His report was not taken as a revelation by the Viennese Medical Society, and the young pioneer was embittered. Ellenberger (1970, p. 448 ff.), however, finds no evidence that Freud was rejected or isolated, and sees Freud's feelings at that time as probably neurotic.

The young Freud continued to use hypnosis in his practice to supplement massage, baths, and the mild kind of electrotherapy then in vogue. He later discontinued the latter, commenting that the only reason he disagreed with those who attributed the effects of electrotherapy to suggestion was that he did not observe any results to explain. This sort of ironic acceptance of reality remained typical of Freud's approach to life and to himself.

By 1895, Freud had lost interest in anatomy. He and Breuer had published *Studies in hysteria,* which marked the beginning of the psychoanalytic school. He wrote no more articles or books on neurology, with the exception of one encyclopedia article in 1897.

It was about this time, too, that Freud became estranged from Breuer and established Fliess as his mentor—this in spite of the fact that Fliess was 2 years Freud's junior and intellectually his inferior. Freud was highly dependent upon Fliess during this most neurotic period of his life. He was overdependent, jealous, sometimes domineering, overly concerned with death, and hypochondriacal.

In 1897, Freud began a full-scale self-analysis. One of its results was the growth of his ability to stand on his own feet. Fliess and Freud had a disagreement in 1900, perhaps over some of Fliess's highly speculative ideas about the periodicity of behavior. Freud later attributed their alienation to an analysis he had made of Fliess's choice of occupation. The final separation followed several years later; Freud had been indirectly responsible for the plagiarism by one of his own patients of Fliess's ideas on bisexuality and had refused first to acknowledge any responsibility and then later to apologize.

Perhaps the greatest milestone in Freud's career was the publication of *The interpretation of dreams* in 1900, 2 years after the death of his father. According to Jones (1953, p. 324) and to Freud's own interpretation, the necessary freeing of the unconscious could occur only after the father was gone. Not long after this he began to gain recognition and soon had gathered around him a group of collaborators. His role became that of the father rather than of the son. Jung, Adler, Rank, and Ferenczi were first disciples and then rebels. Various difficulties in personal interaction usually started the rebellion, and the young group of psychoanalysts was intolerant of disagreement within its ranks. At one time a committee of the faithful was formed composed of Abraham, Eitingon, Ferenczi, Rank, Jones, and Sachs. The committee was to further analytic work. Freud gave each member a setting for a seal ring like the one he wore.

Through the committee and an ever-growing body of publications, Freud became successful and widely known. One of the first marks of his international recognition was G. Stanley Hall's invitation to speak at Clark University's twentieth anniversary celebration in 1909. Freud spoke, as did Jung; among the analysts present were Ferenczi, Jones, and Brill, while Titchener, Cattell, and James were among the famous academic psychologists who attended. James Putnam, a professor of neurology at Harvard University, became a steadfast friend of analysis at this time.

Jung later returned to the United States for further lectures and reported that he had little trouble in getting analytic doctrine accepted if he ceased to emphasize sex so heavily. This widened an already existing breach between Jung and Freud. It is impossible to summarize accurately the reasons for the final break between these two giants of the psychoanalytic movement. Fortunately, their correspondence has now been published, and those who are interested in this fascinating subject can now literally watch Jung's defection pass before their very eyes (See McGuire, 1974).

Freud's recognition and success continued to grow, but his troubles were far from over. He had to deal with almost continuous dissension within the analytic ranks, and to support himself, his wife, their six children, and one sister-in-law. World War I brought hardship and anxiety, as Freud's sons Martin and Ernst were called to the front. Still Freud worked, and his fame grew. When the war ended, he attracted many English and American students who helped to keep him going when Austrian money was of little value. He continued to expand and modify his theories and to regulate the rapid expansion of psychoanalysis. One of his devices for control was his voluminous correspondence, wherein he admonished and praised his followers.

In the fateful year 1923, a cancer was discovered in Freud's mouth. It seems highly probable that Freud's cancer was connected with the fact that he characteristically smoked twenty cigars a day. Parts of the palate and upper jaw had to be removed, necessitating the wearing of a prosthesis to separate the mouth from the nasal cavity and to make eating and talking possible. Freud accepted the series of operations and almost continuous pain that attended that last 16 years of his life with his characteristic blend of realism, pessimism, and fatalism.

Finally, 1938 brought the long-dreaded invasion of Austria by the Nazis. Hitler himself visited the city in triumph. Freud's books were burned, his children detained and questioned by the Gestapo. Still Freud did not wish to leave his home at Berggasse 19, the place at which he had created, founded, and nurtured psychoanalysis. Ernest Jones and Princess Marie Bonaparte, both Freud's dear friends, cajoled and pleaded with Freud on the one hand, and with the Nazis on the other, enlisting the help of many others including Ambassador Bullitt of the United States. Finally both sides were convinced, and the Nazis released Freud after bleeding him of everything they could get their hands on. Freud was required to sign a paper absolving the Nazis of all blame, saying he was perfectly free to stay and continue his work. His only request was that he could add one sentence; he is said to have written "And I can heartily recommend the Gestapo." His ironic humor had not deserted him even in age and extremity!

In England he was welcomed as a hero, and soon made a member of the Royal Society, along with Newton and Darwin. Americans can be proud of the fact that prominent citizens of Cleveland sent him a four-page telegram asking him to settle there, and making all sorts of promises if he did. It is not likely that Freud considered this kind offer seriously. He had a long-standing prejudice against America despite the intense pleasure his visit to Clark University had brought. That visit had unfortunately been accompanied by illness which he attributed to American cooking and accommodations, and Freud felt uncomfortable with the language and manners of the Americans.

Freud had not been in England long before his cancer recurred, and the series of operations and treatments began again. Despite almost continuous pain and discomfort, he worked almost to the end, and died in peace and honor on September 23, 1939. He was spared the knowledge that four of his sisters, who stayed behind in Austria, would be killed by the Nazis.

THE FOUNDING OF PSYCHOANALYSIS

The germ of psychoanalysis appeared in a paper, *Studies in hysteria,* published by Breuer and Freud in 1895. Freud had met the older Breuer in the late 1870s, and they shared a strong scientific interest. Both were interested in hypnotism as a therapeutic device. Breuer had an interesting case, Fraulein Anna O., whom he treated until 1882; that fall he told Freud about it. The highly intelligent girl came to Breuer with multiple symptoms, including paralysis of three limbs, contractures, and a tendency to dual personality. In the course of treatment, it was found that if she related every occurrence of a symptom all the way back to its origin, to Breuer, the symptom would disappear. Anna O. retraced these occurrences while in a kind of transition state between her two personalities. Breuer then began to hypnotize her daily so that she could rid herself of the symptoms faster. She christened the method they had discovered the "talking cure," or "chimney sweeping." The idea of catharsis was very much in the air in Vienna at that time (Ellenberger, 1972), and it is possible that Anna O. and Breuer may have brought that idea from the theatre to the therapy room. Breuer devoted an hour or more a day for over a year to her. Legend, deriving from Freud and Jung through Jones, had it that Breuer and his patient became inordinately fond of each other, and that when Breuer was to terminate the treatment Anna O. went into the throes of a hysterical childbirth; whereupon Breuer fled, taking his by then jealous wife on a second honeymoon during which a real daughter was conceived.

Ellenberger (1972) has discovered that, honeymoon or no, the legend is mostly moonshine. The documented chronology proves that none of Breuer's daughters was conceived at the proper time. More important, Anna O. was far from cured when Breuer stopped treating her, as reported in a previously unknown case history newly discovered by Ellenberger in the sanitarium at Kreuzlingen in Switzerland, where Anna O. was treated after Breuer stopped seeing her. This puts the earliest beginning of psychoanalysis under something of a cloud, since Anna O. has been regarded as a prototype of a cathartic "cure."

Anna O., whose real name turns out to have been Bertha Pappenheim, did later become so well known that Germany devoted a commemorative stamp to her in recognition of her work with children, prostitutes, and Jewish relief. Lucy Freeman (1972) has even written a somewhat novelized biography of her in English. Thus, although Breuer did not cure her completely, she later became well enough to lead a noteworthy life.

Freud was very interested in her case, and urged Breuer to publish it. However, the full-scale *Studies in hysteria* (1895) followed the close of the case (for Breuer) by 13 years, and even a preliminary report took 11 years.

Meanwhile, in 1885, Freud studied with Charcot. Charcot was famous for his treatment of hysteria and other functional nervous diseases by hypnosis. After several months, Freud returned to Vienna and resumed private practice. It was at about this time that he abandoned electrotherapy. He also observed that not all his patients could be hypnotized, and, perhaps feeling that his technique was deficient, he went to study at Nancy with Bernheim for a few weeks. He took along a patient in whom he had been unable to induce a deep trance, but Bernheim also failed. However, Freud was impressed by his observation that posthypnotic suggestions could be carried out, and the suggestion forgotten; he was probably equally impressed with the demonstration that the patient would remember the suggestion after sufficient insistence on the part of the hypnotist.

Freud now began to modify his technique in cases where it was not possible to induce hypnosis. He was determined to save the talking cure; he insisted that the patient would remember the origin of symptoms even though not hypnotized, and he supplemented his insistence with suggestions that the patient would remember when Freud pressed upon his forehead. At this stage, Freud was exerting a great deal of guidance on the patient's processes of association. One patient told him that he was interrupting too much and that he should keep quiet. This suggestion was the final impetus that converted Freud from the hypnotic trance to free association as a method of treatment.

By the time the *Studies* appeared, Breuer and Freud were in possession of many of the ideas that were to provide the basis for psychoanalysis; several of the ideas had come from Breuer's observations of Anna O., and others from Freud's observations of hysterical patients. The first of these ideas was a conviction of the importance of unconscious processes in the etiology of the neuroses. This conviction came partly from the observation that symptoms often seemed to be expressions of events which the patient could not remember or of impulses of which he was unaware. The influence of posthypnotic suggestions, which the subject did not at the moment remember, may have contributed to the belief in the strength of unconscious processes.

Freud was himself convinced by this time that sex plays a dominant role in the psychic aberrations of the neurotic. Breuer did not share Freud's certainty on this point, and their disagreement seems to have resulted in some underplaying of the theme—according to Freud's tastes—in their publication. Charcot had apparently remarked at one time that a certain type of case always has a sexual basis. Freud also claimed that Breuer and a gynecologist named Chrobak had made similar remarks about nervous disorders. Freud himself observed that most of his hysterical patients reported traumatic sexual experiences, often with members of their own families, in their childhood. He concluded that no neurosis is possible in a person with a normal sex life.

The importance of symbolism was also recognized by Freud at this time. Symptoms seemed to be distorted, but symbolic, representations of repressed events or conflicts. In the case of Anna O., the symbolic relation between the origin of the symptoms and the symptoms itself was clear to the patient and to Breuer when the patient was able to recall the origin. The symptoms were thus not arbitrary.

In every case, the situation at the time the symptom originated had involved strong impulses to do something, which had been opposed by forces preventing the girl from carrying out her wish. For example, she might want to cry in the presence of her father because of her grief over his illness and yet be unable to cry for fear he would become upset about his condition. The repressed impulse might later manifest itself, in symbolic form, as an inability to see. The existence of contradictory tendencies was evidence of the importance of conflict in the creation of symptoms and in the production of neuroses in general.

As the preceding discussion implies, an acceptance of the unconscious is intertwined with the notion of repression into the unconscious; undesirable impulses and memories are pushed into the unconscious and are forgotten and unavailable as conscious material under ordinary circumstances. Only through their recovery and working out *(abreaction)* can the patient be cured.

In the quest for the origins of symptoms, for the repressed material represented by the symptoms, Freud was forced further and further back into childhood; his belief in the importance of childhood experiences in the production of neuroses was growing. Many of these childhood experiences were sexual; in hysteria particularly, Freud found reports of early sexual experiences. However, he believed that these experiences gained their traumatic force only after the patient had reached puberty. He had not yet been driven to his later opinions about the early genesis of sexuality in childhood.

The last, and possibly most important, discovery was the transference relation. We have already seen how Breuer became fond of his patient (countertransference); it was also true that she became fond of him. It seemed that the patient transferred to her therapist the feelings that she earlier had for other people, especially her parents. At some stages of the therapeutic relationship, these feelings might be strongly positive, even sexual, in nature; later, the feelings might become as strongly negative. In either case, the patient was able to live through, to work out, the impulses that had earlier been incapable of expression. The transference could thus become one of the most useful tools of the therapist.

On the other hand, transference might strike a chill into the heart of the timid. It may have been Breuer's anxiety about the transference he had elicited in Anna O. that led him to leave the field that he and Freud were starting to open up. There was also the controversy about the importance attributed to sexuality. Breuer, since he could not decide whether sexuality was really so critical or not, chose to leave psychoanalysis to Freud.

FREUD'S SYSTEM

We now leap over the developmental phases to present an extremely abbreviated summary of Freud's system in its later form. We should distinguish between the structure of constructs that Freud developed, with which we will be primarily concerned, and psychoanalytic techniques viewed as therapy or as sources of empirical data. These facets of psychoanalysis need to be separately evaluated; much of the confusion in regard to criticism of psychoanalysis results from a failure to keep them separate. For example, methodological criticisms of the system need not apply to the therapy, and conversely, positive results of the therapy do not necessarily provide support for the system.

It should be understood that Freud did not suddenly develop the ideas to be presented, nor did he always continue to adhere to an idea if it seemed to contradict evidence that he himself gathered in his work. For example, a pronounced modification of his position on hysteria came about after he discovered that in many cases, the traumatic sexual incidents reported by the patients had not occurred at all; yet he had resisted all attempts by others to get him to change his position. R. I. Watson says of this incident:

> A short time after he gave this paper the horrible truth began to dawn on him—these seductions in childhood, in most, but not all instances, had never actually occurred.
>
> A lesser man might have hidden his mistake and tried to forget it. A less clinically acute individual might have "bravely" confessed his error and turned to other more profitable matters. Freud did neither. . . . Was not the very fact that their fantasies took the form of sexual matters evidence that there was a sexual tinge or basis to their thinking, and was he not, consequently, right in emphasizing the sexual basis of their difficulty even though the situations which they had described had actually never taken place? Despite the temporary setback, this "mistake" was actually later to be seen as an advance. (1968, p. 467)

For a scientific investigator, he was extremely insensitive to criticism from the outside, especially from those unsympathetic to psychoanalysis; however, he was sensitive to self-criticism, and his system was accordingly flexible. Seldom did he present his theories as certainties; they were, rather, usually presented as tentative conclusions that seemed to be supported by his clinical data. It is largely his resistance to external criticism and his feeling that experimental support for his notions was not necessary that have given him the reputation of being cocksure and dogmatic about his conclusions.

Freud had a surprising attitude toward the reality of his conceptions. He might, when being self-consciously correct about methodology, admit that they were convenient fictions invented for explanatory purposes, but his usual attitude was that he was dealing with real things. For example, he once used Janet's statement that the unconscious was a "manner of speaking" as an example of Janet's low level of understanding (Jones, 1957, p. 214). Freud apparently regarded the unconscious as a country which he was exploring rather than as a system which he was constructing. Perhaps Freud's background in neurology was conducive to the belief that he was working with *real* structures.

The Psychic Apparatus

As we have already seen, Freud believed that he found two "states" within the "country," the conscious and the unconscious. Different kinds of laws determine what happens in these two states: The unconscious operates according to a set which Freud called the *primary process,* and the conscious according to the *secondary process.* Ordinary logic applies to the latter but not to the former; the mechanisms that can be observed in dreams characterize the action of the primary process. Some of the things that can occur are the *condensation* of several thoughts into a single symbol, the *displacement* of an impulse or affect from one symbol to another, the *timelessness* characteristic of dreams, the *conversion* of an impulse into its opposite, and so on. The illogicality of the dream is characteristic of the primary process as a whole.

Part of the energy for the mental apparatus is called *libido;* its source is in biological tensions, and certainly the most important of these to the mental economy is sexual. Most of the sexual energy derives from the erogenous zones, bodily areas especially sensitive to stimulation. The *id* is the primordial reservoir of this energy and, being unconscious, operates according to the primary process. Various instincts which reside in the id press toward the discharge of their libidinal energy. Each instinct, therefore, has a *source* in biological tensions, an *aim* of discharge in some particular activity, and an *object* which will serve to facilitate the discharge.

The id operates according to the *pleasure principle.* In general, the elimination of tension is what defines pleasurableness, although it is not always clear whether it is the elimination of all tension or the maintenance of a constant level of tension which is pleasurable. Departure from a low level of tension or any heightening of tension is unpleasurable. One should remember that the id operates *only* according to the pleasure principle; it does not, for example, distinguish between the hallucinatory fulfilling of a hunger need and the actual fulfilling of the need. However, the tension does not remain reduced except through contact with objects which are in reality appropriate.

Accordingly, another psychic structure develops and complements the id. It is called the *ego.* It operates according to the laws of the secondary process and, being in contact with reality, operates according to the *reality principle;* that is, it is an evaluative agency which intelligently selects that line of behavior which minimizes pain while maximizing pleasure. The ego is still in the service of the pleasure principle through the reality principle, but sometimes temporarily turns aside the direct gratification of needs in order that their overall gratification will be greater.

As a result of contact with the cultural realities, especially as embodied in the parents, a third mental agency develops. It functions as a suppressor of pleasurable activity in the same way that external agencies did at one time. It has two subsystems—a conscience, which punishes, and an ego ideal, which rewards behavior. The conscience brings about feelings of guilt, and the ego ideal brings about feelings of pride. The *superego* is unlike the ego (which serves the pleasure principle and only postpones gratification) in its attempts to halt completely certain pleasurable activities. The operation of the superego is largely unconscious; that is, a large part of its operation follows the laws of the primary process.

Freud himself came to the conclusion that the instincts active throughout the psychic apparatus could be divided into two groups: the life instincts and the destructive instincts. The latter were more commonly called the *death instincts,* since their aim is the death of the individual. Freud viewed the instincts as conservative; that is, they aim for a return to a previous state and thus explain the *repetition compulsion* which manifests itself in some behavior. Since living matter arises from dead matter, the ultimate previous state must be a state of complete quiescence, of death. The death instincts work for a disintegration of the individual, while the life instincts work for the continued integration of the individual. The death instinct is the part of Freud's theory least frequently accepted by other analysts; many articles written in analytic publications have been unfavorable to this Freudian conception (Jones, 1957, p. 276). The life and death instincts had the advantage for Freud of giving him a polarity, a pair of opposite elements in conflict. Jones (1957, p. 422) points out how fond Freud was of the dualistic mode of thought in preference to monistic or pluralistic conceptions.

The energy in the service of the life instincts was called by Freud the *libido;* no name was given especially to the energy that activates the death instincts. As the individual develops his ego, more and more of the available psychic energy comes under the dominion of the ego rather than of the id, which originally directs it. The ego attaches the energy to psychic representations of external objects; such an attachment is called a *cathexis.* The kind of object cathected depends upon the instinct which has energy available; the distribution of energy over the instincts is flexible. In the original version of the analytic theory, the distribution was assumed to change gradually, so that more and more energy was available for the self-preservative instincts of the ego, and less and less for the sexual instincts of the id. This version made the basis of conflict the self-preservation versus the sexual instincts rather than life versus death.

In the course of an individual's development, there is a stage in which much of the libidinal energy is cathected onto the parent of the opposite sex; in the case of the boy, this leads to the development of the Oedipal conflict. Like the mythical Oedipus, the boy loves his mother. He is also jealous and resentful of his rival, the father. His sexual feelings are directed to the mother, but the child is blocked from direct expression of the instinctual urges toward incest. Because of his impulses, which are repressed, the boy has a fear of castration by the father. It is at this time that the urges toward the mother are repressed into the unconscious, so strongly repressed that all sexual urges enter the latency period. They emerge again at puberty, when the increase in sexual tensions is sufficient to upset the psychic economy and allow the impulses to overcome the repressive forces. The Oedipal conflict was felt by Freud to be a major contribution of psychoanalysis; one of the presuppositions necessary for its acceptance is that sexuality is really developed very early in life.

Treatment of Neurosis

Let us now consider the implications of the psychoanalytic position for the treatment of neurotics. In doing so, we should keep in mind that we are reversing the process that actually occurred; in reality, the theory grew out of the therapy and the observations that attended it, rather than vice versa, as our discussion might erroneously suggest.

In the first place, ordinary methods of gathering information about the genesis of the symptoms will not do. We have seen how unwelcome memories and impulses are repressed by the ego at the behest of reality, or the superego. They are not conscious. They are not even in the in-between zone that Freud called the *preconscious,* where the simple application of sufficient effort may make them conscious. Any attempt at recollecting them will be met by *resistance;* accordingly, a special method, such as hypnosis or free association, is required. Dreams, since they are governed to a considerable extent by the primary process, provide an avenue to knowledge about the unconscious if they are interpreted correctly. Correct interpretation depends upon the knowledge that the function of dreams is to fulfill wishes; since the id does not recognize the difference between hallucinatory and actual satisfaction of wishes, the existing psychic tensions may press toward discharge in dreams. In order to determine the precise meaning of the dream—that is, in order to uncover the hidden (latent) impulses expressed—patients are instructed to give their associations to the elements of their dreams. In this way, dream symbols can be related to their meanings and the repressed material brought to consciousness.

The analysis of resistance to recall of repressed materials is then one of the most difficult and most important tasks of the analyst. If the resistance is too strong, the patient continues to refuse to recognize the existence of the repressed material even when the analyst can present it verbally. It is only when the patient can overcome the inner resistance and accept the analysis that improvement becomes possible. Overcoming the resistance brings the impulses under the control of the ego, where they obey the laws of the secondary process. As the dominion of the ego is enlarged, the ego is strengthened, and the patient's impulses become accessible to rational control. The patient cannot be freed from the rule of the pleasure principle, but more overall gratification can be obtained once the impulses are also made to conform to the reality principle.

The overcoming of the resistance is made possible, at least in some cases, by the transference to the therapist of a considerable portion of the libidinal energy. This energy is therefore available to the therapist for application of counterforce to the resistance. In turn, the transference itself becomes an object of analysis, and it must be overcome before the patient is independent and can be said to be cured.

In overcoming the resistance and tracing the significant repressed materials, the patient must be forced to recall material that goes further and further back into childhood. The childhood years are critical in the development of every individual; if a person becomes fixated at some early stage of sexual development or returns (regresses) to an earlier stage in the face of later trauma, the scene is set for the development of neurosis. The early experiences that are most likely to be punished, and hence repressed, involve sex. Therefore, the significant material that will be recovered will concern sex. Even more specifically, we can say that the Oedipal conflict and its resolution will be central to the analysis, and insight into it by the patient central to recovery.

It is clear in all of this that the symptom is of interest to the Freudian primarily for its symbolic value, as an initial clue that can finally lead the analyst and the patient to the true difficulty. Investigating symptoms to find causes was for many years so much a part of all therapies that it did not even need to be mentioned. It is only in the last 20 years or so, since behavior modifiers began to work *directly* on the elimination of symptoms, that Freud's attitude toward symptoms has been questioned. Are symptoms themselves the problem of the neurotic, or are they only symbols of a deeper-lying problem? That is indeed a fundamental issue, and a clear decision on it would probably help to resolve much of the conflict between psychoanalytic and behavior therapies.

Freud seemed to feel that the iron rule of determinism could be broken if the impulses could be brought under the sway of the secondary process. In this way the patient would achieve *self*-control, rather than remaining under impulse control. Freud was less concerned with the question of determinism within the secondary process, although his followers (including his daughter Anna) have spent a great deal of time in the study of ego processes. For Freud, human hope of improvement lay in becoming truly rational. Insight was not a sufficient condition for being cured, but it was a necessary condition. The insight had to be "deep," that is, there had to be a real emotional acceptance of the analysis, not just an intellectual parroting of words.

This emphasis on rationality by Freud resulted in a rather strange combination of positions on determinism. In most respects he was an arch-determinist. He is famous for his work on the determination of errors in speech and writing, on forgetting, and even on losing objects. He presented evidence that the apparently chance nature of these events conceals the fact that the error reveals the unconscious motivation of the person who has erred, forgotten, or lost something. A published example (Freud, 1938, p. 75) concerns a member of the United Daughters of the Confederacy, who, in concluding her eulogy of Jefferson Davis, said "the great and only President of the Confederate States of America—Abraham Lincoln!" In explaining such "slips" Freud was enlarging the presumed realm of determinism; but in helping his patients to achieve ego control, Freud was trying to free them from its grip.

THE REBELS

Four important early members of Freud's group first occupied a favored position and then disagreed with the Freudian beliefs and established rival analytic factions. They were, in order, Adler, Jung, Rank, and Ferenczi. Their defections have been used by opponents of psychoanalysis to demonstrate either that not all analysts agree among themselves or that Freud was a kind of despotic tyrant who brooked no opposition. As we might expect, the charges were neither wholly true nor wholly false. There were both fundamental agreements and fundamental disagreements among the five men presently being considered. As to the personality factors, these are difficult to assess; in every case, some of the blame can probably be laid at each doorstep. Levinson's research (1978) has thrown an interesting new light on the relationship of Freud to his disciples. Levinson finds that it is typical of young adults that they find a mentor, just as Adler, Jung, Rank, and Ferenczi found Freud. And it is also typical that an intense mentor relationship ends with strong conflict and bad feeling. The younger person finds the mentor critical and demanding, and the older person finds the younger touchy, rebellious, and ungrateful. Thus we have probably tended to think of the successive rebellions of Freud's disciples as unusual, when in fact they are exactly what should have been expected. With this foreword, we now turn to a brief exposition of the four men and the modifications they proposed.

Alfred Adler

Alfred Adler (1870–1937) was a Viennese physician who early attached himself to the Wednesday-night group that started meeting with Freud in 1902 to discuss psychoanalysis. Adler and Stekel were Freud's two oldest followers; they withdrew from the society in successive years (1911 and 1912). Stekel had contributed to the field of symbolism, but, according to Jones (1955, p. 135), had no scientific conscience and formed no school of his own after he left the fold of psychoanalysis.

Adler's case was quite different; he made a greater contribution to psychoanalysis, formulated a partially independent theory of behavior, and set up a rival school.

The difficulties between Freud and Adler became intense after Freud insisted that Jung be made president of the international association; the Viennese were jealous of their positions, since they had been the first followers. Then, the year after the international meetings in 1910, it was decided to hold discussions and debates about Adler's theories. After the discussions, the disagreements about theory seemed obvious, and Adler and his faction resigned from the Wednesday Society before the end of 1911. Adler formed a rival school which he finally named *individual psychology*.

Freud had at first tolerated or even welcomed Adler's contributions. Adler initially stressed organ inferiority in the backgrounds of neurotics. At first blush, this seems a more biological view even than Freud's. However, appearances are deceptive in this case, for Adler emphasized the psychological reaction to either real or *imagined* organ inferiority rather than the biological facts themselves. *Compensation* for this inferiority accounts for the nature of many neurotic symptoms and helps to determine the individual's *life-style,* the way in which he deals with problems in general. The analysis of the compensatory mechanisms was seen by Adler as the major task of both the theory and practice of analysis.

Although Adler emphasized the conflict between masculinity and femininity as very important, his views on sexuality were very different from Freud's. He saw the overcoming of femininity by both males and females ("masculine protest"), rather than sexuality in itself, as the important thing. The will to power was thought to be the most important motivating force in peoples' lives, and sex at times was a symptom of this will, the sex act representing the domination of the female rather than the running off of truly sexual impulses.

The will to power and the need to overcome inferiority arise, according to Adler, because of the conditions of life that universally obtain for human infants.

The infant is not a small sexual animal whose incestuous desires must be repressed, but a small and helpless organism whose every need must be ministered to by relatively powerful adults. Necessarily, then, the infant develops feelings of inferiority relative to these adults and must strive to overcome this inferiority and rise above dependent status. The Oedipal conflict, if it exists at all, should be understood as a conquering of the mother rather than as a direct expression of any infantile sexuality.

Adler thus shifted the emphasis away from inborn biological instincts and energies toward the social relationships within the family as the children grow up; he concluded that the position within the family (such as eldest daughter, second son, youngest child) is extremely important in determining how an individual deals with reality (i.e., life-style). Sibling rivalry is bound to occur and affect the personality. In Adler's theory, we see that the important conflicts often occur between the individual and the environment, rather than within the individual, as Freud had held.

Adler presented a more hopeful view of the human being than the orthodox analysts did. He saw a person not so much as a group of segments at war with themselves but more as an integrated, striving individual. He laid much less emphasis on the uncovering of the unconscious and its dark forces. He perceived the human being as largely conscious and creative, living partly by adherence to a "fictional future," which consists of precepts presently believed in. Such precepts, although not necessarily true, might nevertheless direct behavior, for example, the precept "your reward will be in Heaven."

Adler and his school made therapy a shorter process and, at least sometimes, dispensed with the Freudian couch. Practical applications of the Adlerian theory to educational and social problems helped to popularize the theory, as did the ease with which such terms as *inferiority complex* and *sibling rivalry* were assimilated in the lay language. Adler's theory is generally closer to common sense than Freud's and probably shares the strengths and weaknesses common to such theories.

Carl Jung

Relationship to Freud Carl Gustav Jung (1875–1961) was a Swiss psychiatrist who became interested in Freud's theories after reading his *Interpretation of dreams,* which appeared in 1900. Jung visited Freud and his Wednesday Society in Vienna in 1907, and the two men immediately became strongly attached to each other. Freud soon viewed Jung as the crown prince of the psychoanalytic movement. In 1909, as we have seen, Jung accompanied Freud to America for the Clark University lectures and later returned to America alone to give additional lectures. At the first meeting of the new International Psychoanalytic Association, Freud insisted over the Viennese opposition that Jung be elected president. He wanted a younger man who was not a Jew to head the new movement, for he felt that the resistance to Jews would impede the progress of the analytic movement were a Jew to lead the association. On these grounds, Jung seemed the logical choice. The Viennese, who were nearly all Jews, were jealous of their own priority in the movement and believed that Jung was himself anti-Semitic. But Freud overcame their objections, and Jung was elected.

Soon after, the relationship between Jung and Freud began to weaken. Jung was not performing his presidential duties as well as Freud had expected; he deemphasized sex in his lectures and in his therapeutic analyses, and he changed the concept of libido. Personal frictions were straining the relations between the two men, as they privately accused each other of neurosis, and rivalry developed as both of them nearly simultaneously became interested in the psychology of religion. In January 1913 they agreed to discontinue their personal correspondence. By 1914, Jung had withdrawn completely from the movement. He never resumed his former friendship with Freud, and he soon founded a new school which he called *analytic psychology*.

Basic Attitudes and Methodology Jung had early assumed that there must be some physical changes which account for the development of schizophrenia. In this he was emphasizing a contemporaneous factor rather than a historical factor, as Freud was in the habit of doing. Although Freud at that time agreed with Jung about this particular point, he would not have agreed in general with Jung's emphasis on the present rather than on the past in the study of neuroses. Jung was more like the Gestaltists, and Freud more like the behaviorists, on this issue. Not only did Jung emphasize the *present* as important, but he also believed that one must understand the future, the potentialities, of man in order to make sense when talking about him. Human goals and intentions were to Jung as important in directing human behavior as was personal history. He deplored Freud's study of causality exclusively in terms of the past and thought Freud's theorizing too reductive and mechanistic. Jung later suggested (Jung & Pauli, 1955) a principle called *synchronicity* for those events which occur together in time but which do not cause one another; his archetypes, which are primordial images that entail inherited response tendencies, are supposed to fulfill themselves psychically and physically within the real world at the same time without the two manifestations being causally related. This view sounds like Hume's analysis of causality and contemporaneity, or the doctrine of psychophysical parallelism.

Jung changed his position on scientific methodology as time went on. At first, he was interested in bridging the gap between academic psychology and psychoanalysis via the association experiment. In this way he hoped to make psychoanalysis more scientific. Later, Jung lost interest in "proving" analysis through traditionally conceived experiments. He and his followers turned more to the study of mythology and art as more useful methods of revealing the form of the unconscious. Jung became the most negative of the leading analysts toward the traditional methods of empirical science.

Jung's therapy, in accordance with these basic views, put less stress upon the past of the individual and more upon his present situation and desires for the future. Jung saw the human being as more creative and less a passive recipient of environmental influences than had Freud; Jung was accordingly more optimistic in his psychology. Freud saw Jung's therapy as something that might be expected from a priest, with moral exhortation, appeals to willpower, and an attempt to develop the human yearnings after the divine (Freud, 1938, p. 975). Jung believed that primitive human urges might be channeled into a quest for self-actualization or for the divine; if the energy were not recognized and used properly by the ego, it might so warp a person's functioning that neurosis or psychosis would result.

Basic Energies and Instincts Jung's views about basic human energy were closer to a commonsense conception than Freud's. He regarded the libido as a general biological life energy, not necessarily predominantly sexual. Where Freud saw sexual energy concentrated on different body zones at different stages (oral, anal, phallic, latency, genital), Jung saw the life energy simply manifesting itself in the form which was at the moment most important for the organism, for example, in relation to eating, elimination, and sex. The early concentration of gratification upon the oral zone was accounted for by the relation of the oral zone to eating rather than to the pleasurable sensations (conceived of by Freud as sexual in the broad sense) which arise from oral stimulation. Jung did not like Freud's lumping together of all pleasurable sensations as sexual.

Since he did not conceive of the basic energy as altogether sexual, he was free to reinterpret analytic observations that had previously been assumed to represent sexual strivings. The Oedipal conflict was reinterpreted, as it had been by Adler. This time the nutritive functions, as we might expect, become important in the child's attitude toward the mother. These become overlaid and combined with sexual feelings as the child develops in sexual functioning. Combined with these feelings are certain primitive unconscious predispositions to react toward the mother. The Oedipal relationship is then not based, as Freud thought, almost exclusively on sexuality.

Jung transferred concepts from physics almost directly into dicta about psychic energy. He did not believe that psychic energy can be destroyed any more than physical energy can. If the energy is used in some psychic function, the amount available for that function will decrease, but will reappear in the form of increased energy available for some other function. If the energy disappears from some psychic system, it will reappear in some other. This view is not very unlike Freud's; he, too, talked of the reappearance of unused psychic energy in other forms, as when sexual energy is sublimated and used for artistic creativity. Jung did not believe that the sum of the available psychic energy remains constant, for energy can be exchanged with the external world through such things as muscular work and the ingestion of food. Energy, since it can flow from one psychic system to another, tends to move from the points of higher energy toward the points of lower energy. The system, in short, tends to reach a state of balance, although the tendency is never fully realized. Even were a balance to be reached, it would soon be upset by exchanges between some psychic system and the external world. For example, if most of the available energy were concentrated in the personal unconscious, it would tend to share energy with other systems, such as the ego. Then an exchange with the external world might occur. The ego would further increase the energy supply, and the direction would now be reversed.

Views on Psychic Structures C. S. Hall and Lindzey (1957) have given an excellent thumbnail summary of Jung's position:

> The total personality or psyche, as it is called by Jung, consists of a number of separate but interacting systems. The principal ones are the *ego,* the *personal unconscious* and its *complexes,* the *collective unconscious* and its *archetypes,* the *persona,* the *anima,* or *animus,* and the *shadow.* In addition to these interdependent systems there are the *attitudes* of introversion and extraversion, and the *functions* of thinking, feeling, sensing, and intuiting. Finally, there is the *self* which is the fully developed and fully unified personality. (p. 79)

Jung's ego is something like a lay person's self-conception; it is the conscious mind in contact with reality, and it contains the conscious memories. It is felt to be the center of identity and personality. Jung's ego is not unlike Freud's ego.

The personal unconscious is the region just "interior" to the ego. Since it is in contact with the ego, materials may be repressed into it from the ego. The personal unconscious resembles a blend of Freud's unconscious and preconscious; the contents of the personal unconscious are available to consciousness and contain materials which have come into the unconscious as a result of repression of personal experiences of the individual or of material originating in the collective unconscious.

The collective unconscious lies still deeper than the personal unconscious. In this dark and misty region are those things which human beings have inherited phylogenetically. The things that are inherited are called *archetypes.* Archetypes are predispositions to perceive, act, or think in a certain way. They are formed as a result of the universal human experiences all undergo in their evolution; they are symbols as well as dispositions. Since the presumed experiences are universals, the archetypes are also universals. Jung discovered their existence as a result of his study of the myths and art of several ages and cultures. Certain symbols were common to all, despite the presumed lack of any direct exchange between the cultures. Examples of these universal archetypes are birth, death, the hero, the child, and God.

Four archetypes are better developed than any of the others: the persona, the anima, the animus, and the shadow. These are so well developed that they have become separate personality systems. The *persona* is the mask presented by an individual to society, and is feminine in women and masculine in men. It may or may not serve the function of concealing the real personality.

Balancing the persona will be the *anima,* the feminine part of man, or the *animus,* the masculine part of woman. These archetypes constitute Jung's recognition of human bisexuality. They evolve, like any other archetypes, as a result of universal racial experiences. The anima is the result of man's experiences with woman, and the animus is the result of woman's experiences with man.

The *shadow* consists of that part of the unconscious which was inherited from man's prehuman ancestors; it is the animal instincts. Immoral and passionate impulses emanate largely from the shadow. When these impulses appear in consciousness, they may be expressed or repressed, with the result in the latter case that some of the materials of the personal unconscious originate in the shadow.

A fifth well-developed archetype is the most important one of all. It is the *self.* Jung found this archetype represented in various cultures by a symbol which was called the *mandala* or *magic circle.* It represented human striving for unity, for wholeness, for integration of the personality. Jung made the self, accordingly, a separate system, changing from his earlier conception of the self as equivalent to the whole psyche. The self holds all the other systems together. It apparently strives for oneness of the individual with the world through religious experiences as well as oneness of the psychic systems within the individual. The self can appear only as the other psychic systems become separate enough to require integration, which does not occur until middle age. Some of Jung's disagreements with Freud were based on this "breaking point" in middle age; Jung thought Freud might be essentially correct about the importance of sexual motivation before middle age, but he believed that Freud had simply ignored what happened after this point had been passed, when the self had developed and when sex had become a subsidiary consideration.

The two attitudes toward the world distinguished by Jung, extraversion and introversion, are better known than any other part of his system. In extraversion, most of the individual's attention is directed to the external world; in introversion, the opposite is the case. Usually, the ego and the personal unconscious have opposite attitudes, since both attitudes are always present to some extent somewhere in the personality; the nondominant attitude, then, tends to be repressed. The stronger the conscious expression of one attitude, the stronger the unconscious development of the other. Sometimes an upset allows the libido attached to the unconscious attitude to overwhelm the repression, and the dominant attitude is overcome.

Finally, there are the functions, any one of which may be dominant. Jung's definitions of thinking, feeling, sensing, and intuiting do not differ from the common meanings. He did not think there was anything arbitrary about the statement that there are exactly four functions; it was a statement of fact as far as he was concerned. Generally, two of the functions predominate at the expense of the other two; the latter are then developed unconsciously, just as in the case of the repressed attitude. If an individual is described in terms of function and attitude, we have a sort of typology; thus a feeling-intuiting-introvert might be a prophet or a monk. All functions and both attitudes are necessary for successful living; accordingly, there are no pure types. The whole individual has all these factors in harmony. As pure types are approached, the pathological is approached.

Contribution and Evaluation Jung is especially difficult to evaluate. When Freud was alive, Jung and all other analysts were in his shadow. In addition, it has frequently been pointed out that Jung is difficult to comprehend; as Jones has said (1957): "Then his mentality had the serious flaw of lacking lucidity. I remember once meeting someone who had been in school with him and being struck by the answer he gave to my question of what Jung has been like as a boy: 'He had a confused mind.' I was not the only person to make the same observation" (p. 32).

Although Jones may have been somewhat biased in his estimate because of his friendship with Freud, there does seem to be some justification for his attitude. A reviewer of the English translation of Jung's published works said that Jung's statement about one of his works (1956) seems applicable to many: "It was written at top speed, amid the rush and press of my medical practice, without regard to time or method. I had to fling my material hastily together, just as I found it. There was no opportunity to let my thoughts mature. The whole thing came upon me like a landslide that cannot be stopped" (p. xxiii). A book so written could hardly be easy for the reader. In addition to the style problem, the English-speaking reader had the problem of translation until 1966, when the last of eighteen volumes was translated.

Even when the difficult problem of reading and understanding Jung is passed, many others remain. Jung's dislike for traditional scientific methodology makes his type of persuasion foreign to psychologists who like statistical or laboratory proof. If such proof is demanded, Jung can be dismissed at once.

It is even difficult to find any logical system to evaluate, for Jung was not a systematist. Whatever system there is must be distilled from his writing and then fitted together; Jung has presented no postulates or derivations. In this, he is in the company of the other analysts.

In 1929, Jung himself offered an assessment of the status of psychology, including that of his own system: "Our psychology is the more or less successfully formulated confession of a few individuals, and so far as each of them conforms more or less to a type, his confession can be accepted as a fairly valid description of a large number of people" (reprinted in Hillix & Marx, 1974, pp. 372–373). Jung makes it quite clear that he intends this comment to apply to psychoanalysis as developed by Freud and Adler, as well as to his own system. Thus there would be at least three sorts of people, each reasonably well described and explained by a different psychoanalytic theory.

At first blush, this seems to be a peculiar sort of science, in which there are no general laws. There are only limited laws which apply to an appropriate set of persons. However, Diesing (1971) describes exactly this procedure as one of his four "methods of discovery" in the social sciences. It is part of the holistic method, which begins with concrete data, discovers themes in the data, then constructs typologies (which are theories of limited scope), and finally develops a general theory which accounts for all the types. Within this context, psychoanalysis would be seen as an intermediate stage, which might lead eventually to a general theory of the kind aspired to by most scientists.

Jung has seemed to grow in importance within recent years. He outlived Freud by 22 years, and his works are now available in English. His ideas are novel and provocative. His view of the human being furnishes a refreshing antidote to Freud's. It is optimistic and consistent with the religious point of view. Jung was himself interested in both myths and religions, especially Oriental religions. His position affords a comfortable, compatible resting-place for those who are surfeited with the scientific approach and its results. Jungian psychology is an easy companion for the existentialist (modern variety). The perhaps coincidental fact that interest in these subjects—Oriental religion, mysticism, existentialism—has enjoyed an upsurge has strengthened Jung's position.

It is significant that Jung's scientific training was not as long or intense as Freud's. Thus Jung was able finally to accept a consistently antiscientific view. Freud had faced many fearful tests of courage—childhood sexuality and his own error in believing his patients' stories of sexual episodes, for example—but he never conceived the possibility of flying completely and purposely in the face of organized science. Jung did. That will be his downfall or his salvation. Jung was erudite and enthusiastic, and his followers were loyal and impressed once they understood him. We would not care to bet on what the coming years will do to the popularity of Jung's psychology.

Rank and Ferenczi

These two men can be treated together because they published together and because their defections from Freud were somewhat related to each other. Rank's schism from Freud was earlier, more severe, and more complete than Ferenczi's. Neither has yet assumed the stature of Freud, Adler, or Jung, although both have made significant contributions to the theory or practice of psychoanalysis.

In 1922, Otto Rank (1884–1939) began to present his ideas on birth trauma. In addition, he and Ferenczi were collaborating on a book entitled *The development of psychoanalysis* (1923). The book advocated the possibility of shorter therapy and stirred considerable dissension among analysts later. Even more disturbing was the book Rank wrote alone, *The trauma of birth* (1929). Freud himself reacted quite positively to the book at first, but he was later ambivalent about it. Complicating the picture was Rank's aversion to Jones; Freud apparently did not know whose side to take in these disagreements. A series of declarations of independence by Rank, followed by declarations of friendship, finally resulted in Rank's complete separation from Freud and the orthodox analytic movement.

Initially, Ferenczi showed some hostility to the members of the committee and was disappointed at his treatment at party congresses; he was never elected president by a full congress. However, his final separation from Freud was neither so early nor so dramatic as that of Rank. He simply drifted away from the other analysts, partially because of his therapeutic beliefs. There was little or no real bitterness between him and Freud, at least until very near the end of Ferenczi's life in 1933; by this time Ferenczi's physical illness may have affected his mind (Jones, 1957, p. 176).

Rank's background contributed a professional issue to psychoanalysis. He had come from a technical school to the Wednesday Society and had been encouraged to attend the university. His application of psychoanalysis to cultural developments endeared him to Freud. Rank thereby swayed Freud in favor of lay analysts. Freud had never identified with the medical profession himself and did not see any absolute necessity to study medicine in order to practice analysis.

Rank's more direct contribution was connected largely with the birth trauma. In a sense, Rank was pushing Freud's concern with the early years to its logical conclusion. He saw the neuroses as originating in the trauma of birth, where the child experiences a forcible and painful expulsion from the comfort of the womb into the terrors of the world. This trauma, he believed, is never forgotten. The "separation anxiety" that results from the birth trauma is basic to neurotic symptoms. The clash of will between child and parent that later attends the growing-up process is also important. The job of the therapist, then, is to alleviate both the guilt of the patient over this clash and his anxiety over separation. In order to get the patient to work hard during therapy and in order to ensure that the patient does not become overdependent on the therapist, a definite date is set for the separation of therapist and patient. The therapy is then terminated at the agreed time, and the patient develops in therapy the ability to function alone after this time.

There is one interesting sidelight on Rank's theory. Freud was ordinarily quite opposed to statistical treatment. The only known exception to this occurred when Freud was in a critical mood toward Rank's theory; he suggested (Jones, 1957, p. 68) that he would never have proposed the theory without prior statistical evaluation of the mentalities of those who were firstborn, had difficult births, or were delivered by Caesarean section.

Sandor Ferenczi (1873–1933) made no theoretical modifications as sweeping as Rank's. His chief defections were in therapeutic technique. He shared with Rank the belief that it is not always necessary to exhume the historical origins of neurotic symptoms; thus a briefer therapy should be possible. Ferenczi thought that the warm relationship with the mother was missing in the lives of most of his neurotic patients and that the therapist should supply this missing element. Accordingly, he coddled patients, holding them in his lap and kissing them at times (Jones, 1957, pp. 163–164). Freud saw this as opening the door to therapeutic techniques which could discredit psychoanalysis completely, and Ferenczi was hurt by Freud's doubts. However, he would not be dissuaded from his belief that *acting out* the unconscious problems is the way to mental health, and continued to use his unique therapy until his health became so poor that he could no longer work. Compared to the primal therapy or nude marathon of today, Ferenczi's procedures appear quite conservative. One listens in vain for a new Freud's ironic commentary on the newer procedures.

This concludes the purely expository portion of this chapter. It is in no sense a complete history of psychoanalysis even up to the time of Freud's death in 1939; it is a sample of highlights only. More recent developments will be presented later, but they too must be incomplete. Psychoanalysis is an organic movement that is forever growing; no cross section can give a realistic or a complete picture. However, we now turn to some evaluation of the cross section we have presented here.

In view of the differences between those systems usually called *psychoanalytic,* psychoanalysis cannot be considered a single system. However, there are important commonalities even among the widely divergent systems, and we shall try to keep these commonalities in the focus of the discussion. Wherever we discuss a point which is not common to all systems, Freud's system will be used rather than any of the others. Although the goals and content of psychoanalytic psychology are somewhat different from those of the systems we have treated earlier, we will continue to use the same discussion outline.

Definition of Psychology

Although Freud was not within the tradition of psychology as such, psychoanalysis was to him perhaps the only psychology worthy of the name. He was interested in developing a systematic framework but not in stating definitions. His followers did not differ from him on this point. Freud *distinguished* psychoanalysis at one time by its concern with resistance and transference; at another time he said that the distinguishing mark of an analyst was concern with sexual factors. But these were not definitions. We will follow a similar procedure, describing some salient features of psychoanalysis. This provides a sort of implicit definition of psychology as seen by psychoanalysts. Psychoanalysis is a discipline that began in the study of neurosis through the techniques of hypnosis, dream analysis, and free association. It has emphasized unconscious motivational conditions. It has since broadened its fields and methods of study to include anthropological investigation, laboratory experiments, testing techniques, and the study of normal persons, cultures, and cultural records. Rapaport (1959) makes clear the fact that psychoanalysis does intend to define psychology in a way that allows psychoanalysis to encompass it:

> Finally, in the late thirties, forties, and fifties, the influence of psychoanalysis and of the new psychoanalytic ego psychology expanded to the whole of psychology, first through projective techniques into clinical psychology, then into experimental clinical psychology, and finally into experimental psychology proper. Thus the original claim of comprehensiveness for this theory is gradually being realized. (p. 79)

Several basic assumptions are made by analysts, and these assumptions must be included as a part of the definition of the school; only those who accept some minimum number of them are accepted analysts. These assumptions are next examined.

Basic Postulates

According to Munroe (1955), nearly all varieties of analysts accept four basic assumptions. First, the psychic life is *determined.* Second, the *unconscious* plays a predominant role in determining human behavior, which previously had been thought to follow rational patterns of determination. Third, the most important explanatory concepts are *motivational* (i.e., "dynamic"). Many different behavioral manifestations can be explained by recourse to a single underlying motivational concept; the emphasis is on the purposiveness of action rather than on more mechanical S-R connections. Fourth, the *history* of the organism is of extreme importance in the determination of contemporary behavior.

In addition to these four primary postulates, more orthodox analysts usually accept several others which may be summarized as follows. The basic drive is sexual and has its foundation in the biology of the organism. The manifestation of this primal biological energy is seen in the various instincts. There is a basic conflict of life and death instincts (we have already seen that this is one of the least popular postulates). A structural, topographical model is needed to explain unconscious activity; Freud's id, ego, and superego are the usually accepted structures. Parental relationships to the young child account for the neuroses. The individual goes through various stages of libidinal development—oral, anal, phallic, latency, and genital. The defense mechanisms under the control of the ego protect the individual from psychological harm. Finally, dreams, slips of the tongue, wit, and various errors have symbolic meaning related to repressed sexual content.

Although we have included the above assumptions under the name *postulates,* this term should not be taken literally. Freud was an inductive thinker, at least as he conceived the process. He did not see himself as postulating at all but merely as reporting or summarizing the results of his observations. His reaction to Janet's saying the unconscious was a manner of speaking shows that Freud did not like to have his concepts put on a postulational level. The behavior of many of his followers indicates that they tend to think the same way. This is not necessarily a telling criticism, for it does not matter how concepts are viewed as long as they play a useful part in theory.

Nature of the Data

The basic data of psychoanalysis have been gathered in the therapeutic setting. They are the data of verbal report, or of introspection. The type of introspection is markedly different from the classic type, but the difficulties of the classic type are still present, often in aggravated form. If psychoanalytic introspection is supposed to give information about past events, then the original stimuli for the verbal report occurred months or years previously. Many of the hypotheses of psychoanalysis are about relationships between events in the patient's history and present behavior. In fact, some critics have felt (e.g., Skinner, 1954) that one of the main contributions of psychoanalysis has been its emphasis on the causal importance of events in the life of the individual. Yet these events have been little studied in any direct way. The data are the *present* verbal productions of the patient. Freud was himself puzzled when he found by checking the reports of his patients against the reports of other family members that many of the reported events could not possibly have occurred. He decided that it made no difference whether the event had occurred; the fact that the event had been fantasied made it important for therapy. Ezriel (1951) has argued on the basis of such reasoning that analysis is *not* a historical method. It seems that he is right. The analyst really works on the assumption that *reports* about the past are important; operationally speaking, the analyst has nothing to do with the past of the patient. He studies the personality of the individual through an observation of his interaction with another person (the analyst), not through the reconstruction of the past. Psychoanalysis is a dynamic, not a genetic, method, working with contemporary rather than genetic data.

The relationship between the data and the theory of psychoanalysis is thus far from clear. If the theory is about genetic factors, then most of the data are highly questionable. The past events must be *inferred* from the kind of data collected. We remember from the criticisms of structural psychology that psychologists have generally not been content to trust the human memory for more than a few seconds, even under strictly controlled conditions. If the data are recognized for what they are—appropriate to statements about the present only—then the form of Freudian theory would seem to require modification. This kind of criticism is, of course, less appropriate to Jung or even to Adler, since they recognized more explicitly the importance of the present in their theoretical presentations. Even in their cases, however, many of the hypotheses are about the past—in Jung's case even the phylogenetic past, where no direct data at all are available.

A second difficulty arises necessarily from the nature of the therapeutic relationship. Many of the statements made by the patient must be kept in strictest confidence. Analysts must play the role of therapist during an analytic session and can take the detached role of scientist only after the session is over. They may forget, or select only confirmatory data. What a patient says may be influenced by previous statements of the analyst. Freud himself taught his patients some analytic theory in the therapeutic process, although he did not do so to as great an extent in later years; suggestions may thus have inclined the patient toward those statements which would confirm the theory. The net result is that the data are not generally available. Scientists cannot evaluate their quality. The confirmation by a patient that analysis of, say, a dream is correct is of little value. The patient participates in the interpretation, and agreement or verification could be related more to an unintentional suggestion by the analyst than to correctness of the interpretation. There is no outside source that can confirm or deny the correctness of an analysis.

One might wish to ignore the need for such data and demand only data on the success of therapy. Even data on therapeutic success are seldom available in any quantity. There are, of course, plenty of reports of patients who got better, but there are few studies with control groups, equal in other respects, which are given some other type of therapy or no therapy at all. Each analyst sees so few patients, even over a lifetime of therapy, that it is difficult to get a large sample. Even if one could get such control groups and such samples, it would be extremely hard to show that the individual analyst's application of the theory had been correct or that extraneous factors had not contributed to the outcome. Altogether, it is very difficult to demonstrate a tight logical relationship between the theory and the outcome of therapy. A therapeutic situation does not seem to be the place to prove a scientific theory.

Nevertheless, in one year Dittmann (1966) found five studies of the outcomes of therapy (usually not psychoanalytic therapy). Dittmann's review cannot be used to buttress any statements about psychoanalytic theory or therapy, but it does give some illustrations of the pitfalls involved in such research. One study is particularly instructive (Nash, Frank, Imber, & Stone, 1964). These investigators found, according to Dittmann, "an enormous effect of beginning treatment, an effect which started before any treatment was administered, and seemed unrelated to the type of treatment whether active or inactive medication" (pp. 55–56). When effects like these are prevalent, it is not surprising that the best-intentioned therapists overvalue the effectiveness of their own work.

Bergin and Suinn (1975) provide additional information about the outcomes of therapy. Sloane et al. (1975) found that both behavior theory and psychoanalytically oriented therapy accelerated improvement, as compared with carefully selected control subjects. However, the behavior therapists made just as many interpretations as the psychoanalytic therapists! Further, Lazarus (1971) found that of twenty behaviorists who were themselves in therapy, ten were in psychoanalytic therapy, five in Gestalt therapy, three in bioenergetics, four in existential therapy, and one in group dynamics. None were in behavior therapy! (Since the numbers add to more than 20, we may assume that some therapists were in more than one kind of therapy.) All of this seems to reinforce our point that therapy as it now exists cannot test theory.

Observational data have come in from other situations. Kardiner (1939), Mead (1950), and Malinowski (1950) have gleaned relevant data from primitive societies. These data have sometimes bolstered the system and sometimes necessitated its modification; for example, the data have not supported the supposed universality of the Oedipal complex (Toulmin, 1948).

Hilgard (1952), among others, has reported data from human subjects in laboratory or classroom situations. These data are necessarily fragmentary. They are concerned with isolated portions of psychoanalytic theory, as nearly any closely controlled study must be at this stage. Still absent is the painstakingly detailed longitudinal study which would be needed to give sound underpinning to psychoanalytic genetic assumptions. Pumpian-Mindlin (1952) is typical of those who feel the need for a psychoanalytic institute to carry on such research.

Sears (1943)has reviewed the objective research prior to 1942 which attempts to verify psychoanalytic concepts. Many of these studies have been with animals, and a disproportionately large number have been tests of fixation or regression. Horwitz (1963) points out that psychoanalysts are most often sublimely uninterested in such experiments. Too often the hypotheses investigated are trivial, or the experimental investigator has not taken the trouble to get more than a most superficial knowledge of the theory he is attempting to test. Under these conditions, the attitude of the analyst is certainly understandable. Nevertheless, the experiments are relatively well controlled and indicate a salutary concern with the scientific acceptability of the concepts tested. The overconcern with limited concepts probably indicates a weakness in the theory; most of the analytic statements are too general or too ambiguous to allow easy testing. It is in most cases not possible to test predictions based on derivations from several postulates because there is never any quantitative statement and seldom even any statement of the relative qualitative importance of the several possible factors which might bear on a behavioral outcome. Thus the kinds of data and their relevance to analytic theory are partially limited by the condition of the theory.

Mind-Body Position

Freud was a modern in this respect; he did not much concern himself with the question. Jones (1953, p. 367) has said that passages could be quoted from Freud which would place him in any one of several philosophical mind-body positions; Freud self-consciously declared himself a psychophysical parallelist. He held that psychical processes cannot occur in the absence of physiological processes and that the latter must precede the former. He thus assigned some priority to the material, a priority that may have been held over from his student days when he espoused a radical materialism.

Principles of Connection

Since psychoanalysts are outside academic psychology, it is unnecessary for them to begin with the problem of connection as such. However, their basic method is the free-association method, and one can ask how it happens that the associations are connected in such a way that they provide, as Freud said of the dream, a "royal road to the unconscious." The principles of connection are of several kinds.

First, there are the classic principles of contiguity, similarity, and opposition. The elements that have been contiguous to each other in an individual's experiences tend later to be connected in an associative train. Also, elements which are similar for an individual or which are opposites may evoke or substitute for each other. Although the acceptance of these classic principles makes available a rudimentary learning theory, Rapaport explicitly says (1959): "If we must single out an outstanding limitation of this theory's claim to comprehensiveness, then we should choose its lack of a specific learning theory" (p. 79).

The more important principles of connection are those which relate to motivational factors. In an association, the similarity or opposition may be one of motive or feeling rather than of the objective stimuli. A recognition of this fact enables the analyst to recognize connections which are not apparent to the academic psychologists. The determination of associations by these factors also explains why the patient's "free" associations involve material relevant to the patient's basic problems; these problems beget motives which in turn control the associations.

Still other and more complex principles are needed to explain completely why certain symptoms arise from their problems and why certain manifest content arises from its latent content in the dream. These are the special principles of symbolism which have been mentioned earlier. Distortion, displacement, and condensation are such principles. Finally, there are the defense mechanisms of the ego—rationalization, projection, etc.—which explain the connections between certain overt behaviors and their motivational bases. The complexity of these principles of symbolism and defense is such that they have long been the objects of extended analytic investigation.

Principles of Selection

Motivation provides the key to selection as well as to connection; it seems that in most systems, the principles tend to be simply the obverse of one another. Analysts have emphasized the selectivity exercised in the movement of material into consciousness from the preconscious or unconscious more than the selection of stimuli in the environment. The selection of an idea or memory is dependent upon the dynamic balance between repressive forces and those instinctual forces which strive for the expression of the repressed material. Repression acts selectively to remove material from consciousness, and resistances act to keep the emotionally toned material out. The job of the analyst is to redistribute the libidinal energy available so that the repressive forces of the ego or superego are lessened relative to the expressive forces. Often the libido attached to the repressed material is so strong that it forces its own selection for acting out in disguised form; for example, repressed hostility may be expressed through its projection onto other persons, who are then reported to be hostile. The ego is continuously selecting appropriate repressed materials for such symbolic expression. The principles of connection are also involved in selection; the ego must *select,* according to the principles of *connection,* the symbols that are needed to give vent to repressed impulses.

We see from such examples that a considerable part of Freud's contribution was the detailed development of principles of connection and selection in cases that had previously been regarded as arbitrary and lawless. He extended the principles to the unconscious, where different laws were required, and this extension is at the heart of his system.

Research involving the so-called new look in perception, which is no longer very new, has been concerned with the effects of motivation on the perception of objective stimuli. Such selective perception has been demonstrated in the laboratory and represents an extension of the kind of thinking typical of the analysts. Although the interpretation given the experiments is in doubt (e.g., Goldiamond, 1958), there can be no doubt that variables which were earlier thought inappropriate are now being studied in the perceptual context. An example of the observed results is the finding that more time is required for the perception of a guilt-arousing than a neutral word. The analytic interpretation would be that an ego-defensive mechanism is at work and tends to repress its perception.

CRITICISMS OF PSYCHOANALYSIS

Immorality

The lay and religious publics have been vindictive toward Freud and psychoanalysis because of its alleged irreligiosity, amorality, and emphasis on sex. It has been said that Freud reviled and desecrated religion and childhood. Freud was not personally religious, and he attempted to explain religiosity in natural, scientific terms. It is also true that Freud extended the concept of sexuality into childhood and that he advocated somewhat less repressive attitudes toward sex; he was, for example, in favor of sex education of a realistic sort.

Regardless of what Freud's personal feelings were or of what he said on these subjects, such criticism is altogether irrelevant to the truth or falsity of any scientific hypothesis. If one regards Freud's pronouncements on these subjects as philosophical rather than scientific, then his rejection can be on the grounds of value rather than truth. A reader who does not like the pessimism of Freud as a philosophy of life can reject it for a more optimistic view. Acceptance or rejection will have nothing to do with science.

Origins

Several critics have pointed out relationships between Freud's personality or background and the theory he evolved. For example, some might read Bakan's book (1958) as a denunciation of psychoanalysis, since it points out in a clear and scholarly way the relationship between Jewish mysticism and psychoanalysis, with side excursions into Freud's messianic feelings and their implications for theory. It is no rarity to see the Oedipal part of analysis explained by recourse to Freud's own relationship with his young mother or to see his tendency to oppose traditional views reduced to a reaction to his membership in the Jewish minority.

Ellenberger (1970) suggests that Anna O. was simply a classical case of hysteria, in the sense that her symptoms were the effect of suggestion more than the results of symbolic expressions of traumatic symptoms. If this is true of her and of many other patients (we have indicated above that suggestibility is a pervasive problem), then the foundations of psychoanalysis could be very weak. Freud of course became acutely aware of the possibility that the reports of his patients might be fabrications, but he appears not to have condisered the possibility that part of the symptomatology of the patients might be created by the analyst.

Thus the data of psychoanalysis are not so convincing as most scientific data. Therefore, if a critic explains a part of analytic belief as an outcome of the personal experiences of the theorist, it seems that it should be incumbent upon the defender of analysis to show that the belief also rests upon some firmer foundation of acceptable data.

Theory

No system that we have thus far discussed provides an adequate theory. Psychoanalysis is no exception. There is only a psychoanalytic theory in a very broad sense. There are a large number of empirical generalizations, and there are some parts which constitute rudimentary models. Walker (1957) has outlined very clearly the nature of the unconscious as a scientific model. Rapaport (1959) discusses four separate models and a combined model.

Freud regarded himself as a beginner only, and his system as a beginning only. Perhaps the analogy between psychoanalysis and phrenology (see Dallenbach, 1955) is not so unfair as it would at first appear; both disciplines made important beginnings toward sciences, and Bakan (1968) has defended the virtue of phrenology, so that it is no longer necessary to be offended by an analogy between psychoanalysis and that scientific character of questionable repute.

Since no psychological theory of any scope is completely satisfactory, the only reasonable questions one can ask concern whether a particular theory is likely ever to *become* a good theory. Rapaport (1959) expressed pessimism by doubting that the theory could ever be confirmed by generating and testing predictions. Horwitz (1963) is more optimistic and does not see why this cannot eventually be done. A damning statement, if it continues to be true, was made in a review by Ford and Urban (1967):

> Similarly, although 30 to 40 psychoanalytic articles and books have been examined, they are not emphasized here. Our examination of that literature gives the strong impression that little substantive development is underway. . . . There is little substantive novelty in these writings, and they are likely to be of interest only to follow-

> ers of the particular view represented. . . . These books, the psychoanalytic literature this year, and our reading of that literature during the last few years lead us to the conclusion that the innovative steam has gone out of the psychoanalytic movement. Major theoretical and technical advances in the future will probably come from other orientations, although the theoretical contributions of the past will continue to be influential (p. 333).

As is usual with systems like psychoanalysis, empirical confirmation applies to the limited, confirmable statements rather than to the theory itself. Yet, as Skinner (Hall, 1967) says, "You can't expect a Freudian to say, yes, I will admit that Freud's only contribution was in demonstrating some unusual causal relations between early experience and the present behavior. He loves . . . the various geographies of the mind and all of that stuff" (p. 69).

Farrell (1951) provided a list of propositions which at that time seemed confirmed: that infants obtain pleasure from oral stimulation or genital stimulation, that manual masturbation is more frequent among preschool boys than girls, and that small children exhibit extensive pregenital play. Other propositions he regarded as disconfirmed: that all small girls have penis envy and wish to be boys and that all children exhibit sexual attraction and attachment for the parent of the opposite sex and sexual jealousy of the parent of the same sex. A third class of propositions is regarded as untested or untestable, such as the hypothesis about substitutability of erogenous zones.

Whether or not one agrees with Farrell's classification of these few propositions, his procedure at least illustrates the necessarily piecemeal nature of the confirmation process. It is unrealistic to hope for any real confirmation or disconfirmation of the theory at the present time. We must agree with Farrell that "psychoanalytic theory is, qua theory, unbelievably bad." Although this is true of most psychological theory, analysts seem less concerned with this undesirable state of affairs than most academic psychologists. We have said earlier that theories are nearly always discarded not because they are wrong but because they are improved upon and replaced by superior theories. Kuhn (1962) makes the same kind of point in his discussion of scientific revolutions. Walker (1957) says that psychoanalysis fills the need for a model that will "go anywhere, do anything, and be good at dealing with people" (p. 122). Horwitz (1963) says, along the same lines, that it is the implicit feeling of clinicians "that psychoanalysis is not the best theory of human behavior; it is the *only* theory" (p. 429).

Even if this is the case, and we believe that there is beginning to be reason to doubt it, we are willing to argue that it is time to throw aside tradition and stop giving so much serious concern to psychoanalytic theory *even if there is nothing to replace it.*

A story is told about the mother of many children, who was seen to abandon her infant in a sticky mudhole it had fallen into. Her comment was that it would be easier to get a new one than to clean the old one up. Perhaps that is the case with psychoanalysis. Though Freud was undoubtedly a genius and made contributions of immense importance, he did not leave behind anything enough like a theory for any mortal to be able to make it work. For that reason, it appears that psychoanalytic theory no longer directs psychological research on personality, which is what it should be doing if it is doing anything.

We should say that some recent events indicate a change in this gloomy picture. Silverman (1976) has described two research projects that are providing experimental evidence in support of the fundamental psychoanalytic doctrine that psychopathology is a product of unconscious libidinal and aggressive tendencies. One of these is Silverman's own work, performed at New York University. It involves the presentation of either wishful or aggressive stimuli (e.g., the statement "Cannibal Eats Person"), and the evaluation of consequent behaviors. Most important, control stimuli (e.g., "People Are Walking") are also presented. A large number of experiments in Silverman's laboratory as well as other places have yielded consistently positive results (reliably more behavioral disturbances following the experimental stimuli).

The second project is directed by Reyher at Michigan State University. Stories containing stimuli for socially unacceptable sexual or aggressive impulses are given subjects under hypnotic induction, with key words emphasized in posthypnotic suggestion. Behavioral disturbances are subsequently assessed as a function of presentation of selected stimulus words, certain of which (namely the key words) are related to the impulses and others of which are control (unrelated) cues. Statistically reliable differences in support of the psychoanalytic proposition have also been consistently reported in these studies. Continued success in endeavors like these would force us to reassess the place of psychoanalytic theory in psychology.

Criticisms of Therapeutic Outcomes

Toulmin (1948) said that ". . . if a fully-fledged analytic explanation is not part of a successful cure, we do not regard it as a 'correct' explanation; therapeutic failure is as fatal to an explanation in psychoanalysis as a predictive failure is to an explanation in physics" (p. 29). We must disagree on this point. A psychoanalytic explanation may be correct, but the course of the illness may nevertheless be irreversible because the independent variables which, if manipulated, would result in cure may not be under the control of the analyst. A somewhat analogous challenge might be to ask physicists to change the orbit of Mars and refuse to accept their explanation of the laws of moving bodies if they were unable to do so. The lack of favorable therapeutic outcomes, therefore, may be a basis for criticizing the practicality or usefulness of the therapy, but in itself cannot be a basis for criticism of the theory. The theory could be criticized on the basis of therapeutic outcome only if it could be shown, first, that the theory was applicable and perfectly applied to the case and, second, that the therapist was able to manipulate all circumstances at will.

Lack of Control

This criticism has been implicit in several of the other criticisms. The control we are speaking of here is not the control physicists might lack if they wished to change the orbit of Mars; it is the control of variables in order to isolate the factors at work in any given observation. That is, in the language of experimental psychology, the analyst must work with too many uncontrolled variables. It is not possible to isolate influences on a patient one by one, but one must attempt to disentangle relationships from the complex matrices of lives as patients happen to live them. The analyst cannot be sure that descriptions of the past, or even of the present, are adequate, relevant, or accurate. It is impossible to back up and see what would have happened if events had been changed in some way; one cannot try out the effect of some single manipulation on the patient's future behavior, for there is no way of isolating people from a multitude of other influences. No wonder it has been said that the situation is uncontrolled!

A common answer to this criticism is that the analysts have proceeded through *clinical validation.* This seems to mean that successive confirmations of a theoretical prediction within the clinical setting constitute acceptable demonstrations of the accuracy of the principles involved. Such an argument is basically unsound. We have to know what alternative explanations are possible, and these alternatives must be eliminated by means of appropriate controlled changes in the situation. Otherwise, despite an infinite number of clinical validations, it is possible that the same artifacts continue to give the same outcomes, which happen to be consistent with the theoretical predictions. In reality, it is extremely improbable that clinical validation would ever be as systematic and careful even as we have pictured it; it is difficult to imagine a clinician finding enough cases appropiate to some prediction to permit a repetition of test after test of some good, operationally defined, clear hypothesis.

It is not easy to suggest improved methods for testing psychoanalytic propositions. This is clearly due to the state of the theory. A necessary step involving a huge amount of labor and ingenuity is the improved definition of terms and the formalization of the theory. A prior step, then, would be to try to define operationally the terms that occur in the isolated propositions so that these will be more experimentally testable. Mullahy (1948, pp. 316ff.) has given several examples of the need for clarification and elimination of contradiction. We have already indicated our opinion that the effort required would be misspent.

There are, nevertheless, probably many who will wish to make the effort. For them, we shall suggest the direction that confirmation, or attempted confirmation, of the theory might take.

There are several levels of behavioral observations and corollary realms of discourse involved in analytic theory and its testing. Most of the orthodox observations have been of verbal materials. Investigations at this level of observation might be improved by the use of more objective measures of the verbal behavior of the subject, as with psychological tests of various kinds. Stephenson (1953) has developed a technique, the Q sort, which is a compromise between the usual completely free analytic situation and the more strictly objective type of personality test, and has shown how the technique can be used to test analytic propositions. This technique has the advantage of dealing in a quantitative way with some of the attitudinal dimensions that are related to psychoanalytic theory.

A second level at which psychoanalytic propositions can be investigated is that of everyday life behavior. Social caseworkers can make observations on the real-life characteristics of the individual and relate these observations to the events in therapy. These data would go beyond what is usually available to the analyst. We have already suggested that behavioral observations unrelated to therapy are also needed; although Freud felt that the best way to get information about the psychic apparatus was to study cases in which it was malfunctioning, we also need more information about the genetic events in the lives of normal people.

On a third level of investigation, studies within the therapeutic situation itself might well be improved in terms of both control and sophistication of approach. Horwitz (1963) reports as follows on some of these more ingenious and careful studies:

> The treatment situation, long the subject of post-dictive study, is now becoming the locus of predictive studies. Bellak and Smith (1956) have reported a carefully controlled study of short-term predictions concerning the expected developments in the analytic treatment of patients whose preceding hours had been carefully studied by a group of analyst-predictors who were not themselves treating the patient. Wallerstein, Robbins, et al. (1956, 1958, 1960) have initiated a long-range study of both process and outcome in which a major method is the formulation of predictions prior to beginning treatment. A key feature of this investigation is the formulation of the theoretical assumptive base for each prediction in an effort to validate and extend psychoanalytic theory. (p. 431)

A fourth level at which the propositions need further study is the fully experimental one in which full scientific abstraction and control are reached. Although many analytically inclined people doubt the possibility of testing the propositions in this way, we shall never know unless we try. Furthermore, such investigations would be valuable in their own right, regardless of their bearing on psychoanalytic propositions. It would be surprising if any investigation produced results which were perfectly in keeping with the original speculations that instigated them. If they generally did so, experimentation would become unnecessary.

It is too early to say whether the recent experimental research mentioned above (Silverman, 1976) reflects a trend towards a widespread appreciation and utilization of controlled evidence on psychoanalytic doctrine, rather than the dying gasps of Freudian theory. But if these researchers and others who follow them into the laboratory continue to test fundamental Freudian ideas under appropriately controlled conditions—and find a reasonable degree of support for them—the future of psychoanalytic theory may not be nearly so dark as our previous estimates suggest.

Dogmatism and Cultishness

We have already had some discussion of this point in other connections; for example, we saw the sense in which Freud was dogmatic and the sense in which he was not. We have met the "committee," composed of men who might almost be called disciples; Eitingon, for example, always made a pilgrimage to see Freud on his birthday. There are other points which suggest cultishness: "Only the analyzed can analyze" as though one had to be personally initiated in a trial by fire before one could carry the word.

These characteristics indicate why psychoanalysis from the outside has seemed almost as much a religion as a science. Again, this argument has nothing to do logically with the value of the theory or the therapy, but it has had something to do with the acceptance of the theory by scientists, who feel that science is not a cult. Agreement with a gospel or subjective evaluations of persons should have nothing to do with evaluations of scientific propositions, and psychoanalysts have sometimes seemed to use these criteria.

An interesting form of dogmatism is the criticism by analysts of the detractors of psychoanalysis. A critic who refuses to accept some aspect of psychoanalysis is said to be manifesting resistance. We can find such inherent dogmatism in Freud himself. When he wished to show why Adler was wrong, he said (Freud, 1938): "I shall, therefore, use analysis only to make clear how these deviations from analysis could take place among analysts" (p. 964). No doubt Adler analyzed Freud in return in order to show why Freud had resisted the new ideas.

CONTRIBUTIONS OF PSYCHOANALYSIS

Psychoanalysis is in the paradoxical position of being often rejected as a scientific system and yet accepted as an outstanding contributor to science. Freud is more often regarded as a pioneer, as a prescientist, than as a scientist; he called himself a conquistador. Whatever he is called, he is recognized even by his enemies as a great man and perhaps the greatest genius within psychology. He made contributions to many fields. Let us look at some of his contributions to psychology.

He stimulated thinking about, and observation of, many neglected areas of psychology: the significance of unconscious factors in determining behavior, the widespread importance of sex in normal and abnormal behavior, and the importance of conflict, of childhood, of the irrational, and of the emotional. He personally made acute observations throughout a long life of daily work and contributed hypotheses or facts—we cannot yet tell which are which—about broad areas of human behavior.

He developed highly provocative explanations of kinds of behavior previously considered outside the realm of scientific explanation, such as errors and dreams. The fact that such areas are examined and such explanations developed by a serious worker would have been an important contribution regardless of the eventual correctness or even usefulness of the explanations. A field of study was opened up that was fallow for all practical purposes when Freud touched it.

Even in technique and methodology, where psychoanalysis so often falls short of traditional scientific criteria, Freud either made contributions or reinforced points made by others. His development of the techniques of free association and dream analysis for the study of unconscious processes has been compared with the invention of the microscope for studying cellular processes. Equally important, his emphasis on the study of unconscious processes preceded and reinforced the behaviorist and Gestaltist point that the traditional methods of introspection are altogether inadequate for the development of a complete science of the human being. One could argue that Freud made incidentally a point that became a central thesis of behaviorism. In this sense, psychoanalysis has been the source of a great optimism; psychology is now viewed as a discipline that will certainly become a full-fledged science and develop whatever techniques are necessary. Without Freud, the conviction might have been slower in growing.

Psychoanalysis has contributed much empirical observation. Intensive studies of individual cases are available in the psychoanalytic literature as in no other place. Freud himself published only four case histories of his own patients, but other analysts have contributed, and the distillation of such observations presumably appears indirectly in analytic propositions. C. S. Hall and Lindzey (1957) believe that Freud's use of internal consistency as a method of testing hypotheses was one of his most important contributions to research strategy. As applied within psychoanalysis, internal consistency refers to the checking and cross-checking of a particular hypothesis by means of a large variety of different indicators; homogeneity of results is interpreted as supporting the hypothesis, much as a test is evaluated in terms of the extent to which the separate items can be shown to be positively correlated. Internal consistency becomes important as a research strategy only when there are a great many data on a single case. It makes possible a kind of reliability not otherwise easily obtained.

Another contribution is not easily weighed in a scientific scale. Psychoanalysis has contributed to the popularity of psychology and psychiatry with the lay public. The average person's vocabulary includes analytic words and notions from all schools, and most people use some analytic modes of thinking about the behavior of others—and perhaps occasionally their own. Psychoanalysis has thus revealed the importance of psychology to the lay public in a way that other systems have not. It may be that money and talent are easier to recruit to the science of psychology because of the analytic contribution.

Psychoanalysis presents explanations of normal and neurotic behavior in a language and at a level that people are prone to believe they understand. For better or for worse, it deals with practical situations in an exciting and challenging manner. Its method and theory contrast markedly with the slow, tiresome, painstaking program characteristic of most scientific research and theory construction. Therein lie both its appeal and its weakness.

DIMENSIONAL ANALYSES OF PSYCHOANALYSIS

The reader should again refer to Table 1-2 for the authors' ratings of psychoanalysis on Watson's eighteen dimensions. Three of the dimensions have been found to be difficult to rate, as indicated by large inter-observer discrepancies.

The authors regard Freud, at least, as being clearly mechanistic in his approach. As we have seen, he extended the domain of determinism, and seemed to support the viewpoints of Brücke and the others who made the antivitalistic pact. However, we must admit that he wanted to study psychology as entirely independent of physiology, despite his background in neurology. He also proposed principles of psychic functioning which bore no clear relationship to "mechanical" principles. No doubt these aspects of his approach cause him to be seen as somewhat vitalistic by some.

A second source of disagreement is the rationalistic-irrationalistic dimension. Watson says that he intends this dimension to refer to the extent to which emotional and conative factors intrude on intellectual functioning. If one sticks to this definition, there can be no doubt that Freud's views were irrationalistic; in fact, that is the very core of his contribution. Some, however, might argue that the unique contribution of psychoanalysis was just that it made the *apparently* irrational rational by pointing out the rules by which the psychic apparatus works. In this special sense, psychoanalysis *is* rationalistic, but that is not what Watson meant. It should also be remembered that Freud's whole emphasis was upon human irrationality, a sore point with many of his critics.

Finally, the authors see Freud as a very prototype of dynamicism. He is often described as a, or the, father of dynamic psychology. We have found, however, that some rate psychoanalysis as neutral on this dimension.

The three dimensions that seem most important in characterizing psychoanalysis are unconscious mentalism, determinism, and irrationalism. However, other dimensions like dynamicism are also reasonable choices.

SUMMARY AND CONCLUSIONS

Psychoanalysis deals with the interesting and mysterious, yet practical and important, regions of man's existence. Its adherents have hung together in a kind of cult; psychoanalysis is apparently thoroughly understood by few persons who are not analysts. Still, enough of its theory and practice has filtered out to others so that its terms enrich the lay vocabulary more than the terms from any other psychological system.

Psychoanalysis is more an art, a philosophy, and a practice than a science. The theory is loose and nebulous, sometimes even self-contradictory. The therapy has not demonstrated a greater effectiveness than other kinds of therapy, and only recently has evidence been accumulating that therapy is better than no treatment at all. The data and methodology which gave rise to psychoanalytic theory are markedly inadequate from the point of view of traditional natural science. Analysts have often shown little interest in improving the evidence for the theory. However, analytic theory has changed frequently in response to new observations in therapy, and recently there have appeared the first experimental laboratory tests of fundamental psychoanalytic ideas.

Many of the modern variations on Freud's theory have followed Adler down the path of increased emphasis upon cultural factors, with some compensatory deemphasis of biological factors. Much analytic effort has gone into increased specification of the nature and genesis of ego functioning; it is this area of study which probably gives the most promise of a rapprochement with academic psychology. Jung is typical of those who have placed increasing emphasis upon the unity and the creative potential of the self. The common rejection of the death instinct is typical of the less pessimistic outlook on human nature shown by modern analysts. Psychoanalytic theory has been a powerful force since 1900, and some of its basic ideas are receiving ever wider acceptance. Among these ideas are the unconscious model and the importance of sexuality. There are still several training institutes for analysts within the United States. Yet there are those who say that psychoanalysis is dead or dying. It has glaring systematic and scientific defects.

If psychoanalysis is to remain a viable and unitary force within scientific psychology, these defects must be remedied soon, or it will be displaced by effective competition by theories and therapies growing out of the study of behavior in the academic tradition. However, we have seen that variations on the analytic theme occur even within the therapies of the behavior modifiers, so the disappearance of a psychoanalytic school would not, by any means, indicate the disappearance of the psychoanalytic influence, even within psychology.

We should certainly not derogate the positive contribution of psychoanalysis. It opened up new areas of investigation such as the unconscious and sex; gave impetus to motivational research; pointed to the importance of childhood and genetic factors in the determination of personality; provided valuable and intensive empirical observations; and worked out the nature of the defense mechanisms. All of these contributions are often gratefully accepted by otherwise unfriendly psychologists.

FURTHER READINGS

So much has been written on psychoanalysis that it takes great temerity to present a reading list. The books that follow are good, but are only a tiny fraction of the total number of good books. Jones's three volumes, *The life and work of Sigmund Freud* (1953–1957), are in many ways the best single source on psychoanalysis. These books can be read as absorbing biography and will infuse large quantities of knowledge painlessly into the unwary brain. Jones's formidable volumes have been abridged by Trilling and Marcus (1961). A fine little book which is just what it claims to be is C. S. Hall's *Primer of Freudian psychology* (1954). This book provides a solid basic introduction to Freud's system. C. S. Hall and Lindzey, in their *Theories of personality* (1970), do the same thing for all the important psychoanalytic theorists. Munroe's *Schools of psychoanalytic thought* (1955) is a friendly psychologist's look at psychoanalysis. Ellenberger's *The discovery of the unconscious* (1970) puts all of dynamic psychology in historical and cultural perspective, and is particularly good in showing the contributions of French psychologists like Janet and Charcot, who have been neglected in the present chapter. Bakan's *Sigmund Freud and the Jewish mystical tradition* (1958) is a scholarly and readable account of how Freud's theory was related to his cultural background. *A general introduction to psychoanalysis* (1943) is probably Freud's own most readable work. Rapaport's chapter (1959) has the same kind of systematic aims that we have in the present chapter, but Rapaport is more positive and optimistic about psychoanalysis. He provides a wealth of insights, as well as references which provide a fine directory for still further study. Silverman's (1976) article shows how, with sufficient ingenuity, psychoanalytic theory can be used to direct research.

Part Two

Contemporary Theories

The second part of this book is concerned with more contemporary developments. We will attempt to show the relationships between modern issues and (1) the historical systems, and (2) the philosophy of science.

The first part of the book has been intended to prepare the student to understand the first of these two kinds of relationship. Now we will present a framework for studying theories, derived from the philosophy of science, just as in Part One we provided a framework for understanding the more global problems posed by psychology's historical systems. One of our guiding beliefs is that these global problems are still important even in the most modern developments, but a number of more detailed and specific issues now also demand consideration.

After introducing some theoretical perspective, Part Two presents a selection of theories which have been most influential within American psychology, and which relate most clearly to our historical systems. We do not consider in any detail highly specific theories or models, such as those that deal with color vision or with the learning of verbal materials.

The general theories treated fall naturally into three groups which can be identified more or less with Woodworth's functional schema of stimulus-organism-response. Thus, the so-called stimulus-response theories have been primarily response-centered; the field theories developed from Gestalt psychology, with their emphasis on perception, have been much closer to a stimulus centering; and personality theories concentrate upon the organism and its characteristics. This simple scheme cannot be pushed very far, since no theory deals exclusively with any one category, but it does indicate primary emphases.

The fourth chapter in this part deals with the influences upon psychological theory of mathematical and engineering concepts and procedures. There is little doubt that the rigor and precision so imported are having an increasing and salutary effect on our science.

The epilogue is a survey of some recent systematic and theoretical developments.

Chapter 9

Psychological Theory

THEORY AND OTHER USES OF LANGUAGE

The second part of this book is concerned with the more recent history of psychology. Psychologists have always had a powerful urge to develop theories, and the ideas about what a theory should look like have changed over the years. We should, therefore, examine both the traditional view of what constitutes good theory and some of the criticisms of that view. Armed with an understanding of theoretical problems and controversies, we can better comprehend the transition from the older schools to contemporary psychology.

There is little controversy about the importance of theory. One of our astute theorists, Kurt Lewin, has said, "Nothing is so practical as a good theory." If Lewin had been talking about the practical value of becoming famous, there could be no doubt that he was correct. The most famous figures in every scientific field are its theoreticians: Newton and Einstein in physical theory; Darwin in biology; and Freud, Hull, Skinner, and Lewin himself in psychology, to give just a few examples. But that is not the point Lewin was making; he was opposing the practical and concrete to the useless and abstract.

Theories are necessarily abstract, but abstractions are not useless; probably the dominance of the human being as a species is closely related to the human ability to construct and use abstractions. Mild-mannered Charles Darwin stated his view on the usefulness of scientific abstractions very powerfully in a letter to Henry Fawcett on September 18, 1861: "How odd it is that anyone should not see that all observation must be for or against some view if it is to be of service!"

The most highly respected theories in the most developed sciences are expressed in logical and mathematical language. These theories are often so remote from everyday language and experience that they can be understood only after a long period of preparation. However, the very same thing can be said of any statement in any language. Any English-speaking person who wished to read even a nursery rhyme in Sanskrit (assuming that nursery rhymes exist in Sanskrit) would quickly appreciate the difficulty of interpreting any set of abstract symbols. However, because we learn our native language while we are very young, we tend to forget the backlog of experience and special training that allows us to make sense of its incredible complexity. Scientific theories seem more complex and more abstract partly because we encounter them later.

There are many parallels, then, between scientific theories and the ordinary statements of everyday communication. The cook who concocts, consumes, and communicates a new recipe in everyday language is in many ways similar to a scientist. Both the cook and the theoretician wish to create and share new knowledge. The knowledge is shared via language. The useful recipe and the useful theory must correctly specify the outcome of certain operations, although there are surface dissimilarities between operations like melting butter and, say, creating a powerful magnetic field. Instrumentation is almost certainly involved in both cases, perhaps a blender on the one hand and a cyclotron on the other (or, in psychology, maybe a tachistoscope). Both cooks and scientists may need special training in observation ("Cook until the vegetables are tender but still crisp," or "Continue training until the response rate stabilizes"). Noncooks and nonpsychologists, respectively, might be mystified by such instructions, although the expert might see them as routine. Finally, both the cook and the theoretician appeal to the experience of the observer ("Isn't that yummy?" or "See that blue afterimage floating across your field of view?").

Obviously there are many differences in detail between theoretical and other uses of language, and we will outline some of them later in this chapter. Before we do that, however, let us look further at some of the general problems that must be faced in any study of linguistic activity, and develop a little vocabulary that will be useful in referring to different subareas of linguistic study.

GENERAL PROBLEMS OF LANGUAGE

In a classic article, Stevens (1951) discussed a distinction made earlier by Morris (1938) between three areas of study within the general topic of the use of signs. The general topic, which embraces the three specific areas, was to be called semiotic. The three specific areas were to be called syntactics, semantics, and pragmatics.

Semantics

Let us change Stevens's order and discuss semantics first, which he defines as the study of the relationship of signs to objects. Despite this definition, he later says that meaningful signs must refer to objects *or events.* It is pretty clearly the case that limiting meaningful terms to those that denoted objects would leave us with very little to say! We could point to a desk and a chair, but the meaning of *sit* would remain forever a mystery, since sitting is no object.

Many books have been written on the subject of semantics. It is no simple matter to assign a meaning even to an apparently simple word like *of,* although native speakers of English have a good intuitive notion of what it means. A whole "movement" in the philosophy of science developed around the problem of assigning meaning to scientific concepts. That movement was called *operationism* because Bridgman (1927) insisted that the meaning of a scientific concept must be reducible to a set of operations. Operationism itself, as one proposed solution to the problem of how to establish semantic rules relating signs to objects or events, stimulated a spate of books clarifying, defending, and attacking it. Today the consensus of opinion probably is that operationism was, at best, an incomplete solution to the problem of determining the meaningfulness of statements, and that it may have been too restrictive. Much theoretical activity may occur at a very abstract level, with empirically meaningless signs being manipulated. Only some of the signs need to be coordinated with empirical observations in order that a theory be considered empirically meaningful. If operationism limited the freedom of the theorist to proceed on this basis, it would do science a disservice.

On the other hand, the concept of *operation* may be broadened to include pencil-and-paper operations with purely abstract symbols. Bridgman (1952) did later make it clear that he thought such "abstract" operations were admissible as meaningful. But when such abstract operations are admitted, there seems to be little unique content left to operationism. We are left with Hume's injunction to throw away the metaphysics in our libraries, and to keep only the books involving observation *or* logical reasoning. At the very least, operationism promoted a great concern with semantic problems. Scientists tended to take more care that their terms had a specific empirical meaning, or that they had a defensible rationale for using, within a theory, terms which were not empirically defined. If we have moved beyond operationism, it is because we were forced to move through it. The problems of semantics are not solved, but they are better understood. The student of the history of psychology should recognize a few basic facts about semantics as it relates to psychological theory in particular.

First, definitions are an attempt to assign meanings to terms. A dictionary is a semantic device, one so useful that we have come to think we could hardly do without it. Before there were written dictionaries, there were people to tell other people what oral and written signs meant. There is one difference between these two kinds of "dictionary" that we should dwell upon: the written dictionary is completely insufficient in itself, and the living dictionary is quite sufficient. Other people can clarify the meanings of words through all sorts of nondictionary operations like pointing, demonstrating, and so forth. Without outside reference a dictionary is quite useless. To appreciate this, just try using a dictionary in an unfamiliar foreign language. Although all the words in it are defined, it is no good to you because you have no external referents of any of the words to get you started. You easily use a dictionary in your own language because you already know enough words *independently of the dictionary* so that you can use them to understand the rest.

The language of ancient Egypt could not be translated until the Rosetta stone was discovered in 1799. This stone had parallel inscriptions in Greek and in ancient Egyptian characters; since the Greek was understood, the Egyptian could at last be decoded. Operational definition is the Rosetta stone of scientific theory. Without external definitions of at least some of the terms of a theory, the whole theory stands as devoid of meaning as Egyptian hieroglyphics before the Rosetta stone came to light. However, not all hieroglyphics had to be coordinated with Greek terms; the meanings of other symbols could be determined within the system of hieroglyphics by using internal relationships to deduce the meaings of additional signs, in a way similar to deducing the meaning of an unknown word in English from its context. Modern science allows the theoretician freedom to use some theoretical terms that have no direct relationship to empirical observation, so long as other terms adequately tie the theory to observations.

We will return to some of these same issues in the following sections, since the study of language, like most studies, is in some sense a unity. The issues of semantics are closely related to issues of pragmatics (it is the users of language who relate symbols to things) and to issues of syntactics, which we will now discuss.

Syntactics

Syntactics is the part of the study of language which concentrates on the relationships of symbols to each other. In reality, of course, symbols are related to each other by the users of language; the symbolic relationships that interest users will be determined by the use that can be made of the relationships in understanding and controlling objects and events. Syntactics, however, attempts to isolate from the total study of language a part that includes only the symbols and their manipulation.

Syntactics, then, involves an attempt to deal with abstract systems as such. In a sense, it is a study that turns the world on its head, for the "concrete" objects with which this study deals are the "abstractions" which science is in the habit of using to understand the rest of the world! Syntactics is therefore a clear example of a *metatheory,* since it is a theory about what theories are or what they should be as abstract systems.

Chess, like other games, has some of the properties of the logical and mathematical systems that are used in the development of theories in science. In the case of chess, there is not even an attempt to relate the "symbols" of the system, usually conveniently represented by physical pieces of material, to any "more real" world outside the game of chess. The way chess symbols are represented physically is unimportant, when we consider that chess problems in the newspaper, chess magazine, or computer chess game are represented by marks on paper, rather than by actual pieces. Chess is, therefore, an abstract game. Systems like the algebra of real numbers can be regarded in exactly the same way: as symbolic games with rules for "moves" and the goal of producing new combinations that have aesthetic appeal. In the case of chess, the combinations with the most appeal are clustered under the single name *Checkmate!* In the case of mathematical and logical "games," any new combination has the potential for appeal; however, what seems to be most appealing is the ability to make a sequence of legal "moves" that eventuates in the "proof" of a "conjecture" or important new "theorem."

To learn to play chess, one need only purchase a chess set and a rule book. The book will specify the legal moves. The allowable moves, in fact, define what is meant by a "pawn," a "knight," etc. The outer appearances of the pieces have no significance for the game. The nature of the board and the rules for taking pieces need also to be defined. It is, of course, not enough to know the rules if one wants to be a good player. The "good" moves constitute only a small proportion of the legal moves.

Similar considerations hold for other syntactic games like "Boolean algebra," "Differential topology," "Psychological theory," and so on. The rules of the game can be found in appropriate books, but knowing the rules does not make one a good player. In no case would we want to call the manipulator of symbols a scientist, unless the person used the chess pieces (or theoretical symbols) to model some aspect of the world external to the game. Science in its essence establishes new relationships between symbols and the world outside the symbols. Scientists may invent new symbols with a new syntax, but their work is not finished if they do only that. They are, if they have invented a new system, or proved a new theorem within an established system, "mere" logicians or mathematicians. To become a scientist, one must define symbols, and define operations with the symbols, in terms of objects or events external to the symbolic system. That is, one must work with semantics. To be successful, a scientist must show that a new symbolic-empirical system has some usefulness to "speakers" of scientific language; thus a scientist must be concerned with pragmatics.

Students of syntactics can divorce themselves from such scientific concerns. For them, "the game's the thing." Realizing it or not, the person working on a chess problem is a pure syntacticist. The problem is presented as a position of the pieces on the chessboard, with the somewhat cryptic message "White to move and mate in (some number)." The message and the problem can be decoded in syntactic terms as follows. "You have been presented with an arrangement of symbols that might have arisen from a sequence of moves syntactically allowable (that is, following the rules) within this symbolic system. You are now to demonstrate a sequence (or more than one sequence) of moves, legal under the rules of the syntax, by white, such that, no matter what legal moves are made by black, the sequence (or sequences) terminates with black checkmated."

In chess, the desired configurations of symbols generally have the property that one side or the other is in checkmate. In chess problems, a position is given which can be transformed into the desired position after only a few legal moves. In logic and mathematics, the situation is not terribly different in principle, but in practice the difficulties may be far greater. There is often a desired solution defined, similar to the checkmate of chess; the desired solution in mathematics is often called a *conjecture* or just a problem that needs to be solved. (Conjectures are "proved" rather than solved.) In either case, a mathematician, at least the first mathematician to try to prove a conjecture, is not presented, like the solver of chess problems, with an intermediate position. The mathematician begins at the beginning, with the elements of the system and the rules for their manipulation. Like the chess player, the mathematician may call upon the body of proved theorems within the system (the chess player calls upon his or her knowledge of past games and past problems that have been solved).

A recent example communicates some of the difficulty and excitement of the mathematical version of the syntactic game (Kolata, 1977). A Hungarian mathematician named Paul Erdös was excited enough about a conjecture which he and another mathematician had posed, that he offered $1000 to anyone who could prove it. After 40 years, another Hungarian mathematician, E. Szemerédi, collected the money for his proof, which required 100 typewritten pages! Not surprisingly, it is reported that very few people have read the proof in its entirety. A second, independent proof based on quite different assumptions required "only" 85 pages, and it may be that no one has yet checked *both* proofs!

It is significant that the report we have cited appeared in *Science,* which may seem to contradict our statement that those who concern themselves with "mere" syntactics are not scientists. Usage is not really very important here; symbolic systems are an integral part of scientific activity, and the only reason that it might be useful to classify logicians and mathematicians separately from scientists is that the separation may help us to keep the several aspects of scientific activity conceptually clear. Completely educated scientists, whether psychologists or physicists, cannot afford to neglect the study of the symbolic systems developed by logicians and mathematicians.

Pragmatics

Pragmatics is the study of the relationships between signs and the users of signs. As we have already indicated, semantics and syntactics cannot be studied separately from pragmatics, because signs are related to each other, and to objects and events, only through the mediation of the users of signs. Thus, for example, chess has an unavoidably pragmatic side, despite its abstract character. The complex maneuvers concerning match rules for international championships provide beautiful illustrations of this claim.

Users of signs are trained to think or to do certain things in the presence of certain related sequences of signs. Syntactics tells us what sequences should be regarded as meaningful by the users of the signs. Semantics tells us what the user should think or do in the presence of each meaningful sequence of signs. It might be more accurate to say "Syntactics tries to tell us, etc.," since there is much unfinished business in the realm of language. In any case, the important point is that language cannot be understood as independent of its relationship to users of the language. Perhaps that is one incontrovertible point which can be extracted from Skinner's *Verbal behavior* (1957). For Skinner, language was clearly a matter of stimulus (for a listener) and response (for a speaker), and was to be understood, like any behavior, in terms of the reinforcements which attended linguistic interactions.

That clearly puts the emphasis on pragmatics, which is where an empirical scientist, for example a psychologist, ought to think it belongs. Skinner thinks that we must go out and study how language functions if we wish to understand any aspect of it. His attitude may remind us of the attitude of Thomas Kuhn, who studied the history of science in order to learn about how science proceeded, instead of studying the philosophy of science alone in order to find out how it *ought* to proceed.

Natural languages like English, German, Russian, or Chinese have passed the test of usefulness over many centuries. Languages, like scientific theories, continue to evolve. New words and new usages emerge to cover new situations, and some words become archaic as they are no longer needed. Presumably all of this is a matter of pragmatics in the narrow sense meant here—concerning the relationship of signs to users—as well as of pragmatics in the broader sense of usefulness.

Even the oldest scientific theories are newcomers compared to natural human languages. However, they are subject to the same kinds of tests for usefulness. Simple theories, like simple statements in natural language, are easier to use. There is no doubt that very straightforward pragmatic concern is what accounts for the scientist's preference for the simpler of two alternative hypotheses or theories. Psychological theories that do not allow for the prediction and control of phenomena are less useful than theories which give equal understanding and also allow for prediction and control. Perhaps the decision most characteristic of many modern behaviorists is to concentrate exclusively on the discovery of variables which can be manipulated so as to control outcomes; they base their decision on a belief that true usefulness attaches only to those symbols which tell us how to control outcomes.

This concludes our brief introduction to the areas of study in the field of linguistics as envisioned by Morris and reported by Stevens. Stevens later (1968) characterized science as a "schemapiric" activity; he was once again conveying a picture of science as an activity that establishes relationships between symbols *(schema-)* and empirical observations *(-piric)*. In this chapter we have so far taken the symbol, or schema, as our focus of attention. We now turn to a very brief description of some aspects of scientific activity that are not so directly concerned with language.

Nonlinguistic Features of Science

Nearly every aspect of scientific activity is *ultimately* related in some way to language. Scientists even try to describe every one of their procedures so thoroughly that their observations can be repeated by any other competent observer. However, Kuhn (1970) is one of many who has pointed out that scientists do not usually succeed in conveying their activities that completely via language. The student cannot become a scientist by reading textbooks or even reports, no matter how many. One becomes a scientist by first becoming an apprentice to a practicing scientist one can observe and imitate. The student must learn by watching and doing.

What indescribable things does the neophyte scientist have to learn? One example is learning discriminations. Just as the chef may know when something is properly cooked by observing color, texture, and tenderness, so the scientist must learn what to observe and what observations indicate that the desired outcome is being achieved. In learning what to observe, one is learning to direct attention to relevant features and to ignore others which might seem more important to the uninitiated. This type of learning is sometimes summarized by saying that a scientist has a "trained" or "prepared" mind. Roentgen's mind was prepared when he saw a tube glowing when it should not have been glowing, and he immediately used the observation to discover x-rays. Perhaps one weakness of written reports is the fact that they cannot list everything that should not be seen!

Scientists must learn habits of manipulation, as well as of observation. They must learn what apparatus to use, and how to use it. Occasionally they may need manipulative skills rivaling those of a helicopter pilot. It is difficult to bring about new phenomena without some technical skills, and a part of the business of science is the creation of entirely new phenomena; biologists will probably provide us with a number of examples by recombining genes and producing useful new life forms. (Those which are less useful may also provide fascinating examples of new phenomena.) The world is already replete with examples produced by chemists and physicists and in many cases, brought into being by engineers. The jet plane, the atom bomb, the computer, nuclear power, and plastics spring to mind. Such examples remind us of one undoubted advantage of experimental research over naturalistic observation: naturalistic observation may be a highly effective technique for finding out what *is,* but only experimental research can tell us efficiently what *might be.* The furor about research recombining genetic materials tells us that its friends and its foes share the belief that experimentation will greatly accelerate the rate of development of new life forms.

Finally, science as practiced by human beings may well have a unique character depending in ways that we cannot imagine on our own, certainly nonlinguistic, characteristics as human beings. Francis Bacon put this general problem beautifully, although quite negatively, in his discussion of the various "idols" to which human thought is subject. Bacon pointed out that human thought is not independent of our natures as individuals and as members of human species: "For the mind of man is far from the nature of a clear and equal glass, wherein the beams of things should reflect according to their true incidence; nay, it is rather like an enchanted glass, full of superstition and imposture, if it be not delivered and reduced" (1857, Part 3, p. 276; original pub. 1605). It is almost commonplace today to add that our perceptions (and hence our science based on those perceptions) are not necessarily consistent across different states of awareness. Thus if drugs or training in meditation, for example, produced a different state of awareness, there could be a potential for the construction of a different sort of science tailored to that state of awareness (Blackburn, 1971).

It is already clear that science has tailored itself to the meeting of human needs. People need to stay warm and to control heat for other purposes, so there is a science of thermodynamics; they need to eat, so there are sciences of agronomy and nutrition; they need to heal their wounds and cure their ills, so there are the medical sciences; they need succor and self-understanding, so there is the science of psychology.

Although our discussion only scratches the surface of these issues, it leaves no doubt that the linguistic activities of scientists are balanced by a host of activities and considerations which are not primarily linguistic. And Bacon's idols are worshipped by the theoretician as well as by the observer, and at least as much by the psychologist as by the physicist. However, there is no point in bemoaning the fact that our science is unique to humankind. The possibility of other sciences for other organisms, or even for other times or places in the universe, does not invalidate our science for our time, place, and species.

A PICTURE OF THEORY

Herbert Feigl presents views (1970) which preserve something of the classical view of what scientific theories are, while recognizing modern criticisms of the older picture of theory. In Figure 9–1, we reproduce Feigl's simplified sketch of the nature of scientific theory because we think it provides a clear starting point.

First, let us consider the relationship between Feigl's diagram and the branches of the study of language. Feigl's postulate set, plus the theorems derived from it, is clearly in the province of syntactics. The circles and the triangles representing the elements of the syntactic system are just terms or symbols within the syntactic system.

Feigl's picture of theory is truly classical; he points out that Campbell (1920) developed essentially the same view some time ago. Feigl aptly describes this outlook as "picturesque" in that an "uninterpreted calculus" hovers, or floats freely, above the observation plane.

Chess pieces correspond rather well with the circles in Feigl's calculus. Both the pieces and the elements of Feigl's calculus are defined via rules which relate

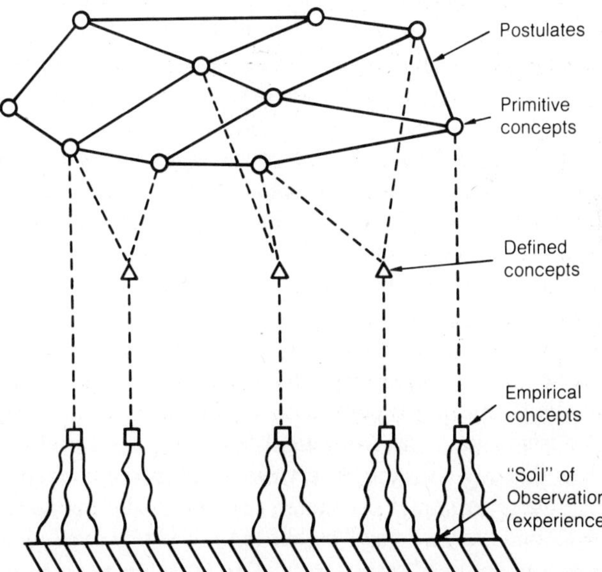

Figure 9-1 A classical view of theory. (Adapted from Feigl, 1970.)

the elements to each other. No element needs any definition relating it to the outside world in order to have meaning; that is, the elements may be made meaningful via strictly *internal* definitions. When we know that a bishop can move along diagonals, cannot jump over pieces of its own color, can take any enemy piece that is within range of a legal move, can be taken by any enemy piece which can move to its position, etc., we know what a bishop means. The activities of the bishop need not be defined in terms of wars, the activities of the stock market, or visual afterimages in order to be meaningful at the level of the game. The meaning is almost purely syntactical. If chess were to be made into a scientific theory, coordinations would have to be established between the elements of the game and empirical concepts. Feigl indicates such coordinations in his diagram by lines linking the hovering syntactical system with empirical concepts.

Thus the elements and rules of the game of chess correspond with the elements of Feigl's calculus and the postulates that connect them. In both cases, the choice of syntactical system can initially be quite arbitrary. New games are frequently invented, and so are new nongame syntactical systems. Most games and most syntactical systems arouse little interest; but sometimes something like calculus comes along and arouses so much interest that there are debates about priority, as to whether Newton or Leibniz deserves most of the credit, or perhaps Newton's teacher, Isaac Barrow. Although the invention of games and of other syntactical systems may be arbitrary, these systems are ultimately selected on the basis of such extrasyntactical considerations as their interest and usefulness.

Exactly the same things can be said about the external definitions of terms of the theory. One could, for example, define a bishop as a blue visual afterimage, and taking of the bishop could become the disappearance of the afterimage. Other pieces could be similarly defined in terms of other visual phenomena, and chess would then furnish the syntactical part of a proposed visual theory. One could question the usefulness of such a theory; considerable ingenuity of definition would seem to be required if the theory were to provide any correct predictions or explanations. However, one should not question the right of the theoretician to define elements at will. We can reject the completed theory if it does not fulfull our criteria of usefulness. We can also refuse even to consider it if we are not satisfied with the clarity of its definitions or its postulates. It does not, however, seem that theories should be rejected on the basis of the content of the postulates or the nature of the definitions.

In Feigl's picture, definition is not portrayed as the kind of one-step process suggested above when we proposed defining a bishop (an element in a "calculus") as a blue afterimage (which seems to belong directly in the "soil" of observation). Rather, Feigl interposes empirical concepts between the abstract system and the soil of observation. The theoretical terms are coordinated with the concepts, rather than directly with the observations. Thus the concepts would themselves seem to have an abstract character. However, such concepts would presumably be developed "from below" rather than "from above" in Feigl's picture. In psychology, a concept like "response rate"might serve as an example. Presumably this concept could be developed independently of any theory about how response rates ought to behave, or of any theory which suggested that response rate ought to be a useful concept. In this sense, then, the concept might be developed "from below," directly as a result of finding such a concept useful for expressing the results of experimentation.

Measurement operations would be used to connect the empirical concept, response rate, to the observations made in an experiment or field study. Thus we are dealing here with one type of operational definition. It is not true that operational definitions are necessarily *restricted* to this type of grass-roots measurement operation, but such measurement constitutes a clear example of one type of operational definition. If the operations for establishing response rate are clearly specified, and if response rate is given no meaning aside from the specified operations, then the operationist would seem to have no reason for objecting to the use of the concept.

A theory builder might then decide that one of the elements in a theory could usefully be defined as, or coordinated with, response rate. He or she would then coordinate other elements from the abstract calculus with other empirical concepts that might influence response rate (or be influenced by response rate). If the calculus truly calculates, the theory builder can go on to make predictions about what the effects of other concepts on response rate ought to be (or, what the effects of response rate on other concepts should be, or both, depending on the structure of the theory). At that point, the theoretician would have a scientific theory which could be "tested" by performing experiments or making observations to see whether or not its predictions were borne out.

Although Feigl's diagram contains some details which we did not discuss in connection with Stevens's picture of the study of language, Feigl does leave one of Stevens's branches of study pretty much out of his account: pragmatics. In order to include it, one needs in the diagram a bemused observer who watches the tentacles of the calculus in their tremulous, though indirect, contact with the empirical world. Actually, the observer is more like a puppeteer, since he is not just observing, but is pulling all the strings. We must not forget that human beings are the creators of the abstract system, the creators of the empirical concepts, and they furnish the soil of observation. Thus it is fitting that human beings also judge the finished products of their imagination (or of all the imaginations participating in the construction of the theory) and approve or reject them, depending on whether or not they meet their needs.

Diesing (1971) defines *theory* as "a model with one or more interpretations." His definition relates very clearly to Feigl's diagram. The calculus corresponds to Diesing's "model" and the whole diagram corresponds to Diesing's "theory." Thus the network interrelating Feigl's calculus to the soil of observation provides Diesing's "interpretation." A theory therefore enables predictions (by manipulating the abstract model), and makes it possible to check on the correctness of the predictions (by making the corresponding manipulations on the "interpretation" and observing the results). In this book, we use the terms *model* and *theory* in a way consistent with Diesing. The reader should recognize that other authors may use these terms in other ways. There is nothing wrong with defining the terms in some other way, but Diesing's definition accords very well with our general discussion and with most usage in the behavioral sciences.

THE OUTLINE FOR REVIEW OF THEORIES

In 1954 a group of psychologists (Estes, Koch, MacCorquodale, Meehl, Mueller, Schoenfeld, & Verplanck) produced a good guide to the evaluation and understanding of theories in psychology. The outline, reproduced in Table 9–1, was intended to guide their evaluation of theories of learning, but there is nothing in it that restricts it to any particular subject matter. We can use Feigl's diagram as a center around which to organize the more detailed questions asked by Estes and his coauthors. We shall refer to the outline as the MLT outline, since the book in which it appeared was *Modern learning theory* (1954). The reader should refer to this outline in reading the following discussion.

I. Structure of the Theory

In this first section MLT asks questions which should lead to a *description* of the whole theoretical enterprise. In the later sections the outline deals with the evaluation and accomplishments of theory. However, some evaluation is implied in the way certain of the earlier questions are phrased. For example, the first complete question is: "Is the data language explicit and theoretically neutral?" The authors of this book, MLT, and the reader no doubt agree that a data language should be explicit, and (with less certainty) that it ought also to be uncontaminated by theoretical presuppositions. The next three questions seem freer of possible implicit criticism and deal with the lower levels of Feigl's diagram, although the last question in this group implies that there may be an effect "from below" on the form of the postulational structure which seems, in Feigl's picture, so blissfully independent of the mundane reality to which it may be connected.

Feigl himself points out that such independence becomes quite illusory if one examines the actual development of scientific theories. The empirical concepts might well be developed first, with the postulate set developed or chosen so that it seemed to fit the concepts (variables) already developed. Thus when MLT asks what influence the choice of variables has on the form of the theory, it is providing a corrective which Feigl also recognizes as necessary.

In asking how the theorist's attitudes affect the coverage of the theory, MLT is recognizing a "pragmatic" issue, in the language of Stevens and Morris. That is, people construct theories, and different people have different "orientative attitudes" which influence the type of theory they are likely to construct. To put this more technically, we might say that different theorists have different metatheories (although these metatheories are not likely to be formally, or even explicitly stated).

In asking about theoretical concepts, the authors continue with their descriptive task. The primitive terms they ask about are the primitive concepts of Feigl's diagram; in both cases, these terms are the most basic terms of the theory, not reducible via definition to any more fundamental terms. Thus their meanings must be fixed via their relationships to other terms of the theory. Presumably the

Table 9-1 Outline for Reviews of Theories

I Structure of the theory

- A Delineation of empirical area
  - 1 Data language
    Is the data language explicit and theoretically neutral?
    How does the theorist relate his empirical variables to the data language?
  - 2 Dependent and independent variables
    How does the selection of variables compare with those of other learning theories?
    What influence does the choice of variables exert upon the form of the theory?
  - 3 Relation between empirical areas covered and orientative attitudes exhibited by the theorist
- B Theoretical concepts
  - 1 Primitive terms
    Are primitive terms of the theory reducible to physical or object language?
    Is the usage of primitive terms fixed by implicit or explicit definitions?
  - 2 Principal constructs
    Do these serve only a summarizing function or are they related by definition or by hypothesis to terms of other disciplines (e.g., physiology)?
  - 3 Relations assumed among constructs
    How are the major theoretical variables interrelated in the foundation assumptions of the theory?
    How are such interrelations constructed from the observation base of the theory?
  - 4 Relations assumed or derived between constructs and experimentally defined variables

II Methodological characteristics

- A Standing of the theory of principal methodological "dimensions"
  - 1 Explicit axiomatization
  - 2 Quantitativeness
  - 3 Consistency and independence of principal theoretical assumptions
  - 4 Use of physical or mathematical models
- B Techniques of derivation
  Are the empirical consequences of the theory developed by informal arguments or formal derivation?

III Empirical content and adequacy

- A Range of data for which interpretation or explanation in terms of the theory has been claimed
- B Specificity of prediction demonstrated
- C Obvious failures to handle facts in the area III-A
- D Tours de force
  Has it been possible to predict new experimental phenomena?
  Have any predictions of this sort been confirmed?
  Does the theory account for facts not predictable from competing theories in the same area?
- E Sensitivity to empirical evidence
- F Programmaticity
- G Special virtues or limitations, techniques which may prove useful outside the context of the specific theory

Source: Estes et al, 1954, pp. xiii, xiv.

"physical or object language" to which the primitive terms might be "reduced" according to the immediately preceding question would, in some sense, constitute a "definition" of the primitive terms. This question refers to a controversy in the philosophy of science, concerning whether the most basic language ought to be an objective ("physical" or "object") language or a subjective language. MLT seems to be suggesting that the objective language is preferable. Bishop Berkeley would not agree.

Next, MLT suggests taking a look at the "principal constructs" (one could equally well say concepts) of the theory. If a construct or concept were to serve "only a summarizing function," then it would have relevance only to the data actually dealt with by the theorist—in the case dealt with by MLT, only to learning data. However, a theorist might wish to hypothesize that the learning variable which was directly coordinated with the construct could also be given a physiological definition in terms of a reverberating neural circuit, a synaptic change, a decrease in cholinesterase activity, or something else. A construct given such hypothetical, additional definitions would be said to have "excess meaning."

It seems to us that there is a tremendous amount of middle ground between constructs with this particular type of excess meaning and constructs that "serve only a summarizing function." If a construct is embedded in a theory, its implicit definition relating it to the other theoretical constructs gives it a great deal of excess meaning not contained in its summarizing of empirical relationships already observed. At the very least, almost all theoretical constructs are assumed to have a timeless, placeless quality; that is, they are assumed to be capable of summarizing the "same" relationship between observables whenever and wherever it occurs.

In more complex theories, a particular construct may play a role in deducing observations of a kind never before made. We are all familiar with the fact that Einstein's theory predicted the bending of light in the vicinity of the sun and the possibility of unleashing the power of the atom. Suggestions that Einstein's constructs ought to have served only a summarizing function seem to be rare. It is safe but unexciting to limit oneself to strictly operationally defined concepts with relevance only to what has already been observed; Darwin's comment, quoted near the beginning of this chapter, says it better than we can.

In asking about the relations assumed among constructs, MLT turns to a detailed examination of the structure of the theory. This requires a study of the structure of the postulates that Feigl has lightly poised in the abstract otherworld. Asking how the interrelationships are constructed from the observation base of the theory again *presumes* the construction of theory from below, rather than from above. The fact that theory is constructed partially from below should not blind us to the fact that theoreticians engage in a great deal of almost purely rationalistic activity. That is, they do learn about logical and mathematical systems, and the theoretical endeavor is a continuous adaptation of these abstract systems to the demands of empirical observations.

Once a theory has been developed, there is also what has been called the *correction from above* in which the theoretician may tell the observer what should be observed and how it should be observed. Without the guidance of relativity theory, it is hard to imagine why experimental physicists would want to look for such an unlikely and apparently trivial thing as a very tiny bending of light in the gravitational field of the sun. Lakatos (1970) describes how Newton continually corrected the observations of Flamsteed, the first Astronomer Royal. As Lakatos says, "One can understand the constant humiliation and slowly increasing fury of this great observer, having his data criticized and improved by a man who, on his own confession, made no observations himself: it was this feeling—I suspect—which led finally to a vicious personal controversy" (pp. 130–131). Kuhn tells us that the practitioners of a paradigm seek facts which should, according to the paradigm, help to reveal the nature of the world. We believe that, without the guidance of a theory or paradigm, one is unlikely to make the most revealing observations. The most successful theoretical development, in psychology as elsewhere, takes place when there is a continuous interaction between abstract and empirical activity.

In the final question about structure, one is invited to examine the definitions that coordinate the theoretical terms in Feigl's diagram with the "empirical concepts" which have presumably been developed independently (at least initially) from the theory.

II. Methodological Characteristics

Here MLT proceeds to ask the kinds of questions that a formal logician would wish to ask about the abstract portion of the theory. The first question is whether or not there *is* any explicit statement of the basic structure of the theory. Until quite recently, the answer to this question for psychological theories was almost always a very simple no.

Exacting theorists seem usually to assume that fully axiomatized systems are desirable. Indeed, it is difficult to disagree with this viewpoint, but full axiomatization is rare, and seldom practical.

To illustrate some of the limitations of the axiomatic approach, we will tell you about the true adventures of Norman, a brilliant young mathematician who was attending graduate school. His mathematical precocity was admired by all who knew him, including his friend, Cleve (the names have, of course, been changed). With respect to women, Norman was a late bloomer. However, Cleve (whose single-minded devotion to women rivaled Norman's to mathematics) introduced Norman to a woman, and Norman attacked the problem thus posed with the same ferocity that he had previously reserved for mathematical puzzles.

A few days later, Cleve described Norman's progress as a seducer. He claimed that Norman had "already worked out all of the axioms and most of the theorems of feminine behavior." If Cleve was correct in his assessment, then something must have gone terribly wrong with Norman's ability to control the inputs to his axiomatic system. Instead of Norman leading the woman to bed, she led him to the altar and, soon after, out of mathematics into applied physics, a field in which there was more assurance of a good income for them and their potential offspring. Cleve, meanwhile, was getting a divorce from his third wife, who got only a property settlement, since Cleve was already paying alimony to the first two wives.

The point is not that there is something wrong with the explication of axiomatic systems; rather, there may be empirical systems so complex that complete axiomatization is presently not feasible. As mathematicians, Cleve and Norman were right to try to apply their techniques to real life, just as psychologists are right to try to apply theirs, including any that they may have borrowed from mathematicians. None of us should be disappointed if our initial attempts, like those of Cleve and Norman, fall short of what we had hoped to achieve. We are temporarily out of our depths with the warm, pulsing, protoplasmic, psychological objects with which our theories must try to cope. Thus readers will find in the following chapters, as in the preceding ones, that rigorous psychological theories are rare jewels, and hence the more to be treasured.

Students of theory are left with two choices if there is no explicit axiomatization: they may either try to extract what seem to be the axioms of the theory for themselves, or they may try to work with an unaxiomatized theory. In the latter case, they must "muddle along" intuitively, perhaps assuming that axiomatization is not necessarily a critical or even a desirable step. It must be admitted that, in the history of psychology this "solution" has been the most common. More recently, however, there has been increasing concern for explicitness; that change to a large extent distinguishes the older, "classical" systems from contemporary theories. As we will see, Clark Hull was psychology's great pioneer and proselytizer in this area; it may well have been Hull's theory that provided the chief inspiration for the writing of *Modern learning theory*. Noam Rashevsky was another great and largely overlooked pioneer, who is only beginning to be posthumously appreciated.

Next, MLT asks about the quantitativeness of the theory. The general meaning of the question is clear; however, it should be noted that while a theory may, in its abstract structure, be highly "quantitative" in that it postulates measurable elements, uses mathematical logic, and so on, the empirical concepts to which the theoretical terms are coordinated may not be quantified. Herbart's old theory (1816) about the interactions of ideas probably falls into this classification. He had an algebra which purported to tell us whether two ideas would inhibit one another, come to consciousness, and so on. Unfortunately, there is no obvious way in which one can quantify (measure) the strength of an idea, let alone several ideas simultaneously, some of which may be unconscious. The opposite situation is also possible; that is, qualitative terms in a theory could be coordinated with quantitative empirical concepts. This situation may be less likely to arise, since the use of quantitative terms in psychological theory tends to be more prestigious, and opportunities to be quantitative are unlikely to be overlooked.

MLT then deals with the purely logical analysis of the structure of the theory. No theorist would want any two of his or her assumptions to be inconsistent. Logicians are fond of pointing out that *anything* can be derived from a pair of inconsistent assumptions. Despite Emerson's assertion that a foolish consistency is the hobgoblin of little minds, consistency *is* desired in formal theory! Independence is also desirable for the sake of neatness; if assumptions are not independent, then there is some redundancy in the theory. Thus the theorist is expected to pay attention to these logical problems, and the critic is quite justified in pointing out any logical shortcomings.

Next, MLT asks about the use of physical or mathematical models. Although there is no necessity for using such models, their use generally makes computation and prediction possible, since physical models behave in predictable ways, and mathematics compute. Human beings also seem to "understand" things better when there is a way of visualizing what is happening, and physical models can be visualized. Even a theorist as seemingly intuitive as Freud made use of models. Rapaport (1959) analyzes Freud's theory in terms of four models: reflex-arc, entropy, Darwinian, and Jacksonian (or neural integration hierarchy). Although these models are looser aggregations than the ones MLT had in mind, they were also intended to aid in understanding and visualizing.

Asking about techniques of derivation also involves logical issues. Less explicit theorists have little choice but to proceed by informal arguments. For example, Freud could probably not rigorously *predict* from, say, his informal model of entropy; but, if he could not *derive* consequences, he could still argue for them. A theorist who has presented an explicit and formal theory may be able to provide formal derivations. In many cases, it will be possible to do so by using the rules of derivation provided for the language in which the theory is stated. Having constructed a mathematical theory, a theorist will take over the techniques of derivation appropriate to the mathematics used. Speaking more globally, the empirical consequences derived should not be inconsistent with the usual rules of grammar and logic, unless the theorist has provided an alternative set of rules for derivation.

III. Empirical Content and Adequacy

In this third main section, MLT gets down to observations, which many people have come to think of as the "real" business of science. This portion of the outline turns our attention away from the abstract portion of the theory—which we can assume for the moment to be a finished product. It is interesting to note that the authors of MLT do *not* ask whether the theory has been confirmed or disconfirmed; they are too sophisticated for that. Asking about both failures and tours de force clearly implies that a theory is not expected to be perfect. If we are satisfied with the ratio of success to failure, then the theory will continue to be used and perhaps modified; if there are too many failures for the successes, the theory will have to be discarded or modified more extensively. Even fairly successful theories are sometimes replaced by theories that are even more successful, or that are more encompassing—which is one way of being more successful.

Sensitivity to empirical evidence has been a central issue for philosophers of science. Theories which are not sensitive to empirical evidence are very unlikely to be scientifically useful. Theories that make predictions are sensitive to empirical evidence, given that the predictions can be checked. Thus theories insensitive to empirical evidence do not make predictions about observables. If a theory makes predictions about events that might *become* observable, it is usually regarded as scientifically acceptable, although it may be regarded for the moment as only an interesting curiosity. If the "events" treated by the theory are in principle not observable, then the theory will probably be rejected as a piece of metaphysics rather than accepted as a part of science.

If a theory is merely programmatic, it is not a theory at all, but merely a program for building a theory. There is nothing wrong with programs, but they are not theories. A programmatic "theory" cannot be evaluated with the logical apparatus provided by this outline. As we said earlier in connection with explicit axiomatization, most psychological theories are indeed lacking in completeness, and thus cannot be completely evaluated as theories. Such a program would bear some resemblance to Kuhn's paradigms, but would be without the predictive power needed to attract adherents and thus to become a genuine paradigm. A program would be likely to include commitments to some of Watson's prescriptive dimensions. It would probably add more specific commitments to experimental procedures and apparatus. Such commitments also occur within paradigms. Examples within psychology would be Freud's commitment to the study of neurotic patients via the method of free association, which we have already examined, and Tolman's commitment to the study of the rat in simple situations, usually the maze. Within Skinner's research program, we see the widespread use of the operant chamber, response rate as the dependent variable, and a number of research preferences as to experimental procedure. At the prescriptive level, Skinner and his followers make a clear commitment to both kinds of objectivism, among other things.

Finally, MLT considers a sort of wastebasket category, "special virtues or limitations," into which leftover tidbits can be thrown along with the garbage. Presumably the tidbits could involve anything from abstract techniques of theory construction to specific techniques of experimentation; however, the word "technique" carries the implication that something more concrete than prescriptive preferences is intended. An example might be the kinds of magazine training procedures developed by operant conditioners, or techniques of shaping, or methods for teaching discriminations without allowing errors to occur.

As a whole, the MLT outline is more in the tradition of the philosophy of science than in that of the history of science. It implies a "normative" view concerned with what science and psychology should be, more than a "descriptive" view of what psychological theory actually has been. This outline, therefore, is the kind of logical tool that Karl Popper would admire more than would Thomas Kuhn. Since there is such a close agreement between the concern expressed in the outline and the picture of theory given us by Feigl, it is clear that both of these views of theory are in the Popperian tradition. Thus when Feigl alludes to criticisms of this classical view, he is referring to the Kuhnian type of criticism, with which we are already familiar.

Critics like Kuhn are prone to point out that science does not develop along the neatly formalized lines that would be implied by Feigl and in MLT. Rather, a very global and inclusive set of procedures (system or paradigm) develops. This system has as prominent elements commitments to doing science in a particular way. These commitments come closer to being metatheory than to being theory, but they are not even explicit or formal enough to be acceptable as metatheory.

Any theories developed as a part of the systematic effort also tend to be informal, incomplete, and, in many cases, expendable. However, fundamental features of a system of psychology will be strongly defended. Proponents of the system, as we have seen, will tend to deny that predictions have failed. The denial may be facilitated by the informality and imprecision of the theories or hypotheses in question. Alternative interpretations of the results of apparently contradictory experiments are especially common. In extremely difficult cases, the outcome of the experiment may be denied as fradulent or the result of inept experimentation. All of this demonstrates that the usual assumption that an experiment can disconfirm a theory is often mistaken. There are too many ways in which the theory can be "saved" by denying the empirical results, or denying their relevance to the theory, or making small ad hoc adjustments in the theory so that it then fits the data.

Despite our agreement with both the criticisms of the traditional view of the nature of theory and with the accompanying description of what actually happens as science proceeds, we believe that some familiarity with the classical view as described by Feigl and outlined in MLT is essential. For one thing, this view is the one which served as the "Platonic ideal" of theory for most of the theorists who were important in psychology. For another, even those who criticize the classical view do not do so because they think the classical sort of theory would be undesirable; they criticize it because it is thought to be too idealized, and hence unattainable.

THE UNFOLDING OF PSYCHOLOGICAL THEORY

As psychology moves gradually toward its paradigmatic phase, the dominant theoretical direction is toward more formal, explicit, and precise theories. In the chapters that follow we will describe Clark Hull's pioneering efforts to construct a rigorous and formal general theory of behavior. Although he did not succeed in producing a lasting theory, he was psychology's most representative "missing link" between systematic thinkers, like Wundt or Titchener, and today's theoretical thinkers, of whom Estes is one example.

Watson says that within any historical period there are likely to be both dominant and counterdominant positions on many prescriptions. Although formal-informal is not a prescription, there is a counterdominant position with respect to the desirability of formal theory in psychology at this time. Part of that opposition comes from the Skinnerian group. This group believes essentially that too much attention devoted to formal theory is likely to divert attention from the main business, empirical study, which will lead to better and more reliable theory than a more rationalistic approach. Skinner and his followers accept a Baconian, inductive approach both to science and to theory construction.

This opposition to formal theory is supplemented by opposition which, for the most part, comes from outside the tradition of academic psychology. The "Third Force" in psychology, made up of a loose alliance of humanists, existentialists, and phenomonologists, tends to reject the formal sort of theory altogether. Formal theorists are seen as modeling themselves slavishly after the admired physical scientists, when psychology should be treated quite differently from physics. This group views the human being as a dynamic and evolving cultural product, the laws of whose behavior are in some sense self-constructed, and potentially variable from time to time and place to place. Any attempt to formalize such fluid laws is foolish and wasteful; we should develop a looser and more human science.

Our own biases lead us to devote more attention to the traditional efforts to develop formal and precise theories. However, we believe that we and the reader should keep an open mind, and be tolerant both of failures to achieve a good formal theory, and of those who reject the whole enterprise.

SUMMARY

The construction of theory in psychology involves the use of language. Hence an understanding of the general nature of the problems of semiotics, which involves syntactics, semantics, and pragmatics, is helpful. But science requires a connecting of language to nonlinguistic elements ("experience" or "reality," depending on one's viewpoint). Feigl's diagram of the classical view of theory is helpful in portraying the scientific connection between language (viewed as an abstract calculus) and experience. Estes et al., in *Modern learning theory,* presented an outline for the review of theories which indicates the main features and most important questions which can be asked about formal theories. The classical view of theory has been criticized as too idealized, particularly in its clean separation of the abstract portion of the theory from its empirical underpinnings. Theory determines and corrects observation and vice versa; the notion of theory-independent soil of experience is therefore questionable. Nevertheless, the classical view of theory is still serviceable as an ideal, and the historical growth of psychological theory has been toward more formal, precise, and limited theories. There is a counterdominant trend which has tended to reject the whole theoretical enterprise as determined by and inherited from the physical sciences. In our preparadigmatic phase, it would be premature to reject any kind of theoretical or antitheoretical viewpoint.

FURTHER READINGS

Marx and Goodson (1976) have collected many useful articles relevant to the concerns of this chapter in their *Theories in contemporary psychology.* Stevens and Feigl present their classical viewpoint there, and Feyerabend and Marx present two versions of the necessary correctives in the light of modern criticism and experience. The introduction to *Modern learning theory* (1954) by Estes et al. is still worth reading as further explanation of their outline. *Criticism and the growth of knowledge,* edited by Musgrave and Lakatos (1970), treats some knotty problems in the philosophy of science and provides a clear connection between general systematic issues and more specific problems in the construction and correction of theories. Stephen Toulmin's *Human understanding* (1972) presents a very attractive view of science as an evolutionary process, using the ideas of variation and selection in a detailed and serious way to apply to the evolution of scientific concepts. Each of these sources presents a multitude of additional sources for those who want an introduction to the world of philosophy of science.

Chapter 10

Varieties of S-R Theory

We must define stimulus and response if we are to define a stimulus-response psychology. It is easy to produce definitions but hard to produce agreement about them. We can at least point out some of the definitional problems and alternative possibilities. The alternative chosen will determine what is taken to be S-R psychology.

One issue is whether the stimulus should be defined independently of the response or as "that which produces a response." We have already seen that Dewey in 1896 deplored the artificial analysis of the reflex into stimulus and response. Skinner (1938) agreed in the sense that he thought it useful to consider a stimulus and a response to be any situational and behavioral aspects of a context that could be shown to enter into an orderly functional relation. J. J. Gibson (1960) was critical of this kind of formulation and pointed to the possibility that it would lead to circularity in some cases (that is, the stimulus might become whatever was needed to bring about the response, leaving no independent term to explain the response). Hocutt (1967) defended the meaningfulness of relational terms of this type. Among Hocutt's examples of such concepts are those of husband and wife, neither of which can be defined independently of the marriage relation. Despite their lack of independence, it remains meaningful to speak of a wife as something like the "female partner in a marriage relationship."

Even if a stimulus is conceptualized initially as independent of responses and is defined in terms of physical energies, it will be of eventual interest only if it does enter into some relationship with a response. It would seem, then, that S-R psychologists need only be careful to have a means of identifying stimuli and manipulating them; they can then ascertain whether the independently identified stimulus enters into relationships with independently identified responses.

A second important question concerns the relative level of molarity of definition of stimulus and response. On the stimulus side, we have encountered a version of this problem in the contrast between the molecular view of the stimulus taken by the structuralists and the molar view taken by the Gestaltists. Brunswik's lens model (see Chapter 11) and his scheme of the organism in its surroundings are clear expositions of some of the possibilities both for stimulus and for response definition. Brunswik's general argument tends toward molar definitions for psychology, at least at the outset. The typical S-R psychologist is probably more molecular than Brunswik would wish, and is in this respect a descendant of the more molecular and analytic associationistic school.

A third definitional question concerns the inclusiveness of the definitions of stimulus and response. Specific questions related to this issue would include: "Is perception a response?" "Is deprivation a stimulus?" "Is an injection of androgens a stimulus?" Because he believes that such things do not fit within the limitations of stimulus and response definitions, Skinner does not think of himself as an S-R psychologist (Evans, 1968, p. 20; Skinner, 1966, p. 12). On the other hand, Kimble (1967), who uses the terms *stimulus* and *response* more inclusively, concludes: "Thus the facts of psychology turn out to be Ss and Rs, a state of affairs which suggests with a certain insistence that the laws of psychology must be reducible to these terms and that an S-R psychology is an inevitability" (p. 76).

Thus there is disagreement about whether one must be an S-R psychologist because there is disagreement about what S and R are. We believe it is useful to regard a stimulus as an event capable of stimulating a receptor. Only stimuli which are related to responses will be of interest, but stimuli must be independently identifiable, or they become mere convenient inventions providing an "explanation" of responses. No position need be taken on the molar level of definition; that is a matter of convenience. We do not believe that S and R should be defined so inclusively that they become indistinguishable from antecedents and consequents; hence we are closer to Skinner than to Kimble on this issue. However, we think it may sometimes be useful to regard inner processes, like perception, as kinds of responses. It may even be advantageous to postulate inner stimuli, provided care is taken to move toward objective identification of such postulated entities. We shall leave definitional problems at this point in favor of an examination of other aspects of S-R theories.

Contemporary S-R theory can be divided into two broad classes which differ in the role accorded the reinforcement, or response-strengthening, process. The first of these classes may be called *S-R reinforcement* theory. Both of the two major subtypes of this theory afford reinforcement a central role, but they interpret the nature of this role differently. Many psychologists, like Hull, have interested themselves in the mechanism of the reinforcement process; some form of "need reduction" has been most often identifed as the necessary and sufficient condition for reinforcement. Others, like Skinner, have stressed the importance of reinforcement without commitment to the underlying nature of the process. This view may be classed as *descriptive* S-R theory, since the fact of reinforcement is accepted in a descriptive or theoretically neutral sense.

The second class of modern S-R theory is generally called *contiguity theory*. Following Guthrie, contiguity theorists hold that all that is essential to learning is contiguity of stimulus and response. Reinforcement, in the sense of presentation of a so-called reinforcing stimulus such as food or money, is important because it changes the stimulus situation and so preserves associations already established. From a historical point of view, modern contiguity theory is a highly refined associationism (see Chapter 3).

The S-R reinforcement theorist is therefore placing the emphasis on the effect of reinforcement upon a connection which has already occurred, much as Thorndike did. The contiguity theorist largely ignores this aspect of reinforcement, attending, however, to the *stimulus* characteristics of reinforcement. Guthrie, for example, was fond of asking what an aversive stimulus made the organism do, and he and the other contiguity theorists also looked closely at what rewarding stimuli made organisms do.

Several writers have suggested combinations of the two major views. These two-factor theories will also be treated briefly. With the exception of Mowrer's version (1960a), they present few new theoretical positions, but rearrange the basic points already present in the two major positions.

All the different S-R theories have a great deal in common, probably more than theories of perception or personality. For one thing, they are all primarily *learning* theories.

Nearly all S-R theories now distinguish between learning and performance (Kimble, 1961), with some variables affecting only the latter, but learning remains central. Because of the important role that learning has played in these theories, it is often very difficult to distinguish between learning theory and general behavior theory. Hull, for example, considered himself a general behavior theorist and thought of learning constructs as central but not exclusive determiners of performance. To most psychologists, however, Hull has been a learning theorist because he has been concerned primarily with behavior *changes*. Similar statements could be made about most of the other theorists discussed in this chapter.

A second characteristic common to all S-R theorists is their neobehaviorism. The most marked difference between modern *neo*behaviorism and Watsonian behaviorism is the greatly increased theoretical sophistication of the former. Watson, Weiss, and Holt had to be content with making gross generalizations based on very limited empirical evidence. Today, however, detailed logical justification as well as empirical evidence is demanded by and of neobehaviorists.

S-R REINFORCEMENT THEORY: THE HULL-SPENCE SCHOOL

The main lines of modern S-R reinforcement theory were laid down by Clark L. Hull. In the development of this systematic effort he had the assistance of many psychologists, notably Kenneth Spence and Neal Miller. Both were associated with him for many years at Yale University, and both helped to determine the way in which Hull's theory developed. Spence especially has been consistently interested in the form of the theory and has trained and sent forth a large number of theoretical devotees. For these reasons we refer to the "Hull-Spence school." Miller not only worked directly with the theory but also extended it to the explanation of personality. This gives him a place in Chapter 12, as well as in this chapter.

Hull's Career

Clark Hull (1884-1952) was born in New York and reared in Michigan. Throughout his childhood and early adult years, he was beset by illnesses, and he suffered from very poor vision all his life. Polio left him crippled in one leg, and he himself believed that much of his motivation derived from his handicap; however, there is some reason to doubt that this is the whole story. His own "idea books" refer to his hope that he might achieve prominence, fully 7 years before he contracted polio (Hays, 1962).

Hull's education was interrupted both by these physical problems and by lack of money; he had to teach both in one-room rural schools and in a Kentucky normal school for various periods. Nevertheless, he managed to earn his bachelor's degree at the University of Michigan, where Pillsbury was a dominant influence, and to complete his doctoral research at the University of Wisconsin. His dissertation was a study of concept formation (Hull, 1920). He was 34 by the time he completed his own personal obstacle course that led him to a Ph.D. His idea books (Hull, 1962) show that he was often concerned that his late start might prevent him from achieving the greatness to which he aspired. At one stage he expected to have only 6 creative years left; then he raised the estimate to 11 upon reading of the advanced ages at which men like Kant and Leibniz had created great works. When he made the 11-year estimate, he actually had 20 productive years left!

After receiving his Ph.D., Hull stayed on at Wisconsin as a member of the psychology staff. One of his early research efforts concerned the effects of tobacco smoking on efficiency of behavior. These much-cited experiments (Hull, 1924) were marked for their especially good control of the sensory factors involved in smoking (such as the warmth of the air produced by a pipe). The control of suggestibility by concealing whether tobacco was actually present presaged Hull's later concern with the general problem of suggestion.

As a result of being assigned a course in tests and measures, Hull surveyed the literature in that field and eventually published an important early text, *Aptitude testing* (1928). He did not continue these activities, however, because of what he later called his "pessimistic view as to the future of tests in this field" (1952, p. 151). Here again Hull himself provides us with good justification for doubting his assessment of his own motives, since he says in an idea book of 1929 that he still plans to do "a grand experiment on a huge scale" (1962, p. 827) with the intention of constructing a universal aptitude battery. Hull's discussions there convey the clear impression that the aptitude work was merely being deferred until later because he thought of it as the kind of work that he could do when he was older and less creative.

Hull's next persistent research interest was in suggestibility. He became involved because he had to present academic lectures and laboratory work to medical students. He spent 10 productive years in research on suggestion, supervising a large number of senior theses. By his own count, some twenty persons engaged in the research, which was reported in thirty-two papers. He has stated that his interest in hypnotic research was not encouraged after he moved to Yale because of medical opposition, which he had not encountered in the Middle West (1952). He published a classic book, *Hypnosis and suggestibility* (1933), at the end of this phase of his research career.

Hull's third and final major research interest was learning theory. He studied Anrep's translation of Pavlov's *Conditioned reflexes* (1927) and became progressively more interested in learning and general behavior theory. In 1929 he became a research professor at Yale's Institute of Psychology (which was shortly to become the Institute of Human Relations). Thenceforth he turned to the development of behavior theory on a full-scale basis. He continued zealous and devoted work on this most important part of his contribution to psychology, despite declining health during the last few years of his life, until his death in 1952. He left behind a band of students as devoted to him as he had been to them.

Development of Hull's System

Hull published a series of brilliantly conceived theoretical papers on conditioning during the 1930s. Perhaps the best known of these was his presidential address before the American Psychological Association, entitled "Mind, mechanism, and adaptive behavior" (1937). The general purpose of these papers, exemplified in the title cited, was to show how basic conditioning principles might be extended to complex behavioral processes. As a methodological, rather than a metaphysical, behaviorist (see Chapter 6), Hull did not deny the existence of mental phenomena. However, he thought mental phenomena *needed explaining,* rather than themselves being useful as explanatory devices. He therefore proposed to give as complete an account of action as possible, and he hoped that this account would someday help to account for consciousness. Hull thought that the behavioral approach to mental phenomena had not had a thorough trial. He wanted to give it a trial that would either succeed or show that the approach could not work.

A brief excursion into the field of verbal rote learning followed this early theoretical work. Here Hull enlisted the aid of a set of mathematicians and logicians, as well as psychologists, and attempted a rigorous quantitative analysis of the kind of rote verbal learing first studied by Ebbinghaus (see Chapter 3). Although the book that emerged from this effort has been hailed as a landmark in the development of scientific psychology, it has been seldom read, less often understood, and unproductive of research. *Mathematico-deductive theory of rote learning* (Hull, Hovland, Ross, Hall, Perkins, & Fitch, 1940) thus remains an idealized but relatively fruitless model of psychological theory construction.

Hull's next major publication, *Principles of behavior* (1943), had quite the opposite effect. Its appearance marked the beginning of an era of psychological research in which Hull became the unquestioned leader of learning research in this country and one of the most controversial figures in the field. In *Principles of behavior* Hull attempted to lay down the framework for a comprehensive theory of all mammalian behavior. He outlined a set of postulates and corollaries, logically interlaced in the hypothetico-deductive style that he had come to consider a model of scientific theorizing.

Although many psychologists did not think the book fulfilled the great promise of Hull's early theoretical papers, *Principles of behavior* nevertheless had an enormous influence on research in the learning area. Hull became by far the most cited writer in the field. Untold numbers of master's theses and doctoral dissertations dealt with tests of various of the implications of Hull's theoretical system. Up to the time of his death in 1952, Hull remained the dominant figure in the field of learning theory.

A major factor in the success of *Principles of behavior* in stimulating research was its detailed spelling out of the postulate-corollary set. Hull deliberately laid the system out in as explicit a manner as possible in order to expedite continuous and persistent empirical checking. This characteristic was probably the most important feature of his systematic endeavor.

In terms of content, perhaps the most important aspect of Hull's theorizing was its attempt to reconcile the basic Thorndikian notion of effect with the conditioning paradigm and methodology of Pavlov (see Chapter 3). In essence, what Hull attempted to do was to incorporate the effect principle—now called *reinforcement*—into a conditioning type of framework. Unlike Watson, he did not think that frequency and recency of response were sufficient principles to account for learning. The emphasis on effect was evident in the last organization of his postulate set. Hull began with introductory postulates that dealt with "unlearned stimulus-response connections" (postulate I) and "stimulus reception" (postulate II). He then stated the key principle of reinforcement, first described as the *law of primary reinforcement,* as follows:

> **Postulate III. Primary Reinforcement**
>
> Whenever an effector activity (R) is closely associated with a stimulus afferent impulse or trace (s) and the conjunction is closely associated with a rapid diminution in the motivational stimulus (S_D or S_G), there will result an increment (Δ) to a tendency for that stimulus to evoke that response. (1952, pp. 5–6)

Immediately following were corollaries dealing with secondary motivation and secondary reinforcement. Postulate IV stated the law of habit formation, utilizing the variable of number of reinforcements.

Hull's last books were *Essentials of behavior* (1951) and *A behavior system* (1952). The latter work attempted to extend the application of quantitative methods within the system and to extend the system to problems of individual behavior. A final contemplated work on social behavior was never begun. As a matter of fact, Hull, who was very ill during his last years, did not live to read the galley proofs of *A behavior system.*

Hullian Methodology

Objectivity Hull was first and foremost a behaviorist. He rejected metaphysical behaviorism, with its denial of consciousness (cf. Chapter 6), but fully and enthusiastically endorsed methodological behaviorism. Hull was considered the archobjectivist of the 1940s by both his followers, who reveled in this identification, and his opponents, who chose it as a point of attack. In pursuing his behavioristic program, Hull tried to use concepts reducible, at least in principle, to physical terms.

Hull (1943) gave physicalistic definitions of stimulus and response; stimulus was defined in part as "stimulus energy in general, e.g., the energy of sound, light, or heat waves, pressure, etc." (p. 407). Koch (1954) does a nice job of showing that Hull's operations with stimuli did not at all conform to his definition. In practice, a stimulus was a part of the environment which the experimenter discriminated and responded to. Thus Hull, like most objectivists, did not really follow physicalistic definitions in his experimental work. However, even his critics have typically found Hull's data language objective enough.

Hull's theory contained a number of explicit intervening variables. Such variables are logical constructs postulated to help in accounting for the relationship between input and output. They correspond to the circles and triangles in Feigl's diagram in Chapter 9. In keeping with his objectivity, Hull made sure that his intervening variables were functions of observable antecedent conditions like number of reinforced trials, stimulus intensity, and hours of deprivation. The intervening variables in their turn entered further equations that determined what the properties of the observed response should be (cf. Figure 10-1). Thus all of Hull's variables were intended to be anchored in both antecedent and consequent conditions. To the extent that the anchoring and the theoretical interrelationships were clearly specified, the intervening variables were assured of having a clear meaning. If theoretical predictions then coincided with observed data, the intervening variables could be said to "summarize" the observed relationships.

Hypothetico-deductive Form Hull was greatly impressed by the elegance of formal mathematical and physical systems, such as those developed by Euclid and Newton. As his interest in developing a general behavior system grew, he determined to model it upon these examples. The result was that he attempted to build a highly formalized and comprehensive behavior theory in a hypothetico-deductive framework. Formal postulates and corollaries were advanced, together with theorems laid down as deductive consequences. Such a system is hypothetico-deductive because it begins with *hypotheses* which are sufficiently well connected in a logical system so that their consequences can be *deduced.* The deductions (theorems) are related by the theorist to statements of empirical observations which should be made under the conditions specified by the theorem. The validity of the empirical statements is then checked by the experiment. If the statements are true, the hypotheses are retained; if they are false, the hypotheses require modification or rejection.

In *Principles of behavior* (1943) Hull laid down sixteen primary principles, as postulates, and a large number of corollaries; in the revision of the system (1951) a total of eighteen postulates and twelve corollaries was produced. In accordance with the hypothetico-deductive procedure that Hull intended to follow, these primary principles were to be used deductively to predict secondary principles, such as the goal gradient and latent learning.

Formulation of Postulates The focal point of Hull's theoretical thinking was the conditioned reflex, as conceptualized by Pavlov. Hull regarded it as a kind of simplified learning situation which was admirably suited for experimental analyses. The findings could then be extended to other, more complex phenomena. Hull made the extension by basing the axioms of his system on experimental findings from conditioning experiments. For example, Hull's postulate II in his final system states the value of the ascending "molar stimulus trace" as a function of time since stimulation in this equation (1952, p. 5):

$$\dot{S}' = 465,190 \times \dot{t}^{7.6936} + 1.0,$$

$\dot{S}'$ reaching its maximum (and termination) when t equals about .450″

Hull stated his equations formally, carefully, and precisely. Although the precision may have been misleading, the symbols introduced were carefully defined, and this equation, as well as the others in postulate II, was based directly on empirical relationships observed in conditioning experiments.

Koch (1954, pp. 70ff.) believes that Hull erred in basing his postulates too directly on data. The history of science suggests that most successful abstract postulates are several steps removed from the function forms seen directly in data. Thus Koch believes that postulates induced from the data of particular experiments have very little chance of being useful in a general theory.

Such use of conditioning experiments as a source of axioms is nevertheless a distinct and critical change from previous behavioristic practice; Watson, for example, used the conditioned reflex grossly, as an element from which more complex behaviors could be directly constructed by chaining elements together. It is clear that Hull's theorizing was a great leap forward in sophistication of theoretical methodology.

Derivation of Theorems An example will illustrate how Hull used some prior empirical knowledge, one or more primary principles (postulates or corollaries), and some deductive derivation combined with a little quantification to produce theorems that could be tested empirically. Consider the problem of the order of elimination of blind alleys in maze learning, as by a rat. It had long been known that the blind alleys closest to the goal are eliminated first, a principle called the "goal-gradient hypothesis" by Hull (1932). Hull put this empirical fact into a logical form by assuming that the response potential of any response is a function of its distance, in time, from the reinforcing event (in this case, the reaching of the food incentive in the goal box). Thus his corollary iii, delay in reinforcement (J), reads (1952): "A. *The greater the delay in reinforcement of a link* *within a given behavior chain, the weaker will be the resulting reaction potential of the link in question to the stimulus traces present at the time*" (p. 126).

This principle, the logical derivation of which was given (1952, Ch. 5), led to a number of empirical predictions, stated as theorems, for multidirectional maze learning (1952, Ch. 9). Among these, for example, were the propositions that a long blind alley, since it entails a greater temporal delay of reinforcement, will be eliminated more quickly than a short blind alley (theorem 104, p. 282) and that the rate of locomotion through the maze will become progressively faster for the later, compared with the early, parts (theorem 110, p. 286). Now it is important to note that neither of these two predictions could be generated directly from the first empirical result itself, the observation of a gradient of error elimination, but could be logically derived from the general principle concerning temporal delay of reinforcement which was developed from the empirical data. Such logical deduction of many new and different empirical predictions from a smaller number of key principles is considered to be a major contribution of a hypothetico-deductive system. Hull's *Behavior system* is full of such derivations, with quantitative calculations, and so is a closer approximation to hypothetico-deductive methodology than the more programmatic *Principles of behavior.*

Hull did not attempt to hold to a static or fixed system. His thinking was extremely fluid, and his formal theory went through an almost continuous series of revisions. He did not take his own quantitative statements too seriously, and said explicitly that he could not be certain of the value of a single parameter in his equations. He thus used the hypothetico-deductive method in the way it was conceived to be used.

Quantitativeness Hull felt very strongly that theoretical progress in psychology would come as a consequence of the successful extension of quantification. His own theory was supposed to be a primarily quantitative one. In *Principles of behavior* Hull's quantification was largely programmatic. Many postulates had no mathematical form or lacked numerical values for the constants. Hull was acutely aware both of the shortcomings of his 1943 system and of the difficulties associated with genuine quantitative statements. He immediately set out to achieve genuine quantification and published five articles which reported on this work. The basic experiment (Felsinger, Gladstone, Yamaguchi, & Hull, 1947; see also Koch, 1954) was a study of latency of response to a manipulandum; latency was measured from the time that a shutter was removed to make the manipulandum available. Thurstone's method of paired comparisons was used to estimate the amount of ${}_{S}E_{R}$ (reaction potential) giving rise to the response.

There are some unavoidable problems associated with the attempt to quantify the variables of any complex theory. Whenever intervening variables which cannot be directly observed are involved in a theoretical chain, rational decisions involving an element of guesswork must be made as to the quantitative interrelationships between all the variables in the theory. There is no escape from this conclusion. Guesses which produce a useful general theory require great creativity, plus some luck. Logan (1959, pp. 303–306) has given a concise example of the general method by which Hull proceeded to combine empirical observations with rational guesses to produce his version of a quantitative behavior theory. A look at Hull's system, which will now be sketched, will show that he would have needed tremendous amounts of both creativity and luck if his quantitative statements were to have the least chance of survival.

Summary of the System

Hullian theory deals with three types of variables: the stimulus (antecedent or input), the intervening (intraorganismic), and the response (consequent or output). The following highly abbreviated account is intended to give something of the general nature and flavor of the system. The basic system is represented diagrammatically in Figure 10-1. For a more detailed exposition the reader is referred to one of the original sources (e.g., Hull, 1943, 1951, 1952) or to a secondary explanatory source (e.g., Hilgard & Bower, 1975; Koch, 1954; Spence, 1951a, 1951b).

The input variables to Hull's theory are such objective factors as number of reinforced trials, deprivation of incentive, intensity of conditioned stimulus, and amount of reward. These various factors are directly associated with processes hypothesized to function within the organism: intervening variables of the first order. Examples are habit strength ($_SH_R$) as a function of number of trials *(N)*, drive *(D)*, as a function of drive condition such as deprivation of incentive *(C_D)*, stimulus-intensity dynamism *(V)* as a function of stimulus intensity *(S)*, and incentive reinforcement *(K)* as a function of amount of reward *(w)*.

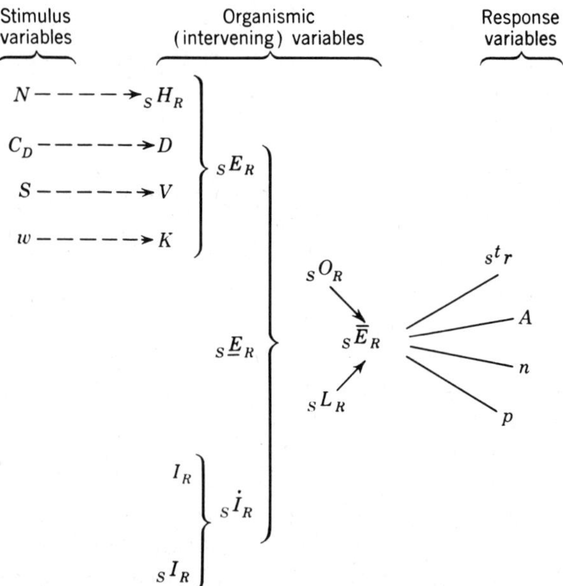

Figure 10-1 Simplified diagrammatic representation of the Hullian system. See text for explanation of symbols and relationships.

Certain of these direct, or first-order, constructs are assumed now to coalesce into a smaller number of second-order intervening variables. The major construct is reaction potential or response evocation (${}_SE_R$), which is a joint function of ${}_SH_R$, D, V, and K. Also to be considered at this level are generalized reaction potential (${}_S\underline{E}_R$), which is a function of the amount of similarity of the present conditioned stimulus to ones previously experienced for which habit strengths have been established, and the aggregate of the negative reaction tendencies (${}_S\dot{I}_R$). The latter construct is a function of reactive inhibition (I_R) and conditioned or learned inhibition (${}_SI_R$), both of which are the direct consequence of work performed in the response.

At the final level, the higher-order intervening constructs then are net reaction potential (${}_S\bar{E}_R$), a function of the two excitatory factors and the one inhibitory factor just mentioned, and two more speculative and less well-specified constructs which modify its action. These are the oscillation (${}_SO_R$) and threshold (${}_SL_R$) of reaction potential. Finally, on the output side, there are four major measures of the effectiveness of reponse: latency (${}_St_R$), amplitude *(A)*, number of responses to extinction *(n)*, and probability of response *(p)*.

A number of stimulus-trace concepts, such as the drive stimulus (S_D) and the fractional goal response (S_G), supplement the theory. They are of primary importance, particularly in some of Spence's (1956) theorizing, but were omitted from our description so that the essentials of Hull's theory could be presented more simply.

Also of great importance, but not included in the summary, are a number of secondary principles which Hull developed in an effort to bridge the gap between the complexities of molar behavior and the abstracted simplicity of his postulate set. Most important among these are the *habit family hierarchy* and the *goal gradient.* The latter was described earlier; *habit family hierarchy* refers to the presumed ordering, according to their relative strengths, of the set of habits that can be elicited in any given stimulus situation.

Systematic Issues

Anyone who aspires to build a theory of behavior like Hull's must face a number of very difficult problems. There is a very low probability that these problems could be solved today, let alone when Hull was alive. However, we can defer criticism of Hull's aspirations until later and look at the nature of the problems which those aspirations led him to face.

One early problem is to decide which independent and dependent variables will be used in the theory. Some guidance is available from experimental practice, but many decisions will remain. For example, will it be profitable to try to predict all response variables from the same theory? Hull emphasized the prediction of latency, amplitude, number of responses to extinction, and probability of responding. Skinner believes that rate of response is the best measure to use; he studies primarily free operants, responses which the animal is free to repeat "at will." Hull studied primarily controlled operants, where-in the experimenter controls opportunities for response emission, as in a runway. His decision to relate his final intervening variable—net generalized reaction potential—to four response measures made it legitimate to ask whether these measures were actually correlated as the theory said they should be. Hull could have avoided embarrassing issues of this kind by making predictions of only one response measure—but he would have lost a great deal of generality in so doing.

Similar problems had to be faced at the level of the intervening variables. For example, there is Hull's decision to have a single excitatory learning construct, $_{S}H_{R}$. If a theorist were working today, he might feel it necessary to have distinct constructs (or distinct theories) for different kinds of learning; for example, food-motivated learning might be distinguished from sex-motivated learning within the theory.

A very general problem connected with the intervening variables concerns what we might call their *reality status.* Hull and his colleagues no doubt had hundreds of discussions about whether it was wise to give the constructs of the theory a physiological interpretation. We have been characterizing Hull's intervening variables as "organismic," which implies some physiological commitment. A more neutral description would be simply that the intervening variables are intratheoretical—which they indubitably are—rather than intraorganismic, which they may or may not be.

Even after the constructs of a system are isolated and their general type decided upon, there remain problems concerning the definition of each construct and the specification of construct interrelationships. As an example of such problems, we might take the innocuous-looking *N,* the number of reinforced trials. What is a reinforced trial?

Hull first specified that if a trial were to be reinforced, it had to be followed by need reduction. There were difficulties with this definition. First, need reduction was likely to be quite slow, and thus did not seem to provide the close temporal contiguity between response and reinforcement expected to be necessary for effective strengthening. Second, it was not easy to know whether or not need reduction had occurred. It could be tempting to postulate need reduction whenever a response had been strengthened. Third, consequences like handling or escape strengthened responses despite the fact that they had no obvious need-reducing properties.

For these and perhaps other reasons, Hull then decided that a reinforcer had to reduce a drive stimulus, rather than a need. This definition had the potential for remedying the first and third difficulties above, but the possibility of circularity remained. Hull had exactly the same sort of problem that Thorndike had encountered with respect to his law of effect, and they needed to resort to the same kind of solution. Any residual looseness in the definition of reinforcement makes the concept of *N* imprecise, and thereby affects all related concepts in the theory.

The specification of construct interrelationships is just as fertile a source of problems. The habit construct, $_{S}H_{R}$, can serve as an example. In Hull's early theory, several imput variables influenced habit. Habit in its turn influenced reaction potential. Since habit was thought to be capable only of slow and continuous change, it was not possible to derive sudden shifts in performance from the theory. Since such shifts occurred in the latent learning experiments (Hilgard & Bower, 1966), a change in the theory was needed. Hull changed the construct interrelationships so that the input variables D (drive) and K (incentive) affected $_SE_R$ (reaction potential) rather than $_SH_R$. It was then possible for the theory to account for the rapid change in response strength which had empirically been observed to occur following changes in deprivation or incentive.

We are not saying that Hull changed the construct interrelationships *in order to* explain latent learning, although there would have been nothing wrong with doing so. Koch (1954) and Hilgard & Bower (1966) agree that the change was actually made so that $_SH_R$ could be more easily quantified.

Hull's precise statement of relationships between constructs helped to create additional controversies. Let us take $_SH_R$ as an example again. Its mathematical relationship to number of trials *(N)* was postulated to be as follows:

$$_SH_R = 1 - 10^{-aN}$$

Trials were assumed to be evenly spaced, and the constant a was thought to be approximately 0.03 in numerical value (Hull, 1951, p. 32).

This clear mathematical statement implies that each trial imparts an increment to the strength of $_SH_R$ and thus indirectly to the tendency to respond. Although this is not truly a continuous function, since N takes only discrete values, Hull's theory was called a *continuity* theory to distinguish it from the view that learning is basically sudden, an all-or-none process. The latter view would be exemplified by the Gestalt position, which was that learning is sudden and insightful and thus noncontinuous. The starkness of Hull's mathematical statements made disagreements stand out nakedly. Controversies like the continuity-noncontinuity controversy and the latent learning controversy raged for years.

Criticisms of the Hullian System

The criticisms of Hull were searching and vehement. As a leading neobehaviorist, he inherited the kind of criticism that had earlier been directed at Watson. Much of this criticism has been based on fundamental methodological or theoretical differences in taste. Nevertheless, the solid critical points lodged against Hull merit attention.

Synthetic Approach As we have seen, Hull attempted to work out a complete and comprehensive theoretical account of mammalian behavior almost at a single stroke. He had to put together the pieces of his puzzle before much necessary research could be done. In Hull's defense, however, it must be said that he started with whatever empirical evidence he could find, and persistently tried to create additional evidence.

Hull wished to emulate the formal elegance of the systems of Euclid and Newton, but lacked much of the background of development which had preceded the construction of these beautifully integrated formal systems. The neatness and elegance of the final product in the case of such formal theory hide the fitfulness of actual development. It may be that theory proceeds faster if initial efforts are not very ambitious. It is now generally conceded that Hull's approach to an exceedingly complex set of problems was too optimistic.

Particularistic Approach Perhaps the most persistent criticism from sympathetic sources has been that Hull relied too much upon certain particular values of critical variables within special experimental circumstances. The problem of generality, always a knotty one in behavior theory, was noted early by Koch (1944, p. 283) in his review of *Principles of behavior;* the point has more recently been made by Hilgard and Bower (1966, p. 186), who have cited the dependence of Hull's system upon particular constants from rat bar-pressing and human eyelid experimentation.

An indication of the extreme particularism of certain aspects of Hull's theorizing, in the sense of dependence upon particular experimental setups, may be seen in his provisional definition of the *wat* (honoring *Watson*) as the unit of reaction potential:

> The wat is the mean standard deviation of the momentary reaction potential ($_SE_R$) of standard albino rats, 90 days of age, learning a simple manipulative act requiring a 10-gram pressure by 24-hour distributed trials under 23 hours' hunger, water available, with reward in the form of a 2.5-gram pellet of the usual dry dog food, the mean being taken from all the reinforcement trials producing the habit strength from .75 to .85 habs inclusive. (1951, p. 100)

The improbability of successful generalization from such particular values of food weight and manipulandum pressure to other variables in animal behavior itself, let alone more complex behavioral functions of higher mammalian forms such as humans, should be quite evident. Thus while Hull's specificity is in some respects admirable, the aspirations of his theorizing seem rather far removed from the actual achievements. Hull himself stated reservations concerning the generality of his theory increasingly in his later writing (cf. Koch, 1954, pp. 167ff.). This is evident in the more cautious tone of his final work (Hull, 1952).

The only reasonable answer to these criticisms is simply that the results will determine the efficacy of the approach. More important, this is also the only answer to the more general criticism made of S-R theorists: that they oversimplify complex behavioral problems. Until we try, we cannot really be sure whether an approach such as Hull's will be adequate to account for the complexities of mammalian behavior, and the only scientific way to be sure is to try.

Logical Weakness Probably the most telling critical attack upon Hull's theory involves the demonstration that his system was not at all the tightly knit, logical one that he intended it to be and that many believed it to be. Hull sometimes failed to build in logically necessary connections between his constructs. A number of careful critical attacks have appeared. Koch's (1954) critique is particularly devastating because of its extremely detailed documentation and logical sophistication (in spite of his unsympathetic and sometimes unfair attitude). The easy testability of construct relationships that Hull envisioned is now seen to be largely illusory. Cotton (1955) gives a persuasive and beautifully worked-out demonstration of the impossibility of making predictions from Hull's theory as it was presented. Difficulties remain even when "friendly" assumptions are made in the attempt to make derivations possible. We are forced to conclude that Hull's theory was logically incomplete.

Two reactions to the growing realization of the logical inadequacy of Hull's theorizing are typical: first, a marked swing to a purely descriptive kind of positivism, such as that provided by Skinner; and second, an intensification of the attention paid to so-called miniature systems, whereby more limited problem areas are more thoroughly attacked. Hull himself showed signs of limiting his approach in *A behavior system* (1952), where he systematically explored problem areas and emphasized the overall system less than previously.

Hull's Contributions

Objective Terminology and Methodology Hull's own life was that of a scientist and scholar, a life of the mind. But in his psychology he determined to start with action, stay with action, and see how far action could carry him. His terms, therefore, were not new names for old concepts. *Reactive inhibition, habit strength, reaction potential*—these words had some of their creator's active vitality, ringing forth with the promise of carrying out the evangelical behavioristic program thrust upon the incredulous world at Watson's psychological revival meeting. The type of methodology implied by these terms will not be forgotten, whatever the fate of the theory in which Hull embedded them.

We believe that Hull's most important contribution to psychology was his demonstration of the value of setting one's sights upon the ultimate goal of a thoroughly scientific and systematic behavior theory. He lived his own scientific life in pursuit of that goal and thereby influenced even those who disagreed most vehemently with the details of his work. Few psychologists have had so deep an effect on the professional motivation of so many researchers. He popularized the strictly objective behavioristic approach as it had never been popularized previously.

New Problem Areas Hull opened new problem areas in a rather peculiar sense. He did not develop important new pieces of apparatus or initiate research in previously untouched areas. Rather, he reconceived ways of viewing problems and suggested new relationships to be studied. He was a theoretical psychologist, as some physicists are theoretical physicists. Unfortunately, he was a theoretician preceded by no Einstein, Newton, Copernicus, or perhaps even Archimedes in the field of psychology. Nevertheless, when he formulated a postulate or derived a theorem from his postulate set, other investigators were prone to perform experiments to test the stated relationships; for example, after Hull stated his belief about the shape of the generalization gradient, research focused on the empirical determination of the gradient. The very attempt to formalize a theory of behavior forced Hull and his followers to see what must be known before the formalization could be completed. Key concepts, such as stimulus, and processes, such as reinforcement, had to undergo intensive examination.

Although Hull was most strongly attacked by cognitive theorists and field theorists (cf. Chapter 11), in one respect his system was more fieldlike than the typical field theory. Hull specified as many of the relevant variables as he could reasonably conceive and also stated their hypothesized mode of interaction (cf. Figure 10-1). Not only is this high degree of theoretical specificity a far cry from the largely speculative utilization of conditioning by the early behaviorists, such as Watson, but it is also a good deal more concrete than anything offered by Hull's critics, who were more prone to counter the Watsonian speculation with their own speculation than to specify the psychological field precisely (cf. Estes, 1954).

Finally, Hull has been criticized by some psychologists of other persuasions for giving too much direction to research effort. He and his system concentrated effort on the solution of those theoretical problems which he believed had to be solved before behavior theory could make significant advances. However, some have felt that we cannot, at the present time, afford to decide the direction of research on formal theoretical grounds. Rather, those empirical areas should be studied which are producing results that are interesting in themselves. We believe that there is value in both views. Fortunately there are large numbers of psychologists available to take both parts; Hull made a great contribution in providing one kind of guidance.

Hull's Place in History

Clark Hull's place in psychological history seems to be assured. He may have been one of those rare people who actively influence their times to such an extent that they can redirect a science. On the other hand, one may prefer the alternative view that this apparent influence is an illusion that results when a person merely moves within the historical stream of events and so actually moves *with* the times.

Whatever the causation, it is true that Clark Hull found psychology still wrestling hard with broad systematic issues, and he left large segments of it wrestling with criticisms of his postulates and theorems. In a sense both kinds of wrestling are misspent. The systematic issues were elusive foes for the psychologist, and Hull's system revealed gaps to the serious student that made criticism almost superfluous. Yet Hull taught psychology a new type of game, one so enthralling that now all but the strictest of positivists want to play some version.

It is paradoxical that Hull changed metatheory by being concerned with theory. His predecessors, the earlier behaviorists, had done their utmost to turn psychology away from verbal issues and toward more empirically meaningful problems. But this never quite came off. Hull brought it off with a positive effect. Hull was certainly deeply and intelligently concerned with metatheory, and his system is the grandest ever attempted in the behavioristic tradition. His distinction and his influence are based on the fact that he did not stop there. His attempt to push on into the tangled unknown where specific issues are resolved was largely unsuccessful. That was inevitable at the time. He did not come back with maps that were likely to be serviceable, but nobody before Hull had even given psychological explorers much of a feel for what a psychological theory should be.

Another paradox is Hull's lack of rigor. His system had the appearance but not the reality. He never had time to smooth out wrinkles. In this he is in the company of all of psychology's greatest figures. If someone in psychology is excessively afraid of being wrong, that person has published no extensive theory. Hull, even while striving for a rigorous statement, had to stand with those who had no such fear. In this rather peculiar way, he carved his niche in history between the systematists and those following him who will construct better behavior theories.

For a time, it seemed that Hull had made of psychology his own private yard. In the early fifties, he was cited far more often than any other psychologist in the *Journal of Experimental Psychology* (Ammons, 1962), and his *Principles of behavior* (1943) was the most frequently cited publication, with its nearest rival cited less than a fourth as often in the *Journal of Experimental Psychology* and three other journals included in the tabulation. Between 1930 and 1950, Hull was regarded as the leading psychological theorist (Coan & Zagona, 1962, p. 319). Recently, however, it would appear that his fall from favor has been rapid. The pendulum of theoretical style has swung rapidly toward primarily inductive procedures, but there are signs that it is swinging back. Mathematical modeling of a less grand scope is becoming popular (see Chapter 13), and there is no denying Hull's priority and early dominance in this type of endeavor.

Hull's Students

Kenneth W. Spence (1907-1967) was the most important successor to Hull, as far as the type of theory Hull was trying to develop is concerned. He took his doctoral training at Yale, where he was strongly influenced by his association with Hull, although he took his degree under Yerkes, and he worked for four years at the Yale Laboratories of Primate Biology in Orange Park. From 1938 to 1964, he was at the University of Iowa, where he worked very actively in research on learning and motivation. In 1964 he moved to the University of Texas, where he remained until his death at the relatively early age of 59. While at Iowa he published a number of theoretical papers with Gustav Bergmann, the philosopher. Spence's major works are *Behavior theory and conditioning* (1956) and *Behavior theory and learning: Selected papers* (1960). The former was based on the 1955 Silliman Lectures at Yale; Spence was the first psychologist to be honored by an invitation to deliver these lectures.

Spence's first important research and theorizing dealt with the problem of discrimination learning (1936; 1937a, 1937b). He produced a classic demonstration of how a conditioning theory involving positive and negative reaction tendencies interacting algebraically can account for the primary data of discrimination and transposition. His tilt with the Gestaltists on the explanation of these phenomena (cf. Chapter 7) is an excellent illustration of opposing approaches to psychological explanation. On one side we see Spence operating in the reductive mode characteristic of associationistic psychology, of S-R psychology as a more modern version of Hull, and of Spence himself. Lloyd Morgan's canon is one of the first principles of theorizing for this tradition. Spence's theorizing on discrimination and transposition serves as an inspiring model of simplicity and clarity for exponents of this general approach. Hull's early work on the derivation of complex behaviors from conditioning was similar in this respect.

While recognizing his debt to basic Hullian theory, Spence was careful to point out the differences between his own theoretical efforts and those of Hull (cf. especially his 1956 book). He was less concerned with the comprehensive formality with which Hull endowed his work and more concerned with the quantification of variables. He did not share Hull's enthusiasm for physiological suggestions and speculations, feeling that until physiology has more to offer psychology, it can most profitably be kept out of behavior theory. He said (1956, p. 57) that he had not accepted the Hullian emphasis on need reduction as the essential component of the reinforcement process; he made no specific physiological assumption about the nature of the action of a reinforcer. Finally, he was much more cautious (1956) than Hull in "hazarding a set of theoretical postulates on the basis of a minimum of empirical data" (p. 58). Spence also pointed out that, on the related question of generality, he intended his own work to be restricted to the particular experimental situations from which his data came. Spence adopted the basic Hullian approach and many of the theoretical constructs, but put less emphasis on the postulational approach and modified some of the postulates that he did accept.

Spence treated the key motivational variables somewhat differently from the way Hull did. Both assumed that there was a multiplicative relationship between motivation and habit in the production of response (reaction potential). Spence, however, theorized that incentive and deprivation factors added to produce motivation; Hull had incentive and deprivation in a multiplicative relationship. Spence's formulation allowed for the occurrence of a response even when either incentive or drive was at zero, as long as the other factor was nonzero. Hull's multiplicative relationship called for a zero value of ${}_SE_R$ when either incentive or drive was zero; it is difficult to embarrass Hull on this point, however, since it is not easy to be certain that drive is completely absent. Neither is it easy to choose between the additive and multiplicative assumptions by doing a parametric study in which D and K are varied. The reason is that K is assumed to be related to fractional anticipatory goal responses and the stimuli produced by them. Thus motivation has a learned component, and the relationship between drive, incentive, and reaction potential is further complicated. The two theories have, in a sense, been given a "side chain" which must be taken into account when making predictions. That is, suppose we are computing ${}_SE_R$ for a response after several trials. Its amount will depend on K. The amount of K will in turn depend on the ${}_SE_R$ of the fractional anticipatory goal responses conditioned to the cues present. Thus we must compute ${}_SE_R$ twice, the first time in the theoretical side chain that determines a value for K.

Spence also took quite a different view of reinforcement from that of Hull. In his later work, he assumed that habit formation was not dependent on reinforcement. He suggested a two-factor learning theory which is precisely reversed from the usual one. Usually, contiguity factors are assumed to account for classical conditioning, and reinforcement for instrumental conditioning. Spence's contiguity explanation for instrumental conditioning does not necessitate any change in the basic form of the theory; it simply changes the definition of what constitutes a trial for the purposes of the theory. For Hull, a trial was a *reinforced* trial. For Spence reinforcement did not matter; it mattered only that the response was performed in the presence of the stimulus. On this matter, Spence's position resembled Tolman's (see Chapter 11); Spence was interested in Tolman's competing theory and was close to Tolman in some of his methodological attitudes (Kendler, 1967).

Following his early development of theory applicable to simple discrimination learning, Spence directed or supervised research projects on eyelid conditioning, latent learning, transposition, secondary reinforcement, and "anxiety" as measured by a questionnaire technique (see Spence, 1960). His work, much of it in collaboration with Janet Taylor Spence, on the relationship between anxiety and learning is widely quoted in articles on personality.

One of Spence's preoccupations in his later work was with the disentanglement of cognitive factors from the results of human eyelid conditioning studies. Earlier work had demonstrated apparent qualitative differences between eyelid conditioning in animals lower than humans and in humans. Human subjects typically extinguished conditioned eyeblinks in a very small number of trials, typically one or two, while animals might continue to make conditioned responses for hundreds of trials. Spence and his students used an ingenious masking task to conceal the true nature of the experiment, thereby apparently eliminating the influence of inhibitory congnitive factors and obtaining extinction behavior in human subjects that paralleled the behavior typically seen in animal subjects (see Spence, 1966).

This last work of Spence's ties in with the history of psychological systems in an interesting way. For one thing, the experimental situation is especially designed to reduce one aspect of the human subjects' functioning to the level of animal functioning. After Darwin, those working in a reductive tradition had often had to face the charge that they were in general trying to reduce human capabilities to the level of animal capabilities. Spence's work on eyelid conditioning thus exemplifies at the experimental level a reductive tendency which too frequently took place only at a theoretical level. At the same time, the attempt at reduction forced a clear recognition of a qualitative difference between human and animal functioning. The differences, like the similarities, have too often remained nebulous and theoretical. In following up on Hull's reductive program, Spence found factors which, at least at this time, cannot successfully be accounted for reductively. He thus, like many honest scientists, made a kind of contribution to those who hold opposing viewpoints about human nature.

Neal Miller (1909–   ) is another of Hull's incredibly productive students and associates. Miller's reputation for empirical investigation is unsurpassed, but he has not neglected limited theory either. He and John Dollard followed up one of Hull's interests, integrating learning theory with psychoanalytic theory, in their book *Personality and psychotherapy* (Dollard & Miller, 1950). This book was probably a direct outgrowth of Hull's seminars of 1936 and 1937 on the relationships between these apparently diverse areas of psychology. In turn, there is little doubt that their book helped to pave the way for later developments in behavior modification.

Miller has also done more than enough work to constitute a successful, complete career in physiological psychology. Some of these studies, and many of his behavioral studies, are reviewed in his article in the Koch series (N. E. Miller, 1959).

Some of Miller's experiments have involved electrical stimulation of brain centers; some, the effects of fistula feeding; and some, preloading the stomach with different substances before the subject eats or engages in instrumental behaviors. Still other studies were examinations of feeding without any nutritive consequences, and several have involved various behavioral effects of drugs.

It is not surprising that Miller has been led to a careful and sophisticated consideration of the starting and stopping of behavior. For one thing, he was aware of the fact that, under certain conditions, electrical stimulation of centers in the brain will be alternatively started and stopped by rats free to do both. For another, he knew that feeding may sometimes be started by brain stimulation or stopped by stomach loading and that feeding may *not* stop when it "should" after hypothalamic brain lesions.

Thinking about "go" and "stop" mechanisms may in turn have helped to lead Miller to his theoretical views on the nature of reinforcement. He was also exposed in 1954 to some of Sheffield's ideas (Haber, 1966, pp. 98ff.). Sheffield suggested that an *increase* in drive, produced directly or indirectly by reward, might account for learning better than the decrease in drive or drive stimulus required by Hull. Hull and Miller would both have, at one time, embraced the view that reinforcement is effective because it reduces the intensity of drive stimuli.

Miller suggested (1963) that reinforcing operations are effective because they activate a "go" mechanism. Responses occurring when the mechanism is activated are intensified and increase in frequency, according to Miller's view. Learning requires only contiguity between stimulus and response, but learning is increased by increases in the intensity or frequency of the pairing. Reinforcement (activation of the "go" mechanism) indirectly increases learning by increasing the opportunity for contiguity to produce learning.

This ingenious proposal is similar to the suggestions of several other theorists. It bears a striking resemblance to Guthrie's theory in that contiguity alone is supposed to suffice for learning (see the discussion later in this chapter). Thorndike's "confirming reaction" is something like Miller's "go" mechanism; the latter, however, is supposed to affect learning indirectly through increasing performance (which is the way Tolman would also have seen the problem), rather than directly through strengthening connections, as Thorndike had suggested. Sheffield's (1954) so-called drive *induction* theory of reinforcement (to contrast with Hull's drive *reduction* theory) is also similar in a number of respects. All these ideas on reinforcement share the feature that they emphasize the reinforcer as stimulus rather than as aftereffect.

Recently, Miller has been involved in a number of studies on whether autonomic responses can be conditioned through operant techniques (N. E. Miller, 1969). This work treats a problem which was central for Hull; we have seen that Hull accepted the Thorndikian principle of effect as a basic condition for learning. Hull had rejected his own earlier tentative commitment to contiguity (as in classical conditioning) as a sufficient condition for learning. Miller's work, which shows that the autonomic system is surprisingly susceptible to modification via effect learning, supports Hull's later formulation, albeit indirectly. This work of Miller's is part of the contemporary excitement about biofeedback, since we ordinarily are not aware of the state of our autonomic nervous system unless we are given artificial feedback. Attempts to condition the autonomic system in human beings via biofeedback have met with mixed success; ironically, replications of Miller's work have also met with what we might call mixed success (Hilgard & Bower, 1975, p. 576). Effects comparable in size to those initially obtained are no longer found, particularly in the area of heart rate changes. The reasons are still being sought.

At about the same time that Miller seemed to be enlarging the scope of behavior which could be modified through reward learning, Brown and Jenkins (1968) reported that key pecking could be shaped simply by illuminating the key prior to food delivery, with no response required of the organism. That is, they were conditioning a voluntary response by using a classical conditioning procedure! We seem to be in danger of losing our traditional distinction between classical and operant conditioning. It may emerge in other guises, for example as a distinction between response-independent and response-dependent schedules (Staddon & Simmelhag, 1971). It may be that somatic and autonomic nervous system activities are never independent, even in curarized animals (Goesling & Brener, 1972).

A number of other psychologists have carried on work in the Hullian tradition. O. H. Mowrer, a student of Hull's, will be discussed later in this chapter because of his contributions to two-factor theories of learning.

Frank Logan, a student of Spence and coworker with Hull, has made important contributions related to the issue of response definition (1956, 1970). Hull, it will be recalled, had a single construct, ${}_SE_R$, which in his theory determined the values of all the dependent response measures—probability, amplitude, number of trials to extinction, etc. Unfortunately, these response measures were typically not highly correlated, as they should be according to the theory. Logan proposed a "micromolar" approach to solve this problem. He suggested that all the properties of responses, like their amplitude and speed, needed to be considered in the definition of what constituted the response under study. A *terms function* could then define how response properties were related to reinforcement. For example, the terms function might require that responses have *low* amplitude in order to be rewarded. In such a case, as learning proceeded, the average amplitude of response would be likely to decrease as the probability of response and its resistance to extinction increased. Such relationships between dependent response measures would be insoluble within the confines of traditional Hullian theory, but would pose no problem for Logan.

Abram Amsel (1965, for example) has also continued work within a Hullian tradition. Amsel's chief interest has been in the analysis of extinction, for which he proposes an account based on the frustrative features of nonreward. Thus we see in Amsel's account an emphasis on the stimulus features of the extinction process. Amsel (1967) has also extended this general type of analysis to discrimination learning. He, like Logan, has succeeded in deriving detailed predictions from his theory. Perhaps the derivation and the confirmation of such predictions are the most fitting reminder of Hull's legacy.

REINFORCEMENT THEORY: SKINNERIAN POSITIVISM

Skinner's Career

B. F. Skinner (1904–) has had a most remarkable career. It is similar to that of Sir Francis Galton in its demonstration of great breadth of interest and exceptional ingenuity of empirical operations. Skinner's contributions have been kaleidoscopic. His lively intellectual curiosity has refused to be contained within the narrow confines of a specialized area. He has concerned himself with an analysis of verbal learning, with missile-guiding pigeons, with teaching machines, and with the control of behavior by scheduled reinforcement. The ingenious apparatus to his credit includes an automatized baby-tending device, used with one of his own children and later marketed commercially. In his leisure time, Skinner has even managed to write a novel on a Utopian theme, *Walden two* (1948b).

Skinner received his doctoral degree from Harvard in 1931. Following several years of postdoctoral fellowships he taught at the University of Minnesota (1936 to 1945) and at Indiana University (1945 to 1947), where he was chairman. He returned to Harvard in 1947. During the 1930s and 1940s Skinner's influence was less than that of Hull and Tolman, but it is now far greater (Coan & Zagona, 1962). His influence on younger psychologists has been especially impressive. Part of the reason for his ascendance is disillusionment with comprehensive theory of the Hullian type. Skinner's positivistic inclinations are at the opposite pole from Hull's fondness for the development of formal theories.

Methodological Emphasis

Skinner is best known for his insistence upon a strictly descriptive, atheoretical approach to behavior research. He has long felt that the state of knowledge in psychology is inadequate to justify elaborate, formal theorizing. Skinnerians often state that when theories are developed and espoused, personal satisfactions from confirmations and disconfirmations, rather than acquisition of facts, tend to become the issue. Skinner believes that more effective progress toward the prediction and control of behavior can be obtained through a careful collection of data. The "functional analysis of behavior" has been his objective. In this, experimental techniques are to be utilized, and the relationships between variables are to be established. Eventually, Skinner holds, sufficient empirical relationships will be established to justify the formation of some limited theories or more comprehensive generalizations, but these must be prepared with caution. Such integrative principles should be allowed to develop, not forced prematurely.

Skinner is not against all theory, and it may be that he believes psychology is more nearly ready for theory now than it was 40 years ago, when he entered the field. At any rate, he has said (Evans, 1968): "But I look forward to an overall theory of human behavior which will bring together a lot of facts and express them in a more general way. That kind of theory I would be very much interested in promoting, and I consider myself to be a theoretician" (p. 88). In fact, Skinner has taken pains to emphasize his interest in theory, subtitling one of his books (1969) *A theoretical analysis* and detailing in its preface the numerous theoretical articles he has written. It is dangerous to overgeneralize with Skinner, just as it is with a Titchener or a Thorndike—or with any great figure in the history of psychology. Brilliant thinkers seldom take positions as extreme as the positions ascribed to them by incautious critics.

A second important methodological emphasis of Skinner has been his insistence upon a thorough analysis of the behavior of a single organism and his disinclination to use large groups of subjects. Large numbers of subjects have too often been used, he contends, to cover up lack of experimental controls; with adequate controls, a single subject, or a very small number of subjects, should be sufficient. The use of large groups, he says, also leads indirectly to other difficulties. When a large group is used, the experimenter usually attends primarily or exclusively to certain statistical properties of the group, rather than to the behaviors of the individuals within it. Individual variations may then be lost, and the statistical measures may not describe the characteristics of *any* of the individuals within the group (Sidman, 1960). Skinner does not believe that such experiments are likely to lead to a science in which prediction and control of the behavior of individual organisms are possible. On the other hand, when large amounts of data from a single animal are collected under stringently controlled conditions, the results will be clearly replicable with other individuals. No statistical techniques will be necessary. In this connection, Skinner claims that as far as he knows no student of his ever "designed an experiment" (Evans, 1968, p. 89).

Third, Skinner has objected particularly to physiological speculation in the guise of theory. He has been against what he has considered excessive and futile physiologizing; when physiological data have more concrete points on which behavioral observations can turn, they should be permitted to influence psychology, but not before. This generally aphysiological attitude has been shared by Spence, and together they have contributed to the prominence of the so-called empty-organism era in recent psychological thinking. Even on this issue, it is easy to overdramatize Skinner's attitude. His opposition to too much physiologizing seems to be largely a matter of self-discipline. He says (Evans, 1968): "I have never said anything against the study of physiology, and I feel that I have done my best to facilitate it by clarifying the problems that the physiologist has to deal with. At the same time, I don't want to borrow support from physiology when my formulation breaks down" (p. 22).

A fourth major methodological characteristic of Skinner has been his emphasis on operant, as compared with respondent, behavior. Skinner early distinguished between responses made in direct response to stimulation (such as classical conditioned responses of a Pavlovian sort) and those emitted by the organism in the absence of any apparent external stimulation (the operant). The eliciting stimuli for the operant are unknown. The free operant is an operant whose emission does not directly preclude successive emissions of the same response; its study has been especially favored by Skinnerians. The free operant is best exemplified in the case of the bar pressing of rats and the key pecking of pigeons. Both animals usually respond in the Skinner box. These boxes are insulated against noise, and temperature and lighting are closely controlled. Data gathered under such controlled conditions tend to be more uniform than the data that are usually available. Skinner has typically used the rate of emission of a response as his dependent variable; the response is a simple one, and the measure, therefore, is relatively uncomplicated. A cumulative recorder which directly produces a cumulative frequency curve of responses, rather than the typical learning curve, has been used to record the data.

The free operant as the object of study, the use of rate as the primary datum, and the cumulative recorder as an instrument—these three, in Skinner's view, constitute a unique combination that makes for progress. Rate becomes a meaningful measure only when free operants are being studied, and the cumulative recorder shows rate characteristics over a long period of time. The experimenter can see what is happening to rate almost as soon as it happens, and can change the procedures if that seems appropriate. Skinner (1966, p. 16) points out how important it was in chemistry to use dull, colorless weight as a measure in order to bring chaos to order in that field of study. He thinks the use of rate as a measure may have similar effects in psychology.

Major Contributions

Shaping One of Skinner's most enduring interests has been in the training of organisms. Quite early in his career, he developed the training technique called *shaping*. Shaping depends upon presenting rewards to the trainee, whether human or animal, contingent upon a graded series of responses approximating the desired response. For example, we might wish to teach a rat to climb a ladder. At first, the animal might be reinforced merely for facing toward the ladder; later, it would be required to move toward the ladder; then, to touch the ladder, then to get on it, and finally to climb the ladder, in each case to receive a reward. Two of Skinner's early associates, Keller and Marian Breland, helped in the development of shaping techniques (Skinner, 1977). They worked with him on what was later called "Project Pigeon" under the auspices of General Mills in Minneapolis. They were well along in teaching pigeons to guide a bomb toward a target when the development of atomic weapons ended the war and removed the urgency from this research. After the project was declassified, a fascinating account was written by Skinner (1960).

One of the many applications of shaping techniques has been in the training of animals for shows. The Brelands themselves left the academic field to become pioneers in the use of operant techniques for this purpose (Breland & Breland,

1951, 1961). Skinner's techniques now find application in virtually every zoo and marine animal show, in the United States, at least.

Superstitious Behavior Skinner found that animals did not need to be rewarded for particular responses in order to develop orderly behaviors. He noted that hungry pigeons developed repetitive behaviors when they were simply given food at regular intervals, regardless of what they did. He called such behaviors *superstitious* (1948a) because of their apparent resemblance to human behaviors like carrying rabbits' feet. When the delivery of reward is not contingent upon the organism's pressing a bar, pecking a key, or engaging in any other specified behavior, the schedule is called *noncontingent* (or *incontingent*). In such a situation some response, which just happens to precede a reinforcement early in the session, will generally be fixated and will predominate in the behavioral repertoire of the animal during the experimental period. This occurs because one or two early reinforcements increase the rate at which the particular response is emitted, thus making more and more likely its occurrence just prior to subsequent reinforcements. The particular response strengthened, such as wing flapping, neck craning, leg raising, etc., varies from one animal to the next. Probably the outcome of this procedure depends on the interaction between the animal's initial repertoire in the situation and the particular schedule of reinforcement delivery. Herrnstein (1966) reports on a study in which the animal is first taught a response on a fixed-interval schedule and then is shifted to a noncontingent schedule; this procedure gives experimenters control over the animal's repertoire, at least in that it allows them to specify which response shall be of highest frequency when the noncontingent condition is initiated. Under these conditions, Herrnstein found that the high-frequency response was maintained at a rate well above the operant level over the course of many sessions. This result, however, probably depends on the relationship between the contingent conditions and the noncontingent conditions, since Edwards, West, and Jackson (1968) found that response rates fell fairly rapidly when noncontingent conditions were instituted.

Killeen (1978) showed that pigeons are capable of distinguishing between reinforcements delivered on a noncontingent basis and those delivered on a contingent basis. Presumably the change in behavior which would occur when they were shifted from one kind of schedule to another would depend upon the value of changing. That is, very effortful responding might undergo a more rapid decline than less effortful responding when noncontingent conditions were instituted.

Staddon and Simmelhag (1971) published a paper which showed that the careful study of superstitious behaviors may be very instructive. They studied the occurrences of several behaviors in a noncontingent reinforcement situation. They found, among other things, that highly characteristic sequences of behaviors occurred. Component parts of these sequences never occurred "out of position." Their work tends to highlight the stimulating aspects of the reinforcer, since "interim" behaviors repeatedly occurred, but *not* in close proximity to the delivery of the reinforcer.

Schedules of reinforcement There is no absolute difference between the noncontingent situation and the contingent situation. Skinner has noted that the link between response and reinforcement in most operant work is simply a temporal relationship; as he says (1966): "The response produces food only in the sense that food follows it—a Humean version of causality" (p. 14). He is also aware that superstitious behaviors arise from response-reinforcement relationships not specified by the experimenter, and he has generalized this thinking to contingent conditions (1966): "It is characteristic of most contingencies that they are not precisely controlled, and in any case they are effective only in combination with the behavior which the organism brings to the experiment" (pp. 20–21).

Thus Skinner's concern with superstitious behavior is related quite directly to his even earlier and still continuing work on the problem of reinforcement scheduling in operant conditioning. His early emphasis on intermittent reinforcement (1938) culminated in the exhaustive volume *Schedules of reinforcement* (Ferster & Skinner, 1957). He worked first with the rat in the Skinner box, subsequently with the pigeon in a comparable chamber, and ultimately with human subjects. Use of children as subjects in operant conditioning studies involving various reinforcement schedules has become a very important feature of behavioral research, involving psychologists of varying degrees of adherence to Skinnerian principles.

A number of examples may be cited from everyday-life situations to illustrate the effectiveness of intermittent reinforcement in controlling behavior. One of the most apt is the control of behavior exercised by the occasional payoff of the slot machine or by other gambling devices. Examination of other situations indicates that reinforcement is characteristically scheduled intermittently, rather than continuously, as it has more typically been scheduled in learning experiments. Thus the child's behavior produces approbation in the parent, but not invariably; the student succeeds on examinations, but also fails or misses particular items; and the typical fisherman returns home empty-handed from a very large proportion of his trips.

In laboratory investigations of the effects of different schedules of reinforcement, four major types have been used. These are *fixed interval* (FI), in which the first response made after some fixed period of time is reinforced; *variable interval* (VI), in which the first response made after some variable period of time is reinforced; *fixed ratio* (FR), in which the first response made after some fixed number of responses is reinforced; and *variable ratio* (VR), in which the first response made after some variable number of responses is reinforced. The two variable schedules (VI and VR) and the fixed-ratio schedule (FR) characteristically produce remarkably steady and high rates of responding. The FI schedule ideally produces more cyclical cumulative performance curves featuring bursts of responses just preceding the usual reinforcement time, with pauses or very low rates of response immediately following reinforcement. This pattern of responding gives the cumulative curve its so-called scalloped appearance.

Schoenfeld, Cumming, and Hearst (1968) have suggested a classification scheme for schedules of reinforcement in terms of strictly temporal variables; the critical properties of schedules dealt with were the length of the period during which reinforcement was available and the total "cycle length," which included the period of unavailability as well as the period of availability. If the animal responded during the period of availability, the reinforcement was delivered; during the remainder of the period, responding produced no results. They found a general response-rate increase when, for a fixed cycle time, reinforcement availability time was increased. Conversely, rates tended to decrease when the reinforcement availability time decreased.

This work and Skinner's own thinking would seem to be pointing toward a description of contingencies couched in more basic terms than those currently used. Describing a schedule as "fixed-interval fifteen-seconds" leaves out critical properties of the relationship between reinforcement delivery and the organism's behavior. It also encourages a distinction between such a schedule and a fixed-ratio twenty-five-response schedule, whether or not such a distinction is important in a particular context. Finally, the similarities which may exist between intermittent reinforcement schedules and free food delivery on a noncontingent basis may tend to be obscured. A general description in terms of more basic properties of the various schedules as they relate to the organism's responses should make it possible to describe all the types of schedules in a single framework that also encompasses a description of noncontingent schedules.

A complete description of a reinforcement schedule would require the precise specification of the terms function which related Logan's micromolar type of response description to the reinforcement parameters. The amount, probability, and delay of reinforcement would need to be specified for every response of interest. Working out the details of such a descriptive framework for schedules is a tremendous undertaking, but it may ultimately be necessary. The currently used schedules, despite their large number and considerable complexity, constitute only a small proportion of the schedules that could be generated within such a framework.

Verbal Behavior Another of Skinner's interests has been systematic thinking about verbal behavior. His conceptualization of the important human behavioral problem of language has been influential in the field. This interest culminated in publication of a major work, *Verbal behavior* (1957). According to Skinner's interpretation, language as verbal behavior is basically similar to other behavior and can be best understood when viewed in this general conceptual framework.

Skinner characterizes verbal behavior as behavior whose reinforcement is mediated by another organism that has been specifically conditioned to mediate such reinforcements. Verbal operants, like other operants, are recognized because of a relationship to an antecedent condition, typically a controlling stimulus. An example of a functional relationship between an antecedent variable and a verbal response would be one's writing "chair" as a response to the object on which one sits. Such responses are called *tacts* by Skinner because their controlling variable is *contact* with an object, event, or property of an object or event. If a person says "coffee" because he or she is deprived of that substance, that person is to Skinner emitting a *mand* because of his or her *demand* for the appropriate reinforcer. Skinner believes that the appropriate course of investigation of language involves just the functional analysis of the relationship between antecedents and verbal behavior. The organism makes no real contribution to verbal behaving, but is best regarded as a locus through which variables act.

Although, as we will see, Skinner's analysis has come in for severe criticism, there is little doubt that it has been influential. Skinner's break with conventional accounts preceded, and without doubt was partially responsible for, the several successful attempts to teach the rudiments of human language to chimpanzees. We will discuss these efforts later, since they are not part of Skinner's own work.

Behavioral Technology Skinner's Utopian *Walden II* of 1948 revealed his interest in applying behavioral technology in the interests of the betterment of society. Much later, *Beyond freedom and dignity* (1971) challenged our society to do something about itself by using the behavioral techniques discovered by Skinner and others. No doubt Skinner was being deliberately provacative when he suggested that freedom and dignity, two of America's most holy cows, are in the way of progress toward a better world. We will reserve comment on whether those cows belong on the street or on the table. However, we do believe that Skinner had the attention of the nation, for the book was on the best-seller list, and evoked strong opposition from no less a personage than then Vice President Spiro Agnew (Goodall, 1972). We have seen no rush to apply Skinner's ideas in this case.

Many other ideas have been taken more seriously. For example, Skinner usually receives credit for the great contemporary interest in programmed learning, much of which he probably deserves. We might consider the following, quoted in Boring and Lindzey, (1967):

> In a window of the little apparatus showed a four-choice question to which students responded by pressing the key corresponding to the answer they thought right. If it was, the next question turned up, but if not, they had to try again until they did find the righı answer—meanwhile a counter kept a cumulative record of their tries. Moreover (two features no device since has had) if a lever were raised, the device was changed into a self-scoring and rewarding testing machine: whatever key was pressed, the next question turned up, but the counter counted only rights; also when the set on a reward dial was reached, a candy lozenge was automatically presented. . . . (p. 322)

This quotation is not from Skinner's autobiography, but from Pressey's, and the machine described was exhibited in 1925. However, teaching machines did not catch on until much later. It is interesting to ask why. The machines themselves have undergone changes, but some highly successful ones are very simple—no more complex than Pressey's much earlier machine. Modern exponents of programmed learning would probably insist that the materials are now better organized and that the technical features of this organization are responsible for the current much greater success of programmed learning.

It is, nevertheless, interesting to contemplate the possibility that the reason for Skinner's success in popularizing this approach to learning, where Pressey had failed thirty years earlier, is that Skinner had better reasons to believe that the technique ought to work. Further, he had a cohesive and enthusiastic group of followers, and Pressey did not. The principles of operant conditioning were working in the control of animal behavior, and concurrent efforts indicated that they would work for the control of human behavior. Thus a *Zeitgeist* was developing within which programmed learning could thrive. It was probably Pressey's fate to be a little too far ahead of his time in 1925.

Similar considerations apply to Skinner's role in the development of the behavior-modification movement. Kalish (1977) is one of those who have pointed out that most of the concepts central to behavior modification were developed by Thorndike, Pavlov, or J. B. Watson. Yet the use of behavior-modification techniques remained rare, and there was no "movement" before Skinner was there to lead the movement. Now the books on the subject are legion, and studies are countless. Ullman and Krasner (1965) provided one of the earlier summaries, reporting a host of cases in which operant techniques were used to modify the behaviors of patients ranging from disturbed children to psychotic adults. Skinner has participated in and nurtured this development from the beginning; yet his really critical role has been providing the intellectual justification.

Criticisms of Skinner

Positivism Skinner's positivism has invited attack. Critics have maintained that Skinner is deluding himself if he believes theory has no value. Theory is inevitable. Every experiment and observation is in some way planned, based on hunches or ideas; therefore, say the critics, it is better to bring the presuppositions into the open and formalize them. Then they can be recognized and critically evaluated rather than hidden. In addition, formal theory in the older sciences has afforded a generality which Skinner's fact gathering alone can never achieve.

Further, the *efficiency* of the atheoretical approach has been questioned. The book *Schedules of reinforcement* (1957) has been used as an example of the dangers of too inductive and positivistic an approach. It summarizes about 70,000 hours of continuously recorded behavior of individual pigeons, during which time the pigeons emitted approximately one-quarter of a billion responses. The data are presented in a total of 921 separate figures with almost no interpretive, or even summarizing, comment. This procedure accords well with Skinner's (1959a) belief that the scientist should be brought into direct contact with data, but it does not agree so well with the scientific temperament of those whose immediate interests are in general principles.

Skinner has several replies available. First, he is not antitheoretical; he is only against certain types of theories, either those which are premature or those which are attempts to avoid the necessity for empirical work or for genuine explanation. He does believe that theories may guide investigators into unprofitable efforts to confirm or disconfirm theories, when they might better devote themselves to the exploration of interesting empirical situations. Theories should be primarily inductive, not based on logical guesses. Theories *should* be an end product of scientific endeavor, but they should be proposed only as the data are ready to support them. Second, Skinner would probably insist that presuppositions need to be kept to a minimum. Premature speculation, even if it is not misleading, is a waste of time. In the worst cases, it will be misleading, a waste of time both directly and indirectly, and a source of personal involvement and controversy.

Peripheralism This kind of argument against Skinner has two major facets. One involves his aphysiological bias; this is largely a matter of taste. If one prefers not to think in physiological terms, surely this is one's privilege. The other involves his refusal to posit intervening processes of a psychological sort (such as Hull's habit strength or inhibition, Spence's incentive motivation, and the like). Here too the issue is one of personal preference, but difficulties arise when one side attempts to force its views on the other.

We have already noted in passing Skinner's own contention that he is not against real physiological psychology. He is against only the practice of taking refuge in physiological terminology when behavioral accounts break down. The use of merely verbal explanations, whether physiological, mentalistic, or anything else, is discouraged by Skinner.

In some cases, Skinner or his followers may have waxed too enthusiastic in their efforts to purify psychological language by eliminating terms like *emotion, motivation,* and *perception.* These much-abused terms may be highly variable in meaning and yet might still have some core of useful meaning. If so, the critics would hve a legitimate claim that certain problems were being neglected because of a positivistic insistence on purity of language. The reply might be that the problems of nature eventually insist that attention be paid to them. Meanwhile, there are plenty of problems suggested by concepts with demonstrated meaningfulness. Would the critic rather devote time to issues that are assuredly meaningful or to problems with no clear meaning?

Excessive Extrapolation Skinner has often gone well beyond his data, as in his proposals about complex human problems in *Science and human behavior* (1953). On this issue he seems to be somewhat vulnerable. The whole spirit of his methodology seems to revolve around the notion of sticking close to already observed facts. Yet his generalizations to human behavior very clearly go far beyond the observations of the laboratory.

Cook (1963) has criticized Skinnerians for too literal an application of techniques appropriate in the operant conditioning chamber to programmed learning. For one thing, there is a great deal of evidence that humans need *not* make an overt response in order to learn, and in fact often do better if no overt response is required (Hillix & Marx, 1960; Rosenbaum & Hewitt, 1966; Rosenbaum & Schutz, 1967). Further, they often do as well when they are told in advance what the correct response is (prompted) as they do when they are reinforced after making the correct response. Both these errors in the application of operant techniques to humans are specific instances of the general criticism of premature extrapolation.

The best-known criticism of Skinner's extrapolations is by Chomsky (1959). In his famous thirty-two-page review of *Verbal behavior,* Chomsky analyzes Skinner's formulation with great care and criticizes it with great effectiveness. He devotes a great deal of attention to the terms *stimulus, response,* and *reinforcement,* since these are critical terms in Skinner's account of verbal behavior. Serious problems arise with the use of each of the three terms as they are employed in the analysis of verbal behavior. We shall note here only some difficulties with the use of *reinforcement.*

Chomsky notes that, in bar-pressing experiments, the reinforcer is an identifiable stimulus and that statements about reinforcement therefore have a meaningful referent, which in turn makes it meaningful to use the concept of reinforcement in the explanation of behavior. Chomsky contends that the extension to the explanation of verbal behavior is, however, completely unjustified. In support of his argument, he cites from Skinner a number of examples in which *reinforcement* does *not* refer to an identifiable stimulus. Skinner often uses automatic self-reinforcement (not identifiable as a stimulus!) as an explanation of why verbal behavior is maintained. Future reinforcements are also appealed to, as when a writer is said to be reinforced because of the effect his work will have upon future generations. Chomsky says of such usage (1959): "In fact, the term is used in such a way that the assertion that reinforcement is necessary for learning and continued availability of behavior is likewise empty" (p. 37).

Chomsky's review is reiminiscent of Koch's review of Hull's work. Both are extremely sophisticated, careful, and thorough reviews. Both attack specific issues with great force and accuracy. Yet from one point of view both reviews are unjust. The reason is that Hull and Skinner were both being programmatic. Neither believed that he was correct in detail; in fact, it was Hull's explicit intention to set up hypotheses which could be proved wrong by others. However, Chomsky would probably reply that the defects in detail in Skinner's account are so great that the whole program becomes meaningless. At present, there seems to be much more interest in pursuing Chomsky's program than in pursuing Skinner's.

Nevertheless, Skinner's work on verbal behavior is quite defensible. Bem and Bem (1968), although they are not highly impressed with Skinner's viewpoint, indicate the direction such a defense might take. In comparing Skinner's *Verbal behavior* and Lenneberg's *Biological foundations of language* (1967), they say: "Both works, in short, constitute plausibility arguments for particular views of verbal behavior" (p. 497). Skinner clearly stated that this was the way in which he viewed his analysis of verbal behavior, and he could easily extend this argument to his other extrapolations. If they are accepted as merely suggestions stemming from his conceptual framework, they may serve at least as an intellectual stimulant. The extent to which simple principles can be applied to apparently complex situations and processes is an empirical problem and cannot be safely prejudged.

Skinner is confident that the pendulum of opinion will swing back and award the victory to him:

> What the psycholinguists miss is any conception of a functional analysis as opposed to a structural analysis of verbal behavior. . . . They lean very heavily on the mentalistic psychology, and they are going to be let down because there is no such psychology. But as I said earlier, now they are postulating innate ideas, and that is next to worthless, if not a little bit comical. But I am in no real hurry, I have had my say. I am not interested in arguing with them at all. When all their mythical machinery finally grinds to a halt and is laid aside, discarded, then we will see what is remembered fifty or a hundred years from now, when the truth will have all been brought out in the open. (M. H. Hall, 1967, pp. 69–70)

MacCorquodale agrees with Skinner. After chastising Chomsky for what he sees as misunderstanding Skinner's purpose, MacCorquodale says:

> Unfortunately for his purposes, Chomsky did not grasp the differences between Skinnerian and Watsonian-Hullian behaviorism, and his criticisms, although stylistically effective, were mostly irrelevant to *Verbal Behavior.*
>
> He was simply wrong. This is a *great* book. (1969, p. 841)

Environmentalism Skinner's position in *The behavior of organisms* (1938) was often interpreted as quite environmentalistic. He put a good deal of stress on the ubiquity of learned behaviors, and seemed to have great faith in the power of operant procedures—a faith which has been for the most part justified by events.

However, the Brelands in the course of training many species of animals made some observations that led them to depart to some extent from Skinnerian views on operant conditioning. The Brelands noted (1961) numerous incidents of failure to teach the operant behaviors desired. For example (see Breland & Breland, 1966, pp. 67–68), raccoons, pigs, squirrel monkeys, and other animals often have trouble letting go of a token which they are learning to insert into a food dispenser, much as humans insert coins into machines. The Brelands believed that more primitive food-related behaviors were activated on earlier trials and that these more primitive behaviors interfered with the performance of the operant response. They described this "instinctive drift" as follows:

> The general principle seems to be that wherever an animal has strong instinctive behaviors in the area of the conditioned response, after continued running the organism will drift toward the instinctive behavior, to the detriment of the conditioned behavior and even to the delay or preclusion of the reinforcement. (1961, p. 684)

The Brelands, although they were nurtured by Skinner in the environmentalistic tradition which has been a common feature of the behavioristic outlook, have been prominent among psychologists partly responsible for the swing toward nativism, which the ethologists initiated and which is evident in American psychology today.

Lockard (1971) has documented that part of the nativistic trend which is most closely related to animal behavior, detailing some of the contributions of the Brelands and of ethologists like Lorenz and Tinbergen. Lockard's conclusions come through clearly in statements like the following:

> Scientifically speaking, only two pieces of information were needed to bring behavior into the modern synthesis of the new biology: the fact that behavior has a genetic basis, thus making it heritable and therefore subject to natural selection; and the fact that behavior, or rather, particular behaviors, are adaptive—that they bear intimate relationships to particulars of the environment such that some kind of advantage results. The genetic basis of hundreds and hundreds of particular behaviors has been demonstrated beyond doubt, and the adaptive significance of particular behaviors has been demonstrated in hundreds of cases. (p. 171)

Another student of Skinner's, R. J. Herrnstein (1977a, 1977b) also interpreted the findings of the Brelands as contradicting Skinner's views. Fortunately for Skinner, he is still here to stem what Herrnstein called the "rising tide of anti-Skinnerianism" (p. 593), and we do not need to guess what Skinner's reply would be to critics of his environmentalism.

His first retort is that his extreme environmentalism does not exist. Skinner's position on the issue has no doubt shifted over the years, just as everyone else's has, or should have. However, there is no denying that Skinner published a fairly extensive article many years ago (Skinner, 1966) devoted to the phylogeny and ontogeny of behavior—and he very clearly recognized the important role played by phylogeny at that time. Skinner simply refuses to go overboard in either direction (1977): "Phylogeny and ontogeny are friendly rivals and neither one always wins" (p. 1009).

Skinner points out examples in which learned behaviors intrude on instinctive behaviors, and concludes that "civilization has supplied an unlimited number of examples of the suppression of the phylogenic repertoire of the human species by learned behavior. In fact, it is often the very function of a culture to mask a genetic endowment" (p. 1007). Clearly Skinner needs no defense from us on this point; he is more than capable of taking care of himself.

Neglect of Statistics Skinner and his followers are usually not interested in statistical tests. Their attitude has probably been best presented by Sidman (1960). The preferred methodology within this tradition involves intensive and carefully controlled investigation of a small group of subjects. The search is for reliable functional relationships, and reliability is established by demonstrating the same functional relationship in several *individual* organisms, preferably under several different conditions. The statistical approach more typically uses larger groups of subjects and examines quantitative indices of the group's performance. Skinner does not believe that we are likely to arrive at laws which will help us predict and control the behavior of the individual unless we look at individuals. The issue is, like the more general issues, debatable, but the Skinnerians have certainly forced some important questions into the spotlight, where they can be more carefully considered. Some aspects of operant methodology are unquestionably useful, and on some issues concerning the relationships between group and individual functions the Skinnerians can be demonstrated to be correct. Those who advocate an overtly statistical approach are probably correct when they maintain that Skinnerians must make some statistical decisions, for example, about whether rate of responding has stabilized and about whether experimental manipulations have reliably been shown to have produced an effect.

Skinner's Role in Contemporary Systematic Psychology

The extent of Skinner's systematic contributions to modern experimental psychology is nicely summarized in the formal citation accompanying the American Psychological Association's Distinguished Scientific Contribution Award granted him in 1958. This citation is as follows:

> An imaginative and creative scientist, characterized by great objectivity in scientific matters and by warmth and enthusiasm in personal contacts. Choosing simple operant behavior as subject matter, he has challenged alternative analyses of behavior, insisting that description take precedence over hypotheses. By careful control of experimental conditions, he has produced data which are relatively free from fortuitous variation. Despite his antitheoretical position, he is considered an important systematist and has developed a self-consistent description of behavior which has greatly increased our ability to predict and control the behavior of organisms from rat to man. Few American psychologists have had so profound an impact on the development of psychology and on promising younger psychologists. *(American Psychologist,* 1958)

Whereas in the period 1945 to 1950 there was no more enthusiastic band of psychologists than those working actively within the Hull-Spence systematic framework, today the same thing can be said of the Skinnerians, as they are often called. In addition to the group with Skinner at Harvard, there has been for years a tightly knit group trained under Fred Keller and William Schoenfeld at Columbia University. Skinnerian psychologists, resenting the orthodox restrictions of the American Psychological Association's journals (particularly the unwritten regulations concerning sample size and statistical tests), established the *Journal for the Experimental Analysis of Behavior* as their journal in 1958. Skinnerian techniques are almost universally accepted for some purposes even by opponents of the Skinnerian viewpoint. Young psychologists eager to help make the study of behavior an exact science continue to flock to the Skinnerian banner, often to the discomfiture of those holding opposing views. The popular press is coming to recognize Skinner as the greatest contemporary behaviorist (e.g., *Time,* 1969) and his theoretical views as a serious competitor to Freud's. He has revivified and extended the strictly behavioral position. As one reviewer put it (MacLeod, 1959): "Watson's spirit is indestructible. Cleansed and purified, it breathes through the writings of B. F. Skinner" (p. 34).

We do not think Skinner should or would be displeased with that assessment.

CONTIGUITY THEORY: GUTHRIAN ASSOCIATIONISM

Guthrie's Career

Edwin Guthrie (1886–1959) was for several decades the leading exponent of a simple contiguity principle of learning. Throughout a long period, while first one and then another opposing school developed, Guthrie held steadfast to a small number of strict associationistic principles. This patience has finally paid off in the modern appearance of statistical models of learning based largely upon the Guthrian pattern. However, Guthrie's own contribution has remained that of a prophet and overseer more than that of an active experimentalist or detailed theorist.

Guthrie remained at one school, the University of Washington, throughout his entire academic career (1914 to 1956). He had less than the usual formal training in psychology, having been trained instead in philosophy and mathematics. He took his doctoral degree in 1912 at the University of Pennsylvania after having earned degrees earlier at the University of Nebraska. With one major exception (Guthrie & Horton, 1946), he preferred writing and argumentation to experimentation. His several books, especially *The psychology of learning* (1935, rev. 1952) and *The psychology of human conflict* (1938), are full of persuasive anecdotal supports for his general associationistic principles, but contain little controlled evidence.

Watson's doctrines so influenced Guthrie that he became a thoroughgoing behaviorist, although he differed from Watson on many points of theory. Guthrie's interest in psychology was apparently kindled during his graduate training by the philosopher E. A. Singer. He has stated that his year's collaboration on a textbook with the psychologist Stevenson Smith (S. Smith & Guthrie, 1921) gave him "invaluable training" in psychology. He retained his early interest in problems of philosophy of science throughout his career; his final major work (Guthrie, 1959) shows a continuing interest in general methodological questions, such as the relationship between logic, language, and scientific progress.

Guthrie's Basic Principles

Guthrie believed that a few primary principles are sufficient to account for the fundamental facts of learning. His most famous principle is popularly referred to as *one-trial learning.* Guthrie held that S-R associations, as the basis of learning, are established by contiguity per se in a single pairing of stimulus and response. He early stated this principle as follows (1935): "A combination of stimuli which has accompanied a movement will on its recurrence tend to be followed by that movement" (p. 26). A related principle is (1942): "A stimulus pattern gains its full associative strength on the occasion of its first pairing with a response" (p. 30). Guthrie offered a final simplified version (1959): "What is being noticed becomes a signal for what is being done" (p. 186). This statement reflects his concern with the active role of the organism (the old problem of attention). In his final paper he also placed increased emphasis on the problem of patterning in stimulus complexes (cf. Guthrie, 1959, pp. 186ff.).

His early distinction between acts and movements enabled Guthrie to hold to his basic one-trial-learning principle and still account for the fact that behavior change typically requires repeated pairings of cue and response before it can be reliably predicted that the response will occur in the presence of the cue. According to Guthrie, the basic connections are between stimuli and movements, but *acts,* rather than movements, are usually measured. An example of an act would be serving a tennis ball into the service court; every separate muscular movement which was necessary would serve well as an example of what Guthrie means by a movement. While observable in principle, these movements are not easily noticed and are generally overlooked in theorizing. However, anyone who has ever had tennis lessons is aware of the fact that these movements must sometimes be considered and carefully learned, especially when complex coordinations are involved.

This does not mean that movements are equivalent to the contractions of individual muscles. In a sense what Guthrie means by movement is itself a kind of behavioral result; it is a result in terms of what is happening to a part of the organism, but it is not a result in terms of the environment. It is not the most molecular level of description which could be used. As Guthrie says (1959): "A description of the action of the individual muscles concerned would be hopeless confusion" (p. 183).

The situation is similar on the stimulus side. Guthrie regarded a complex stimulus as a collection of a great many stimulus components, with not all components present on every occasion. The net results of this complexity of stimulus and response components is that many presentations of the gross stimulus and many occurrences of the gross response (the act) are required before satisfactory regularity can be found in the behavior being measured. This is so because large numbers of the stimulus and response components need to be involved in the conditioning process. If exact replications of stimuli and responses could be achieved, single presentations would be sufficient to produce perfect conditioning.

For Guthrie, the process of conditioning is as follows: Aspects of the total stimulus situation present on a given trial become associated with a successful movement, that is, one which is part of the sequence constituting the successful "act." The successful movement causes movement-produced stimuli, which, along with external stimuli present in the environment as it may be altered by the movement, are associated with a subsequent successful movement. This chain of movements linked by movement-produced stimuli constitutes an act. When the act is terminated, it must result in the removal of the relevant stimuli if it is to be retained. Otherwise, other movements would become associated with the same stimuli.

On a subsequent trial in which different aspects of the total stimulus situation are present, the subject will engage in random behaviors until he again performs the act successfully. The movements constituting the act on that occasion are consequently associated with the stimulus complex present during the second trial. This associative process will recur on additional trials until successful movements are conditioned to all aspects of the stimulus situation. When this point is reached, conditioning is complete, and the act will occur smoothly, whatever aspect of the stimulus situation happens to be present.

Finally, it should be noted that Guthrie thought learning occurs through pure contiguity of stimulus and response. This might be considered a misguided view of the process of forming associations, since it is obvious that reinforcers have an important role in learning. Guthrie had no need to deny that reinforcers are effective; his theory simply accounted for their effectiveness in an ingenious and different way. The reinforcer was presumed to change the stimulus situation in which the response had just been made. The original stimulus situation (pre-reinforcer) therefore cannot be disconnected from the response just made and connected to a new response; the connection is thus preserved because of the stimulus change produced by the presence of the reinforcer. Unlearning, or extinction, is really the learning of different responses to the same stimulus, according to Guthrie. He is therefore able to present a beautifully parsimonious and consistent picture of both learning and extinction.

Evaluation of Guthrie

Guthrie's views have been most directly supported in the laboratory by his own investigation of stereotypy in the cat's behavior in the puzzle box (Guthrie & Horton, 1946) and by two investigations of Voeks (1948, 1954). Guthrie did not himself present any highly formalized theory; he stated (1959) that he did not think psychology was yet advanced enough to justify such theory. Voeks (1950) has nevertheless published a useful formalization of Guthrie's position. Her postulate of postremity, for example, states that only the last response made to a stimulus remains conditioned. Guthrie had said the same thing, but had made no effort to state it formally or to combine it with other postulates to form a system from which deductions could be made.

Although Guthrie did not leave any comprehensive theory, it is interesting to examine some experiments designed to test his statement that the last reponse made is the one that will be preserved and made again on the next presentation of the same cue. Voeks (1948) found that human subjects learning mazes made the postreme response on later trials far more often than the response which had previously been most frequent. Postremity won out over frequency in predicting responses for fifty-six out of fifty-seven subjects, in cases where the two principles made opposing predictions. Seward, Dill, and Holland (1944), however, found that subjects in a multiple-choice situation usually made the response made earliest, rather than latest, to a particular cue (color). It would thus appear from these two studies that the principle of postremity works sometimes, but not always—a statement which is true with disturbing frequency when applied to psychological principles.

The most searching criticism of Guthrie's theory has been offered by Mueller and Schoenfeld (1954). They have indicated that the simplicity of Guthrian notions is more apparent than real and has been achieved only at the expense of failure to be explicit about key problems. They have also suggested that Guthrie has developed no real system at all, in contrast to the leading alternative theorists. He has been satisfied with repeating, over the years, certain of the key assumptions with which he started. Finally, they have raised some serious questions concerning the interpretation of the Guthrie and Horton (1946) data on sterotypy of behavior. Their treatment should be consulted, along with Guthrie's final authoritative paper (1959), by anyone interested in evaluation of Guthrian theory.

Guthrie's success in maintaining his position as a leading learning theorist is surprising in view of the relative paucity of experimental support his theory received. This success has probably been due to a combination of several factors. Foremost among these is the apparent simplicity of his theory compared with the leading alternatives, such as Hull's. There is no difficulty in grasping at least the basis of Guthrie's views, and this simplicity appeals to many psychologists. A second factor has been the difficulty experienced by opposing theorists in presenting evidence which clearly contradicts the Guthrian theory. Finally, there is the fact that Guthrie and some of his adherents, notably Sheffield, have been consistently able to point to weaknesses and contradictions in the alternative accounts. Hull's need-reduction principle has been a special target (e.g., Sheffield, 1948; Sheffield, 1949; Sheffield & Roby, 1950; Sheffield, Wulff, & Backer, 1951). The fact that these successful attacks depend upon the greater predictive specificity of the alternative accounts does not seem to have reduced the effectiveness of the Guthrian attack. A consequence of this success in criticism has been that Guthrie's theory has remained a formidable alternative account, even though its laurels may have been won on largely negative grounds.

Despite these limitations, Guthrie has been more than merely an astute critic and propounder of simple generalizations supported by fluent anecdotal stories. He is one theorist who has stood by his theoretical guns, consistently espousing a contiguity principle as the basis of all learning. He has supported his emphasis on movements as the theoretical response elements by experimental studies of stereotypy and has shown how well stereotypy observed by other experimenters can be subsumed by his theoretical analyses. Guthrie has demonstrated the theoretical roles that can be played by mediating mechanisms like movement-produced stimuli. This ingenious mechanism is much like Hull's fractional anticipatory goal response in that both serve as the forgers of links in the chain of behavior. Finally, Guthrie has not said much because he did not believe he had enough information to say much. Thus he has made a small target. In 1958, the year before his death, Guthrie, the consistent psychologist, received the American Psychological Foundation Gold Medal Award in recognition of his distinguished contributions. These contributions have not stopped with his death; William K. Estes has modeled his statistical association theory on Guthrian principles. The Estes theory is discussed in Chapter 13, along with other mathematical developments.

Two-Factor Theories

It has been clear for a long time that the Thorndikian and the Pavlovian procedures for studying learning differ in the operations employed. In the Pavlovian procedure, the unconditioned stimulus follows the conditioned stimulus, whatever the subject in the experiment does. In the Thorndikian procedure, the reward is presented only if the subject has previously engaged in the behavior required by the experimenter. This basic difference in procedure implies some corollary distinctions. In the Pavlovian paradigm, the conditioned stimulus, which comes to elicit the conditioned response if learning occurs, is an identifiable stimulus and is manipulated by the experimenter. The unconditioned stimulus elicits an identifiable unconditioned response. The unconditioned response in the Pavlovian studies was always, or nearly always, an involuntary response mediated by the autonomic nervous system. The conditioned response typically bears a close relationship to the unconditioned response, if it is not identical to it as measured in the experiment. The Thorndikian procedure is different in all the above respects: There is no experimentally identified conditioned stimulus; the response elicited by the reward is not of great interest, nor do the experimental arrangements "force" the performance of the unconditioned response to the reward; the response to be learned may not be at all related in form to the response made to the reward; and the responses of interest are mediated by the "voluntary" nervous system.

A consideration of these operational differences between Pavlovian (classical) conditioning and Thorndikian (instrumental) learning leads one fairly naturally to question whether different laws of behavior modification are involved in the two situations. For example, one might ask whether stimulus associations, as in Pavlovian conditioning, and stimulus-response associations, as emphasized by the Thorndikian procedure, are formed by different basic processes. Rescorla and Solomon (1967), in their review of the literature on two-factor learning theories, state that three different sets of variables are usually implicated by those who think they are two basically different processes. The three sets are the class of responses affected by the process, the effective reinforcers involved, and the results of the learning process. The most common distinction based on response characteristics has been that classical conditioning involves autonomic responses, while instrumental learning involves somatic (skeletal) responses, but a number of other distinctions have also been suggested. It is more difficult to find a basis for distinguishing the kinds of reinforcers, but it has been suggested that the "rewards" used in instrumental learning have to have an affective character, while Pavlovian reinforcers do not; again, several bases for a distinction between the reinforcers have been proposed. Finally, among the several possible distinctions between the "products" of learning is the suggestion that classical conditioning involves stimulus-stimulus connections, while instrumental learning produces stimulus-response connections. There is no highly convincing empirical evidence that compels adherence to any of these theoretical distinctions, but there is not sufficient evidence to reject them either.

The most popular theoretical strategy has been an attempt to reduce the two operationally different procedures to a common theoretical framework which can explain both. Hull, for example, accepted the laws of Pavlovian conditioning as basic, but modified the most common conception of the process in his emphasis on the necessity for drive reduction to occur if learning is to be successful. The more complex, and therefore less popular, solution is to assume that there are two different processes involved and to propose a theory which relates the two processes. If this approach is chosen, it is natural to assume that classical conditioning involves contiguity as a basic process and that instrumental learning involves reward as a basic component.

Kimble (1961) reports that Miller and Konorski presented an early version of two-factor theory in 1928, and that they were followed into the field by Schlosberg (1937) and by Skinner (1938). Skinner's distinction between type S and type R conditioning has since become part of the jargon of our discipline; the former was essentially Pavlovian, and the latter Thorndikian. Skinner was far more interested in the Thorndikian, operant variety, and he held the evidence for pure Pavlovian conditioning to be questionable.

Mowrer later became, and has remained, the best-known two-factor theorist because of the tightness of his reasoning, the empirical work which buttressed his suggestions, and the length and number of his publications on the subject (1947, 1951, 1954). He contrasted conditioning and solution learning. The acquisition of emotions, meaning, attitudes, and the like is mediated through simple contiguity of stimuli—conditioning. Overt instrumental learning—solution learning—occurs through reinforcement, or law-of-effect learning. Since Mowrer was originally a strong Hullian reinforcement theorist, his shift was an important one. His interpretation was criticized by his earlier collaborator, Neal Miller (1951), among others.

A suggestion for a different kind of two-factor theory has been made by Spence in his Silliman Lectures (1956). As he pointed out, one might develop his suggestions into a two-factor theory "exactly the opposite of the well-known two-factor theory espoused by Schlosberg, Mowrer, and others" (p. 151). Reinforcement would thus be accorded a determining role in the case of classically conditioned responses, which are emphasized in Spence's systematic theorizing, rather than in that of instrumental behavior.

By far the most ambitious two-factor theory has been provided by Mowrer (1956, 1960a, 1960b) in a drastic revision of his earlier two-factor theory. Actually, this theory is no longer "two-factor" in the original sense; Mowrer has come to accept now only conditioning or sign learning as the single basic learning process; solution learning is regarded as a special, derived case of conditioning. It is still a two-factor theory, however, in the sense that it stresses two *types of reinforcement. Decremental reinforcement* refers to the need-reducing type of process stressed by Thorndike and Hull in their theories; *incremental reinforcement* refers to the growth of "fear" with consequent avoidance behavior from excessive stimulation.

The present theory was developed mainly by means of an extension of the secondary-reinforcement principle. Mowrer assumes that when a hungry animal obtains food, response-produced stimuli become conditioned as secondary reinforcers—as "promising" stimuli which arouse "hope." In this "feedback theory of habit," as Mowrer calls it, hope is thus conditioned in fundamentally the same manner as fear is conditioned in aversive learning. The parallelism is stated by Mowrer (1960b): "A conditioned stimulus not only makes the subject salivate: it also makes him *hopeful,* just as surely as a stimulus which has been associated with the onset of pain makes a subject *fearful*" (p. 8).

It is too early to say whether learning will eventually be subsumed under a single set of laws, under two sets, or under several. Rescorla and Solomon (1967) cite a number of empirical studies which demonstrate interactions between classical and instrumental conditioning. Changes in rate of instrumental responding can be produced by the introduction of conditioned stimuli previously used in the Pavlovian context. Such empirical demonstrations obviously do not prove that there are two kinds of learning, but they do show that it is profitable to study the relationships between situations in which stimulus *contiguity* is arranged (Pavlovian) and situations in which a response-reinforcement *contingency* is arranged. Two-factor theories may not turn out to be "correct," but they have the virtue of encouraging the study of such relationships.

Two-factor theories should also help us to remember that it is always the organism, and not some "autonomic learning system" or "somatic learning system" that is involved in the learning process. Kendon Smith (1954) early suggested that autonomic conditioning might occur only as a by-product of somatic learning, and is therefore in a sense an artifact. Theorists like Neal Miller tried to eliminate this possibility by showing that animals learn autonomic responses even though they are under the influence of curare, which is supposed to block all somatic responses. But Black (1967) reports that instrumental avoidance learning also occurs under curare, even though the avoidance response could not occur during the learning session! And Goesling and Brener (1972) have shown that the effects of somatic learning prior to curarization were manifested in autonomic learning *after* curarization. Considering all these complexities—and there are cognitive effects to be added—it indeed seems best to suspend judgment about the number of fundamental types of learning while we hope for future clarification.

SUMMARY AND CONCLUSIONS

In this chapter we have surveyed some S-R theories. In the main, these are neobehavioristic and concentrate on the problem of learning. They are distinguished on the basis of their treatment of the problem of reinforcement.

The reinforcement theory of Clark L. Hull represents a combination of the Thorndikian law of effect and the Pavlovian conditioning paradigm. This hypothetico-deductive system is highly formalized. It is by far the most ambitious theoretical and systematic effort of its kind. Compared with Watson, Hull was a sophisticated theorist, much concerned with logical as well as experimental specifications and empirical tests; he was a methodological, rather than a metaphysical, behaviorist. In spite of, or even perhaps partly because of, his high aspirations, Hull's direct systematic influence has declined markedly in recent years. This decline has been a function both of the fundamental faults found in his system and of the increasing popularity of the positivistic psychology of B. F. Skinner.

Skinner has been much less interested in formal theory than Hull. He believes that theory should develop inductively and be determined by data, rather than from postulates which then determine what data are gathered. Skinner does seem to have either moderated or clarified his position, beginning from what seemed to be an antitheoretical position and developing toward a positive attitude toward certain limited types of theory.

In keeping with his metatheoretical beliefs, Skinner has maintained an atheoretical, descriptive view of reinforcement. His research has been some of the most provocative and stimulating to be found in psychology. His interests have ranged freely from baby boxes to Utopian communities.

The major opposition within the S-R camp to the various reinforcement theories has been provided by the contiguity theorists, who hold to some kind of associationistic principle. They argue that reinforcement operates mainly to protect S-R connections formed through contiguity per se. E. R. Guthrie has been the most influential contiguity theorist over several decades. Within the past decade, however, the basic Guthrian contiguity principle has been cast in mathematical form by W. K Estes and his associates. Their use of mathematical models has given a strong impetus to empirical research as well as to theoretical development.

A number of two-factor theories have also been developed. These have historically attempted to combine the reinforcement and contiguity positions. The most recent of these, by O. H. Mowrer, does offer something of a novel approach. It involves two kinds of reinforcement, both based upon the conditioning or contiguity principle.

An important conclusion to be drawn from the wide variety of theoretical approaches outlined is that no one procedure can be guaranteed in advance to be more productive than any other. Rather, all kinds of empirical and theoretical endeavors are to be encouraged, as long as the fundamental requirements of scientific procedure are met. Each approach that is given a thorough trial will help to motivate and organize research. Which kind of research will eventually be seen to be most significant must await the verdict of history.

FURTHER READINGS

For an understanding of Hull's system, the most useful of his books are probably *Principles of behavior* (1943) and *A behavior system* (1952). His 1937 paper on conditioning theory, cited in the text, indicates the fundamental development of his thinking, and his autobiographical statement (1952) is unusually frank in detailing personal factors in his career. Spence's adaptation of Hullian theory is presented in his *Behavior theory and conditioning* (1956) and in the volume of collected writings, *Behavior theory and learning* (1960). Of Skinner's many papers and books, the most important sources are his beginning text, *Science and human behavior* (1953), and his collected writings, *Cumulative record* (1959b). Two particularly influential books by psychologists writing in the Skinnerian framework are Keller and Schoenfeld's *Principles of psychology* (1950), which presents an integrated set of principles based on operant conditioning, and Sidman's *Tactics of scientific research* (1960), which is a persuasive elaboration of the positivistic approach to experimentation. Guthrie is represented by his two basic books, *The psychology of learning* (1935) and *The psychology of human conflict* (1938). Koch's *Psychology: A study of a science* (Vol. 2, 1959), contains two papers on the Hullian system and its derivatives (by Logan and Miller), Guthrie's final systematic effort, Skinner's "Case history in scientific method," and an excellent detailed account of statistical theories by Estes. *Theories of learning,* by Hilgard and Bower (1975), describes all the above S-R theories in impressive detail.

Chapter 11

Varieties of Field Theory

Several psychological theorists have been called *field theorists* because of an analogy between their theories and the field theories of physics. We have already seen in Chapter 7 that Robert Oppenheimer (1956), who presumably understood the nature of field theory very well, questioned the usefulness of the analogy. In the published version of his speech to the American Psychological Association, he put the matter quite politely:

> But probably between sciences of very different character, the direct formal analogies in their structure are not too likely to be helpful. Certainly what the pseudo-Newtonians did with sociology was a laughable affair; and similar things have been done with mechanical notions of how psychological phenomena are to be explained. . . . I know that when I hear the word "field" used in physics and in psychology I have a nervousness that I cannot entirely account for. (pp. 133–134)

As psychologists, we shall of course be quick to consider the possibility that we have here simply the case of an effete physicist throwing up a defense of his own territory. However, we might quickly find ourselves unduly swelling the ranks of the effete if we put all those who question this particular analogy into those ranks. For example, one of our own (psychologist William K. Estes) said in connection with his examination of Kurt Lewin's theory:

> Now we may ask what are the distinguishing characteristics of the enterprises which claim or at least permit the appellation field theory? It should be noted first of all that most of the attributes claimed by field theorists and sympathetic reviewers tend to vanish or at least become non-differentiating upon critical scrutiny. It is not clear to the present writer in what technical sense the term field theory is especially applicable to the systems of Lewin, Koffka, Köhler, or Tolman. The term field has been taken over from physics, but it is not easy to find a basis for the presumed analogy between field theories of physics and the so-called field theories of psychology. (1954, pp. 318–319)

Estes goes on to point out that many of the adjectives that are supposed to describe field theories in psychology apply equally well to S-R theories, for example, *dynamic* and *multiply determined.*

Two points can be extracted from the objections of Oppenheimer and Estes. First, there *is* no close technical or formal relationship between the field theory of physics and the field theory of psychology. We shall see that Lewin developed the most formalized field theory in psychology and that it used an altogether different formal system and an altogether different set of variables from those used by any extant field theory in physics.

The second point is that the metatheoretical program which was supposed to direct the efforts of field theorists in psychology did not produce theories which bore the distinctive marks of the metatheory. A detailed examination of this point would carry us too far from our purpose here, and Estes (1954) has already documented this assertion.

What, then, is there left to discuss about field theory? There are three things. First, we can examine the analogy at the *metatheoretical* level between the field theories of physics and those of psychology, since there seems to be no valid analogy at a more technical level. Second, we can discuss the nature of the theories which have been called *field theories* in psychology, regardless of whether they are really any more fieldlike (in the sense of physics) than their competitors. Third, we can review representative empirical work done by field theorists to see what effect a field-theoretical viewpoint has on observations. We shall try to take a friendly look at field theory, and to assess it more in terms of its own aspirations than in terms of those of outside critics. We believe that field theorists in psychology have made extremely important theoretical, methodological, and empirical contributions. A close look at both their contributions and criticisms of them is clearly justified.

THE METATHEORETICAL ANALOGIES

Einstein's special relativity theory of 1905, and his general relativity theory of 1915, had unparalleled impacts on the view of the world held by physicists and philosophers alike. Related developments in quantum theory have further revolutionized man's world view. The awe with which these contributions are sometimes viewed is revealed by Gillispie (1960), who says: "And Lorentz lacked only that ultimate quality of something like divinity in Einstein's mind, which would take the same evidence and quite transform the shape of the world that physics sees in nature" (p. 506).

Even before the formulation of Einstein's special theory, Maxwell's field theory evoked great admiration. Under the circumstances, it was natural and desirable that the developing science of psychology try to emulate its more established fellow scientists by borrowing the lessons learned in the transformation from classical physics to relativity theory, the most prestigious representative of physical field theory.

The philosophy of relativity theory is a sea in which every man can find water beyond his depth. We must, nevertheless, try to extract from it those features which were taken over in the metatheoretical attitudes of field theorists in psychology.

Einstein's relativity theory, as modified by Minkowski, places events in a four-dimensional space-time field. The description of events is "holistic" in this and in other field theories in the sense that the theory inextricably interrelates the variables in describing the "trajectory" of events through this four-dimensional field. This general holistic property of field theories is taken over by field theorists in psychology as part of their metatheoretical equipment, whether or not it ever becomes visible as a characteristic of their theories.

A second supposed property of physical field theory, its dynamic character, is more controversial; that is, it is not agreed that relativity theory, at least, is really dynamic in the sense that it admits of change in a degree greater than the more "mechanistic" theories of classical physics. It has been argued that relativity theory provides for a complete and *static* view of existence, with past and future stretched out along the temporal dimension just as the sun and stars are arrayed in the spatial dimensions. Whether or not one agrees with this position (see Fraser, 1966, pp. 417–454, for both sides of the argument), it is hard to see why field theories in physics might be regarded as more dynamic than non-field theories. In psychology, "dynamic" has come to have a quite different connotation involving motivation, especially unconscious motivation, in addition to the more nearly physical meaning emphasizing change.

Field theories in physics do generally provide for continuity, for example, in space and time. The field properties may therefore change continuously, and this continuity of change—a mathematical continuity—may somehow connote dynamicism. It is, at least superficially, peculiar that Gestalt theory gave rise to a noncontinuity view of learning despite the close relationship of Gestalt metatheory to its precursors in physical field theory.

Einsteinian theory set sharp limits to the range of causality. Events which were too distant in space-time could not interact; no causal factors could propagate faster than the speed of light in a vacuum. The paths of the planets were reconceived as being along the shortest paths in the curved space produced by the presence of other bodies. There was no longer a gravitational attraction per se, since in some cases that attraction would have to take place instantaneously over vast distances. The field in which the planet moved at the time produced the movement of the planet. Action at a distance was no longer required. Psychological field theorists seem usually to have taken a position consistent with such restrictions on causal relationships. They accept the so-called contemporaneity principle, which states that only events coexisting at the same time can be causally related.

Apart from these metatheoretical considerations, there has been a high degree of commonality of theoretical content among field theories. Most important here are the widely shared interest in problems of perception and cognition and the correlated tendency to utilize perceptual and cognitive processes as explanatory factors. This is hardly surprising in view of the close relationship between modern field theories and classical Gestalt psychology, which was concerned primarily with similar emphases.

Principally, but by no means exclusively, field theory as used in psychology has come to refer to the metatheory of Kurt Lewin; his system is therefore the first described in the present chapter. The unique combination of behaviorism and Gestalt psychology achieved in the purposivism of E. C. Tolman is included as the second important specimen of field theory. The increasingly influential thinking of Egon Brunswik is next described. Then we turn to an examination of the contributions of Roger Barker, who combines ideas of Lewin with those of Brunswik in some unique investigations. Finally, other systematists (K. S. Lashley and J. R. Kantor) whose work may be classified as falling within some kind of field-theoretical classification are more briefly described.

LEWIN'S VECTOR FIELD THEORY

The contributions to psychological theory made by Kurt Lewin (1890–1947) have been among the most significant of recent decades. On the one hand, Lewin was a brilliant researcher. Even his severest critics recognize him as a most ingenious experimenter; the series of experimental studies which he directed while at the University of Berlin in the 1920s is a model of theoretical creativity and imagination combined with appropriate methodology. Throughout his career he remained a strong advocate of the primacy of directive theory in research, and he is best known for his development of the motivational, or vector, system of psychology, most commonly referred to as *field theory.*

Although Lewin was associated with an active center of Gestalt psychology at Berlin, he retained little formal identification with the orthodox group, and his systematizing went well beyond the usual confines of the school. As a matter of fact, there was no formal relationship between his theories and those of the Gestaltists. In a letter to Köhler that constitutes the preface to his book *The principles of topological psychology,* Lewin probably expresses his relationship to Gestalt psychology most succinctly: "I have tried my best to destroy the myth that Gestaltists do not attack each other" (1936, p. viii). Thus Lewin was a sort of half-Gestaltist, and perhaps felt most a member of the group when he was criticizing it! Lewin's early efforts were concerned largely with motivational problems of the individual subject, which led to an interest in problems of personality organization; his later efforts were concerned mainly with a wide variety of problems in social psychology, including his initiation of the group-dynamics movement and his assistance in the development of *action research* (i.e., research directed at producing social changes). In between, he was peripherally concerned with problems such as the nature of learning, cultural factors in personality structure, and child development. But in all these diverse areas Lewin brought to bear on critical issues the same fundamental approach: an emphasis always upon the psychological, rather than the simple environmental, factors in the situation (or field). This emphasis is related to the earlier Gestalt distinction, most explicitly made by Koffka, between the "behavioral" and the "geographical" environments. The crux of the distinction is that the effective meaning of the environmental conditions depends upon more than merely physical attributes; that is, a description in terms of such factors alone is inadequate. An individual's *perception* of the physical attributes determines how that individual will react.

Lewin's Career

Kurt Lewin was born in Prussia and received his higher education at the Universities of Freiburg, Munich, and Berlin (Ph.D., 1914). He was thus present during the formative years of the Gestalt movement. After a 5-year interlude of military service, he returned to Berlin and remained in various academic capacities until 1932, when he came to the United States. He spent that year as visiting professor at Stanford and the following 2 years at Cornell. The decision to establish permanent residence in this country was made as a consequence of the rise of Nazi power in Germany, where his Jewish ancestry became a handicap. Lewin went to the Child Welfare Station of the State University of Iowa as professor of child psychology in 1935 and finally to Massachusetts Institute of Technology in 1944. In this last appointment he was director of the Research Center for Group Dynamics, a movement which he had only fairly well started at the time of his death in 1947.

Marrow, in his biography *The practical theorist* (1969), describes Lewin as an enthusiastic, charming, and intellectually scintillating man. He was as far from the popular image of the German professor as Wundt and Titchener were close to it. Marrow describes him as being so democratic that he was a sort of natural American. He was very close to his students, and prone to make unannounced visits to their homes. Through them, as well as through his own research and conceptualization, he has left an indelible mark on American social psychology.

Roger Barker reported to Marrow that Lewin never had any conception of when to stop once he had begun a stimulating discussion. Only the excuse that he had to get home to his wife saved Barker from complete exhaustion on many occasions. Perhaps that level of intensity accounts in part for Lewin's tragically early death of a heart attack when he was only 56.

Lewin's major publications were in the form of journal reports and contributions to various collections of papers. His own papers have been collected in four small volumes. The first two of these, *A dynamic theory of personality* (1935) and *Principles of topological psychology* (1936), represent the earlier European phase of his career; the last two collections, *Resolving social conflicts* (1948) and *Field theory in social science* (1951), relate to the later American phase.

Topology and Hodological Space

Lewin selected topology, a relatively new geometry, as providing a mathematical model upon which he could base his conceptual representation of psychological processes. In brief, topology is a geometry in which spatial relationships are represented in a strictly nonmetrical manner. Positional relationships between areas or regions are maintained in spite of various kinds of changes in size and shape. The primary concern is with the connections between bounded regions and with their spatial relationships; for example, one area will remain inside another throughout a wide variety of stretchings and distortions. (See Brown, 1936, for a relatively simplified introduction to Lewin's use of the topological geometry.) Lewin felt that such positional relationships were the best way to conceptualize the structure of psychological relationships. There was, however, one serious limitation to topology: its lack of directional concepts. To represent the psychological concept of direction, Lewin then invented a new qualitative geometry (1938), which he named *hodological space* (from the Greek *hodos,* translated as "path"). He developed the characteristics of such a space that he felt were necessary for an adequate representation of the dynamic factors, usually called *vectors,* in psychological relationships.

Cartwright (1959, pp. 61–65) reports that recent researchers have substituted a new mathematical tool, the linear graph, for Lewin's topology plus hodology. On the planar maps which Lewin usually used to represent his life spaces, no more than four regions can have mutual boundaries. This limits the complexity of structure which can be represented on a two-dimensional, planar map. On a linear graph, an indefinite number of points (which replace regions in the life space) can be mutually interconnected. The linear graph also allows for the representation of asymmetrical relationships, as when movement can occur from region A to region B, but not back. There is no natural way to represent these asymmetries on the map.

Life Space

Lewin's objective in adapting and even inventing such geometries was to clarify his conceptualization of the psychological field, or *life space.* The life space is most simply defined as the totality of effective *psychological* factors for a given person at some particular time. It consists of a number of differentiated *regions,* which represent significant conditions in the person's life. Although the totality of factors is emphasized in definitions such as the above, in actual practice only the most relevant ones are ordinarily included in diagrammatic presentations of the life-space concept.

Let us illustrate Lewin's distinction between physical and psychological representations by a relatively simple example from his writing. Figure 11-1*a* shows the physical situation, and Figure 11-1*b* shows the psychological representation, where a goal object (toy) is placed out of reach within a circular area. Direct physical approach to the goal via path w_1 is not possible, but psychological locomotion, via path w_2, is effective if mother can be persuaded to obtain the toy. Although the example pictured involves a physical barrier, the same psychologi-

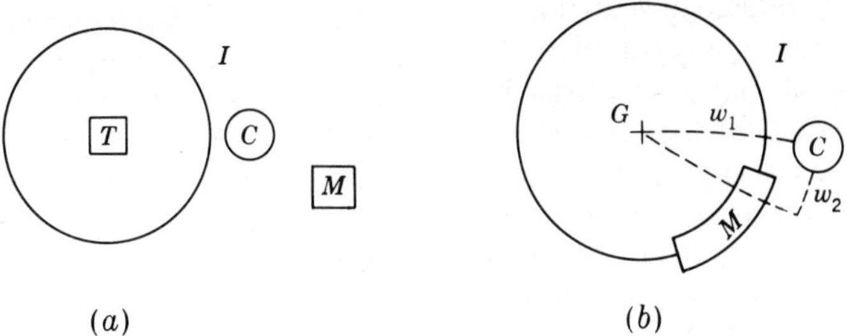

Figure 11-1 Situation in which a young child wishes to reach a toy that lies inside a circular barrier: (a) physical situation; (b) psychological situation. *C*, child; *T*, toy; *I*, barrier; *M*, mother; *G*, goal; w_1, w_2, paths. (*Source:* Lewin, 1936, p. 147.)

cal situation might obtain with a barrier produced by verbal restriction involving the toy, especially for an older child. Or, in somewhat similar situations, the barrier might consist of more strictly personal or intraorganismic factors such as politeness in a child trained not to take things without asking or timidity or even fear in some other child. In these cases the physical picture would show no barrier, but the psychological representation, for this slice of the life space, might look very much like that shown in the figure.

A somewhat more comprehensive example of a typical life space is shown in Figure 11-2. Here Lewin depicted a series of locomotions involving a particular occupational choice for a young man. Lewin (1936) pointed out that the passing of the college entrance examinations, while not a physical locomotion, represents a "real change of position in the quasi-social . . . life space. . . . Many things are now within his reach which were not before" (p.48). It is this kind of crossing from one region to another that is emphasized in the life-space schema.

Important dimensions of the life space, as Lewin conceptualized it, are its temporal and reality characteristics. As children grow older, not only does their life space become increasingly differentiated into regions as a function of maturity and expanding personal problems, but it also develops temporal and reality-irreality dimensions. For example, children begin to plan for the future as well as to respond more effectively in longer time units. Further, they begin to use imagery and fantasy and thus to live, in some degree, on an irreality level; there they are less restricted in behavior by the usual barriers of the real world.

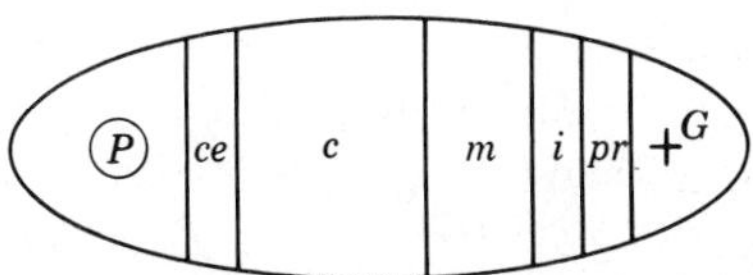

Figure 11-2 Situation of a boy who wants to become a physician. *P*, person; *G*, goal; *ce*, college entrance examinations; *c*, college; *m*, medical school; *i*, internship; *pr*, establishing a practice. (*Source:* Lewin, 1936, p. 48)

The reality dimension is illustrated in Figure 11-3, in which Lewin showed three levels of this variable in the life space.

Lewin considered this dimension highly significant in a psychological analysis, and so it was given considerable attention in his work. Lewin did not believe that an absolute reality or irreality dimension was tenable because of the continually changing field of experiences; that is, what at one instant may be considered absolute reality may be altered by new events and experiences. Furthermore, as the individual matures, the reality-irreality dimension broadens and becomes more differentiated (1936, p. 204).

Perhaps the most widely known Lewinian contribution within the life-space framework is his conceptualization of conflict. He stated that there are three basic types of conflicts producing frustration: approach-approach, approach-avoidance, and avoidance-avoidance. Approach-approach conflict occurs when an individual desires to achieve two goals, only one of which is obtainable (e.g., one has two invitations for the same evening). Approach-avoidance conflict is characterized by a goal which is both desired and undesired (e.g., one desires the money but not the effort entailed in a proffered job). An avoidance-avoidance conflict is present when anticipated consequences are both undesirable (e.g., one must accept an unwanted invitation or offend an esteemed friend). This type of conflict is characterized by a vacillation between the alternatives or by an attempt to escape the situation ("leave the field").

One misinterpretation of Lewin's life space occurs often enough to demand discussion. This is that the life space is the same as the phenomenal world of the person who occupies the life space. That is not true. Lewin intended the life space as a representation of the factors which influenced the behavior and perception of the individual. Some of these factors might be quite unconscious. Thus the life space is a conceptual device in the service of the scientist. The phenomenology of

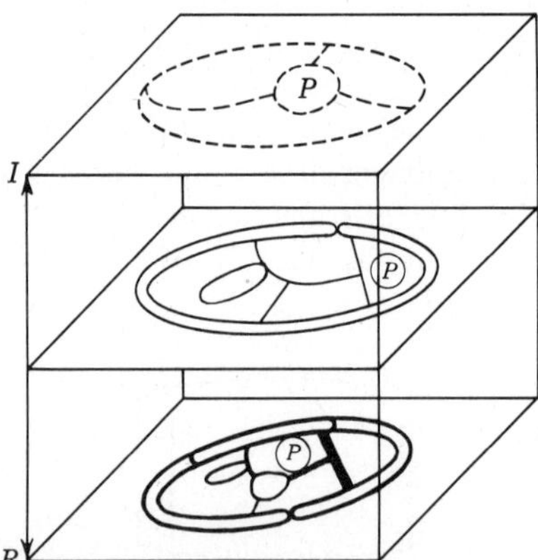

Figure 11-3 Representation of different degrees of reality by an additional dimension of the life space. *R*, more real level; *I*, more irreal level; *P*, person. In a level of greater reality the barriers are stronger, and the person *P* is more clearly separated from the environment. (*Source:* Lewin, 1936, p. 200.)

the individual may be either close to or rather distant from the life space as conceptualized by the psychologist. Although the life space is intended to represent the *concrete* reality in which the individual is immersed, it also shares an *abstract* quality with theories like Hull's.

Lewin's System

It is impossible to describe any single integrated system constructed by Lewin (such as that described for Hull in Chapter 10). This is mainly because Lewin never attempted to produce such an integrated system; when not concerned with methodological problems in field theory, he worked on a variety of different problems. All of them involved somewhat the same general type of working assumptions and procedures and to a great extent the same constructs. However, no serious attempt was made by Lewin to coordinate these concepts into one systematic framework (cf. Cartwright, 1959).

The series of researches involving Lewin's assumption of the *tension system* has been selected as the best example of his work; in some respects it comes close to being an integrated system. A continuing series of experimental studies, some of them described below, was based upon implications of this central concept. Lewin himself has provided a theoretical account of these researches, emphasizing the formal assumptions and derivations (Lewin, 1940, pp. 13–28; 1944, pp. 4–20). Our treatment follows this account as well as the more informal description given by Deutsch (1954, pp. 199ff.).

The background for Lewin's development of the construct of the tension system goes back to his first psychological research (1917). He was interested in refining some of Ach's (1910) earlier research on the strength of the will. The general procedure here was to establish associations of nonsense syllables through repeated pairings and then to evaluate the strength of the voluntary factor, manipulated by instructions, by opposing it to the habitual tendency. (See Hilgard, 1956, pp. 258ff., for a description of this research and the theoretical rationales.) Lewin finally rejected Ach's attempt to supplement the association factor with such new constructs as set and determining tendency, in the tradition of the Würzburg school, to which Ach belonged (see Chapter 4). He felt that Ach had not gone far enough in his interpretation. Rather than accept *both* association and voluntary factors, Lewin simply assumed two voluntary factors. He pointed out that association per se provided no motive power. That power had to be accounted for in some other way; as he later put it:

> Dynamically, an "association" is something like a link in a chain, i.e., a pattern of restraining forces without intrinsic tendency to create a change. This property of a need or quasi-need can be represented by coordinating it to a "system in tension." By taking this construct seriously and using certain operational definitions, particularly by correlating the "release of tension" to a "satisfaction of the need" (or "reaching of the goal") and the "setting up of tension" to an "intention" or to a "need in a state of hunger," a great many testable conclusions were made possible. (1940, p. 14)

The first formal effort to test the tension-system proposition thus developed by Lewin was the doctoral-dissertation research done by Zeigarnik (1927) under his supervision. Her experiments were based on the assumptions that (1) tension systems would be established in a subject when given simple tasks to perform and (2) if such tension systems were not dissipated, as would normally occur with the completion of the tasks, their persistence would result in a greater likelihood of subsequent recall by the subject of the names of the tasks. Her results in a variety of experiments substantially confirmed this prediction, since interrupted tasks were generally better recalled by subjects than completed tasks. There has been an extensive experimental literature (cf. Alper, 1948; Deutsch, 1954) concerning this interesting phenomenon, the so-called Zeigarnik effect.

The next experimental test of the tension-system construct was performed by Ovsiankina (1928). She showed that subjects would voluntarily resume interrupted activities more often than they would return to activities that had been completed.

Following the confirmatory results of these first two studies, further experimental tests were performed. Among the better known of these are the studies of Lissner (1933) and Mahler (1933) on the role of substitute activities as effective discharger of tension; of Hoppe (1930) and J. D. Frank (1935) on success and failure, especially as these are related to the "level of aspiration" expressed by the subject; and of Karsten (1928) on "psychical satiation," which concerns the problem of the reduction in performance of an activity as a function of the continued repetition of the activity. A summary of these and other related studies is provided by Lewin (1935, pp. 239ff.). Although we do not have space here to present a further development of Lewin's contributions to research and theory via the tension-system construct, its fruitfulness is well attested by the manner in which these concepts and problems have been used in personality theory (cf. Deutsch, 1954).

Lewin's later concern with systematic problems of social psychology may be illustrated by his interesting, and somewhat unusual, wartime research on food habits of people (Lewin, 1943b; see also Lewin, 1951, chap. 8). Here Lewin raised first the question of why people eat what they do. Interaction of psychological factors (e.g., cultural tradition, individual preference) and nonpsychological factors (e.g., food availability, cost) was investigated in the framework of a so-called channel theory. According to this viewpoint, most of the food that appears on the table is eventually eaten by someone or other in the family group, so that the primary question reduces to the particular channels by which food is obtained for family use. The two major sources of food in this country during World War II were store purchases and gardening (minor channels were country buying, home baking and canning, and the like). Lewin emphasized the role of the "gatekeeper"—ordinarily the housewife—as the individual who determines for each channel how much of each foodstuff shall be procured and taken through the various stages of preparation for consumption (in the case of home gardening, of course, more steps are necessary before the final usable products are available for the table).

The psychology of the gatekeeper, as Lewin phrased it, thus became a focal point of this research. Although several interesting questions were asked in the pursuit of the problem, we shall outline only one that received considerable empirical attention. That is the question of the most effective procedure for changing opinions. Here attention centered on individual versus group procedures. Lewin pointed out (1951, chap. 10) that an a priori expectation might well be that single individuals, being "more pliable" than groups of like-minded persons, should be easier to convince. An opposite conclusion, however, is supported by the preponderance of much research (on a variety of social problems, such as alcoholism and prejudices, as well as food habits). Once the group standards themselves are changed, as by group rather than individual discussions, individual opinions are much more readily altered.

One illustrative study concerned increased consumption of fresh milk. No pressure was used in the individual or group discussions, and equal time was spent in each case. The results showed clearly that compliance by housewives with the requested change was greater following the group procedure. Similar results were found for other types of foodstuffs (such as evaporated milk and orange juice) and for quite different social problems (such as increased productivity among factory workers). A public commitment to a new course of action seems generally to produce more permanence of changed attitudes or behaviors. In some cases, the degree of change may even increase over a period of time following the experimental manipulations; when this happens there is said to be a "sleeper effect."

This research is a good example of the way in which Lewin's work combined theoretically important questions with practically significant problems and procedures. Food acceptability was of practical importance when Lewin started this research during wartime, and as the world's population increases, the problem promises to become of permanent practical significance. More generally, group processes are important to man's sense of well-being, and to his very survival. The contemporary upsurge in interest in such activities as T groups can be traced, to a very great extent, directly to the work of Lewin (see, for example, Bradford, Gibb, & Benne, 1964).

Criticisms of Lewin

Most of the criticism of Lewin has been related to his field-theoretical approach. London (1944) has charged that Lewin misappropriated and misused topological concepts. London claimed that in his purported use of topology Lewin had merely borrowed the terminology and certain of the gross conceptualizations from this geometry and failed to use anything like the full set of fundamental topological relationships. In answer to this objection, Lewin argued that all that can legitimately be required of psychologists who attempt to apply a mathematical model is that they coordinate some of the conceptual relations with empirical processes (1951): "There can be no other meaning and no other proof of the applicability of these geometries to psychology than the fruitfulness of predictions based on such coordination" (p. 22). The issue between London and Lewin can be efficiently stated as: "Does the topological model appropriated by Lewin retain enough of its logical structure so that it retains any deductive power?" If it does not, London's criticism is well taken, and there really are no predictions based on the coordination of topology and psychology. The totality of the evidence seems to indicate that Lewin's predictions were based on informal arguments and prior observations, rather than on deductions within topology. Even if this judgment is correct, however, the topological analogy may have had a good deal of motivational and heuristic value for Lewin and his students. Marrow (1969) says that they often carried on animated discussions in Lewin's home with the aid of a litter of paper and colored pencils, used to make topological diagrams! Such procedure is obviously valuable, even if it lacks formal rigor.

Another criticism, voiced even by some who are strongly sympathetic to Lewin (Deutsch, 1954), as well as by less friendly critics, has been that he has failed to specify which of several possible interpretations he intended for key terms, such as *person,* of key relationships, such as *person* to *life space.* A related but much more fundamental criticism (Estes, 1954) has been that Lewin has generally failed to indicate the empirical basis of his psychological concepts, such as life space, in spite of his admirable emphasis upon the necessity for strict operational coordinating definitions of concepts.

A corollary to the above stricture is the objection that Lewin in his emphasis upon the central cognitive aspects of behavior has tended to ignore the motor aspects. Field theorists generally, with their perceptual or cognitive orientation, have tended to undervalue the response side of the S-O-R formulation.

In a much-cited criticism, Brunswik has gone even further, holding that Lewin's "encapsulation into the central layer" means that his life space "is post-perceptual and pre-behavioral" (1943). Lewin's reply to this particular comment has been that he did not think that psychology needs to study the objective physical and sociological factors which do not have implications for behavior. However, he was willing to include the study of those objective factors which are potential determiners of the life space; this kind of study he called *psychological ecology* (Lewin, 1943a). Cartwright's paper contains a carefully detailed formulation of this problem of the "boundary zone" of the life space (1959, pp. 69ff.).

Critical evaluations of the more technical aspects of Lewinian field theory may be found in Leeper (1943) and Cartwright (1959). Comprehensive reviews by Deutsch (1954) and Escalona (1954) cover the contributions of his work to social psychology and child psychology, respectively.

Finally, a serious objection to Lewin has been that he failed to make his general conceptual system sufficiently precise and specific so that it can be disconfirmed by experimental test. To quote Estes:

> This informal development of coordinating definitions in use enables the theorist to give plausible accounts of concrete situations, but with no possibility of having the theory refuted by the outcome of the behavioral situation, since the correspondence between theoretical and empirical terms is adjusted in accordance with the empirical findings and is never formally incorporated into the system. Flexibility is obtained at the cost of testability. (1954, p. 332)

It is necessary to recognize the important distinction between Lewin's effective experimental-theoretical research on specific problems, emphasized in the following section, and his theoretical efforts, criticized in the preceding paragraph for their lack of adequate empirical specification. In particular, the life-space schemata seem to be of limited value in setting up experiments. They serve as pedagogic devices and provide a general stimulating effect for the experimenter. Although it is impossible to identify the sources of a thinker's influence with certainty, it seems likely that Lewin's tremendous contemporary influence stems less from his formal theorizing than from his informal theorizing and the associated empirical work.

Lewin's Contributions

Lewin has few peers as a creative conceptualizer *and* an ingenious experimenter. It was largely this ability to implement his theoretical insights with concrete empirical situations that accounts for his preeminence. This ability was apparently based, at least in part, upon insightful observations of the everyday-life scene. For example, his conceptualization of the tension system in relation to memory (cf. the Zeigarnik effect, described above) is said to have been suggested by his observation that waiters in Berlin restaurants had a remarkably accurate memory for the detailed amount of each bill—but only until it was paid (G. W. Hartmann, 1935, p. 221).

Lewin's specific contributions to psychological theory were of great scope and depth. He developed concepts and experimental techniques, such as level of aspiration, that have enjoyed widespread acceptance in the fields of personality and motivation. These contributions to personality theory have had a strong, continuing influence.

Finally, Lewin's pioneering efforts in the field of social psychology would be sufficient to guarantee him a lasting and prominent place in the history of psychology. His early research in social psychology in this country is exemplified by the pioneer studies (Lewin, 1939; Lippitt, 1940; Lippitt & White, 1943) on behavior in social climates that were experimentally manipulated. For example, leadership techniques were experimentally varied in boys' clubs (laissez-faire, democratic, autocratic), and various behaviors, such as aggression, were correlated with different social climates that resulted (Lippitt & White, 1943). These studies not only opened up an important new area of social research but also had some influence upon educational and social practices (Cartwright, 1959).

The final phase of Lewin's research, concerned mainly with group dynamics, found him taking more of an administrative and supervisory role and leaving to others the detailed working out of hypotheses and collection of data. In *Resolving social conflicts* (1948), Lewin reported on various experimental efforts to change social behavior in real, everyday-life situations (such as interracial factory workshops). It is unfortunate that his relatively early death prevented further contributions to this kind of research program.

The lines of work started by Lewin certainly did not stop with his death. He was one of those rare individuals who are in tune with the times 25 to 50 years after they are no longer alive. The problems connected with social influence and leadership are still under active study. Field observations, which so often gave Lewin his inspiration, are fast gaining respectability as a source of psychological information (Willems & Raush, 1969). His concern, late in life, with psychological ecology must have provided part of the impetus for Barker's work resulting in a book on precisely that topic (1968). Even his attempt to find parallels between different fields, best seen in his general attitude toward field theory and his attempt to use mathematical formalism, may have, at the least, provided part of the general background for the development of general systems theory (see Buckley, 1968, for papers in this area). To say that Kurt Lewin was one of the germinal figures for modern psychology is praise too faint.

Few psychologists have been as eager as Lewin to contribute to the solutions of social problems. Part of his practical interest is traceable to his own personal experiences. He had been in the German army in World War I and had experienced the disaster that was postwar Germany. His own mother died as a victim of the Nazis during World War II, and he felt the long arm of anti-Semitism even in the United States. It was a Jewish religious group concerned with the elimination of prejudice that funded the Research Center for Group Dynamics which Lewin founded at MIT. Circumstance and temperament seemed to combine in him to form a unique combination of theoretician and man of action. No wonder, then, that his interests encompassed leadership and prejudice, and that he devoted so much attention and ingenuity to methods of changing behavior.

So great was the effect of Lewin as a human being and as an investigator that it is hardly hyperbole to describe American social psychology as a Lewinian development. However, Lewin's theory and the earlier Berlin developments were almost completely abandoned. He had changed his own interests in his later years, and the early work was not easily accessible, not to mention not easily understood, in the United States. A book by de Rivera (1976) may change this situation. He has collected the early Berlin dissertations, related them to the theoretical background, and added theoretical suggestions of his own. If empirical work by de Rivera or by others is stimulated anew, even the previously neglected interests of Lewin may enjoy a renaissance.

COGNITIVE FIELD THEORY: TOLMAN'S PURPOSIVE BEHAVIORISM

The important contribution of Edward C. Tolman (1886–1959) to the development of behaviorism has already been noted (Chapter 6). The emphasis which he early placed on a *molar* interpretation of behavior as *purposive* (1932) persisted throughout his long and illustrious career. Although Tolman cannot be said to have developed a definitive theory, his system of psychology, with its primarily cognitive, or S-S, position on learning, has been extremely influential. He has been the most acceptable of the major avowed behaviorists to nonbehavioristically oriented psychologists. His system represents the seemingly paradoxical combination of important elements of behaviorism and Gestalt psychology. His primary orientation has been stimulus-centered, or cognitive, rather than S-R; in his later papers especially (e.g., 1949a) he has not only professed a deep-seated admiration for the field-theoretical views of Kurt Lewin but also adopted a Lewinian position with regard to fundamental theoretical problems. For these reasons, Tolman is treated here as a kind of field theorist.

Tolman's Career

Edward Tolman was born in Massachusetts and took an engineering degree at the Massachusetts Institute of Technology. He switched to psychology and received his M.A. in 1912 and his Ph.D. in 1915 from Harvard. He served as an instructor in psychology at Northwestern University from 1915 to 1918. Tolman then moved to the University of California, where he established a rat laboratory. During World War II he served for 2 years (1944 and 1945) in the Office of Strategic Services. In 1950, at the age of 64, Tolman demonstrated his patriotism in a different way by leading the fight against the state loyalty oath. During the next 3 years, while the issue was being resolved, Tolman held appointments at the University of Chicago and at Harvard. His humanness, which made him beloved by his students, shows through even in the conclusion to his final published statement:

> I have liked to think about psychology in ways that have proved congenial to me. Since all the sciences, and especially psychology, are still immersed in such tremendous realms of the uncertain and the unknown, the best that any individual scientist, especially any psychologist, can do seems to be to follow his own gleam and his own bent, however inadequate they may be. In fact, I suppose that actually this is what we all do. In the end, the only sure criterion is to have fun. And I have had fun. (1959, p. 152)

Tolman the man was thus something of a maverick and a dissenter. We shall see, too, that the system he produced refuses to fit itself easily into the usual categories.

Tolman's System

Tolman's system was loosely formulated in his first and most important book, *Purposive behavior in animals and men* (1932). At the time he was working on it, little effort was expended to organize the major ideas into an integrated system. Predictions about experimental outcomes were not related to one another in a logically rigorous manner. Tolman was long considered a programmatic theorist. MacCorquodale and Meehl (1954) formalized his major principles in much more rigor and detail. In his final work, Tolman himself presented a more organized picture of his system (1959). We shall present here only a brief summary of his most salient principles; readers who want the clearest presentation of a Tolmanian system should refer to MacCorquodale and Meehl.

The primary principle in Tolman's systematic thinking about behavior is that in its purposive or adaptive activities, the organism uses environmental objects and develops *means-end readinesses* with regard to them and their role in relation to his behavior. This phrase is but one of many awkwardly compounded terms which Tolman coined early in his career and used consistently in his writing; this one is particularly emphasized in his "Principles of purposive behavior" (1959). The term is roughly synonymous with *cognitions* or *expectancies.* It refers to the kind of learning which Tolman felt was central to behavior—sign learning. Briefly put, the organism learns "what leads to what." Like the Gestalt theorists, Tolman felt that the actual behavior is relatively unimportant; the primary determiners of action are central, not peripheral, as the typical S-R theorist would hold.

In his statement of 1959 Tolman presented a schema for each of five representative situations: simple approach to food, simple escape from electric shock, simple avoidance of electric shock, choice-point learning, and latent learning.

These five paradigms suggest several aspects of Tolman's late thought. First, a superficial similarity to the Hullian system is evident. To some extent this logical interrelating of concepts was induced by the form of presentation requested by the editor of the book. This kind of formalization may also have been encouraged by the earlier effort of MacCorquodale and Meehl, who had put Tolman's thinking into a near-Hullian form. However, Tolman had used a comparable, though much simpler, tabular arrangement much earlier (e.g., 1936, 1938).

Second, and more important, Tolman's final formulation illustrates the central role played in his theory by the cognitive constructs. Here a little explanatory detail is in order. Two major cognitive constructs are involved. The means-end readiness is a relatively pure acquired cognitive disposition—pure in the sense that it endures independently of the present motivational state of the organism; that is, the organism may know where food is whether or not it is hungry. The expectation, on the other hand, is the concrete product of the means-end readiness—a cognitive event that applies directly and specifically to the present situation. Tolman summed up the two concepts:

> A means-end readiness, as I conceive it, is a condition in the organism, which is equivalent to what in ordinary parlance we call a "belief" (a readiness or disposition) to the effect than an instance of this *sort* of stimulus situation, if reacted to by an instance of this *sort* of response, will lead to an instance of that *sort* of further stimulus situation, or else, that an instance of this *sort* of stimulus situation will simply by itself be accompanied, or followed, by an instance of that *sort* of stimulus situation. Further, I assume that the different readinesses or beliefs (dispositions) are stored up together (in the nervous system). When they are concretely activated in the form of expectancies they tend to interact and/or consolidate with one another. And I would also assert that "thinking" as we know it in human beings, is in essence no more than an activated interplay among expectancies resulting from such previously acquired readinesses which result in new expectancies and resultant new means-ends readinesses. (1959, pp. 113–114)

Tolman conceded the weakness of this formulation in terms of specific empirical measures. He recognized the difficulty of implementing such constructs operationally, but at the same time repeatedly pointed to what he saw as a comparable weakness in the Hull-Spence r_g–s_g construct (see Chapter 10).

Although the concept of cognition, however phrased, is the key one in Tolman's system, he considered other types of concepts and other kinds of learning. In his effort (1949b) to cover the major types of learning processes, he pointed to the following six "types of connections": *cathexes,* which represent the affective properties acquired by objects (similar to Lewin's *valence*); *equivalence beliefs,* which are the cognitive representations of subgoals, secondary reinforcers, or impending disturbances; *field expectancies* (earlier called *sign-Gestalt-expectations*), which are representations of the environment that make possible latent learning, shortcuts, etc.; *field-cognition modes,* which are the higher-order functions that produce field expectancies through perceptual, memorial, or inferential processes; *drive discriminations,* which are the demonstrated abilities of animals to behave differentially under different deprivation conditions; and *motor patterns,* which are the responses and combinations of responses (skills) themselves.

Tolman made only the sketchiest effort to indicate the kinds of laws, or empirical relationships between variables, that might relate to these various kinds of learning. No laws were suggested, for example, for the important field-cognition modes or for drive discriminations. A simple contiguity principle, following Guthrie, was accepted for motor patterns. Hullian need reduction was considered to be at least partially responsible for cathexes and equivalence beliefs. And no definitive interpretations were offered for the key concept of field expectancies, although the reinforcement principle here was specifically denied more than an incidental role.

Tolman's (1951b) model contained three major constructs: the *need system,* closely related to orthodox drive notions; the *behavior space,* closely related to Lewin's life space, described earlier in this chapter; and the *belief-value matrix,* which consists of hierarchies of learned expectations concerning environmental objects and their roles in relation to behavior.

These brief sketches of Tolman's approach should indicate the essentially tentative and preliminary nature of his system. He seldom felt certain enough of his ground to suggest lawful relationships, or even logical relationships, between the variables of his system. Tolman was himself acutely aware of the questionable status of some aspects of his system (1959): ". . . I think the days of such grandiose, all-covering systems in psychology as mine attempted to be are, at least for the present, pretty much passé. . . . I have an inveterate tendency to make my ideas too complicated and too high-flown so that they become less and less susceptible to empirical test" (pp. 93–94).

Tolman did not produce the kind of system he did because of his metatheoretical principles or his methodological ignorance, but because he was the kind of person he was. In his early works (1936, 1938), he had specified in some detail the particular variables which he felt were significant ones in behavior and had indicated the kind of "standard" experimental situation in which their values might be determined. He was also early concerned with a prototype of experimental design intended to identify the functional interrelationships of independent, intervening, and dependent variables. Thus Tolman espoused a strict empirical methodology designed to uncover lawful relationships between variables, but he did not always carry his beliefs over into practice. The amount of tedium involved may well make such a program impractical for anyone to carry out. Certainly it was not Tolman's kind of fun.

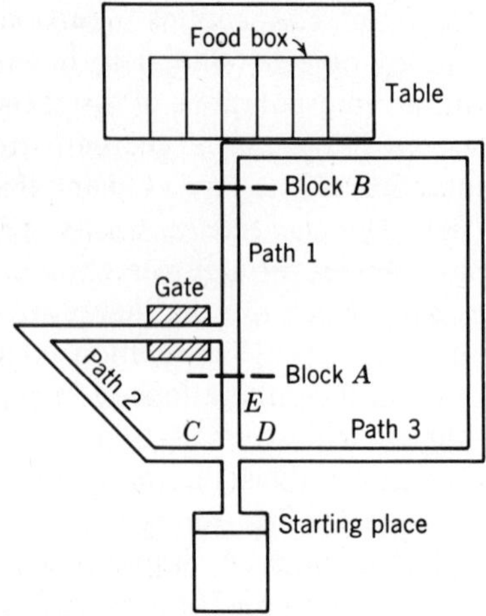

Figure 11-4 Maze used to test insight in rats. The paths become established as a hierarchy according to length, path 1 preferred to path 2, and path 2 preferred to path 3. If path 1 is closed by block A, the rats run by path 2. If path 1 is closed by block B, the rats run by path 3 if they have insight that the barrier closes path 2 as well as path 1. (*Source:* Tolman & Honzik, 1930, p. 223.)

Tolman's Experimentation

The kind of experimental research performed by Tolman is well illustrated by an early study on insight learning in the rat (Tolman & Honzik, 1930). An elevated maze with three alternative paths to the goal box was used, as shown in Figure 11-4. The three paths varied in length. In preliminary training path 1, the shortest, was sometimes blocked, and the animals then learned to use the next shortest, path 2. It will be noted that paths 1 and 2 share the final part of the direct runway to the goal box. During training trials the block had been placed close to the starting place, well before the common segment of paths 1 and 2. For the test trials the block was moved to position B, toward the end of the common segment and close to the goal box. According to the insight prediction the animal would now turn to path 3, rather than to previously preferred path 2, since this was also blocked. A noninsight type of simple S-R view would presumably predict the mechanical running off of the next strongest response in the hierarchy established in training, that of running down path 2. Most of the animals tested in the study chose path 3, thus supporting Tolman's cognitive or expectancy position.

Modifications of this early experiment have been reported a number of times (cf. Hilgard & Bower, 1975, p. 154). Although insight occurred in some cases, apparently minor changes in apparatus or arrangements sometimes produced a failure of insight. Deutsch (1960) developed a structural model, superficially unlike Tolman's rough models, which made predictions about when insight should or should not occur. An experiment by Deutsch and Clarkson (1959) used the same basic procedure as Tolman and Honzik, with familiarization trials followed by blocking of routes to goal boxes. The predictions of the Deutsch model were confirmed. This situation is highly reminiscent of Spence's earlier improvement of predictions with respect to the occurrence or nonoccurrence of transposition (see Chapter 7). In both cases we see genuine progress. Other ideas of Tolman's may have helped point in the direction of progress. In the Deutsch-Clarkson "non-insightful" condition, the animals experienced frustration in the goal box, and Tolman and Gleitman (1949) had showed that rats were quite capable of avoiding the route to a box in which they had been shocked, even though the shock did not follow *running* to the box. Perhaps, in a loose system like Tolman's, we can always find another idea or another experiment to account for new results.

Even more characteristic of Tolman's research is the latent learning experiment, originated by Blodgett (1929) in the California laboratory. The fundamental problem here is whether reward (or reinforcement) is essential for learning to occur. As a cognitive theorist, defining learning in terms of perceptual rather than response factors, Tolman insisted that learning will occur in the absence of reward but simply will not be demonstrated until the appropriate motivational conditions obtain.

In a typical latent-learning experiment, designed to test Tolman's cognitive position, a hungry animal is permitted access to a learning device, such as a maze, without being rewarded by food in the goal box. After a certain number of such trials, on which numerous errors are made and limited overt learning evidenced, the animal finds food in the goal box for the first time. The subsequent test trials generally show a remarkably improved performance, indicating that the animal had been learning something about the maze on the earlier trials but had not been motivated to perform appropriately (i.e., to take the true path to the goal box and avoid the blind alleys). When reward is introduced, the performance of such experimental animals quickly approximates that of controls which have had the same number of trials, all reinforced by food.

Although there is still some controversy on this issue, especially about the various subtle sources of reinforcement now suspected to operate (e.g., removal of the animal from the maze), the majority of the results seem to support Tolman's original position. (See Kimble, 1961; MacCorquodale & Meehl, 1951; and Thistlethwaite, 1951, for reviews of the pertinent literature.)

Criticisms of Tolman

The most persistent criticism of Tolman's work has already been indicated: his failure to develop a logically integrated theory. In this respect certain of his own comments may be instructive. For example, in refusing to comment on a requested distinction between his use of immediate data language and construct language, Tolman noted (1959) that "I myself can neither get very interested in nor completely understand such more refined logical distinctions" (p. 149). Apparently his lack of interest in problems of logical relationships at least partly accounts for the programmaticity of his systematizing.

One particular and important criticism which Tolman has shared with Lewin is that he has paid insufficient attention to the problem of relating overt behavior to cognition and similar central states. Guthrie, for instance, has commented (1935) that Tolman leaves the rat "buried in thought" (p. 172). This weakness in

Tolman's system may be seen as part of the overall inadequacy of specification, discussed above.

Finally, as a representative of a kind of commonsense approach to behavior, Tolman has come in for a variety of criticisms from the more tough-minded type of psychologist. An obvious point of attack has involved his alleged mentalism, largely as a result of the kind of language Tolman has used and the centralist nature of his constructs. In answer to such attacks, he has stoutly and persistently defended his basic behaviorism. Even the more sympathetic of Tolman's critics, however, have entertained some doubt on this score. Thus MacCorquodale and Meehl have noted (1954) "a certain affinity for the dualistic" even while not meaning "even to suggest that he is anything else [than a behaviorist] consciously or unconsciously" (p. 185). In considering this criticism Tolman had at least a partial explanation, if not justification, to offer in terms of his initial exposure to objectivism. He has stated (1959) that ". . . although I was sold on objectivism and behaviorism as *the* method in psychology, the only categorizing rubrics which I had at hand were mentalistic ones. So when I began to try to develop a behavioristic system of my own, what I really was doing was trying to rewrite a commonsense mentalistic psychology . . . in operational behavioristic terms" (p. 94).

Tolman's Contributions

In spite of the undeniable programmaticity of his systematizing, Tolman has had a great influence upon the course of psychology over the past four decades. We shall describe several general forms of this influence and then mention some more specific contributions.

Tolman's role in leavening the behavioristic loaf in its early, formative period was a most significant one. Although his emphasis on a molar point of view and an acceptance of purposiveness was never quite accepted by some behaviorists, nevertheless this kind of interpretation served to make the system more readily understandable and acceptable to many others. Tolman thus saved for the consideration of the science of psychology concepts which might otherwise have been discarded completely because they were not easy to define operationally. The verdict of history has clearly favored Tolman, particularly in the case of "purpose"; the science of cybernetics has objectified and precisely defined what it is for a machine to have a purpose, so that there are few left in or out of psychology who would now maintain that the concept cannot be objectified.

The influence of his cognitive learning system has also been very great. For two decades Tolman's cognitive position offered the major alternative to the Hullian need-reduction theory. As a matter of fact, much of the learning experimentation and literature was directly concerned with one attempt or another to pit cognitive theory against reinforcement theory. Thus in reviewing the learning literature for the first issue of the *Annual Review of Psychology,* Melton (1950) could say that ". . . these past twenty years of experimental-theoretical development have been increasingly under the influence of the opposed theoretical systems of Tolman and Hull" (p. 9).

We have already mentioned Tolman's longtime associate at the University of California, David Krechevsky (later Krech) as a contributor to the cognitive tradition (Chapter 7). His hypotheses about hypotheses in rats agreed nicely with Tolman's viewpoint. Levine (1970) worked out much more detailed accounts of just how hypotheses ought to be related to prior experience in human subjects, and how they should then control behavior. An ingenious series of experiments were in excellent agreement with his predictions—and with Tolmanian thinking!

An important influence may be attributed to Tolman's long-standing support of the rat as a laboratory animal and appropriate subject for even the field-theoretical and centralist thinking which he espoused. Such use of this favored laboratory animal by Tolman was undoubtedly responsible for a large amount of the acceptance generally accorded "rat psychology" in spite of the strong opposition of many psychologists. His position on this issue was very clearly and forcefully stated in his delightful (1945) essay. Here Tolman, always humorous and self-effacing, is at his best. The concluding sentences are especially noteworthy:

> What, by way of summary, can we now say as to the contributions of us rodent psychologists to human behavior? What is it that we rat runners still have to contribute to the understanding of the deeds and the misdeeds, the absurdities and the tragedies of our friend, and our enemy—*homo sapiens?* The answer is that, whereas man's successes, persistences, and socially unacceptable divagations—that is, his intelligences, his motivations, and his instabilities—are all ultimately shaped and materialized by specific cultures, it is still true that most of the formal underlying laws of intelligence, motivation, and instability can still be studied in rats as well as, and more easily than, in men.
>
> And, as a final peroration, let it be noted that rats live in cages; they do not go on binges the night before one has planned an experiment; they do not kill each other off in wars; they do not invent engines of destruction, and, if they did, they would not be so inept about controlling such engines; they do not go in for either class conflicts or race conflicts; they avoid politics, economics, and papers in psychology. They are marvelous, pure, and delightful. And, as soon as I possibly can, I am going to climb back again out on that good old phylogenetic limb and sit there, this time right side up and unashamed, wiggling my whiskers at all the silly, yet at the same time far too complicated, specimens of *homo sapiens,* whom I shall see strutting and fighting and messing things up, down there on the ground below me. (p. 166)

Of many particular contributions that Tolman made, two early ones need to be mentioned. One is his invention (1936) of the intervening-variable paradigm, later adopted and much more thoroughly implemented by Hull (see Chapter 10). An intervening variable is an intraorganismic function (e.g., hunger) that is postulated to account for a particular kind of behavior (e.g., eating) in a certain stimulus situation (e.g., presentation of food object after one day of food deprivation). Although Tolman had apparently intended a purely summary usage of the intervening variable, he eventually renounced such a usage for the less strictly operational "hypothetical construct" (cf. Marx, 1963, chaps. 1, 5). He later stated (1959): "My intervening variables are generally speaking mere temporarily believed-in, inductive, more or less qualitative generalizations which categorize and sum up for me various empirically found relationships" (p. 97). He further observed (1959) that they are not "primarily neurophysiological . . . but are derived rather from intuition, common experience, a little sophomoric neurology, and my own phenomenology" (pp. 98ff.).

Tolman is generally credited with having made the first effective distinction in the psychological literature between learning and performance. He early pointed out that learning alone is not sufficient to produce the learned behavior, that the motivational conditions must also be appropriate. The distinction between learning and performance has been a most important one in the development of learning theory and research. Tolman credited Blodgett, who performed the first latent-learning experiment, for having forced this distinction on him and also noted (1959, p. 149) that Lashley had anticipated him.

Tolman must also be credited with helping to open up several significant areas of research. The most important are probably the latent-learning problem, which deals with the necessity of the reinforcement principle in learning; the transposition problem, which concerns the dependence of learning upon relative as contrasted with absolute cues; and the continuity-noncontinuity issue, which involves the question of whether each single reinforcement or nonreinforcement has an effect in learning. Each of these problem areas relates directly to the theoretical opposition between Hull and Tolman. While the large-scale systematic issues posed by these two views are no longer of prime concern to learning theorists, many of the particular problem areas developed in the theoretical controversy not only have produced much valuable research, but also are still themselves of first importance in learning research. In this way Tolman, like Hull, has had a great and continuing influence on experimental-theoretical psychology.

Finally, we should mention Tolman's influence through his students. Z. Y. Kuo has already been mentioned as an early behaviorist; his last publication in English (1967) had this to say about Tolman:

> My major professor, the late E. C. Tolman, exerted a great influence on me; although I was never an adherent of his psychological views, his exceptional tolerance and the way he encouraged his students to develop and express views that opposed his own greatly strengthened the skeptical attitude toward everything I read that I had acquired earlier in China. In a joking, yet approving matter, Tolman often said to other students in my presence: "Kuo has an Oedipus complex against all authorities and a strong tendency toward negativism." (p. viii)

Kuo's comments on Tolman came 44 years after he had left Berkeley to return to China. Little more need be added regarding students' opinions of Tolman.

FIELD THEORY OF ACHIEVEMENT: BRUNSWIK'S PROBABILISTIC FUNCTIONALISM

The probabilistic functionalism developed and propounded by Egon Brunswik (1903–1955) is difficult to categorize within the simplified theoretical framework which we have used for expository purposes in the present volume. Certainly

Brunswik was not an S-R theorist, although under the influence of Tolman and others he very definitely moved in the direction of behaviorism after he came to this country. It is equally certain that he was in no obvious way a field theorist of the sort that Lewin represented. Although his research on the perceptual constancies was often related to orthodox Gestalt psychology, Brunswik himself (1949, p. 57) explicitly denied any such historical or conceptual relationship.

We have categorized Brunswik as a field theorist primarily because he so persistently and successfully considered the totality of interacting factors in his attempt to establish a meaningful systematic framework within which to evaluate psychological systems and behavioral problems. In this respect he outdid even Lewin, especially with his explicit emphasis upon distal, as compared with proximal, antecedent and consequent conditions. Furthermore, his insistence upon a representative, rather than merely a systematic, design for experimentation likewise indicates a deep concern for all the interacting factors involved in the determination of behavior. These statements should be clearer after the reader has grasped some of the basic points that Brunswik attempted to make and to implement in his own research.

Brunswik's Career

Egon Brunswik was born in Hungary, where he received an unusually varied education. After being trained in engineering and passing the first state examination, he shifted to the study of psychology at the University of Vienna. There he was much influenced by contacts with the logical positivists, in the Vienna Circle. He studied psychology under Karl Bühler, taking his doctorate in 1927. In the meantime he passed the state examination for teaching mathematics and physics.

Following several years of various academic appointments, a critical turning point in Brunswik's career occurred during the 1933–1934 academic year. E. C. Tolman, visiting in Vienna, met and was quite impressed with Brunswik. Two years later Brunswik received a Rockefeller Fellowship and, largely at Tolman's instigation, was invited to serve as visiting lecturer and research fellow in psychology at the Berkeley campus of the University of California. In 1937, he returned to Berkeley as an assistant professor. He stayed there until 1955 when, after years of illness, he ended his own life.

Brunswik's Research

Brunswik is best known in psychology for his research on visual constancy factors, usually referred to as *thing constancy.* This research program was well begun in Europe and was a major factor in attracting Tolman to Brunswik. The heart of Brunswik's thing-constancy research is the dichotomy between the physical nature of an object and its sensory representation. The extent to which the perceptual effect tends to approximate the more remote physical (distal) or the more immediate sensory (proximal) value is the fundamental problem of this kind of research. For example, consider a wooden table. As a distal object, the table has a certain determinate physical length; as a proximate object it also has a certain length, equivalent to the physical distance delimited on the appropriate receptor surface of the subject. It is the physical, or distal, dimension that remains relatively stable while a wide variety of other conditions, such as distance or angle of view, directly affect the proximal dimension.

The major finding of Brunswik's thing-constancy research was that there is almost inevitably a compromise in experience, or—more operationally—in the subject's reported judgment, between the distal and the proximal dimensions. Normally the subject tends to approximate more closely the distal, or real, characteristics of the object in spite of the various distorting conditions: hence the term *thing constancy.* The index of the distal influence (Thouless's "regression to the real") is called the *Brunswik ratio.* This ratio is unity when constancy is perfect—that is, when perceived factors such as size, shape, and brightness are independent of distance, angle of tilt, luminous flux, or other proximal variables. On the other hand, when the proximal (in this case, retinal) stimulus completely determines the perception, the Brunswik ratio is 0. Thus the ratio reflects, on a scale ranging from 0 to 1, the degree to which the distal (object) aspects of the stimulus situation determine perception.

In subsequent research Brunswik extended this basic methodology to new problems. First, within the area of perception, he brought into his experiments such variables as monetary value. For example, in one experiment (Brunswik, 1934, pp. 147–150; see also Brunswik, 1956, p. 78) the experimenter asked subjects to make comparisons between cards containing varying numbers of coins of varying sizes and monetary value. In accordance with the basic principle repeatedly demonstrated in the simpler research, judgments of equality between stimuli were compromised to some extent by each of the three variables. Later, under the influence of Tolman and American neobehaviorism Brunswik came to concern himself with instrumental behavior as well as perception (cf. the early collaborative paper, Tolman & Brunswik, 1935). Brunswik had noted that organisms could use varying cues to arrive at the same knowledge of an object; Tolman had noted that organisms could use various behavioral means to reach the same ends. The two joined their ideas in a paper, and expressed their common core of ideas in the concept of *vicarious function,* which meant that cues or behaviors could act vicariously for each other.

Brunswik (1939b) also attacked the problem of what is now called *partial* or *intermittent reinforcement.* The all-or-none reward situation almost invariably used in American learning experimentation up to that time Brunswik felt to be quite unrepresentative of normal situations. Accordingly he varied the proportion of reward to total trials in the two ends of a standard T maze. The rat subjects cooperated and expressed preferences that were roughly correlated with degree of probability of reward in the two ends. This research is related, conceptually, to the earlier work in perception in that the primary concern is again with the degree to which the subject normally achieves a kind of constancy relationship.

Brunswik's System

The probabilistic functionalism which Brunswik came to feel most adequately systematizes psychological problems was a fairly direct and logical outgrowth of

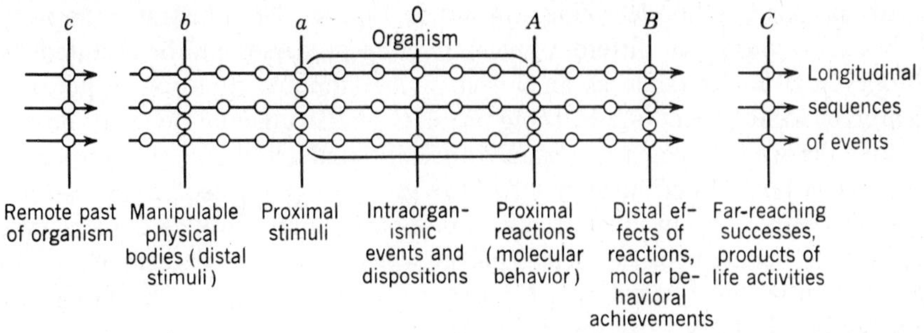

c b a 0 Organism A B C

Longitudinal sequences of events

Remote past of organism · Manipulable physical bodies (distal stimuli) · Proximal stimuli · Intraorganismic events and dispositions · Proximal reactions (molecular behavior) · Distal effects of reactions, molar behavioral achievements · Far-reaching successes, products of life activities

Figure 11-5 Scheme of the organism in its surroundings. (*Source:* Brunswik, 1939a, p. 37.)

the research program outlined above. Brunswik's system is *probabilistic* since it holds that the perceptual and behavioral goals in the natural environment are related usually in an equivocal and rarely in a univocal manner to cues and responses. The system is a *functionalism* since it is concerned primarily with the degree of success, or achievement, in perception and instrumental behavior.

An illustration of Brunswik's systematic thinking is his conceptual framework (1939a) in which a succession of temporally and spatially ordered "levels" or "layers" of variables is envisioned. These range from the temporally most remote (those furthest back in the past of the individual) through manipulable physical objects (distal stimuli) to the outer physical areas of the organism (proximal stimuli) and thence to intraorganismic functions and states; on the response side, a comparable array is conceptualized, from proximal reactions through distal effects (achievements in regard to environmental objects) to long-range successes and ultimate products of the individual's life-span. These relations are represented in Figure 11-5. Brunswik used his conceptual framework in the analysis, or characterization, of psychological systems. For example, both structural and Gestalt psychologists, according to Brunswik's analysis of the situation, confined themselves primarily to the study of the relationships between proximal stimuli (level *a* in the scheme) and intraorganismic events and dispositions (level O). Classical behaviorism studied *a*-*A* relationships for the most part. Psychoanalysis would be described as concentrating on *c*-O relationships. The concentration of a functionalism or a molar behaviorism would tend to be on *b*-*B* relationships (the O level may enter into nearly any systematic position).

Leeper (1966), in a generally balanced and friendly critical review of Brunswik's contribution, points out that Brunswik was prone to take too simple a view of what others were doing. Thus each of the groups referred to in the previous paragraph might find something objectionable in Brunswik's description of their efforts. However, his characterizations demonstrate an important and unique feature of his thought: he integrated history, theory, methodology, and research into one conceptual structure. In this respect he is perhaps more reminiscent of Freud than of anyone else we have studied, although the nature of their syntheses was quite different.

Brunswik's lens model (1952), shown in Figure 11-6, illustrates the way in which a great variety of different but interacting processes can be initiated from a single focal factor (such as an object in the stimulus situation in perception research or some aspect of a learning problem in instrumental behavior research) and also the way in which a similarly differentiated array of response processes mediated within the organism may focalize into a single perceptual or instrumental achievement. For an illustrative commonplace application of the lens model, consider the behavior of a baseball player who is attempting to catch a high fly ball (the "initial focal variable"). A number of different perceptual cues emanate from the ball in flight—its speed, height, etc.—and must be quickly taken into account by the fielder estimating its trajectory and ultimate destination. Such "stray causes" as the direction and force of the wind and position of the sun may also need to be taken into account. On the response side, the fielder needs to mobilize energies so movement toward the ball can be timed properly and avoid interference from other stray causes such as teammates, fences, and the like. "Stray effects" would then be exemplified by collisions with other fielders, bumping into fences, etc. An ultimate instrumental achievement such as catching a difficult fly ball (the "terminal focal variable") is thus seen as dependent upon the successful coordination of a variety of "process details" on both the perceptual and the response sides.

Leeper (1966, p. 423) has suggested that Brunswik's thinking would be better represented by a two-lens model, rather than the single-lens model he actually used. The single lens was fine so long as Brunswik was concerned only with focusing cues in bringing about a stable central representation of the object. However, if the focusing of different behaviors on goal attainment is also to be

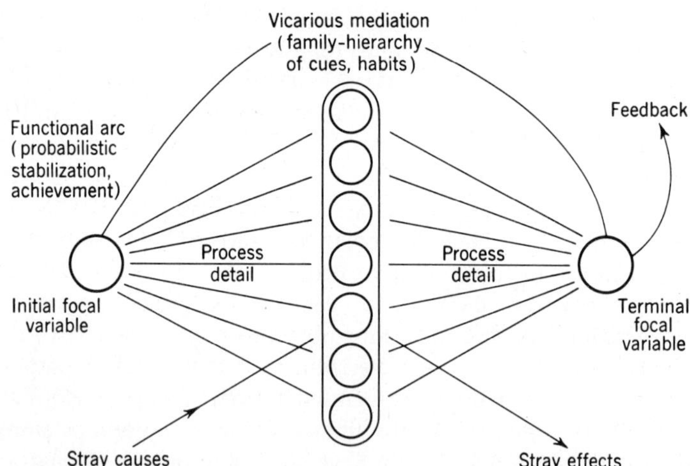

Figure 11-6 The lens model: Composite picture of the functional unit of behavior. (*Source:* Brunswik, 1952, p. 20.)

represented, a second lens is needed, with the central response between them, the distal stimulus on the left, and the distal achievement on the right.

Brunswik felt that the double-convex model represents the manner in which an organism is able to mobilize its functions so as to maximize its utilization of cues emanating from distal stimuli and achieve a reasonable amount of success in its control of the environment. He felt that problems of distal relationships need to be studied first, before problems of mediation by intraorganismic detail processes are investigated. He criticized those who used intervening variables, and in particular the Gestaltists, for moving in toward the center of the organism when he thought they should be moving outward into the environment. Postman and Tolman (1959) have made it clear, however, that Brunswik had no absolute prejudices against physiology, but felt that psychology's original duty lay with distal investigations. In this Brunswik's position was remarkably close to Skinner's.

Hursch, Hammond, and Hursch (1964) followed up Brunswik's suggestion that the relationships represented in the lens model could be more precisely studied by using multiple correlation methods. Their techniques make it possible to determine how well a subject could do on the basis of various ecological cues and how well the subject actually is using the available cues. They show how their analysis can be applied to a case of probability learning and to a case of clinical inference. Although some additional experiments have used this type of analysis (for example, C. R. Peterson, Hammond, & Summers, 1965; Summers & Hammond, 1966), it is probable that the use of this particular derivation of Brunswik's thought has by no means reached its peak of popularity. With the increased respectability of naturalistic studies and the tremendous interest in ecology in general, it seems inevitable that applicable statistical techniques will be much in demand.

A major reason why Brunswik felt that problems involving particular mechanisms should wait until the fundamental achievement principles are worked out is the high degree of substitutability among such mechanisms. On the instrumental side, this may be simply illustrated by the variety of particular responses (habits) which a rat can use to depress a bar, or which a cat can use to tip a pole, and thereby open a restraining door, as in the Guthrie and Horton (1946) experiment. In these cases, the terminal—focal—effect is the same regardless of the particular mechanism used.

The same relationship of interchangeability among mechanisms may be illustrated, on the perceptual side, by the variety of cues that mediate visual depth perception (cf. Postman & Tolman, 1959, pp. 511ff.). The distal stimulus here is represented as a focal point, shown on the left in the double-convex lens model of Figure 11-6. A variety of different kinds of physical energies, represented by the diverging lines of the lens model, serve to produce the proximal distance cues (retinal disparity, accommodation, convergence, linear perspective, and the like), which are represented by circles in the center of the model. Intraorganismic mediating processes relate each proximal cue to the terminal perceptual event, in this case the distance judgment.

Several interesting points are suggested by this kind of analysis. The *ecologi-*

cal validity of cues (or habits) is defined as the degree of correlation between each such proximal condition and the value of the distal stimulus. For example, the ecological validity of retinal disparity is generally higher than that of accommodation or convergence as a cue to distance. This means simply that retinal disparity is a more effective cue, correlating more highly with physical distance. But it is not essential; other cues can substitute for it and mediate depth perception. In its normal adjustment to the flux of events in the environment the organism needs to have considerable flexibility with regard to which cues (or habits) are given the greatest weight. The necessarily probabilistic nature of the terminal focal events (perceptual and instrumental) is clearly indicated by this analysis. As Brunswik has put it:

> The general pattern of the mediational strategy of the organism is predicated upon the limited ecological validity or trustworthiness of cues. . . . This forces a probabilistic strategy upon the organism. To improve its bet, it must accumulate and combine cues. . . . No matter how much the attainment is improved, however, distal function remains inherently probabilistic. (1955a, p. 207)

Brunswik's Emphasis on Representative Design

Perhaps the most far-reaching aspect of Brunswik's conceptual formulation was his increasing emphasis on the necessity for psychology to use what he called *representative,* rather than systematic, design in its experimentation (Brunswik, 1956). This emphasis follows directly out of the probabilistic functionalism which he developed. As long as rigorous control of variables is practiced, in the orthodox systematic design used by most psychologists, there will be serious limitations on the degree to which experimental results are representative of the natural behavior of the subject. In order to permit a more adequate analysis of the organism's achievements in relation to the environment—seen by Brunswik from his functionalistic position as the primary problem for psychology—a wider sampling of effective variables must be utilized, even if this means less rigorous control in the usual sense.

As a corollary of this position, the highly general laws aimed at in orthodox systematic research would need to be replaced by statistical statements in which only probabilities values can be expressed. Such statistical expressions concern the probabilities with which the various conditions sampled are found to correlate with the achievements of the organism in dealing with the environment. In representative designs correlational techniques thus replace the statistical tests of differences that are usual in systematic designs.

Although the positive side of these methodological proposals seems reasonably clear, since they follow directly from Brunswik's own research program, his criticisms of the orthodox type of systematic design may require further specification. Brunswik felt that any experiment which deals with only one variable at a time, in the classic manner, is hopelessly inadequate to present a realistic picture of the organism's behavior. Although the recent trend toward multivariate design was considered to be a step in the right direction, it has been nonetheless a small and seriously limited one. Furthermore, the variables ordinarily manipulated are

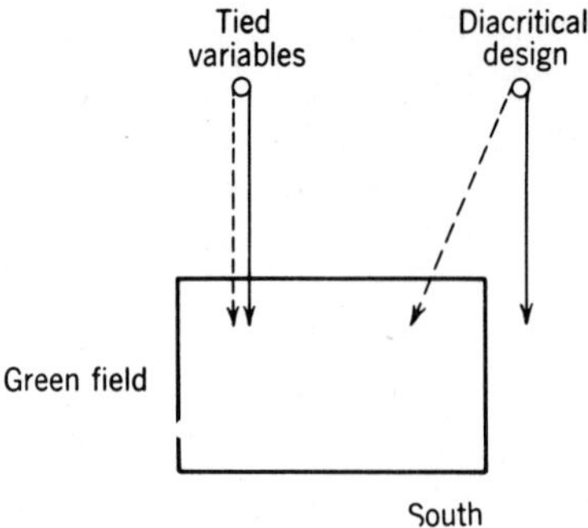

Figure 11-7 Systematic design in the study of behavior constancy. See text for explanation. (*Source:* Brunswik, 1955a, p. 194.)

proximal rather than distal ones, in the conceptual framework described above; from Brunswik's point of view, this places the emphasis on the wrong kind of investigation.

Brunswik was also highly critical of the way in which variables are artifically "tied" and "untied," as well as "interlocked," in the orthodox systematic design. Although a detailed specification of these problems is beyond the scope of the present book, the general point here is that a truly representative design should permit a freer kind of covariation among factors (see Postman & Tolman, 1959, pp. 516ff., for an especially clear presentation of this argument). This point may be illustrated by a relatively simple example which Brunswik (1955a, pp. 194ff.) developed on the basis of a problem earlier suggested by E. B. Holt (1915). Imagine a flock of birds flying (1) over a green field (dashed line) and (2) southward (solid line). As shown in Figure 11-7, these two variables are confounded, or tied. Merely returning the birds to point 0 does not resolve the confounding, nor does adding new subjects from the same population. The typical technique used to untie these two variables in systematically designed experimentation is called *diacritical* by Brunswik. It is indicated in Figure 11-7 by the movement of the birds to a new position, so that the two alternative interpretations may be clearly separated, that is, have different consequences (birds either fly to the green field and not directly south or fly south and thereby miss the green field). But, Brunswik pointed out:

> We soon discover that southwardness is still tied to such factors as the general area of start, temperature and other climatic conditions, topographic landmarks, magnetic cues, and so forth; and so is the greenness of the field to its squareness or size. What we have accomplished in diacritical design is to separate or "split" an original encompassing cluster into two subclusters of tied variables; but we have not really "isolated" our variable as it may have seemed at first glance, and therefore are not yet entitled to speak of its attainment as a constant function. (1955a, p. 195)

For Brunswik the only satisfactory solution to this kind of problem would be a truly representative design in which a more adequate sampling of situational variables is possible. A partial solution would not be enough. A simple example of the inadequacy of such artificial untying of variables, in systematic design, has been provided by Brunswik (1956, p. 27). In an experiment on judgment of personality traits, subjects are placed in identical bodily positions and given identical clothes to wear. While this experimental procedure controls for the influence of these two variables, it also makes impossible the assay of any normal interaction between the personality traits estimated and such factors as body tone and dressing habits. This typical experiment is thus incompletely designed, according to Brunswik. For completeness, one would need to include a much wider range of important variables in the behavior sampling (e.g., have subjects take different positions or wear different clothes).

The problem posed is indeed like the problem posed for the pollster asked to assess public opinion. The pollster would like to sample the whole population, but that is impractical. He therefore settles for a "representative sample" of the population. In the same way, the experimenter might like to sample all the variables, and all the interrelationships between variables, in order to arrive at psychological laws. It would then be possible to use a systematic design, which would indicate all the interrelationships between variables. Such a procedure is far more difficult even than sampling a complete population. Thus the experimenter, too, must take a sample, and the most useful sample to take is not one that is arbitrarily chosen, but one that characterizes the variables and their values and interactions *as they occur in the actual environment.* Even if we could do a complete systematic experiment, we would not know what organisms would do until we studied the situations to which they would be exposed. Thus representative designs are necessary in principle as well as in practice.

Brunswik's Contribution to Psychology

Brunswik's logical analysis of design problems is almost certain to have more influence upon the future course of psychological science than is typical of such logical endeavors. Already there is evidence that his position is being implemented far outside the experimental study of perception in which it started. An outstanding example of this is K. R. Hammond's (1954, 1955) demonstration of the importance of considering representative design in clinical psychology. Research on the diagnostic use of test scores is criticized for not sampling adequately the personality characteristics of the examiners themselves and the situational variables involved in the test administration. As a matter of fact, frequently the range of examiners is severely limited, such as to a single person, for the express purpose of eliminating variability in results. Such application of the typical systematic design unfortunately has not prevented investigators from generalizing their results, at least implicitly, to a presumably wide range of examiners and situations, as well as to a population of tested individuals (the representativeness of whose selection in sampling is generally explicitly considered). Some extension of the principles of more representative design to other experimental and clinical situations would seem to be indicated, regardless of the extent to which one accepts Brunswik's strictures of orthodox systematic design.

It is quite possible to accept Brunswik's plea for more representative designs without denying the value of orthodox designs where the latter are appropriate. Leeper (1966) thinks Brunswik did himself a disservice by overstating the case against systematic experimentation. In medical research, for example, one may be quite concerned with the effects of curative agents on particular diseases, and systematic design is appropriate, sufficient, and efficient in answering the questions that arise. However, in this as in other issues, Brunswik saw the one-sidedness of psychological research as so extreme that he probably felt that he must state the case for other procedures is just as extreme a fashion.

Other criticisms of Brunswik's methodological points have centered on his apparent opposition to research on mediational mechanisms and his apparent assumption of a basic nonuniformity or nonuniversality in behavioral laws (cf. Hilgard, 1955; Postman, 1955). We have already encountered the attempt by Postman and Tolman (1959) to clarify Brunswik's attitude on the study of mediational mechanisms. On the second point, Brunswik has taken pains to say that he did not think that behavioral laws are fundamentally probabilistic but only that their establishment is necessarily limited to statistical or probabilistic expression. As he has put it: "The crucial point is that while God may not gamble, animals and humans do, and that they cannot help but to gamble in an ecology that is of essence only partly accessible to their foresight" (1955b, p. 236).

With the increasing influence of ethology on psychology, some of Brunswik's methodological points begin to look almost prophetic. However, ethology and comparative psychology show signs of beginning to fit together in harmony, just as we believe that systematic and representative design principles are destined to fit together. The pendulum must swing much farther before it will reach a point that would please Brunswik, but it is still swinging. We might wonder why it has taken so long. Hammond (1966, p. vi) suggests one reason: it is that, in the United States, Brunswik had but one student who completed a dissertation with him. Tolman (1966) tells us that Brunswik had to curtail his contacts in his last years, and Leeper (1966) bemoans the fact that Brunswik worked too much alone. Hammond's memorial volume, which contains the three papers just cited among several others, is helping to bring Brunswik's contributions to the attention of psychology. Brunswik's condensed and difficult writing does not help with that task!

Eventually, however, Brunswik will be recognized for the great thinker he was. He was deeply admired by the students who knew him, though perhaps they would not, or dared not, do dissertations with him. And besides his methodological contributions, Brunswik contributed substantially to our understanding of perceptual constancies. He started the study of probability learning. He demonstrated how one might weave all one's work into a single piece. These achievements insure him a prominent place in the history of psychology.

BARKER'S ECOLOGICAL PSYCHOLOGY

Roger G. Barker (1903–) is one of the few psychologists who have behaved as if they had ever heard of Egon Brunswik. Hammond (1966, p. 317n) describes one of Barker's papers as a unique reconciliation of Brunswik's environmentalism with Lewin's interest in central processes. Although Barker's work seems to reflect a far more Brunswikian than Lewinian methodology, the characterization does seem to fit Barker's book *Ecological psychology* (1968) at least as well as it does the earlier paper.

Barker seems to have combined Brunswik's attitude toward data collection with Lewin's type of interest. Brunswik collected much of his data in the natural environment, but he was primarily interested in perception. Lewin and his students collected much of their data in contrived stiuations, but they were interested primarily in motivational and social variables. Barker collected his data in natural field settings, but he concentrated on the behavioral—often social—responses of his subjects. And Barker and his students and coworkers have looked as closely at the environment as they have at the people in the environment. His results are the most convincing argument that could be made for the value of proceeding as he has done.

Barker's Career

Barker never had the advantages attached to being a member of two cultures, as Brunswik and Lewin had. He received all his academic degrees from Stanford University (Ph.D., 1934). He met Lewin when Lewin came as a visiting professor in 1932, and later took a postdoctoral fellowship with him at Iowa. Their association led to their publication of the classic laboratory study of frustration and regression in children (Barker, Dembo & Lewin, 1941), of which we shall have more to say later. After serving as an instructor at Harvard from 1937 to 1938, an assistant professor at the University of Illinois from 1938 to 1942, an associate professor at Stanford from 1942 to 1945, and a professor at Clark University from 1945 to 1947, Barker settled down as a professor at the University of Kansas. Barker and his colleague, Herbert F. Wright, established the Midwest Psychological Field Station in Oskaloosa, Kansas, in 1947. Barker's place in this volume is based largely on his first 20 years of work at the Midwest Station and at a station established in 1954, operated on a periodic basis, in Leyburn, Yorkshire, England. Comparisons between the findings at the two stations contribute to the fascination of the findings of Barker and his coworkers.

Barker's Research

Although Barker has made methodological discoveries and contributions to our theoretical attitudes, these have grown so naturally out of his research that we are justified in putting all of our emphasis there, just as he has done. We have seen that Barker has close conceptual and personal ties to Lewin. In some respects, their research too went in similar directions after they left Iowa. Lewin had been forced to take a close look at the "social ecology" when he was doing research on how food finds its way to the table. Lewin, however, tended to pull people out of their natural settings for his study and manipulation, and Barker did not.

Barker felt that Brunswik tended to overemphasize the disordered and probabilistic nature of the environment. However, at other times Brunswik's intuitive evaluations were prophetic of the empirical findings of Barker, as when he said:

> Ecological generality of experimental or statistical results may thus be established along with populational generality. In fact, proper sampling of situations and problems may in the end be more important than proper sampling of subjects, considering the fact that individuals are probably on the whole much more alike than are situations among one another. (Brunswik, 1956, p. 39)

Barker actually went out and sampled situations and subjects in the ecologies of Kansas and Yorkshire. When he reported, 22 years after Brunswik's statement, what he had found, he did not have to guess, as Brunswik had. Barker's summary was:

> The environment is seen to consist of highly structured, improbable arrangements of objects and events which coerce behavior in accordance with their own dynamic patterning. When, early in our work at the Field Station, we made long records of children's behavior in real-life settings in accordance with a traditional person-centered approach, we found that some attributes of behavior varied less across children within settings than across settings within the days of children. We found, in short, that we could predict some aspects of children's behavior more adequately from knowledge of the behavior characteristics of the drugstores, arithmetic classes, and basketball games they inhabited than from knowledge of the behavior tendencies of particular children (Ashton, 1964; Barker & Gump, 1964; Raush et al., 1959, 1960). It was this experience that led us to look at the real-life environment in which behavior occurs, with the methodological and theoretical consequences that are reported in this book. (1968, p. 4)

One can only be grateful that Barker and his coworkers were led to look closely at this "real-life environment in which behavior occurs," for the results of that work have the kind of sturdy, unselfconscious beauty seen in the well-fed Hereford cows admired around Oskaloosa, Kansas. The data presented by Barker to illustrate molar units of individual behavior exemplify the general sturdy empiricism of the approach. Five-year-old Maud Pintner is in Clifford's Drugstore

> Maud sat at the fountain waiting to order the treat her mother had promised her. On the stool next to Maud was her two-year-old brother, Fred; her mother sat beside Fred.
>
> 2:48 P.M. From her jeans pocket Maud now took an orange crayon. She brushed it across her lips as if it were a lipstick.
>
> Maud then leaned over, sliding her arms along the counter, as she watched a man serve a strawberry soda to his blond, curly-headed, three-year-old girl.
>
> Maud seemed fascinated by the procedure; she took in every detail of the situation. (1968, p. 146)

From this, two molar units of behavior, called *behavior episodes,* were abstracted: *pretending to use lipstick* and *watching girl eat soda.* The isolation of these units, which might at first appear to be a simple task, is both difficult and of critical importance if effective fieldwork is to be done. Barker (1968) says of behavior episodes: "Like crystals and cells that also have distinguishing attributes and limited size-ranges, behavior episodes have as clear a position in the hierarchy of behavior units as the former have in the hierarchies of physical and organic units" (p. 146).

Barker favors the gathering of data uncontaminated by the operation of the psychologist on the situation; the psychologist in the field can act simply as a transducer (and hence gathers T data, rather than the O data gathered by the psychologist who also operates in the situation). Barker illustrates the possible misleading conclusions that may be drawn from O data. His strictures are made doubly impressive by the fact that he uses his own classic study as the horrible example! Barker says:

> Experiments have provided basic information about the consequences for children of frustration, as defined and contrived in the experiments, e.g., Barker et al. (1941). But Fawl, who did *not* contrive frustration for his subjects, but studied it in transducer records of children's everyday behavior, reported (Fawl, 1963, p. 99):
>
> The results . . . were surprising in two respects. First, even with a liberal interpretation of frustration fewer incidents were detected than we expected. . . . Second . . . meaningful relationships could not be found between frustration . . . and consequent behavior such as . . . regression . . . and other theoretically meaningful behavioral manifestations.
>
> In other words, frustration was rare in children's days, and when it did occur it did not have the behavioral consequences observed in the laboratory. It appears that the earlier experiments simulated frustration very well as defined and prescribed in theories, but the experiments did not simulate frustration as life prescribes it for children. (1968, pp. 144–145)

Brunswik would no doubt have loved to have the Fawls-Barker commentary as an example of the weaknesses of systematic design. However, we should not *equate* Barker's preference for T data with Brunswik's preference for representative design. Brunswik did not say that data should actually be gathered in an undisturbed environment, and his research was not at all identical with Barker's. Brunswik did follow subjects around in their daily routines, but he disturbed and manipulated those routines whenever he wished.

Nevertheless, Brunswik's and Barker's attitudes converge in suggesting the need for a thorough study of the ecology in which human beings grow and behave. Barker has not hesitated to make this point forcefully and directly. He says that it is strange and ironic that we know the percentage of each element to be found in the earth's crust, but do not have similar knowledge about man's *behavioral* surroundings. Barker makes his contribution to this effort by cataloging the "behavior settings" of Oskaloosa, Kansas (the Midwest Psychological Field Station). His appendix lists 220 behavior settings, from abstract and title company offices to X-ray laboratories. These are all public behavior settings; one misses, for example, Maud Pintner's living room and awaits the Masters and Johnson of Oskaloosa, Kansas, to fill in the ecological picture.

In order to survey behavior settings, Barker had first to define a behavior setting—to discover or invent its identifying attributes. We shall list only the first three of seven attributes. First, a behavior setting consists of one or more standing patterns of behavior. Barker says that such patterns are clearly located in time and space, and he gives basketball games, worship services, and piano lessons as examples. Second, a behavior setting consists of standing patterns of behavior and milieu. That is, the setting includes the surroundings as well as the behavior, and the surroundings may be man-made (such as buildings) or natural (such as trees). Third, the milieu is circumjacent to the behavior—that is, the milieu surrounds the behavior, rather than vice versa. The interested reader is invited to consult Barker (1968) for the remaining defining characteristics, as well as for the details of other aspects of his data and theory.

Finally, Barker considers the interactions between behavior settings and the behaviors of the people who inhabit them. We might expect him to see the behavior setting as a field, and the persons in it as particles, on the basis of an analogy with physics. Instead, he borrows an almost opposite analogy from Heider and likens the behavior setting to a "thing" and the people who inhabit it to a "medium." An example of a thing is a stone, which can be thrown into a pond, the medium. The medium, although it has characteristics of its own, is more flexible than the thing and so adapts itself to it. People in general adapt themselves to behavior settings, partially because of the intervention of "environmental force units." But those are another part of the story, and we cannot tell it all. We shall conclude with the comment that Barker's work combines in a rare way the imaginative approach of the field theorist with the persistent empiricism which seems to have become connected more often with the image of the associationistic psychologist. Both his descriptive schemes and his theory of behavior settings show great promise for stimulating further work in ecological psychology. The availability of usable descriptive categories makes Barker one of the few psychologists rich enough to throw away the following tidbits, among others, on a single page (1968, p. 141): Disturbances occur in a child's experience at a median rate of 5.4 per hour, half of the disturbances being occasioned by adults; the units of the Midwest children are shorter on the average than those of comparable "Yoredale" children; the Yoredale children receive four times as frequent devaluative input from adults as do the Midwest children.

Barker's Contributions

It would be a serious injustice to regard Barker as a follower of Lewin and Brunswik who had simply worked out some elements of their programs. He cites each of them as often to reveal their errors as to express appreciation for their guidance. For example, one of Barker's most insistent themes is that the environment is organized into unique and unlikely patterns. Describing it as chaotic or probabilistic leads us in exactly the wrong direction. It turns out that the texture of the environment is highly patterned, and that this structured environment coerces our behavior. Humans do not ingeniously organize a "blooming, buzzing confusion"; they respond appropriately and sometimes apparently unwillingly to a surrounding structure.

Barker (1969) has repeatedly called for the creation of tools appropriate to the task of studying the interdependence of human beings and their environment.

We need three things that are in too short supply: archives, field stations, and statistical techniques that are appropriate to naturalistic studies. All of these things seem to be coming into existence at the present time, and Barker must deserve some of the credit for that.

Although Barker has not to date produced any encompassing theory, he has shown us that a field-theoretical orientation need not lead to mere fuzzy thinking and nonempirical research. His study of Maud Pintner applying lipstick should help us to see that the gigantic flywheel of our society is not just James's habits, but may also be in part Barker's behavior settings.

LASHLEY'S NEUROPSYCHOLOGY

Karl S. Lashley (1890-1958) cannot be easily assigned to any single, simple category. We have already met him in Chapter 6, since he was one of the most enthusiastic of the early behaviorists. He belongs in this chapter also, however, since as his career developed, he moved more and more in the direction of a kind of field theory and could be found increasingly on the Gestalt or field-theory side of particular theoretical issues.

Lashley did his graduate work at the University of Pittsburgh and Johns Hopkins University, receiving his Ph.D. in psychology in 1914 at the latter school. His major teaching appointments were at the Universities of Minnesota and Chicago and at Harvard. He then became director, in 1942, of the Yerkes Laboratory of Primate Biology, the world-renowned chimpanzee-research station at Orange Park, Florida. In this capacity he retained his professorship at Harvard because the two institutions were then administratively related.

Lashley's earliest research was performed in collaboration with the biologist H. S. Jennings and the behaviorist John B. Watson at Johns Hopkins. His research interests ranged quite widely, from problems concerning the inheritance of size in paramecia to cerebral factors in migraine headaches in humans (see Beach, Hebb, Morgan, & Nissen, 1960, for these and many of his other papers). However, the problem of brain function related to behavior was his most important and most persistent interest and the one for which he is best known.

Lashley's interest in brain function was formed early in his training, but it was only in 1917, when he became associated with the eminent neurophysiologist Franz, that he embarked upon the line of research using ablation of the rat brain as a technique to determine localization of function.

It is unfortunate that those who do not know Lashley's work well almost inevitably remember him for two vague principles with catchy names—*mass action* and *equipotentiality*. Even these names are not remembered precisely, for here is Lashley's statement of his famous principles:

> *Equipotentiality of parts.* The term "equipotentiality" I have used to designate the apparent capacity of any intact part of a functional area to carry out, with or without reduction in efficiency, the functions which are lost by destruction of the whole. This capacity varies from one area to another and with the character of the functions involved. It probably holds only for the association areas and for functions more complex than simple sensitivity or motor co-ordination.

> *Mass function* I have already given evidence . . . that the equipotentiality is not absolute but is subject to a law of mass action whereby the efficiency of performance of an entire complex function may be reduced in proportion to the extent of brain injury within an area whose parts are not more specialized for one component of the function than for another. (1929, p. 25)

A careful reading of these principles makes any comment on their vagueness (and even some possible circularity) unnecessary. Krech (1962), in his excellent review of the problem of cortical localization, credits Lashley with being aware of his own vagueness in stating these principles; Lashley stated the principles vaguely because the state of knowledge about brain mechanisms was vague!

Why, then, should Lashley be remembered? Pierre Flourens had reached similar conclusions on the basis of the results of similar ablations about 100 years earlier. Lashley's unique contribution was that he brought far better, more analytic *behavioral* techniques into cooperation with the available physiological techniques. Lashley was not limited to the study of the effects of operations on naturally occurring behaviors; he experimentally created behaviors in mazes and discrimination problems, and he studied their retention and reacquisition after carefully planned ablations. His methodology was brilliant for his time, and his techniques excellent. He had been anticipated to some extent by his teacher, Franz, much as Isaac Newton was anticipated in the development of calculus by his teacher, Isaac Barrow; both pupils went far beyond their teachers.

There is no doubt, despite the vagueness of his statements, that Lashley strongly opposed the common belief in localization of function. The problem is by no means settled, but the "final" decision on this problem will probably favor more localization than Lashley believed likely. We still understand too little of the structure of behavior to know what a unitary "function" is; until we know, it is difficult to attack the localization problem. Lashley made a tremendous contribution to the beginning of the attack on the critical behavioral side of the question.

The extent to which Lashley was recognized by the physiologist as well as the psychologist is suggested by the tribute paid him by the neurologist Stanley Cobb, who said (Beach et al., 1960) that in the early days at Hopkins, Lashley "fascinated us by the breadth of his interest and by his flair for ingenious and adventurous experimentation" (p. xvii). Cobb added (Beach et al., 1960): "During the next forty years, Lashley was to be the psychologist most frequently chosen by neurologists and psychiatrists to come to their meetings to give a paper or to discuss the papers of others (p. xviii)." He concluded by saying (Beach et al., 1960): "And so, in paying Karl Lashley our homage, we claim at least a tithe of his work for neurology!" (p. xx).

But it is, of course, not only for his neurological contributions that Lashley is honored in psychology. In a twin introduction to the memorial volume of Lashley's selected papers (Beach et al., 1960), E. G. Boring reviewed his systematic contributions to psychological theory. The field-theoretical flavor of Lashley's interpretations is illustrated in certain quotations selected by Boring. For example, Lashley wrote that ". . . it is the pattern and not the localization of energy on the sense organ that determines the functional effect" (p. 492); and referring to brain action, that ". . . all of the cells of the brain are constantly active and are participating, by a sort of algebraic summation, in every activity" (p. 500).

Lashley's field-theoretical orientation is illustrated also by his position in support of a pattern, or relational, interpretation of transposition learning rather than the S-R, or connectionistic, position. In his presidential address to the American Psychological Association in 1930, he attacked the simple connectionistic view. He later presented a novel alternative to the orthodox S-R interpretation of generalization and discrimination learning. The Lashley-Wade hypothesis is that differential training on several values of a stimulus dimension is necessary for generalization to occur, denying the fundamental S-R assumption that reinforcement of a single stimulus value produces a generalization gradient whereby similar values of the stimulus automatically gain similar but reduced potency to elicit the conditioned response. The controversy thus created has stimulated a good deal of research. Kimble (1961, pp. 369ff.) presents one review of the issue. Terrace (1966) more recently reached a conclusion which favors Lashley and Wade: "A differential reinforcement procedure is necessary for the typical generalization gradient to emerge" (p. 339). Finally, Kalish (1969) reached something of a compromise position after a thorough and thoughtful review of the evidence.

Lashley made still other experimental and methodological contributions. For the former, his researches on visual discrimination and on the analysis of the visual cortex (see Beach et al., 1960) are perhaps the best examples; for the latter, his invention of the jumping stand, which forces an animal such as a rat to step or leap from a platform to one of two discriminable doors, is probably the most important contribution. This new experimental device enormously facilitated discrimination learning in the rat, presumably by forcing the animal to attend more directly to the relevant visual cues. Among the many subsequent users of the device, Norman R. F. Maier should be mentioned in the present context. Not only was he responsible for the most controversial use of the jumping stand (1938, 1949); but he also has been a strong supporter of the field-theoretical position (e.g., Maier & Schneirla, 1935).

In conclusion, it is fitting to quote Boring's final tribute to Lashley's scientific perspicacity (Beach et al., 1960): "The impressive thing about the papers in this volume is the way in which discovery leads speculation, not speculation discovery" (p. xvi).

Kantor's Interbehaviorism

Jacob Robert Kantor (1888–) was born in Pennsylvania and educated at the University of Chicago, receiving his Ph.D. in 1917. He was an instructor in philosophy and psychology for two years at the University of Minnesota and then for 3 years at the University of Chicago following his obtaining the doctoral degree. In 1920, he went to teach at Indiana University and served as professor of psychology there from 1923 until his retirement. Kantor has been a consistent and prolific writer. A number of years ago his bibliography included eighty-eight items, several of which were multivolume books. His scholarship was further attested by his publication of eighty-three book reviews, and nothing can be more certain than that, by now, all of these numbers have increased. Kantor became our choice for the grand old man of American psychology with the death of E. G. Boring in 1968. Like Boring and Woodworth before him, Kantor has remained active even though he retired formally. For example, the second volume of his historical study, *The scientific evolution of psychology,* appeared in 1969. Also, Kantor and Smith (1975) have published a general textbook based on his theory.

Kantor has been first and foremost a logical analyst and critic of the general scientific scene, with special reference to psychology. His major concern for over half a century has been, as he put it, "smoothing the path of psychology toward its goal of natural science" (1958, p. 223). Two favorite targets have been (1) "mental fictions" as represented in theoretical constructions within psychology and (2) major tenets of physiological psychology. These and related "errors" he attributed to the widespread acceptance in our culture of the dualistic heritage and the resultant failure of many scientists to look closely at their data. He has felt that the problems produced by the dualistic heritage are especially aggravated in psychology. Skinner, at least, appreciated Kantor's criticism of the surviving mentalism in psychology (1967): "Another behaviorist whose friendship I have valued is J. R. Kantor. In many discussions with him at Indiana I profited from his extraordinary scholarship. He convinced me that I had not wholly exorcised all the 'spooks' in my thinking" (p. 411). This comment may amuse us, as we picture a "better" behaviorist than Skinner. It should also instruct us, as we are reminded that there is no contradiction between being a strict methodological behaviorist and taking a field-theoretical position.

Kantor does not have a system in the sense that Hull, or even Tolman or Lewin, had. Kantor has been above all else a metatheoretician, emphasizing a broad philosophical approach to behavior problems rather than specific solutions to such problems. He has written on physiological psychology (1947), language (1936), logic (1945, 1950, 1953), and history (1963, 1969), but has not concentrated his efforts in any one field in a way that might have made him preeminent in a particular area. He has offered what he calls a "formal logical system" (1958, p. ix). This last-mentioned book was prepared, as he noted, in order to present his ideas more efficiently and to avoid an excess of duplication from earlier works.

The heart of Kantor's logical system is the notion of the interbehavioral field, which is an interaction between the "response functions" of the organism and the "stimulus functions" of the environment. These two basic factors must always be considered together, in Kantor's view. The properties of the interaction between organism and stimulus are built up largely in the history of the interbehavioral relation. Both biological and cultural factors need to be considered.

Except perhaps for a lessened enthusiasm for S-R psychology, Kantor's critical views have changed little throughout the course of his long career, beginning with the publication of his *Principles of psychology* in 1924. He has continued to stress the psychological field and its constantly changing interactions, and he is included in this chapter for that reason. This aspect of his views is related to Dewey's views as expressed in the famous paper on the reflex arc, and even to the

Gestalt doctrine of emergence. Kantor, however, would be anxious to distinguish his views from those of the Gestalt psychologists and most other field theorists, since he saw remnants of mentalistic fictions in their views.

Kantor's stress on holism led him to criticize the doctrine of localization of function (1947, pp. 80ff.) and to see language and logic as instances of the many products of, and participants in, interbehavioral relations. He also saw clearly that environmental objects participate importantly in social relationships (1929); his views in this respect are consistent with those of Barker, whom we have just discussed.

Many papers by Kantor and by sympathetic students (on whom he has had a remarkably strong and lasting influence) can be found in the journal *Psychological Record,* which Kantor founded. There is some evidence that Kantor's influence may be increasing, despite his failure to found an active experimental school; N. W. Smith (personal communication) has found that Kantor's work was cited about twice as often in the ten-year period ending in 1966 as it had been in the preceding 10-year period. Perhaps psychology, at last, is ready to acknowledge this tough old critic.

SUMMARY AND CONCLUSIONS

The views of six theorists of "field" persuasion, and the work of several theorists with related attitudes, have been surveyed in this chapter. These theorists generally emphasize patterns of organization at the expense of discrete connections. Following from this general attitude are a general tendency to study molar variables and a tendency to resort to field observations in order to get the overall view of behavior and behavior laws.

The field-theoretical view has a tendency to drive people away from simple cause-and-effect thinking because of the large number of potential variables in fields or wholes. Some experimenters have been repelled by field theory because it tends to lose them in a maze of complexity and may paralyze empirical investigations. This follows from the insistence on the importance of such a large number of variables, with their potentially complex interactions. Research may further appear difficult because of the initially vague, nonoperational character of some field concepts, for example those of Lewin. Yet the metatheoretical points made by theorists like Lewin and Brunswik are extremely persuasive.

On an abstract level, the way out of the impasse may be indicated by people like Kantor, who retains a general field orientation while providing a strong antidote for subjectivity and the dualism that may be associated with it. Concretely, the way out has been demonstrated by Lewin, Brunswik, and Barker, all of whom carried out ingenious and productive research which was initially inspired by a field-theoretical viewpoint. We might regard Barker, in particular, as having taken on a kind of S-R coloration because his careful and persistent observations are the sort of thing we usually associate with associationistic researchers. Willems (1969) presents a way of thinking about research activities which should help us to reconcile our cognitive dissonance in such cases. He puts research in a two-dimensional space. One dimension is degree of manipulation of antecedent conditions. The other is degree of imposition of units. Field theorists have tended to do research which is low on both dimensions, while S-R theorists have tended to do research that is high on both dimensions. Willems' space forces us to recognize that there is a continuity between types of research activities, and there is plenty of room in the two-dimensional space for everyone. Contemporary investigators tend to be occupying many interesting intermediate positions in the space, as well as the traditional niches.

Still further rapprochement is represented by the increasing popularity of multivariate analysis, which combines the rigor typical of the S-R psychologist with the attempt to deal with complex interrelationships, which is demanded by the field theorist.

Brunswik and Barker were the field theorists most particularly insistent on the value of naturalistic, ecological study of the organism in its environment. Certainly such studies provide unique opportunities for discovering naturally occurring systems of interrelated variables, and they prevent the investigator from "wasting" time studying variables that do not have relevance to the world as it exists. However, an *exclusive* concern with naturalistic studies might prevent investigators from studying potential but nonexistent systems which could be artifically created with great benefit to humankind. As humans construct more and more of their own environment, the charge of "artificiality" of psychological studies may become less and less significant.

The first of the field theories considered was that presented by Kurt Lewin. Lewin's contributions have included a brilliant series of experimental attacks upon motivation and personality factors and the initiation of the group-dynamics movement; theoretically, however, he is best known for his conceptualization of life space. The second field theory considered was that of E. C. Tolman, who early espoused a molar, purposive behaviorism. His experimental and conceptual innovations leavened the behavioristic doctrine and gave cognitive psychology an experimental basis; for a time Tolman offered what seemed to be a clear contrast to Hullian, S-R doctrines. The third theory was Egon Brunswik's probabilistic functionalism, which offered alternatives to many otherwise unquestioned methodological assumpitons in perception and learning.

Briefer consideration was given to Barker's ecological psychology, Lashley's neurophysiological theory, and Kantor's interbehaviorism.

One major strength of field theory comes from the fact that it has unhesitatingly attacked problems avoided by orthodox S-R theory. On the one hand, these have involved central functions. Lewin, Tolman, and Lashley represent this concern (cf. Hebb, 1949; G. A. Miller, Galanter, and Pribram, 1960). On the other hand, we see field theorists moving away from the periphery of the organism out into the environment. Brunswik, Barker, and Kantor represent this direction of movement.

FURTHER READINGS

The most painless introduction to Lewin is through Morrow's *The practical theorist* (1969). That will instruct the reader as well as entertain, and lead to as many further works by Lewin himself as desired. De Rivera's book *Field theory as human science: Contributions of Lewin's Berlin group* (1976) is the most important supplement to Morrow's work. Critiques and reviews by Leeper (1943), Estes (1954), Deutsch (1954), and Cartwright (1959) will balance the picture.

Tolman is well represented by his early *Purposive behavior in animals and men* (1932); his *Collected papers in psychology* (1951a); and his final statement (1959). The formalization of Tolman's system by MacCorquodale and Meehl (1954) is well worth reading, partly because it shows the reader how the enterprise of formalization can be carried out.

There is no easy way to understand Brunswik's thinking, but the best place to start has to be Hammond's *The psychology of Egon Brunswik* (1966). It contains, and leads to, papers by Brunswik. Brunswik's *Perception and the representative design of psychological experiments* (1956) contains the heart of his methodological contribution. Brunswik's system is also intensively treated by Postman and Tolman (1959). Barker puts his own best foot forward in his interesting and readable *Ecological psychology* (1968). Lashley is well represented by *The neuropsychology of Lashley,* edited by F. A. Beach et al. (1960). Kantor's *Interbehavioral psychology* (1958) is the best introduction to his systematic thinking.

Chapter 12

Varieties of Personality Theory

Personality theory is a kind of behavior theory. However, personality theories do have some characteristics that set them apart as special subvarieties of behavior theory. The very word *personality* indicates that personality theories have been based primarily on the study of persons. In most personality theories, individual differences among persons are regarded as a very significant source of variance in behavior. Information about the unique characteristics of persons would therefore be necessary to making accurate predictions about behavior.

However, Sechrest (1976) regards the emphasis on individual differences as mistaken. He points out that, paradoxically, most theorists have operated from theories that postulate universal characteristics of all individuals, such as Freud's developmental states or Adler's striving for superiority.

Whether or not the emphasis is mistaken, personality theories have paid close attention to individual idiosyncracies. These in turn shade over into the maladaptive behaviors of the neurotic and the bizarre behaviors of the psychotic. It is not surprising that most of our prestigious theories of personality have been born in the clinic and the counseling room. Confusion sometimes reigns about where personality theory stops and the study of abnormal psychology begins. The answer is that personality theory never stops; it aims to account for all behavior, normal or abnormal.

Thus a second general property of personality theories is their attempt to be complete. For many of the everyday problems of human behavior, the only theories complete enough to apply are personality theories. But no theory that aims to be encompassing can be very formal or make very specific predictions. For these and related reasons, Levy (1970) suggests that we stop talking about theories of personality and start talking about "conceptions" of personality. We agree with Levy's logic, but we have seen that the same logic can be applied to most psychological theories of all kinds. All of our so-called theories are deficient in many ways, with the possible exceptions of some modern minitheories. Personality theories are a little more deficient because they attempt more.

There is great diversity of opinion and of emphasis on several issues connected with the study of the person. The first is the very basic set of opinions concerning the amount of variance which is attributed to persons, as compared with the amount attributed to situations. In the last chapter, we saw that Brunswik and Barker agreed that behavior could be predicted to a great extent from knowledge of the situation, regardless of the person in the situation. Rogers, who emphasizes the tendency of the person to develop capacities "from within" (he calls this *self-actualization*), probably best represents the opposite extreme—he is the greatest optimist about the extent of the ability of individuals to determine their own fate. In this respect Rogers is close to the existentialists, who believe that all individuals have irrevocable responsibility for their own choices. S-R theorists generally emphasize the influence of the situation, or stimulus, and show less interest in the unique characteristics of the individual person. These theorists have a related tendency toward denying the generality and permanence of "traits" of personality; for example, it would be characteristic of S-R theorists to deny that honesty is a general trait or that it is likely to be a permanent characteristic of a particular person. This is consistent with the so-called empty-organism approach, which places little reliance either on assumed physiological functions or on assumed personality structures such as traits or attitudes. In this sense, S-R theories are general behavior theories, *not* personality theories in any restricted sense. However, we shall discuss one S-R theory below, partly to emphasize the continuity between behavior theories and more representative theories of personality.

There has been some response to the question about the relative contribution of individuals and situations. Sechrest (1976) makes a plea for more experimentation which combines subject and experimental variables in the same design so that both sources of variability, plus their interactions, can be studied. He sees a trend toward interactionism in current theories of personality. This refers to the proposition that behavior is jointly determined by the individual and the situation. Sechrest says that one difficulty is that there is no taxonomy of situations which can guide research and theory of this kind. That shortcoming is one of the central concerns of the previous chapter, particularly in connection with the work of Roger Barker. The relationship between the problems posed by field theory and those posed by personality theory shows that different approaches to psychology can complement each other. The problems of human and animal behavior are the same, and can be attacked from different viewpoints. Thus solutions to problems are likely to help theorists of all kinds.

Still another question concerns the extent to which personality structure—whatever form it takes—is determined by nativistic factors and the extent to which it is determined by learning. The so-called self theorists are more likely to make a place in their scheme for nativistic factors than the S-R theorists, who quite naturally insist on the importance of learning. An emphasis on learning, however, does not *necessarily* preclude a recognition of nativistic factors. As one example, Skinner (1974) has described J. B. Watson's environmentalism as stupid. To some, this may be surprising because of Skinner's own reputation as an environmentalist. There may have been some tendency for both Watson and Skinner to be stereotyped as antinativistic because both men attended primarily in their work to environmental influences. But the modern belief, accepted by most theorists of all kinds, is that *both* nativistic and environmental factors are *always* critical to every behavior.

The striving of personality theorists for completeness may become more and more distinctive because theorists in other areas of psychology are *less* enamored of attempts to develop "grand theories" than they used to be. Increasingly they limit themselves to partial or full explanations of things like one-trial learning by the method of paired associates in lists of nonsense syllables, auditory threshold effects, or some other closely circumscribed area.

The other distinguishing characteristics of personality theory are related to its usual attempt at comprehensiveness. First, the functional nature of personality theory should be noted. Theories of personality focus upon an understanding of the development, survival, and general adjustment of the organism. Second, an emphasis on motivational ("dynamic") processes is characteristic of such theories. Third, the object of study is the whole person within the natural habitat. On this point, the study of personality clearly separates itself from the experimental tradition in psychology, which has typically advocated the study of more limited aspects of behavior. Fourth, personality theories are characteristically integrative, whereas much of psychology has moved in the direction of more specialized explanatory attempts. Fifth, personality theories frequently have rebelled against the prevailing psychological thought of the times. Certainly Freud's psychoanalytic theory offered dissenting explanatory principles at the time of its inception. More recently, Gordon Allport has persisted in advocating the basic principles he felt necessary for an adequate theory of personality even when he seemed to stand alone. The fact that much of personality theory has developed outside the mainstream of academic psychology—frequently as a result of clinical observation—may account, in part, for its taking the highroad while the rest of psychology proceeded along the low road.

Thus we find in personality theories concern with variables typically left out of more limited theories. Psychoanalysis opened up the study of the unconscious determinants of behavior and offered a model of the structure of personality; Chapter 8 contains a more complete discussion of the empirical areas whose study was initiated by psychoanalysis. This personality theory and others have pointed to the need for detailed study of dynamic (motivational) variables, individual differences, heredity, biological factors, child and developmental psychology, abnormal and social psychology, and all the interrelationships between these and other fields. Every one of this formidable array of fields plays an important role in any complete theory of personality.

Implied in the preceding discussion of the characteristics of personality theory are both its weaknesses and its strengths. The personality theorist is faced with a dilemma composed of, on the one hand, mounting needs to predict and control human behavior and, on the other hand, a distressing scarcity of knowledge about the basic laws needed for the task. Consequently, the structure of personality theory tends to be loosely cemented for lack of sufficient cohesive material in the form of empirical observables. The major weakness of such theory, and the shortcoming at which criticism is continually leveled, is its disproportion of explanatory principles in relation to the amount of empirical data at hand. Similarly, personality theories frequently fail to distinguish clearly between that which they assume and that which is empirically testable. Consequently, the derivation of predictions and empirical hypotheses from these theories is severely hampered.

In spite of these problems, however, there has been a good amount of research in the area of personality. Adelson (1969), in his review of a year's literature, said that an extremely modest estimate of the year's volume is 500 citations; he references 210 of them in his paper. Dahlstrom, in his 1970 review, refers to 366 articles from some presumably larger set. Sechrest (1976) disclaims any attempt to review all of the research of the previous year in the field of personality. It is clear that his concern is with the significance of the research, rather than with its quantity. Most of the research is probably little read and less remembered.

The problem is neither a lack of data nor a lack of technical sophistication in experimental design. The primary problem seems to be the low degree of relationship between the empirical studies and any general theoretical framework; thus progress does not seem to be cumulative. Even in this respect, perhaps one should not be too pessimistic. C. S. Hall and Lindzey (1970), after examining seventeen theories of personality, conclude that twelve of them have been responsible for generating a considerable amount of research. Their comment was:

> It is reassuring that, in spite of the limitations of theories of personality as generators of research, the large majority of such theories has been accompanied by a considerable quantity of research. Whatever procedural limitations may inhere in these investigations, the fact remains that they document the interest of the theorists in examining the effectiveness of their theories in the face of empirical data. It is hard to believe that in the long run this attitude will not lead to progressive changes that will result in more effective theories. (p. 595)

It is encouraging to encounter optimism about the future of personality theories, for they are sometimes weak even in the area of their greatest strength—completeness. Few theories have attempted to handle all the areas considered essential to a comprehensive theory. Table 12-1, adapted from C. S. Hall and

Table 12-1 Dimensional Comparison of Theories of Personality

Interdisciplinary emphasis

	Purpose	Unconscious determinants	Reward	Contiguity	Learning process	Formal analysis	Personality structure	Heredity	Early developmental experience	Continuity of development	Organismic emphasis	Field emphasis	Uniqueness	Molar units	Homeostatic mechanisms	Psychological environment	Self-concept	Group membership determinants	Biology	Social science	Multiplicity of motives	Multiple mechanisms
Freud	H	H	H	M	M	M	H	H	H	H	M	L	M	M	H	H	H	M	H	H	L	H
Jung	H	H	M	L	L	M	H	H	M	L	H	L	M	M	H	H	H	L	H	L	M	H
Adler	H	M	L	L	L	M	M	H	H	H	M	H	H	M	H	M	H	H	M	H	L	L
Horney	H	H	M	L	M	L	M	L	M	M	M	M	M	M	H	M	H	H	L	H	L	L
Fromm	H	M	M	L	M	M	M	L	M	M	M	M	M	M	H	M	M	H	L	H	L	M
Sullivan	H	M	M	H	M	M	M	L	M	H	M	H	M	M	L	H	M	H	M	H	M	M
Lewin	M	L	M	L	M	H	M	L	L	L	L	H	H	L	H	H	M	H	L	M	H	M
Allport	H	L	L	M	M	M	H	M	L	L	H	M	H	H	H	M	H	L	H	L	H	M
Murray	H	H	M	L	L	M	H	M	H	H	H	H	H	M	H	H	M	M	H	H	H	H
Angyal	H	M	L	L	M	H	M	M	L	H	H	H	M	M	H	H	H	L	M	L	L	M
Goldstein	H	L	L	L	M	M	L	M	L	L	H	M	M	M	H	H	M	L	H	L	L	L
Sheldon	L	M	L	L	L	L	H	H	L	H	H	L	H	L	L	L	L	L	H	L	L	M
Cattell	M	M	M	M	M	L	H	H	M	M	L	M	M	M	L	L	H	M	M	L	H	H
Dollard and Miller	L	M	H	M	H	H	L	L	H	H	L	L	L	L	L	L	L	M	M	H	M	M
Skinner	L	L	H	M	H	H	L	M	M	H	L	L	L	L	L	L	L	L	L	L	L	L
Rogers	H	L	L	L	L	M	L	L	L	L	H	M	M	H	H	H	H	M	L	M	L	L
Binswanger and Boss	H	L	L	L	L	L	L	M	L	L	M	H	H	H	M	H	M	L	M	L	L	L

Key: H, high (emphasized); M, moderate; L, low (deemphasized).
Source: C. S. Hall & G. Lindzey, *Theories of personality* (2d ed.), New York, Wiley, 1970, p. 592.

Lindzey, indicates their evaluation of the degree of attention paid to various factors by the personality theorists they review in their book. Even the most comprehensive theories pay little attention to some issues.

And what of the positive functions of personality theory? Curiously, its strengths often derive from the same characteristics which harbor its weaknesses. Through its rebelliousness and its attempts at integration and completeness, it has drawn attention to previously neglected problem areas. Motivation, which only recently has received widespread attention from psychologists, has long been heralded by personality theorists as basic to the understanding of behavior. In addition, personality theories have generated empirical investigation. If we allow ourselves a slightly less hardheaded attitude for a moment, we can find still other virtues in personality theories (or conceptions, if you prefer). Every important point of view adds something persuasive to our stock of knowledge about human behavior. The degree of understanding we attain helps to sustain our belief in the ultimate ability of psychology to cope with important human problems, despite the frequent imperfection and imprecision of the understanding. Finally, it is for some questions "the only answer in town," and it has become an American tradition to play the only game in town, even if it's a little questionable.

S-R Theories

Two S-R positions are included in the summary of Table 12-1: the theory of Dollard and Miller, and that of Skinner and his followers. It is said that Skinner pays little attention to fifteen of the twenty-two areas considered important by Hall and Lindzey, and that Dollard and Miller ignore ten. Freud is said to ignore but two. We think this is some indication that S-R theories are really not personality theories in the traditional sense; their organism is too empty. Nevertheless, the skeptical temper of our times has led many psychologists to ask whether personality theories help more in understanding personality than S-R theories, which can be at least partially applied to personality. The success of behavior modifiers in working with clinical problems has lent some credence to this view and has helped to justify the inclusion of Skinner, especially, among the personality theorists. However, we have treated Skinner and his views in Chapter 10, and his views on personality are very close to his views on behavior in general. We shall therefore simply refer the reader to our earlier discussion for Skinner's "theory of personality," just as we do for Lewin, Freud, and some other early psychoanalysts.

We shall therefore take Dollard and Miller's theory as our "specimen S-R theory of personality." These authors, like the Skinnerians, have tried to develop an account of personality based on experimental data, and with a minimum number of concepts in addition to the basic principles of learning and behaving. This type of theory is also less concerned with assessment and more concerned with change than is the classical type of personality theory.

Dollard and Miller's S-R Theory.

John Dollard (1900–) and Neal Miller (1909–) began their collaboration at Yale's newly formed Institute of Human Relations in the 1930s. The institute—an innovation in cooperation among the behavioral sciences of psychology, psychiatry, sociology, and anthropology—provided an environment both receptive to psychoanalytic investigation and strongly influenced by Hull. We have already mentioned in Chapter 10 that Hull was himself interested in exploring the relationship between his concepts and those of Freud, and he conducted a seminar on the topic in the academic year 1936–1937. Dollard and Miller conducted research at the institute and soon started a series of joint publications. The first effort (with other coauthors) was *Frustration and aggression* (Dollard et al., 1939), in which S-R concepts were applied to the problem of frustration. Shortly thereafter Miller and Dollard (1941) published a volume on social learning that provided a basic S-R framework in which complex behavior problems could be conceptualized. They subsequently explicated their joint theorizing further in *Personality and psychotherapy* (Dollard & Miller, 1950). Dollard remained at Yale, where he became a professor emeritus in 1969. Miller moved from Yale to Rockefeller University in 1966.

Aside from their joint theoretical effort, Dollard and Miller have contributed to different areas of psychology. Both received laboratory and clinical training. However, Dollard's work has been less centered on experimental problems than Miller's. Dollard received his Ph.D. in sociology at the University of Chicago and has taught both anthropology and sociology at Yale. Further training at the Berlin Psychoanalytic Institute crystallized his interest in psychoanalysis. Dollard has consistently dedicated himself to the unification of the social sciences and has published in the areas of anthropology and sociology (e.g., 1937). During World War II he conducted a psychological analysis of military behavior, published as *Fear in battle* (1943).

Miller took his Ph.D. at Yale and, shortly thereafter, became a Social Science Research Council traveling fellow. During his stay in Europe, he underwent training analysis at the Vienna Institute of Psychoanalysis. Miller directed psychological research for the Army Air Force during the war years and then returned to Yale. He is characteristically a careful experimentalist and theorist, having conducted numerous studies on drive acquisition, reinforcement, conflict, the effects of drugs and physiological variables on behavior, and the operant conditioning of autonomic responses.

In their work Dollard and Miller came closer to a complete theory of personality than any other S-R theorists, though Guthrie (1938) and Skinner (1953) have generalized their findings freely to the human case. Lundin (1969, 1977) provides a full explanation of the Skinnerian approach to personality. Mowrer (1950) has also been interested in personality as well as in learning; however, none of these psychologists have developed an integrated S-R personality theory as thoroughly as Dollard and Miller have.

Dollard and Miller (1950; N. E. Miller, 1959) have not found the Hullian system, upon which their personality theory is ultimately based, adequate to the task without considerable interpretation. Both authors are interested in psychoanalytic theory as well as in S-R theory, and their interpretation takes the line of a reduction of many psychoanalytic concepts to S-R terms (e.g., N. E. Miller, 1948). Their aim is to combine the assets of the two systems; they need the scope of psychoanalytic theory in order to have anything like the desired coverage of dependent and independent variables. Where in Hull does one find a discussion of neurotic guilt or anxiety? At the same time, they prefer the greater precision of statement and degree of empirical confirmation found within the confines of Hullian theory. The drawing of precise parallels between theories as different as psychoanalysis and Hullian theory is always difficult, perhaps sometimes impossible. Yet Dollard and Miller have made an attempt at integration that is stimulating and worthwile, though in their system it is possible to see the outlines of two distinct subsystems.

There are systematic similarities between psychoanalysis and Hullian theory which make a partial amalgamation easier than might at first appear. A version of the law of effect is found in both. Freud speaks of maintaining a fixed tension level or reducing the tension level as a goal of the organism. Hull speaks of drive reduction, or a reduction in the intensity of a drive stimulus, as a condition which strengthens behavior. Both formulations seem essentially the same on this point. There are also similarities in the attitude toward learning. Hull's basic learning construct, ${}_SH_R$, is conceived of as building up through repeated practice and staying at a high level; once ${}_SH_R$ builds up, it is not destroyed. If the behavior which reflected ${}_SH_R$ stops, this happens because there is opposition to it by inhibitory factors or because there is no motivation left for the behavior. This account of learning, with its assumption of the permanence of the effects of experience, is in this way much like Freud's; he also seemed to believe that early experiences leave ineradicable effects, though the effects might not be easily seen because of repression, a concept which here plays the same role as Hullian inhibition.

The heart of the Dollard-Miller account is learning, or habit formation. They point out four significant features of the learning process: drive, cue, response, and reward. They give as an example a child looking for concealed candy in a room containing bookshelves. The initial *drive* is the hunger for candy; the *cues* are the instructions for playing the game plus the stimuli from the room; varied *responses* are made until the candy is found behind a book; and the response of moving the appropriate book is reinforced by finding and eating the candy *reward.* If the game continues with the candy in the same place each time, the drive gradually decreases; the significant cues for the child become just those helpful in making the correct response, and the response is now made more quickly and strongly. In this way *habits* are reinforced. These habits, which are environmentally acquired, are regarded as the basic and enduring elements of personality.

Dollard and Miller have not borrowed only the simplest concepts from Hull's (1943) theory; they have found a use for the hierarchy of responses, secondary reinforcement, the generalization gradient, and other more complex theoretical notions. They have also shown great ingenuity in relating concepts to simpler ones, thereby "explaining" what is involved. Their attempt to handle the problems of symbolic behavior is particularly valuable.

One of the contributions which Dollard and Miller have made, then, is the integration of two originally separate—if not opposed—theories in such a way that it becomes reasonable to apply the results of laboratory investigations with animals to practical human problems. Though Hull intended his theory to have such applications, he never personally took time to show how they could be made. Two such human problems which Dollard and Miller have treated are fear and conflict.

Fear in the neurotic human being may seem an irrational thing. Dollard and Miller, however, believe that this irrationality is a matter of appearance only; we as observers of irrational human behavior arrive upon the scene too late to observe the development of the fear, and we often do not know enough of the laws that determine the learning and spread of fear. Consider, in an analogous situation, a rat that is placed in a white box and shocked. If allowed to escape through a door to a black box, the rat will quickly learn to fear the white one. Futhermore, it will continue to respond in order to escape the white box even when there is no longer any shock present. The fear may even spread (generalize) to similar boxes. If we had not observed the learning process but only the fearful animal in a harmless white box, we should consider its fear irrational. Similarly, if we did not understand the process of generalization, we should consider fear of a *light gray* box irrational even if we had observed the process.

Dollard and Miller have given an equally stimulating account of the nature of conflict. Their analytic approach involves at least five assumptions derived from theory or from empirical observations. They assume that (1) the tendency to approach a goal increases as the distance to the goal decreases, (2) the tendency to avoid a negative stimulus (punishment) increases as the distance to it decreases, (3) the gradient for negative stimuli is steeper than the gradient for positive stimuli, (4) changes in drive increase or decrease the *level* (not the slope) of the appropriate gradients, (5) if two responses (say, approach and avoidance) compete at any point, the one associated with the stronger tendency will occur. Empirical studies of this model have typically involved white rats, shock, food, and a spatial scale, but the model has been freely applied to quite different situations, such as bachelors contemplating marriage. Summaries of experimental research on this problem have been provided by Miller (1944, 1958b). He has also reviewed the relationship between the experimental results on conflict and the conduct of psychotherapy in a short chapter (1964) which also examines other implications of modern behavior theory for psychotherapy. Finally, his work on the operant conditioning of autonomic responses (1969) has exciting implications for the acquisition and treatment of psychosomatic disorders. If the results can be replicated, refined, and successfully applied to human problems, they will need to be incorporated into the conceptual schemes of all personality theories.

This short sketch should be enough to indicate that the original contribution of Dollard and Miller shares the strengths and weaknesses of S-R theory more than it does those of psychoanalytic theory. Their approach tends toward analysis and the application of laboratory principles to human behavior. They take Hullian theory as the methodological model; psychoanalytic theory is used because it is based on the content, the observations, they wish to explain. Dollard and Miller seem to be molding psychoanalytic *content* into S-R *form*. In doing so, it may be argued, they incorporate the elementaristic weakness of S-R theory. Their "personalities" become bundles of habits without the consistency and purposefulness which most other personality theorists see as guiding human behavior. In choosing a theory which treats learning much more thoroughly than other determinants of behavior, Dollard and Miller take a more environmentalistic position than many theorists think is justifiable.

Despite any such criticism, the Dollard-Miller theory has earned an important place in the history of personality theory. Skinner and the behavior modification movement have followed them through the door they opened. It is now respectable for therapists of all persuasions to apply concepts and procedures modeled after the outcomes of laboratory experiments. Dollard and Miller in effect claimed that anything the psychoanalyst could talk about, they could talk about; and they made the claim by example. Their case was convincing to many, especially to those who preferred the language of S-R reinforcement theory to the language of psychoanalysis. Perhaps most of those who accepted this argument concluded that there was no sense in retaining the language and procedures of psychoanalysis, and discarded it altogether. For these people, Miller and Dollard had not gone far enough.

Interest in the details of the Dollard-Miller theory has waned, for both the component theories on which their efforts were based have fallen into disrepute. Hull's theory no longer dominates the field of learning, and Freud's is under attack in the field of personality. Dollard and Miller have turned their own attention to other matters. They have neither updated their theory nor concentrated on demonstrating its applicability in clinical or educational settings. Thus the field belongs to the followers of Skinner rather than to the followers of Hull. Nevertheless, Dollard and Miller deserve a tremendous amount of credit for indicating the character, the scope, and the feasibility of synthesizing laboratory-derived and clinic-derived concepts in a theory of personality. *Personality and psychotherapy* was a milestone, as yet perhaps too little appreciated, in the history of psychology.

TRAIT AND FACTOR THEORIES

In addition to comprehensiveness, personality theories have another characteristic which generally sets them apart from other theories of behavior: Nearly all personality theories have within them a concept which serves to explain and emphasize the *consistency* of behavior per se. Nonpersonality theories typically predict such consistency only insofar as there is consistency of circumstances; that is, the same response should be observed only if the external stimuli are the same, if they are equivalent because experiences with each were the same, or if they are related closely enough via generalization to produce the same response. Obviously, the *ifs* in the preceding sentence give the S-R theorist enough latitude to predict some consistency of behavior, but most personality theorists have not been content with this. They insist that the behavior is the same, or is consistent, because the behaving individual is the same. We pointed out at the beginning of this chapter that classic personality theorists generally maintain that much of the variance in behavior is attributable to individual differences; the corollary to this is that much of the consistency in behavior is attributable to *individual sameness*—that is, the same individual is behaving at different times or in different situations.

Two general classes of personality theory, not ordinarily categorized together, are alike in that they both give primary attention to the problem of consistency in behavior, albeit in markedly different ways. These are the trait theories best exemplified by the views of G. W. Allport, and the factor theories, represented by the work of Eysenck and R. B. Cattell.

The trait theorist believes that the job of the personality theorist is to isolate and describe certain properties of the individual which underlie and determine overt behavior, thereby giving the individual's behavior a consistent, integrated direction. These properties are called *traits,* and the traits may be very general, influencing all or nearly all the individual's behavior, or very specific, in which case only behavior in certain kinds of situations is influenced by the trait.

The factor theorist derives concepts (factors) from a statistical analysis of consistency observed in test performance. Like traits, factors may be general or specific, and may be arranged in hierarchies with the most encompassing factors (or traits) at the top and the most specific and limited at the bottom.

Allport's Trait Theory

Gordon Willard Allport (1897–1967) was educated in a variety of fields and continued his interest in many of them. He received his A.B. at Harvard in economics, taught sociology and English in Istanbul, returned to Harvard for his Ph.D., and subsequently studied at three European universities—Berlin, Hamburg, and Cambridge. While in Europe Allport developed his persisting interest in international affairs. As a by-product of his stay abroad, he became one of the major interpreters of German psychology in the United States.

Allport taught in the Department of Social Ethics at Harvard upon returning to the United States and then moved for a short time to Dartmouth. In 1930 he returned to Harvard, where he remained until his death in 1967. At Harvard he helped to form the Department of Social Relations, in which psychologists, sociologists, and anthropologists combined their talents. Allport received high professional honors in 1963, when he received the gold medal of the American Psychological Foundation, and in 1964, when he received the American Psychological Association's award for distinguished scientific contributions.

Allport's publications reflect his diversity of interests and his recognition of the complexity and uniqueness of human behavior. A former editor of the *Journal of Abnormal and Social Psychology,* Allport wrote on subjects ranging from *The individual and his religion* (1950a) to *The psychology of radio* (G. W. Allport & Cantril, 1935). His major works in the area of personality theory are *Personality: A psychological interpretation* (1937), *The Nature of personality: Selected papers* (1950b), *Becoming: Basic considerations for a psychology of personality* (1955), *Personality and social encounter: Selective essays* (1960), and *Pattern and growth in personality* (1961). Many of his important papers have been collected in *The person in psychology: Selected essays* (1968). Finally, in the area of test construction, Allport collaborated with his brother Floyd in the development of the *A-S reaction study* (G. W. Allport & Allport, 1928), and with P. E. Vernon to produce *A study of values* (1931).

Allport recognized that there are many factors which determine behavior. These form a hierarchy from most specific to most general, as follows: Conditioned reflex, habit, attitude, trait, self, and personality. The more general factors typically dominate the more specific ones. The most general factor, personality, was defined by Allport as follows (1937): "Personality is the dynamic organization within the individual of those psychophysical systems that determine his unique adjustments to his environment (p. 48)."

As Allport developed his thought, he incorporated more and more of the humanistic attitude, at the expense of the more functional attitude with which he had begun. From the beginning he had been influenced by the personalism of the German psychologists William Stern and Eduard Spranger. Allport followed them in emphasizing the unity and creativity of the individual. As time passed, Allport accepted ideas from others, like Abraham Maslow, who stressed the human tendency to self-actualize and rise above animal nature. A definition of personality which placed the stress on "mere" adjustment to the environment was really contradictory to Allport's core beliefs. Accordingly, years later Allport (1961) redefined personality as "The dynamic organization within the individual of those psychophysical systems that determine his *characteristic behavior and thought*" (p. 28; italics ours). This definition in turn is very consistent with Allport's own behavior and thought in relationship to personality theory.

Despite the dominating position of personality in the hierarchy of factors, Allport believed that the most profitable level for the personality theorist to study is the trait. He gave it its best-known definition (1937): "A generalized and focalized neuropsychic system (peculiar to the individual), with the capacity to render many stimuli functionally equivalent, and to initiate and guide consistent (equivalent) forms of adaptive and expressive behavior" (p. 295).

This comprehensive definition, though vague, points out clearly the role of the trait as a determiner of consistency in behavior and reveals Allport's emphasis on individuality as well as his interest in adaptive and expressive behavior. His studies of expressive behavior (G. W. Allport & Vernon, 1933) have afforded evidence for consistency. Expressive behavior is that aspect of behavior which is related to an individual's own style of behaving rather than to the function of the behavior in adaptation; for example, two individuals writing or saying the same words in response to a question may do so in quite different ways, their individual ways expressing their own personalities.

Allport and Vernon studied the expressive aspects of several types of behavior, obtaining thirty-eight measures. They determined that there was satisfactory reliability for the measures when the behavior was repeated and when the same behavior was measured from different muscle groups. Then they examined the intercorrelations of their thirty-eight measures to see whether a few general traits of factors might account for the observed intercorrelations. They concluded that three general factors were indicated by the data: one was a kind of motor expansiveness indicated chiefly by the extensiveness of responses such as writing; a second was called the *centrifugal group factor,* related to distance from the individual's center and having to do with outward tendency and extroversion; and the third had to do with emphasis, as indicated by gestures made while speaking, writing pressure, and so on.

Typically, Allport did not rest content with the group aspect of the study. He and Vernon then proceeded to an intensive study of four individuals and concluded that the expressive measures were quite congruent with the subjective estimates of personality study. This part of the study is typical of both the strength and the weakness of Allport's approach; the results are suggestive and provocative and yet somewhat unconvincing because of their subjectivity and the lack of specific predictions.

There are several aspects of Allport's psychology which deserve comment, aside from his definition and study of traits. Allport emphasized the complexity and individuality of behavior, together with the multiplicity of its determinants. Accordingly, he was not attracted by the aseptic laboratory studies which some others have used in the construction of their theories of personality. He felt very strongly that studies of group tendencies in a search for universal laws were overemphasized in American psychology; such studies he called *nomothetic.* Allport wished to foster intensive studies of the individual via methods which would reveal the uniqueness of that individual and thereby make it possible to predict his behavior; this approach he called *idiographic.* When Allport (1937) imported into personality discussions this nomothetic-idiographic distinction (originally made by Windelband [1921], a philosopher), he stirred up controversy (Skaggs, 1945) and further discussions of the issues (see Beck, 1953; Eysenck, 1954; Falk, 1956). Allport had struck a nerve.

The nomothetic-idiographic distinction is complex, and we cannot discuss all the issues here. Allport's point has been made in the sense that intensive study of individuals is now regarded as necessary. We have seen that even Skinner and his followers have arrived at this conclusion, but their reasons for doing so are diametrically opposed to those advanced by Allport. The operant conditioner studies the individual case intensively to make sure that every individual follows the same behavioral laws; that is, individual differences are studied to make sure they do not interfere with the functional relationships revealed by *every* individual in the experiment. The operant conditioner studies individuals to exclude them from laws; Allport would have us study individuals so that we can understand them in their uniqueness. In his detailed study of "Jenny" (1965), for example, Allport defends his idiographic approach by claiming to be able to predict her future behavior because of its consistency with what she had done in the past. Such limited generality over time would seem to be all the truly idiographic scientist can aspire to. Traditional science has generally sought laws with the widest possible range of generality; although every condition studied has some unique features, the scientist has attempted to abstract from unique situations those features which are general. Few psychologists have been willing to abandon this view for Allport's more idiosyncratic perspective.

R. R. Holt (1962), who did one of the later and more thorough analyses of the issue raised by Allport, tries to lay the whole issue to rest. First he shows how the idiographic opposition to natural science (characterized at that time as nomothetic) arose within the romantic movement. Holt then examines each idiographic assumption systematically and concludes that the phrase *idiographic science* is self-contradictory. However, he does *not* embrace the conclusion that science is therefore nomothetic:

> The nomothetic conception of science must be rejected as a caricature of what any contemporary scientist does. The only way to justify the application of the term nomothetic to the natural science of the present is to change the definition of the term so much that it no longer resembles its original meaning, and becomes an unnecessary redundancy . . . the nomothetic is as dead a duck today as the idiographic, and neither term adds anything to contemporary philosophy of science. (pp. 399–400)

Allport's thinking in another area was more widely accepted. Psychoanalytic theory made it fashionable to emphasize past experiences and unconscious influences in the determination of behavior. Allport provided a needed antidote by pointing out the necessity for determination of present behavior by present influences and by insisting that, in normal people at least, conscious influences on behavior are far more powerful than unconscious ones. It follows that the verbal report an individual gives for behaving a certain way is likely to be the best single source of information about those reasons. In addition, the conscious *intentions* of an individual provide a better indication of future behavior than any searching into the past (see especially G. W. Allport, 1955).

Allport's ideas on the functional *autonomy* of motives (Allport, 1937) have inspired more criticism (see Bertocci, 1940, for an early example) than any other single one of his ideas. Behavior, according to this view, may persist independently of the motive originally responsible for its occurrence. No other biological or primary motive need replace the original one; the behavior, once it has become functionally autonomous, may be engaged in for its own sake only. The old track star who in college ran for adulation or for pay may continue to run years afterward when there is no motive, external to the behavior itself, for continuing.

It is easy to see that such a concept invites critical attack. Allport cannot be saying that all behavior becomes functionally autonomous, or extinction could never be observed. He should then give an account of why some behaviors or motives become autonomous and some do not. This Allport attempted to do (1961). His account of the reasons for functional autonomy seems to constitute a moderation of his original position. For one class of autonomous behaviors, he accepts an account in terms of fairly traditional mechanisms, like unusual resistance to extinction. For the second class, he maintains that the behaviors continue because they are consistent with the acquired structure of the person. It seems that Allport's later position is more congruent with the views of learning theorists. Allport has again succeeded in drawing attention to a serious problem by somewhat overstating his case. Most psychologists would now at least agree that one should pay attention to the contemporary dynamics of any given behavior; one cannot rely exclusively on an account of the motives active when the behavior was originally acquired.

We have pointed out ways in which Allport sometimes opposed prevailing opinion. Yet in many ways Allport's theory is a prototype of most personality theory. He emphasizes structure and hierarchical arrangement of personality. He stresses the complexity and individuality of personality and the multiple determination of behavior. He opposes laboratory methods and nomothetic studies, preferring some looseness of conceptualization to oversimplification. For the tough-minded, these are serious defects; for the more tender-minded, the same attitudes are sources of inspiration and wisdom.

After treating Allport's contribution, Sahakian (1977) concludes that the future of personalistic psychology is assured. This appears to be a sound conclusion, and certainly Allport was an American pioneer in personalistic psychology. He became part of the Third Force of of psychologists who were neither behaviorists nor Freudian analysts. Before it was recognized or named, Allport was leading personality psychologists in the very direction that movement was later to take. He was a humanist, emphasized human freedom and creativity, and accepted a generally phenomenological methodology. In short, he was a quiet and unintentional leader of what has become a broad and current movement. Paradoxically, the fact that he studied normal persons, founded no school, and fits so well into the current *Zeitgeist,* conspired to make him nearly disappear as a distinct entity. Allport's innovative ideas will continue to have their influence, but their association with his name may well come to be forgotten by those who use them.

Factor Theories

Factor theories are conceptually related to Allport's trait theory, though historically more closely related to a statistical technique called *factor analysis* (Spearman, 1931). The search of the factor analyst leads to something which accounts for an observed consistency of behavior, that is, a something much like Allport's traits. The rigor of the method of search, however, tends to set factor theory apart from trait theory and give it a kinship in spirit with S-R theories, though the two proceed toward the goal of precision via very different paths (Cattell, 1959).

Factor theories are more closely related to a particular method of study than other personality theories are. To understand them we must know something of the reasoning behind factor analysis as a statistical technique. In order to make the discussion concrete, we shall relate factor analysis to the study of intelligence, the context in which it actually developed.

We may look at the problem in this way. Say that we have observed, in a gross way, that some people consistently stand higher than others on some loosely defined dimension which we shall call *intelligence.* We understand little about either the dimension or the reasons for individual variations in amount of intelligence. Assume now that we are able to agree on a large number of measures of behavior which are related to this gross intelligence dimension. We can then find out how each of a large number of people scores on each of the measures. If there is a tendency for people who score high on one test also to score high on every other test, it is clear that these high-scoring people must possess a higher-than-usual amount of some general factor which plays a role in determining all the test scores. If smaller subgroups of the tests have a larger relationship than can be accounted for by the general factor, then there is a group factor present which underlies performance on just these groups of related tests. Any remaining variation in test scores must be attributable to factors useful only on the single test or to "errors" or unique circumstances surrounding the administration of the test. Burt (1941) has given a full description of these various types of factors.

There are generally several ways in which the tests can be associated so that mathematically reasonable factors can be isolated. In selecting a single one from the several available factor accounts of the observed correlations, a decision must be based upon some variety of psychological acumen.

Once the factors have been determined, the measures, or tests, can be looked at again. For an individual measure, we can ask how much its value has been determined by the general factor, how much by each of the group factors involved, and how much by specific and error factors. The pattern of determination for the measure is called the *factor loading,* or *saturation,* of the measure.

Finally, we can reexamine the gross concept, intelligence, and answer questions about its composition, its nature, and its usefulness as a concept. The outcome of the factor analysis will have suggested new ways to test intelligence and to conceive of intelligence; it may at this stage appear that intelligence is not what we thought it was or that our measures were not good measures of that which we wish to continue to call *intelligence.*

Although our discussion has been concerned with the more orthodox type of factor analysis in which scores from many individuals are analyzed, it is also possible to apply factor analysis to the correlations between different tests taken repeatedly by a single individual. Stephenson (1953, 1961) has combined factor analysis with his Q sort to obtain information about the unique attitudinal organization of individual persons. His subjects are required to make judgments concerning both themselves and others in a wide variety of situations, in order to provide data for the factor analysis. In this application of factor analysis to an individual, successive scores by a single individual can be treated as though they were made by different persons.

At this point it should be clear that factor analysis is a complex, sophisticated, and fascinating method for the study of multiple variables. As such, it is clearly applicable to the study of personality. But it, like any other method in any science, is no substitute for ingenuity and insight. It will not produce hypotheses of interpretations. Furthermore, it is important to remember that the results of a factor analysis can be no better than the data that are fed into it (see Anastasi, 1958, pp. 335ff., for a simple, well-reasoned discussion of this problem).

Eysenck's Factor Theory Hans Jurgen Eysenck (1916–), a German by birth, left his homeland during the rise of the Nazis and has spent most of his life in England. After taking his Ph.D. at the University of London, Eysenck served as a hospital psychologist during World War II. He then returned to the University of London and became director of the psychological department at the Institute of Psychiatry, where he conducted research in institute hospitals. Eysenck is presently associated with the University of London and serves as senior psychologist at two hospitals. During visits to the United States, he has taught briefly at the Universities of Pennsylvania and California.

Eysenck's contributions to personality theory are exemplified by *Dimensions of personality* (1947), *The scientific study of personality* (1952b), *The structure of human personality* (1953), *The dynamics of anxiety and hysteria: An experimental application of modern learning theory to psychiatry* (1957), his editorship of the comprehensive *Handbook of abnormal psychology* (1961), *The causes and cures of neurosis* (1965), of which Rachman is coauthor, and *The biological basis of personality* (1967). Eysenck's interests have been quite broad, encompassing aesthetics, attitudes, humor, and politics.

As an outstanding contemporary factor theorist, Eysenck tends to be tough-minded and operational in approach. He puts little credence in the dimensions of personality which have been initiated from outside the framework of quantitative method. His general attitude, with which most of those in the "behavior modification movement" enthusiastically agree, is well expressed in the following quotation (Eysenck & Rachman, 1965): "Learning theory does not postulate . . . 'unconscious' causes, but regards neurotic symptoms as simply learned habits; there is no neurosis underlying the symptom, but merely the symptom itself. *Get rid of the symptom (skeletal and autonomic) and you have eliminated the neurosis*" (p. 10).

The basic structure of Eysenck's theory is not unlike Allport's. He too recognizes a hierarchial arrangement of consistencies from least to most: the specific response, the habitual response, the trait, and the type. The trait is an observed consistency of action tendencies, while the type is a constellation of traits. Most of Eysenck's interest is directed to the types, though much of his research is necessarily concerned with traits; one cannot constellate regularities in behavior without first discovering them. Eysenck, with his operational orientation, does not accept traits unless they have been operationally validated.

In his early research on 700 neurotic soldiers, Eysenck (1947) uncovered two fundamental underlying variables, or typal polarities: introversion-extraversion and neuroticism. The first of these is recognized by Eysenck as the introversion-extraversion earlier proposed by Jung as a basic personality dimension. It is different chiefly because it was extracted by Eysenck from the intercorrelations of a large number of ratings and classifications available on a large number of people. A major result of this study was that the neurotic type was found to be inferior in nearly every respect: intellectually, physically, emotionally, and especially with respect to the ability to sustain motivation.

Personality for Eysenck is divided, in the classic British tradition, into areas or sectors: the cognitive or intellectual, the conative, the affective, and the somatic. For the first three of these areas Eysenck is willing to suggest underlying general factors. For the first, of course, it is intelligence. Neuroticism is, in a sense, a conative or character defect, since it represents an inability to persist in the face of obstacles. Introversion-extraversion is a general factor in the affective area.

Later Eysenck (1952b) discovered a third type, psychotocism, in a study of hospitalized mental patients and normal subjects. Somehow this does not seem surprising. Psychotics, like neurotics, tended to do more poorly than normals, though by no means on all tests. They were distinguished from normals and neurotics by a number of specific behavioral deficiencies.

Eysenck has made a methodological contribution which promises to be important. It is called the *method of criterion analysis* (1950). The method is simply a stipulation that the factor analyst should begin with two groups which are known to differ on some hypothesized underlying factor. Eysenck's normal and psychotic subjects would provide an example. When the measures are obtained from the two groups, only those which discriminate between the groups can justifiably be assumed to relate to the hypothesized factor. If Eysenck's criterion analysis is used, it ensures that the investigator will plan the investigation carefully in advance; it will not be possible simply to administer a haphazard truckload of tests to a randomly selected flock of subjects and let the factors fall where they may.

Eysenck has been an extremely controversial figure. He is the kind of person who, if in India, might try to live on raw hamburger. He is a clinical psychologist who has characterized psychotherapy as a loose art form and has seriously questioned whether it does any good (1952a). Eysenck's forthright behavior has not endeared him to all his colleagues, who have not hesitated to apply the same high standards to his work that he has applied to theirs. Serious questions have been raised about both the empirical and the theoretical aspects of his research. It has been frequently noted that the evidence for his assertions is typically meager; he has also been criticized for overlooking alternative interpretations of his data in the absence of adequate controls to eliminate such factors (e.g., cf. Jensen, 1958, p. 300).

Eysenck's criticisms of orthodox therapies and his insistence on reliable outcome evaluations, together with his general hardheadedness, have probably tended to endear him to those who take the S-R approach. However, they find his factor-analytic approach, and the typology which he bases on the results, less attractive. His insistence on the importance of biological factors in personality also strikes a jarring note for the S-R psychologist. Altogether, we do not look forward to Eysenck's winning a popularity contest, no matter who the respondents are. We would guess that Eysenck does not put popularity high on his list of goals.

Nevertheless, Eysenck's influence on persoanlity theory has been substantial, and his research looks very promising. He has tended to toughen thinking without eliminating valuable methods of observation. He has applied quantitative methods to the data of the clinic; this has been one of the crying needs of personality research. He has been quite as willing to eliminate a concept as to accept it; yet he is not at all antitheoretical. If these techniques result in further integration of the relatively fragmentary factors thus far isolated and tested, they will have made a most significant contribution to personality theory.

Cattell's Factor Theory Raymond Bernard Cattell (1905–) was born and educated in England, where he was recognized as a leader in the field of personality research before coming to the United States. Cattell took his Ph.D. at the University of London and held both academic and clinical positions at that institution in close succession. His later career has been characterized by broad interests, encompassing both of these areas of psychology.

In the United States, Cattell has taught at Columbia Teachers College, Clark University, Harvard, and the University of Illinois. He is now professor emeritus at Illinois, and Resident in the Department of Psychology at the University of Hawaii. His major works include *Personality and motivation structure and measurement* (1957) and three handbooks which he edited and to which he contributed chapters: *Handbook of multivariate experimental psychology* (1966), *Handbook of modern personality theory* (1970), and, with R. M. Dreger, another *Handbook of modern personality theory* (1977). Besides much other work in personality theory, Cattell has to his credit work in the areas of measurement (1936, 1946) and experimental and social psychology (1952). Cattell has authored three widely used tests: The Culture Free Test of Intelligence (1944), The O-A Personality Test Battery (1954), and The 16 Personality Factor Questionnaire (1950). These are only a few of the tests with which Cattell has been involved; Cattell and Warburton (1967) list over 400 tests devised by Cattell and his students!

Like Eysenck, Cattell is intellectually indebted to the factor analysts; this is not surprising, since he studied under Spearman, who developed the essential ideas for factor analysis, which he applied to the study of intelligence. Cattell's general personality theory shows similarities to McDougall's in its tendency to look for underlying dimensions of behavior; more directly, Cattell borrows McDougall's notion of the self-regarding sentiment. Cattell's developmental theory is markedly Freudian.

Cattell combines the qualities of tough-minded factor theorists like Eysenck with the qualities of more traditional personality theorists who stress comprehensiveness. His theory is therefore at once extensive and, in part, quantitative in emphasis and content. Eysenck has a far stronger tendency to limit himself to concepts derived from factor studies; Cattell sometimes allows himself more range in order to make his theory inclusive and to avoid ignoring data from other sources.

Cattell (1950) has defined personality as "that which permits a prediction of what a person will do in a given situation" (p. 2). This definition is consistent with our contention that a theory of personality is really identical with a general theory of behavior, for Cattell's definition would fit theories of behavior. However, we should by no means conclude that Cattell's theory is just another S-R theory of behavior. Cattell (1977a) unambiguously describes the S-R paradigm of all behavioristic psychology as simpler but emptier than his own, and adds, "Most early use of the S-R element by the *reflexologists,* from Pavlov through Watson, omitted completely any term for the organism and its properties" (p. 24).

Traits are Cattell's basic elements of personality. He explicitly recognizes that traits are concepts used to explain observed consistencies of behavior, and he agrees with Allport and Eysenck that there are many levels of generality of traits, some applying only to particular individuals or circumstances, and others applying to very large groups. He has been concerned mainly, however, with the intraindividual organization of traits.

The chief distinction made by Cattell is between *surface traits* and *source traits.* The former are based simply on observed behaviors that occur together, while the latter underlie the surface traits, determining observed behavior consistencies through particular combinations. There is a rough correspondence between Eysenck's trait and Cattell's surface trait, and Eysenck's type and Cattell's source trait. The latter pair is in both cases more stable and more general, and both investigators have concentrated their interest more intensively upon such general factors.

Cattell also recognizes two kinds of traits according to their origins: constitutional and environmental-mold traits. He has performed some ingenious research in an attempt to discover to what extent traits are determined via these two influences. For example, in one study (Cattell, Blewett, & Beloff, 1955) a personality test was administered to identical twins, to fraternal twins, to siblings reared together and apart, and to unrelated subjects. The test measured traits established as significant personality factors in earlier factor studies. Study of the results obtained with subjects who thus differed to varying degrees in both hereditary and environmental similarity allowed the investigators partially to evaluate the relative contributions of heredity and environment to the factors studied. Such research is noteworthy within the personality area for its logical consistency and coordination with earlier research, as well as for its ingenuity.

Different names are assigned to source traits that have different origins. Dynamic source traits with constitutional origins are called *ergs;* those with environmental origins are called *metaergs.* Both determine patterns of behavior because they consist of motivational predispositions toward environmental objects. Metaergs are further subdivided into attitudes, interests, and sentiments. Sentiments are the most stable class.

The most powerful sentiment of all is the self sentiment. Cattell, like other personality theorists, introduces the self to explain the consistency that seems to suffuse all the behavior of an individual. Thus the self sentiment acts on all other sentiments and may strengthen or inhibit the tendency to action aroused by other sentiments. There are two selves, the real and the ideal. These have their obvious meaning, the former being the most realistic estimate we could make of ourselves, and the latter the person we would ideally like to be.

The development of personality depends upon the evolution of ergs and metaergs and the organization of the self through the process of learning. Cattell accepts both contiguity and reinforcement as principles of learning. Learning is conceived of as occurring via a series of stages, each involving alternative outcomes called *crossroads* by Cattell.

The framework within which personality development takes place is the social context. Cattell has turned his talents to the description of this context as well as to the description of personality. The dimensions of social institutions combine to form an analog to individual personality, the *syntality* of the institution. In several studies (e.g., Cattell, 1949; Cattell & Wispe, 1948) he has found factors which he believes are useful for the description of families and nations. The use of a variety of measures to derive social factors is still another example of Cattell's originality and enterprise.

Cattell has made greater efforts to synthesize his concepts explicitly than most personality theorists have. One example of this is his *dynamic lattice* (1950), which diagrammatically interrelates the ergs, sentiments, and attitudes which constitute the most important elements of a personality structure. This lattice portrays the connections between ergs (e.g., sex, protection, and security) and sentiments (e.g., toward a spouse), which are in turn related to attitudes (e.g., toward a spouse's hairstyle). In addition, elements at the same level may be interrelated (e.g., sentiments regarding one's spouse and one's bank account).

Finally, Cattell suggests an explicit way to combine information about an individual in order to predict what that individual will do in a specific situation. This is done through the *specification equation:*

$$R = s_1T_1 + s_2T_2 + s_3T_3 + \ldots + s_nT_n$$

Here s_1 represents the "weighting" of trait number 1 (T_1) in the situation in question, etc. The form of the equation is a simple linear sum. Cattell and Butcher (1968) have shown how this equation can be applied in the prediction of things like academic performance, which is a degree of specificity achieved by few, if any, competing theories of personality. However, Cattell recognizes (1977a) that the specification equation may need further development, and shows how it can be achieved by successive analysis and study of the intraorganismic and intrasituational determinants of performance, and by recognizing the effect of behavior on a person's perception of the situation. Further, the situation's effect on the traits of the organism is incorporated.

Allport, Eysenck, and Cattell have developed theories which have considerable logical similarity. All three men are alike in their vigor and iconoclastic tendencies—traits which psychology presently needs, especially in personality theory. Allport was very different from the other two in attitude and in method of study, having had little sympathy for factor analysis or for the massive experiment. Eysenck and Cattell have shown unusual aptitude for originating experimental designs that wed quantitative methods to the study of personality. Thus the methodological dissimilarity of the three theorists is as striking as their logical similarity. Despite the current disagreements about which factors have really been found, we agree with the judgment of Corsini (1977b):

> . . . the work of Raymond B. Cattell, Hans J. Eysenck, J. P. Guilford, F. C. Thorne, and L. L. Thurstone, who have worked generally in the statistical tradition established by Charles Spearman in the early 1900s, holds more promise for eventual convergence than do clinical systems. (p. 427)

Among these psychologists, Cattell has been the most productive, persistent, and systematic. Madsen (1977) characterizes the whole body of work covered in

Cattell's latest massive handbook as *Cattellian personality theory.* Thus there is some indication that this approach is attracting adherents, and may produce cumulative progress even after Cattell himself leaves the field. The fact that recognition has come so belatedly may reflect how difficult it is to love so complex an approach, rather than any conceptual weaknesses. Cattell and Eysenck are nearly alone in that they have accepted stringent scientific criteria for personality theory without ignoring the personalistic questions raised by the traditional theories.

ORGANISMIC THEORIES

Many personality theorists start from a point of view systematically close to that of the Gestalt psychologists. Murphy, Rogers, Goldstein, Angyall, Maslow, Lecky, Murray, and Sheldon are members of this class. Any or all of these men might be included as organismic theorists. The decisions must be based on the extent to which a holistic, Gestalt orientation toward the individual is a *central* feature of their personality theories. Quite arbitrarily, we are choosing Goldstein and Sheldon as organismic theorists and omitting the rest or treating them in a separate section. The choice of Goldstein needs no justification; Sheldon would often be put in another class because the really central feature of his theory is his preoccupation with constitutional influences on personality; he does, however, espouse a general organismic point of view, and his interest in organic effects qualified him as an organismic theorist in the popular meaning of the term.

Goldstein's Holistic Theory

Kurt Goldstein (1878–1965) established his reputation as a neuropsychiatrist in Europe before coming to this country in 1935. Having received his medical degree from the University of Breslau, he associated himself with the Psychiatric Hospital at Königsberg. At an early age, Goldstein became a professor of neurology and psychiatry and director of the Neurological Institute at the University of Frankfurt. He later held a similar position at the University of Berlin.

During World War I, Goldstein conducted the fundamental studies of brain-injured soldiers which laid the groundwork for his organismic theory (1942) and his most significant publication, *The organism* (1939). It is peculiarly ironic that Goldstein, who devoted much of his early professional life to studying and caring for injured German soldiers, should have been forced to leave Nazi Germany, first for Amsterdam and then for the United States.

In the United States, Goldstein held academic and clinical positions in a variety of institutions, in addition to maintaining a private neuropsychiatry and psychotherapy practice in New York City for many years. He delivered the William James Lectures at Harvard, discussing human nature in the light of psychopathology (1940), and was associated with the New York Psychiatric Institute, Tufts Medical School in Boston, Columbia University, Brandeis University, City College of New York, and the New School for Social Research. Goldstein died in 1965, and his posthumously published autobiography (1967) summed up the history of his intellectual development literally from beginning to end.

Aside from his theoretical and clinical work, Goldstein published works on language disturbances (1948) and, with Gelb (1920), on the Gestalt problem of figure-ground relationships. Although Goldstein denied any direct ties with Gestalt psychology, there are some close analogies between his thinking and theirs. In the case of figure-ground relationships, Goldstein saw each act of an individual as influenced by and as influencing the whole organism at the time of its occurrence. This is similar to the Gestalt point about figure and ground in perception. The principal and outstanding feature of ongoing activity is figure, just as the outstanding feature of perception is figure. In an organism's behavior, those features which are related to the strongest drives stand out.

The normal organism is structured but flexible, capable of tailoring its behavior to fit the needs of the ongoing stimulus situation. Its behavior can be understood only as part of an organic unity; the significance of its behavior can be assessed only as a contribution to the ongoing goal of the organism.

For Goldstein, the goal of the organism is unitary. It is self-actualization. Self-actualization sums up all the needs of the organism. A sexually driven organism actualizes itself in coitus, and a hungry one in eating; but the self-actualization of the complex human adult is expressed in many less organically driven acts.

Self-actualization has become an extremely crucial part of the conceptions of Abraham Maslow and Carl Rogers. Maslow was directly influenced by Goldstein. Interestingly, Goldstein developed the idea through study of damaged organisms, brain-injured soldiers. Maslow continued to develop the idea by studying highly successful, unusually self-actualized people. Rogers' therapy relies heavily upon the patient's ability to self-actualize, given a favorable environment.

Goldstein believed that the strongly organized organism is capable of choosing a favorable environment or manipulating an unfavorable one to some extent. It is thus not the victim of blind forces or the pawn of fortuitous stimulus situations. But no organism is insulated from environmental effects; it must thus come to terms with its environment. Only through accepting those terms of the environment which cannot be avoided or changed can the organism continue in its attempt to actualize itself. This aspect of Goldstein's thinking puts him close to the phenomenologists and existentialists—a similarity which Goldstein himself did not fail to note when, in his eighties, he wrote about his life (1967, pp. 161–164).

Organismic theorists tend to avoid analysis; Goldstein was no exception. If it is necessary to study every behavior event within the context of the whole organism, it is tempting to stay on the level of generality without coming to terms with the problem of specificity of prediction. In this Goldstein was again no exception. His central concept, self-actualization, leaves one uncertain of the defining characteristics of such behavior and wondering whether there is much behavior which is not in some sense self-actualizing.

It may seem peculiar that Goldstein was led to his holistic view by brain-injured patients, who are not altogether whole. But he found that the behavior of a patient with a brain injury could be understood only by examining the whole matrix of the patient's behavior. What at first appears to be a direct result of injury might, upon closer examination, turn out to be a quite indirect reaction stemming from an attempt to fit the results of injury into the mosaic of life. The same physical injury might lead to a variety of behavior syndromes, depending upon the patient's circumstances and personality structure. A specific deterioration in some ability may lead a patient to be generally more sensitive, less self-confident, and more withdrawn; if one did not know this, one might uncritically attribute various performance decrements to direct results of injury rather than to these indirect manifestations.

With his background of clinical experience, it is natural that Goldstein should have preferred the intensive study of the individual to the group approach. Through this approach, Goldstein made his best-known discovery: The most characteristic difference between patients with extensive brain injury and normal individuals is that the former have lost the abstract attitude. Their ability to do concrete things and to react to concrete situations may be relatively unimpaired, but their ability to abstract is likely to be extremely limited. For example, brain-injured patients may be unable to make statements that are obviously contrary to fact, such as "the moon is green." They cannot abstract common properties of dissimilar objects, such as a radio and a newspaper. This lack of abstract ability permeates their behavior. Goldstein and Scheerer (1941, 1953) developed tests to determine the extent to which abstract behavior is impaired; these tests therefore help to diagnose brain damage.

Goldstein was an example of an organismic theorist at his observational, clinical best. He was self-consciously antiexperimental, sharing the organismic belief that by thus restricting conditions and controlling behavior, we lose the significance which the activity might have in its natural context. But Goldstein was shrewd and industrious in taking advantage of the wealth of material which paraded before him in his psychiatric practice.

Although he was extremely ingenious in his own observations, Goldstein did not make important methodological contributions. Neither was his holistic theory itself whole enough to endure long as a distinguishable theory or conception of personality. Nevertheless, his ideas about the nature of self-actualization play such a central role in many popular conceptions of personality—indeed, throughout the humanistic movement—that Goldstein will not be soon forgotten.

Sheldon's Typology

William H. Sheldon (1899–   ) is a trained physician, as his theoretical efforts to relate behavioral and body components might indicate. After receiving both his Ph.D. and his M.D. from the University of Chicago, he interned at a children's hospital. Sheldon taught at the University of Chicago, Northwestern University, and the University of Wisconsin before continuing his studies with 2 years of psychiatric training abroad. His visits with Jung, Freud, and Kretschmer contributed directly to his later theorizing, which owes most to constitutional theorists such as Kretschmer and Viola, but which also shows resemblances to Freudian, and particularly Jungian, theory.

At Harvard, Sheldon entered into a collaborative relationship with experimentalist S. S. Stevens, who brought to Sheldon's work a new sophistication in procedure and measurement. Together they published the basic works in constitutional psychology: *The varieties of temperament: A psychology of constitutional differences* (1942) and *The varieties of human physique: An introduction to constitutional psychology* (1940).

Sheldon's writing has been characterized by concern for the identification of, and relationships between, structural and temperamental factors, particularly as applied to the problem of delinquency (1949b). He has written a somatotyping guide, *Atlas of men: A guide for somatotyping the adult male at all ages* (1954). Always the taxonomist, Sheldon ventured away from personality theory temporarily, only to produce *Early American cents* (1949a)—a classification of coins!

Sheldon's road has not been an easy one. American psychology generally has been unfriendly to the idea that constitutional factors are important influences on behavior. Our democratic ideals and, more specifically, the extreme environmentalism of John B. Watson have made us unwilling to believe that innate predispositions really have a directive influence on our personality. Further, Sheldon has strewn a number of unnecessary boulders in his own path. He has suggested that we should make sure that only those constitutionally endowed with the best qualities of human temperament reproduce. Reproduction, he says, should be left to specialists. Visions of Nazi pogroms and of a specialized reproductive group, like termite queens, continually pregnant, are enough to turn many against Sheldon's conception without a second glance.

Despite this resistance, it has remained obvious to the person in the street that there are associations between constitutional factors and personality. To the naïve observer, the fat man appears jolly; the skinny kid with glasses remains a withdrawn bookworm. It is not surprising, then, that the man who reinforced these long-held popular beliefs is one of the better-known theorists.

Sheldon is also well known to the beginning psychology student, perhaps because he stands out among the personality theorists as a man who has said something comprehensible to the beginning student. Regrettably, Sheldon has sometimes been presented as having made ludicrous or incautious statements. He may have advocated something unpopular or capable of misinterpretation, but not something ludicrous.

Sheldon's system is a modern version of statements running back at least as far as Hippocrates, who believed that there were associations between body fluids and temperaments and that there were two basic types of physique: short and fat or long and thin. Ernst Kretschmer, many years later, added a third body type—the muscular—between the two extremes and designated them as follows: pyknic, short and squatty; athletic, broad and muscular; and asthenic, tall and thin. He studied the relationship between these three types and the varieties of psychoses. Sheldon's continuity with his typological forebears has probably also contributed to his difficulty in getting a completely open-minded hearing from American psychologists. Hippocrates and his bilious temperaments are all too easy to laugh at, and some of this attitude toward humors has generalized to

Sheldon. Psychology has been suspicious of typology as too easy a solution; even the description of personality in terms of patterns of traits is not above suspicion. Those familiar with the sad history of phrenology recognize both its similarity to trait psychology and its similarity to constitutional typology, for do not both phrenology and constitutional typology assess personality from physical measurements? It is easy to understand the rockiness of Sheldon's professional path. Fortunately, Sheldon seems well equipped to dish out punishment as well as to take it. He has written pungent criticisms of others, in addition to defending his own position.

Sheldon's contributions have been primarily an elaboration and tightening of Kretschmer's basic physical types and further empirical work in relating these types to behavioral variables. An important difference exists between his work and earlier theorizing, such as Kretschmer's. Sheldon has recognized that any given individual is marked by some *degree* of each type and thus is in this sense always a blend of types rather than a pure type.

Sheldon's attempt to establish a constitutional interrelationship between behavior and body build is anchored in the belief that the outward physical appearance (phenotype) is determined and guided by a hypothetical biological process (morphogenotype). Measurement of the physique is utilized by Sheldon in an attempt to evaluate indirectly the function of the morphogenotype. The obtained data fall into three categories of body types: endomorphy, mesomorphy, and ectomorphy.

This trichotomy was determined by evaluating 4,000 standardized photographs taken from three angles—front, back and side. These were sectioned into seventeen parts (Sheldon, 1940, p. 55), from which anthropometric measurements could be obtained. Sheldon is thus unique among personality theorists in being able to work with variables that can be, and have been, measured with a ruler. After analyzing the data, Sheldon concluded that all the physical characteristics could be grouped into three components according to the presumed embryonic origin of most of the individual's tissue in the outer (ectomorphic), middle (mesomorphic), or inner (endomorphic) layer.

The endomorph tends to be soft, fleshy, and round; the mesomorph is square, tough, muscular, dense, and athletic; the ectomorph is tall, thin, fragile, and small-boned. Endomorphs are massive in relation to their surface area; mesomorphs intermediate; and ectomorphs more exposed to the world because of their high proportion of surface area to mass.

Besides the primary components of body type there are several which are classified as secondary. These are dysplasia (disharmony between the body parts), gynandromorphy (bisexuality denoted by the physique), and texture (as of hairiness of the body) (1940, p. 7).

According to Sheldon, the three primary components of physique correspond to three components of temperament: visceratonia, somatotonia, and cerebrotonia. The visceratonic individual loves comfort, food, and affection, and is good-natured. The somatotonic person is active, vigorous, and aggressive. The cerebrotonic individual is a bookish, sensitive, shy individual who withdraws from social contacts.

If we assume that there are such identifiable components of constitution and of personality, are the two related or not? Sheldon (1942, p. 400) found a remarkably high correlation between the components that one would expect to find associated: endomorphy-visceratonia; mesomorphy-somatotonia; and ectomorphy-cerebrotonia. These correlations are all about .80! Personality theorists seldom find their expectations so gratifyingly corroborated.

It is easy to be dubious about Sheldon's components of personality, since they seem so close to lay stereotypes, until one discovers that the clusters of traits were derived from careful correlational studies using a large number of original traits rather than from the depths of the armchair (Sheldon, 1944, pp. 526–549). Sheldon's components of personality are each defined by twenty related traits (Sheldon, 1942, p. 26).

Sheldon seems to be on safe ground when he maintains that, descriptively, the postulated correlations exist. However, other experimenters generally find that the correlations are lower than those obtained by Sheldon (Child, 1950; Lindzey, 1967, Sanford, 1953, Seltzer, Wells, & McTernan, 1948). The inflated correlations between temperament and physique could be attributed to a "halo effect" since both sets of ratings were done by the same person; that is, there was no attempt at blind analysis. Although in *The varieties of temperament* (1942, pp. 411–425) Sheldon made an effort to justify his position, his attempt in no way negates the possibility that a subjective bias may have contaminated the results. The procedure, despite the possibility of subjectivism, remained unaltered.

An additional criticism has been made by Lubin (1950), who discovered that some of the coefficients found in the tables of intercorrelation among the temperamental traits (Sheldon, 1942, pp. 506–511) are not mathematically possible.

Sheldon has also been attacked because he assumes that genetic, strictly biological factors account for the observed correlations. If Sheldon really maintained that these direct biological influences were *the* reason for the correlations, he would be open to attack. He does not; he recognizes, as do his detractors, that different cultural expectations or differential rewards related to different body builds might account for the observed personality differences. For example, a boy who is muscular by nature probably finds more reward in athletics than an endomorphic type. The rewards of sport would then increase both active competitive behavior and the accumulation of muscle tissue. Sheldon admits that, although the morphogenotype is invariant, the phenotype (from which measurements are taken) does fluctuate because of cultural and other influences. This admission forces him to relinquish partially his grasp on his basic theoretical relationship between the constitution and temperament. He says that the crucial relationship is between the morphogenotype and the temperament. The phenotype is only an attempt to measure the morphogenotype; this measurement is the best we have to date, despite its inexactness. It seems to us that operational criteria are highly applicable to this issue. Operationally, the morphogenotype has no meaning not exhausted by the measures of phenotype. The notion of morphogenotype may be lent *credibility* by analogy with other genetic characteristics, but no genetic observations directly justify the theoretical use of the morphogenotype. Therefore, we suggest, on grounds of parsimony, that the stated relationships be restricted to those holding between observed properties.

Sheldon is less willing to recognize the possibility that exclusively environmental factors, such as diet, might explain the observed relationships. However, Anastasi (1958) has pointed out that "Habitual overeating does lead to the accumulation of fat tissue. It is interesting to note in this connection that recent literature in abnormal psychology as well as in psychosomatic medicine contains many references to 'psychological overeating' resulting from frustration and other emotional problems" (p. 182).

Anastasi has also stated (1958) that "The original identification of the three temperamental components . . . can likewise be questioned because of inadequacy of data" (p. 177). That is, in the original study there were only thirty-three male college subjects, and although further attempts were made to revise the original twenty-two traits, the procedure for doing so was clearly dependent upon the original study and its results.

A major asset of Sheldon's theory is that it has kept public the fact that there is some type of relationship between physique and temperament; at the present time, however, we cannot ascertain its direction. Does the physique direct the temperament, or does the temperament determine the physique; or, more logically, is it a two-way process whose exact interrelations have not yet been ferreted out? Several studies have found that delinquent boys are very often mesomorphs (Glueck & Glueck, 1956; Epps & Parnell, 1942; Gibbens, 1963). Why, precisely, should that be?

History seems to be rendering the verdict that Sheldon's theory should be used primarily to provide such interesting footnotes—surprising minor relationships between physique and temperament. Shontz (1977) reports that he could turn up only four studies between 1968 and 1975 that related somatotypes and personality profiles. Sheldon himself appeared in print only once since 1954 in a major publication (Sheldon, Lewis, & Tenney, 1969). It is not likely that Sheldon's theory will be of much current interest in another 10 years. There are, however, two factors that could make this judgment mistaken. The first is that the Hafner Publishing Company reissued five of Sheldon's major works in 1970. The second is a generally renewed interest in the genetics of behavior, as reflected in the growth of ethology and sociobiology. We simply doubt that Sheldon's typology will share in this resurgence.

NEOANALYTIC PERSONALITY THEORIES

There are several closely related theories of personality that owe a great deal to psychoanalytic theory. Though they are by no means identical, their similarity of background and emphasis justified their treatment under a single heading. The term *neoanalytic* is used to reflect their basic psychoanalytic framework as well as their modification of such principles in one way or another.

Karen Horney, Erich Fromm, Harry Stack Sullivan, and Henry Murray all developed their own personality theories as improvisations on the primary Freudian, Adlerian, and Jungian themes (see Chapter 8). In these newer theories social factors are emphasized. In playing up social factors, there has been a concomitant tendency to deemphasize biological factors. It is the relative neglect of the instinctive which sets these theories apart from Freudian analytic theory and which keeps at least the first three from having any basic commonality with Jungian theory.

All four of these theorists, and Sullivan especially, have contributed to the theory of ego functioning. This emphasis on ego functioning has been regarded as a strong point by sympathizers; on the other hand, some Freudians have regarded it as evidence that the theories represent an elaboration of Freudian theory rather than any really original contribution. Regardless of basic originality, each of these theorists has said unique things about the relationship of the individual to his society.

Horney's Social Theory

The training and contributions of Karen Horney (1885–1952) were entirely within the field of psychoanalysis, although she represented an important outbranching from orthodox psychoanalytic theory. German by birth, Horney studied medicine at the University of Berlin and received her psychoanalytic training at the Berlin Psychoanalytic Institute, where she was analyzed by Karl Abraham and Hans Sachs, and where she remained from 1918 until 1932. She became one of the early emigrants to the United States. When she arrived here during the Depression, she found that American neuroses refused to conform to the Freudian model; they concerned economics more often than sex. That finding helped to lead her away from biological and toward social factors in neurosis.

In the United States, Horney served as associate director of the Chicago Psychoanalytic Institute, taught at the New York Psychoanalytic Institute, and conducted a private practice in psychotherapy. Her efforts to break away from orthodox psychoanalysis led to the formation of the Association for the Advancement of Psychoanalysis and the American Institute of Psychoanalysis, of which she was dean.

Horney's theoretical emphasis is reflected in the titles of three of her works on personality theory: *Neurotic personality of our times* (1937), *Our inner conflicts* (1945), and *Neurosis and human growth* (1950). Her theory is further explicated in *New ways in psychoanalysis* (1939) and *Self-analysis* (1942).

Horney's social theory flies the banner of *basic anxiety.* This essential factor in personality development (Horney, 1937) is "the feeling a child has of being isolated and helpless in a potentially hostile world" (p. 79). Horney's concept of helplessness as experienced by the infant does not have the universal flavor that Adler assigned to it. It provides a predisposition for the future development of pathological conditions; it does not lead to a striving for superiority, but merely accentuates a predilection for security.

The home environment and the social structure within the family receive by far the most emphasis in Horney's theory. In this structure and the child's reaction to it Horney believed she had the key to the development of an individual's personality structure. The predominant reason that basic anxiety develops from parent-child relationships is the absence of genuine love and affection, and this can almost invariably be traced to neurotic parents. It should be noted, however, that Horney defines neurosis as any deviation from normal, efficient behavior; the term is not used in a pathological context unless so indicated.

The child responds to basic anxiety by developing some strategy of behavior, *neurotic trends,* in an attempt to overcome it. It is this character structure arising from the reaction to basic anxiety which accounts for neurotic symptoms; it is *not,* as Freud said, a frustration of the sexual instinct. Horney maintained that sexual difficulty is the result and not the cause of conflicts. Furthermore, it is not a compulsion to repeat experiences based on unchanged, repressed childhood experiences (Horney, 1939): "There is no such thing as an isolated repetition of isolated experiences; but the entirety of infantile experiences combines to form a certain character structure, and it is this structure from which later difficulties emanate" (p. 9).

The child also develops an idealized self-concept by internalizing the aspirational levels and ethics of others in the culture. This concept develops without regard for the child's own potentialities or limitations. Consequently, attempting to realize these ideational concepts, the child is curtailed both by personal limitations and by limitations imposed by the existing culture. In other words, a person's basic conflict is between self-realization and self-idealization. The idealized self becomes a crutch for neurotic persons. They come to believe that they *are* their idealized picture. This solution brings a temporary reduction of anxiety, but in the long run increases it. The attempts of neurotics to live up to their idealized, unrealistic picture of themselves result in new conflicts and consequently greater tension. The only real conflict which Horney recognized is that of the present situation and the demands it makes upon the individual.

The devices the individual uses to face conflicts (neurotic trends) are generally unrealistic and lead to some degree of neurotic behavior. These may be classified into two categories: (1) those which have their roots in the early developmental period of the child and which demonstrate a discernible etiology and (2) those which are a reaction to some situational stress and are usually transitory (Munroe, 1955). A vicious circle develops once these neurotic trends are initiated. Anxiety causes the original behavior, which in turn, because of its inadequacy, leads to further anxiety that initiates another cycle.

Attempting to find security, a person uses three types of behavioral patterns, moving toward people, against them, or away from them (Horney, 1945). Fundamental to these three types of behavior are the need for affection, the need for self-sufficiency, and the need to exploit people. In respect to the type of behavior a person selects there are corresponding personality types: compliant, aggressive, and detached. Again one must be cautioned not to assume that an individual uses only a single type. Vacillating from one situation to another, a person uses the one most efficient for the specific situation. However, if one pattern is used exclusively, regardless of the situation, that is an index of neurosis.

The compliant individual relies upon other people; is ostensibly loving, kind, and loyal; and finds personal criticism devastating. Cynicism, a philosophy of the survival of the fittest, and extreme independence characterize the aggressive personality. The detached individual is perfectionistic, uncreative, and has a paucity of interpersonal relationships.

Horney emphasized only two of the many unconscious defense mechanisms: Rationalization and externalization. Rationalization is used in the Freudian sense except that it is explained in the context of the social theory of Horney; that is, it is concerned with the whole organism and is not related to Freud's instinctual personality components. Externalization is merely a more general term for projection. The whole organism participates in an attempt to explain *every* motive and action externally, not just the undesirable ones.

Horney was optimistic about the possibility of avoiding neurotic reactions, as one tends to be when one believes that social factors are of preponderant importance. A secure and loving home would be insurance against the development of a neurotic character structure. Those, like Freud, who emphasize biological factors find it harder to be optimistic; if conflict is based on hereditary factors, change can come but slowly. Horney's more hopeful views have been welcomed by many as a relief from the oppressive pessimism of the orthodox Freudian assumptions. She has attempted to point the way to better families, to better societies, and, through them, to better people. Despite her long-term association with the training of analysts, Horney never formed a cohesive school of followers, nor did her theoretical views inspire research directly. As time passes, Horney's important contributions will probably become less associated with her name and more a part of the general *Zeitgeist* of psychology.

Fromm's Escape-from-Freedom Theory

Erich Fromm (1900–) was born and trained in Germany. He studied sociology and psychology at the Universities of Munich, Frankfurt, and Heidelberg, where he took his Ph.D. His psychoanalytic training was conducted mainly at the Berlin Psychoanalytic Institute.

Fromm cannot be clearly identified by his affiliation with any one institution, although he has lectured at the Chicago Psychoanalytic Institute and has taught at numerous universities and institutes in this country since he emigrated here in 1933. Since 1951 he has been a professor at the University of Mexico; he is also the director of the Mexican Psychoanalytic Institute. He is said to spend some time during each summer in New York City, although his primary residence is in Mexico City.

Escape from freedom (1941), *Man for himself* (1947), and *The sane society* (1955)—Fromm's major contributions to personality theory—probably have drawn more cross-scientific and public attention than the works of any other neo-Freudian.

Fromm's primary interests lie in the larger segments of society as they affect the individual (Fromm, 1955, 1961b). As a matter of fact, Fromm is a greater admirer of Marx (Fromm, 1961a) than of Freud (Fromm, 1959) and might as accurately be labeled a Marxist personality theorist as a Freudian personality theorist (see C. S. Hall & Lindzey, 1970, p. 130). Such a labeling, however, does not fit well into the categorization system of American psychology!

However he is classified, Fromm believes that our political organizations no longer provide the firm direction and secure framework which they did when the units of political organization were smaller and people had less freedom to determine their own fate. Today, people suffer from a feeling of insecure aloneness engendered by their lack of a framework; that is, people desire to actualize their self-potential and develop a feeling of belongingness.

Fromm's basic premise that an individual attempts to escape from freedom and return to a more secure existence first gained public notice through his *Escape from freedom.* Children's physical condition at birth and shortly thereafter makes their survival dependent upon their environment in general and upon their mothers in particular. Children are soon weaned from early postnatal surroundings and gradually achieve more and more independence. However, the accompanying amount of strength necessary to augment their independence and to cope with the elements of society is conspicuously lacking. Moreover, human beings alone have the power to reason and imagine, and with the acquisition of this power they have lost the animal's ability to react instinctively, intimately, and directly to nature. Thus people find themselves in a unique position of being separated from their fellows by political conditions and from the rest of nature by being human. Their first reaction to this situation is to try to recapture their earlier form of security. Upon finding this physically impossible and socially inefficient, they attempt other means. The two most common solutions are *authoritarianism* and *humanism.*

Broadly defined, authoritarianism is that which externally imposes a set of principles on society. It may be exemplified by a totalitarian state, or dictatorship, or belief in a supreme being. This solution is inadequate because it does not permit individuals an opportunity to realize their potentialities. Frustration and hostility against the imposed conditions are then mobilized.

Fromm believes that humanism is a better solution. All the actualities of human life have a chance to develop through love of fellow human beings and mutual cooperation. In a humanistic society, all would be brothers and sisters, and no one would be alone.

Fromm identified four ways of escaping the isolation and insecurity prevalent in modern society. He referred to them as types of orientation, or relatedness. They are receptive, exploitative, hoarding, and marketing. In addition, there is the healthy, or productive, orientation. No person exhibits a pure orientation. However, it is possible to manifest one type so that it subordinates all others.

The receptive orientation (Fromm, 1947) "is often to be found in societies in which the right of one group to exploit another is firmly established" (p. 79). Individuals with this type of orientation sacrifice everything in order to maintain their identification with the group or the leader. They expect to receive something gratis, and when adversity occurs they are extremely rebellious and aggressive, exhibiting behavior not unlike that of a spoiled child.

The philosophy of "might makes right" characterizes exploitative individuals. The value which they place upon an object is directly proportional to the value which others place on it. They would feel no compunction about taking some object for no other reason than that it is highly prized by another.

The hoarding orientation is what one might expect it to be: frugal, impecunious, and miserly. Security is evaluated in terms of tangible physical wealth.

The last orientation, marketing, is relatively new and is associated with the advent of modern capitalism. Here the emphasis is centered upon such superficial objectives as keeping up with the Joneses and social climbing.

Fromm (1964) later added the biophilous type, who is in love with life. If love of life is frustrated, the person may become necrophilous (attracted to death).

As society now stands, it is absolutely necessary to warp the individual to fit the needs of society. Though human beings will always have to fit into human society, Fromm sees hope in a society which would give each individual a chance to develop into a fully human creature. Fromm has named his ideal society a *humanistic communitarian socialism.* His desperate concern for the development of such a society, born at least partly out of his own flight from Nazism, has put him in the forefront of the science of psychology, which is only now undergoing its social awakening. Every conception of the human being has implications for the kind of society in which people can live comfortably. We have encountered Skinner's attempt to specify the nature of a Utopian society, and his attempt to tell us how to get "beyond freedom and dignity." Few psychologists have devoted as high a percentage of their efforts to specifying the significance of politics for persons and persons for politics as Erich Fromm. It should be one of our missions to study this problem, and Fromm has tried to point the way.

Murray's Need-Press Theory

Henry Murray (1893–) was a rigorously trained, productive biological scientist before turning to psychology. His academic degrees include an A.B. from Harvard in history, an M.D. from Columbia's College of Physicians and Surgeons, and an M.S. in biology from Columbia. Murray subsequently completed a surgical internship at Columbia's Presbyterian Hospital, taught physiology at Harvard, conducted embryological research at the Rockefeller Institute for Medical Research, and then journeyed to England to take his Ph.D. in biochemistry at Cambridge University.

While in Europe, a visit with Jung dramatically shifted Murray's interest to depth psychology. Shortly thereafter he took a position in academic psychology at Harvard and directed the Psychological Clinic there. He was on leave with the Office of Strategic Services during World War II, after which he returned to Harvard as a professor at the Psychological Clinic annex, where he remained until his retirement as professor emeritus in 1962. Murray's psychoanalytic training came under the direction of Franz Alexander and Hans Sachs; Murray paid his debt to psychoanalysis by helping found the Boston Psychoanalytic Society and by stimulating widespread interest in psychoanalytic research among his students. C. S. Hall and Lindzey (1970, p. 166) regret that Murray's conversations have not been preserved, since the richness of his thought and contribution is not fully represented in his published work. We shall see, however, that his published contributions are considerable! Murray, like another maverick, Gordon Allport, received the two highest awards his profession has to offer: the Distinguished Scientific Contribution Award of the APA and the Gold Medal Award of the American Psychological Foundation.

The Thematic Apperception Test (1943), which Murray developed, has become one of the most widely used empirical tools of clinicians and personality theorists. His major theoretical work is *Explorations in personality* (1938). However, his *Assessment of men* (Office of Strategic Services, 1948), written as a result of his work in the Office of Strategic Services during World War II, is also considered a significant contribution to the area of personality assessment. As an intellectual sideline, Murray has engaged in a 25-year study of Herman Melville and has published an analysis (1951) of the psychological meaning of the novel *Moby Dick.*

One cannot read Murray (e.g., 1959) without receiving the impression that he is deeply preoccupied with the notions of process and field. Yet Murray is too well rounded to deny the importance of a controlled and reductive approach to psychology. The reductive approach is certainly foreign to Murray's own nature, for he sees too vividly the interactions that occur among all the processes that constitute a system. The system, to Murray as to the Gestaltist, is the unit to be studied. Only systems maintain their boundaries and provide the hope for that stability which is so rare in nature but so necessary to scientific study. Murray sees science as operating not primarily with stable structures but with processes which may, with some probability, be predictable.

Murray has said of himself (1959): "But at no time, to the annoyance of my friends, was I a good Jungian, a good Freudian, a good Adlerian, or a good schoolman of any breed" (p. 13). Despite this independence of thought, Murray is close to Freud in many basic attitudes as well as in some of the details of his theory. Two of these attitudes are a belief in the great importance of the early history of the organism and an emphasis on the physiological processes accompanying the behavioral events in which the psychologist is interested. Murray allows for more changes of the personality by later events than Freud did. However, Murray still recognizes the possibility that the effects of infantile experiences may be so great that they lead to various complexes in adulthood. On the physiological issue, Murray is one with Freud in recognizing the independence of the science of psychology from that of physiology, while at the same time pointing out that there is a relationship of dependence between the two types of events: without physiological processes, there can be no psychological processes. Some particular dominant configuration of processes in the brain always accompanies a particular conscious process.

Another theme in Murray's theorizing is his recurrent clear statement that the concepts of his theory are constructions, hypothetical entities, not reality. Murray is not the kind of person who believes that nailing a name onto the flow of process can make it hold still or behave like a convenient structure that the scientist can then deal with complacently. Murray is more like someone who builds a transparent map with rough lines and shadings, through which reality can be viewed more conveniently, building and rebuilding systems of classification, analyzing and reanalyzing processes as understanding is enriched. Murray's theory could be called a tool as much as a description.

Murray has presented one of the most elaborate taxonomies of needs (1938). He does not attempt to talk about needs as things isolated from the context of behavior. Although needs are related to internal states, they are also related to the presence of valued external stimuli which impel to action (presses). The need directs behavior to objects which can lead to a desired state; though this state may often involve the reduction of tension, it may sometimes involve an increase in tension. Murray does not believe that the normal person always seeks the numbness of no tension. Most needs have as accompaniments certain emotions and feelings.

Murray has redefined Freud's term *cathexis* to describe need-related objects; an object may have a positive or negative cathexis according to its ability to press the individual into responses of approach or avoidance. The individual's feeling for the object is called a *sentiment.* Cathexis and sentiment therefore refer to the same relationship between person and object; one is applicable when we are concerned with the properties of the object, the other when we are concerned with the properties of the person. Thus Murray has subdivided Freud's concept of cathexis into two parts.

Needs are interrelated as well as embedded in ongoing processes. Some needs are subsidiary to more global, superordinate needs, and the satisfaction of the subsidiary need is not an end in itself but only a step toward the greater satisfaction. Different needs may occur in the individual at the same time, in which case a conflict is engendered; one of the needs will be or become the strongest, in which case it is called *prepotent,* and will demand satisfaction before the concurrent needs can be attended to.

Closely related to Murray's acceptance of possible needs for tension increase in his description of two types of needs which do not involve a Thorndikian type of effect. He adds to the Thorndikian type of need *process needs* and *modal needs.* Process needs are needs to do; for example, the adult may need to exercise, or the infant may need to babble. Modal needs are needs to perfect some behavior and differ from process needs only in that the need to improve is involved.

Murray's thoroughness in his treatment of needs is also reflected in his full discussion of significant units of behavior. He has relatively little use for a formulation as molecular as S-R. His most analytic unit is the *proceeding,* which is an interaction involving a person and an object or a person and a person; the interaction must be long enough to be of dynamic significance. The proceeding need not be overt; it may be a daydream or plan.

Proceedings may follow one another in a coherent fashion, in which case they may constitute another unit, a *serial.* The serial involves planning and organization, and its nature imposes direction upon the proceedings which constitute it. A marriage is an example of a serial. Proceedings, and therefore serials, may overlap and intertwine; all of us are involved in many endeavors in a single day or even hour.

A *thema* is another of Murray's behavioral units. It lays more emphasis upon the press and need which determine the behavior in question and therefore is a more analytic and theoretical unit than the more descriptive proceeding. The thema, like the proceeding, may be serially organized. The thema is less fixed in scope than the proceeding and may persist over a longer period of time.

A serial program may also be considered a unit of behavior, but it lays emphasis upon the plans of the individual. He may plan a life goal, for example, college graduation, which involves a very large number of subgoals before it can be accomplished. A subgoal might be passing a course or completing a major.

We can see that Murray puts realism before precision, and creativity before compulsion, in his theory of personality. Though many of his ideas are basically psychoanalytic, there can be no doubt whatever that he is a thinker who is not afraid to modify or innovate whenever he feels that the evidence is in his favor. He has also devised new methods for getting evidence, as we know from his Thematic Apperception Test (TAT) (1943) and from the ingenuity of his wartime work in assessing men for special assignments (Office of Strategic Services, 1948).

C. S. Hall and Lindzey (1970) evaluate Murray's theory and his research as being out of tune with the times: "There is too much of the poet and too little of the positivist in his make-up" (p. 205). Murray has never shown a great desire to be in tune with the times and has had enough independent resources so that he has not had to be. His espousal of unpopular viewpoints may, as he thought, have been responsible for keeping him from getting tenure until he was 55. At any rate, he was recently concerned that he might have achieved too much respectability (1967): "In due course the practice of introspection and the concept of motive force, in altered forms and disguised by fresh labels, surreptitiously regained their lost respectability; and after World War II, Freudian theory *in toto* overran large areas of American psychology as Napoleon overran Europe. . . . Murr found himself occupying a position of discomforting respectability" (p. 295).

Unfortunately, even the attractiveness of Murray's iconoclasm and the persuasiveness of his writing have not inspired much research to test his theory. This is in stark contrast to the fact that his Thematic Apperception Test has been involved in literally hundreds of experiments. At least Murray's concept of "thema" has proved its heuristic value! However, unless more research related to his general outlook is forthcoming, we do not expect interest in Murray's conception of personality to continue for long. Corsini (1977b, p. 410) reports that Murray is working on his theory, however, and a major publication might infuse new life into his system.

Sullivan's Interpersonal Theory

Harry Stack Sullivan (1892–1949) was first and foremost a psychiatrist, although his contribution to psychology through his personality theory is undeniable and he was also influential as a scientific statesman and educator. After receiving his M.D. from the Chicago College of Medicine and Surgery, Sullivan became a medical officer for the Federal Board for Vocational Education. He was later affiliated with the U.S. Public Health Service; with Saint Elizabeth's Hospital in Washington, D.C.; and with the University of Maryland medical school, where he conducted investigations of schizophrenia.

As a scientific statesman, Sullivan served as consultant for the Selective Service System and the UNESCO Tensions Project. He helped plan the International Congress of Mental Health. He also edited *Psychiatry,* a journal whose publication was stimulated mainly by the need to publicize Sullivan's theory.

Neuropsychiatrist William Alanson White exerted a permanent influence upon Sullivan, who later was president of the William Alanson White Foundation and founded and directed its training institution, the Washington School of Psychiatry. The influences of Sigmund Freud and Adolph Meyer are also discernible in Sullivan's theory. Sullivan published only one book in the area of personality theory, *Conceptions of modern psychiatry* (1947). After his death, he became much more influential; that is, five books based on his notes and recorded lectures have been published (1953, 1954, 1956, 1962, 1964).

The interpersonal theory of Sullivan is less exclusively analytic than that of Horney or Fromm. Although Sullivan acknowledged intellectual indebtedness to Freud, his theory bears a closer resemblance to Adler's. Much of Sullivan's thinking is related to that of thinkers who have a nonanalytic approach, for example, William Alanson White, Adolph Meyer, and George Herbert Mead. Moreover, Sullivan's closer relationship to psychiatry and to academicians (particularly social scientists) has resulted in a greater acceptance of his theory and may have something to do with its fuller statement (Sullivan, 1953); these features of his theory have, in turn, led to greater acceptance among clinicians.

Personality as defined by Sullivan (1953) is "the relatively enduring pattern of recurrent interpersonal situations which characterize human life" (p. 111). That is, it is regarded as an intervening variable inferred from an individual's behavior in relation to other people and objects. Personality exists only in interpersonal relationships. It follows that personality cannot be studied unless more than one person is interacting, although one of the persons need not be physically present; a person's interactions may be with an image, dream, fictional character, and the like. Sullivan has not entirely rejected the influences of heredity and biological factors; in fact, he has acknowledged their importance during infancy and at puberty. He proposed a hierarchy of physiological needs from which tension arises, which must be dissipated by satisfying the needs. However, he held that distinctively human characteristics are interpersonally developed and may directly affect the physiological needs.

Sullivan stated that three processes are evidenced in the development of the personality: dynamisms, personifications, and cognitive processes. A dynamism is a prolonged behavior pattern which is revealed in characteristic interpersonal relationships. Dynamisms may also be described as classes of habits or personality traits which characterize an individual; toward certain people an individual may display a dynamism of hostility or of friendliness, depending upon habitual behavior toward them. The self dynamism is the individual's self-image as perceived through social interactions.

Personifications are images that individuals hold of other people or of themselves. They are often products of an individual's infancy. If they remain intact so that they influence future opinion toward people, they are called *eidetic personifications.* An example of this might be a child's attitude toward a domineering father; this personification could influence responses toward other authority figures. However, when an image occurs solely in connection with a particular situation, only the word *personification* is used. A stereotype is any personification which is held by a group of people. It is interesting to note that these are in some ways a socialized and conscious version of Jung's archetypes.

Cognitive processes are subdivided into three classes: *prototaxic, parataxic,* and *syntaxic.* In the prototaxic mode, the individual simply experiences directly, without connecting the raw feelings or attaching meaning to them. It is not unlike what has been called a "stream of consciousness": all the thoughts, visions, ideas, sensations, and perceptions occurring at any given moment. This is followed by the parataxic mode, in which the individual connects experiences as they occur and regardless of their logical relations: casual relationships between nonrelated events and experiences. Logical connections are accomplished in the syntaxic mode by the use of *consensually validated* symbols. Consensual validation is a Sullivanian concept which refers to any symbol to which a particular meaning has become attached and agreed upon by a number of people. It is used chiefly for communication, and words are the most common example of such symbols.

Sullivan proposed six stages in the development of the individual. These are roughly delineated into age groups corresponding to maturational levels. However, the importance of maturation is limited in the degree to which it enables the individual to achieve a new and higher level of interpersonal relationships.

Sullivan noted that in personal development it is often apparent that certain entities are outside the individual's realm of awareness. Three major reasons may be posited for this: selective inattention, disassociation, and parataxic distortion. Selective inattention is merely the unwillingness to perceive in the immediate environment that which contradicts one's own beliefs. Disassociation is approximately what the Freudians refer to as *repression.* Parataxic distortion occurs when personal and autistic meanings, rather than the socially validated meanings, accrue to a symbol and influence an individual's thinking.

In sum, Sullivan held that individuals function because they need to secure satisfaction; their basic needs are not instinctual or biological, as Freud would have us believe, but are based on interactions with people.

Sullivan's theory did not attract much criticism. Several books on personality theory which discussed his theory contained none at all (e.g., C. S. Hall & Lindzey, 1970; Levy, 1970; Maddi, 1968). Past experiences with theories which escaped criticism should make the sophisticated reader suspicious; it is likely that such theories either say nothing testable, or that they say nothing particularly interesting. Certainly Sullivan's system contains no outlandishly salient features (such as penis envy) that invited criticism in alternative systems like Freud's. Sullivan also incorporated originally antagonistic views into his system, and that may have blunted criticism. However, we believe it is most likely that interest in

Sullivan's theory simply no longer runs high. There was never much of a program of empirical research connected with the theory, and there is no reason to expect that to change now that Sullivan has been dead for 30 years; he did not have a band of devoted followers to carry on his work, although there can be no question that many were influenced by him.

In summary, Sullivan helped to add the needed social dimension to the basically biological theory of Freud. He was also the only social psychological theorist of his day who extended the Freudian developmental stages beyond puberty. Like all other personality conceptions, Sullivan's had shortcomings in the areas of completeness and specificity. He was nevertheless a relatively comprehensive theorist who had significiant influence. His strength was that he could accommodate what Freud had been saying with what the socially oriented theorists had been saying. His influence will continue to be seen in the work of cognitively and socially oriented personality theorists. The probable fate of Sullivan's theory is poignantly expressed by Corsini (1977a) who listed his among theories regarded as worthwhile, but which could not be covered in the space available.

THE THIRD FORCE: MASLOW AND ROGERS

Abraham Maslow recognized two points of view which had been dominant as descriptions of the human being: the objective, behavioristic, mechanistic, and the orthodox Freudian psychoanalytic view. He then clustered a group of other viewpoints as a "third force" distinct from the first two in a number of ways. We shall capitalize and abbreviate Maslow's entity in this discussion as psychology's TF.

The TF was influenced by a number of previous lines of development. Maslow himself mentions Goldstein, Freud, and his own experimental training at the University of Wisconsin as important influences on him. However, the three streams most often mentioned as converging in TF psychology are humanism, phenomenology, and existentialism. We will therefore devote some attention to each of these three precursors before turning to a brief description of the contributions of our two examples of TF psychologists.

For the phenomenologists, the first question was the nature of human knowing. Thus their interests would be classified as fundamentally epistemological. Edmund Husserl (1859–1938) and his associate Martin Heidegger (1889–1976) found that human consciousness was critical to human knowing. Their philosophical development was an attack on the question of just how to approach the phenomena of consciousness so as to arrive at correct knowledge. The phenomenological method regards the phenomena of consciousness as beyond doubt; they may not give us correct information *about* anything, but as themselves these phenomena are not to be questioned.

From this description it should be clear that phenomenology derives from philosophy, and has a long historical development prior to Husserl. We have encountered Descartes and Kant, two philosophers who rested knowledge upon an experiential base, and Berkeley, who equated being and experience. Husserl was a student of both Brentano and Stumpf, and his phenomenology derives partially from their teaching. The contributions of Husserl and Heidegger involved the detailed working out of the methods and implications of phenomenology. We have already seen that Gestalt psychology was more phenomenological than the introspective psychology of Wundt and Titchener. The Gestaltists were using an approach compatible with Husserl's when they attempted to keep their study of experience free of preconceptions. Husserl wished to achieve purity in his description of phenomena through something called the *phenomenological reduction.* The reduction is supposed to require the observer to describe consciousness, rather than the external world. This sounds like a discussion of Titchener's stimulus error, but Husserl would of course shy away from any assumption that the contents of consciousness should be *analyzed.*

It has been doubted by many that Husserl's reduction could be attained; even Heidegger rejected it. There has been continuing discussion within the phenomenological tradition about precisely *how* phenomena were to be treated; but there has been agreement that phenomena *must* be treated. That is really all that is necessary for our present discussion.

Phenomenology shades over into existentialism. The existentialists are all phenomenologists, but the reverse is not true. The concern of the phenomenologist is with human knowledge, but the concern of the existentialist is with the implications of that knowledge for human action. Thus only those phenomenologists who follow the existentialists out beyond epistemology become existentialists.

Søren Kierkegaard (1813–1855) is usually mentioned as the pioneer developer of existential philosophy. He was deeply concerned with the problems posed by human existence, particularly with the conflict posed by the human desire for eternal life and awareness of one's own mortality. This led Kierkegaard to a consideration of existential dread, which has been a key concept for later existentialists.

The viewpoints of Kierkegaard and Husserl were combined and transformed by Heidegger. His seminal book *Being and time* (1962; originally *Sein und Zeit,* 1927) was instrumental in introducing existentialism to psychology and psychiatry (Misiak & Sexton, 1973). Heidegger suggests that human beings can achieve an "authentic" existence only after fully acknowledging the inevitability of their own death and return to nothingness.

Jean-Paul Sartre (1905–) is one of the most pessimistic of the existentialists, as well as perhaps the best-known. His examination of the meaning of human existence in *Being and nothingness* (1956; originally *L'Etre et le neant,* 1943) convinced him that there was no meaning. People are absurd, the world is absurd, and there is no God. People are, however, free to make choices; in fact, they are *condemned* to make choices, and in those choices they create themselves.

We should not leave the impression that existentialism is necessarily deeply pessimistic or atheistic. Presumably those who find pessimism in the phenomena will be pessimists, and those who do not will be otherwise. Maslow (1968) has spoken of yea-saying and nay-saying existentialists, and both varieties are certainly logical possibilities. So far, the existing specimens tend to be somewhat somber.

The third stream in the TF is humanism. Its tendency is to be as upbeat as existentialism is downbeat. Humanism has been an ancient and diffuse philosophy whose chief tenet is that the human being is the central concern in our universe. We will make no attempt to summarize its history as a movement. Humanism has recognized that human consciousness seems to be one of the human being's most distinguishing characteristics. Hence this third stream coalesces with the other two in focusing its attention on the phenomena of consciousness and their significance for people.

Maslow's Humanism

Abraham Maslow (1908–1970) was the person most responsible for turning the interests of psychology toward the Third Force, at least in the United States. He was trained as a research psychologist at Wisconsin under Harlow, and began his professional life as a behaviorist. Although he later abandoned behaviorism, he never abandoned many of the scientific attitudes inculcated during his training. He tried to expand the boundaries of science, but never suggested that the study of the human being could succeed without its help.

Maslow taught at Brooklyn College from 1937 until 1951, when he moved to Brandeis. He became a Resident Fellow at the W. Price Laughlin Foundation in Menlo Park, California in 1969 and died there in 1970.

The year 1954 was a critical one for Maslow and for the development of humanistic psychology. In that year he published *Motivation and personality,* a book in which he began to express his humanistic convictions to a large audience. He also wrote his first general outline of humanistic psychology, and sent it to the people on his mailing list; he corresponded regularly with a number of people who shared ideas similar to his.

In 1961 Maslow was instrumental in founding the *Journal of Humanistic Psychology,* and he served as one of its three editors. The American Association for Humanistic Psychology was founded the next year. In the year of Maslow's death, the American Psychological Association approved the formation of a Division of Humanistic Psychology, and the First International Conference on Humanistic Psychology met in Amsterdam. Without Maslow's leadership, probably none of these events would have happened when they did.

In some ways Maslow serves as a bridge between the old behavioral psychology and the "new" humanistic psychology. His concept of a hierarchy of motivation symbolizes this bridging function beautifully. Maslow thought that humans have a hierarchy of needs, beginning with physiological needs at the bottom and moving up to safety needs, then love and belonging needs, followed by esteem needs, and finally needs for self-actualization at the top. According to Maslow's account, higher needs do not take over until lower needs are satisfied. A hungry person, or one in severe pain, would not be concerned for safety until the dominating physiological need had been satisfied. Esteem would not be important until the need for love and belonging had been satisfied. Finally, self-actualization would not be a need—and hence self-actualizing behaviors would not occur—until all lower needs were under control.

Maslow derived his ideas from the study of superior individuals. He thought that prior theories had been weak because they had studied weak individuals. He decided to study superior people, not neurotics or psychotics, in order to form his conceptions of human potentialities. Maslow quickly found that many of his superior subjects reported "peak experiences," almost mystical moments which transcended their usual experiences and produced tremendous feelings of well-being.

We thus see Maslow's bridge between human biological and animal needs at the bottom and the peak experiences which accompany self-actualization at the top. There is no doubt, however, that Maslow's mature interests lay at the top of his pyramid of needs. The titles of his books tell us that: *Toward a psychology of being* (2d ed., 1968) and *The farther reaches of human nature* (1972). Maslow was a humanistic optimist who looked forward to the future and upward to human potentialities more than backward to the past and downward to the human's animal nature.

We can see clear evidence of similarities to phenomenology and existentialism in Maslow. He saw the nature of our experience as central. For him we are indeed free, but Maslow saw our freedom as a blessing that allowed us to self-actualize, not as a curse in a meaningless existential vacuum. The psychology of Maslow, like that of James before him, seems in tune with the American temperament. Perhaps it is also significant that modern existentialism, like the story of Hamlet, had its origin in Denmark. The optimists among us will be hoping that Maslow's optimism will defeat Kierkegaard's pessimism among proponents of our Third Force.

Rogers' Person-Centered Theory

At the 1977 convention of the American Psychological Association, four symposia were arranged to honor Carl Rogers (1902–   ) on the occasion of his seventy-fifth birthday. As reported in *Science* on October 7, Rogers, his daughter Natalie, and the other participants brought their chairs down on the floor with the audience, announced that they weren't giving their prepared papers, and proceeded to have an informal interchange with the audience. It terminated with a standing ovation and a singing of "Happy birthday." Such is the unconditional positive regard in which Rogers is held by his admirers.

It has not always been so. Rogers, like many other theorists in this chapter, came into the esteem of American psychologists somewhat by the back door. He was at first interested in scientific agriculture, which he encountered during his boyhood days on a farm (see Rogers, 1959, 1967a, for autobiographical information). Rogers subsequently attended the University of Wisconsin and Union Theological Seminary before terminating his education at Columbia Teachers College, where he took his Ph.D. and fell under the philosophical influence of John Dewey. Columbia also provided Rogers's first introduction to clinical psychology; he grew better acquainted with the field during his internship at the psychoanalytically oriented Institute for Child Guidance. While there he felt a definite conflict between psychoanalytic theory and the Thorndikian statistical influence which had prevailed at Columbia.

Rogers served as director of the Rochester Guidance Clinic, finding stimulation in the eclectic staff there. Their constant search for effective treatment was a problem Rogers turned to in *The clinical treatment of the problem child* (1939). He then shifted to academic psychology, teaching at Ohio State University, the University of Chicago, and the University of Wisconsin, but remained active in clinical activities. Rogers received the American Psychological Association's Distinguished Contribution Award in 1956. At Wisconsin, Rogers became progressively more disillusioned with what he thought were unduly stultifying rules imposed in the name of high standards by the psychology department. In 1963, he resigned from the department; in January, 1964, he joined the staff of the Western Behavioral Sciences Institute in San Diego, California, as a resident fellow; in 1968 he became a resident fellow at the Center for Studies of the Person in the same city.

The major stimulus for Rogers's personality theory came from his clinical therapeutic work, although he was strongly influenced by psychoanalyst Otto Rank. Rogers first advanced his views on personality in *Counseling and psychotherapy: Newer concepts in practice* (1942). That book was followed by his major theoretical work, *Client-centered therapy* (1951). He further explained his position in his chapter in Koch's *Psychology: A study of a science* (1959). Several of his more important papers were edited and collected in his *On becoming a person* (1961), and his most extensive research effort was published later (1976b). In a comprehensive textbook Rogers (1975) updated his ideas on client-centered psychotherapy in the chapter he contributed; and among many other recent publications is a summary of his latest thought (Holdstock & Rogers, 1977). As judged by his publications, Rogers is getting faster as he gets older.

A central feature of Rogers's theory is the belief that people are self-directive and self-actualizing. The therapy which Rogers developed is based on the assumption that patients have a self structure which they themselves must change if improvement is to occur. Rogers believes that his observations demand both this kind of therapy and a concept of self like the one he evolved.

To Rogers, the self is a structure compounded out of the experiences which individuals are able to attribute to their own bodies or to the results of their own behavior; the self, then, is a self-picture, or self-awareness. The experiences come with value tags attached; that is, some aspects of the self-picture are positive, while others are negative. The self regulates behavior, for behavior that is not consistent with the self-picture does not occur or is not fitted into the self-picture.

Though Rogers was at times subjected to psychoanalytic influences, he tends to reject the analytic emphasis on unconscious processes. He does recognize the possibility that self-inconsistent behaviors will occur as a result of unconscious influences, but he still feels that understanding of an individual can occur most easily if the therapist can enter the phenomenal field that appears to the patient. For Rogers, the consciousness of the individual contains most of what is needed for understanding his personality. Patients may, however, need to be helped to become more open to their own experiences. The encounter group has become one way of achieving this openness.

The self-picture is not supposed to be a static thing; although its structure has some stability, it can at times assimilate new experiences in such a way that the structure changes and the particular type of experience is subsequently experienced more easily. The threatened self is rigid and rejecting, but the secure self is fluid and tolerant. This single statement is the conceptual basis for Rogers's nondirective theraphy. Rogers's client-centered therapy has now been reconceptualized as a person-centered *approach* (Holdstock & Rogers, 1977), partially to emphasize its applicability outside, as well as inside, helping relationships.

There are three essential requirements for therapy conducted according to the person-centered approach. First, the therapist should have an accurate empathic understanding of the patient. Second, the therapist should truly care for, that is, have unconditional positive regard for, the patient. Third, the therapist must respond as a whole person, not just as a therapist, and behave in a fashion that is real, genuine, and congruent with feelings actually being experienced. There has been some disagreement about which of these three therapist attitudes is "really" the most important. Rogers has suggested that their relative importance depends upon the life situation of the patient, and his suggestion seems very plausible.

Person-centered therapy sets a situation in which patients can incorporate changes into their self structure because the self is never threatened and reports of experiences are at no time rejected or devalued by the therapist. Studies have shown that, in therapeutic circumstances, the patients' conceptions of themselves and their ideal selves came into closer agreement (Butler & Haigh, 1954; Rudikoff, 1954, pp. 85–98). Whether the change occurs in the self-picture as such or in the ideal self, the observed changes in therapy should be helpful. The individual's experiences would be more easily assimilated as long as the real self was accepted as a satisfactory structure in relation to the ideal. The self would be less threatened and more subject to adjustment as necessitated by life experiences.

Rogers, in the tradition of Goldstein and Maslow, believes that the unhampered human organism strives to actualize, enhance, and maintain itself. The possible lines of actualization are laid down by heredity, and the organism has, as a part of its native equipment, a creative urge. Human beings, however, cannot actualize themselves effectively unless they can symbolize their experiences and choose the path that leads to self-enhancement.

It is the failure to symbolize all experience which makes Rogers's distinction between the objective world and the world as perceived by the individual so important. Individuals respond to the world as they perceive it rather than directly to the objective world; thus it is essential for their adjustment that the two worlds be as similar as possible.

Carl Rogers is a clinician's clinician. He has spent much of his professional life in his role as therapist, and his theory could hardly be other than closely related to his therapy. We should not expect the theory to be simple, static, dogmatic, or complete. It is the opposite of all these. His theory is, and will be, inductive.

A surprising aspect of Rogers' theory is its strong emphasis upon conscious processes. Like Snygg and Combs (1949), he holds that the experienced world as available to the consciousness of the individual plays the dominant role in determining the individual's behavior. Rogers thus stands with Allport, among others, in stemming the psychoanalytic tide, which seems today to run less strongly toward the depths of the unconscious. That Rogers's views on the current status of psychoanalysis do not differ widely from ours is apparent from one of his statements describing a stay at the Center for Advanced Study in the Behavioral Sciences at Stanford:

> Another important influence was my contact with Erik Erikson, a splendid person whose very appearance is therapeutic, and several other psychoanalysts, foreign as well as American. From them I learned what I had strongly suspected—that psychoanalysis as a school of thought is dead—but that out of loyalty and other motives, none but the very brave analysts mention this fact as they go on to develop theories and ways of working very remote from, or entirely opposed to, the Freudian views. (1967a, p. 372)

Rogers differs from the psychoanalysts not only in that he assigns a small role to unconscious processes but also in that Rogers's self is a less differentiated entity than the psychoanalyst's mental apparatus. In fact, Rogers has been more concerned with personality *change* than with personality. It seems to us that he has contributed far more to therapeutic theory than to personality theory. Even when he discusses personality, his attention focuses on personality *development, breakdown,* or *functioning* (see Rogers, 1959, pp. 221–235), rather than on personality *structure.*

It is interesting to compare Rogers with Skinner, as we have compared him with Freud. Rogers and Skinner are usually regarded as being at opposite poles. American psychologists seem to regard getting Rogers and Skinner on the same symposium as better sport than baiting bears, and anyone who can succeed in setting up the game is assured of a huge audience and a lively time (see Rogers, 1956; Wann, 1964). Nevertheless, the contrast is in some respects overdrawn. Skinner himself says (quoted in Evans, 1968):

> The whole thing is a question of method. That's the crux of my argument with Carl Rogers; I'd like people to be approximately as Rogers wants them to be. I want independent people, and by that I mean people who don't have to be told when to act or who don't do things just because they've been told they're the right things to do. . . . We agree on our goals; we each want people to be free of the control exercised by others—free of the education they have had, so that they profit by it but are not bound by it, and so on. (pp. 67–68)

Rogers in turn says of Skinner's work:

> To avoid misunderstanding, let me say immediately that I concur with the idea that the theory of operant conditioning, its development and its implementation, has been

> a creative achievement. It is a valuable tool in the promotion of certain types of learning. I do not denigrate the contribution it has made. . . . Let me also say that I have a great personal respect for Fred Skinner. (Evans, 1975, p. 131)

Skinner and Rogers, despite many disagreements on *method,* have some common attitudes even in that area. Neither seeks to discover the details of the unconscious mental apparatus. Neither is greatly concerned to uncover the origins of the patient's symptoms in the past. Both would pay attention to current verbalizations, although the attitude toward the verbalizations would be different. Even some of Rogers's prescriptions can be translated into operant language, and the translation approved by Skinner. For example, Rogers, in outlining the necessary conditions for therapy, says a requirement is "That two persons are in *contact.*" Skinner could agree that only if the patient behaves in the presence of the therapist can the therapist effectively change the patient's behavior. Rogers: "The therapist is *experiencing unconditional positive regard* toward the client." Skinnerian translation: "An organism which is showing a behavior deficit may be encouraged to behave if free reinforcement follows every identifiable behavior emitted." Finally, both Skinner and Rogers are optimistic about the possibilities for improving the lot of humankind.

We have no desire to gloss over the divisions between Rogers and Skinner (and thereby to ruin psychology's favorite spectator sport), and we have no illusions that Skinner and Rogers will suddenly experience unconditional positive professional regard for each other. However, it is worthwhile to note their fundamental agreements as well as their equally fundamental disagreements.

The fact that Rogers has shied away from the postulation of complex inner structures has made his ideas more amenable to empirical attack than the ideas of some other personality theorists. C. S. Hall and Lindzey (1970, p. 538) report a rather amusing finding from Rogers's (1967b) extensive study of therapy with schizophrenics. Several rating scales were being applied to the therapeutic interaction, and their reliability was being evaluated. One scale was to measure "unconditional positive regard," one of Rogers's key constructs (see, for example, 1959): "Putting this in simpler terms, to feel unconditional positive regard toward another is to 'prize' him (to use Dewey's term, recently used in this sense by Butler)" (p. 208).

Unfortunately, there was a *negative* correlation between the therapists' evaluation of the therapeutic interaction and the evaluations by patients or by independent raters. This is embarrassing enough in its implications concerning a therapist's ability to judge whether a therapeutic relationship is worth saving, but it becomes even more embarrassing if the finding is attributed to unconscious defenses on the part of the therapists!

It is to the credit of Rogers and his theory that they can be embarrassed. Few theories of personality are explicit enough to be tested, and the exponents of those which are that explicit seldom test them. Rogers has tried.

Rogers has turned his attention largely to intensive group experiences with normal individuals, thus starting to explore yet another field. He is using the same phenomenological, existential approach that he was using before those labels came into American psychology. His concern with groups, like his earlier work, fits perfectly into the Third Force. Rogers, with Maslow, was a leader in the humanistic movement. With Maslow's death, Rogers became *the* leader. Near the end of his autobiography, Rogers says (1967a): "I want to have *impact.* I am not a person who is ambitious in the ordinary sense. . . . But it is important to me to have influence. I want what I do to *count,* to make a difference somewhere" (p. 380). Rogers has his wish. He counts. How high history will carry him now depends on the fate of our Third Force. It could be high indeed.

SUMMARY AND CONCLUSIONS

We have discussed five categories of personality theories: S-R theories (Miller and Dollard), trait and factor theories (Allport, Eysenck, and Cattell), organismic theories (Goldstein and Sheldon), Neoanalytic theories (Horney, Fromm, Murray, and Sullivan), and the Third Force (Maslow and Rogers). Salient characteristics of each of these types of theory have been examined.

Except for S-R theories, all of them are typical personality theories in that they focus on the organism. All are typical personality theories in the sense that Levy (1970) meant when he said that there really are no theories of personality; there are only *conceptions* of personality. We made a similar point when we characterized them as "points of view" (Marx & Hillix, 1973, p. 410). None of the supposed theories have achieved the completeness and specificity to qualify as a true *theory* of personality. However, most have completeness as a goal, and are intended to apply to the practical business of understanding and helping people.

Seventy-eight personality theories were included in what Corsini (1977b) described as his partial list. The list does not include Asian and Soviet conceptions, which are included in Corsini's own book. No doubt there are many other omissions; Shakespeare, Shaw, and Dostoevsky could have been included along with Sartre, who might very well have been included as an existentialist theorist. The point is that the criteria for having a theory of personality have been neither clear nor restrictive. Partially because of this, many of the earlier viewpoints drop from view as their creators age, become inactive, or die. Because conceptions of personality typically lack logical cohesiveness, ideas can be borrowed without borrowing the total conception. Thus it may be easier to borrow an idea from Adler and forget its source than to borrow one from Titchener, and forget how it fit into *its* original framework. In any case, there seems to be a fast turnover in personality theories, but some good ideas from each survive in slightly altered forms in new theories.

What will be the fates of the classes of theories we have discussed? We have already indicated our belief that psychoanalytic theory is of very questionable validity. The organismic and Third Force theorists have a good point of view in many respects, but their theories still lack a clear structure. The trait theories do not rest on a very secure empirical foundation, unless they are also factor theories. The S-R theories have a solid foundation, but they say very little about the person.

It is our guess now, as it was in 1973, that Cattell's theory is the one most likely to survive. It is carefully worked out and supported by "hard" data. It is reasonably comprehensive and flexible. It has not yet had enough input from the clinic and the therapy situation, but perhaps that will come.

As a general point of view, however, the Third Force is now most popular. That is partly because Maslow included so much when he characterized everything besides behaviorism and traditional psychoanalysis as part of his "third force." The Third Force is borrowing freely from all sources, including behavioristic psychology. One indication of this is that the American Humanist Association gave B. F. Skinner its "Humanist of the Year" award for 1972! That is one of the more hopeful signs of mutual understanding and appreciation that we have seen in our field.

Research related to limited problems continues in personality as in other fields. It may be that an entirely new theory, or even a new *type* of theory, will arise out of the dust of this empiricism. We are confident that future theories will continue to incorporate the work of the laboratory with the work of the clinic. Such rapprochement will signal the maturing of the scientific study of personality.

FURTHER READINGS

Hall and Lindzey's *Theories of personality* (1970) is still a very good general source. In the Corsini text, *Current personality theories* (1977b), the individual chapters are written by people who are very conversant with the theories they are treating; good examples are the chapter on Rogers, coauthored by Rogers himself, and the chapter on existential personality theory, coauthored by Maddi, who is not only the author of a general textbook in the field, but also an existential theorist in his own right. It is not surprising to find a book edited in this fashion accurate, but it is somewhat surprising to find it lucid. These two books provide an excellent overview, and their bibliographies contain hundreds of references. In the text, we have mentioned some of the most important sources of information about each individual theorist. Cattell and Dreger's *Handbook of modern personality theory* (1977) deserves special mention because it gives a comprehensive and very up-to-date picture of one line of development, but could not be suggested as a general reading for the nonspecialist. The easiest way to get a picture of almost contemporary research is to consult the latest volume of the *Annual Review of Psychology,* which has been published long enough now to be a historical source as well. For even later research, journals like the *Journal of Personality* or *Journal of Personality and Social Psychology* will give the student a foothold into the other journal literature.

Chapter 13

Engineering and Mathematical Influences on Psychology

Psychology has undergone many revolutions. Revolution in a science becomes more difficult as the body of established knowledge increases, and psychology is developing enough confidence in its own internal worth so that it can react more coolly to new developments in other fields of knowledge. Nevertheless, psychology has undergone, over the past 30-odd years, a change in its point of view because of a technical explosion in the field of engineering. In retrospect, we see the genesis of this change in the field of mathematics, with the first relevant development occurring over 100 years ago.

For the past few years, engineering has been increasingly concerned with the handling of information. In the more distant past, engineers were most interested in the production of devices whose chief output was work or heat or material. Today, engineers have turned their attention to devices that carry on humanlike activities, devices for data processing. Such devices are not entirely new, having developed over centuries from abacus to adding machine, but the scope of successes is now of a different order of magnitude. We must recognize that today is the age of automation, while yesterday was not. The names of computers become household words, with the Eniac overshadowed by the Illiac, the Illiac by the Univac, and it in its turn by the Cray-1. This latest giant among computers is so fast that the speed of light had to be carefully considered as a limiting factor in its design, and the longest wire in the machine was kept to 3.5 feet in length to minimize transmission times along the wires. Its compact design produces so much heat in a small volume that the whole computer is literally designed around its own refrigerator. Although no figures on its speed were given (*Science,* Jan. 27, 1978), it is said to be 5 times as fast as the next fastest supercomputer, and its basic operations must be measured in, at most, billionths of a second.

As we have become more familiar with the computer, our attitudes seem to have undergone a kind of splitting. Most of the time, the computer is regarded tolerantly as a convenience or a relatively mild threat to privacy or to the opportunity to cheat on income taxes. On the other hand, sometimes the popular imagination readily accepts projections of the controversy about the inherent goodness or evil of humans themselves into the computer. Thus the computer HAL in the movie *2001* becomes the incarnation of evil before its consciousness is taken away via the removal of a few critical panels. But one couldn't ask for nicer fellows than the robots of *Star Wars,* C3P0 and R2D2. Both good and evil computers are possible. They, like humans themselves, are flexible enough to take on the characteristics that their construction and programming dictate. Also like humans, they can be given the ability to construct the details of their own programming, with the potentialities for good and evil that we know exists in that possibility!

What has this to do with psychology? Perhaps a great deal, but we will discuss only some more limited aspects of the human being–computer relationship in this chapter. The center of our interest is in what the replacement or simulation of human function via the computer can tell us about human function. Trying to have a computer speak or recognize speech is likely to force us to learn more about how humans speak and recognize speech. If a computer is to be given a humanlike memory, we must understand what "humanlike" means. And indeed, recent progress in the fields of language and memory seems to be fast, and may be nearing the stage of very significant understanding. The comparative psychology of the human being and the machine is developing across the disciplinary line that divides psychology and engineering, just as the comparative psychology of human being and animal developed out of biology and psychology about a century ago.

This new comparative psychology is related to the use of mathematical models, but it is more than that. It is a very far cry from the hodological space of Lewin (see Chapter 11) to the computer program which recognizes digits as they are spoken to a sensing device. The really serious and practical consideration of how a human function can be performed mechanically lends interest, urgency, and precision to the task of describing the process. Engineers who want to automate a function force psychologists to recognize that they do not really know how the function is carried out. The actual testing of theory in devices gives an immediate knowledge of results which discourages fuzzy thinking. A computer also gives a theory a very thorough test. Its speed and "stupidity" combine to make it possible to test all the implications of almost any logical system programmed into it. Thus it is likely that a computer will examine conditions which a theorist will not think of, or will think irrelevant. Incompleteness and error may well be revealed in such a thorough examination.

Our emphasis on the speed and thoroughness of computers should not lead us to the conclusion that it is only the devices per se which are important for psychology. They are associated with a conceptual sharpening which attends the application of computers to the simulation of, replacement of, or improvement on, human functions. Further, computers are not just fast and thorough. With sophisticated programming, they become quite flexible. They remain, at the most basic level, mere "number crunchers"; but, on the surface, they become capable of complex performances and complex decisions that appear not to be mathematical at all. Thus in composing music, playing chess, or interpreting sentences in a natural language, the computer may appear to have transcended its fundamentally mathematical construction.

THE ROLE OF THE COMPUTER

There are two types of computers: analog and digital. The analog computer is designed to accept continuous variables as inputs and give outputs that are also continuous functions. The human being may behave like an analog computer in a number of respects; even the individual neural cells may show continuous variations over a range of values, rather than behaving strictly in an all-or-none manner. Nevertheless, there has been more general intellectual interest in digital computers, and our attention will be confined to them.

The digital computer is so named because its inputs and outputs can take on only digital values, with no fractional values between numbers. We can therefore specify exactly the range of numbers that can be represented in a register of a particular digital computer. A representative register might hold ten decimal digits. An overwhelming majority of digital computers are electronic. The electronic digital computer can be quickly adapted to new problems without gross physical changes; the programs, or sequences of instructions to be performed, are changed. The presence of a program of operation distinguishes computers from calculators. The human operator "instructs" a simple calculating machine, one instruction at a time, by hitting keys. The operator instructs a computer, many instructions at a time, by writing down a sequence of operations which the computer is to carry out. Then, once the computer starts, it proceeds through the whole programmed task without outside intervention. It is this independence from the human operator which allows the computer to be so fast, for example, to add 1,000,000 numbers per second. Any figures that are given on speeds achieved by computers quickly become too conservative; computers have been quadrupling their speeds every 5 years, and there is so far no indication that the curve is leveling off. It is no wonder that machines which perform such computational miracles capture the imagination.

It is not their speed, however, which makes computers of unique importance to psychology. Their speed makes them wonderful labor-saving devices and helps the psychologist, as it helps every other scientist. Data-reduction problems that would have taken years without a computer may take minutes with a computer, though writing the program may now take years. Problems that could not previously have been attacked can now be studied. However, this in itself would have no more theoretical significance than would the invention of an automatic cage-cleaning machine that made it possible to do more animal research. The fact that humans have created the computer in their own image makes the computer uniquely fascinating to the psychologist. A computer is humanlike, of course, in a functional rather than in a structural sense. We do not care whether the computer operates in a way which physically apes the human being, as long as the answers are "correct," that is, the same answers that a human would give to the same questions. This requires that the computer be the same as a human in some logical sense.

N. Wiener (1948) and Von Neumann (1958) pointed to a logical similarity between humans and computer even in the basic elements of their information-processing systems. That is, the classic view of the human neuron had it either responding completely or not responding at all (the "all-or-none" law), just as the computer element was either in one state or in another (usually called "on" versus "off" or "0" versus "1"). Physically, computer elements are larger, faster, fewer, and simpler—at the moment. La Brecque (1970) reports: "Today, microminiaturization has superceded miniaturization, and 100,000 integrated circuits can easily be placed on a single, half-dollar-sized silicon wafer . . . other research aims at developing even more tightly integrated devices, some nearly as compact as the bioelectric system of the human brain (p.8)." We should emphasize, however, that any physical similarity between computer elements and human neurons is unrelated to logical similarity, which is our main concern here.

Over a hundred years ago, George Boole (1854) developed an algebra which has turned out to be very useful in computer design. It is a two-valued logic, based on the notion that elements are either in or out of a set. This computer logic was developed by Boole as an expression of the laws of *human* thought; he had no intention of writing logic which would apply to *mechanized* thinking. Ironically, the symbols for *or, and, not,* etc., in Boole's algebra found their direct analogs in the "OR gate", "AND gate", etc., in the digital computer. Boole's algebra is, therefore, an abstract model which can be coordinated either with human or with machine decision processes.

Digital computers use a two-valued number system which is compatible with Boolean algebra and with the two-valued character of computer elements. This so-called binary (two-valued) number system is worth looking at because of its almost universal use in digital computers and because an understanding of binary numbers is necessary for an understanding of information measures. The binary equivalents for the decimal numbers are 0 = 0, 1 = 1, 10 = 2, 11 = 3, 100 = 4, 101 = 5, 110 = 6, 111 = 7, 1000 = 8, and 1001 = 9. It is clear that only one of two things can occur in a particular binary column, 0 or 1. It takes more space on paper to write a given number in binary notation than it does to write it in our familiar decimal notation. However, binary numbers can be represented physically with simpler, more reliable, and cheaper elements. Perhaps animal brains were designed with the same requirements in mind! Certainly nearly all current computers operate internally with binary numbers, although the computer user need not always be aware of that fact when interacting with the computer.

The digital computer is able to do complex things because complex, apparently nonmathematical operations can be broken down into millions of elementary operations that are expressible in Boolean algebra. Alternative inputs and alternative outputs (courses of action) can be numbered. Such numbers can be manipulated in any way desired, compared, and decisions made based on the outcomes of these manipulations. Thus an Internal Revenue Service computer could reject an income-tax return if its information about an individual's income did not agree with information on the return. A military computer could aim a gun at a point obtained by computing the path of a ship, airplane, or missile.

One of the authors vividly remembers one of his early encounters with the apparent intelligence of a computer. He was entering his version of a new program into a computer which already contained a program called a *compiler.* Compilers translate new programs from the language in which they are written into a language which the computer can use more directly. They check the new program for its adherence to certain rules before undertaking the translation.

In the case under consideration, the date of the computer run was supposed to be entered at the very beginning. It was not. When the run button was pushed, the lights blinked momentarily, and then the computer typed out, seemingly wearily, the query "Date?" on its automatic typewriter. Thus chastened, your programmer entered the date and again pushed the run button. The computer, following the dictates of its earlier program, examined the supposed new program which had been fed in and started revealing a stream of human errors, typing out indignant comments like "Undefined routine jumped to from Cell 27624." Several pages later the typewriter fell into a moody silence; one may imagine the computer waiting for a more intelligent programmer to give it a more reasonable program to compile.

After this exercise in projection (into the "indignant," "moody" computer), we hasten to say that the computer was not programmed to be either indignant or moody, and therefore we do not seriously propose that it experienced those emotions. A computer's sequence of operations is completely fixed by a set of operations prepared by a human computer programmer. Because of this, those with conservative viewpoints toward computer capabilities may maintain that computers are not capable of intelligent behavior, since they are merely slavishly following instructions.

One should not accept the conservative view too incautiously, since "what the computer is told to do" may be something like "learn to do this task better." For example, Samuel (1963) wrote a program instructing a computer how to play checkers and how to improve its game. After some practice, the computer played Robert W. Nealy, one of the country's strongest players. His comment, in part, was:

> Up to the 31st move, all of our play had been previously published, except where I evaded "the book" several times in a vain effort to throw the computer's timing off.

> At the 32-27 loser and onwards, all the play is original with us, so far as I have been able to find. It is very interesting to me to note that the computer had to make several star moves in order to get the win, and that I had several opportunities to draw otherwise. That is why I kept the game going. The machine, therefore, played a perfect ending without one misstep. In the matter of the end game, I have not had such competition from any human being since 1954, when I lost my last game. (Wooldridge, 1968, p. 105)

Wooldridge believes that such computer behavior is adequate evidence of intelligence. Readers can make their own decision as to the adequacy of the evidence. The evidence could, of course, be multiplied with examples of behaviors of other types—chess playing, musical composition, and the like—but the other examples exhibit essentially the same principles.

Some have suggested (e.g., Newell, Shaw, & Simon, 1958; Newell & Simon, 1961) that computer programs can constitute a theory of intelligent *human* behavior. However, there is a great danger in jumping to the conclusion that because a computer program operates in some particular way, so does the human being. The computer program is like the more traditional mathematical model in this sense; each may allow the correct prediction to be made, but neither is likely to describe how human beings accomplish what they do.

Without its program, the computer "knows" nothing. The human worker who is given inadequate or incomplete instructions may manage to muddle through somehow or may even fall back on previous knowledge or experience and do perfectly well. It is quite likely that neither worker nor instructor will be able to say precisely and completely how the job was done. It is because of this that the absolute literalness of the usual computer may be an advantage. If a computer is required to do a task with a program which is *in any way* incomplete, it simply cannot proceed. Imagine that some learning theorist is programming a computer to produce "behavior" that would be predicted from a theory. The theorist may discover that some of the thoughts involved are not sufficiently explicit to be written in the program, although until that time the theory had seemed perfectly clear. It may happen that, when the program runs, the results do not conform with empirical findings in several unusual cases which the theorist had previously not bothered to examine. In short, the stupidity of the unprogrammed computer demands complete foresight on the part of any person who wants the computer to do anything; no human taskmaster would be likely to exact such explicitness of statement. Yet the computer, once programmed, is so fast that it can afford to examine difficult conditions and is so rigid and thorough that it examines even those conditions which the human being would dismiss as "obviously" irrelevant for the purposes at hand (but which may turn out to be not only relevant but also critical).

The simulation of human functions is likely to lead the psychologist or engineer to take a particular series of steps. In any particular case, the series of steps is likely to be disjointed, unrelated, and undirected. It may be recognized only later, or perhaps never, that any simulation of human function was accomplished. However, if the process is self-conscious, the steps may occur as follows:

A function needs to be carried out—for example, the detection of a target on a radar display. Human being and device are regarded as substitutable for each other. The human is observed as the task is performed; the behavior involved is described precisely. A new program is written or a new device constructed, or both. The behavior of the new "robot" may then be compared with human behavior.

Each of the steps in this process is likely to be interesting and instructive for the science of psychology. The precise description, however, may well be the most useful. Often improvements in the description will be forced by failures in the attempted simulation. For example, attempts to program computers to understand language using an S-R approach or transformational grammars have failed persistently. Winograd (1972) solved a version of this problem by giving the computer a detailed model of the particular "world" about which the computer was to talk. His experience in simulation focuses our attention upon the way our own understanding of language depends upon extralinguistic considerations, specifically upon our ability to understand in some other way the world to which the language refers. This will in turn force us to consider how we can have a "world model" which is not expressed in ordinary linguistic terms. In this way, our thinking about ourselves is forced through a series of elaborations and clarifications.

An increasing range of human functions can be performed by inanimate devices. The more complex functions are carried out less well; we have seen that computers can play checkers (a relatively simple game) at an extremely high level of competence. Chess, which is more complex, is played less well; Simon (1970) says: "No program yet plays expert, or even Class A, chess, but Greenblatt's program, perhaps the strongest in the field today, has won a Class C American Chess Federation rating on the basis of its performance in tournaments (against humans). This would place it, I am confident, well above the median strength of *Science*-reading chess players" (pp. 630–631).

How far can computer simulation be carried? There are two kinds of answers that can be given to this question. The first, empirical, answer is "Wait and see." Extrapolating from the first 30 years, one would guess that the trend is going quite a way, until eventually it will include expert chess, good translation of natural languages, etc. Ten years ago the first flush of enthusiasm about translators had been dashed by the initial failures, and it appeared that success, if it ever came, would be in the distant future. Now, however, we would guess that good machine translations will be routinely carried out within the reasonably foreseeable future.

The second kind of answer to "How far can it go?" is a logical one derived from mathematical and logical reasoning. There are three key logical findings which have an important bearing on the extent to which a machine may be expected to simulate a man. The first finding was by Turing (1937; see Arbib, 1964, for a discussion of this "second kind of answer"). To put it very crudely, what Turing showed was that *any* well-defined input-output relationship can be simulated by a simple type of machine (which came, of course, to be called a

Turing machine). Thus any findings of S-R psychology could be simulated by a machine if those "findings" were in the form of well-defined S-R relationships. The second discovery was by McCulloch and Pitts (1943), who showed that the functions of a digital computer could be carried out by a nerve net, and vice versa. Thus it is reasonable to suppose that the logic of operation of the human nervous system can be simulated exactly by a computer. The third finding was by Kurt Gödel in 1931 (see Arbib, 1964, for an account in English). He proved a characteristic of formal systems which Arbib (1964) summarizes as follows: "His theorem states that *any* adequate consistent arithmetical logic is incomplete, i.e., there exist true statements about the integers which cannot be proved within such a logic" (pp. 122–123). Gödel's theorem has been used to argue that there are limits on the extent to which human thought can be simulated by computers. The argument goes something like this: Digital computers are logical machines. As such, they are covered by Gödel's theorem. Human beings are not logical machines; hence they are not covered and thus not limited. Thus machines cannot completely simulate man.

We disagree that Gödel's theorem applies to computers but not to humans. The theorem says nothing about how the logical system is represented—whether by transistors or by neurons, for example—and thus seems to have no force limiting the extent of simulation. In any case, we, in keeping with the usual scientific practice, are far more impressed by empirical demonstrations of ability to simulate human behavior than by deductive proofs that simulation is or is not likely to be possible.

There is no indication that the computer is losing its fascination as a model for the human being. George's *The brain as a computer* (1973) is one of many recent books exploring one or another facet of the computer model. Pask (1975) concentrates on learning and performance, but is in the same tradition. Hilgard and Bower (1975) continue their practice, begun in 1966, of including a chapter on information-processing models in their standard text on theories of learning.

In considering limitations on simulation, it is difficult to ignore the one final question: Can computers be conscious? Psychologists seem mostly to have ignored this question, perhaps as too redolent of the philosophical tradition from which we see ourselves as emancipated. However, for those who find it meaningful, there is hardly a larger question. Scriven (1963) decided that the question was meaningful, and the answer, yes. His solution to deciding whether or not a computer was conscious sounds simple. Just teach it to understand the question: "Are you conscious?" and ask the question. If the computer says yes, take its word for it.

A computer programmer would probably like to know a few more details before starting to write a program enabling a computer to understand the question. We would prefer a somewhat different approach. Progress in science has usually depended upon breaking down questions into smaller parts. We would begin by asking, "What are the properties of entities that we call conscious?" The answers include contact with the outside world, possession of an inner model of that world, ability to communicate, possession of a model of the self, ability to initiate behavior, and understanding of various relationships between self, others, and the outside world. This is probably not an exhaustive list, and better analyses no doubt exist. However, an entity possessing these properties might be conscious or close to it. To our knowledge, nobody is trying to create a conscious computer. The usual science-fiction script has one coming into being accidentally. That could well happen, but it seems likelier to occur as a result of malice aforethought (advance planning?). A nice new group of ethical questions will be introduced with the first conscious computer. Will it be alive? Only when it is conscious? What rights will it have? Should it be given the ability to replicate itself? We can envision the first philosopher-computers speculating in their existential voids, and the first computeristic computers optimistically striving to actualize their potentialities—which, according to present indications, may be great indeed. All of this will happen if consciousness is simply a matter of a logical interrelationship between parts. If consciousness is a matter of the physical constituents of which entities are made, then computers will never be conscious until they are constructed of protoplasm, or are living, or until consciousness is poured onto them, like the icing on a cake.

It is time to return to two presently formulated approaches which are related to engineering and psychology. The first is information theory (see Attneave, 1959; Garner, 1974). The second is detection theory (Green & Swets, 1974; Egan, 1975). In this chapter we will look at each theory in broad perspective.

Both these theories grew in intimate association with engineering problems. Shannon (1951) did his work on information theory at Bell Telephone Laboratories, and no doubt much of the impetus for his work came from the desire of Bell Telephone to develop better devices for the transmission of information. Detection theory has emanated in large part from the Electronic Defense Group at the University of Michigan, and devices for detection are certainly desired products of this group. To date, a human being is likely to be a part of such a detection device.

INFORMATION THEORY

Information Measures

According to Norbert Wiener, no one person can be credited with the development of a measure of information (1948): "This idea occurred at about the same time to several writers, among them the statistician R. A. Fisher, Dr. Shannon of the Bell Telephone Laboratories, and the author" (p. 18). However, Shannon has worked most persistently on the theoretical development of information theory and has most widely disseminated information theory through his publication of both theory and data (e.g., Shannon, 1951; Shannon & Weaver, 1949). We may therefore give Shannon the primary credit.

The argument that underlies the definition of an information measure can be presented rather simply as long as we remain content with an approximate and intuitive treatment. Shannon was, as we have said, concerned with actual communication systems, containing at least a transmitter, communication channel, and receiver. What was desired was a measure of the capacity of channels to carry information. Shannon described one such measure.

First, assume that only a limited number of alternatives can be communicated via any communication system. For example, assume an English-speaking radio announcer is transmitting messages from a set of one-word messages limited to the words of the English language. What the announcer does in speaking is to choose from all the possible words a single word to transmit. Until the word is spoken, a person at the receiver is uncertain what word will be spoken, but does know that one of the set of English words will be chosen. The process of information transmission can be regarded as a process of reducing uncertainty. If there is no uncertainty remaining after a message is sent and received, then the amount of information transmitted is the same as the amount of uncertainty that existed initially. It seems reasonable to make the amount of uncertainty proportional to the number of possible messages that might conceivably be sent; the more alternatives there are, the harder it would be to guess which would be sent.

Shannon noted that it would be possible to number all the alternatives using the binary number system. If there were sixty-four alternative messages, any of which might be sent, we would number them in binary notation from 000000, through 000001, etc., to 111111. A six-place binary number is needed to cover the alternatives that would be coded by decimal 00 through 63.

If we have N columns of binary numbers, we can designate 2^N different alternatives. In the present case, $2^6 = 2 \times 2 \times 2 \times 2 \times 2 \times 2 = 64$. Shannon lets the number of columns of binary digits required to number the alternative messages equal the number of units of information. These units of information are called *bits,* an abbreviation for *bi*nary dig*its*. If you are told which of sixty-four possible alternatives is true, you have received six bits of information.

Let us recall how this measure of information relates to logarithms. In the case we just examined, 6 is the *logarithm* of 64, since we took 2 as the *base* for the logarithm. That is, a logarithm is the *power* to which we raise some base in order to obtain the number in question. We can write in the conventional mathematical notation $\log_2 64 = 6$; that is, the logarithm to the base 2 of 64 equals 6. We can, therefore, find the number of bits involved in selecting one of a set of equally probable alternatives by taking the logarithm to the base 2 of the number of alternatives. The number of bits is usually symbolized by H, and thus we can write $H = \log_2 N$.

The use of the simple definition of the number of bits, $H = \log_2 N$, is justified only if every message in the set of alternative messages is equally likely to occur. It seems intuitively obvious that the occurrence of unlikely events is more informative than the occurrence of very probable events. Thus, "man bites dog" is newsworthy, while "dog bites man" is not. The difference in information content as a function of the probability of occurrence of a particular alternative is considered in the more general formula, $H = \log_2 1/P$, where P is the probability that the message would have occurred. If an honest die comes up 4, the occurrence of this event transmits $\log_2 1/\frac{1}{6}$ bits $= \log_2 6$ bits $= 2.58$ bits. If the die is heavily loaded, the occurrence of a 4 may transmit almost no information.

A die that always comes up 4 transmits $\log_2 1/1 = 0$ bits of information when it turns up 4.

On the morning before these words were written, one of us tested the notion that very low probability messages require large amounts of information in order to be transmitted. Upon arising, he lay down on the bedroom floor to do his usual few morning situps, normally an occasion only for a few grunts. However, as his wife walked past, he said quite slowly and distinctly, "A lion on a bicycle just delivered the newspaper." His wife stopped, turned, and, failing as anticipated to receive the message, said, "What?" He repeated even more slowly and clearly, with no other change of expression, "A lion on a bicycle just delivered the newspaper." This time a look of suppressed consternation crossed her face, and she said, "Why! What do you mean?" A message had apparently been received, but it was still not the one contained in the words. She had more probably received the message, "My husband has gone all the way over at last." In this particular instance, the real message was, "He's trying out one of his hypotheses again."

Often the occurrence of a sequence of messages may present problems very similar to a gradual transition from a situation like throwing a fair die to one like throwing a loaded die; that is, the occurrence of a particular message in the first position may change the probabilities in the next position and so on through the whole series of messages. Language is an excellent example of this kind of relationship between the messages in a sequence. In English, the letter *T* is very likely to be followed by an *H* and not at all likely to be followed by an *L*. The effect of 100 letters on the 101st is so great that the 101st carries somewhere between 0.6 and 1.3 bits of independent information (it is not practical to make exact determinations). If every letter were equally probable, the occurrence of a letter or space at position 101 would carry $\log_2 27 = 4.76$ bits. It is clear, then, that a given amount of information transmitted via the English language is shared among many symbols. To put it another way, each symbol really carries *less* than the maximum information which it would be capable of carrying.

Systems of this kind are called *redundant,* and English would seem to be about three-fourths redundant. Redundancy is not all bad; if the information transmitted is shared among words, the *information* may be available even though part of the message is missed. For example, the blank in *psychol gy* can easily be filled in with an *o,* for the remaining letters give us sufficient information, and in effect we still have the whole message. If we reflect on the frequency with which children respond with "Huh?" to an attempt at communication, we shall no doubt be grateful for all the redundancy English contains. Children's difficulties probably come from a lack of well-learned alternatives from which they can select the message intended. It is seldom a problem in hearing, but hearing is not the same as understanding the message.

Empirical Studies

With this brief background, we can look at the psychological application of information measures and of the point of view afforded by information theory.

We can ask how great the human channel capacity is, and some answers have been given. Pierce and Karlin (1957) have reported one of the highest rates of continuous transmission. They had subjects read words aloud as rapidly as possible from a fixed vocabulary. The sequences of words were random; thus it was easy to calculate the amount of information involved in reading words, and information was not lost to the usual sequential effects. About 45 bits per second were transmitted.

For a time it seemed that the rate of information transmission of the human channel might be almost independent of the nature of the transmission task, but it now appears that this is far from true. In reading words the information rate equals information per word times words per unit of time. Since information per word equals $\log_2$ (vocabulary size), larger vocabularies would have to be read more slowly than small vocabularies if the information-transmission rate were to remain constant. However, Pierce and Karlin—and, earlier, Sumby and Pollack (1954)—found that reading speed does not decrease markedly with increases in the size of the vocabulary. For a fixed number of syllables per word, the transmission rate in bits increases almost as fast as the logarithm of vocabulary size.

In the reading task, subjects transmitted information continuously. It is also possible to have subjects observe a single brief presentation of a stimulus and then have them respond at leisure to what was observed. Here the measure is a measure of a kind of "absorption" rate rather than of what we would intuitively feel should be called a "transmission" rate. It may be considered a measure of the channel capacity of the sensory channel involved. G. A. Miller (1956) has reviewed the evidence from a number of studies of human abilities to discriminate between stimuli varying along some single dimension. Judgments of pitch, loudness, pointer position, and square size are examples of the tasks involved. Surprisingly, the number of values of stimuli which can be discriminated accurately is small, Miller's "seven plus or minus two"! This number is much smaller than the number of just-noticeable differences along these scales. The subject's task is very different in the situation Miller is discussing and in the situation where just-noticeable differences are being determined. In the latter case, a reference is presented so that the subject need only discern a difference. In studying information transmission, the subject is required to state which of several alternatives was presented; no reference is present and an "absolute" discrimination must be made. Very surprisingly, the number of absolutely discriminable values is insensitive to the spacing along the scale of the chosen values, at least to a considerable extent (Attneave, 1959, pp. 67ff.). Garner (1960) has indicated, however, that more information is transmitted by rating scales which use larger numbers of values; the total information transmitted may increase with the number of scale values up to 20.

Several experiments (Klemmer & Frick, 1953; Pollack & Ficks, 1953; Pollack & Klemmer, 1954) indicate that increasing the number of stimulus dimensions increases the number of bits that can be assimilated at a single observation. Klemmer and Frick, for example, got a transmission value for eight-dimensional stimuli of 7.8 bits, as compared with a value for single-dimensional stimuli of about 3 bits. Quastler, Osborne, and Tweedell (1955) investigated the best combination of number of scales and number of divisions and found that five or six scales, each divided into five or six scale positions, could be arranged to transmit 12 bits per look. Using three symbols in conjunction with a dial increased transmission to 17.6 bits.

MacKay (1952, 1969) made a distinction between two kinds of information content of stimuli which is useful in talking about this set of results. He called the information carried by the different values along a single scale the *metron content,* and the information carried by the different dimensions the *logon content.* It appears that the useful metron content, then, is limited to about eight values, and additional information can best be carried by increasing the logon content.

Information measures are useful in the study of memory as well as in the study of human information transmission. For example, Pollack (1954) found that immediate memory span is approximately constant at about seven units whether the units are binary numbers containing only 1 bit of information per digit, decimal numbers containing $\log_2 10 = 3.32$ bits, or letters of the alphabet containing 4.76 bits. It occurred to S. K. Smith and Miller (1952) that the information span might be increased for the smaller units if they were coded into units containing more information; then the larger units would be remembered and decoded back into the smaller units as they were reproduced. Binary digits could easily be coded three at a time as follows: 000=0; 001=1; 010=2; 011=3; 100=4; 101=5; 110=6; and 111=7. The code would then be remembered and finally reconverted into binary digits upon demand. For example, the stimulus digits 111011100010001 would be converted to 73421, which would be remembered easily. If the conversion-reconversion process were perfectly efficient, the memory span for binary digits would be increased threefold. Empirically, the improvement is not quite that marked.

Information measures have found further application in the description of the perceptual process. Attneave (1954) and Hochberg and McAlister (1953) pointed out the applicability of information measures to Gestalt concepts. For example, they noted that good figures contain less information. It is easier to predict the continuation of a line from a knowledge of previous portions of the line in a good figure than in a poor one. One can fill in a circle from a knowledge of any short arc, or a triangle from a knowledge of its three corners. Such figures are highly organized, redundant, and good. Similar informational descriptions can be given for many other Gestalt principles of organization. Information measures are more precise as measures of organization and accordingly should help to bring the heretofore qualitative Gestalt principles more fully into the province of quantitative psychology.

Garner (1962) discusses some of the difficulties in making a translation of Gestalt concepts into information terms; the problem arises because the Gestalt principles are supposed to apply to *single* stimuli, whereas information concepts are designed to apply to the characteristics of sets of stimuli. Later, Garner (1966) made a persuasive case for regarding stimuli as representatives of members of a class. He regarded perceiving as analogous to knowing the structure and organization of *sets* of stimuli. His series of experiments provides an excellent example of the usefulness of the viewpoint provided by information theory, even though very little of the technical apparatus of the theory was used.

Posner (1964) is among those who have made extensive use of the information-processing view of human behavior. He suggests, for example, that such tasks can usefully be categorized as conservation tasks (in which the goal is to transmit information exactly as it is received, as in memory tasks), reduction tasks (as in addition of numbers, in which the goal is to map multiple stimuli into a single response), and creation tasks (in which the goal is to make multiple responses to a single stimulus, as in multiple associations). Posner finds predictable empirical relationships between the amount of information transformation required and the adequacy of behavior; for example, reaction time increases as the amount of information reduction increases. Fitts and Posner (1967) organized their book, *Human performance,* largely around the information model.

Neisser (1964) has conducted a series of studies of the process of searching for target words, numbers, faces, and the like in a background of similar items. He finds that the search process does not demand that all the information be processed fully and that different tasks may require several different levels of information analysis, from extremely gross to extremely careful. This conclusion can be reached because of the extremely different rates of examination of information under different conditions. One of Neisser's more interesting and counterintuitive findings is that experienced scanners can search for multiple targets as quickly as they can search for single targets. For example, an experienced searcher can search a list for one of four names as quickly as for a single name.

Sternberg (1966) has developed an ingenious technique for studying the process of scanning *memory,* rather than external stimuli. A subject, having memorized a sequence of symbols, is asked to give a "yes" response if a newly presented symbol was in the remembered sequence and to give a "no" response if it was not. Subjects are required to respond as quickly as possible. The time required for responding is an apparently linear increasing function of the number of items held in memory, and it is the same whether the symbol is present in the remembered set or absent from it. Sternberg concludes that the search process consists of serial comparisons between the "new" item and those held in memory and that the search is exhaustive even though a match is found.

Townsend (1974) has extended Sternberg's work, and paid special attention to the interesting claim that the processing in short-term memory was serial and exhaustive. Townsend concluded that a large class of serial and self-terminating models could indeed be eliminated, but it is too soon at this point to be sure of any single model. Serial and parallel models can produce identical predicted performances with some parameter settings.

The foregoing has been a brief summary of some of the early work using information measures and concepts. We have ignored such important problems as the determination of the amount of information transmitted when the transmitter and receiver are not always in agreement. Attneave (1959) and many others who have written books devoted to information theory give methods for calculating transmitted information from a knowledge of the inputs, outputs, and their relationships. We cannot deal with these more technical problems here, but we hope that the diversity of areas in which information theory plays a part has been indicated.

The strength of information theory is that its measure does not specify in any way whatever the nature of the message. It can be applied to things as different as binary digits, musical notes, and hormone flow from one part of the body to another. The generality is based on the simple but ingenious insight that any finite set of alternatives can be coded by numbering the alternatives. This same possibility is the basis for the variety of abilities which a digital computer can display. The generality of information theory makes it a very useful device for unifying the points of view of different sciences, for example, psychology and biology. One could ask, for example, whether the quantity of information which could be stored in a given number of RNA molecules is sufficient to represent a picture of a given size to a given resolution. Before information measures were available, such a question would have been considered nonsense.

During its formative years, information theory was regarded as a tremendously exciting development, perhaps one which would revolutionize psychology. It is now regarded as one of our basic mathematical tools, like algebra or calculus. It is clear from our discussion that we believe information theory has proved its worth and will have a useful future. Further, we believe that near-paradigmatic status is being achieved by those psychologists who are organizing their activities around computers and information theory, just as it is by those subsumed under the umbrella of "behavior modification." Psychologists in both groups have achieved the ability to solve a significant class of problems, and both groups are attracting adherents because of the apparent promise of their respective *approaches* to problem solving. We are more confident that the apparent paradigm of the behavior modifiers is a *psychological* paradigm, but linguists and cognitive theorists might not agree with us on this point.

DETECTION THEORY

During World War II, engineers developed a theory of detection which would apply to the detection of targets by radar receivers. Tanner and Swets (1953, 1954) and M. Smith and Wilson (1953) took over the mathematical treatment and applied it to human detection. These theorists and many others have since extended the theory.

Egan (1975) describes signal detection theory (SDT) as a combination of decision theory and distribution theory. We will describe a little of the decision theory aspect of SDT, and just touch on the distribution theory aspect, in an attempt to indicate the power and range of the theory.

SDT thus involves statistical decision theory. A detection involves a decision based on statistical considerations rather than a simple statement of the form, "Yes, I heard the signal," or "No, I did not hear the signal." Detection theory regards the experiment which attempts to determine a sensory threshold as a game between subject and experimenter. According to this view, the subject would always claim to have heard the signal, having heard it or not, if it were known in advance that it would be presented. This does not mean that subjects should simply be regarded as dishonest; it means that there is no sharp division between detecting and not detecting a signal, and the subject must therefore always make a decision based on probabilistic rather than on certain information. Subjects should make the best decision possible based on the information available, whatever the source of the information.

Since decisions must be based on probabilistic rather than on certain information, they are often influenced by the values or costs that may be associated with making them and being right or wrong in the decision. The values and costs associated with being right or wrong about each possible decision determine a *payoff matrix*. If there are only two possible decisions—for example, "Yes, a signal was presented," or "No, a signal was not presented"—the payoff matrix will have only four entries. An example is given in Table 13-1. According to the matrix, the subject gains 10 units (say, 10 cents) for saying the signal was presented when it was, but loses 5 units (5 cents) for saying it was not when it was. An incorrect decision when a signal was not presented entails a 1-cent loss, but a 1-cent gain results from a correct decision. It is intuitively clear that, given this payoff matrix, cases where the probability that a signal was presented is about equal to the probability that no signal was presented should be resolved in favor of signal. More will be gained if this turns out to be right than will be lost if it is wrong; putting it another way, more can be gained by saying "yes" correctly than by saying "no" correctly.

If at first this theory seems not to apply to real-life situations, consider some interesting examples of decision making under uncertain conditions, where values and costs are obviously involved.

Case 1 You are at a party, and you think you detect a possible sign of interest on the part of an attractive person of the opposite sex. The circumstances are such that there will be appreciable embarrassment if you are mistaken.

Case 2 Your wife thinks she hears a burglar downstairs. You do not think it is a burglar. Could you be looking at different value-cost matrices?

Case 3 An airline pilot on his landing approach glimpses something ahead through the haze of wispy clouds. Evasive action will frighten passengers and crew and strew carry-on baggage all around the cabin.

Table 13-1 Payoff Matrix for Detection Experiment

	Subject's decision	
Signal presented?	yes	no
Yes	10	-5
No	-1	1

Another factor combines with the payoff matrix in biasing decisions. This is the advance, or a priori, probability that a signal will be presented. Again our intuition tells us that if we know in advance that signals will be presented in nine intervals out of ten, we should say "signal presented" in uncertain cases. The a priori probability, in conjunction with the payoff matrix, determines a criterion—a number—usually called *beta,* with which a number derived from the sensory observation should be compared in order to make the best decision. If the number derived from the sensory input exceeds the criterion, the ideal observer says "signal"; if it does not, the ideal observer says "no signal."

The criterion value is chosen so that some function is maximized. It is assumed that the ideal observer wishes to make decisions such that the greatest gain will be obtained, the most correct decisions made, or some other desirable goal achieved. W. W. Peterson, Birdsall, and Fox (1954) have discussed possible goals and have developed for each the equations which combine the a priori probabilities and payoff matrix to determine the optimum criterion value.

Two probabilities must be computed in order to derive the most useful number from the sensory observation. The first is the probability that *if* a signal had been presented, the observed sensory input would have occurred. The second is the probability that the observed sensory input would have occurred if no signal had been presented. The first probability is then divided by the second to form the *likelihood ratio.* This likelihood ratio is compared with the criterion in order to reach an optimal decision, as outlined above. It can be shown that the likelihood ratio contains all the information an observer needs to make an optimal decision. This fact vastly simplifies the decision process, as compared, say, with the necessity to remember exactly what the detailed signal was.

The reader may be wondering at this point what sense it can possibly make to consider the probability that a sensory input would occur if no signal were presented. Such a probability becomes reasonable on the assumption that there is always random stimulation, or noise, present in any sensory system. The name generally given to a sensory system within detection theory is *receiver.* As far as a receiver is concerned, there are two kinds of noise. One comes from the outside world, and the other from the receiver's own workings. In case the receiver is a human observer, the internal noise is usually called *neural* noise. Such internal noises can never be completely eliminated, even if it were possible to eliminate completely noise at the receiver input. The origin of the noise, as far as the performance of the detector is concerned, is irrelevant. Any noise will degrade the performance of the system. Most people have had the experience of hearing unearthly noises emanating from the television set, to which they respond, "Was that the set [internal noise] or the station [external noise]?" The reader by this time should also have noted the possibility that the "unearthly noise" might have been produced by, say, a rock music group—which gives us all the elements for a detection problem, if it is assumed that rock music groups produce signals.

The determination of the necessary probabilities for the computation of a likelihood ratio is not a trivial accomplishment. It is this determination which distinguishes detection theory from decision theory in general. This is where distribution theory comes into the picture. One must determine the nature of the distributions from which the likelihood ratio is to be determined. One basic difficulty in associating a likelihood ratio with a sensory input is that inputs may be given as continuous wave forms, while statistical decision theory is intended to work with discrete numerical measurements. If the wave form has certain properties, it can be characterized, without loss of information, by a limited number of measurements. The number of measurements required depends on the highest frequency present in the wave form (W) and the length of time (T) over which the wave form is to be measured; the number of measurements required is exactly $2WT$. Still other difficulties have to be overcome before the signal and noise can meaningfully be compared; the reader who is interested in the details of this problem may consult Licklider (1959). Green and Swets (1974) also treat this problem, as well as other psychologically relevant aspects of detection theory, in their excellent book.

Figure 13-1 is a general block diagram of the ideal observer as visualized in detection theory. Let us now examine an experimental situation in conjunction with this block diagram in order to get a clearer idea of how detection theorists think about signal detection.

Two general types of situations usually are treated. An observer must say either whether or not a signal was presented within a single fixed time interval, or which of several specified intervals contained a signal, knowing that one of them did. It is simpler to talk about the former situation, although it is easier to relate the theory to the latter. In the multiple-interval case, the subject's best strategy is just to choose the interval containing the sensory event with the largest likelihood ratio; the a priori probabilities, the payoff matrix, and hence the criterion are the same for all the intervals. Subject errors in assessing or combining the criterion factors therefore do not affect the decision.

In the other case, in which the subject must say whether or not a signal occurred in a single interval, a number of types of errors may occur. The subject might not use the correct a priori probabilities, might not use the correct payoff matrix, might not try to maximize the desired quantity, or might not combine the

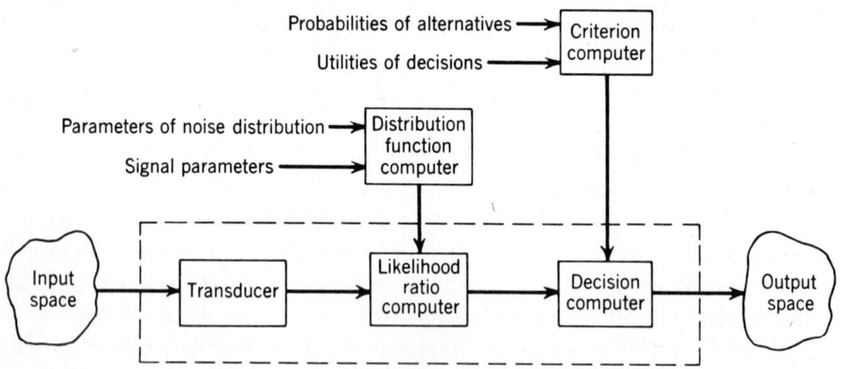

Figure 13-1 Block diagram of ideal observer in detection theory. (*Source:* Tanner, 1961.)

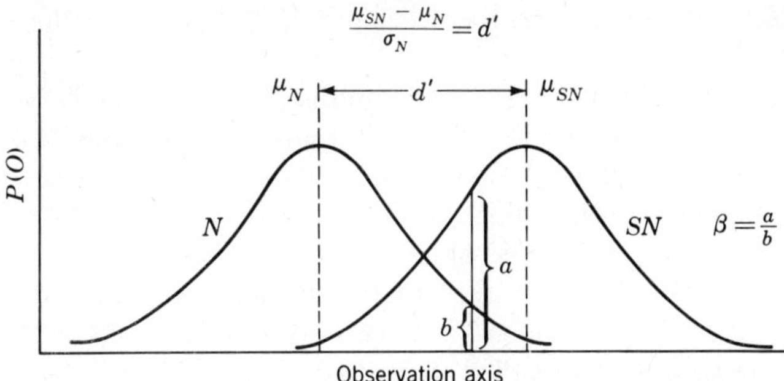

Figure 13-2 A visualization of some concepts of the theory of signal detectability. See text for explanation.

factors correctly to do so. In addition, subjects under either condition may not compute the likelihood ratio correctly.

We shall consider the block diagram as it relates to the single-interval case. It is simplest to assume that the distribution-function computer is given the signal-plus-noise and the noise-alone distributions so that these need not be computed from experience. The distributions must be available so that the likelihood ratio can be computed from its two component probabilities. The signal-plus-noise distribution gives the probability that any given observation would occur on a signal trial. The noise-alone distribution gives the probability that any given observation would arise on a noise-alone trial.

The a priori probabilities that signal plus noise, or noise alone, will be presented on a particular trial are needed by the criterion computer. The payoff matrix would also be necessary to its computation of the criterion. These quantities would be combined so that some goal would be best achieved, and the criterion computed.

With the distributions and the criterion in hand, the ideal observer is ready to begin its observations. An input is presented within an interval. The observer takes the sample through its transducer, which performs the necessary measurements. The output of the transducer is fed into the likelihood computer along with the distribution functions for the two distributions. This information is sufficient for the likelihood-ratio computer to compute its output. The decision computer needs only to compare the likelihood ratio with the criterion computed by the criterion computer in order to make its decision.

Figure 13-2 illustrates some other concepts of SDT. This figure is based on the assumption that sensory events can be represented along a unidimensional "observation axis." The observations might represent, for example, very faint sounds at the left and very loud sounds at the right end of the axis. Both the N (noise alone) events and the SN (signal plus noise) events are assumed to distribute normally with equal variances. That is, the relative probabilities of occurrence of values along the observation axis are represented by normal probability distributions. We have chosen these assumptions for the sake of simplicity of exposition. The axis and distributions needed for application to a particular detection problem would depend on the actual distributions of the events being modelled.

In our case, the measure of detectability of the signal, d', is the distance between the means of the N and SN distributions, with the units of d' taken to be the standard deviation of the N distribution. We must also compute the criterion value for the likelihood ratio, which we recall is called *beta* (β). We can then find some point along the observation axis at which the ordinate of the SN distribution (a in the figure) divided by the ordinate of the N distribution (b) will equal the criterion value of the likelihood ratio (β). For this case, all observations to the right of that point should be called *signal* and all observations to the left of that point *noise.* Since the two distributions overlap, even an ideal, perfect observer will only "hit" the signal when it occurs *and* the observation associated with signal occurrence happens to fall to the right of the cutoff. The observer will mistakenly say that the signal is presented, even though noise alone is presented (this is called a *false alarm*), if the noise produces an observation to the right of the cutoff. The total probability of a hit is thus given by the area under the SN curve which is to the right of the cutoff. Similarly, the probability of a false alarm is the area under the N curve which is to the right of the cutoff.

The observer is free to move the cutoff to either the right or the left. Moving it to the right will result in fewer false alarms, but also in fewer hits. Moving it to the left will result in more hits, but also in more false alarms. We shall see in a moment how movement of the criterion traces out a "receiver operating characteristic" curve. At this point, we should note that the sensitivity (measured by d') and the criterion (β) are separated by detection theory; thus measures of sensitivity are more likely to remain constant over situational changes that might affect a subject's criterion setting.

A perfect performance would be defined by the observation that the subject always said "signal" when a signal was in fact presented and never said "signal" when noise alone was presented. As we have seen, a perfect performance would be possible only if the N and SN distributions had no overlap. The goodness of imperfect performances must always be described as a certain relationship between the probability of a hit, $P_s(S)$, and the probability of a false alarm, $P_s(N)$. Since $P_s(S)$ and $P_s(N)$ can be determined from the value of d', the reverse computation, plus certain assumptions, will give d' if one knows $P_s(S)$ and $P_s(N)$. This is indeed fortunate when d' is to be computed for the human observer, for in this case it is not possible to measure the noise distribution which is presented to the distribution-function computer or, for that matter, to measure the signal-plus-noise distribution. The neural noise cannot be directly measured. Instead, the experimenter computes what d' would have to be in order that the ideal observer duplicate the observed values of $P_s(S)$ and $P_s(N)$. The required d' can then be compared with the higher value of d' computed from whatever physical measures the ideal observer would use. Actual observers can never perform better than (and probably never quite as well as) the ideal observer. Thus the theory is "normative" in that it allows us to say how well an observer "ought" to do. Further, the theory allows us to postulate that an ideal observer is limited to less-than-perfect information, and it also allows us to compare this limited performance with that of a human observer; if the limited ideal is very like the human, there is some possibility that the human is actually processing sensory information under the same limitation that we have imposed on our ideal observer.

The *d′* values so far obtained for human observers have shown good consistency for a given individual over a considerable range of values of a priori probability and payoff matrix. It is this consistency which represents perhaps the greatest victory of detection theory, for this consistency cannot be achieved by the traditional theory based on thresholds. The threshold has been found to vary with conditions. Corrections for guessing cannot eliminate inconsistencies in threshold. Psychophysicists were coming to regard thresholds as significant only under the specified conditions in which the threshold had been determined. The *d′* measure, with its greater generality, escapes this limitation. If *d′* has been determined for a particular pair of values $P_s(S)$ and $P_s(N)$, then the pairing of other values of $P_s(S)$ and $P_s(N)$ can be given with greater generality (for a particular subject, as values in the payoff matrix and a priori probabilities are changed).

The ability to do this derives from the fact that *d′* determines a receiver operating curve, or ROC. Figure 13-3 shows a set of such curves. The diagonal line represents chance performance; we note that an observer who gives no false alarms cannot ever correctly call out "signal." However, an observer willing to call "signal" each time will always be correct *if* the signal is presented and always

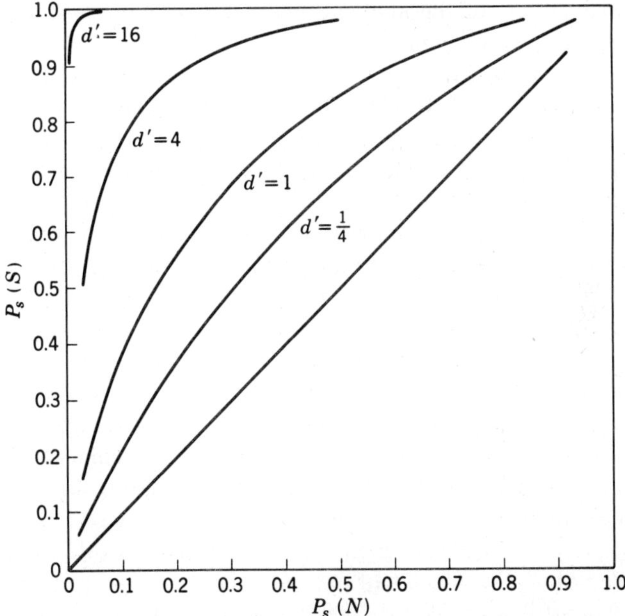

Figure 13-3 Receiver operating curves of varying values of *d′*. (*Source:* Peterson et al., 1954.)

incorrect if the noise is presented. The diagonal line is the only possible ROC if d' equals 0; as d' increases, the ROC moves further from the diagonal line. There is never any sudden shift to a new level of responding as the signal and noise are made more discriminable, as a naïve view of the threshold concept might suggest. Swets (1961) reviewed several versions of threshold theory and showed that the modifications required to bring threshold theory into line with empirical results may so complicate it that it begins to look quite similar to detection theory. Swets (1964) has also collected many of the experimental papers on detection theory into an easily available set of readings.

Detection theory has been useful for predicting results in sensory psychology, particularly in vision and audition (Carterette & Cole, 1962). This is not surprising, since the theory was developed for handling "sensory" problems. An unexpected bonus, however, has been the application of detection theory to problems in memory, beginning with Egan (1958) and continuing to the present (e.g., Banks, 1970; Lockhart & Murdock, 1970). As we have mentioned, the theory has close relationships to the more general theory of statistical decisions and therefore applies in part to games and to statistical testing. Detection theory thus has surprisingly broad application, and its future importance in psychology seems assured. New techniques are being developed which make it possible to apply traditional tests of significance to the parameters of detection theory (Dorfman & Alf, 1968, 1969), thus integrating it even more closely with traditional statistics. Green and Swets (1974) provide an invaluable bibliography of empirical research using SDT. The bibliography is classified by subjects, among them attention, medical diagnosis, memory, personality, and many others. It would be hard to find a better overview of the applications of SDT than browsing through their bibliography and then referring to the articles that struck one's fancy.

Now let us summarize some of the concepts presented so far in this chapter. The primary datum for the detection theorist is a *decision* made by the observing organism (or observing equipment). The observer is playing a game (in the mathematical sense) and trying to win, rather than describing a sensory experience. If the organism has information that the a priori probability that a tiger is present is equal to 1.00, the organism does not even listen to present stimuli; it does not introspect—it runs. The observer in the psychophysical experiment is regarded as a similar expression of a tendency for an adjustive organism to use whatever information *should* be related to a decision, with no prejudice that all relevant information is given on a sensory channel on a particular trial. This point of view resembles the functionalist point of view in its emphasis on adaptation, and it is behavioristic in its acceptance of the overt decision as the significant experimental datum. It is modern in its use of a mathematical system as a model; it shows the impact of another modern influence of mathematics on psychology in its relationship to game theory (see Birdsall, 1953). Its realm of relevance is limited, and its specificity is often very high; yet the theory has sufficient generality so that experimental results which had seemed to disagree can be related in a consistent and meaningful way. Despite the fact that the theory is specific and hence sensitive to experimental results, it is not so rigid that it must fall whenever any deviation of experiment from theory occurs; it can be modified to accommodate, to some extent, new and unexpected results.

Both detection theory and information theory represent what may be considered a new middle of the road for psychological theory. They strike a balance between specificity and generality, and between sensitivity and flexibility. Both bodies of theory are quite rigorous compared with the theory and systems of yesteryear, and neither takes all psychological knowledge for its province. Both theories have runners that cross into other gardens; or, to be more accurate, their roots are actually in engineering gardens and their runners in psychology. Finally, they are not isolated from each other or from other theories in terms of the people interested in them, the disciplines involved, or the problems treated. On one level of generality, they have much in common. Both theories deal with signals in a mathematical way, both originated in the study of equipment, and both apply in a most satisfying manner to the study of human beings. Both are heavy in considerations of probabilities of messages or signals, respectively. Neither is divorced from the study of cybernetics—here one could note again Wiener's discussion of information measures in his book entitled *Cybernetics* (1961). As we saw earlier, computers play a role in the thinking of all who are interested in these areas. In fact, there is a very broad sense in which "information theory" or "information-processing theories" can be used to mean those theories which use concepts from all the fields discussed so far in this chapter: statistical communication theory (information theory in the narrow sense), computer simulation, detection theory, and cybernetics (which we did not discuss). All these theories must come together in the complete robot. If a complete robot existed, it would be a walking model of human behavior.

MATHEMATICAL MODELS IN LEARNING THEORY

The Usefulness of Mathematics

Mathematics has always been a tool of the scientist. It has been said that mathematics lends to science rigor, precision, richness, logic, and other highly valued properties. We have ourselves said many laudatory things about two mathematical developments, information theory and detection theory. It is not surprising that psychology, which has been a sort of scientific second cousin, should turn increasingly to mathematics as a gateway to respectability. However, mathematics cannot be guaranteed to be such a gateway; before turning to some additional inroads of mathematics into psychology, let us consider briefly what mathematics can and cannot be expected to do.

Logic and mathematics are very closely related. We can say, at the very least, that any mathematical system has formal postulates at its foundations. These postulates are such that further statements (theorems) can be derived from them via rules for logical deduction. Mathematical theorems are thus derived from the postulates for the particular mathematical system.

Consider a mathematical system that can be used as a model for a physical system. New statements that are valid within the mathematical system can be generated. If these new statements turn out to be true of the physical system, the mathematical model is at that point a successful model. If the mathematically valid statement does not fit the physical system, the model fails. The possibility of checking statements in this way is the basis of the hypothetico-deductive approach and is what makes the effort to construct and interpret models of any kind worthwhile. We should remember that empirical observations do not test models; they test theories, which are models plus their empirical interpretations. Models are only abstract systems, and their validity as abstract systems is a question of logic, not of observation.

There are two opposite directions from which theorists might come to relate a mathematical system to an empirical system. They might apply existing mathematics to the empirical system without changing the mathematics. This is not an unusual procedure; detection theory, for example, took a mathematical framework and specialized it to apply to several areas of psychological investigation. Some degree of specialization is nearly always necessary, even though no real mathematical innovation is needed. The mathematical system would be complete, with postulates and most theorems worked out, in this case.

Rashevsky (e.g., 1948) suggested many examples of mathematical application that were largely lost on psychologists during his lifetime. He confined himself primarily to the application of existing mathematics to physiological and psychological problems. He appears not to have been in sufficiently close contact with an experimental program for his ideas to have been given an adequate test. Only now, belatedly, is he receiving recognition, primarily in the field of mathematical biology. Despite the amount of time that has passed since he made his primary contribution, it is still too early to say just how important his contribution will turn out to be for psychology.

A theorist might begin from the other direction and try to begin with an empirical area and construct whatever model would fit that area. Hull and his collaborators (Hull, Hovland, Ross, Hall, Perkins & Fitch, 1940) seem to have made an attempt of this kind. The postulational structure that was necessary to encompass the area of rote learning was so formidable that the model has aroused more amazement than interest on the part of psychologists. The model was too complex and unwieldy to be of much use, even if it had provided significant predictive advances over those possible from simpler empirical generalizations. The lesson of history seems to be that viable mathematical models must be both relatively simple and in a continuing intimate interchange with experimental results. As psychologists become more sophisticated mathematically, the requirement for simplicity may be relaxed, but the second requirement is not likely to become less stringent for a long time.

Mathematics is useful to science because it provides convenient and conventional deductive apparatus for prediction and generalization. There are many general types of mathematics as well as many possible models within a given type. One does not need to ask whether it is appropriate to use mathematics because the ability to predict and generalize is useful and because mathematics, conceived of very broadly, is just a tool for accomplishing these functions. Whether some new tools need to be invented for psychology's use remains to be seen.

One new development in mathematics that has excited the imagination of psychologists is called *catastrophe theory* (Thom, 1975). The name comes from the sudden, or catastrophic, changes with which this type of mathematics deals. In order to talk about catastrophe theory, we must make a distinction between the dynamics of a system and the equilibrium conditions of a system. A mathematical description of system dynamics tells us how the state of a system would change with time. A description of system equilibria tells us the states in which a system would rest; roughly, if we know the stable equilibria of a system, we know where the system will be after it has had time to "settle down."

Catastrophe theory deals most directly with equilibrium conditions. Stable equilibria are called *attractors* because when a system is in a state in the attractive neighborhood of such an equilibrium, it will, in the long run, be found very near to the equilibrium point. Interestingly, very dramatic changes in the eventual state of a system may be produced by moving its initial position a very tiny distance, if doing so results in moving the system from the attractive neighborhood of one attractor into the attractive neighborhood of another, perhaps quite distant, attractor.

Thom has described precisely, although only qualitatively, how these catastrophic changes in state can occur. He has thereby considerably increased the mathematician's ability to deal with discontinuities. For this reason, psychologists and others are quite interested in applying Thom's mathematics as a model for psychological and sociological phenomena, which often seem to undergo significant and sudden changes as a result of very small changes in input to the system. For example, all reversible figures seem to change radically from one manifestation to the other, with no stable perception in between. The famous old lady–young lady figure never looks middle-aged.

E. C. Zeeman (1976), a mathematician, is in the forefront among those who have suggested applications of catastrophe theory to psychology. He has proposed models for aggression in dogs, for prison riots, and for the misestimation of driving speed caused by alcohol, as well as for less immediately psychological topics like heartbeat and nerve impulse. So far, the applications suggested have been somewhat reminiscent of those of the field theorists in their looseness and consequent failure to coerce conviction. After their many past disappointments with programmatic theories, psychologists are not in a mood to accept interpretations of models when the coordinations between model and empirical observation are suspect. Nevertheless, Thom's model has fascinating properties, and Zeeman has given us, at the least, sketches of how interpretation of the model in psychology might proceed. It will be interesting to see whether catastrophe theory in 10 years will have become a useful tool like information theory and detection theory, or merely a curiosity.

However history decides the fate of catastrophe theory, we believe that all psychology students who neglect mathematics are agreeing to run their life's intellectual race on crutches. Platt (1962), in his discussion of creativity, supports this point of view: "The third component of intellectual prowess is the use of the best available equipment. It is the nylon tents and oxygen tanks, and the easy donkey train as far as possible, that make the difference in climbing Everest. A man should lose no opportunity to upgrade his intellectual manipulative equipment; that is, the symbolic apparatus with which he does his mental operations" (p. 123).

Mathematics and Measurement

Some people confuse mathematics and measurement, but the two are to a considerable extent independent. Measurement, as far as we are concerned, is a process that establishes a correspondence between mathematical systems and empirical systems. Manipulations within the abstract system of mathematics are possible whether any correspondence exists or not. Traditional measurement established a correspondence between some number system (usually the real numbers) and some property of an empirical system (like the deflection of a needle on an appropriate meter applied to a point in a physical system). Coombs (1964) has shown that the correspondence between numbers resulting from measurement operations and empirical events is not simple, direct, or free of assumptions.

It is clear that the problem of measurement is inextricably intertwined with the problem of constructing mathematical models, though measurement is not necessarily part of mathematics per se. As we shall see later in studying the model of Estes, it is not necessary that all abstract elements be measured directly, but measurement in the sense of establishment of correspondences between model and empirical data is nevertheless an absolutely essential part of the process of modeling.

Properties of Mathematical Models

There is no single criterion defining what a mathematical model is. A single functional relationship between two variables can be considered a mathematical model, since it provides a method of deducing values of one variable from values of another. This function may hold only for a highly restrictive situation, as for rote learning of digits presented at a fixed rate under rigidly specified conditions, and only given several parameters of the equation.

At the other extreme, we might consider all the mathematical apparatus of Newtonian mechanics as another mathematical model. Here the model is of enormous scope and is far more complex.

One dimension of models, then, is their scope. In psychology we see at one extreme Ebbinghaus's empirical learning curve (see Hilgard, 1956) and at the other, Hull's theory of mammalian behavior (e.g., Hull, 1952). A related dimension is complexity. Though simplicity is desirable, it is not legitimate to criticize a model because of complexity, for it may be that even a complex model is the simplest one possible.

Another dimension of models has to do with their origins; the most common question asked is whether a portion of the model was derived empirically or rationally. Further questions then concern the adequacy of whatever grounds are produced. These are all legitimate questions, but they cannot have any bearing on the adequacy of the model. If the model had been, like commandments, simply handed to the theorist, there would be no formal grounds for criticism. The critic might justifiably be either skeptical or jealous (depending on his religious beliefs), but the final verdict on the model should in every case depend on its empirical adequacy rather than on its source.

Another broad category of dimensions is the mathematical and logical adequacy of the model. The model should meet the usual criteria, such as independence and consistency of assumptions, and the necessary correspondence between model and data must be established in order that mathematical operations be justified.

It is not likely to be easy to evaluate either the relative logical merits of a model or the degree of empirical verification of predictions made through the use of the model. Most models can make particular predictions with only a particular probability, and competing models may make the same prediction with a greater or lesser probability. It is not a simple matter to relate hypotheses to empirical outcomes; some excellent papers have been devoted to this problem (e.g., Watanabe, 1960). It will suffice for our purposes to say that a successful model must have predicted all outcomes to which it applies with some probability greater than zero and that in general, the higher the probability and the greater the number of outcomes predicted, the better the model.

A final property of mathematical models is the type of mathematical or logical system used. Lewin's work, discussed earlier in Chapter 11, is one illustration that the usual kind of mathematics taught in algebra and calculus courses is not the only type which has been tried in application to psychology. Thom's theory, which we have just discussed briefly, is another. Like Lewin's theory, Thom's is a derivative of topology. Also like Lewin's, it is encountering difficulties with quantification, which is no doubt related to the fact that topology does not deal with quantitative relationships. However, quantitative mathematics also play a role in Thom's theory, and the difficulties with quantification may be overcome. Science has shown an undeniable preference for models whose elements are quantifiable. However, there may be phenomena which do not lend themselves to quantification. There is no a priori reason to prefer one type of mathematics to another. The type of mathematics to be preferred in psychology will be determined on other than a priori, logical grounds. It is clear that a model cannot be successful without diligent and prolonged effort. There is no ready panacea either in new and esoteric or in old and established mathematics.

A Representative Model

W. K. Estes has been a highly successful pioneer among contemporary psychologists who have attempted to use mathematical models for learning (see also Chapter 10). His first statement of the preliminary version of his statistical association model was published in 1950. The scope of the effort that has gone into the development of his model is reflected in a comprehensive article (1959a). The present chapter can consider only some of the orienting attitudes involved, the basic assumptions underlying the model, and a sample of the techniques involved.

Estes is one of an increasing number of psychologists who are willing to pledge allegiance to the basic methods of the older sciences, especially physics.

His orientation is quantitative, operational, physicalistic—generally hardheaded. This orientation seems typical of those who are or have been in the business of constructing mathematical models.

Estes is frankly behavioristic. His general orientation toward learning theory is similar to Guthrie's. His is an S-R theory which considers a stimulus to be decomposable into elements and which considers the termination of a situation a reinforcing event; it is a contiguity theory.

In this last respect, Estes' recent position is less clear than his initial one. He has said (1959b): "In brief, our answer to the question 'reinforcement or contiguity?' is simply, 'both.' Whether we can have our cake and eat it and still not grow fat is a much more difficult question" (p. 405). In spite of this apparent hedging, Estes leaned toward contiguity assumptions. He later (1959a, 1960; Estes, Hopkins, & Crothers, 1960) made a radical shift in the basic assumptions underlying his statistical association learning theory. The newer theory, backed by experimental results from human paired-associate learning, regards learning as an all-or-none process. The stimulus pattern to be learned either is or is not associated with the correct response on a particular trial. There is a certain probability that the association will be forgotten, so that a correct response on one test will be followed by an incorrect response on a subsequent test. (As yet, it is not certain whether the correct-incorrect series should be attributed mostly to forgetting or to change in the stimulus pattern.) If the correct association is not learned on a particular trial, there seems to be no increase over the chance probability that a correct response will be made on a subsequent test.

Despite the drastic revision in basic assumptions that has occurred, we have elected to present Estes' more classic version of statistical association theory. It was the first of a long series of limited learning theories using mathematical models, and it illustrates how such theories are developed as clearly as any later theory. Hilgard and Bower (1975) provide one of several sources of information about more recent developments in mathematical modeling in learning theory.

Estes (1950) treated learning as a fundamentally statistical process. The stimulus is conceived of as a set of stimulus elements. Not all elements are available on any given trial; that is, on any given trial, the organism samples some proportion of the total set of elements. If an element is sampled on a trial, and some reinforced response terminates the trial, that element will be conditioned (connected) to that response as a result of that single pairing. Any stimulus element can be connected to only one response at a time. Extinction occurs, then, whenever the stimulus elements become connected to some other response instead of to the previously reinforced one. The response measure used is probability of response, which is certainly in keeping with the generally statistical approach.

A critical question that must be answered concerns what proportion of stimulus elements is sampled by the organism on a particular trial. Let us ignore for a moment the problem of how this proportion is determined and assume that we know it. We shall call this proportion *theta* (θ). The question then is, "What effect will a single trial have on the probability of making a specified response?"

To answer this question, we must consider the possible "states" of the elements. At any moment, each element will be in one of two states: either conditioned to the response in question, or conditioned to some other response. Let X represent the number of elements conditioned to the response in question. If S is the total number, then there will be $S - X$ elements conditioned to some other response. Consider what this implies for a situation in which the response in question always occurs last and terminates a trial, that is, a correction procedure in which the trial does not end until the subject makes the correct response and is reinforced.

What number of elements do we expect to have conditioned as the result of a single reinforced trial? It would be the total number of initially unconditioned elements, $S - X$, times the probability that any element would be conditioned on a trial, θ. To take a simplified example with only a finite number of elements, suppose there are 100 elements, 80 of which are not conditioned, with $\theta = 0.05$. Then the expected number of elements conditioned as a result of one trial would be 4. A "difference equation" in which ΔX represents the number of elements changed (conditioned) on each trial therefore reads $\Delta X = \theta(S - X)$.

The probability of response is taken to be equal to X/S. Thus we can write a difference equation in terms of the change in *probability,* rather than in terms of the change in number of elements conditioned, simply by dividing both sides of the preceding equation by S to obtain $\Delta P = \theta(1 - P)$. With this equation in hand, we can always say what, on the average, the probability of response would be if we know the probability of response on the previous trial. If P_n is the probability of the response on the nth trial and P_{n+1} is the probability of response on the next trial, then $P_{n+1} = P_n + \theta(1 - P_n)$. This is Estes' basic learning equation.

Given this background, a general equation for the probability of response on any trial can be derived, provided θ and the probability of response on the first trial are given. One can begin by noticing that the probability that an element is connected on a given trial is exactly the same as 1 minus the probability that it is not connected. The probability that an element is not connected at any time is the same as the probability that it was not connected on trial 1, and that it missed every chance to be connected on trials prior to the current trial. If P_1 represents the probability of response on the first trial, we can then write $P_n = 1 - (1-P_1)(1-\theta)^{n-1}$. The last term is, of course, the probability that an element will fail to be connected on previous trials. This equation has provided a good fit to acquisition data obtained from rats in runways, T mazes, and bar-pressing experiments (see Estes, 1959b).

There are still a few points that should be explained. First, there is the question of determining θ, the proportion of elements sampled. The determination cannot be made directly by any sort of observation of a stimulus sampling process. No correspondence is established between the theoretical stimulus elements and observable elements of any experimentally defined stimulus. Even if such a correspondence existed, it is hard to visualize how one could determine what proportion of elements an organism sampled on a given trial. The determination of θ must, then, be indirect. That value of θ is chosen which provides the best fit of the theoretical curve to acquisition data. At this stage, the model becomes, for the moment, superfluous; that is, if success in fitting a curve to data were *all* the model provided, the theorist would be no better off than if he had started out directly in quest of a curve. However, if the value of θ obtained from a part of a set of data yields a good fit to the remainder, that is a gain over mere curve fitting. If values of θ obtained in one situation apply to others, that is a substantial gain. We saw in the earlier part of this chapter that the measure of separation, d', used in the theory os signal detectability, provides this kind of predictability from situation to situation, whereas the threshold as a measure did not. Estes, similarly, has found that values of θ generalize to some extent over changes in situation.

This concludes our sketch of some mathematical and engineering developments. The field is already enormous and growing almost as fast as the capabilities of computers are growing. It is showing signs of becoming paradigmatic science in the sense Kuhn intended.

SUMMARY AND CONCLUSIONS

A coherent group of ideas emanating from engineering and mathematics is serving to organize a new attitude toward parts of psychology. The organizing concepts are information transmission, decision and detection theory, feedback, and the ideas involved in the computer simulation of human function. In the present chapter, some basic concepts of information theory and detection theory have been presented. An indication of the relationships between computer technology and these theoretical developments has been given.

Finally, Estes' statistical learning theory was sketched. His theory is a distant relative of detection theory and information theory; only the use of statistical and mathematical models relates them.

Mathematical psychology burst out of its adolescence contemporaneously with the development of computer technology in the 1950s and 1960s. It now has its own multivolume handbook (Luce, Bush, & Galanter, 1963–1965), its own collections of readings (e.g., Atkinson, 1964), a choice of introductory textbooks (Coombs, Dawes, & Tversky, 1970; Restle & Greeno, 1970; Levine & Burke, 1972), and its own *Journal of Mathematical Psychology.* A new tradition seems to be well established.

FURTHER READINGS

It is still difficult to suggest readings in mathematical psychology for the average psychologist because our level of mathematical literacy remains low. Until it rises, we could well begin by reading *Plans and the structure of behavior* (1960) by G. A. Miller, Galanter, and Pribram, which shows how the feats of the computer have freed the psychological theorist to consider new cognitive types of explanations. Wooldridge, in *Mechanical man* (1968), ranges even further, in an even more popular tone. G. A. Miller's *Mathematics and psychology* (1964) is a beautifully chosen short paperback collection of articles covering the broad features of the subject—factor analysis, detection theory, information theory, and computers are all represented to some extent, as are mathematical learning theories and other topics with a longer history. Garner's *Uncertainty and structure as psychological concepts* (1962) is not mathematically demanding and illustrates how useful the point of view of information theory can be in psychological experiments and theories. Attneave's little book, *Applications of information theory to psychology: A summary of basic concepts, methods, and results* (1959), is still a model of concise clarity which should be read by every psychology major. The going is rougher in Green and Swets' *Signal detection theory and psychophysics* (1974), but it tends to be that way with detection theory. Egan (1975) tries to ease the way in his *Signal detection theory and ROC analysis.* Estes is represented in the G. A. Miller collection cited above. Finally, we suggest further reading on a subject that we did not even cover, game theory. The reason is that the topic is important and the author of *Two-person game theory* (1969) and *N-person game theory* (1970), Anatol Rapoport, is one of those rare writers who combine brilliance and the patience necessary to bring mathematical topics to basically nonmathematical readers. He deserves our attention.

EPILOGUE

Some Extrapolations from Psychology's Present to Its Future

PSYCHOLOGY AND SOCIETY

Our previous, generally optimistic, predictions about the continued growth and health of psychology have proved, so far, to be correct. From a base of 20,000 members, fellows, and associates of the American Psychological Association in 1963, when the first edition of this book appeared, our national association had grown through 30,000 in 1970, had gone to 42,000 in 1976, and will be approaching the neighborhood of 50,000 by the time this book appears. In the United States, psychology continues to be one of the most popular academic majors. However, our rate of growth, expressed in terms of percentage of initial membership, has begun to decline slightly. It now appears that there will *not* be more psychologists than people by the year 2000, after all. We would guess that psychology will be getting close to a steady state by that time, with as many retiring from the profession as are entering it. We can hope that our steady state in this country will be compensated for by growth in the developing nations, but at the moment that hope has little foundation.

Thus it appears to us that psychology in its second century of formal existence, beginning in 1979, is entering a period of stability and respectability. The exciting old fights between psychology and psychiatry, and the internecine warfare between clinicians and experimentalists, seem to be losing a lot of their spirit.

Psychologists even seem to be winning some respect from their more distant academic neighbors, like the chemists and physicists, as they become more capable of using and criticizing their methods.

In some respects our relationship to the larger society has also improved. The anti-intellectual, antiacademic, antiscientific attitudes which were widespread 10 years ago have diminished. There is less talk about generation gaps and the perils posed by the establishment; perhaps there is even too much conservativism and too much reliance on scientific and technological solutions to our problems. In any case, the tensions related to the radicalism of the sixties, in which psychology shared, are no longer a significant energizing and dividing force.

This is not to say that we do not have serious problems in our relationship to the larger society. Funding for universities and research institutes is being held down, which restricts growth and productivity. However, that is a problem shared by all academic disciplines, and psychology should, in the long run, move closer to equity in receiving its share of funding. We have another problem shared only with the human sciences; that is, how can we best reconcile our need to do research with the protection of the rights of subjects? We still trace much of society's concern back to the Milgram experiments of 1963, and we continue to believe that these experiments were widely misunderstood (we have heard many times that Milgram administered shocks to his learners, which he did not). Further, the objections were perhaps as often based on the unflattering picture of conformity which emerged as on the methods by which it was discovered. Despite the strange genesis of the widespread concern with the rights of subjects, the problem is real and does deserve continuing attention. Psychology departments continue to be in the midst of controversy about the treatment of subjects, and we must continue to be vigilant if we wish to avoid ever more stringent controls.

Finally, we continue to wrestle with a problem which is almost exclusively ours. Testing has been one of psychology's most important sources of bread and butter for many years, and it has been under continuing attack in recent years as prejudicial. A protracted court case in California, in progress as we write (1978), illustrates the severity of the problem. Several parents are suing the state for using intelligence tests, on the grounds that minority students are unjustifiably placed in "slow" classes on the basis of test results. The outcome of this case and of similar cases will obviously have significance for our profession.

Psychologists have been furnishing a number of services to the larger society for a long time. In addition to testing, there have been counseling and clinical services. Group training and experiences have been provided and continue to be popular. Now schools are starting to use psychological work with evoked potentials to diagnose both visual and auditory deficiencies in young children. Behavioral technology is coming into widespread use with retarded children and, in the form of individualized instruction, even with college students. Behavior modification techniques are being used by special clinics, for example for weight reduction or smoking control, operated partly or exclusively by nonpsychologists for profit. This trend toward capitalizing on psychological techniques is due to continue and broaden, perhaps to include treatment of phobias, and, as we learn more, treatment of alcoholism and drug addiction. This is always what happens as a science establishes some secure principles, and is therefore a sign of progress in psychology. Industrial psychologists are also using the same general techniques; one, to our knowledge, now guarantees to meet the goals contracted in advance with the firm being consulted, or his services cost nothing.

The trend, therefore, seems to be for psychologists to extend their interests and services beyond individuals to groups and organizations. Our success so far is quite limited; compare the examples above to the significance of, say, rehabilitating 100% of the prison population, returning all psychotics to a useful and happy life, and eliminating poverty and war. We cannot deny these as ultimate human goals, to which we are just beginning to contribute significantly. We hope and predict that psychology will progress from a creep to a crawl toward those objectives during the next 20 years. If it does, we can enter the twenty-first century with greater hope.

METATHEORETICAL DEVELOPMENTS

Tolerance for a variety of viewpoints seems to be spreading in psychology. Behaviorists, psychoanalysts, and Third Forcers exist, almost amicably, side by side. The computer modelers are an identifiable, and so far unnamed, fourth force whose contributions and significance will rise tremendously during the next 20 years. Theoretically and practically significant breakthroughs in computer understanding, language, and "conscious" behaviors are difficult to predict, but the stage is set for shocks like those we received when Washoe started creating sentences in American Sign Language, and other chimps started looking away so that they couldn't "hear" a request for a share of their delicacy. The resurgence of interest in the evolutionary perspective will synthesize every aspect of psychology in the long run, although it will take some time before the relationships between, say, phenomenology and behavioral pharmacology are clarified. Signs of synthesis may now be appearing as fast as signs of fragmentation in psychology. Ten years ago, that was clearly not the case.

The philosophical controversy surrounding Kuhn's statements on scientific procedures appears to be subsiding. No doubt there has been a gain in sophistication for everyone as a result of the interchange. Popper, whose views are generally quite different from Kuhn's, said that Kuhn had forced him to see that something like "normal science" played a larger role than he had previously realized. If Kuhn's investigations of science encourage psychologists to undertake empirical investigations of scientific activity, we can look forward to learning more about "the context of discovery" via such future investigations.

THEORETICAL AND EMPIRICAL TRENDS

The trend toward the development of more precise theories is continuing. A generally "tight" logical and mathematical approach is assuming greater importance, but there is some indication that more encompassing theories might make a comeback. Let us look at just one possible example.

In 1973 we noted a nativistic trend. At that time, the forceful statement that there were "biological boundaries" to learning was fairly new. Now that general attitude is so well accepted as to be no longer controversial. What is now controversial is the extent to which human social behavior has a genetic basis. A related issue is the extent to which psychology can be integrated through the application of an evolutionary perspective.

One of the potentially most significant books published in the last decade is Edward Wilson's *Sociobiology* (1975). Wilson presents a wealth of evidence indicating that evolutionary considerations are correlated in interesting and possibly illuminating ways with animal social behavior. Plausible, but unproved, extensions to human social behavior are suggested. Wilson's theses are attractive enough that scientific and political opposition to the sociobiological approach has been quick to appear.

There seems to be no question that both heredity and environment contribute to every behavior. In that sense, there is nothing to argue about. There is no convincing way to establish that some particular percentage of the variance in a behavior is attributable to environmental variance and some other percentage to genetic variance; the figures would change as the variances of environment and of genetic constitution changed. Thus there is not even a quantitative argument that makes any sense. What can the argument be about?

One guess might be that certain of our "higher" behaviors had seemed to preclude a genetic account. Specifically, one might conclude that "unselfish" or "altruistic" behaviors should not evolve if the rule of evolution is "survival of the fittest." Those individuals that behaved most selfishly, putting their own reproductive potential above all other considerations, would at first thought seem to be most likely to have their genes represented in the next and subsequent generations. Hence, the argument goes, if altruism exists, it must be some sort of "higher" function, developed despite evolutionary considerations, and in conflict with them.

However, a little thought reveals exceptions to the rule of selfishness. For example, the genes of a mother would benefit any time she made a sacrifice of her reproductive potential which was more than compensated for by an increase in the reproductive potential of her young. On the balance sheet of the great evolutionary bookkeeper, her altruistic behavior would in such cases be marked on the profit side of the ledger, and such altruistic behaviors should increase. Genes predisposing to an appropriate degree of "mother love" thus have an advantage, particularly in older mothers whose own reproductive potential is low. The same logic applies, with modifications, to fathers, and even to more distant relatives. However, the evolutionary referee would penalize us for wrong decisions. If the ratio of genetic benefits to genetic costs is not high enough, the selfish player is awarded some free throws.

The point of all this is that sociobiologists have been able to specify conditions under which altruism ought to be favored by evolution; this opens the door to specifying conditions under which genes, if such exist, for *any* observed behavioral tendency might evolve. Circumstances might be hypothesized which favored the development of originality, martyrdom, kindness, curiosity, or any other characteristic which at first blush might seem impossible to account for from an evolutionary perspective. Of course, the same could still be said for selfishness, timidity, cannibalism, greed, or any characteristic that we might find less desirable and more consistent with the "law of tooth and claw." Genes in themselves are not selfish or altruistic, greedy or generous. They are simply there to be counted. Genes which in their particular combinations and in their particular environment reproduce in the greatest numbers are declared, provisionally, winners in the game of survival.

It has therefore become feasible to try to reconcile all human behaviors within an evolutionary perspective. We cannot yet know that any such attempt will succeed, but it seems likely that a generally functional psychology will enjoy a renaissance during the coming years.

The recent furor about recombinant-DNA research gives us another perspective on beliefs about the power of genetic determinism. There is a great resistance to attempts to exaggerate the power of genes to influence human behavior. At the same time, there seems to be little resistance to exaggerating the likelihood that changing heredity artificially may produce dangerous new forms of life! Fortunately for those who wish to do the research, the fears of evil forms are countered by hope that highly beneficial organisms can be created, and that defective human genetic programs might in the distant future be correctible. Before that time comes, we expect such research to produce significant information for psychologists about genetic effects on behavior.

We also continue to believe that work with simple model systems, for example with gastropods, will eventually pay off by giving us a clear understanding of the fundamentals of operation of complex nervous systems. It is by no means easy to work with the several thousands of large neurons present in a sea hare, but it is far easier than trying to ferret out basic principles among the several billions of smaller neurons present in the human central nervous system. Good pharmacological, anatomical, physiological, chemical, and behavioral work with a variety of such simple systems is still in its early stages. We see no reason to doubt that the payoff in principles of neural operation will be less than the harvest of knowledge about genetics taken from the lowly fruit fly.

In conclusion, we think there are signs of maturity in our science and profession. There will be no shortage of the trivial and irrelevant during the next decades, but there may be the beginning of a broad synthesis. We are becoming more tolerant of our diversity, and there is a growing suspicion that there may yet be unity in it.

REFERENCES

Ach, N. *Über den Willensakt und des Temperament: Ein experimentelle Untersuchung.* Leipzig: Quelle & Meyer, 1910.

Adelson, J. Personality. *Annual Review of Psychology,* 1969, **20,** 217–252.

Allport, F. H. *Social psychology.* Boston: Houghton Mifflin, 1924.

Allport, G. W. *Personality: A psychological interpretation.* New York: Holt, 1937.

Allport, G. W. *The individual and his religion.* New York: Macmillan, 1950.(a)

Allport, G. W. *The nature of personality: Selected papers.* Reading, Mass.: Addison-Wesley, 1950.(b)

Allport, G. W. *Becoming: Basic considerations for a psychology of personality.* New Haven, Conn.: Yale University Press, 1955.

Allport, G. W. *Personality and social encounter: Selected essays.* Boston: Beacon Press, 1960.

Allport, G. W. *Pattern and growth in personality.* New York: Holt, 1961.

Allport, G. W. *Letters from Jenny.* New York: Harcourt, Brace & World, 1965.

Allport, G. W. *The person in psychology: Selected essays.* Boston: Beacon Press, 1968.

Allport, G. W., & Allport, F. H. *A-S reaction study.* Boston: Houghton Mifflin, 1928.

Allport, G. W., & Cantril, H. *The psychology of radio.* New York: Harper, 1935.

Allport, G. W., & Vernon, P. E. *A study of values.* Boston: Houghton Mifflin, 1931.

Allport, G. W., & Vernon, P. E. *Studies in expressive movement.* New York: Macmillan, 1933.

Allport, G. W., & Vernon, P. E. *A study of values.* (Rev. ed.) Boston: Houghton Mifflin, 1951.

Alper, T. G. Memory for completed and incompleted tasks as a function of personality: Correlation between experimental and personality data. *Journal of Personality,* 1948, **17,** 104–137.

American Psychologist, 1958, **13,** 735.

Ammons, R. B. Psychology of the scientist. II. Clark L. Hull and his "idea books." *Perceptual and Motor Skills,* 1962, **15,** 800–802.

Amsel, A. On inductive versus deductive approaches and neo-Hullian behaviorism. In B. B. Wolman (Ed.), *Scientific psychology.* New York: Basic Books, 1965. Pp. 187–206.

Amsel, A. Partial reinforcement effects on vigor and persistence. In K. W. Spence and J. T. Spence (Eds.), *The psychology of learning and motivation.* Vol. 1. New York: Academic Press, 1967.

Anastasi, A. *Differential psychology.* (3rd ed.) New York: Macmillan, 1958.

Anderson, R. J. Attribution of quotations from Wundt. *American Psychologist,* 1971, **26,** 590–593.

Angell, J. R. The relations of structural and functional psychology to philosophy. *Philosophical Review,* 1903, **12,** 243–271.

Angell, J. R. *Psychology: An introductory study of the structure and function of human consciousness.* New York: Holt, 1904.

Angell, J. R. The province of functional psychology. *Psychological Review,* 1907, **14,** 61–91.

Angell, J. R. Behavior as a category of psychology. *Psychological Review,* 1913, **20,** 255–270.

Angell, J. R., & Moore, A. W. Reaction time: A study in attention and habit. *Psychological Review,* 1896, **3,** 245–258.

Arbib, M. *Brains, machines, and mathematics.* New York: McGraw-Hill, 1964.

Ardrey, R. *The territorial imperative.* New York: Atheneum, 1966.

Ardrey, R. *The social contract.* New York: Atheneum, 1970.

Asch, S. E., Hay, J., & Diamond, R. M. Perceptual organization in serial rote-learning. *American Journal of Psychology,* 1960, **73,** 177–198.

Ashton, M. An ecological study of the stream of behavior. Master's thesis, University of Kansas, 1964.

Atkinson, R. C. *Studies in mathematical psychology.* Stanford, Calif.: Stanford University Press, 1964.

Attneave, F. Some informational aspects of visual perception. *Psychological Review,* 1954, **61,** 183–193.

Attneave, F. *Applications of information theory to psychology: A summary of basic concepts, methods, and results.* New York: Holt, 1959.

Bacon, F. *The works of Francis Bacon: Philosophical writings.* Boston: Houghton Mifflin, 1857 (originally published 1605).

Bacon, F. *The new organon, and related writings.* F. H. Anderson (Ed.), Indianapolis: Bobbs-Merrill, 1960 (originally published 1620).

Bain, A. *The senses and the intellect.* London: Parker, 1855 (Republished: 1886.)

Bain, A. *The emotions and the will.* London: Parker, 1859.

Bakan, D. *Sigmund Freud and the Jewish mystical tradition.* Princeton, N.J.: Van Nostrand, 1958.

Bakan, D. Is phrenology foolish? *Psychology Today,* 1968, **1,** 44–51.

Banks, W. Signal detection theory and human memory. *Psychological Bulletin,* 1970, **74,** 81–99.

Barker, R. G. *Ecological psychology.* Stanford, Calif.: Stanford University Press, 1968.

Barker, R. G. Wanted: An eco-behavioral science. In E. P. Williams & H. L. Raush (Eds.), *Naturalistic viewpoints in psychological research.* New York: Holt, Rinehart, Winston, 1969, Pp. 31–43.

Barker, R. G., Dembo, T., & Lewin, K. Frustration and regression: A study of young children. *University of Iowa Studies in Child Welfare,* 1941, **18,** 1.

Barker, R. G., & Gump, P. V. *Big school, small school.* Stanford, Calif.: Stanford University Press, 1964.

Beach, F. A., Hebb, D. O., Morgan, C. T., & Nissen, H. W. (Eds.) *The neuropsychology of Lashley: Selected papers of K. S. Lashley.* New York: McGraw-Hill, 1960.

Beck, S. J. The science of personality: Nomothetic or idiographic? *Psychological Review,* 1953, **60,** 353–359.

Becker, R. J. Outstanding contributors to psychology. *American Psychologist,* 1959, **14,** 297–298.

Bekhterev, V. M. *Objektive Psychologie: Oder Psychoreflexologie, die Lehre von den Assoziationsreflexen.* Leipzig: G. G. Teubner, 1913. (Trans from the original 1910 Russian ed.) (Republished: London, Jarrolds Publishers, 1933.)

Bellak, L., & Smith, M. B. An experimental exploration of the psychoanalytic process. *Psychoanalytic Quarterly,* 1956, **25,** 385–414.

Bem, D. J., & Bem, S. L. Nativism revisited: Review of E. H. Lenneberg's *Biological foundations of language, Journal of the Experimental Analysis of Behavior,* 1968, **11,** 497–501.

Bergin, A. E. & Suinn, R. M. Individual psychotherapy and behavior therapy. In M. R. Rosenzweig & L. W. Porter (Eds.), *Annual Review of Psychology,* Vol. 26. Palo Alto, Calif.: Annual Reviews, 1975.

Bergmann, G. The contribution of John B. Watson. *Psychological Review,* 1956, **63,** 265–276.

Berkeley, G. *An essay toward a new theory of vision.* Dublin: Jeremy Pepyat, 1709.

Berkeley, G. *Principles of human knowledge.* Oxford: Oxford University Press, 1710.

Bertocci, P. A. A critique of G. W. Allport's theory of motivation. *Psychological Review,* 1940, **47,** 501–532.

Beveridge, W. I. B. *The art of scientific investigation.* New York: Vintage Books, 1957.

Birdsall, T. An application of game theory to signal detectability. Technical Report 20, Electronic Defense Group, University of Michigan, 1953.

Black, A. H. Operant conditioning in curarized dogs. *Conditional Reflex,* 1967, **2,** 158.

Blackburn, T. R. Sensuous-intellectual complementarity in science. *Science,* 1971, **172,** 1003–1007.

Blodgett, H. C. The effects of the introduction of reward upon the maze performance of rats. *University of California Publications in Psychology,* 1929, **4,** 113–134.

Boice, R. Heroes and teachers. *Teaching of Psychology,* 1977, **4**, 55–58.

Boole, G. *An investigation of the laws of thought.* New York: Dover, 1854.

Boring, E. G. *The physical dimensions of consciousness.* New York: Appleton-Century-Crofts, 1933.

Boring, E. G. A psychological function is the relation of successive differentiations of events in the organism. *Psychological Review,* 1937, **44,** 445–461.

Boring, E. G. *A history of experimental psychology.* New York: Appleton-Century-Crofts, 1950.

Boring, E. G. A history of introspection. *Psychological Bulletin,* 1953, **50,** 169–187.

Boring, E. G. Cognitive dissonance: Its use in science. *Science,* 1964, **145,** 680–685.

Boring, E. G., & Lindzey, G. (Eds.) *A history of psychology in autobiography.* New York: Appleton-Century-Crofts, 1967.

Bradford, L. P., Gibb, J. R. & Benne, K. D. *T-group theory and laboratory method: Innovation in re-education.* New York: Wiley, 1964.

Breland, K., & Breland, M. A field of applied animal psychology. *American Psychologist,* 1951, **6,** 202–204.

Breland, K., & Breland, M. The misbehavior of organisms. *American Psychologist,* 1961, **16,** 681–684.

Breland, K., & Breland, M. *Animal behavior.* New York: Macmillan, 1966.

Brentano, F. *Psychologie von empirischen Standpunkte.* Leipzig: Meiner, 1874, and Heiner, 1955, New ed.

Breuer, J., & Freud, S. *Studien über Hysterie.* Vienna: Franz Deuticke, 1895.

Bridges, Katherine M. B. Emotional development in early infancy. *Child Development,* 1932, **3,** 324–341.

Bridgman, P. W. *The logic of modern physics.* New York: Macmillan, 1927.

Bridgman, P. W. *The nature of some of our physical concepts.* New York: Philosophical Library, 1952.

Bringmann, W. G., Balance, W. D. G., & Evans, R. B. Wilhelm Wundt 1832–1920: A brief biographical sketch. *Journal of the History of the Behavioral Sciences,* 1975, **2,** 287–297.

Brown, J. F. On the use of mathematics in psychological theory, *Psychometrika,* 1936, **1,** 7–15; 77–90. Also in M. H. Marx (Ed.), *Psychological theory: Contemporary readings.* New York: Macmillan, 1951, Pp. 233–256.

Brown, J. F., & Voth, A. C. The path of seen movement as a function of the vector-field. *American Journal of Psychology,* 1937, **49,** 543–563.

Brown, P. L. & Jenkins, H. M. Auto-shaping of the pigeon's key-peck. *Journal of the Experimental Analysis of Behavior,* 1968, **11,** 1–8.

Brožek, J. Soviet psychology. In Marx, M. H., & Hillix, W. A., *Systems and theories in psychology.* New York: McGraw-Hill, 1973. Pp. 521–548.

Brunswik, E. *Wahrnehmung und Gegenstandswelt.* Vienna: Franz Deuticke, 1934.

Brunswik, E. The conceptual focus of some psychological systems. *Journal of Unified Science,* 1939, **8,** 36–49. Reprinted in M. H. Marx (Ed.), *Psychological theory: Contemporary readings.* New York: Macmillan, 1951. Pp. 131–143.(a)

Brunswik, E. Probability as a determiner of rat behavior. *Journal of Experimental Psychology,* 1939, **25,** 175–197.(b)

Brunswik, E. Organismic achievement and environmental probability. *Psychological Review,* 1943, **50,** 255–272.

Brunswik, E. Discussion: Remarks on functionalism in perception. *Journal of Personality,* 1949, **18,** 56–65.

Brunswik, E. The conceptual framework of psychology. *International Encyclopedia of Unified Science,* 1952, **1,** No. 10. Pp. 1–102.

Brunswik, E. Representative design and probabilistic theory in a functional psychology. *Psychological Review,* 1955, **62,** 193–217.(a)

Brunswik, E. In defense of probabilistic functionalism: A reply. *Psychological Review,* 1955, **62,** 236–242.(b)

Brunswik, E. *Perception and the representative design of psychological experiments.* Berkeley: University of California Press, 1956.

Brunswik, E., & Kamiya, J. Ecological cue-validity of "proximity" and of other Gestalt factors. *American Journal of Psychology,* 1953, **66,** 20–32.

Buckley, W. (Ed.) *Modern systems research for the behavioral scientist: A sourcebook.* Chicago: Aldine, 1968.

Burnham, J. C. On the origins of behaviorism. *Journal of the History of the Behavioral Sciences,* 1968, **4,** 143–151.

Burt, C. L. *The factors of the mind.* New York: Macmillan, 1941.

Buss, A. *Psychology: Man in perspective.* New York: Wiley, 1973.

Butler, J. M., & Haigh, G. V. Changes in the relation between self-concepts and ideal concepts consequent upon client-centered counseling. In C. R. Rogers & Rosalind F. Dymond (Eds.), *Psychotherapy and personality change: Coordinated studies in the client-centered approach.* Chicago: University of Chicago Press, 1954. Pp. 55–76.

Butterfield, H. *The origins of modern science: 1300–1800.* (Rev. ed.) New York: Macmillan, 1957.

Campbell, N. R. *Physics: The elements.* Cambridge, Mass.: Cambridge University Press, 1920.

Capretta, P. J. *A history of psychology in outline.* New York: Dell, 1967.

Carr, H. A. *Psychology: A study of mental activity.* New York: Longmans, 1925.

Carr, H. A. Teaching and learning. *Journal of Genetic Psychology,* 1930, **37,** 189–219.

Carterette, E. C., & Cole, M. Comparison of the receiver-operating characteristics for messages received by ear and eye. *Journal of the Acoustical Society of America,* 1962, **34,** 172–178.

Cartwright, D. Lewinian theory as a contemporary systematic framework. In S. Koch (Ed.), *Psychology: A study of a science.* Vol. 2. *General systematic formulations, learning and special processes.* New York: McGraw-Hill, 1959. Pp. 7–91.

Cattell, R. B. *A guide to mental testing.* London: University of London Press, 1936.

Cattell, R. B. *The culture free test of intelligence.* Champaign, Ill.: Institute of Personality and Ability Testing, 1944.

Cattell, R. B. *Description and measurement of personality.* New York: Harcourt, Brace & World, 1946.

Cattell, R. B. *A guide to mental testing.* (Rev. ed.) London: University of London Press, 1948.

Cattell, R. B. The dimensions of culture patterns by factorization of national character. *Journal of Abnormal and Social Psychology,* 1949, **44,** 443–469.

Cattell, R. B. *Personality: A systematic theoretical and factual study.* New York: McGraw-Hill, 1950.

Cattell, R. B. *Factor analysis: An introduction and manual for psychologist and social scientist.* New York: Harper & Row, 1952.

Cattell, R. B. *The O-A personality test battery.* Champaign, Ill.: Institute of Personality and Ability Testing, 1954.

Cattell, R. B. *Personality and motivation structure and measurement.* New York: Harcourt, Brace & World, 1957.

Cattell, R. B. Personality theory growing from multivariate quantitative research. In S. Koch (Ed.), *Psychology: A study of a science.* Vol. 3. *Formulations of the person and the social context.* New York: McGraw-Hill, 1959, Pp. 257–327.

Cattell, R. B. (Ed.) *Handbook of multivariate experimental psychology.* Chicago: Rand McNally, 1966.

Cattell, R. B. (Ed.) *Handbook of modern personality theory.* Chicago: Aldine, 1970.

Cattell, R. B. The grammar of science and the evolution of personality theory. In R. B. Cattell and R. M. Dreger (Eds.), *Handbook of modern personality theory.* New York: Wiley, 1977. Pp. 3–42.(a)

Cattell, R. B. A more sophisticated look at structure: Perturbation, sampling, role and observer trait-view theories. In R. B. Cattell & R. M. Dreger (Eds.), *Handbook of modern personality theory.* New York: Wiley, 1977. Pp. 166–220.(b)

Cattell, R. B. Structured learning theory, applied to personality change. In R. B. Cattell & R. M. Dreger (Eds.), *Handbook of modern personality theory.* New York: Wiley, 1977. Pp. 433–472.(c)

Cattell, R. B., Blewett, D. R., & Beloff, J. R. The inheritance of personality. *American Journal of Human Genetics,* 1955, **7,** 122–146.

Cattell, R. B., & Butcher, H. J. *The prediction of achievement and creativity.* Indianapolis: Bobbs-Merrill, 1968.

Cattell, R. B., & Dreger, R. M. (Eds.), *Handbook of modern personality theory.* New York: Wiley, 1977.

Cattell, R. B., & Warburton, F. W. *Objective personality and motivation tests.* Urbana: University of Illinois Press, 1967.

Cattell, R. B., & Wispe, L. G. The dimension of syntality in small groups. *Journal of Social Psychology,* 1948, **28,** 57–78.

Chance, P. After you hit a child, you can't just get up and leave him; you are hooked to that kid. *Psychology Today,* 1974, **7,** 76–84.

Child, I. L. The relation of somatotype to self-ratings on Sheldon's temperament traits. *Journal of Personality,* 1950, **18,** 440–453.

Chomsky, N. Review of *Verbal behavior* by B. F. Skinner. *Language,* 1959, **35,** 26–58.

Coan, R. W., & Zagona, S. V. Contemporary ratings of psychological theorists. *Psychological Record,* 1962, **12,** 315–322.

Cole, M., & Maltzman, I. (Eds.), *A handbook of contemporary Soviet psychology.* New York: Basic Books, 1969.

Comte, A. *The positive philosophy.* (Trans. by H. Martin) London: G. Bell, 1896 (1824).

Conant, J. B. *On understanding science: A historical approach.* New Haven, Conn.: Yale University Press, 1947.

Conant, J. B. *Harvard case histories in experimental science.* Cambridge, Mass.: Harvard University Press, 1957.

Cook, J. O. "Superstition" in the Skinnerian. *American Psychologist,* 1963, **18,** 516–518.

Coombs, C. H. *A theory of data.* New York: Wiley, 1964.

Coombs, C. H., Dawes, R. M., & Tversky, A. *Mathematical psychology: An elementary introduction.* Englewood Cliffs, N.J.: Prentice-Hall, 1970.

Corsini, R. J. (Ed.), *Current personality theories.* Itasca, Ill: Peacock, 1977.(a)

Corsini, R. J. A medley of current personality theories. In R. J. Corsini (Ed.), *Current personality theories.* Itasca, Ill: Peacock, 1977. Pp. 399–431.(b)

Cotton, J. W. On making predictions from Hill's theory. *Psychological Review,* 1955, **62,** 303–314.

Crannell, C. W., Wolfgang Köhler. *Journal of the History of the Behavioral Sciences,* 1970, **6,** 267–268.

Dahlstrom, W. G. Personality. *Annual Review of Psychology,* 1970, **21,** 1–48.

Dallenbach, K. M. Phrenology versus psychoanalysis. *American Journal of Psychology,* 1955, **68**(4), 511–525.

Darwin, C. *Expression of emotions in man and animals.* (2nd ed.) London: J. Murray, 1872.

Darwin, C. *Origin of species.* (2nd ed.) London: Collier, 1909 (originally published 1859).

Davis, R. C. Physical psychology. *Psychological Review,* 1953, **60,** 7–14.

Dawkins, R. *The selfish gene.* New York: Oxford University Press, 1976.

Dennis, W. (Ed.) *Readings in the history of psychology.* New York: Appleton-Century-Crofts, 1948.

de Rivera, J. *Field theory as human science: Contributions of Lewin's Berlin group.* New York: Halsted Press, 1976.

Deutsch, M. Field theory in social psychology. In G. Lindzey (Ed.), *Handbook of social psychology.* Reading, Mass.: Addison-Wesley, 1954. Pp. 181–222.

Deutsch, J. A. *The structural basis of behavior.* Chicago: University of Chicago Press, 1960.

Deutsch, J. A., & Clarkson, J. K. Reasoning in the hooded rat. *Quarterly Journal of Experimental Psychology,* 1959, **11,** 150–154.

Dewey, J. *Psychology.* New York: Harper, 1886.

Dewey, J. The reflex arc concept in psychology. *Psychological Review,* 1896, **3,** 357–370.

Dewey, J. Psychology and social practice. *Psychological Review,* 1900, **2,** 105–124.

Diesing, P. *Patterns of discovery in the social sciences.* Chicago: Aldine-Atherton, 1971.

Diserens, C. M. Psychological objectivism. *Psychological Review,* 1925, **32,** 121–152.

Dittman, A. J. Psychotherapeutic processes. *Annual Review of Psychology,* 1966, **17,** 57–78.

Dollard, J. *Caste and class in a Southern town.* New Haven, Conn.: Yale University Press, 1937.

Dollard, J. *Fear in battle.* New Haven, Conn.: Yale University Press, 1943.

Dollard, J., Doob, L. W., Miller, N. E., Mowrer, O. H., & Sears, R. R. *Frustration and aggression.* New Haven, Conn.: Yale University Press, 1939.

Dollard, J., & Miller, N. E. *Personality and psychotherapy: An analysis in terms of learning, thinking, and culture.* New York: McGraw-Hill, 1950.

Dorfman, D. D., & Alf, E., Jr. Maximum likelihood estimation of parameters of signal-detection theory: A direct solution. *Psychometrika,* 1968, **33,** 117–124.

Dorfman, D. D., & Alf, E., Jr. Maximum-likelihood estimation of parameters of signal-detection theory and determination of confidence intervals-rating method data. *Journal of Mathematical Psychology,* 1969, **6,** 487–496.

Duncker, K. On problem solving. (Trans. by L. S. Lews from the original 1935 ed.) *Psychological Monographs,* 1945, **58**(270).

Ebbinghaus, H. *Über das Gedachtnis,* 1885. (Reprinted as *Memory.* [Trans. by H. A. Ruger & C. E. Busenius.] New York: Teachers College, 1913.)

Edwards, D. D., West, J. R., & Jackson, V. The role of contingencies in the control of behavior. *Psychonomic Science,* 1968, **10,** 39–40.

Egan, J. P. *Recognition memory and the operating characteristic.* Technical Report No. AFCRC-TN-58-51, AD-152650, Indiana University, Hearing and Communication Laboratory, 1958.

Egan, J. P. *Signal detection theory and ROC analysis.* New York: Academic Press, Harcourt Brace Jovanovich, 1975.

Ellenberger, H. Fechner and Freud. *Bulletin of Menninger Clinic,* 1956, **20,** 201–214.

Ellenberger, H. *The discovery of the unconscious.* New York: Basic Books, 1970.

Ellenberger, H. F. The story of "Anna O": A critical review with new data. *Journal of the History of the Behavioral Sciences,* 1972, **8,** 267–279.

Ellis, W. D. *A source book of Gestalt psychology.* New York: Harcourt, Brace & World, 1938.

Epps, P., & Parnell, R. W. Physique and temperament of women delinquents compared with women undergraduates. *British Journal of Medical Psychology,* 1942, **25,** 249–255.

Escalona, S. K. The influence of topological and vector psychology upon current research in child development: An addendum. In L. Carmichael (Ed.), *Manual of child psychology.* (2nd ed.) New York: Wiley, 1954. Pp. 971–983.

Esper, E. A. Max Meyer in America. *Journal of the History of the Behavioral Sciences,* 1967, **3,** 107–131.

Estes, W. K. Toward a statistical theory of learning. *Psychological Review,* 1950, **57,** 94–107.

Estes, W. K. Kurt Lewin. In W. K. Estes et al., *Modern learning theory.* New York: Appleton-Century-Crofts, 1954. Pp. 317–344.

Estes, W. K. Component and pattern models with Markovian interpretations. In R. R. Bush & W. K. Estes (Eds.), *Studies in mathematical learning theory.* Stanford, Calif.: Stanford University Press, 1959. Pp. 9–52.(a)

Estes, W. K. The statistical approach to learning theory. In S. Koch (Ed.), *Psychology: A study of a science.* Vol. 2. *General systematic formulations, learning and special processes.* New York: McGraw-Hill, 1959. Pp. 380–491.(b)

Estes, W. K. Learning theory and the new "mental chemistry." *Psychological Review,* 1960, **67,** 207–223.

Estes, W. K., Hopkins, B. L., & Crothers, E. J. All-or-none and conservation effects in the learning and retention of paired associates. *Psychological Review,* 1960, **60,** 329–339.

Estes, W. K., Koch, S., MacCorquodale, K., Meehl, P. E., Mueller, C. G., Jr., Schoenfeld, W. N., & Verplanck, W. S. *Modern learning theory.* New York: Appleton-Century-Crofts, 1954.

Evans, R. B. E. B. Titchener and his lost system. *Journal of the History of the Behavioral Sciences,* 1972, **2,** 168–180.

Evans, R. I. *B. F. Skinner: The man and his ideas.* New York: Dutton, 1968.

Evans, R. I. *Carl Rogers: The Man and his ideas.* New York: Dutton, 1975.

Eysenck, H. J. *Dimensions of personality.* London: Routledge, 1947.

Eysenck, H. J. Criterion analysis: An application of the hypothetico-deductive method of factor analysis. *Psychological Review,* 1950, **57,** 38–53.

Eysenck, H. J. The effects of psychotherapy. *Journal of Consulting Psychology,* 1952, **16,** 319–324.(a)

Eysenck, H. J. *The scientific study of personality.* London: Routledge, 1952.(b)

Eysenck, H. J. *The structure of human personality.* New York: Wiley, 1953.

Eysenck, H. J. *The psychology of politics.* London: Routledge, 1954.

Eysenck, H. J. *The dynamics of anxiety and hysteria: An experimental application of modern learning theory to psychiatry.* New York: Praeger, 1957.

Eysenck, H. J. (Ed.) *Handbook of abnormal psychology.* New York: Basic Books, 1961.

Eysenck, H. J. *The biological basis of personality.* Springfield, Ill: C.C. Thomas, 1967.

Eysenck, H. J., & Rachman, S. *The causes and cures of neurosis.* San Diego: Knapp, 1965.

Ezriel, H. The scientific testing of psychoanalytic findings and theory. *British Journal of Medical Psychology,* 1951, **24,** 26–29.

Falk, J. L. Issues distinguishing idiographic from nomothetic approaches to personality theory. *Psychological Review,* 1956, **63,** 53–62.

Farrell, B. A. The scientific testing of psychoanalytic findings and theory. *British Journal of Medical Psychology,* 1951, **24,** 35–41.

Fawl, C. L. Disturbances experienced by children in their natural habitats. In R. G. Barker (Ed.), *The stream of behavior.* New York: Appleton-Century-Crofts, 1963. Pp. 99–126.

Fechner, G. T. *Elemente der Psychophysik.* Leipzig: Breitkopf & Härtel, 1860.

Feigl, H. The "orthodox" view of theories: Remarks in defense as well as critique. In M. Radner & S. Winokur (Eds.), *Analyses of theories and methods of physics and psychology.* Minneapolis: University of Minnesota Press, 1970.

Feigl, H., Scriven, M., & Maxwell, G. (Eds.) *Minnesota studies in the philosophy of science.* Vol. 2. Minneapolis: University of Minnesota Press, 1958.

Ferenczi, S., & Rank, O. *The development of psychoanalysis.* (Trans. by Caroline Newton) New York: Nervous and Mental Disease Publishing, 1925, 1956.
Ferster, C. B., & Skinner, B. F. *Schedules of reinforcement.* New York: Appleton-Century-Crofts, 1957.
Fisher, R. Biological time. In J. T. Fraser (Ed.), *The voices of time.* New York: George Braziller, 1966. Pp. 357–382.
Fitts, P. M., & Posner, M. I. *Human performance.* Belmont, Calif.: Brooks/Cole, 1967.
Ford, D. H., & Urban, H. B. Psychotherapy. *Annual Review of Psychology,* 1967, **18,** 333–372.
Frank, J. D. Some psychological determinants of the level of aspiration. *American Journal of Psychology,* 1935, **47,** 285–293.
Fraser, J. T. *The voices of time.* New York: George Braziller, 1966.
Freeman, L. *The story of Anna O.* New York: Walker, 1972.
Freud, S. *The interpretation of dreams.* New York: Modern Library, 1950 (originally published 1900).
Freud, S. The history of the psychoanalytic movement. In A. A. Brill (Ed. & Trans.), *The basic writing of Sigmund Freud.* New York: Random House, 1938.
Freud, S. *A general introduction to psychoanalysis* (Trans. by J. Riviere) Garden City, N.Y.: Doubleday, 1943.
Fromm, E. *Escape from freedom.* New York: Holt, 1941.
Fromm, E. *Man for himself.* New York: Holt, 1947.
Fromm, E. *The sane society.* New York: Holt, 1955.
Fromm, E. *Sigmund Freud's mission.* New York: Harper, 1959.
Fromm, E. *Marx's concept of man.* New York: Ungar, 1961.(a)
Fromm, E. *May man prevail? An inquiry into the facts and fictions of foreign policy.* Garden City, N.Y.: Doubleday, 1961.(b)
Fromm, E. *The heart of man.* New York: Harper & Row, 1964.
Galton, F. *Hereditary genius: an inquiry into its laws and consequences.* New York: Appleton, 1883 (1869).
Garner, W. R. Rating scales, discriminability and information transmission. *Psychological Review,* 1960, **67,** 343–352.
Garner, W. R. *Uncertainty and structure as psychological concepts.* New York: Wiley, 1962.
Garner, W. R. To perceive is to know. *American Psychologist,* 1966, **21,** 11–19.
Garner, W. R. *The processing of information and structure.* New York: Wiley, 1974.
Garner, W. R., Hake, W. H., & Eriksen, C. W. Operationism and the concept of perception. *Psychological Review,* 1956, **63,** 149–159.
Gates, A. I. Connectionism: Present concepts and interpretations. *Yearbook of National Society of the Study of Education,* 1942, **41,** Part II, 141–164.
Geissler, L. R. The measurement of attention. *American Journal of Psychology,* 1909, **20,** 473–529.
Gelb, A., & Goldstein, K. *Psychologische Analysen Hirnpathologischer Faelle.* Leipzig: Barth, 1920.
George, F. H. *The brain as a computer.* New York: Pergamon, 1973.
Gibbens, T. C. N. *Psychiatric studies of Borstal lads.* London: Oxford, 1963.
Gibson, J. J. The concept of stimulus in psychology. *American Psychologist,* 1960, **15,** 694–703.
Gibson, J. J. *The senses considered as perceptual systems.* Boston: Houghton Mifflin, 1966.
Gillispie, C. C. *The edge of objectivity.* Princeton, N.J.: Princeton University Press, 1960.
Glueck, S., and Gleuck, E. *Physique and delinquency.* New York: Harper, 1956.
Goesling, W. J., & Brener, J. Effects of activity and immobility conditioning upon subse-

quent heart-rate conditioning in curarized rats. *Journal of Comparative and Physiological Psychology,* 1972, **81,** 311–317.

Goldiamond, I. Indicators of perception. I. Subliminal perception, subception, unconscious perception. *Psychological Bulletin,* 1958, **55,** 373–411.

Goldstein, K. *The organism.* New York: American Book, 1939.

Goldstein, K. *Human nature in the light of psychopathology.* Cambridge, Mass.: Harvard University Press, 1940.

Goldstein, K. *After-effects of brain injuries in war.* New York: Grune & Stratton, 1942.

Goldstein, K. *Language and language disturbances.* New York: Grune & Stratton, 1948.

Goldstein, K. Kurt Goldstein. In E. G. Boring, & G. Lindzey (Eds.), *A history of psychology in autobiography.* Vol. 5. New York: Appleton-Century-Crofts, 1967. Pp. 145–166.

Goldstein, K., & Scheerer, M. Abstract and concrete behavior: An experimental study with special tests. *Psychological Monographs,* 1941, **53,** No. 2.

Goldstein, K., & Scheerer, M. Tests of abstract and concrete thinking. A. Tests of abstract behavior. In A. Weidler (Ed.), *Contributions toward medical psychology.* New York: Ronald Press, 1953. Pp. 702–730.

Goodall, K. Tie line. *Psychology Today,* 1972, **5,** 24–28.

Graham, C. H. Visual perception. In S. S. Stevens (Ed.), *Handbook of experimental psychology.* New York: Wiley, 1951. Pp. 868–920.

Graham, C. H. Sensation and perception in an objective psychology. *Psychological Review,* 1958, **65,** 65–76.

Green, D. M., & Swets, J. A. *Signal detection theory and psychophysics.* New York: Krieger, 1974.

Gulliksen, H. Louis Leon Thurstone, experimental and mathematical psychologist. *American Psychologist,* 1968, **23,** 786–802.

Guthrie, E. R. *The psychology of learning.* New York: Harper & Row, 1935.

Guthrie, E. R. *The psychology of human conflict.* New York: Harper & Row, 1938.

Guthrie, E. R. Conditioning: A theory of learning in terms of stimulus, response and association. *Yearbook of National Society of the Study of Education,* 1942, **41,** Part II, 17–60.

Guthrie, E. R. *The psychology of learning.* (Rev. ed.) New York: Harper & Row, 1952.

Guthrie, E. R. Association by contiguity. In S. Koch (Ed.), *Psychology: A study of a science.* Vol. 2. *General systematic formulations, learning and special processes.* New York: McGraw-Hill, 1959. Pp. 158–195.

Guthrie, E. R., & Horton, G. P. *Cats in a puzzle box.* New York: Holt, 1946.

Haber, R. N. (Ed.) *Current research in motivation.* New York: Holt, Rinehart & Winston, 1966.

Haley, A. *Roots.* Garden City, N.Y.: Doubleday, 1976.

Hall, C. S. *A primer on Freudian psychology.* Cleveland: World Publishing, 1954.

Hall, C. S. & Lindzey, G. *Theories of personality.* New York: Wiley, 1957.

Hall, C. S., & Lindzey, G. *Theories of personality.* (2nd ed.) New York: Wiley, 1970.

Hall, G. S. *Adolescence.* New York: Appleton, 1904.

Hall, G. S. *Jesus, the Christ, in the light of psychology.* Garden City, N.Y.: Doubleday, 1917.

Hall, G. S. *Senescence: The last half of life.* New York: Appleton, 1922.

Hall, M. H. An interview with "Mr. Behaviorist" B. F. Skinner. *Psychology Today,* 1967, **1,** 20–23, 68–71.

Hammond, K. R. Representative vs. systematic design in clinical psychology. *Psychological Bulletin,* 1954, **51,** 150–159.

Hammond, K. R. Probabilistic functioning and the clinical method. *Psychological Review,* 1955, **62,** 255–262.
Hammond, K. R. (Ed.) *The psychology of Egon Brunswik.* New York: Holt, 1966.
Harlow, H. F. Primate learning. In C. P. Stone (Ed.), *Comparative psychology.* Englewood Cliffs, N.J.: Prentice-Hall, 1951. Pp. 183–238.
Harrower, M. R. Organization in higher mental processes. *Psychologische Forschung,* 1932, **17,** 56–120.
Hartley, D. *Observations on man, his duty, and his expectations.* London: W. Eyres, 1749.
Hartmann, G. W. *Gestalt psychology.* New York: Ronald Press, 1935.
Hays, R. Psychology of the scientist. III. Introduction to "Passages from the 'idea books' of Clark L. Hull." *Perceptual and Motor Skills,* 1962, **15,** 803–806.
Hearst, E. Discrimination learning as the summation of excitation and inhibition. *Science,* 1968, **162,** 1303–1306.
Hebb, D. O. *The organization of behavior.* New York: Wiley, 1949.
Hebb, D. O. A neuropsychological theory. In S. Koch (Ed.), *Psychology: A study of a science.* Vol. 1. *Sensory, perceptual, and physiological formulations.* New York: McGraw-Hill, 1959. Pp. 622–643.
Heidbreder, E. *Seven psychologies.* New York: Appleton-Century-Crofts, 1933.
Heidegger, M. *Being and time.* New York: Harper & Row, 1962.
Heider, F. Gestalt theory: Early history and reminiscences. *Journal of the History of the Behavioral Sciences,* 1970, **6,** 131–139.
Helson, H. The psychology of Gestalt. *American Journal of Psychology,* 1925, **36,** 342–370, 454–526.
Helson, H. The psychology of Gestalt. *American Journal of Psychology,* 1926, **37,** 25–62, 189–223.
Helson, H. The fundamental propositions of Gestalt psychology. *Psychological Review,* 1933, **40,** 12–32.
Helson, H. Why did their precursors fail and the Gestalt psychologists succeed? *American Psychologist,* 1969, **24,** 1006–1011.
Henle, M. Some problems of eclecticism. *Psychological Review,* 1957, **64,** 296–305.
Henle, M. (Ed.) *The selected papers of Wolfgang Köhler.* New York: Liveright, 1971.
Herbart, J. F. *A textbook of psychology.* (Trans. by M. K. Smith.) New York: Appleton, 1891. Pp. 9–19. Original German Edition: *Lehrbuch der Psychologie,* Konigsberg und Leipzig, 1816.
Herrnstein, R. J. Superstition: A corollary of the principles of operant conditioning. In W. K. Honig (Ed.), *Operant behavior: Areas of research and application.* New York: Appleton-Century-Crofts, 1966, Pp. 33–51.
Herrnstein, R. J. The evolution of behaviorism. *American Psychologist,* 1977, **32,** 593–603.(a)
Herrnstein, R. J. Doing what comes naturally: A reply to Professor Skinner. *American Psychologist,* 1977, **10,** pp. 1013–1016.(b)
Herrnstein, R. J., & Boring, E. G. *A source book in the history of psychology.* Cambridge, Mass.: Harvard University Press, 1965.
Hilgard, E. R. Experimental approaches to psychoanalysis. In E. Pumpian-Mindlin (Ed.), *Psychoanalysis as science.* Stanford, Calif.: Stanford University Press, 1952. Pp. 3–45.
Hilgard, E. R. Discussion of probabilistic functionalism. *Psychological Review,* 1955, **62,** 226–228.
Hilgard, E. R. *Theories of learning.* (Rev. ed.) New York: Appleton-Century-Crofts, 1956.

Hilgard, E. R., & Bower, G. H. *Theories of learning.* (3rd ed.) New York: Appleton-Century-Crofts, 1966.

Hilgard, E. R., & Bower, G. H. *Theories of learning.* (4th ed.) New York: Appleton-Century-Crofts, 1975.

Hillix, W. A., & Marx, M. H. Response strengthening by information and effect in human learning. *Journal of Experimental Psychology,* 1960, **60,** 97–102.

Hillix, W. A., & Marx, M. H. (Eds.), *Systems and theories in psychology: A reader.* St. Paul: West, 1974.

Hochberg, J. E. Effects of the Gestalt revolution: The Cornell symposium on perception. *Psychological Review,* 1957, **64,** 73–84.

Hochberg, J., & McAlister, E. A quantitative approach to figural "goodness." *Journal of Experimental Psychology,* 1953, **46,** 361–364.

Hocutt, M. On the alleged circularity of Skinner's concept of stimulus. *Psychological Review,* 1967, **74,** 530–532.

Hofstadter, R. *Social Darwinism in American thought.* Boston: Beacon Press, 1955.

Holdstock, T. L., & Rogers, C. R. Person-centered theory. In R. J. Corsini (Ed.), *Current personality theories.* Itasca, Ill: Peacock, 1977.

Holt, E. B. *The Freudian wish and its place in ethics.* New York: Holt, 1915.

Holt, E. B. *Animal drive and the learning process.* New York: Holt, 1931.

Holt, R. R. Individuality and generalization in the psychology of personality. *Journal of Personality,* 1962, **30,** 377–404.

Hoppe, F. Erfolg und Misserfolg. *Psychologische Forschung,* 1930, **14,** 1–62.

Horney, K. *Neurotic personality of our times.* New York: Norton, 1937.

Horney, K. *New ways in psychoanalysis.* New York: Norton, 1939.

Horney, K. *Self-analysis.* New York: Norton, 1942.

Horney, K. *Our inner conflicts.* New York: Norton, 1945.

Horney, K. *Neurosis and human growth.* New York: Norton, 1950.

Horwitz, L. Theory construction and validation in psychoanalysis. In M. H. Marx (Ed.), *Theories in contemporary psychology.* New York: Macmillan, 1963, Pp. 413–434.

Hull, C. L. Quantitative aspects of the evolution of concepts. *Psychological Monographs,* 1920, **28,** (no. 123).

Hull, C. L. The influence of tobacco smoking on mental and motor efficiency. *Psychological Monographs,* 1924, **33**(No. 3), 1–160.

Hull, C. L. *Aptitude testing.* Yonkers, N.Y.: World, 1928.

Hull, C. L. *Hypnosis and suggestibility: An experimental approach.* New York: Appleton-Century, 1933.

Hull, C. L. Mind, mechanism, and adaptive behavior. *Psychological Review,* 1937, **44,** 1–32.

Hull, C. L. *Principles of behavior.* New York: Appleton-Century-Crofts, 1943.

Hull, C. L. *Essentials of behavior.* New Haven, Conn.: Yale University Press, 1951.

Hull, C. L. *A behavior system.* New Haven, Conn.: Yale University Press, 1952.

Hull, C. L. Psychology of the scientist. IV. Passages from the "idea books" of Clark L. Hull. *Perceptual and Motor Skills.* 1962, **15,** 807–882.

Hull, C. L., Hovland, C. L., Ross, R. T., Hall, M., Perkins, D. T., & Fitch, F. G. *Mathematico-deductive theory of rote learning.* New Haven, Conn.: Yale University Press, 1940.

Hume, D. *A treatise on human nature.* London: Longmans, 1886 (1739–1740).

Hume, D. *An enquiry concerning human understanding.* (2nd ed.; L. A. Selby-Bigge [Ed.]) Oxford: Clarendon Press, 1902 (1748).

Hunter, W. S. The problem of consciousness. *Psychological Review,* 1924, **21,** 1–31.
Hunter, W. S. Psychology and anthroponomy. In C. Murchison (Ed.), *Psychologies of 1925.* Worcester, Mass.: Clark University Press, 1926 (Ch. IV). Pp. 83–107.
Hursch, C. J., Hammond, K. R., & Hursch, J. L. Some methodological considerations in multiple-cue probability studies. *Psychological Review,* 1964, **71,** 42–60.
Irvine, W. *Apes, angels, and Victorians.* New York: Time-Life, 1963.
James, W. A. *The principles of psychology.* New York: Holt, 1890. Vols. I, II.
James, W. A. *Talks to teachers on psychology and to students on some of life's ideas.* New York: Holt, 1899.
James, W. A. *The varieties of religious experience.* New York: Holt, 1902.
Jensen, A. Personality. *Annual Review of Psychology,* 1958, **9,** 295–322.
Joncich, G. E. L. Thorndike: The psychologist as a professional man of science. *American Psychologist,* 1968, **23,** 434–446.
Jones, E. *The life and work of Sigmund Freud.* New York: Basic Books, Vol. 1, 1953; Vol. 2, 1955; Vol. 3, 1957.
Jones, M. C. A laboratory study of fear: The case of Peter. *Pedagogical Seminary,* 1924, **31,** 308–315.
Jones, M. C. Albert, Peter, and John B. Watson. *American Psychologist,* 1974, **29,** 581–583.
Jung, C. G. *Symbols of transformation.* New York: Random House, 1956.
Jung, C. G., & Pauli, W. *The interpretation of nature and the people.* New York: Random House, 1955.
Kalish, H. I. Stimulus generalization. In M. H. Marx (Ed.), *Learning processes.* New York: Macmillan, 1969. Pp. 205–298.
Kalish, H. I. Conditioning and learning in behavior modification. In M. H. Marx & M. E. Bunch (Eds.), *Fundamentals and applications of learning.* New York: Macmillan, 1977, Pp. 455–490.
Kantor, J. R. *Principles of psychology.* Vol. 1. New York: Knopf, 1924.
Kantor, J. R. *Principles of psychology.* Vol 2. New York: Knopf, 1926.
Kantor, J. R. *An outline of social psychology.* Chicago: Follett, 1929.
Kantor, J. R. *An objective psychology of grammar.* Bloomington: Indiana University Press, 1936. (Republished: Bloomington, Ind., Principia Press, 1952.)
Kantor, J. R. *Psychology and logic.* Vol. 1. Bloomington, Ind.: Principia Press, 1945.
Kantor, J. R. *Problems of physiological psychology.* Bloomington, Ind.: Principia Press, 1947.
Kantor, J. R. *Psychology and logic.* Vol. 2. Bloomington, Ind.: Principia Press, 1950.
Kantor, J. R. *The logic of modern science.* Bloomington, Ind.: Principia Press, 1953.
Kantor, J. R. *Interbehavioral psychology.* Bloomington, Ind.: Principia Press, 1958.
Kantor, J. R. *The scientific evolution of psychology.* Vol. 1. Bloomington, Ind.: Principia Press, 1963.
Kantor, J. R. *The scientific evolution of psychology.* Vol. 2. Bloomington, Ind.: Principia Press, 1969.
Kantor, J. R., & Smith, N. W. *The science of psychology: An interbehavioral survey.* Chicago: Principia, 1975.
Kardiner, A. *The individual and his society.* New York: Columbia University Press, 1939.
Karsten, A. Psychische Sattigung. *Psychologische Forschung,* 1928, **10,** 142–154.
Katona, G. *Organizing and memorizing.* New York: Columbia University Press, 1940.
Kawash, G., & Fuchs, A. H. A factor analysis of ratings of five schools of psychology on prescriptive dimensions. *Journal of the History of the Behvaioral Sciences,* 1974, **10,** 426–437.

Keller, F. S., & Schoenfeld, W. N. *Principles of psychology.* New York: Appleton-Century-Crofts, 1950.

Kendler, H. H. Kenneth W. Spence. *Psychological Review,* 1967, **74,** 335–341.

Killeen, P. R. Superstition: A matter of bias, not detectability. *Science,* 1978, **199,** 88–90.

Kimble, G. A. *Hilgard and Marquis' conditioning and learning.* New York: Appleton-Century-Crofts, 1961.

Kimble, G. A. *Foundations of conditioning and learning.* New York: Appleton-Century-Crofts, 1967.

Klemmer, E. T., & Frick, F. C. Assimilation of information from dot and matrix patterns. *Journal of Experimental Psychology,* 1953, **45,** 15–19.

Koch, S. Review of C. L. Hull, *Principles of behavior. Psychological Bulletin,* 1944, **41,** 269–286.

Koch, S. C. L. Hull. In W. K. Estes et al., *Modern learning theory.* New York: Appleton-Century-Crofts, 1954, Pp. 1–176.

Koch, S. (Ed.) *Psychology: A study of a science.* New York: McGraw-Hill, 1959–1963. 6 vols.

Koffka, K. *Principles of Gestalt psychology.* New York: Harcourt, Brace, 1935.

Köhler, W. *Die physischen Gestalten in Ruhe und im stationaren Zustand.* Erlangen: Weltkreisverlag, 1920.

Köhler, W. *The mentality of apes.* New York: Harcourt, Brace, 1925.

Köhler, W. Some Gestalt problems. In W. D. Ellis (Ed.), *A source book of Gestalt psychology.* London: Routledge & Kegan Paul, 1938. Pp. 55–70.

Köhler, W. Kurt Koffka. *Psychological Review,* 1942, **49,** 97–101.

Köhler, W. Gestalt psychology: An introduction to the new concepts in modern psychology. New York: Liveright, 1947.

Köhler, W. The present situation in brain physiology. *American Psychologist,* 1958, **13,** 150–154.

Köhler, W. *The task of Gestalt psychology.* Princeton, N.J.: Princeton University Press, 1969.

Kolata, G. B. Structure in large sets: Two proofs where there were none, *Science,* 1977, **195,** 767–768.

Krantz, D. L. Schools and systems: The mutual isolation of operant and non-operant psychology as a case study. *Journal of the History of the Behavioral Sciences,* 1972, **8,** 86–102.

Krech, D. Cortical localization of function. In L. Postman (Ed.), *Psychology in the making.* New York: Knopf, 1962. Pp. 31–72.

Krechevsky, I. "Hypotheses" in rats. *Psychological Review,* 1932, **39,** 516–532.

Kuhn, T. S. *The structure of scientific revolutions.* Chicago: University of Chicago Press, 1962.

Kuhn, T. S. *The structure of scientific revolutions.* (2nd ed.) Chicago: University of Chicago Press, 1970.

Kulpe, O. *Outlines of psychology, based upon results of experimental investigation.* (Trans. by E. B. Titchener) New York: Macmillan, 1895.

Kuo, Z. Y. The nature of unsuccessful acts and their order of elimination. *Journal of Comparative Psychology,* 1922, **2,** 1–27.

Kuo, Z. Y. A psychology without heredity. *Psychological Review,* 1924, **31,** 427–448.

Kuo, Z. Y. The genesis of the cat's response to the rat. *Journal of Comparative Psychology,* 1930, **11,** 1–35.

Kuo, Z. Y. Ontogeny of embryonic behavior in Aves. I. The chronology and general nature of the behavior of the chick embryo. *Journal of Experimental Zoology,* 1932, **61,** 395–430.(a)

Kuo, Z. Y. Ontogeny of embryonic behavior in Aves. IV. The influence of embryonic movements upon the behavior after hatching. *Journal of Comparative Psychology,* 1932, **14,** 109–122.(b)

Kuo, Z. Y. Ontogeny of embryonic behavior in Aves. II. The mechanical factors in the various stages leading to hatching. *Journal of Experimental Zoology,* 1932, **62,** 453–489.(c)

Kuo, Z. Y. Ontogeny of embryonic behavior in Aves. V. The reflex concepts in the light of embryonic behavior in birds. *Psychological Review,* 1932, **39,** 499–515.(d)

Kuo, Z. Y. Ontogeny of embryonic behavior in Aves. III. The structural and environmental factors in embryonic behavior. *Journal of Comparative Psychology,* 1932, **13,** 245–271.(e)

Kuo, Z. Y. Further study of the behavior of the cat toward the rat. *Journal of Comparative Psychology,* 1938, **25,** 1–8.

Kuo, Z. Y. *The dynamics of behavior development.* New York: Random House, 1967.

LaBrecque, M. Very short circuits. *The sciences,* 1970, **10,** 8–10.

Lakatos, I. Falsification and the methodology of scientific research programmes. In A. Musgrave & I. Lakatos (Eds.), *Criticism and the growth of knowledge.* New York: Cambridge University Press, 1970. Pp. 91–195.

Land, E. H. Experiments in color vision. *Scientific American,* 1959, **200,** 84–99.

Lashley, K. S. The behavioristic interpretation of consciousness. *Psychological Review,* 1923, **30,** 329–353.

Lashley, K. S. *Brain mechanisms and intelligence.* Chicago: University of Chicago Press, 1929.

Lashley, K. S. Cerebral control versus reflexology: A reply to Professor Hunter. *Journal of General Psychology,* 1931, **5,** 3–20.

Lashley, K. S., Chow, K. L., & Semmes, J. An examination of the electrical field theory of cerebral integration. *Psychological Review,* 1951, **58,** 123–136.

Lauer, Q. *Phenomenology: Its genesis and prospect.* New York: Harper & Row, 1965.

Lazarus, A. A. *Behavior therapy and beyond.* New York: McGraw-Hill, 1971.

Leeper, R. W. *Lewin's topological and vector psychology.* Eugene: University of Oregon Press, 1943.

Leeper, R. W. A critical consideration of Egon Brunswik's probabilistic functionalism. In K. R. Hammond (Ed.), *The psychology of Egon Brunswik.* New York: Holt, Rinehart, Winston, 1966. Pp. 405–454.

Lenneberg, E. H. *The biological foundations of language.* New York: Wiley, 1967.

Levine, G. & Burke, C. J. *Mathematical model techniques for learning theories.* New York: Academic Press, 1972.

Levine, M. Human discrimination learning: The subset sampling assumption. *Psychological Bulletin,* 1970, **74,** 397–404.

Levinson, D. J. Growing up with the dream. *Psychology Today,* 1978, **11,** 20.

Levy, L. *Concepts of personality: Theories and research.* New York: Random House, 1970.

Lewin, K. Die psychische Tatigkeit bei der Hemmung on Willensvorgängen und der Grundgestz der Assoziation. *Zeitschrift für Psychologie,* 1917, **77,** 212–247.

Lewin, K. *A dynamic theory of personality.* (Trans. by K. E. Zener & D. K. Adams) McGraw-Hill, 1935.

Lewin, K. *Principles of topological psychology.* (Trans. by F. Heider & G. Heider) New York: McGraw-Hill, 1936.

Lewin, K. *The conceptual representation and measurement of psychological forces.* Durham, N.C.: Duke University Press, 1938.

Lewin, K. Field theory and experiment in social psychology: Concept and methods. *American Journal of Sociology,* 1939, **44,** 868–896.

Lewin, K. Formalization and progress in psychology. *University of Iowa Studies in Child Welfare,* 1940, **16,** 9–42.

Lewin, K. Defining the "field at a given time." *Psychological Review,* 1943, **50,** 292–310.(a)

Lewin, K. Forces behind food habits and methods of change. *Bulletin of the National Research Council,* 1943, **108,** 35–65.(b)

Lewin, K. Constructs in psychology and psychological ecology. *University of Iowa Studies in Child Welfare,* 1944, **20,** 1–29.

Lewin, K. *Resolving social conflicts.* New York: Harper & Row, 1948.

Lewin, K. *Field theory in social science.* New York: Harper & Row, 1951.

Licklider, J. C. R. Three auditory theories. In S. Koch (Ed.), Psychology: A study of a science. Vol. 1. *Sensory, perceptual, and physiological formulations.* New York: McGraw-Hill, 1959. Pp. 41–144.

Lindzey, G. Behavior and morphological variation. In J. N. Spuhler (Ed.), *Genetic diversity and human behavior.* Chicago: Aldine, 1967. Pp. 227–240.

Lippitt, R. An experimental study of authoritarian and democratic group atmospheres. *University of Iowa Studies in Child Welfare,* 1940, **16,** 43–195.

Lippitt, R., & White, R. K. The "social climate" of children's groups. In R. G. Barker, J. S. Kounin, & H. F. Wright (Eds.), *Child behavior and development.* New York: McGraw-Hill, 1943. Pp. 485–508.

Lissner, K. Die Entspannung von Bedurfnissen durch Ersatzhandlungen. *Psychologische Forschung,* 1933, **18,** 218–250.

Lockard, R. B. Reflections on the fall of comparative psychology: Is there a message for us all? *American Psychologist,* 1971, **26,** 168–179.

Locke, J. *An essay concerning human understanding.* Vol. 2. (Reprinted from the 20th London ed.) Boston: David Carlisle, 1803 (originally published 1690).

Lockhart, R. S., & Murdock, B. B. Memory and the theory of signal detection. *Psychological Bulletin,* 1970, **74,** 100–109.

Logan, F. A. A micromolar approach to behavior theory. *Psychological Review,* 1956, **63,** 73–80.

Logan, F. A. The Hull-Spence approach. In S. Koch (Ed.), *Psychology: A study of a science.* Vol. 2. *General systematic formulations, learning and special processes.* New York: McGraw-Hill, 1959. Pp. 293–348.

Logan, F. A. *Fundamentals of learning and motivation.* Dubuque, Iowa: Brown, 1970.

London, I. D. Psychologists' misuse of the auxiliary concepts of physics and mathematics. *Psychological Review,* 1944, **51,** 42–45.

Lorenz, K. *On aggression.* New York: Harcourt, Brace & World, 1966.

Lorge, I. D. (Comp.) Edward L. Thorndike's publications from 1940 to 1949. *Teachers College Record,* 1949, **51,** 42–45.

Lubin, A. A note on Sheldon's table of correlations between temperamental traits. *British Journal of Psychology and Statistics,* 1950, **3,** 186–189.

Luce, R. D., Bush, R. R., & Galanter, E. *Handbook of mathematical psychology.* Vols. 1–3. New York: Wiley, 1963–1965.

Lundin, R. W. Behaviorism: Operant reinforcement. In R. J. Corsini (Ed.), *Current personality theories.* Itasca, Ill: Peacock, 1977. Pp. 177–202.

MacCorquodale, K. B. F. Skinner's *Verbal behavior:* A retrospective appreciation. *Journal of the Experimental Analysis of Behavior,* 1969, **12,** 831–841.

MacCorquodale, K., & Meehl, P. E. On the elimination of cul entries without obvious reinforcement. *Journal of Comparative & Physiological Psychology,* 1951, **44,** 367–371.

MacCorquodale, K., & Meehl, P. E. Edward C. Tolman. In W. K. Estes et al., *Modern learning theory.* New York: Appleton-Century-Crofts, 1954. Pp. 177–266.

MacKay, D. M. The nomenclature of information theory. In H. von Foerster (Ed.), *Transactions of the eighth conference on cybernetics: Circular causal and feedback mechanisms in biological and social systems.* New York: Josiah Macy, Jr., Foundation, 1952. Pp. 222–235.

MacKay, D. M. *Information, mechanism, and meaning.* Cambridge, Mass.: M.I.T. Press, 1969.

Macleod, R. B. Review of B. F. Skinner, *Cumulative record. Science,* 1959, **130,** 34–35.

Maddi, S. R. *Personality theories: A comparative analysis.* Homewood, Ill.: Dorsey Press, 1968.

Madsen, K. B. The formal properties of Cattellian personality theory and its relationship to other personality theories. In R. B. Cattell and R. M. Dreger (Eds.), *Handbook of modern personality theory.* New York: Wiley, 1977. Pp. 721–743.

Mahler, V. Ersatzhandlungen verschiedenen Realitatsgrades. *Psychologische Forschung,* 1933, **18,** 26–89.

Maier, N. R. F. Experimentally produced neurotic behavior in the rat. Paper presented at the meeting of the American Association for the Advancement of Science, Richmond, 1938.

Maier, N. R. F. *Frustration: The study of behavior without a goal.* New York: McGraw-Hill, 1949.

Maier, N. R. F., & Schneirla, T. C. *Principles of animal psychology.* New York: McGraw-Hill, 1935.

Malinowski, B. *Argonauts of the western Pacific.* New York: Dutton, 1950.

Marrow, A. J. *The practical theorist: The life and work of Kurt Lewin.* New York: Basic Books, 1969.

Marx, M. H. Spread of effect: A critical review. *Genetic Psychology Monographs,* 1956, **53,** 119–186.

Marx, M. H. Gradients of error-reinforcement in a serial perceptual-motor task. *Psychological Monographs,* 1957, **71,** 1–20.(a)

Marx, M. H. Gradients of error-reinforcement in normal multiple-choice learning situations. *Journal of Experimental Psychology,* 1957, **54,** 225–228.(b)

Marx, M. H. (Ed.) *Theories in contemporary psychology.* New York: Macmillan, 1963.

Marx, M. H., & Goodson, F. E. (Eds.), *Theories in contemporary psychology.* New York: Macmillan, 1976.

Marx, M. H., & Hillix, W. A. *Systems and theories in psychology.* (2nd ed.) New York: McGraw-Hill, 1973.

Maslow, A. H. *Motivation and personality.* New York: Harper, 1954.

Maslow, A. H. *Toward a psychology of being.* (2nd ed.) New Jersey: Van Nostrand-Reinhold, 1968.

Maslow, A. H. Self-actualizing and beyond. In A. H. Maslow (Ed.), *The farther reaches of human nature.* New York: Viking Press, 1972.

Masterman, M. The nature of a paradigm. In I. Lakatos & A. Musgrave (Eds.), *Criticism and the growth of knowledge.* London: Cambridge University Press, 1970. Pp. 59–89.

Maturana, H. R., Lettvin, J. Y., McCulloch, W. S., & Pitts, W. H. Anatomy and physiology of vision in the frog (Rana pipiens). *Journal of Genetic Physiology,* 1960, **43,** 129–175.
McCulloch, W. S., & Pitts, W. A logical calculus of the ideas immanent in nervous activity. *Bulletin of Mathematical Biophysics,* 1943, **5,** 115–133.
McDougall, W. *Physiological psychology.* London: Dent, 1905.
McDougall, W. *Psychology: The study of behavior.* London: Williams & Norgate, 1912.
McGeoch, J. A. The formal criteria of a systematic psychology. *Psychological Review,* 1933, **40,** 1–12.
McGeoch, J. A. Letters to Charles Mullett. Unpublished, 1934.
McGeoch, J. A. *The psychology of human learning.* New York: Longmans, 1942.
McGeoch, J. A., & Irion, A. L. *The psychology of human learning.* (2nd ed.) New York: Longmans, 1952.
McGuire, W. (Ed.) *The Freud/Jung letters.* Princeton, N.J.: Princeton University Press, 1974.
Mead, M. *Coming of age in Samoa.* New York: Morrow, 1928. (Republished: Garden City, N.Y., Doubleday, 1950.)
Meehl, P. E. On the circularity of the law of effect. *Psychological Bulletin,* 1950, **47,** 52–57.
Melton, A. W. Learning. *Annual Review of Psychology,* 1950, **1,** 9–30.
Meyer, M. *The fundamental laws of human behavior.* Boston: R. G. Badger, 1911.
Meyer, M. *The psychology of the other one.* Columbia: Missouri Book Store, 1921.
Mill, J. *The history of British India.* New Delhi: Associated Publishing House, 1972 (1818).
Mill, J. *Analysis of the phenomena of the human mind.* Vol. 1. London: Longmans, 1829.
Mill, J. S. *A system of logic.* London: Longmans, 1843. (Republished: 1956.)
Miller, G. A. The magical number seven, plus or minus two: Some limits on our capacity for processing information. *Psychological Review,* 1956, **63,** 81–87.
Miller, G. A. *Mathematics and psychology.* New York: Wiley, 1964.
Miller, G. A., Galanter, E., & Pribram, K. H. *Plans and the structure of behavior.* New York: Holt, 1960.
Miller, N. E. Experimental studies in conflict. In J. McV. Hunt (Ed.), *Personality and the behavior disorders.* Vol. 1. New York: Ronald Press, 1944. Pp. 431–465.
Miller, N. E. Theory and experiment relating psychoanalytic displacement to stimulus-response generalization. *Journal of Abnormal and Social Psychology,* 1948, **43,** 155–178.
Miller, N. E. Comments on multiple-process conceptions of learning. *Psychological Review,* 1951, **58,** 375–381.
Miller, N. E. Central stimulation and other new approaches to motivation and reward. *American Psychologist,* 1958, **13,** 100–108.
Miller, N. E. Liberalization of basic *S-R* concepts: Extensions to conflict behavior, motivation, and social learning. In S. Koch (Ed.), *Psychology: A study of a science.* Vol. 2. *General systematic formulations, learning and special processes.* New York: McGraw-Hill, 1959. Pp. 196–292.
Miller, N. E. Some reflections on the law of effect produce a new alternative to drive reduction. *Nebraska symposium on motivation.* Lincoln: University of Nebraska Press, 1963. Pp. 65–112.
Miller, N. E. Some implications of modern behavior theory for personality change and psychotherapy. In P. Worchel & D. Byrne (Eds.), *Personality change.* New York: Wiley, 1964. Pp. 149–175.
Miller, N. E. Learning of visceral and glandular responses. *Science,* 1969, **163,** 434–445.

Miller, N. E., & Dollard, J. *Social learning and imitation.* New Haven, Conn.: Yale University Press, 1941.

Misiak, H., & Sexton, V. S. *Phenomenological, existential, and humanistic psychologies: A historical survey.* New York: Grune & Stratton, 1973.

Morgan, C. L. *Introduction to comparative psychology.* London: W. Scott, 1891. (2nd ed., 1899.)

Morris, C. W. Foundations of the theory of signs. *International Encyclopedia of Unified Science,* 1938. Pp. 63–75.

Morris, D. *The naked ape.* New York: McGraw-Hill, 1968.

Mowrer, O. H. On the dual nature of learning: A re-interpretation of "conditioning" and "problem solving." *Harvard Educational Review,* 1947, **17,** 102–148.

Mowrer, O. H. *Learning theory and personality dynamics.* New York: Ronald Press, 1950.

Mowrer, O. H. Two-factor learning theory reconsidered with special reference to secondary reinforcement and the concept of habit. *Psychological Review,* 1956, **63,** 114–128.

Mowrer, O. H. Review of R. S. Woodworth, *Dynamics of behavior. Contemporary Psychology,* 1959, **4,** 129–133.

Mowrer, O. H. *Learning theory and behavior.* New York: Wiley, 1960.(a)

Mowrer, O. H. *Learning theory and the symbolic processes.* New York: Wiley, 1960.(b)

Mueller, C. G., Jr., Schoenfeld, W. M. *Edwin R. Guthrie.* In W. K. Estes et al., *Modern learning theory.* New York: Appleton-Century-Crofts, 1954. Pp. 345–379.

Mullahy, P. *Oedipus: Myth and complex.* New York: Hermitage House, 1948.

Müller, G. E. Komplextheorie und Gestalttheorie: Ein Beitrag zur Wahrenemungspsychologie. *Göttingen,* 1923.

Munroe, R. *Schools of psychoanalytic thought.* New York: Holt, 1955.

Murchison, C. (Ed.) *A history of psychology in autobiography.* Vols. 1–3. Worchester, Mass.: Clark University Press, 1930–1936.

Murphy, G. *Historical introduction to modern psychology.* New York: Harcourt, Brace & World, 1949.

Murray, E. Peripheral and central factors in memory: Images of visual form and color. *American Journal of Psychology,* 1906, **17,** 225–247.

Murray, H. A., et al. *Explorations in personality.* New York: Oxford University Press, 1938.

Murray, H. A. *Manual of thematic apperception test.* Cambridge, Mass.: Harvard University Press, 1943.

Murray, H. A. *Assessment of men.* New York: Holt, Rinehart and Winston, 1948.

Murray, H. A. In nomine diaboli. *New England Quarterly,* 1951, **24,** 435–452. (Reprinted in *Princeton University Library Chronicle,* 1952, **13,** 47–62.)

Murray, H. A. Preparations for the scaffold of a comprehensive system. In S. Koch (Ed.), *Psychology: A study of a science.* Vol. 3. *Formulations of the person and the social context.* New York: McGraw-Hill, 1959. Pp. 7–54.

Murray, H. A. Henry A. Murray. In E. G. Boring & G. Lindzey (Eds.), *A history of psychology in autobiography.* Vol. 5. New York: Appleton-Century-Crofts, 1967. Pp. 283–310.

Musgrave, A., & Lakatos, I. (Eds.) *Criticism and the growth of knowledge.* New York: Cambridge University Press, 1970.

Nafe, J. P. The psychology of felt experience. *American Journal of Psychology,* 1927, **39,** 367–389.

Nash, E. H., Frank, J. D., Imber, S. D., & Stone, A. R. Selected effects of inert medication on psychiatric outpatients. *American Journal of Psychotherapy,* 1964, **18,** Suppl. 1, 33–48.

Natsoulas, T. Concerning introspective "knowledge." *Psychological Bulletin,* 1970, **73,** 89–111.

Neisser, U. Visual Search. *Scientific American,* 1964, **210,** 94–102.

Newbury, E. Current interpretation and significance of Lloyd Morgan's canon. *Psychological Bulletin,* 1954, **51,** 70–74.

Newell, A., Shaw, J. C., & Simon, H. A. Elements of a theory of human problem solving. *Psychological Review,* 1958, **65,** 151–166.

Newell, A., & Simon, H. A. The simulation of human thought. In W. Dennis et al. (Eds.), *Current trends in psychological theory.* Pittsburgh: University of Pittsburgh Press, 1961. Pp. 152–179.

Office of Strategic Services Assessment Staff. *Assessment of men.* New York: Holt, 1948.

Olds, J. Physiological mechanism of reward. In M. R. Jones (Ed.), *Nebraska symposium on motivation.* Lincoln: University of Nebraska Press, 1955. Pp. 73–139.

O'Neil, W. M. Realism and behaviorism. *Journal of the History of the Behavioral Sciences,* 1968, **4,** 152–160.

Oppenheimer, R. Analogy in science. *American Psychologist,* 1956, **11,** 127–135.

Orbison, W. D. Shape as a function of the vector field. *American Journal of Psychology,* 1939, **52,** 31–45.

Ovsiankina, M. Die Wiederaufnahme unterbrochener Handlungen. *Psychologische Forschung,* 1928, **11,** 302–379.

Pask, G. *The cybernetics of human learning and performance.* London: Hutchinson, 1975.

Pavlov, I. P. The scientific investigation of the psychical faculties or processes in the higher animals. *Science,* 1906, **24,** 613–619.

Pavlov, I. P. *Conditioned reflexes.* London: Oxford University Press, 1927.

Pavlov, I. P. *Lectures on conditioned reflexes.* New York: Liveright, 1928.

Pavlov, I. P. The reply of a physiologist to psychologists. *Psychological Review,* 1932, **39,** 91–127.

Pavlov, I. P. *Lectures on conditioned reflexes.* Vol. 2. *Conditioned reflexes and psychiatry.* (Trans. & ed. by W. H. Gantt) New York: International Publishers, 1941.

Pavlov, I. P. *Selected works.* (Trans. by S. Belsky; ed. by J. Gibbons, under supervision of Kh. S. Koshtoyants) Moscow: Foreign Languages Publishing House, 1955.

Perky, C. W. An experimental study of imagination. *American Journal of Psychology,* 1910, **21,** 422–452.

Peterson, C. R., Hammond, K. R., & Summers, D. A. Optimal responding in multiple-cue probability learning. *Journal of Experimental Psychology,* 1965, **70,** 270–276.

Peterson, W. W., Birdsall, T. G., & Fox, W. C. The theory of signal detectability. *Transactions of Professional Group on Information Theory, Institute of Radio Engineers,* 1954, PGIT-4, 171–212.

Pierce, J. R., & Karlin, J. E. Reading rates and the information rate of a human channel. *Bell System Technical Journal,* 1957, **36,** 497–516.

Platt, J. R. *The excitement of science.* New York: Houghton Mifflin, 1962.

Polanyi, M. Life's irreducible structure. *Science,* 1968, **160,** 1308–1312.

Pollack, I. The assimilation of sequentially-encoded information. *HFORL Memo Report,* TR-54-5, 1954.

Pollack, I., & Ficks, L. Information on multidimensional auditory displays. *Journal of the Acoustical Society of America,* 1953, **25,** 765–769.

Pollack, I., & Klemmer, E. T. The assimilation of visual information from linear dot patterns. *Air Force Cambridge Research Center, Technical Report,* 1954, **54,** 16.

Popper, K. R. Normal Science and its dangers. In A. Musgrave & I. Lakatos (Eds.), *Criticism and the growth of knowledge.* New York: Cambridge University Press, 1970. Pp. 51–58 .

Posner, M. I. Information reduction in the analysis of sequential tasks. *Psychological Review,* 1964, **71,** 491–504.

Postman, L. The probability approach and nomothetic theory. *Psychological Review,* 1955, **62,** 218–225.

Postman, L. Spread of effect as a function of time and intraserial similarity. *American Journal of Psychology,* 1961, **74,** 493–505.

Postman, L., & Tolman, E. C. Brunswik's probabilistic functionalism. In S. Koch (Ed.), *Psychology: A study of a science.* Vol. I. *Sensory, perceptual, and physiological formulations.* New York: McGraw-Hill, 1959, Pp. 502–564.

Prentice, W. C. H. The systematic psychology of Wolfgang Köhler. In S. Koch (Ed.), *Psychology: A study of a science.* Vol. 1. *Sensory, perceptual, and physiological formulations.* New York: McGraw-Hill, 1959. Pp. 427–455.

Pumpian-Mindlin, E. (Ed.) *Psychoanalysis as science.* Stanford, Calif.: Stanford University Press, 1952.

Quastler, H., Osborne, J. W., & Tweedell, K. Human performance in information transmission. III. University of Illinois Report R-68, Control Systems Laboratory, 1955.

Rank, O. *The trauma of birth.* New York: Harcourt, Brace, 1929.

Rapaport, D. The structure of psychoanalytic theory: A systematizing attempt. In S. Koch (Ed.), *Psychology: A study of a science.* Vol. 3. *Formulations of the person and the social context.* New York: McGraw-Hill, 1959. Pp. 55–183.

Rapoport, A. *Two-person game theory.* Ann Arbor: University of Michigan Press, 1969.

Rapoport, A. *N-person game theory.* Ann Arbor: University of Michigan Press, 1970.

Rashevsky, N. *Mathematical biophysics.* (Rev. ed.) Chicago: University of Chicago Press, 1948.

Raush, H. L., Dittman, A. T., & Taylor, T. J. Person, setting, and change in social interaction. *Human Relations,* 1959, **12,** 361–378.

Raush, H. L., Dittman, A. T., & Taylor, T. J. Person, setting and change in social interaction. II. A normal control study. *Human Relations,* 1960, **13,** 305–332.

Razran, G. Stimulus generalization of conditioned responses. *Psychological Bulletin,* 1949, **46,** 337–365.

Reinforcement therapy: short cut to sanity? *Time,* 1969, **94**(2), 52–54.

Rescorla, R. A., & Solomon, R. L. Two-process learning theory: Relationships between Pavlovian conditioning and instrumental learning. *Psychological Review,* 1967, **74,** 151–182.

Restle, F., & Greeno, J. C. *Introduction to mathematical psychology.* Reading, Mass.: Addison-Wesley, 1970.

Roback, A. A. *A history of American psychology.* New York: Library Publishers, 1952.

Rogers, C. R. *The clinical treatment of the problem child.* Boston: Houghton Mifflin, 1939.

Rogers, C. R. *Counseling and psychotherapy: Newer concepts in practice.* Boston: Houghton Mifflin, 1942.

Rogers, C. R. *Client-centered therapy: Its current practice, implications, and theory.* Boston: Houghton Mifflin, 1951.

Rogers, C. R. Some issues concerning the control of human behavior. (Symposium with B. F. Skinner) *Science,* 1956, **124,** 1057–1066.

Rogers, C. R. A theory of therapy, personality, and interpersonal relationships, as developed in the client-centered framework. In S. Koch (Ed.), *Psychology: A study of a science.* Vol. 3. *Formulations of the person and the social context.* New York: McGraw-Hill, 1959. Pp. 184–256.

Rogers, C. R. *On becoming a person.* Boston: Houghton Mifflin, 1961.

Rogers, C. R. Carl R. Rogers. In E. G. Boring & G. Lindzey (Eds.), *A history of psychology in autobiography.* Vol. 5. New York: Appleton-Century-Crofts, 1967. Pp. 341–384.(a)

Rogers, C. R. (Ed.) *The therapeutic relationship and its impact: A study of psychotherapy with schizophrenics.* Madison: University of Wisconsin Press, 1967.(b)

Rogers, C. R. Client-centered psychotherapy. In A. M. Freedman, H. I. Kaplan, & B. J. Sadock (Eds.) *Comprehensive textbook of psychiatry II.* Baltimore: Williams & Wilkins, 1975.

Romanes, G. J. *Animal intelligence.* London: Kegan Paul, Trench, Trubner, 1886.

Rosenbaum, M. E., & Hewitt, O. J. The effect of electric shock on learning by performers and observers. *Psychonomic Science,* 1966, **5,** 81–82.

Rosenbaum, M. E., & Schutz, L. J. The effects of extraneous response requirements on learning by performers and observer. *Psychonomic Science,* 1967, **8,** 51–52.

Ross, D. *G. Stanley Hall: The psychologist as prophet.* Chicago: University of Chicago Press, 1972.

Rubin, E. *Syncopleoede figurer.* Kobenhavn: Gyldendalske Boghandel, 1915.

Ruckmick, C. A. The use of the term function in English textbooks of psychology. *American Journal of Psychology,* 1913, **14,** 99–123.

Rudikoff, E. C. A comparative study of the changes in the concepts of the self, the ordinary person, and the ideal: Eight cases. In C. R. Rogers & R. F. Dymond (Eds.), *Psychotherapy and personality change: Coordinated studies in the client-centered approach.* Chicago: University of Chicago Press, 1954. Pp. 85–98.

Russell, B. *A history of western philosophy.* New York: Simon & Schuster, 1945.

Sahakian, W. S. *History and systems of psychology.* New York: Wiley, 1975.

Sahakian, W. S. Personalism. In R. J. Corsini (Ed.), *Current personality theories.* Itasca, Ill: Peacock, 1977. Pp. 153–175.

Samuel, A. L. Some studies in machine learning using the game of checkers. In E. Feigenbaum & F. Feldman (Eds.), *Computers and thought.* New York: McGraw-Hill, 1963. Pp. 71–105.

Sanford, R. N. Physical and physiological correlates of personality structure. In C. Kluckhohn, H. A. Murray, & D. Scheider (Eds.), *Personality in nature, society, and culture.* (2nd ed.) New York: Knopf, 1953. Pp. 100–103.

Sarton, G. *A guide to the history of science.* Waltham, Mass.: Chronica Botanica, 1952.

Sartre, J. P. *Being and nothingness.* (Trans. by H. Barnes) New York. Philosophical Library, 1956.

Schaub, A. deV. On the intensity of images. *American Journal of Psychology,* 1911, **22,** 346–368.

Schlosberg, H. The relationship between success and the laws of conditioning. *Psychological Review,* 1937, **44,** 379–394.

Schoenfeld, W. N., Cumming W. W., & Hearst, E. On the classification of reinforcement schedules. In A. C. Catania (Ed.), *Contemporary research in operant behavior.* Glenview, Ill.: Scott, Foresman, 1968. Pp. 113–118.

Schultz, D. P. *A history of modern psychology.* New York: Academic Press, 1969.

Scriven, M. The mechanical concept of mind. In K. M. Sayre & F. J. Crosson (Eds.), *The modeling of the mind: Computers and intelligence.* Notre Dame, Ind: University of Notre Dame Press, 1963. Pp. 243–254.

Sears, R. R. *Survey of objective studies of psychoanalytic concepts.* New York: Social Science Research Council, 1943.

Sechenov, I. M. *Reflexes of the brain.* Cambridge, Mass.: M.I.T. Press, 1965 (1863).

Sechrest, L. Personality. *Annual Review of Psychology.* Palo Alto, Calif.: 1976, **27,** 1–27.

Sechrest, L. Personal constructs theory. In R. J. Corsini (Ed.), *Current personality theories.* Itasca, Ill: Peacock, 1977. Pp. 203–241.

Seltzer, C. C., Wells, F. L., & McTernan, E. B. A relationship between Sheldonian somatotype and psychotype. *Journal of Personality,* 1948, **16,** 431–436.

Seward, J. P., Dill, J. B., & Holland, M. A. Guthrie's theory of learning: A second experiment. *Journal of Experimental Psychology,* 1944, **34,** 226–238.

Sexton, V. & Misiak, H. (Eds.) *Psychology around the world.* Monterey, Calif.: Brooks-Cole, 1976.

Shannon, C. E. Prediction and entropy of printed English. *Bell System Technical Journal,* 1951, **30,** 50–64.

Shannon, C. E., & Weaver, W. *The mathematical theory of communication.* Urbana: University of Illinois Press, 1949.

Sheffield, F. D. Avoidance training and the contiguity principle. *Journal of Comparative and Physiological Psychology,* 1948, **41,** 165–167.

Sheffield, F. D. "Spread of effect" without reward or learning. *Journal of Experimental Psychology,* 1949, **39,** 575–579.

Sheffield, F. D., & Roby, T. B. Reward value of a non-nutritive sweet taste. *Journal of Comparative and Physiological Psychology,* 1950, **43,** 471–481.

Sheffield, F. D., Wulff, J. J., & Backer, R. Reward value of copulation without sex drive reduction. *Journal of Comparative and Physiological Psychology,* 1951, **44,** 3–8.

Sheffield, F. D. *A drive-induction theory of reinforcement.* New Haven: Yale University, 1954 (mimeographed MS., personally distributed).

Sheldon, W. H., with the collaboration of S. S. Stevens & W. B. Tucker. *The varieties of human physique: An introduction to constitutional psychology.* New York: Harper & Row, 1940.

Sheldon, W. H., with the collaboration of S. S. Stevens. *The varieties of temperament: A psychology of constitutional differences.* New York: Harper & Row, 1942.

Sheldon, W. H. Constitutional factors in personality. In J. McV. Hunt (Ed.), *Personality and the behavior disorders.* New York: Ronald Press, 1944. Pp. 526–549.

Sheldon, W. H. *Early American cents,* 1793–1814. New York: Harper & Row, 1949.(a)

Sheldon, W. H., with the collaboration of E. M. Harth & E. McDermott. *Varieties of delinquent youth: An introduction to constitutional psychiatry.* New York: Harper & Row, 1949.(b)

Sheldon, W. H., with the collaboration of C. W. Dupetuis & E. McDermott. *Atlas of men: A guide for somatotyping the adult male at all ages.* New York: Harper & Row, 1954.

Sheldon, W. H., Lewis, N. D. C., & Tenney, A. M. Psychotic patterns and physical constitution: A thirty-year follow-up of thirty-eight hundred psychiatric patients in New York State. In D. V. Siva Sankar (Ed.), *Schizophrenia: Current concepts and research.* Waterbury, N.Y.: PJD Publications, 1969. Pp. 838–912.

Sherrington, C. S. *The integrative action of the nervous system.* London: Constable, 1906. (Republished with a new foreword and a bibliography of Sherrington's publications: New Haven, Conn.: Yale University Press, 1947.)

Shipley, T. (Ed.) *Classics in psychology.* New York: Philosophical Library, 1961.

Shontz, F. C. Constitutional theories of personality. In R. J. Corsini (Ed.), *Current personality theories.* Itasca, Ill: Peacock, 1977 Pp. 303–333.

Sidman, M. *Tactics of scientific research.* New York: Basic Books, 1960.
Silverman, L. H., Psychoanalytic theory: "The reports of my death are greatly exaggerated." *American Psychologist,* 1976, **9,** 621–637.
Simon, H. A. Letters. *Science,* 1970, **169,** 630–631.
Skaggs, E. B. Personalistic psychology as a science. *Psychological Review,* 1945, **52,** 234–240.
Skinner, B. F. *The behavior of organisms.* New York: Appleton-Century-Crofts, 1938.
Skinner, B. F. "Superstition" in the pigeon. *Journal of Experimental Psychology,* 1948, **38,** 168–172.(a)
Skinner, B. F. *Walden two.* New York: Macmillan, 1948.(b)
Skinner, B. F. *Science and human behavior.* New York: Macmillan, 1953.
Skinner, B. F. Critique of psychoanalytic concepts and theories. *Scientific Monthly,* 1954, **79,** 300–305.
Skinner, B. F. *Verbal behavior.* New York: Appleton-Century-Crofts, 1957.
Skinner, B. F. A case history in scientific method. In S. Koch (Ed.), *Psychology: A study of a science,* Vol. 2, *General systematic formulations, learning and special processes.* New York: McGraw-Hill, 1959, Pp. 359–379.(a)
Skinner, B. F. *Cumulative record.* New York: Appleton-Century-Crofts, 1959.(b)
Skinner, B. F. Pigeons in a pelican. *American Psychologist,* 1960, **15,** 28–37.
Skinner, B. F. Operant behavior. In W. K. Honig (Ed.), *Operant behavior: Areas of research and application.* New York: Appleton-Century-Crofts, 1966. Pp. 12–32.
Skinner, B. F. B. F. Skinner. In E. G. Boring & G. Lindzey (Eds.), *A history of psychology in autobiography.* New York: Appleton-Century-Crofts, 1967. Pp. 385–413.
Skinner, B. F. *Contingencies of reinforcement: A theoretical analysis.* New York: Appleton-Century-Crofts, 1969.
Skinner, B. F. *Beyond freedom and dignity.* New York: Knopf, 1971.
Skinner, B. F. *About behaviorism.* New York: Knopf, 1974.
Skinner, B. F. Herrnstein and the evolution of behaviorism. *American Psychologist,* 1977, **32,** 1006–1012.
Sloane, R. B., Staples, F. R., Cristol, A. H., Yorkston, N. J., & Wipple, K. *Psychotherapy versus behavior therapy.* Cambridge, Mass.: Harvard University Press, 1975.
Smith, C. S. Matter versus materials: A historical view. *Science,* 1968, **162,** 637–644.
Smith, K. Conditioning as an artifact. *Psychological Review,* 1954, **61,** 217–225.
Smith, M., & Wilson, E. A model of the auditory threshold and its application to the problem of the multiple observer. *Psychological Monographs,* 1953, **67,** No. 9. Pp. 1–35.
Smith, N. K. *The philosophy of David Hume.* London: Macmillan, 1949.
Smith, S., & Guthrie, E. R. *General psychology in terms of behavior.* New York: Appleton, 1921.
Smith, S. K., & Miller, G. A. The effects of coding procedures on learning and memory. Quarterly progress report of Research Laboratory of Electronics, M.I.T., to Air Force Human Resources Research Laboratories, 1952.
Snygg, D., & Combs, A. W. *Individual behavior.* New York: Harper & Row, 1949.
Sokal, M. M. The unpublished autobiography of James McKeen Cattell. *American Psychologist,* 1971, **26,** 626–635.
Spearman, C. E. *Creative mind.* New York: Appleton, 1931.
Spence, K. W. The nature of discrimination learning in animals. *Psychological Review,* 1936, **43,** 427–449.

Spence, K. W. Analysis of the formation of visual discrimination habits in chimpanzees. *Journal of Comparative Psychology,* 1937, **23,** 77–100.(a)

Spence, K. W. The differential response in animals to stimuli varying within a single dimension. *Psychological Review,* 1937, **44,** 430–444.(b)

Spence, K. W. Continuous vs. non-continuous interpretations of discrimination learning. *Psychological Review,* 1940, **47,** 271–288.

Spence, K. W. The methods and postulates of "behaviorism." *Psychological Review,* 1948, **55,** 67–78. (Reprinted in M. H. Marx [Ed.], *Theories in contemporary psychology.* New York: Macmillan, 1963. Pp. 272–286.)

Spence, K. W. Theoretical interpretations of learning. In C. P. Stone (Ed.), *Comparative psychology.* (3rd ed.) Englewood Cliffs, N.J.: Prentice-Hall, 1951. Pp. 239–291.(a)

Spence, K. W. Theoretical interpretations of learning. In S. S. Stevens (Ed.), *Handbook of experimental psychology.* New York: Wiley, 1951. Pp. 690–729.(b)

Spence, K. W. *Behavior theory and conditioning.* New Haven, Conn.: Yale University Press, 1956.

Spence, K. W. *Behavior theory and learning: Selected papers.* Englewood Cliffs, N.J.: Prentice-Hall, 1960.

Spence, K. W. Cognitive and drive factors in the extinction of the conditioned eye blink in human subjects. *Psychological Review,* 1966, **73,** 445–458.

Spencer, H. *The principles of psychology.* New York: Appleton, 1855.

Spencer, H. *The study of sociology.* Ann Arbor: University of Michigan Press, 1961. (originally pub. 1873).

Sperry, R. W., & Miner, N. Pattern perception following insertion of mica plates into visual cortex. *Journal of Comparative and Physiological Psychology,* 1955, **48,** 463–469.

Sperry, R. W., Miner, N., & Myers, R. E. Visual pattern perception following subpial slicing and tantalum wire implantations in the visual cortex. *Journal of Comparative and Physiological Psychology,* 1955, **48,** 50–58.

Staddon, J. E. R., & Simmelhag, V. L. The "superstition" experiment: A reexamination of its implications for the principles of adaptive behavior. *Psychological Review,* 1971, **78,** 3–43.

Stephenson, W. *The study of behavior: Q-technique and its methodology.* Chicago: University of Chicago Press, 1953.

Stephenson, W. Scientific-creed—1961: Philosophical credo, abductory principles, the centrality of self. *Psychological Record,* 1961, **11,** 1–18.

Sternberg, S. High speed scanning in human memory. *Science,* 1966, **153,** 652–654.

Stevens, S. S. Psychology and the science of science. *Psychological Bulletin,* 1939, **36,** 221–263.

Stevens, S. S. (Ed.) *Handbook of experimental psychology.* New York: Wiley, 1951.

Stevens, S. S. Measurement, statistics, and the schemapiric view. *Science,* 1968, **161,** 849–856.

Stout, G. F. *Analytic psychology.* New York: Macmillan, 1902.

Sullivan, H. S. *Conceptions of modern psychiatry.* Washington, D.C.: William Alanson White Psychiatric Foundation, 1947.

Sullivan, H. S. *The interpersonal theory of psychiatry.* New York: Norton, 1953.

Sullivan, H. S. *The psychiatric interview.* New York: Norton, 1954.

Sullivan, H. S. *Clinical studies in psychiatry.* New York: Norton, 1956.

Sullivan, H. S. *Schizophrenia as a human process.* New York. Norton, 1962.

Sullivan, H. S. *The fusion of psychiatry and social science.* New York: Norton, 1964.

Sumby, W. H., & Pollack, I. Short-time processing of information. HFORL Report TR-54-6, 1954.

Summers, D. A., & Hammond, K. R. Inference behavior in multiple-cue tasks involving both linear and nonlinear relations. *Journal of Experimental Psychology,* 1966, **71,** 751–757.

Swets, J. A. Is there a sensory threshold? *Science,* 1961, **134,** 168–177.

Swets, J. A. (Ed.) *Signal detection and recognition by human observers: Contemporary readings.* New York: Wiley, 1964.

Tanner, W. P., Jr. Physiological implications of psycho-physical data. *Annals of the New York Academy of Science,* 1961, **89,** 752–765.

Tanner, W. P. & Swets, J. A. A new theory of visual detection. Technical Report 18, Electronic Defense Group, University of Michigan, 1953.

Tanner, W. P., & Swets, J. A. A decision-making theory of visual detection. *Psychological Review,* 1954, **61,** 401–409.

Terrace, H. S. Stimulus control. In W. K. Honig (Ed.) *Operant behavior: Areas of research and application.* New York: Appleton-Century-Crofts, 1966. Pp. 271–344.

Thistlethwaite, D. A. A critical review of latent learning and related experiments. *Psychological Bulletin,* 1951, **48,** 97–129.

Thom, R. *Structural stability and morphogenesis: An outline of a general theory of models.* (Trans. by D. H. Fowler.) Reading, Mass.: Benjamin, 1975.

Thorndike, E. L. *The elements of psychology.* New York: A. G. Seiler, 1905.

Thorndike, E. L. *Animal intelligence.* New York: Hafner, 1911.

Thorndike, E. L. *Educational psychology.* Vol. 2, *The psychology of learning.* New York: Teachers College, 1913.

Thorndike, E. L. *Human learning.* New York: Century, 1931.

Thorndike, E. L. *The fundamentals of learning.* New York: Teachers College, 1932.

Thorndike, E. L. An experimental study of rewards. *Teachers College Contributions to Education.* 1933, No. 580.(a)

Thorndike, E. L. A theory of the action of the after-effects of a connection upon it. *Psychological Review,* 1933, **40,** 434–439.(b)

Thorndike, E. L. *The psychology of wants, interests, and attitudes.* New York: Appleton-Century-Crofts, 1935.

Thorndike, E. L. E. L. Thorndike. In C. Murchison (Ed.), *A history of psychology in autobiography.* Vol. 3. Worcester, Mass.: Clark University Press, 1936. Pp. 263–270.

Thorndike, E. L. *Selected writings from a connectionist's psychology.* New York: Appleton-Century-Crofts, 1949.

Thorndike, E. L., & Rock, R. T., Jr. Learning without awareness of what is being learned or intent to learn it. *Journal of Experimental Psychology,* 1934, **17,** 1–19.

Thorndike, E. L., & Woodworth, R. S. The influence of improvements in one mental function upon the efficiency of other functions. *Psychological Review,* 1901, **8,** 247–261, 384–395, 553–564.

Titchener, E. B. The postulates of a structural psychology. *Philosophical Review,* 1898, **7,** 449–465. As reported by W. Dennis (Ed.), *Readings in the history of psychology.* New York: Appleton-Century-Crofts, 1948. Pp. 366–376.

Titchener, E. B. *An outline of psychology.* New York: Macmillan, 1899.

Titchener, E. B. *Text-book of psychology.* New York: Macmillan, 1910.

Titchener, E. B. Prolegomena to a study of introspection. *American Journal of Psychology,* 1912, **23,** 427–488(a)

Titchener, E. B. The schema of introspection. *American Journal of Psychology,* 1912, **23,** 485–508.(b)

Titchener, E. B. *Systematic psychology: Prolegomena.* New York: Macmillan, 1929.

Tolman, E. C. A behaviorist's definition of consciousness. *Psychological Review,* 1927, **34,** 433–439.

Tolman, E. C. *Purposive behavior in animals and man.* New York: Appleton, 1932.

Tolman, E. C. The determiners of behavior at a choice point. *Psychological Review,* 1938, **45,** 1–41.

Tolman, E. C. A stimulus-expectancy need-cathexis psychology. *Science,* 1945, **101,** 160–166.

Tolman, E. C. The psychology of social learning. *Journal of Social Issues, Supplement Service,* 1949, **3,** 5–18.(a)

Tolman, E. C. There is more than one kind of learning. *Psychological Review,* 1949, **56,** 144–155.(b)

Tolman, E. C. *Collected papers in psychology.* Berkeley: University of California Press, 1951.(a)

Tolman, E. C. A psychological model. In T. Parsons & E. A Shils (Eds.), *Toward a general theory of action.* Cambridge, Mass.: Harvard University Press, 1951. Pp. 279–361.(b)

Tolman, E. C. Principles of purposive behavior. In S. Koch (Ed.), *Psychology: A study of a science.* Vol. 2. *General systematic formulations, learning and special processes.* New York: McGraw-Hill, 1959. Pp. 92–157.

Tolman, E. C. Eulogy: Egon Brunswik: 1903–1955. In K. R. Hammond (Ed.), *The psychology of Egon Brunswik.* New York: Holt, Rinehart and Winston, 1966. Pp. 1–12.

Tolman, E. C., & Brunswik, E. The organism and the causal texture of the environment. *Psychological Review,* 1935, **42,** 43–77.

Tolman, E. C., & Gleitman, H. Studies in learning and motivation. *Journal of Experimental Psychology,* 1949, **39,** 810–819.

Tolman, E. C., & Honzik, C. H. "Insight" in rats. *University of California Publications in Psychology,* 1930, **4,** 215–232.

Toulmin, S. The logical status of psychoanalysis. *Analysis,* 1948, **9,** 23–29.

Toulmin, S. *Human understanding.* Vol. 1. Princeton, N.J.: Princeton University Press, 1972.

Townsend, J. T. Issues and models concerning the processing of a finite number of inputs. In B. H. Kantoqitz (Ed.), *Human information processing: Tutorials in performance and cognition.* New York: Wiley, 1974. Pp. 133–185.

Trilling, L., & Marcus, S. (Eds.) *The life and work of Sigmund Freud.* By E. Jones. Garden City, N.Y.: Doubleday, 1961.

Turing, A. M. On computable numbers, with an application to the Entscheidung's problem. *Proceedings of the London Mathematical Society,* 1937, **42,** 230–265; 1937, **43,** 544–546. Also in M. Davis (Ed.), *The undecidable.* Hewlett, N.Y.: Raven Press, 1965.

Turner, M. B. *Philosophy and the science of behavior.* New York: Appleton-Century-Crofts, 1967.

Turner, M. B. *Realism and the explanation of behavior.* New York: Appleton-Century-Crofts, 1971.

Twitmyer, E. B. Knee jerk without stimulation of the patellar tendon. *Psychological Bulletin,* 1905, **2,** 43–44. (Abstract)

Ullman, L. P., & Krasner, L. *Case studies in behavior modification.* New York: Holt, Rinehart, and Winston, 1965.

Underwood, B. J. *Experimental psychology.* New York: Appleton-Century-Crofts, 1949; rev. ed., 1966.

Underwood, B. J. *Psychological research.* New York: Appleton-Century-Crofts, 1957.

Underwood, B. J., & Ekstrand, B. R. Studies of distributed practice: XXIV. Differentiation and proactive inhibition. *Journal of Experimental Psychology,* 1967, **74,** 574–580.

Voeks, V. W. Postremity, recency, and frequency as bases for prediction in the maze situation. *Journal of Experimental Psychology,* 1948, **38,** 495–510.

Voeks, V. W. Formalization and clarification of a theory of learning. *Journal of Psychology,* 1950, **30,** 341–362.

Voeks, V. W. Acquisition of S-R connections: A test of Hull's and Guthrie's theories. *Journal of Experimental Psychology,* 1954, **47,** 137–147.

Von Neumann, J. *The computer and the brain.* New Haven, Conn.: Yale University Press, 1958.

Walker, N. Science and the Freudian unconsciousness. In T. Reik (Ed.), *Psychoanalysis and the future.* New York: National Psychological Association for Psychoanalysis, 1957. Pp. 117–124.

Walls, G. L. "Land! Land!" *Psychological Bulletin,* 1960, **57,** 29–48.

Wann, T. W. (Ed.) *Behaviorism and phenomenology.* Chicago: University of Chicago Press, 1964.

Washburn, M. F. *The animal mind.* New York: Macmillan, 1908.

Watanabe, S. Information-Theoretic aspects of inductive and deductive inference. *IBM Journal of Research & Development,* 1960, **4,** 208–231.

Watson, J. B. Image and affection in behavior. *Journal of Philosophy,* 1913, **10,** 421–428.(a)

Watson, J. B. Psychology as the behaviorist views it. *Psychological Review,* 1913, **20,** 158–177.(b)

Watson, J. B. *Behavior: An introduction to comparative psychology.* New York: Holt, 1914.

Watson, J. B. *Psychology from the standpoint of a behaviorist.* Philadelphia: Lippincott, 1919.

Watson, J. B. *Behaviorism.* New York: Norton, 1925.

Watson, J. B. Experimental studies on the growth of the emotions. In C. Murchison (Ed.), *Psychologies of 1925.* Worcester, Mass.: Clark University Press, 1926. Pp. 52–53.(a)

Watson, J. B. Recent experiments on how we lose and change our emotional equipment. In C. Murchison (Ed.), *Psychologies of 1925.* Worcester, Mass.: Clark University Press, 1926. Pp. 59–81.(b)

Watson, J. B. *Psychology from the standpoint of a behaviorist.* (3rd ed.) Philadelphia: Lippincott, 1929.

Watson, J. B. *Behaviorism.* (Rev. ed.) New York: Norton, 1930.

Watson, J. B. J. B. Watson. In C. Murchison (Ed.), *A history of psychology in autobiography.* Vol. 3. Worcester, Mass.: Clark University Press, 1936. Pp. 271–281.

Watson, J. B. *Behavior: An introduction to comparative psychology.* New York: Holt, Rinehart, & Winston, 1967.

Watson, J. B., & McDougall, W. *The battle of behaviorism.* New York: Norton, 1929.

Watson, R. I. *The great psychologists from Aristotle to Freud.* Philadelphia: Lippincott, 1963.

Watson, R. I. Psychology: A prescriptive science. *American Psychologist,* 1967, **22,** 435–443.

Watson, R. I. *The great psychologists from Aristotle to Freud.* (Rev. ed.) Philadelphia: Lippincott, 1968.

Watson, R. I. *The great psychologists.* (3rd ed.) Philadelphia: Lippincott, 1971.

Weiss, A. P. Relation between structural and behavior psychology. *Psychological Review,* 1917, **34,** 301–317.

Weiss, A. P. *A theoretical basis of human behavior.* Columbus, Ohio: Adams, 1925.

Weiss, P. 1 + 1 ≠ 2 (one plus one does not equal two.) In G. C. Quarton, T. Melnechuk, & F. O. Schmitt (Eds.), *The neurosciences.* New York: Rockefeller University Press, 1967. Pp. 801–821.

Wellek, A. The impact of the German immigration on the development of American psychology. *Journal of the History of the Behavioral Sciences,* 1968, **4,** 207–229.

Wertheimer, M. Experimentelle Studien über das Sehen von Bewegung. *Zeitschrift für Psychologie,* 1912, **61,** 121–165.

Wertheimer, M. Untersuchungen zur Lehre von der Gestalt. II. *Psychologische Forschung,* 1923, **4,** 301–350.

Wertheimer, M. The general theoretical situation. In W. D. Ellis (Ed.), *A source book of Gestalt psychology.* New York: Harcourt, Brace & World, 1938. Pp. 12–16.

Wertheimer, M. *Productive thinking.* New York: Harper & Row, 1945.

Wheeler, R. H. *The science of psychology.* (2nd ed.) New York: Crowell, 1940.

Whytt, R. *An essay on the vital and other involuntary motions of animals.* (2nd ed.) Edinburgh: J. Balfour, 1763.

Wiener, N. *Cybernetics, or Control and communication in the animal and the machine.* Cambridge, Mass.: Technology Press [c1948], New York: Wiley, 1948.

Wiener, N. *Cybernetics, or Control and communication in the animal and the machine.* (2nd ed.) Cambridge, Mass.: M.I.T. Press, 1961.

Willems, E. P., & Raush, H. L. (Eds.) *Naturalistic viewpoints in psychological research.* New York: Holt, 1969.

Wilson, E. O. *Sociobiology: The new synthesis.* Cambridge, Mass.: Harvard University Press, 1975.

Windelband, W. *An introduction to philosophy.* (Trans. by J. McCabe) London: T. Fisher Unwin, 1921.

Winograd, T. *Understanding natural language.* New York: Academic Press, 1972.

Woodworth, R. S. *Dynamic psychology.* New York: Columbia University Press, 1918.

Woodworth, R. S. Four varieties of behavior. *Psychological Review,* 1924, **31,** 257–264.

Woodworth, R. S. *Experimental psychology.* New York: Holt, 1938.

Woodworth, R. S. Reinforcement of perception. *American Journal of Psychology,* 1947, **60,** 119–124.

Woodworth, R. S. *Contemporary schools of psychology.* New York: Ronald Press, 1948.

Woodworth, R. S., & Schlosberg, H. *Experimental psychology.* New York: Holt, 1954.

Woodworth, R. S. *Dynamics of behavior.* New York: Holt, 1958.

Woodworth, R. S., & Sheehan, M. R. *Contemporary schools of psychology.* New York: Ronald Press, 1964.

Wooldridge, D. E. *Mechanical man: The physical basis of intelligent life.* New York: McGraw-Hill, 1968.

Wundt, W. *Lectures on human and animal psychology.* (Trans. by J. E. Creighton & E. B. Titchener.) New York: Macmillan, 1894.

Wundt, W. *Principles of physiological psychology.* (Trans. by E. B. Titchener.) New York: Macmillan, 1910.

Wundt, W. *Völkerpsychologie.* Vols. 1–10. Leipzig: Engelmann, 1900–1920.

Yerkes, R. M. *Chimpanzees: A laboratory colony.* New Haven, Conn.: Yale University Press, 1943.

Young, T. On the theory of light and colours. In the *Philosophical Transactions* of the Royal Society of London, 1802, p. 20.

Zeeman, E. C. Catastrophe theory. *Scientific American*, 1976, **234**(4), 65–83.

Zeigarnik, B. Das Behalten erledigter und unerledigter Handlungen. *Psychologische Forschung,* 1927, **9,** 1–85. (Trans. and cond. as "On finished and unfinished tasks" in W. D. Ellis [Ed.], *A source book of Gestalt psychology.* New York: Harcourt, Brace & World, 1938. Pp. 300–314.)

GLOSSARY

Abacus A manual computational device using beads that slide on rods; though of ancient origin, an abacus may be used for some operations by an expert at a speed as great as that of a desk calculator.

Abreaction A process of emotional release that occurs with the reliving of past experiences (psychoanalytic); the basic mechanism in catharsis ("talking-out cure").

Abstraction Process of stripping away of concrete properties of objects and events to reduce them, conceptually, to their essential properties.

Action research Scientific investigations designed to effect changes in the real world, as in factories or military organizations (Lewin).

Act psychology A school of psychology that stressed mental processes rather than the contents of consciousness (Brentano).

Adaptive act Carr's primary unit of behavior, which involves three phases: (1) a motivating stimulus, (2) a sensory situation, and (3) a response that alters the situation to satisfy the motivating conditions.

Adder A device for adding numbers; the adders in electronic digital computers are almost without exception designed to add binary numbers because the adding equipment is much simpler to build for base-2 arithmetic.

Afferent stimulus interaction Hull's postulate that stimuli interact in such a manner that the resulting behavior is more than a mere summation of the behavioral effects of the stimuli taken separately.

Afterimage The lingering sensation following the removal of stimulation; usually noted in connection with visual stimulation.

All-or-none law Classic principle that a neuron responds completely or not at all.

Analog Having the property of continuous functions, as in the analog computer.

Anal stage The period in an individual's development which is marked by interest in the anal region and which has certain concomitant effects on personality that may be characteristic of the adult individual if fixation at this stage occurs (Freud).

Analysis Separation into constituent parts; conceptually, as in science, as well as physically.

Analytic psychology Name given Carl Jung's version of psychoanalysis.

And A commonly used connective in Boolean algebra, $C = A \cdot B$ may be read: "C is true if and only if *A and B* are both true."

Anecdotal method The use of casually observed events as scientific data.

Anima A well-developed archetype representing the *feminine* characteristics in men (Jung).

Animus A well-developed archetype representing the *masculine* characteristics in women (Jung).

Anthropomorphism The attributing of human characteristics or capacities to other things, especially infrahuman species.

Anthroponomy A term advocated by Hunter as a name for the "science of human behavior."

Antimosaic hypothesis The theoretical view opposed to the structuralist bundle hypothesis.

Antiquarianism Emphasis on the past for its own sake.

Apperception A clear and vivid perception.

Approach-approach conflict A conflict which occurs when an individual desires to achieve two goals, only one of which can be obtained (Lewin).

Approach-avoidance conflict A conflict which is characterized by one anticipated goal which is both desired and not desired (Lewin).

Archetype Inherited predisposition to perceive or act in a certain way (Jung).

Associationism The view that mental complexity is produced via learned associations of simple sensations and ideas.

Asthenic The body type identified by Kretschmer as tall and thin.

Attensity Clearness of sensation which varies with attention rather than with the objective characteristics of the stimulus (Titchener).

Attention Focusing of consciousness.

Attractor A stable equilibrium condition in a system (catastrophe theory).

Authoritarianism External imposition of social principles.

Autonomic nervous system Network of nerves and nerve centers serving mainly the viscera and primarily mediating involuntary activities.

Avoidance-avoidance conflict A conflict which is present when two anticipated consequences are both undesirable (Lewin).

Axiom A self-evident truth; a proposition not susceptible to proof or disproof.

Bandwidth The effective frequency range of a signal, or to which a particular instrument or channel responds; for example, a particular filter may have a bandwidth of 100 cycles per second.

Basic anxiety The feeling a child has of being isolated and helpless in a potentially hostile world (Horney).

Behavior Bodily responses, overt and covert; the primary subject matter of psychology as ordinarily defined in the United States.

Behavior episode A molar response sequence of limited size range which has constancy of direction and equal potency throughout its parts (Barker).

Behaviorism Generally, the systematic position that all psychological functions can be explained in terms of muscular reactions and glandular secretions, and *nothing more*; therefore, the objective study of the stimulus and response aspects of behavior (Watson). Specifically, (1) methodological (empirical) behaviorism: The view that behavior is all that scientists can study and that strictly objective techniques are therefore required, as in all other natural sciences; and (2) metaphysical (radical) behaviorism: The philosophical position that there is no mind—a kind of physical monism.

Behavior space Totality of factors affecting behavior for a given individual—similar to Lewin's "life space" construct (Tolman).

Belief-value matrix Hierarchies of learned expectations concerning environmental objects and their roles in relation to behavior (Tolman).

Belongingness, principle of The proposition that items are more easily associated if they are related in a recognizable way (Gestalt).

Beta Numerical criterion relating to the a priori probability that a signal will be presented in a perceptual judgment situation, and to the values and costs of possible outcomes.

Binary Two-valued, as in the Boolean logic underlying the operation of the digital computer.

Binary number A number to the base 2; in any place the value of the coefficient can be one of only two values, 0 or 1.

Birth trauma The emotional experience of the infant ending its prenatal life (emphasized by Rank as having subsequent effects on personality).

Bit Unit of information, in information theory; abbreviation of "*bi*nary digi*t*."

Bond Connection of stimulus and response; hypothetical linkage used to account for the formation of associations.

Boolean algebra Two-valued logic, based on the assumption that any given element is either in or out of a set; the logical basis for the operation of the digital computer (Boole).

Brunswik ratio Relationship of distal (real or physical) to proximal (sensory) representations of an object, indicating degree to which physical attributes determine any given perception.

Bundle hypothesis The assumption that complex perceptions are a group of simple perceptions.

Canalization The development of a single preferred means of satisfying a need (Murphy).

Catastrophe theory Mathematical propositions concerning sudden changes in the equilibrium conditions of systems, possibly exemplified in psychological phenomena (e. g., aggression, perceptual judgments).

Catharsis The psychoanalytic principle of releasing tension and anxiety by emotionally reliving experiences; originally described as the "talking-out cure" (Breuer and Freud).

Cathexis The investing of psychic energy in some object, person, or thing (Freud, Tolman).

Causality Conceptualization of the determination of events by prior events.

Centralism A viewpoint which stresses brain functions in the explanation of psychological phenomena.

Centrifugal group factor The tendency to make gestures away from the body; an expressive factor in Allport's theory of personality.

Cerebrotonia A pattern of temperament characteristic of a bookish, shy, and sensitive individual (Sheldon).

Circular conditioned response A conditioned response sequence in which each successive response serves as a stimulus for the ensuing response.

Client-centered therapy Active encouragement of patients to do and say what they wish so as to facilitate growth and self-actualization (Rogers).

Clinical validation The demonstration of a theoretical principle through successive confirmations within the same clinical setting from which it was derived.

Coded Transformed into other than the original form; for example, the letters of the alphabet might be coded by transforming each into a unique decimal number, which in turn might be coded into binary numbers, which finally might be coded as holes in a punched card.

Cognitive Pertaining to the mental process involved in achieving awareness or knowledge of an object.

Cognitive dissonance Incongruity between two sets of belief systems, resulting in change of attitude or other behavior so as to minimize the discrepancy.

Cohesive forces The tendency of excitations in the cortex to attract one another (Gestalt).

Collective unconscious That part of a person's unconscious which is inherited phylogenetically and is common to all members of the species (Jung).

Common fate Gestalt principle which holds that visual perception tends to group objects together when they seem to be moving in the same direction.

Compensation Development in those areas in which an individual feels inferior, and the attempt to overcome this inferiority.

Compile To translate a program written in a problem language into the language of machine instructions; the problem language is designed to be more natural for the programmer to use than the machine language.

Complex A potentially debilitating belief system held by an individual in spite of contradictory objective evidence.

Computer A device, usually electronic, which carries out a sequence of operations under the control of a stored program of operation.

Conative Purposeful; having to do with motivation.

Condensation The representation of more than one latent element by a single manifest dream element (psychoanalysis).

Conditioned reflex A response that has come to be elicited by an initially ineffective stimulus after that stimulus has been presented together with an initially effective (unconditioned) stimulus.

Conditioning, classical Relatively simple associative learning in which the reinforcement follows the presentation of a neutral stimulus, whether or not the response to be learned occurs.

Conditioning, instrumental Learning in which the opportunity to engage in one behavior (e.g., eating, observing, or sexual activity) is made contingent upon the performance of the response to be learned (e.g., pressing a bar or passing a test). See **Conditioning, operant.**

Conditioning, operant Instrumental conditioning in which the subject "emits" the learned response in the absence of any particular eliciting stimulus (Skinner); the free operant is a response whose emission leaves the subject in a position to make further such responses (e.g., pressing a bar in a box, as contrasted with running down a runway).

Conditioning, respondent Classical conditioning, in which there is an eliciting stimulus and in which reinforcement occurs independently of the performance of the response.

Confirming reaction A cerebral function hypothesized by Thorndike as the physiological basis of reinforcement through reward.

Conflict The simultaneous operation of two or more contradictory tendencies; the condition resulting therefrom.

Connectionism The school of psychology which considers a stimulus-response connection or bond to be the basis of all or most behavior.

Conscious Aware of one's own mental activities.

Conscious mentalism Attention to thinking activities (R. I. Watson).

Consciousness State of awareness of one's own mental activities.

Consensual validation Validation of a symbol or word by agreement on its meaning by a number of people (Sullivan).

Conservation of energy, principle of The proposition that energy is neither created nor destroyed in physical systems but is only transferred into other forms and hence "conserved."

Construct A concept that represents relationships between objects or events.

Contemporaneity, principle of The proposition that only present factors influence present behavior; the past influences behavior only as it is represented in the present (Lewin).

Contentual objectivism Viewing psychological data behaviorally (R. I. Watson).

Contentual subjectivism Viewing psychological data as mental activities or structures (R. I. Watson).

Context theory of meaning The view that the meaning of anything results from the context in which it occurs in consciousness (Titchener).

Contiguity Nearness in time and/or space.

Contingent schedule of reinforcement Systematic presentation of reinforcer following some specified response.

Continuity Principle of learning emphasizing small, smooth steps in response changes rather than large discontinuous increments.

Continuum A variable whose values are continuous, that is, such that another value can always be found between any two given values.

Control (1) The method by which extraneous variation is eliminated in science, permitting a less ambiguous assignment of cause-and-effect relationships. (2) The exerting of influence over some variables(s).

Controlled variable A condition whose differential influence on the dependent variable in an experiment is eliminated. This is sometimes achieved by eliminating all variations in the controlled variables (for example, by eliminating the influence of sex by using only one sex) and sometimes by equating the values of the controlled variable for each value of the independent variable (for example, by putting equal numbers of men and women in each group).

Copernican theory Contemporary astronomical view that the earth revolves around the sun.

Corollary A proposition that follows directly from another which has been proved or postulated; a natural consequence which follows, without additional effort, from an action.

Correlation A relationship between two or more variables so that a change in one occurs whenever a change occurs in the other; the degree to which two or more variables are so related.

Creative synthesis The proposition that new characteristics emerge from the combination of elements into wholes (Wundt).

Criterion analysis, method of A method of factor analysis in which two groups known to differ in some hypothesized underlying factor are selected; test batteries are administered, and only those tests which differentiate between groups are submitted to factor analysis (Eysenck).

Cybernetics The study of communication and control in animal and machine (Weiner). Control is typically achieved by feeding back information about the results of past activities as input, as in thermostats which control furnaces, or as in various homeostatic mechanisms in animals. Sweating and shivering are temperature-dependent examples in humans that parallel the action of the thermostat.

d′ Measure of detectability of a signal, in detection theory.

Darwinism Principle of organic evolution systematically propounded by Charles Darwin in 1859.

Data Empirical observations and the records thereof in protocols.

Data processing The manipulation of data, generally for the purpose of making them more comprehensible by revealing hidden relationships.

Decoded Converted back into a form which had been coded into some other form; for example, if letters of the alphabet were *coded* into numbers, the numbers would be *decoded* into letters of the alphabet.

Deduction A type of reasoning in which one proceeds from a set of given statements, via transformation rules, to generate further valid statements. The classic example goes from the premises "All humans are mortal" and "Socrates is a human" to the conclusion "Socrates is mortal."

Deductivism Emphasis on primacy of deductive investigations (R. I. Watson).

Defense mechanism Unconscious adaptive behavioral device whereby an individual tries to adjust to some real or fancied psychological threat.

Delayed response A response whose performance is permitted only after some set duration of time following the original presentation of the relevant stimuli.

Dependent variable The variable in an experiment whose values are treated as potentially being a function of the values of the independent variable; in psychology, the dependent variable measured is usually some feature of the subject's responses.

Detection theory The theory which treats problems in sensitivity to signals. It is a branch of statistical decision theory and is often called the theory of signal detectability (TSD) or signal detection theory (SDT). Using this theory, it is possible to separate criterion considerations from sensitivity considerations.

Determining tendency A predisposition to behave in a particular manner.

Determinism An assumption that all phenomena can be explained by natural law in a cause-and-effect manner; the view that all events are therefore explicable entirely in terms of relevant antecedent events.

Developmentalism Emphasis on longitudinal changes (R. I. Watson).

Diacritical design The division of intertwined variables into subclasses in an attempt to separate the effects of variables (Brunswik).

Digital Concerning discrete rather than continuous values, as in a digital computer.

Dimension An ordered variable with continuously changing values (exemplified by each of R. I. Watson's eighteen prescriptions).

Dimensional analysis The structuring of a total situation into specific continua which are measurable.

Discrimination The process of differentiating between objects or actions; the ability to point to a difference.

Displacement The temporary substitution of a secondary goal for a primary one (psychoanalytic).

Distal effects Alterations of the environment which result from an organism's responses.

Distal stimuli Objects in the environment which produce stimuli at the receptor surfaces of the organism (the latter are proximal stimuli).

Distribution theory Logic underlying the determination of probabilities, as of a given observation arising from signal-plus-noise or noise alone, needed for computation of likelihood ratios in signal detection.

Double-alternation task An experimental design in which the responses must be AABB.

Double-aspect view The metaphysical position in which both mind and body are assumed to be a function of one underlying reality.

Dramatization Children's play activities which emulate adult behavior (Sullivan).

Drive *(D)* A construct used by Hull to indicate a condition of the organism resulting from a deprivation which increases the organism's activity toward a particular class of stimuli.

Drive discriminations The demonstrated ability of organisms to behave differentially under different deprivation conditions.

Dualism The metaphysical position in which both mind and body are assumed to exist.

Dynamic Relating to the motivational forces underlying behavior, as stressed by, for example, psychoanalysis.

Dynamicism Emphasis on change and change-producing processes.

Dynamism A habitual way of responding toward others (Sullivan).

Dynamic lattice Diagrammatic representation of interrelationships among ergs, sentiments, and attitudes in R. B. Cattell's personality theory.

Dysplasia Disharmony or disproportion between body parts (Sheldon).

Eclecticism The selection of what seems best from various systems, theories, or procedures.

Ecological validity The extent to which cues aid an organism's accomplishing a successful interaction with the environment (Brunswik).

Ecology, psychological The study of those parts of the environment which play an important role in an individual's life space (Lewin).

Ectomorphy A body type characterized as tall, thin, and small-boned (Sheldon).

Effect, law of The proposition that strengthening of stimulus-response connections, as measured by the increased probability of the occurrence of a response in a particular stimulus situation, results from the action of reward following a response (satisfying aftereffects, as formulated by Thorndike); the original corollary proposition that punishing aftereffects produce a weakening of responses was subsequently discarded by Thorndike.

Effect, spread of The proposition that reinforcement by reward tends to strengthen erroneous responses in close temporal and/or spatial contiguity (Thorndike).

Ego (1) The self. (2) That part of mental activity which is conscious and in close contact with reality (psychoanalytic).

Ego-defense mechanism Any unconscious process which protects the individual from unpleasant reality; an irrational manner of dealing with anxiety (psychoanalytic).

Element The irreducible unit into which all conscious states can be broken down (Titchener).

Elementarism The methodological bias that mental and behavioral states and processes should be analyzed as far as possible into their constituent components (structuralism); strongly attacked by Gestalt psychology.

Emergentism The view that unique properties emerge in combinations of elements, properties not predictable from knowledge of the elements per se. Life and mind, according to this view, would not be completely reducible to physical principles.

Empathy The sympathetic awareness of an emotional state in another person.

Empirical Relating to facts and sensory experience; denotes reliance on observation.

Empiricism (1) The school of philosophical thought that believes all knowledge originates in experience. (2) A methodology that emphasizes data and minimizes theoretical inference.

Encounter group Extended meeting in which members are encouraged to say and do more or less as they please in order to break down interpersonal barriers and facilitate personal insight and growth.

Endomorphy A body type characterized as soft, fleshy, and round (Sheldon).

Entropy In physics, the energy of a physical system which is unavailable for work; in information theory, the average information content of a symbol emitted by a source.

Environment Totality of energies impinging on an organism from within as well as without.

Environmentalism The doctrine that emphasizes environmental factors as crucial determinants of behavior.

Epiphenomenalism The metaphysical position in which mind is assumed to be a noncausal by-product of body.

Epistemology A branch of philosophy concerned with the acqusiition and the validity of knowledge.

Equilibrium Stable or resting condition in a system.

Equipotentiality, principle of The principle stating that within cerebral areas performing the same function, all parts are equally capable of carrying on that function (Lashley).

Equivalence belief A hypothesized state of an organism as a result of which it behaves as though a subgoal were the goal (Tolman).

Erg An underlying motivational trait having a hereditary origin (Cattell).

Erogenous zones Different zones or regions of the body which are especially sensitive to manipulation (psychoanalytic).

Ethology The study of animal behavior via observation in the field.

Eugenics The science that attempts to improve humankind by selective breeding so as to maximize desirable genetic characteristics.

Evolution, organic The theory that gradual changes in plants and animals resulting from cumulative environmental influences account for the development of today's diverse species from some simpler common ancestor(s) (Darwin).

Exercise, law of The proposition that performance of a response improves subsequent performance through practice alone.

Existential psychology (1) The name often given to structuralism because it treated the elements of consciousness as existent. (2) The school of personality theorists who stress the individual's self-understanding. The term derives from existentialism in philosophy; there the emphasis is on the concrete events in experience and the free will of human beings to choose how they wish to live their lives.

Expectancy Anticipation of some relationship, such as between two particular stimulus events or a stimulus and a response (Tolman).

Experience Conscious (mental) processes.

Experience, immediate Conscious processes in their own right, as studied directly in structural psychology (Wundt).

Experience, mediate Conscious processes regarded as an avenue to the external "real" world (and used, indirectly, in physics) (Wundt).

Exploitative orientation A means of escaping insecurity by obtaining objects valued by others (Fromm).

Expressive behavior That aspect of behavior which is related to an individual's own style of behaving rather than to the behavior's adaptive function (Allport).

External explanation Interpretation of some phenomenon in terms of principles extrinsic to its own function.

Exteroceptor A sense organ or receptor directly stimulated by energy sources outside the body (e.g., the eye).

Extrasensory perception (psi) Responsivity to external events that is not mediated by any known sense modality.

Extraversion The mode of responding to the world in which the person's attention is directed toward the external world (Jung).

Fact A verbal statement accepted by a certain group at a particular time.

Factor A basic condition or variable that is singled out for investigation.

Factor analysis A statistical technique utilizing sets of correlations; used to extract the underlying dimensions or factors which account for the observed relationships between scores.

Factor theory Personality theory which emphasizes the isolation of factors by the statistical analysis of test performances.

False alarm Identification of noise as signal, in detection theory.

Feedback In an energy system, the part of the output energy that is returned to the system to regulate further output.

Fictional future The plans and aspirations a person has for the future and presently believes in (Adler).

Field-cognition modes A combination of thinking, perceiving, and remembering on the part of the organism which gives rise to a specific way of knowing some characteristic of the environment (Tolman).

Field expectations A set of the organism that a particular response to a certain cue or stimulus will produce a particular situation or consequence (Tolman).

Field observation (study) Scientific research carried out in a real-life situation such as a school, factory, or home.

Field theory Any psychological theory which attempts to utilize fields of force analogous to those in physics as an explanation for psychological data.

Figure-ground A general property of perception; the figure is that which stands out and is attended to, while the ground is that which surrounds the figure and is secondary to it.

Film color A transparent color which is not substantial and lacks definite localization.

Fixation (1) Perseveration of a particular response. (2) The persistence of immature behavior or thought processes accompanied by a lack of normal development (psychoanalytic).

Fractional antedating goal response An implicit goal response which occurs progressively earlier in the response chain, thus providing stimuli which may become conditioned to ensuing responses (Hull, Spence).

Free association (1) An unrestrained sequence of ideas or thought. (2) The technique of having a subject respond with unrestricted verbalizations for clinical purposes (psychoanalytic).

Free operant See **Conditioning, operant.**

Frequency, law of The proposition that learning is a function of the frequency of occurrence of a response.

Functional autonomy The performance of a task for its own sake; the drive state is thus independent of the need which gave rise to it (Allport).

Functionalism The psychological system that stresses the function or utility of behavior in adapting to the environment (Angell, Carr, Woodworth).

Generalization (1) The process of extending results or conclusions beyond their initial observational basis. (2) The function whereby a particular conditioned response is made to some stimulus that is similar to the conditioned stimulus (stimulus generalization) or a conditioned stimulus elicits a response similar to the conditioned response (response generalization).

Generalization gradient The orderly differences in effectiveness with which stimuli that have not previously occurred in the conditioning procedure elicit a response, as a function of their similarity to the conditioned stimulus.

Genital stage The final psychosexual stage in the individual's development, in which the individual desires sexual relations with members of the opposite sex (Freud).

Gestalt A figure or configuration which is a whole greater than the sum of its parts and which, if analyzed into its parts, is destroyed.

Gestalt psychology The psychological system that stresses the phenomenological study of molar stimulus and response units, with emphasis placed on the primacy of wholes and on the existence of brain fields and configurations (Wertheimer, Koffka, Köhler).

Gestaltqualität Patterns of time and space that are presumed to inhere in the mind and so are independent of physical elements; emphasis thereon is often considered the immediate precursor of Gestalt psychology (von Ehrenfels).

Goal gradient The progressive increment in response strength that occurs as a function of closeness to the goal (Hull).

Gynandromorphy Refers to bisexuality as denoted by the physique (Sheldon).

Hab A unit of learning invented to quantify habit strength ($_SH_R$); equal to 1 percent of the physiological maximum (Hull).

Habit A learned response to some stimulus or situation.

Habit family hierarchy The ordering by strength of the total set of responses which may occur in a given stimulus situation (Hull).

Habit strength ($_SH_R$) An intervening variable representing learning; a function of (1) number of reinforcements, (2) amount of reinforcement, (3) time between stimulus and response, and (4) time between response and reinforcement (Hull, 1943); in the final Hullian system (1951, 1952) only (1) was retained as a determiner.

Hallucination A false perception for which appropriate external stimuli are absent.

Hedonism The philosophical belief that behavior is directed at the attainment of pleasure and the avoidance of pain.

Heisenberg principle A mathematical proof that exact simultaneous measurement of the position and the momentum of a single electron is impossible.

Historicist One who wants to understand each period of the past primarily in terms of then-existing phenomena, rather than in terms of present values and knowledge.

Hit Identification of a signal when it occurs, in detection theory.

Hodological space A qualitative geometry of spatial relations invented by Lewin which used vectors to represent dynamic psychological factors.

Holistic Referring to the theoretical position stressing that an organism must be studied as a whole since the whole is different from the sum of its constituent parts.

Humanism The general position that human needs and values should primarily determine the focus and direction of scientific inquiry and interpretation, especially in the behavioral and social sciences.

Hypnosis Technique whereby a respected person can so effectively manipulate another person's attention that a trancelike condition of extremely heightened suggestibility develops.

Hypochondria A neurosis which is characterized by excessive concern for one's health.

Hypothesis (1) A prediction concerning the relationship between variables. (2) A tentative explanation.

Hypothetical construct A construct whose meaning goes beyond summarizing the relationship between the antecedent (stimulus) and consequent (response) conditions which it represents.

Hypothetico-deductive method A method of theory construction which starts with a few general postulates from which testable theorems and corollaries are derived by rigorous deduction, and then tests the derivations empirically.

Hysteria The manifestation of such bodily symptoms as anesthesia and paralysis as the result of psychic trauma or conflict.

Id A psychic structure or process which is the original reservoir of psychic energy and operates according to the pleasure principle (Freud).

Ideal observer An abstract mathematical construct within detection theory; the behavior of this construct defines the optimal behavior achievable within specified situations amenable to the necessary mathematical treatment.

Ideomotor action The belief that an idea, unless inhibited by other ideas, will lead directly to motor action (James).

Idiographic Referring to an individual case or event and to the methodology that stresses understanding individual events rather than seeking general laws.

Idiographicism Emphasis on intensive investigation of individuals for the sake of understanding them as unique cases (R. I. Watson).

Image The relatively faint reproduction in consciousness of a previous sensation (Titchener).

Imageless thought Mental processes or functions which elude introspective analysis.

Incentive Goal object.

Independent variable The factor whose influence (on the dependent variable) is determined in an experiment.

Indeterminism Denial that all events are explicable in terms of antecedent events ("causes").

Individual differences The totality of diversity exhibited by living organisms in various biological, behavioral and social measurements.

Individual psychology The version of psychoanalysis developed by Alfred Adler.

Induction A mode of logic which proceeds from specific statements to general conclusions.

Inductivism Emphasis on primacy of inductive investigations (R. I. Watson).

Inferiority complex The feeling an individual has as the result of real or imagined deficiencies (Adler).

Information Whatever reduces uncertainty (information theory); the receipt of an information-bearing message reduces uncertainty or ignorance by reducing the number of alternative possible messages or by biasing their probabilities so that the remaining uncertainty is reduced.

Information processing The sensory reception, coding, manipulation, storing (in memory), and retrieval of environmental cues and patterns of stimulation by an organism or a machine.

Information theory The mathematical theory which deals with the coding, decoding, and transmission of messages.

Inhibition, conditioned The hypothesized acquisition of inhibitory properties by a stimulus through its repeated association with reactive inhibition.

Inhibition, reactive The hypothesized explanation for the decrement of a learned response owing to the effortfulness of the activity (Hull).

Insight (1)A sudden understanding of a previously insoluble problem. (2) A sudden reorganization of the perceptual field (Gestalt).

Instinct (1) An innate, complex, stereotyped mode of behaving. (2) Need (Freud).

Instinct, death The wish of an organism to return to an inorganic state (Freud).

Instinct, life The desire of the organism to maintain a balance between the anabolistic and catabolistic forces of the body—to maintain life (Freud).

Instructions Specifications of computer operations to be performed; for example, a computer might have approximately sixty basic instructions to which it can respond, all the more complex functions carried out by the computer being synthesized from these basic instructions.

Intelligence (1) Adaptive ability of individuals as exhibited by how successfully they adjust to their environment. (2) "What intelligence tests measure."

Interactionism The metaphysical position in which mind and body are assumed to be two separate but interacting entities.

Interbehaviorism Field theory with emphasis on the interaction between stimulus and response functions (Kantor).

Internal explanation Interpretation of some phenomenon in terms of its own intrinsic functions.

Interoceptor A sense organ or receptor within the organism sensitive to stimuli within the body.

Intervening variable A construct which abstracts the relationship between antececent (stimulus) and consequent (response) conditions, with no meaning beyond this relationship.

Introspection A generic term for any method which relies upon the subjective report of the subject.

Introversion The mode of responding to the world in which one's attention is directed toward oneself (Jung).

Irradiation The phenomenon of generalization, with the implication of spreading excitatory brain functions (Pavlov).

Irrationalism Acceptance of primacy of emotion in thought.

Isomorphism The 1:1 relationship assumed to hold between brain fields and experience (Gestalt).

J curve The graphic description of the distribution of responses when some social institution influences behavior in a particular direction so that scores pile up markedly at one end of the scale (F. Allport).

Kinesthetic Pertaining to the sense of body movement or position.

Kymograph A revolving drum which makes graphic records; often used in recording respiration and other physiological processes.

Laboratory Any place where scientific investigations are performed, with special regard for observations under controlled conditions (experiments).

Lamarckian evolution The doctrine of the inheritance of acquired characteristics: The use or disuse of organic structures results in changes which are passed on to the organism's offspring.

Latent learning Learning which is not yet reflected in performance (Tolman).

Law (1) A statement of a regular and predictable relationship between empirical variables. (2) A well-accepted theoretical proposition.

Learning Real or potential change in behavior attributed to training or experience.

Lens model Conceptualization of the interaction of the functional variables affecting behavior (Brunswik).

Level of aspiration The performance level which an individual expects to reach in a given situation and by which he or she judges a performance as a success or failure (Lewin).

Libido Energy in the service of the life instincts (Freud).

Life space The totality of effective psychological factors for a given person at a particular moment in time (Lewin).

Life-style The particular manner which an individual develops in order to deal with reality (Adler).

Likelihood ratio The ratio of the probability that an observed event would occur given one hypothesis to the probability that it would occur given some second hypothesis; within detection theory, the hypotheses are most commonly that "a signal was presented" and that "noise alone was presented."

Linear graph A graph representing an equation of the first degree between two variables.

Linear perspective A monocular depth cue in which parallel lines tend to converge.

Lloyd Morgan's canon Law of parsimony applied to comparative psychology: "In no case may we interpret an action as the outcome of the exercise of a higher psychical faculty, if it can be interpreted as the outcome of the exercise of one which stands lower on the psychological scale."

Logon content Information carried by different scales or dimensions (MacKay).

Logic A set of rules of formal reasoning procedures.

Logical positivism A philosophical movement headed by Schlick to rid philosophy of metaphysics and to establish a science of science.

Mandala The magic circle found in many religious cults which Jung believed to be symbolic of the human being's striving for unity.

Manic-depressive insanity A psychotic disorder characterized by marked emotional cycles from extreme elation to marked depression.

Marketing orientation A means of escaping insecurity by emulating the social group in which one lives (Fromm).

Masculine protest The desire of both males and females to overcome femininity (Adler).

Mass action, principle of The principle which states that brain tissues function with an effectiveness which depends on the mass of undisturbed tissue (Lashley).

Materialism The metaphysical position in which a single underlying physical reality is assumed.

Mathematical models Calculational systems based on some mathematical formulation; may be applied to empirical problems.

Measurement Use of numbers (quantification) to express the values of variables and their effects.

Means-end readiness A state of selective readiness which endures independently of the present motivational state of the organism and which leads to the acquisition of certain expectancies more readily than others (Tolman).

Mechanism (1) A purposive response or set of responses (Woodworth). (2) Assumption that life processes are entirely explicable in terms of physiochemical functions.

Mechanistic explanation Interpretation of phenomena in terms of known or presumed machinelike functions.

Mediational mechanisms Processes whose effects, as on behavior, are produced indirectly (by mediation) rather than directly.

Memory (1) Retention of information by an organism or machine. (2) System which retains the information.

Mental activity The generic term for adaptive behavior (Carr).

Mental chemistry The doctrine that simple ideas coalesce to form new, more complex ideas and lose their individual identity (John Stuart Mill).

Mentalism (See **Conscious mentalism.**)

Mental mechanics The doctrine which states that a complex idea is no more than the simple ideas from which it is formed, which maintain their individual identity (James Mill).

Mental retardation Chronic reduction of adaptive (intellectual) abilities in an organism.

Mesomorphy A body type characterized as tough, muscular, and athletic (Sheldon).

Metaerg An underlying motivational trait acquired through environmental influence (Cattell).

Metaphysics A branch of philosophy concerned with the identification and understanding of ultimate reality; "above physics."

Metatheory A set of general rules governing the construction of a theory; a theory about theory.

Methodological objectivism Use of techniques open to verification by another observer (R. I. Watson).

Methodological subjectivism Use of techniques not open to verification by another observer (R. I. Watson).

Method, scientific The fundamental process by which all science proceeds; it is characterized by conceptual analysis and controlled observation.

Metron content Information carried by varying values along a single scale (MacKay).

Mind Collective name for totality of an individual's thinking and perceptual activities.

Mind-body problem The puzzle generated by the apparent concomitant operation of mental (conscious) and physical (bodily) functions, and the question how their relationship may be best understood.

Modal need The need to perfect some type of behavior (Murray).

Model Abstract system with logical determinants that can be tested empirically only when their elements have been "interpreted" in terms of observable events.

Model, deterministic Any theoretical position which stresses the complete predictability of a response when antecedent conditions are known.

Model, mathematical learning Any learning theory expressed in mathematical form.

Model, stochastic Any model in which one uses the stochastic assumption, i.e., that in a long series of trials, the probability of an outcome approaches the true probability of that outcome.

Molar Referring to large units of study.

Molarism Preference for large units of description in psychological data (R. I. Watson).

Molecular Referring to small units of study.

Molecularism Preference for small units of description in psychological data (R. I. Watson).

Monad The element of all being, which is indestructible, uncreatable, immutable, and active (Leibniz).

Monism A metaphysical position in which only one basic reality is assumed, either mind or body.

Morphogenotype A hypothetical unchanging biological characteristic of the organism which determines both body type and temperament (Sheldon).

Morphology The study of biological forms and structures.

Motivation Activating conditions that underlie behavior and mental functions.

Motor conditioned response A voluntary (striped-muscle) response that has been conditioned to some initially ineffective stimulus. (See also **Conditioning.**)

Motor patterns Responses and combinations of responses.

Movement-produced stimuli (mps) Stimuli originating in the movements of the organism (Guthrie).

Nativism The doctrine which emphasizes hereditary factors in the development of an organism, rather than environmental ones.

Naturalism View that natural phenomena can be completely interpreted by principles yielded by study of those phenomena without recourse to any external principles (R. I. Watson).

Naturalistic view In history, the view that the course of events is determined by the *Zeitgeist* and historical forces, rather than by great men (Boring).

Naturalistic observation Study of phenomena in their normal state, without experimental or other interference.

Need Some deficit or want in an organism.

Need reduction Principle that satisfaction of need is crucial in learning (Hull).

Need system Totality of motivational factors affecting an individual (Tolman).

Neoanalytic Referring to relatively new versions of psychoanalysis, rather than to the initial orthodox ones, such as Freudian.

Neobehavioristic Referring to the relatively new versions of behaviorism, in contrast to the early Watsonian.

Neural noise Extraneous internal neural activity in an observer.

Neuroticism A fundamental personality variable along which individuals can be ordered; the neurotic is generally identified as inferior (Eysenck).

Neurosis A class of personality disorders which are characterized by extreme anxiety and whose symptoms are not usually severe enough to require hospitalization.

Neurotic trend The particular approach an individual uses in an attempt to avoid conflict and find security (Horney).

Noise Anything (e.g., meaningless sounds) which interferes with a signal being transmitted.

Nomothetic Referring to the attempt to discover laws that apply generally to classes of organisms.

Nomotheticism Emphasis on laws applicable to more than a single individual (R. I. Watson).

Non-Euclidean geometry A geometry using a different set of axioms from those of Euclidean geometry; the most famous example is the geometry used in relativity theory, which rejects the Euclidean postulate concerning parallel lines.

Nonsense syllable A "meaningless" item most often composed of two consonants separated by a vowel (CVC); developed by Ebbinghaus to reduce variations in learning rate which might otherwise result from differences in prior experience with the materials used for experimentation on human verbal learning and memory.

Noncontingent schedule of reinforcement Presentation of reinforcer without regard to the occurrence of some specified response.

Noncontinuity Principle of learning in which large, discontinuous increments in response strength are emphasized rather than small continuous steps.

Normal science The type of science practiced during the period of relatively unquestioned acceptance of a framework ("paradigm") in which scientists work (Kuhn).

Objective set Perspective that focuses on objects and events as they are seen by others rather than on one's own subjective biases.

Objectivism (See **Contentual objectivism, Methodological objectivism.**)

Observation Empirical noting of objects and events.

Occam's razor (See **Parsimony, principle of.**)

Occasionalism A philosophical position on the mind-body issue in which two separate processes are assumed and are correlated by divine intervention.

O data Behavioral observations made with active intervention of an operator—hence, O (Barker).

Oedipal conflict The feeling of hostility of the child toward the parent of the same sex and love for the parent of the opposite sex (Freud).

Operant behavior Responses characterized by their effect on the environment and for which there is usually no known or manipulated eliciting stimulus (Skinner).

Operant conditioning Conditioning of emitted behavior by establishing a contingency (reinforcement schedule).

Operationism A movement intended to clarify the language of science; an operational definition is any definition in which the meaning of a term is strictly determined by a corresponding set of operations (Bridgman).

Or A connective used in writing Boolean algebraic equations; typically the inclusive or is used, and $C = A + B$ would then mean "C is true if A is true or if B is true, or if both A and B are true."

Oral stage The first period in an individual's psychosexual development; marked by interest in the oral region (Freud).

Organic evolution (See **Evolution.**)

Organ inferiority (See **Inferiority complex.**)

Organism The individual considered as an integrated totality.

Organismic Pertaining to any point of view which stresses studying the behavior of the whole organism rather than its parts.

Orienting reaction (OR) Attentional response, perceptual, physiological, and postural, to novel stimuli.

Paradigm A more or less inclusive framework of concepts, assumptions, and methods within which some scientific enterprise is carried out ("normal" science) (Kuhn).

Parameter (1) A constant in an equation; the values of the constants determine which curve of a family will represent the relationship between the dependent variable and the independent variable or variables. Parameters in equations would be expected to correspond to the values at which controlled variables have been set in an experiment. (2) Less precisely, a parameter is a particular value of a variable; for example, one might say that the value of the stimulus *parameter* was changed in order to produce novelty in the experiment.

Parapsychology A branch of psychology which studies extrasensory phenomena, or those which do not fall within the range of known sensory modalities.

Parataxic Cognitive or emotional systems which are not adequately related to other systems; they then constitute logic-tight compartments (Sullivan).

Parsimony, principle of The scientific principle that the simpler of two hypotheses should be accepted, other things being equal. It does not negate the acceptance of complex explanations if the data require them. (Also called *William of Occam's razor* and, in comparative psychology, *Lloyd Morgan's canon.*)

Partial reinforcement Schedule of reinforcement in which reinforcement is provided intermittently rather than continuously following some given response.

Payoff matrix The pattern of gains (values) and losses (costs) related to being right or wrong in judgments, as in perceptual responses to signals.

Peak experience Quasi-mystical moments transcending normal consciousness and producing extreme feelings of well-being (Maslow).

Penis envy The repressed female desire to possess a penis; the female form of castration anxiety (Freud).

Perception Meaningful apprehension of the environment by means of sense organs.

Performance Actual behavior; may be contrasted with learning, which refers to behavior potential.

Peripheralism The explanation of psychological phenomena emphasizing muscular action and other distal events rather than the functioning of the central nervous system.

Permutations All the possible arrangements of a certain number of different items; each arrangement is called a *permutation.*

Persona A well-developed archetype which represents a human being's social self (Jung).

Personal equation Correction for individual differences in reaction times exhibited by astronomers observing stellar transits.

Personalistic view The belief that the course of history is determined by great individuals and their unique contributions (Boring).

Personality Unique way in which traits, attitudes, aptitudes, and the like are organized in an individual.

Person-centered theory Belief that people are essentially self-directive and self-actualizing and should be encouraged to act on their own (Rogers).

Personification The attribution of human characters to nonhuman entities.

Personification, eidetic A personification which persists and influences a person's opinion of others (Sullivan).

Phallic stage The period in an individual's development when the Oedipus complex develops; marked by interest in the penis (Freud).

Phenomenalism The metaphysical position in which neither mind nor body is considered real and only ideas resulting from sensory impressions are held to exist.

Phenomenology A method of observation in which experiential data are accepted in a more or less naïve manner, without any attempt at analysis.

Phenotype (1) A bodily characteristic, as contrasted with the underlying hereditary factor (genotype). (2) The physique of an individual (Sullivan).

Phi phenomenon The name given by Wertheimer to the perception of apparent motion generated by stationary stimuli. *Pure* phi occurs when motion is seen, but no *object* is seen in motion.

Phrenology The belief that mental characteristics can be determined by examining the contours of the skull (Gall).

Physicalism The philosophical position that all scientific propositions are ultimately reducible to the language of physical science.

Physiologizing Advancing physiological explanations and conjectures in the absence of definite physiological knowledge.

Physiology Study of the functions of the various organ systems of the body.

Pleasure principle Principle that considers only the immediate satisfaction of instinctual desires; governs the development of the id (Freud).

Pluralism A philosophical position on the mind-body issue in which multiple entities or processes are assumed.

Positivism A metatheoretical and general scientific position that emphasizes parsimony and operationism in data language and eschews theorizing and inferential commitment; any method designed to produce *positive* knowledge.

Postremity, postulate of The proposition that the last response made in a particular stimulus situation is the one most likely to occur on the next occasion of that stimulus situation; a primary postulate in one formalization of Guthrie's contiguity theory of learning (Voeks).

Postulate (1) A fundamental assumption not meant to be tested. (2) A theoretical proposition used within a given logical framework and tested indirectly by means of its empirical implications.

Practitioner One who is engaged in some professional service function after being more or less intensively trained at a relatively high level of responsibility.

Pragmatics Study of the relationships between signs and their users (Morris).

Pragmatism Validation of a principle through its utility; the philosophical position that that which is useful is true.

Prägnanz, law of The Gestalt principle that a figure will be perceived in its best possible form.

Preconscious That part of mental activity which consists of materials not presently conscious but readily recallable (psychoanalysis).

Preparadigmatic science Diffuse and tentative beginnings of a science prior to the clear formation of a generally accepted set of concepts, assumptions, and methods (Kuhn).

Prescription The manner in which some given group of psychologists tends to answer psychology's most fundamental and persistent questions, as ordered on a continuum, with positive and negative polar extremes (R. I. Watson; p. 8).

Presentist One who wants to understand the past as it relates to present problems so as better to understand and cope with them.

Press The environmental forces acting upon the individual (Murray).

Primary memory image A lingering memory trace postulated to maintain a sensation for a relatively short duration of time, permitting an accurate introspective report (Titchener).

Primary process Process whose aim is direct and immediate instinctual satisfaction, mediated by the id (psychoanalysis).

Primary qualities Those qualities which are alleged to inhere within the object and to be independent of the perceiver, such as size and shape (Locke).

Primitive term A term which is not defined by any more basic term within a theory.

Probabilistic functionalism Egon Brunswik's position, which emphasizes that both the correctness of perception and the effectiveness of action are only probable. The adaptive, functional relating of distal stimuli to distal effects of responses on the environment is seen as the task of the organism.

Proceeding A person's interaction with an object or another person, of sufficient duration to have dynamic significance (Murray).

Process need A need for activity per se (Murray).

Program A sequence of instructions that can be carried out by a computer.

Programmatic Lacking in systematic specificity.

Projection A defense mechanism in which individuals attempt to externalize their own values, faults, and ideas (psychoanalysis).

Proprioceptor A sense organ or receptor sensitive to the position or the movement of the body (e.g., vestibular canal).

Protensity Temporal duration of a sensation or an image (Titchener).

Prototaxic Referring to a cognitive process in which individuals experience directly without attaching meaning to their sensations; an infantile type of perception (Sullivan).

Proximal reactions The peripheral motor responses of the organism, without regard for the consequences on the environment (Brunswik).

Proximal stimuli Stimuli as they are when they impinge upon the organism (Brunswik).

Psychic apparatus The various mental structures (id, ego, superego, and the like) hypothesized by Freud to account for normal and maladjusted behavior.

Psychical satiation A reduction in performance of an activity as a function of the continued repetition of the activity.

Psychoanalysis (1) A school of psychology developed by Sigmund Freud which places a great deal of emphasis upon unconscious motivation, conflict and symbolism. (2) A type of psychiatry stressing the free-association technique and long-term, deep psychotherapy.

Psychogenesis The origin and development of mind or behavior.

Psychometrist A person skilled in the administration and scoring of mental tests.

Psychopathology Abnormal behavior.

Psychophysical parallelism The metaphysical position in which mind and body are independent and yet perfectly correlated entities.

Psychophysics The scientific study of the relationship between stimuli and sensations.

Psychotherapy Techniques for alleviating maladjustment.

Psychoticism A fundamental personality dimension along which individuals can be ordered, identified by various behavioral deficits (Eysenck).

Ptolemaic theory Ancient astronomical view that the earth is the center of the universe.

Purism Seeking knowledge for its own sake (R. I. Watson).

Purposivism The doctrine that behavior is more than purely mechanical and that it is directed toward some goal.

Puzzle box An enclosure which prevents an organism from reaching a goal until a particular device is manipulated (Thorndike).

Pyknic Short and squatty body type (Kretschmer).

Q sort A personality inventory, utilizing factor analysis, in which subjects evaluate their own personalities by sorting into different piles statements which apply to them (Stephenson).

Qualitative Referring to that which can be distinguished or identified as different in kind.

Qualitativism Stress on knowledge that focuses on differences in kind or essence (R. I. Watson).

Quantification The process of establishing relationships between empirical objects of study and numbers.

Quantitative Referring to that which can be distinguished or identified as different in number or amount.

Quantitativism Stress on measured knowledge (R. I. Watson).

Rationalism The philosophical position which maintains that truth can be found only through pure reason.

Rationalization A form of projection in which individuals attempt to find justifiable causes for their actions (psychoanalysis).

Reaction potential (sEr). A construct that indicates the degree of strength of a particular response (Hull).

Reaction time, motor Latency of response made with attention to the response rather than to the stimulus onset.

Reaction time, sensory Latency of response made with attention to the stimulus onset rather than to the response.

Readiness, law of The principle which states that when a conduction unit is ready to conduct, conduction by it is satisfying, providing nothing is done to alter its action (Thorndike).

Reality principle The principle of action imposed by the demands of the environment on the ego, leading to the eventual satisfaction of libidinal drives in such a way that the organism continues to exist (Freud).

Receiver Name for a sensory system in signal detection theory.

Receiver operating characteristic (ROC) curve A function relating the probability of a "hit" (correct report of detection) to the probability of a "false alarm" (incorrect report of detection), in detection theory.

Recency, law of The principle stating that, other things being equal, that which is best remembered is that which was most recently learned.

Receptive orientation A means of escaping insecurity by strong identification with a group or its leader (Fromm).

Reduction screen An opaque screen with one or two small eye holes, used so that a subject can view stimuli without knowledge of the surrounding illumination.

Reductionism The position holding that complex phenomena should be understood through analysis (reduction) into simpler components.

Redundant Containing repetitious information; redundant transmission systems carry information which is less than the system could potentially carry.

Reflex An involuntary, stereotyped response of a body part to a stimulus.

Reflex arc The simplest functional unit in the nervous system, composed of a receptor, synapse, and effector.

Reflexologist Critical term used by those (E.g., R. B. Cattell) who wish to stress the oversimplification of the S-R position.

Relfexology The school of psychology which holds that reflexes and combinations of reflexes are the basis of all behavior (Bekhterev).

Regression The return to a former state or condition.

Reinforcement Any process by which a response is strengthened; generally assumed to involve more than mere contiguity of stimulus and response elements.

Relativity theory Presumption of a four-dimensional space-time field for natural phenomena (Einstein).

Repetition compulsion An irrepressible desire to repeat some act over and over (Freud).

Representative design An experimental approach allowing a large representative sample of variables to change together in a random but known fashion, thus better "representing" the effects of the existing combinations of variables and values (Brunswik).

Repression The unconscious removal of unpleasant thoughts or events from consciousness (Freud).

Resistance Opposition by a patient to the recall of past events, presumably because of unconscious repression (psychoanalysis).

Respondent behavior Response characterized by its identification with a specific eliciting stimulus (Skinner).

Response Any behavior resulting from some stimulus.

Restraining forces Brain excitations preventing the unrestrained action of cohesive forces; usually the result of present stimulation (Gestalt).

Retinal disparity A visual depth cue resulting from the slight difference between the two retinal images in binocular vision.

Retroactive inhibition The interference by a second task with the retention of a previously learned task.

Retrospection Introspection on a past event.

Revolution, scientific Radical and fundamental changes in the framework within which a particular science operates, resulting in a new "paradigm" (Kuhn).

Reward An object or activity that satisfies some motivating condition; often assumed to be necessary for learning (as in Thorndike's law of effect or Hull's S-R behavior system).

ROC See **Receiver operating characteristic curve.**

Routine A computer program or part of a program, generally so named because it is designed to carry out a specific function (for example, finding square roots); the word *routine* is ordinarily used if the portion of the program is on the main line of the program, whereas the work *subroutine* is used for units which are called upon periodically from the main program.

Salivary conditioning Process whereby the salivary response becomes attached to some initially ineffective stimulus; see also **Conditioning.**

Scaling The construction of an ordered system of measurement to represent any phenomenon.

Schedule, fixed-interval (FI) A program of reinforcement in which reinforcement is given for the first response made after some fixed period of time.

Schedule, fixed-ratio (FR) A program of reinforcement in which reinforcement is given after some fixed number of responses.

Schedule, reinforcement A program indicating how the presentation of some reinforcing stimulus is arranged.

Schedule, variable-interval (VI) A program of reinforcement in which reinforcement is given for the first response made after some variable period of time.

Schedule, variable-ratio (VR) A program of reinforcement in which reinforcement is given after some variable number of responses.

Schemapiric Description of science as involved in establishing relationships between symbols (schema-) and empirical observations (*-piric*). (Stevens).

Schizophrenia A psychotic disorder characterized by disturbances of the thought processes and lack of contact with reality.

School A collection of adherents to a particular systematic position, with varying degrees of temporal and spatial contiguity.

Science The enterprise by which human beings obtain ordered knowledge about natural phenomena, working with a particular methodology (controlled observation and analysis) and set of attitudes (skepticism, objectivity, etc.).

Science, applied That part of science which is concerned with investigations believed to have immediate practical utility.

Science, pure That part of science which is concerned only with the discovery of new facts and the development of theories without regard for the immediate utility of such knowledge.

Secondary process Conscious activity of the ego guided by external reality; it is thus distinguished from the primary-process activity of the id (psychoanalysis).

Secondary qualities Those qualities alleged to inhere not within the object but within the perceiver, such as color (Locke).

Secondary reinforcement The strengthening of a response by presentation of a stimulus that does not itself have any direct need-reducing properties, but which has occurred contiguously with such a need-reducing stimulus (the primary reinforcer).

Second signal system Pavlov's name for the complex (secondary) signal system, language, with ordinary conditioning as the first signal system.

Self (1)An existing picture of an individual's past behavior and experiences as the individual perceives it. (2) A summary name for a set of psychological processes, usually including evaluative and attitudinal functions, involving an individual and that individual's relationship to the world. (3) Construct developed by individuals to account for the integrity and continuity of their experiences.

Self-actualization Full realization of one's potential.

Semantics Study of the relationship of signs to objects (Morris).

Semiotic Study of the uses of signs and symbols, including three major components (semantics, syntactics, and pragmatics) (Morris).

Sensation A conscious experience which cannot be further analyzed (Titchener).

Sentiment An individual's feeling for a given object or event (Murray).

Sensory isolation Removal of all or almost all stimulation from an individual for a set period of time.

Separation anxiety Severe emotionality resulting from birth trauma and basic to neurotic symptoms (Rank).

Serial A group of proceedings which follow one another in a coherent fashion, involving planning on the part of the organism and providing direction and meaning (Murray).

Set A predisposition or determining tendency.

Shadow A well-developed archetype inherited from the human being's prehuman ancestors; the animal instincts (Jung).

Shaping A technique used to produce a desired behavioral pattern by selectively reinforcing responses that approximate it or are a part of it.

Sibling rivalry Competition among offspring (Adler).

Signal detection theory See **Detection theory.**

Sign A cue that signals the appearance of some other object or event.

Sign learning Learning of the relationships between signs—what leads to what (Tolman).

Sign significate (sign Gestalt) An object which gives rise to the expectation that a particular response will lead to a goal (Tolman).

Simplicity See **Parsimony.**

Skepticism A refusal to accept propositions without what is considered irrefutable evidence.

Skinner box An operant conditioning chamber; a box provided with a device which the organism can manipulate to produce some type of reinforcement.

Solipsism The philosophical view that one can be certain of nothing but one's own experience, so that the existence of an external world becomes a mere assumption.

Solution learning Overt instrumental learning or problem solving (Mowrer).

Somatic nervous system Network of nerves and nerve centers serving the striped musculature of the body and primarily mediating voluntary activities.

Somatotonia An active, aggressive personality pattern supposed to be associated with the mesomorphic body type (Sheldon).

Somatotype A ratio of body measurements which represents an individual's body type (Sheldon).

S-O-R Stimulus-organism-response.

Source trait Underlying determinant of observed behavioral consistency in an individual.

Specification equation Technique of combining information about an individual to permit specific behavioral predictions, developed in R. B. Cattell's personality theory.

Spread of effect Hypothesis that errors occurring in proximity to rewarded responses also acquire some degree of strengthening, relative to more distal errors, from the reward function (Thorndike).

State variable A hypothesized condition of the organism which is the result of a past interaction of the organism and the environment, such as deprivation or drug treatment.

Statistical decision theory A theory that specifies how probabilistic decisions, as in perceptual judgments, should be decided.

Staticism Emphasis on cross-sectional or enduring rather than developmental factors (R. I. Watson).

Stimulus Any environmental energy that impinges on an appropriate sense organ.

Stimulus error Paying attention to the properties of the stimulus rather than to the characteristics of the sensation (Titchener).

Stimulus field The totality of stimuli that act on the organism at any given moment (Gestalt).

Stimulus generalization The process whereby some initially ineffective stimulus, not itself used in conditioning, becomes effective in eliciting some response after the conditioning of that response to a stimulus that is similar along some dimension.

Stimulus-intensity dynamism The principle that reaction potential or response amplitude increases monotonically with the intensity of the stimulus (Hull).

Stimulus pool The total population of stimuli from which different samples may be drawn (Estes).

Stimulus-response (SR) psychology A position whose conceptual framework depends on stimuli and responses.

Stimulus trace The activity in the nervous system which results from stimulation (Hull).

Structuralism The system that stresses the analysis of consciousness into elements through the method of introspection (Wundt, Titchener).

Subjective idealism The metaphysical position in which a single underlying mental or spiritual reality is assumed.

Subjectivism The tendency to base belief on one's own perception and thinking. See also **Contentual subjectivism and Methodological subjectivism.**

Sublimation The permanent substitution of a secondary goal for a primary one (Freud).

Superego The psychic structure or process which represents external values, particularly as inculcated by parents. It is roughly equivalent to the conscience (Freud).

Supernaturalism Natural phenomena can be completely interpreted only by assuming some external (transcendent) principles (R. I. Watson).

Superstitious behavior Learned responses whose strength depends on adventitious contiguity of the behavior and the reinforcing stimulus (Skinner).

Surface color Color seen as lying on the surface of an object.

Surface trait Overtly observed behavioral consistency in an individual (R. B. Cattell).

Symbol Anything that "stands for" or "means" something else.

Symptom Behavioral manifestation of some underlying disorder, such as neurosis or psychosis.

Synchronicity The occurrence of events at the same time but without causal relation (Jung).

Syntactics Study of the linguistic relationships among symbols (Morris).

Syntality The dimensions or traits of a social institution, analogous to the traits of an individual (Cattell).

Syntaxic Referring to a cognitive process in which thoughts and ideas become connected in a logical fashion (Sullivan).

System Ideally, an organization and interpretation of the data and theories of a subject matter, with special assumptions (postulates), definitions, and methodological biases. In psychology, the actual "systems" were primarily sets of suggestions about how to construct a psychology.

Systematic design Classic experimental methodology utilizing rigorous control of variables (Brunswik).

Tabula rasa Blank tablet; usually refers to the doctrine that the mind at birth is blank and is developed through sensory experience.

Talking cure Improvement in adjustment presumably effected by emotional release achieved when one tells one's troubles (also called catharsis, "cleansing") (Freud).

TAT Thematic Appreception Test. A projective device involving making up stories from pictures and permitting personality assessment (Murray).

Taxis See **Tropism.**

T data Behavioral observations made directly as though by a transducer (hence *T*) rather than an operator (Barker).

Technician One trained to provide technical services for the practitioner or scientist.

Teleology The explanation of behavior in terms of its ultimate utilities, in the absence of evidence that these are actually determining factors.

Tension system A motivational factor in which some particular act or set of acts acquires directive influence in behavior until dissipated (Lewin).

Terminal focal event An achievement of the organism, which may be either perceptual or instrumental (Brunswik).

T group See **Encounter group.**

Thema A unit describing behavior in terms of the press and need which are involved (Murray).

Theorem A statement derived from postulates through the rules of deduction; in science, a statement to be subjected to direct empirical testing.

Theory (1)A group of laws deductively connected. (2) Generalizations beyond the data which are used to bridge gaps in knowledge and to generate research. (3) A model plus one or more interpretations.

Theta The proportion of stimulus elements sampled by an organism on any given learning trial (Estes).

Thing constancy The principle that the perceptual character of an object remains essentially stable in spite of wide variations in its sensory representation (Brunswik).

Third Force Amalgam of humanism, phenomenology, and existentialism recently envisioned (initially by Maslow) as an alternative to behaviorism and orthodox psychoanalysis, the two leading historical forces in American psychology.

Topology A nonmetric and nondirectional geometry of spatial relationships in which boundaries are the critical factors and a variety of transformations may be achieved; used by Lewin as a model for representation of behavior functions. (See also **Hodological space.**)

Trait A generalized and focalized neuropsychic system (peculiar to the individual) with the capacity to render many stimuli functionally equivalent and to initiate and guide consistent (equivalent) forms of adaptive and expressive behavior (Allport).

Trait theory Personality theory which emphasizes the isolation of factors accounting for consistency and integration of behavior.

Traits, constitutional Traits having an innate origin (Cattell).

Traits, environmental-mold Consistencies in behavior which are acquired through environmental influences, especially social institutions (Cattell).

Traits, source Underlying general predispositions which account for observed consistencies in behavior (Cattell).

Traits, surface Observed consistencies in behavior (Cattell).

Transducer A device that changes energy from one form to another. A radio receiver is a transducer that changes electromagnetic energy into acoustic energy; the human retina transduces light energy into the electrochemical energy of the nerve impulse.

Transference The shifting of emotion from an object or person to the psychoanalyst during therapy (Freud).

Transposition experiment An experiment in which a subject is trained to respond to one of two stimuli which stand in a particular relationship to each other (for example, the stimulus associated with reward is *larger than* the stimulus not associated with reward). During later test trials, typically the stimulus previously rewarded is paired with a stimulus which has the relationship to it which it previously had to the other training stimulus (i.e., the other test stimulus is now *larger than* the previously rewarded stimulus). The question is whether the subject will respond to the relationship (demonstrate transposition) by choosing the new larger stimulus or will respond to absolute stimulus properties by choosing the old, previously rewarded stimulus.

Trial and error Apparently unplanned but nonetheless not random attempts at problem solving.

Tropism A forced movement which is a direct function of stimulation, as when a plant turns toward the sun. Now more often refers to plants, with *taxis* the equivalent for animals.

Turing machine A conceptual device designed to simulate any clearly defined input-output relationship.

Two-factor learning theory Any theoretical position in which two separate learning processes are considered essential in the acquisition of behavior.

Typology A systematic classification of individuals into distinct categories according to types or kinds that have been hypothesized.

Uncertainty That property of a set of alternatives which determines its information content; the amount of uncertainty in a set of messages or alternatives is the same as the amount of information transmitted in reducing that uncertainty to zero. Analogous to entropy in physical systems (see **Information**).

Unconscious The collective term for mental activities of which the person is not aware (psychoanalysis).

Unconscious inference The drawing of a conclusion, as in perception, in the absence of any reasoning process of which one is aware (Helmholtz).

Unconscious mentalism Lack of attention to thinking activities (R. I. Watson).

Utilitarianism Seeking knowledge for its applicability to practical problems (R. I. Watson).

Valence The attactiveness of objects; can be positive or negative (Lewin).

Variable Usually, any condition or property that may change and be assigned a number. (See also **Controlled, Dependent, Independent,** and **Intervening variable.**)

Vector Directional force hypothesized to underlie behavioral relationships (Lewin).

Vicarious function The substitution of one means for another in order to achieve some result (Tolman and Brunswik).

Visceratonia A comfort-loving personality pattern associated with the endomorphic body type (Sheldon).

Vitalism The philosophical position that life cannot be explained entirely in terms of physicochemical principles.

Volumic color Color seen as occupying volume, as in the case of colored smoke.

Voluntary Carried out with conscious intention.

Weber-Fechner law In the more sophisticated form presented by Fechner, a law stating that the intensity of a sensation is proportional to the logarithm of stimulus intensity.

Weber's law A psychophysical law which states that a noticeable change in a stimulus intensity is always a constant proportional part of the original stimulus.

Zeigarnik effect The name for the finding that tasks which are not completed are better remembered than tasks which are completed (Lewin).

Zeitgeist Spirit of the times.

Acknowledgments

The authors wish to thank the following copyright owners, authors, and publishers for permission to reprint excerpts from copyrighted material:

THE AMERICAN ASSOCIATION FOR THE ADVANCEMENT OF SCIENCE

Boring, E. G. When is human behavior predetermined? *Scientific Monthly*, 1957, **84**, 189–196.

Smith, C. S. Matter versus materials: A historical view. *Science*, 1968, **162**, 637–644.

THE AMERICAN JOURNAL OF PSYCHOLOGY

Murray, E. Peripheral and central factors in memory: Images of visual form and color. *American Journal of Psychology*, 1906, **7**, 227–247.

THE AMERICAN PSYCHOLOGICAL ASSOCIATION

Coan, R. W. Dimensions of psychological theory. *American Psychologist*, 1968, **23**, 715-722.

Guthrie, E. R. Psychological facts and psychological theory. *Psychological Bulletin*, 1946, **43**, 1–20.

AMERICAN SCIENTIST

Skinner, B. F. The experimental analysis of behavior. *American Scientist*, 1957, **45**, 343–371.

ANNUAL REVIEWS, INC.

Adelson, J. Personality. *Annual Review of Psychology*, 1969, **20**, 217–252.

Ford, D. H. & Urban, H. B. Psychotherapy. *Annual Review of Psychology*, 1967, **18**, 333-372.

APPLETON CENTURY CROFTS, EDUCATIONAL DIVISION, MEREDITH CORPORATION

Boring, E. G. *The physical dimensions of consciousness*. New York: Appleton-Century-Crofts, 1933.

Boring, E. G. *A history of experimental psychology*. New York: Appleton-Century-Crofts, 1950.

Boring, E. G., & Lindzey, G. (Eds.) *A history of psychology in autobiography*. New York: Appleton-Century-Crofts, 1967.

Estes, W. K., Koch, S., MacCorquodale, K., Meehl, P. E., Mueller, C. G., Jr., Schoenfeld, W. N., & Verplanck, W. S. *Modern learning theory*. New York: Appleton-Century-Crofts, 1954.

Heidbreder, E. *Seven psychologies*. New York: Appleton-Century-Crofts, 1933.

Thorndike, E. L. *Selected writings from a connectionist's psychology.* New York: Appleton-Century-Crofts, 1949.

Turner, M. *Philosophy and the science of behavior.* New York: Appleton-Century-Crofts, 1967.

BASIC BOOKS, INC.

Jones, E. *The life and work of Sigmund Freud.* Vol. 3. New York: Basic Books, 1957.

Nagel, E. The nature and aim of science. In S. Morgenhesser (Ed.), *Philosophy of science today.* New York: Basic Books, 1967.

BOLLINGEN FOUNDATION

Jung, C. G. *Symbols of transformation.* New York: Random House, 1956.

BUREAU OF PUBLICATIONS, TEACHERS COLLEGE, COLUMBIA UNIVERSITY

Thorndike, E. L. *Educational psychology.* Vol. 2. *The psychology of learning.* New York: Teachers College, 1913.

CLARK UNIVERSITY PRESS

Murchison, C. (Ed.) *A history of psychology in autobiography.* Vol. 3. Worcester, Mass.: Clark University Press, 1936.

Watson, J. B. What the nursery has to say about instincts. In C. Murchison (Ed.), *Psychologies of 1925.* Worcester, Mass.: Clark University Press, 1926.

Watson, J. B. Recent experiments on how we lose and change our emotional equipment. In C. Murchison (Ed.), *Psychologies of 1925.* Worcester, Mass.: Clark University Press, 1926.

E. P. DUTTON & CO., INC.

Evans, R. I. *B. F. Skinner: The man and his ideas.* New York: Dutton, 1968.

HARVARD UNIVERSITY PRESS

Bridgman, P. W. *The way things are.* Cambridge, Mass.: Harvard University Press, 1959.

HOLT, RINEHART AND WINSTON, INC.

James, W. *The principles of psychology.* New York: Holt, 1890.

HOUGHTON MIFFLIN COMPANY

Platt, J. R. *The excitement of science.* Boston: Houghton Mifflin, 1962.

J. B. LIPPINCOTT COMPANY

Watson, R. I. *The great psychologists from Aristotle to Freud.* (Rev. ed.) Philadelphia: Lippincott, 1968.

THE MACMILLAN COMPANY

Bridgman, P. W. *The logic of modern physics.* New York: Macmillan, 1927.

Horwitz, L. Theory construction and validation in psychoanalysis. In M. H. Marx (Ed.), *Theories in contemporary psychology.* New York: Macmillan, 1963.

Wundt, W. *Principles of physiological psychology.* New York: Macmillan, 1904.

McGRAW-HILL BOOK COMPANY

Prentice, W. C. H. The systematic psychology of Wolfgang Köhler. In S. Koch (Ed.), *Psychology: A study of a science.* Vol. 1. *Sensory, perceptual, and physiological formulations.* New York: McGraw-Hill, 1958.

Tolman, E. C. Principles of purposive behavior. In S. Koch (Ed.), *Psychology: A study of a science.* Vol. 2. *General systematic formulations, learning and special processes.* New York: McGraw-Hill, 1959, pp. 92–157.

Wooldridge, D. E. *Mechanical man: The physical basis of intelligent life.* New York: McGraw-Hill, 1968.

W. W. NORTON & COMPANY, INC.

Watson, J. B. *Behaviorism.* New York: Norton, 1925. Rev. ed., 1930.

Watson, J. B., & McDougall, W. *The battle of behaviorism.* New York: Norton, 1929.

PHILOSOPHICAL LIBRARY, INC.

Bridgman, P. W. *The nature of some of our physical concepts.* New York: Philosophical Library, 1952.

THE PHILOSOPHICAL REVIEW

Titchener, E. B. The postulates of a structural psychology. *Philosophical Review*, 1898, **7**, 449–465.

PSYCHOLOGY TODAY

Hall, M. H. An interview with "Mr. Behaviorist" B. F. Skinner. *Psychology Today*, 1967, **1**, 21–23, 68–71.

ROCKEFELLER UNIVERSITY PRESS

Weiss, A. P. 1 + 1 = 2 (one plus one does not equal two). In G. C. Quarton, T. Melnechuk, & F. O. Schmitt (Eds.), *The neurosciences.* New York: Rockefeller University Press, 1967.

THE RONALD PRESS

Woodworth, R. S., & Sheehan, M. R. *Contemporary schools of psychology.* New York: Ronald Press, 1964.

SIMON & SCHUSTER, INC.

Russell, B. *A history of Western philosophy.* New York: Simon & Schuster, 1945.

SPRINGER-VERLAG OHG

Harrower, M. R. Organization in higher mental processes. *Psychologische Forschung*, 1932, **17**, 56–120.

STANFORD UNIVERSITY PRESS

Barker, R. G. *Ecological psychology.* Stanford, Calif.: Stanford University Press, 1968.

THE UNIVERSITY OF CHICAGO PRESS

Kuhn, T. S. *The structure of scientific revolutions.* Chicago: University of Chicago Press, 1962.

Lashley, K. S. *Brain mechanisms and intelligence.* Chicago: University of Chicago Press, 1929.

VINTAGE BOOKS, RANDOM HOUSE, INC.

Beveridge, W. I. B. *The art of scientific investigation.* New York: Vintage Books, 1957.

JOHN WILEY & SONS, INC.

Hall, C. S., & Lindzey, G. *Theories of personality.* New York: Wiley, 1957.

The authors also wish to thank the following authors and publishers for permission to reproduce figures and quotations from their publications:

THE AMERICAN JOURNAL OF PSYCHOLOGY

Orbison, W. O. Shape as a function of the vector field. *American Journal of Psychology*, 1939, **52**, 31–45.

THE AMERICAN PSYCHOLOGICAL ASSOCIATION

Brunswik, E. Representative design and probabilistic theory in a functional psychology. *Psychological Review*, 1955, **62**, 193–217.

Coan, R. W. Dimensions of psychological theory. *American Psychologist*, 1968, **23**, 715–722.

McGeoch, J. A. The formal criteria of a systematic psychology. *Psychological Review*, 1933, **40**, 1–12.

INSTITUTE OF ELECTRICAL AND ELECTRONIC ENGINEERING

Peterson, W. W., Birdsall, T. G., & Fox, W. C. The theory of signal detectability. *Transactions of Professional Group on Information Theory, Institute of Radio Engineers*, 1954, PGIT-4, 171–212.

McGRAW-HILL BOOK COMPANY

Lewin, K. *Principles of topological psychology.* (Tr. by F. Heider & G. Heider.) New York: McGraw-Hill, 1936.

THE NEW YORK ACADEMY OF SCIENCES

Tanner, W. P., Jr. Physiological implications of psychophysical data. *Annals of the New York Academy of Science*, 1961, **89**, 752–765.

UNIVERSITY OF CALIFORNIA PRESS

Tolman, E. C., & Honzik, C. H. *Insight in rats.* Berkeley: University of California Press, 1932.

THE UNIVERSITY OF CHICAGO PRESS

Brunswik, E. The conceptual framework of psychology. *International Encyclopedia of Unified Science*, 1952, **1**, 1–102.

UNIVERSITY OF MINNESOTA PRESS

Feigl, H. The "orthodox" view of theories: Remarks in defense as well as critique. In M. Radner & S. Winokur (Eds.), *Analyses of theories and methods of physics and psychology.* Minneapolis: University of Minnesota Press, 1970.

W. P. VAN STOCKUM

Brunswik, E. The conceptual focus of some psychological systems. *Journal of Unified Science*, 1939, **8**, 36–49.

JOHN WILEY & SONS, INC.

Hall, C. S., & Lindzey, G. *Theories of personality.* (2d ed.) New York: Wiley, 1970.

Index

Page numbers in *italic* indicate bibliography references.